8000
AMAZING
THINGS
you should know

8000
AMAZING
THINGS
you should know

Miles
KeLLy

First published in 2006 by Miles Kelly Publishing Ltd
Harding's Barn, Bardfield End Green, Thaxted, Essex, CM6 3PX, UK

Copyright © Miles Kelly Publishing Ltd 2006

This edition printed 2016

2 4 6 8 10 9 7 5 3 1

PUBLISHING DIRECTOR Belinda Gallagher

CREATIVE DIRECTOR Jo Cowan

COVER DESIGNER Simon Lee

PICTURE RESEARCH MANAGER Liberty Newton

PRODUCTION Elizabeth Collins, Caroline Kelly

REPROGRAPHICS Stephan Davis, Jennifer Cozens,
Thom Allaway, Anthony Cambray

ASSETS Lorraine King

ISBN: 978-1-78617-081-1

Printed in China

British Library Cataloguing-in-Publication Data
A catalogue record for this book is available from the British Library

All images from the Miles Kelly Archives

Made with paper from a sustainable forest

www.mileskelly.net

CONTENTS

Contents

SPACE 18-75

Contents

PLANET EARTH 76-133

Contents

WILD ANIMALS 134-191

Contents

HUMAN BODY 192-249

Contents

SCIENCE 250-307

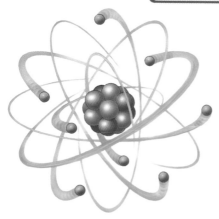

Contents

BUILDINGS & TRANSPORT 308-365

Contents

WORLD GEOGRAPHY 366-423

Contents

PLANTS 424-481

INDEX 482-511

Introduction

This incredible reference resource provides knowledge, fascination and inspiration on every page. Its 800 subject panels contain facts that will inform, amaze and entertain. You can discover space, planet Earth, the world of animals, the human body – and much much more. Learn from fascinating facts like these:

• *Mars' volcano Olympus Mons is the biggest in the Solar System. It covers the same area as Ireland and is three times higher than Mount Everest.*

• *Factories in the Chinese city of Benxi make so much smoke the city is invisible to satellites.*

• *The Arctic beetle can survive in temperatures below -60°C.*

• *The reproductive system is the only body system that can be surgically removed without killing you.*

Read on to discover the other 7997 facts in *8000 Things You Should Know.*

Using this book

The organization of *8000 Things You Should Know* brings surprises and interest to every page. The book is divided into eight broad areas.

On each double-page spread there are three or four subject panels. Each panel contains ten key facts and is identified with a highlighted subject symbol. Look at each individual section contents to find out what they mean.

The subjects are organized so that you will find interest and variety throughout the book. Use the subject symbols, the contents page and the index to navigate

Headings tell you which of the eight areas of the book you are in

Ten key facts are provided in each subject panel. There are 800 panels making 8000 facts in all

Veins
- Veins are
- Unlike ar
  the heart
  need from
- When blo
  blue colour
  blood carrie
- The only ve
  four pulmor
  lungs the sh
- The two larg
  that flow into
- Inside most l
  make sure tha

  At any

Teeth
▼ Teeth have long roots
but they sit in a fleshy ri
tooth is a living ma·
of den·

Space
- Space probes
  unmanned spa
- The first suc
  Mariner 2, w
- Mariner 10
- Vikings 1 a
- Voyager 2
  of the Sola
  Saturn (19
- Most pre
  passing
- To save
  probes
  them e

  NA

1000 Things You Should Know About Space

40

Jupiter
- **Jupiter** is the biggest planet in the Solar System – twice as heavy as all the other planets put together.
- **Jupiter has no surface** for a spacecraft to land on because it is made mostly from helium gas and hydrogen. The massive pull of Jupiter's gravity squeezes the hydrogen so hard that it is liquid.
- **Towards Jupiter's core,** immense pressure turns the hydrogen to solid metal.
- **The Ancient Greeks** originally named the planet Zeus, after the king of their gods. Jupiter was the Romans' name for Zeus.
- **Jupiter spins right round** in less than 10 hours, which means that the planet's surface is moving at nearly 50,000 km/h.

Great Red Spot

! NEWS FLASH !
The Galileo space probe reached Jupiter and its moons in the year 1995.

- **Jupiter's speedy spin makes** its middle bulge out. It also churns up the planet's metal core until it generates a hugely powerful magnetic field (see magnetism), ten times as strong as the Earth's.
- **Jupiter has a Great Red Spot** – a huge swirl of red clouds measuring more than 40,000 km across. The scientist Robert Hooke first noticed the spot in 1644.
- **Jupiter's four biggest moons** were first spotted by Galileo in the 17th century (see Jupiter's Galilean moons). Their names are Io, Europa, Callisto and Ganymede.
- **Jupiter also has 17 smaller moons** – Metis, Adastrea, Amalthea, Thebe, Leda, Himalia, Lysithea, Elkar, Ananke, Carme, Pasiphaë and Sinope and 5 recent discoveries.
- **Jupiter is so massive** that the pressure at its heart makes it glow very faintly with invisible infrared rays. Indeed, it glows as brightly as 4 million billion 100-watt light bulbs. But it is not quite big enough for nuclear reactions to start, and make it become a star.

◄ Jupiter is a gigantic planet, 142,984 km across. Its orbit takes 11.86 years and varies between 740.9 and 815.7 million km from the Sun. Its surface is often rent by huge lightning flashes and thunderclaps, and temperatures here plunge to –150°C. Looking at Jupiter's surface, all you can see is a swirling mass of red, brown and yellow clouds of ammonia, including the Great Red Spot.

H

There are diagrams
throughout the book

Subject symbols appear on
every panel. Look for the ones
that are highlighted

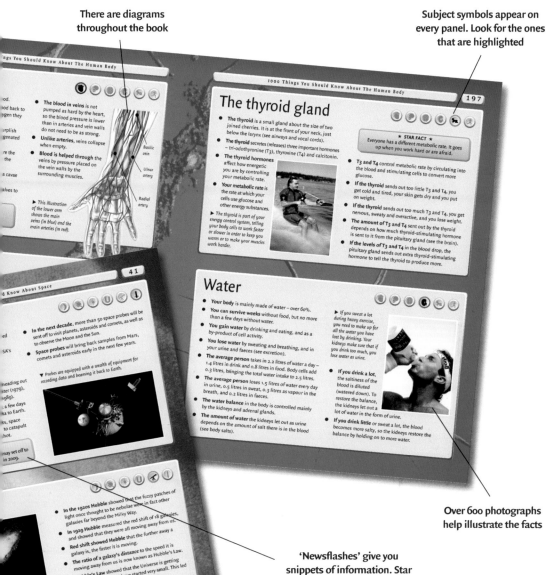

- **The blood in veins** is not pumped as hard by the heart, so the blood pressure is lower than in arteries and vein walls do not need to be as strong.
- **Unlike arteries**, veins collapse when empty.
- **Blood is helped through** the veins by pressure placed on the vein walls by the surrounding muscles.

▶ This illustration of the lower arm shows the main veins (in blue) and the main arteries (in red).

Basilic vein

Ulnar artery

Radial artery

od.
od back to
gen they

rplish
genated

re the
the

a cavae

alves to

The thyroid gland

- **The thyroid** is a small gland about the size of two joined cherries. It is at the front of your neck, just below the larynx (see airways and vocal cords).
- **The thyroid secretes** (releases) three important hormones – tri-odothyronine (T3), thyroxine (T4) and calcitonin.
- **The thyroid hormones** affect how energetic you are by controlling your metabolic rate.
- **Your metabolic rate** is the rate at which your cells use glucose and other energy substances.

▶ The thyroid is part of your energy control system, telling your body cells to work faster or slower in order to keep you warm or to make your muscles work harder.

★ STAR FACT ★
Everyone has a different metabolic rate. It goes up when you work hard or are afraid.

- **T3 and T4** control metabolic rate by circulating into the blood and stimulating cells to convert more glucose.
- **If the thyroid** sends out too little T3 and T4, you get cold and tired, your skin gets dry and you put on weight.
- **If the thyroid** sends out too much T3 and T4, you get nervous, sweaty and overactive, and you lose weight.
- **The amount of T3 and T4** sent out by the thyroid depends on how much thyroid-stimulating hormone is sent to it from the pituitary gland (see the brain).
- **If the levels of T3 and T4** in the blood drop, the pituitary gland sends out extra thyroid-stimulating hormone to tell the thyroid to produce more.

- **In the next decade**, more than 50 space probes will be sent off to visit planets, asteroids and comets, as well as to observe the Moon and the Sun.
- **Space probes** will bring back samples from Mars, comets and asteroids early in the next few years.

▼ Probes are equipped with a wealth of equipment for recording data and beaming it back to Earth.

ed

SA's

heading out
ter (1979),
989).
a few days
ta to Earth.
ts, space
to catapult
hot.

may set off to
in 2009.

Water

- **Your body** is mainly made of water – over 60%.
- **You can survive weeks** without food, but no more than a few days without water.
- **You gain water** by drinking and eating, and as a by-product of cell activity.
- **You lose water** by sweating and breathing, and in your urine and faeces (see excretion).
- **The average person** takes in 2.2 litres of water a day – 1.4 litres in drink and 0.8 litres in food. Body cells add 0.3 litres, bringing the total water intake to 2.5 litres.
- **The average person** loses 1.5 litres of water every day in urine, 0.5 litres in sweat, 0.3 litres as vapour in the breath, and 0.2 litres in faeces.
- **The water balance** in the body is controlled mainly by the kidneys and adrenal glands.
- **The amount of water** the kidneys let out as urine depends on the amount of salt there is in the blood (see body salts).

▶ If you sweat a lot during heavy exercise, you need to make up for all the water you have lost by drinking. Your kidneys make sure that if you drink too much, you lose water as urine.

- **If you drink a lot**, the saltiness of the blood is diluted (watered down). To restore the balance, the kidneys let out a lot of water in the form of urine.
- **If you drink little** or sweat a lot, the blood becomes more salty, so the kidneys restore the balance by holding on to more water.

- **In the 1920s Hubble** showed that the fuzzy patches of light once thought to be nebulae were in fact other galaxies far beyond the Milky Way.
- **In 1929 Hubble** measured the red shift of 18 galaxies, and showed that they were all moving away from us.
- **Red shift** showed Hubble that the further away a galaxy is, the faster it is moving.
- **The ratio of a galaxy's distance** to the speed it is moving away from us is now known as Hubble's Law.
- **Hubble's Law** showed that the Universe is getting bigger – and so must have started very small. This led to the idea of the Big Bang.
- **The figure given** by Hubble's law is Hubble's constant and is about 40 to 80 km/sec per megaparsec.
- **In the 1930s Hubble** showed that the Universe is isotropic (the same in all directions).
- **Hubble space telescope** is named after Edwin Hubble.

nents was to show that
.laxies.

3) was an American who
and Oxford, and was also
.urned to astronomy.
ntury, astronomers thought
.here was to the Universe.

Over 600 photographs
help illustrate the facts

'Newsflashes' give you
snippets of information. Star
facts are strange-but-true

1000
THINGS
YOU SHOULD KNOW ABOUT

SPACE

KEY

 Earth, Sun and Moon

 Planets

 Stars

 Universe

 Astronomy

 Space travel

Small stars

- **Small stars** of low brightness are called white, red or black dwarves depending on their colour.

- **Red dwarves** are bigger than the planet Jupiter but smaller than our medium-sized star, the Sun. They glow faintly, with 0.01% of the Sun's brightness.

- **No red dwarf** can be seen with the naked eye – not even the nearest star to the Sun, the red dwarf Proxima Centauri.

- **White dwarves** are the last stage in the life of a medium-sized star. Although they are even smaller than red dwarves – no bigger than the Earth – they contain the same amount of matter as the Sun.

- **Our night sky's brightest star**, Sirius, the Dog Star, has a white dwarf companion called the Pup Star.

◀ Black dwarves are stars that were either not big enough to start shining, or which have burned up all their nuclear fuel and stopped glowing, like a coal cinder.

- **The white dwarf Omicron-2 Eridani** (also called 40 Eridani) is one of the few dwarf stars that can be seen from the Earth with the naked eye.

- **Brown dwarves** are very cool space objects, little bigger than Jupiter.

- **Brown dwarves** formed in the same way as other stars, but were not big enough to start shining properly. They just glow very faintly with the heat left over from their formation.

- **Black dwarves** are very small, cold, dead stars.

- **The smallest kind of star** is called a neutron star.

Life

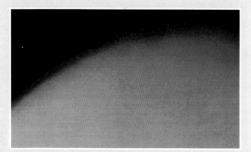

▲ Saturn's moon Titan has plenty of evidence of organic (life) chemicals in its atmosphere.

- **Life is only known** to exist on Earth, but in 1986 NASA found what they thought might be fossils of microscopic living things in a rock from Mars.

- **Life on Earth** probably began 3.8 billion years ago.

- **The first life forms** were probably bacteria which lived in very hot water around underwater volcanoes.

> **! NEWS FLASH !**
> Microscopic organisms have been found in rock deep underground. Could similar organisms be living under the surface of Mars or Titan?

- **Most scientists** say life's basic chemicals formed on Earth. The astronomer Fred Hoyle said they came from Space.

- **Basic organic (life) chemicals** such as amino acids have been detected in nebulae and meteorites (see meteors).

- **Huge lightning flashes** may have caused big organic molecules to form on the young Earth.

- **Earth is right for life** because of its gas atmosphere, surface water and moderately warm temperatures.

- **Mars is the only** other planet that once had water on its surface – which is why scientists are looking for signs of life there.

- **Jupiter's moon Europa** probably has water below its surface which could spawn life.

Space suits

- **Space suits protect astronauts** when they go outside their spacecraft. The suits are also called EMUs (Extra-vehicular Mobility Units).

- **The outer layers** of a space suit protect against harmful radiation from the Sun and bullet-fast particles of space dust called micrometeoroids.

- **The clear, plastic helmet** also protects against radiation and micrometeoroids.

- **Oxygen is circulated** around the helmet to stop the visor misting.

- **The middle layers** of a space suit are blown up like a balloon to press against the astronaut's body. Without this pressure, the astronaut's blood would boil.

- **The soft inner lining** of a space suit has tubes of water in it to cool the astronaut's body or warm it up.

- **The backpack** supplies pure oxygen for the astronaut to breathe, and gets rid of the carbon dioxide he or she gives out. The oxygen comes from tanks which hold enough for up to 7 hours.

- **The gloves** have silicone-rubber fingertips which allow the astronaut some sense of touch.

- **Various different gadgets** in the suit deal with liquids – including a tube for drinks and another for collecting urine.

- **The full cost** of a spacesuit is about $11 million although 70% of this is for the backpack and control module.

◄ *Space suits not only have to provide a complete life-support system (oxygen, water and so on), but must also protect against the dangers of space.*

Newton

- **Isaac Newton** (1642-1727) discovered the force of gravity and the three basic laws of motion.

- **Newton's ideas** were inspired by seeing an apple fall from a tree in the garden of his home in Lincolnshire.

- **Newton also discovered** that sunlight can be split into a spectrum made of all the colours of the rainbow.

- **Newton's discovery of gravity** showed why things fall to the ground and planets orbit the Sun.

- **Newton realized** that a planet's orbit depends on its mass and its distance from the Sun.

- **The further apart** and the lighter two objects are, the weaker is the pull of gravity between them.

- **To calculate** the pull of gravity between two objects, multiply their masses together, then divide the total by the square of the distance between them.

- **This calculation** allows astronomers to predict precisely the movement of every planet, star and galaxy in the Universe.

- **Using Newton's formula for gravity**, astronomers have detected previously unknown stars and planets, including Neptune and dwarf planet Pluto, from the effect of their gravity on other space objects.

- **Newton's three laws of motion** showed that every single movement in the Universe can be calculated mechanically.

▶ *Newton's theory of gravity showed for the first time why the Moon stays in its orbit around the Earth, and how the gravitational pull between the Earth and the Moon could be worked out mathematically.*

Nebulae

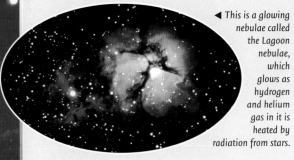

◀ *This is a glowing nebulae called the Lagoon nebulae, which glows as hydrogen and helium gas in it is heated by radiation from stars.*

- **Nebula** (plural nebulae) was the word once used for any fuzzy patch of light in the night sky. Nowadays, many nebulae are known to be galaxies instead.

- **Many nebulae** are gigantic clouds of gas and space dust.

- **Glowing nebulae** are named because they give off a dim, red light, as the hydrogen gas in them is heated by radiation from nearby stars.

- **The Great Nebula of Orion** is a glowing nebula just visible to the naked eye.

- **Reflection nebulae** have no light of their own. They can only be seen because starlight shines off the dust in them.

- **Dark nebulae** not only have no light of their own, they also soak up all light. They can only be seen as patches of darkness, blocking out light from the stars behind them.

- **The Horsehead nebula** in Orion is the best-known dark nebula. As its name suggests, it is shaped like a horse's head.

- **Planetary nebulae** are thin rings of gas cloud which are thrown out by dying stars. Despite their name, they have nothing to do with planets.

- **The Ring nebula** in Lyra is the best-known of the planetary nebulae.

- **The Crab nebula** is the remains of a supernova that exploded in AD 1054.

Extraterrestrials

- **Extraterrestrial (ET)** means 'outside the Earth'.

- **Some scientists** say that ET life could develop anywhere in the Universe where there is a flow of energy.

- **One extreme idea** is that space clouds could become sentient (thinking) beings.

- **Most scientists** believe that if there is ET life anywhere in the Universe, it must be based on the chemistry of carbon, as life on Earth is.

- **If civilizations like ours** exist elsewhere, they may be on planets circling other stars. This is why the discovery of other planetary systems is so exciting (see planets).

- **The Drake Equation** was proposed by astronomer Frank Drake to work out how many civilizations there could be in our galaxy – and the figure is millions!

- **There is no scientific proof** that any ET life form has ever visited the Earth.

- **SETI** is the Search for Extraterrestrial Intelligence – the program that analyzes radio signals from space for signs of intelligent life.

- **The Arecibo radio telescope** beams out signals to distant stars.

> ★ STAR FACT ★
> The life chemical formaldehyde can be detected
> in radio emissions from the galaxy NGC 253.

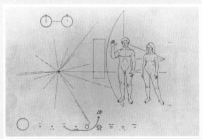

▲ *The space probes Pioneer 10 and 11 carry metal panels with picture messages about life on Earth into deep space.*

H-R diagram

- **The Hertzsprung-Russell (H-R) diagram** is a graph in which the temperature of stars is plotted against their brightness. The temperature of a star is indicated by its colour.

- **Cool stars** are red or reddish-yellow.

- **Hot stars** burn white or blue.

- **Medium-sized stars** form a diagonal band called the main sequence across the graph.

- **The whiter and hotter** a main sequence star is, the brighter it shines. White stars and blue-white stars are usually bigger and younger.

- **The redder and cooler** a star is, the dimmer it glows. Cool red stars tend to be smaller and older.

- **Giant stars and white dwarf stars** lie to either side of the main sequence stars.

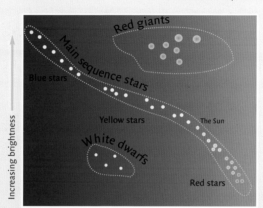

Red giants

Main sequence stars

Blue stars

Yellow stars

The Sun

White dwarfs

Increasing brightness

Red stars

Increasing temperature

- **The H-R diagram** shows how bright each colour star should be. If the star actually looks dimmer, it must be further away.

- **By comparing a star's** brightness predicted by the H-R diagram with how bright it really looks, astronomers can work out how far away it is.

- **The diagram** was devised by Ejnar Hertzsprung and Henry Russell.

The Milky Way

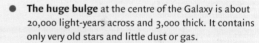

- **The Milky Way** is the faint, hazy band of light that you can see stretching right across the night sky.

- **Looking through binoculars,** you would see that the Milky Way is made up of countless stars.

- **A galaxy** is a vast cluster of stars, and the Milky Way is our view of the galaxy we live in, called the Galaxy.

- **The Milky Way Galaxy** is one of billions in space.

- **The Galaxy** is 100,000 light-years across and 1,000 light-years thick. It is made up of 100 billion stars.

- **All the stars** are arranged in a spiral (like a giant Catherine wheel), with a bulge in the middle.

- **Our Sun** is just one of the billions of stars on one arm of the spiral.

- **The Galaxy** is whirling rapidly, spinning our Sun and all its other stars around at 100 million km/h.

- **The Sun** travels around the Galaxy once every 200 million years – a journey of 100,000 light-years.

- **The huge bulge** at the centre of the Galaxy is about 20,000 light-years across and 3,000 thick. It contains only very old stars and little dust or gas.

- **There may be a huge black hole** in the very middle of the Galaxy.

▼ *To the naked eye, the Milky Way looks like a hazy, white cloud, but binoculars show it to be a blur of countless stars.*

The Universe

- **The Universe** is everything that we can ever know – all of space and all of time.

- **The Universe** is almost entirely empty, with small clusters of matter and energy.

- **The Universe** is probably about 15 billion years old, but estimates vary.

- **One problem** with working out the age of the Universe is that there are stars in our galaxy which are thought to be 14 to 18 billion years old – older than the estimated age of the Universe. So either the stars must be younger, or the Universe older.

- **The furthest galaxies** yet detected are about 13 billion light-years away (130 billion trillion km).

- **The Universe** is getting bigger by the second. We know this because all the galaxies are zooming away from us. The further away they are, the faster they are moving.

◀ *The Universe is getting bigger and bigger all the time, as galaxies rush outwards in all directions.*

- **The very furthest galaxies** are spreading away from us at more than 90% of the speed of light.

- **The Universe** was once thought to be everything that could ever exist, but recent theories about inflation (see the Big Bang) suggest our Universe may be just one of countless bubbles of space-time.

- **The Universe** may have neither a centre nor an edge, because according to Einstein's theory of relativity (see Einstein), gravity bends all of space-time around into an endless curve.

> ★ **STAR FACT** ★
> Recent theories suggest there may be many other universes which we can never know.

Black holes

▲ *This is an artist's impression of what a black hole might look like, with jets of electricity shooting out from either side.*

- **Black holes** are places where gravity is so strong that it sucks everything in, including light.

- **If you fell** into a black hole you'd stretch like spaghetti.

- **Black holes form** when a star or galaxy gets so dense that it collapses under the pull of its own gravity.

- **Black holes** may exist at the heart of every galaxy.

- **Gravity shrinks** a black hole to an unimaginably small point called a singularity.

- **Around a singularity**, gravity is so intense that space-time is bent into a funnel.

- **Matter spiralling** into a black hole is torn apart and glows so brightly that it creates the brightest objects in the Universe – quasars.

- **The swirling gases** around a black hole turn it into an electrical generator, making it spout jets of electricity billions of kilometres out into space.

- **The opposite of black holes** may be white holes which spray out matter and light like fountains.

> ★ **STAR FACT** ★
> Black holes and white holes may join to form tunnels called wormholes – and these may be the secret to time travel.

Mercury

- **Mercury is the nearest planet** to the Sun – during its orbit it is between 45.9 and 69.7 million km away.

- **Mercury is the fastest orbiting** of all the planets, getting around the Sun in just 88 days.

- **Mercury takes 58.6 days** to rotate once, so a Mercury day lasts nearly 59 times as long as ours.

- **Temperatures** on Mercury veer from -180°C at night to over 430°C during the day (enough to melt lead).

- **The crust and mantle** are made largely of rock, but the core (75% of its diameter) is solid iron.

- **Mercury's dusty surface** is pocketed by craters made by space debris crashing into it.

- **With barely 20% of Earth's mass**, Mercury is so small that its gravity can only hold on to a very thin atmosphere of sodium vapour.

- **Mercury is so small** that its core has cooled and become solid (unlike Earth's). As this happened, Mercury shrank and its surface wrinkled like the skin of an old apple.

- **Craters on Mercury** discovered by the USA's *Mariner* space probe have names like Bach, Beethoven, Wagner, Shakespeare and Tolstoy.

★ STAR FACT ★
Twice during its orbit, Mercury gets very close to the Sun and speeds up so much that the Sun seems to go backwards in the sky.

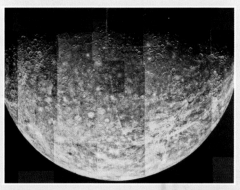

▲ *Mercury is so close to the Sun that it is not easy to see. The first time astronomers had a clear view of it was when the Mariner 10 space probe flew past it in 1974.*

Mercury's surface is covered with impact craters

The largest feature on Mercury is a huge impact crater called the Caloris Basin, which is about 1,300 km across and 2 km deep

Most of the craters were formed by the impact of debris left over from the birth of the solar system, about 4 billion years ago

The surface is wrinkled by long, low ridges which probably formed as the core cooled and shrunk

▶ *Mercury is a planet of yellow dust, as deeply dented with craters as the Moon. It does have small polar icecaps, but the ice is pure acid.*

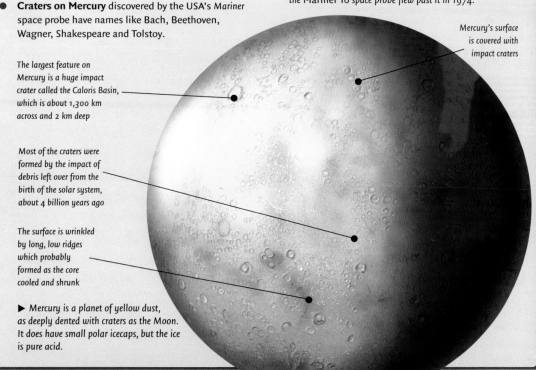

Copernicus

- **Until the 16th century** most people thought the Earth was the centre of the Universe and that everything – the Moon, Sun, planets and stars – revolved around it.

- **Nicolaus Copernicus** was the astronomer who first suggested that the Sun was the centre, and that the Earth went round the Sun. This is called the heliocentric view.

- **Copernicus was born** on 19 February 1473 at Torun in Poland, and died on 24 May 1543.

- **Copernicus had an extensive** education at the best universities in Poland and Italy. He studied astronomy and astrology, medicine and law.

- **Copernicus described his ideas** in a book called *De revolutionibus orbium coelestium* ('On the revolutions of the heavenly spheres').

- **The Roman Catholic Church** banned Copernicus's book for almost 300 years.

- **Copernicus's ideas** came not from looking at the night sky but from studying ancient astronomy.

- **Copernicus's main clue** came from the way the planets, every now and then, seem to perform a backward loop through the sky.

- **The first proof** of Copernicus's theory came in 1609, when Galileo saw (through a telescope) moons revolving around Jupiter .

- **The change in ideas** that was brought about by Copernicus is known as the Copernican Revolution.

▶ 'The Earth,' wrote Copernicus, 'carrying the Moon's path, passes in a great orbit among the other planets in an annual revolution around the Sun.'

Day and night

- **When it is daylight** on the half of the Earth facing towards the Sun, it is night on the half of the Earth facing away from it. As the Earth rotates, so the day and night halves shift gradually around the world.

- **The Earth turns eastwards** – this means that the Sun comes up in the east as our part of the world spins round to face it.

◀ The Sun comes up to bring the dawn, as the Earth turns your part of the world around to face its light. It sets again at dusk, as the Earth goes on revolving, spinning your part of the world away from the sunlight again.

> ★ STAR FACT ★
> One day on Venus lasts 5,832 Earth hours!

- **As the Earth turns**, the stars come back to the same place in the night sky every 23 hours, 56 minutes and 4.09 seconds. This is a sidereal day (star day).

- **It takes 24 hours** for the Sun to come back to the same place in the daytime sky. This is is the solar day, and it is slightly longer than the star day because the Earth moves 1 degree further round the Sun each day.

- **On the other planets**, the length of day and night varies according to how fast each planet rotates.

- **One day on Mercury** lasts 59 Earth days, because Mercury takes almost two months to spin around.

- **A day on Jupiter** lasts less than 10 hours because Jupiter spins so fast.

- **A day on Mars** is 24.6 hours – much the same as ours.

- **A day on the Moon** lasts one Earth month.

Moon landings

- **The first Moon landing** was by the unmanned Soviet probe *Lunar 9*, which touched down on the Moon's surface in 1966.
- **The first men to orbit** the Moon were the astronauts on board the US *Apollo 8* in 1968.
- **On 20 July 1969** the American astronauts Neil Armstrong and Edwin (Buzz) Aldrin became the first men ever to walk on the Moon.
- **When Neil Armstrong** stepped on to the Moon for the first time, he said these famous words: 'That's one small step for a man; one giant leap for mankind.'
- **Twelve men have landed** on the Moon between 1969 and 1972.

◄ In 1969, Neil Armstrong was the first to walk on the Moon.

- **The Moon astronauts** brought back 380 kg of Moon rock.
- **A mirror was left on** the Moon's surface to reflect a laser beam which measured the Moon's distance from Earth with amazing accuracy.
- **Laser measurements** showed that, on average, the Moon is 376,275 km away from the Earth.
- **Gravity on the Moon** is so weak that astronauts can leap high into the air wearing their heavy space suits.
- **Temperatures** reach 117°C at midday on the Moon, but plunge to -162°C at night.

Constellations

- **Constellations are patterns of stars** in the sky which astronomers use to help them pinpoint individual stars.
- **Most of the constellations** were identified long ago by the stargazers of Ancient Babylon and Egypt.
- **Constellations are simply patterns** – there is no real link between the stars whatsoever.
- **Astronomers today** recognize 88 constellations.
- **Heroes and creatures of Greek myth**, such as Orion the Hunter and Perseus, provided the names for many constellations, although each name is usually written in its Latin form, not Greek.
- **The stars in each constellation** are named after a letter of the Greek alphabet.
- **The brightest star in each constellation** is called the Alpha star, the next brightest Beta, and so on.
- **Different constellations** become visible at different times of year, as the Earth travels around the Sun.

- **Southern hemisphere constellations** are different from those in the north.
- **The constellation of the Great Bear** – also known by its Latin name Ursa Major – contains an easily recognizable group of seven stars called the Plough or the Big Dipper.

▼ Constellations are patterns of stars that help astronomers locate stars among the thousands in the night sky.

Dark matter

- **Dark matter** is space matter we cannot see because, unlike stars and galaxies, it does not give off light.
- **There is much more dark matter** in the Universe than bright. Some scientists think 90% of matter is dark.
- **Astronomers know about dark matter** because its gravity pulls on stars and galaxies, changing their orbits and the way they rotate (spin round).
- **The visible stars in the Milky Way** are only a thin central slice, embedded in a big bun-shaped ball of dark matter.
- **Dark matter** is of two kinds – the matter in galaxies (galactic), and the matter between them (intergalactic).
- **Galactic dark matter** may be much the same as ordinary matter. However, it burnt out (as black dwarf stars do) early in the life of the Universe.
- **Intergalactic dark matter** is made up of WIMPs (Weakly Interacting Massive Particles).
- **Some WIMPs** are called cold dark matter because they are travelling slowly away from the Big Bang.

- **Some WIMPs** are called hot dark matter because they are travelling very fast away from the Big Bang.
- **The future of the Universe** may depend on how much dark matter there is. If there is too much, its gravity will eventually stop the Universe's expansion – and make it shrink again (see the Big Bang).

▼ *A galaxy's bright stars may be only a tiny part of its total matter. Much of the galaxy may be invisible dark matter.*

Orbits

▲ *Space stations are artificial satellites that orbit the Earth. The Moon is the Earth's natural satellite.*

- **Orbit means 'travel round',** and a moon, planet or other space object may be held within a larger space object's gravitational field and orbit it.
- **Orbits may be circular,** elliptical (oval) or parabolic (conical). The orbits of the planets are elliptical.
- **An orbiting space object** is called a satellite.

- **The biggest-known orbits** are those of the stars in the Milky Way Galaxy, which can take 200 million years.
- **Momentum** is what keeps a satellite moving through space. Just how much momentum a satellite has depends on its mass and its speed.
- **A satellite orbits** at the height where its momentum exactly balances the pull of gravity.
- **If the gravitational pull** is greater than a satellite's momentum, it falls in towards the larger space object.
- **If a satellite's momentum** is greater than the pull of gravity, it flies off into space.
- **The lower a satellite orbits,** the faster it must travel to stop it falling in towards the larger space object.
- **Geostationary orbit** for one of Earth's artificial satellites is 35,786 km over the Equator. At this height, it must travel around 11,000km/h to complete its orbit in 24 hours. Since Earth also takes 24 hours to rotate, the satellite spins with it and so stays in the same place over the Equator.

Venus

- **Venus** is the second planet out from the Sun – its orbit makes it 107.4 million km away at its nearest and 109 million km away at its furthest.

- **Venus shines like a star** in the night sky because its thick atmosphere reflects sunlight amazingly well. This planet is the brightest thing in the sky, after the Sun and the Moon.

- **Venus is called the Evening Star** because it can be seen from Earth in the evening, just after sunset. It can also be seen before sunrise, though. It is visible at these times because it is quite close to the Sun.

- **Venus's cloudy atmosphere** is a thick mixture of carbon dioxide gas and sulphuric acid, which are belched out by the planet's volcanoes.

- **Venus is the hottest planet** in the solar system, with a surface temperature of over 470°C.

- **Venus is so hot** because the carbon dioxide in its atmosphere works like the panes of glass in a greenhouse to trap the Sun's heat. This overheating is called a runaway greenhouse effect.

> ★ STAR FACT ★
> Pressure on the surface of Venus is 90 times greater than that on Earth!

- **Venus's thick clouds** hide its surface so well that until the Russian *Venera 13* probe landed on the planet in 1982, some people thought there might be jungles beneath the clouds.

- **Venus's day** (the time it takes to spin round once) lasts 243 Earth days – longer than its year, which lasts 224.7 days. But because Venus rotates backwards, the Sun actually comes up twice during the planet's yearly orbit – once every 116.8 days.

- **Venus is the nearest** of all the planets to Earth in size, measuring 12,102 km across its diameter.

▼ *Venus's thick clouds of carbon dioxide gas and sulphuric acid reflect sunlight and make it shine like a star, but none of its atmosphere is transparent like the Earth's. This makes it very hard to see what is happening down on its surface.*

▲ *This is a view of a 6km-high volcano on Venus' surface called Maat Mons. It is not an actual photograph, but was created on computer from radar data collected by the Magellan orbiter which reached Venus in the 1980s. The colours are what astronomers guess them to be from their knowledge of the chemistry of Venus.*

Galileo

- **Galileo Galilei** (1564-1642) was a great Italian mathematician and astronomer.

- **Galileo was born** in Pisa on 15 February 1564, in the same year as William Shakespeare.

- **The pendulum clock** was invented by Galileo after watching a swinging lamp in Pisa Cathedral in 1583.

- **Galileo's experiments** with balls rolling down slopes laid the basis for our understanding of how gravity makes things accelerate (speed up).

- **Learning of the telescope's invention**, Galileo made his own to look at the Moon, Venus and Jupiter.

★ **STAR FACT** ★
Only on 13 October 1992 was the sentence of the Catholic Church on Galileo retracted.

◄ One of the most brilliant of scientists of all time, Galileo ended his life imprisoned (in his villa near Florence) for his beliefs.

- **Galileo described his observations** of space in a book called *The Starry Messenger*, published in 1613.

- **Through his telescope** Galileo saw that Jupiter has four moons (see Jupiter's Galilean moons). He also saw that Venus has phases (as our Moon does).

- **Jupiter's moon and Venus's phases** were the first visible evidence of Copernicus' theory that the Earth moves round the Sun. Galileo also believed this.

- **Galileo was declared a heretic** in 1616 by the Catholic Church, for his support of Copernican theory. Later, threatened with torture, Galileo was forced to deny that the Earth orbits the Sun. Legend has it he muttered *'eppur si muove'* ('yet it does move') afterwards.

Earth's formation

▲ Earth and the Solar System formed from a cloud of gas and dust.

- **The Solar System** was created when the gas cloud left over from a giant supernova explosion started to collapse in on itself and spin.

- **About 4.55 billion years ago** there was just a vast, hot cloud of dust and gas circling a new star, our Sun.

- **The Earth probably began** when tiny pieces of space debris (called planetesimals) began to clump together, pulled together by each other's gravity.

- **As the Earth formed**, more space debris kept on smashing into it, adding new material. This debris included ice from the edges of the solar system.

- **About 4.5 billion years ago**, a rock the size of Mars crashed into the Earth. The splashes of material from this crash clumped together to form the Moon.

- **The collision** that formed the Moon made the Earth very hot.

- **Radioactive decay** heated the Earth even further.

- **For a long time** the surface of the Earth was a mass of erupting volcanoes.

- **Iron and nickel melted** and sank to form the core.

- **Lighter materials** such as aluminium, oxygen and silicon floated up and cooled to form the crust.

Distances

- **The distance to the Moon** is measured with a laser beam.

- **The distance to the planets** is measured by bouncing radar signals off them and timing how long the signals take to get there and back.

- **The distance to nearby stars** is worked out by measuring the slight shift in the angle of each star in comparison to stars far away, as the Earth orbits the Sun. This is called parallax shift.

- **Parallax shift** can only be used to measure nearby stars, so astronomers work out the distance to faraway stars and galaxies by comparing how bright they look with how bright they actually are.

- **For middle distance stars**, astronomers compare colour with brightness using the Hertzsprung-Russell (H-R) diagram. This is called main sequence fitting.

◄ *Estimating the distance to the stars is one of the major problems in astronomy.*

- **Beyond 30,000 light-years**, stars are too faint for main sequence fitting to work.

- **Distances to nearby galaxies** can be estimated using 'standard candles' – stars whose brightness astronomers know, such as Cepheid variables (see variable stars), supergiants and supernovae.

- **The expected brightness of a galaxy** too far away to pick out its stars may be worked out using the Tully-Fisher technique, based on how fast galaxies spin.

- **Counting planetary nebulae** (the rings of gas left behind by supernova explosions) is another way of working out how bright a distant galaxy should be.

- **A third method** of calculating the brightness of a distant galaxy is to gauge how mottled it looks.

Spacecraft

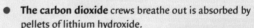

- **There are three kinds of spacecraft** – artificial satellites, unmanned probes and manned spacecraft.

- **Spacecraft** have double hulls (outer coverings) to protect against other space objects that crash into them.

- **Manned spacecraft** must also protect the crew from heat and other dangerous effects of launch and landing.

- **Spacecraft windows** have filters to protect astronauts from the Sun's dangerous ultraviolet rays.

- **Radiators** on the outside of the spacecraft lose heat, to stop the crew's body temperatures overheating the craft.

- **Manned spacecraft** have life-support systems that provide oxygen to breathe, usually mixed with nitrogen (as in ordinary air). Charcoal filters out smells.

- **The carbon dioxide** crews breathe out is absorbed by pellets of lithium hydroxide.

- **Spacecraft toilets** have to get rid of waste in low gravity conditions. Astronauts have to sit on a device which sucks away the waste. Solid waste is dried and dumped in space, but the water is saved.

- **To wash**, astronauts have a waterproof shower which sprays them with jets of water from all sides and also sucks away all the waste water.

★ STAR FACT ★
The weightlessness of space means that most astronauts sleep floating in the air, held in place by a few straps.

▶ *The US space shuttle, the first reusable spacecraft, has made manned space flights out into Earth's orbit and back almost a matter of routine.*

The Earth

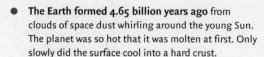

- **The Earth is the third planet** out from the Sun, 149.6 million km away on average. On 3 January, at the nearest point of its orbit (called the perihelion), the Earth is 147,097,800 km away from the Sun. On 4 July, at its furthest (the aphelion), it is 152,098,200 km away.

- **The Earth is the fifth largest planet** in the solar system, with a diameter of 12,756 km and a circumference of 40,024 km at the Equator.

- **The Earth is one of four rocky planets**, along with Mercury, Venus and Mars. It is made mostly of rock, with a core of iron and nickel.

- **No other planet in the solar system** has liquid water on its surface, so Earth is uniquely suitable for life. Over 70% of Earth's surface is under water.

- **The Earth's atmosphere** is mainly harmless nitrogen and life-giving oxygen, and it is over 700 km deep. The oxygen has been made and maintained by plants over billions of years.

- **The Earth formed 4.65 billion years ago** from clouds of space dust whirling around the young Sun. The planet was so hot that it was molten at first. Only slowly did the surface cool into a hard crust.

- **The Earth's orbit** around the Sun is 939,886,400 km long and takes 365.242 days.

- **The Earth is tilted** at an angle of 23.5°. Even so, it orbits the Sun in a level plane, called the plane of the ecliptic.

- **The Earth is made up** of the same basic materials as meteorites and the other rocky planets – mostly iron (35%), oxygen (28%), magnesium (17%), silicon (13%) and nickel (2.7%).

> ★ STAR FACT ★
> The Earth is protected
> from the Sun's radiation
> by a magnetic field
> which stretches 60,000 km
> out into space.

▼ The Earth looks mostly bright blue from space – this is due to the unique presence of water on its surface.

▲ Most of the Earth's rocky crust is drowned beneath oceans, formed from steam belched out by volcanoes early in the planet's history. The Earth is just the right distance from the Sun for surface temperatures to stay an average 15°C, and keep most of its water liquid.

Comets

▲ *Comet Kahoutek streaks through the night sky.*

- **Comets are bright objects** with long tails, which we sometimes see streaking across the night sky.

- **They may look spectacular**, but a comet is just a dirty ball of ice a few kilometres across.

- **Many comets orbit the Sun**, but their orbits are very long and they spend most of the time in the far reaches of the solar system. We see them when their orbit brings them close to the Sun for a few weeks.

- **A comet's tail** is made as it nears the Sun and begins to melt. A vast plume of gas millions of kilometres across is blown out behind by the solar wind. The tail is what you see, shining as the sunlight catches it.

- **Comets called periodics** appear at regular intervals.

- **Some comets reach speeds** of 2 million km/h as they near the Sun.

- **Far away from the Sun**, comets slow down to 1,000 km/h or so – that is why they stay away for so long.

- **The visit of the comet Hale-Bopp** in 1997 gave the brightest view of a comet since 1811, visible even from brightly lit cities.

- **The Shoemaker-Levy 9 comet** smashed into Jupiter in July 1994, with the biggest crash ever witnessed.

- **The most famous comet** of all is Halley's comet.

Giant stars

- **Giant stars** are 10 to 100 times as big as the Sun, and 10 to 1,000 times as bright.

- **Red giants** are stars that have swollen 10 to 100 times their size, as they reach the last stages of their life and their outer gas layers cool and expand.

- **Giant stars have burned** all their hydrogen, and so burn helium, fusing (joining) helium atoms to make carbon.

- **The biggest stars** go on swelling after they become red giants, and grow into supergiants.

- **Supergiant stars** are up to 500 times as big as the Sun, with absolute magnitudes of -5 to -10 (see star brightness).

- **Pressure in the heart** of a supergiant is enough to fuse carbon atoms together to make iron.

- **All the iron in the Universe** was made in the heart of supergiant stars.

- **There is a limit to the brightness** of supergiants, so they can be used as distance markers by comparing how bright they look to how bright they are (see distances).

- **Supergiant stars** eventually collapse and explode as supernovae.

▶ The constellation of Cygnus, the Swan, contains the very biggest star in the known Universe – a hypergiant which is almost a million times as big as the Sun.

★ **STAR FACT** ★
The biggest-known star is the hypergiant Cygnus OB2 No.12, which is 810,000 times as bright as the Sun.

Eclipses

- **An eclipse** is when the light from a star such as the Sun is temporarily blocked off by another space object.

- **A lunar eclipse** is when the Moon travels behind the Earth, and into the Earth's shadow (Earth is between the Moon and the Sun).

- **Lunar eclipses happen once or twice** every year and last only a few hours.

- **In a total lunar eclipse**, the Moon turns rust red.

- **There wil be total lunar eclipses** on 3 March 2007 and 28 August 2007.

- **A solar eclipse** is when the Moon comes between the Sun and the Earth, casting a shadow a few kilometres wide on to the Earth's surface.

- **In a total eclipse of the Sun**, the Moon passes directly in front of the Sun, completely covering it so that only its corona can be seen (see the Sun).

- **There are one or two solar eclipses every year**, but they are visible only from a narrow strip of the world.

▲ *During a total solar eclipse of the Sun, the Moon blocks out everything but the Sun's corona.*

- **There will be total solar eclipses** on 29 March 2006 and 1 August 2008.

- **Solar eclipses are possible** because the Moon is 400 times smaller than the Sun, and is also 400 times closer to the Earth. This means the Sun and the Moon appear to be the same size in the sky.

Star brightness

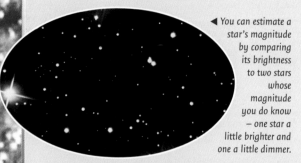

◀ *You can estimate a star's magnitude by comparing its brightness to two stars whose magnitude you do know – one star a little brighter and one a little dimmer.*

- **Star brightness** is worked out on a scale of magnitude (amount) that was first devised in 150 BC by the Ancient Greek astronomer Hipparchus.

- **The brightest star** Hipparchus could see was Antares, and he described it as magnitude 1. He described the faintest star he could see as magnitude 6.

- **Using telescopes and binoculars**, astronomers can now see much fainter stars than Hipparchus could.

- **Good binoculars** show magnitude 9 stars, while a home telescope will show magnitude 10 stars.

- **Brighter stars than Antares** have been identified with magnitudes of less than 1, and even minus numbers. Betelgeuse is 0.8, Vega is 0.0, and the Sun is -26.7.

- **The brightest-looking star** from Earth is Sirius, the Dog Star, with a magnitude of -1.4.

- **The magnitude scale only** describes how bright a star looks from Earth compared to other stars. This is its relative magnitude.

- **The further away a star is,** the dimmer it looks and the smaller its relative magnitude is, regardless of how bright it really is.

- **A star's absolute magnitude** describes how bright a star really is.

- **The star Deneb** is 60,000 times brighter than the Sun. But because it is 1,800 light-years away, it looks dimmer than Sirius.

Herschel

- **William Herschel** (1738-1822) was an amateur astronomer who built his own, very powerful telescope in his home in Bath, England.

- **Until Herschel's time**, astronomers assumed there were just seven independent objects in the sky – the Moon, the Sun, and five planets.

- **The five known planets** were Mercury, Venus, Mars, Jupiter and Saturn.

- **Uranus**, the sixth planet, was discovered by William Herschel in 1781.

- **At first, Herschel** had thought that the dot of light he could see through his telescope was a star. But when he looked more closely, he saw a tiny disc instead of a point of light. When he looked the next night, the 'star' had moved – this meant that it had to be a planet.

◀ William Herschel was one of the greatest astronomers. With the help of his sister Caroline, he discovered Uranus in 1781. He later identified two of the moons of Uranus and Saturn.

- **Herschel wanted to name** the planet George, after King George III, but Uranus was eventually chosen.

- **Herschel's partner** in his discoveries was his sister Caroline (1750-1848), another great astronomer, who catalogued (listed) all the stars of the northern hemisphere.

- **Herschel's son John** catalogued the stars of the southern hemisphere.

- **Herschel himself added** to the catalogue of nebulae.

- **Herschel was also the first** to explain that the Milky Way is our view of a galaxy shaped 'like a grindstone'.

Rockets

- **Rockets** provide the huge thrust needed to beat the pull of Earth's gravity and launch a spacecraft into space.

- **Rockets burn propellant** (propel means 'push'), to produce hot gases that drive the rocket upwards.

- **Rocket propellant** comes in two parts – a solid or liquid fuel, and an oxidizer.

- **Solid fuel** is a rubbery substance that contains hydrogen, and it is usually used in additional, booster rockets.

- **Liquid fuel** is usually liquid hydrogen, and it is typically used on big rockets.

- **There is no oxygen in space**, and the oxidizer supplies the oxygen needed to burn fuel. It is usually liquid oxygen (called 'lox' for short).

- **The first rockets** were made 1,000 years ago in China.

- **Robert Goddard** launched the very first liquid-fuel rocket in 1926.

- **The German V2 war rocket**, designed by Werner von Braun, was the first rocket capable of reaching space.

▶ Unlike other spacecraft, the space shuttle can land like an aeroplane ready for another mission. But even the shuttle has to be launched into space on the back of huge rockets. These soon fall back to Earth where they are collected for reuse.

★ STAR FACT ★
The most powerful rocket ever was the *Saturn 5* that sent astronauts to the Moon.

Satellites

- **Satellites are objects** that orbit planets and other space objects. Moons are natural satellites. Spacecraft sent up to orbit the Earth and the Sun are artificial satellites.

- **The first artificial satellite** was *Sputnik 1*, launched on 4 October 1957.

- **Over 100 artificial satellites** are now launched every year. A few of them are space telescopes.

- **Communications satellites** beam everything from TV pictures to telephone calls around the world.

- **Observation satellites** scan the Earth and are used for purposes such as scientific research, weather forecasting and spying.

- **Navigation satellites** such as the Global Positioning System (GPS) are used by people such as airline pilots to work out exactly where they are.

- **Satellites are launched** at a particular speed and trajectory (path) to place them in just the right orbit.

- **The lower a satellite's orbit**, the faster it must fly to avoid falling back to Earth. Most satellites fly in low orbits, 300 km above the Earth.

- **A geostationary orbit** is 35,786 km up. Satellites in geostationary orbit over the Equator always stay in exactly the same place above the Earth.

- **Polar orbiting satellites** circle the Earth from pole to pole about 850 km up, covering a different strip of the Earth's surface on each orbit.

▼ One of the many hundreds of satellites now in Earth's orbit.

Hipparchus

▲ Some of Hipparchus' knowledge of stars came from the Sumerians who wrote on clay tablets

- **Hipparchus of Nicaea** was a Greek astronomer who lived in the 2nd century BC, dying in 127 BC.

- **Hipparchus created the** framework for astronomy.

- **Hipparchus's ideas** were almost lost until rescued by roman astronomer Ptolemy and developed into a system that lasted 1500 years until they were overthrown by the ideas of Copernicus.

- **Ancient Babylonian records** brought back by Alexander the Great from his conquests helped Hipparchus to make his observations of the stars.

- **Hipparchus was the first astronomer** to try to work out how far away the Sun is.

- **The first star catalogue**, listing 850 stars, was put together by Hipparchus.

- **Hipparchus was also the first** to identify the constellations systematically and to assess stars in terms of magnitude (see star brightness).

- **Hipparchus discovered** that the positions of the stars on the equinoxes (21 March and 21 December) slowly shift round, taking 26,000 years to return to their original place. This is the 'precession of the equinoxes'.

- **The mathematics of trigonometry** is also thought to have been invented by Hipparchus.

Mars

- **Mars** is the nearest planet to Earth after Venus, and it is the only planet to have either an atmosphere or a daytime temperature close to ours.

- **Mars is called the red planet** because of its rusty red colour. This comes from oxidized (rusted) iron in its soil.

- **Mars is the fourth planet** out from the Sun, orbiting it at an average distance of 227.9 million km. It takes 687 days to complete its orbit.

- **Mars is 6,786 km** in diameter and spins round once every 24.62 hours – almost the same time as the Earth takes to rotate.

- **Mars's volcano Olympus Mons** is the biggest in the solar system. It covers the same area as Ireland and is three times higher than Mount Everest.

- **In the 1880s**, the American astronomer Percival Lowell was convinced that the dark lines he could see on Mars's surface through his telescope were canals built by Martians.

> **★ STAR FACT ★**
> The 1997 Mars Pathfinder mission showed that many of the rocks on Mars's surface were dumped in their positions by a huge flood at least 2 billion years ago.

- **The Viking probes** found no evidence of life on Mars, but the discovery of a possible fossil of a micro-organism in a Mars rock (see life) means the hunt for life on Mars is on. Future missions to the planet will hunt for life below its surface.

- **The evidence is growing** that Mars was warmer and wetter in the past, although scientists cannot say how much water there was, or when and why it dried up.

- **Mars has two tiny moons** called Phobos and Deimos. Phobos is just 27 km across, while Deimos is just 15 km across and has so little gravity that you could reach escape velocity (see take off) riding a bike up a ramp!

▼ Mars's surface is cracked by a valley called the Vallis Marineris – so big it makes the Grand Canyon look tiny.

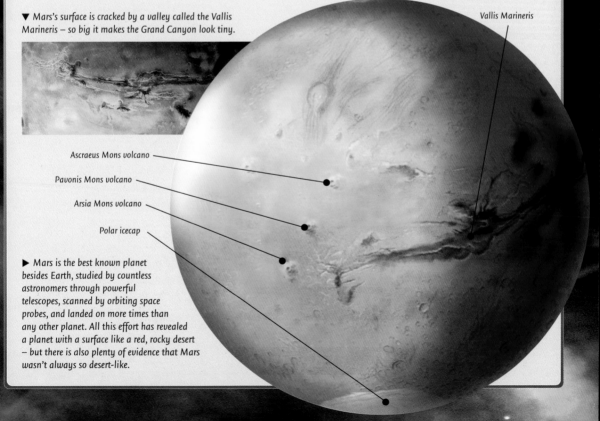

Vallis Marineris

Ascraeus Mons volcano

Pavonis Mons volcano

Arsia Mons volcano

Polar icecap

▶ Mars is the best known planet besides Earth, studied by countless astronomers through powerful telescopes, scanned by orbiting space probes, and landed on more times than any other planet. All this effort has revealed a planet with a surface like a red, rocky desert – but there is also plenty of evidence that Mars wasn't always so desert-like.

Light

- **Light is the fastest thing** in the Universe, travelling at 299,792,458 metres per second.
- **Light rays always travel** in straight lines.
- **Light rays change direction** as they pass from one material to another. This is called refraction.
- **Colours** are different wavelengths of light.
- **The longest light waves** you can see are red, and the shortest are violet.
- **Light is a form** of electromagnetic radiation (see magnetism and radiation), and a light ray is a stream of tiny energy particles called photons.
- **Photons of light** travel in waves just 380 to 750 nanometres (millionths of a millimetre) long.
- **Faint light** from very distant stars is often recorded by sensors called CCDs (see observatories). These count photons from the star as they arrive and build up a picture of the star bit by bit over a long period.

- **The electromagnetic spectrum** (range) includes ultraviolet light and X-rays, but light is the only part of the spectrum our eyes can see.
- **All light is given out by atoms**, and atoms give out light when 'excited' – for example, in a nuclear reaction.

▼ Stars send out huge amounts of light and other radiation as they are heated within by stupendously big nuclear reactions.

Magnetism

- **Magnetism is a force** that either pulls magnetic materials together or pushes them apart.
- **Iron and nickel** are the most common magnetic materials. Electricity is also magnetic.
- **Around every magnet** there is a region in which its effects are felt, called its magnetic field.
- **The magnetic field** around a planet or a star is called the magnetosphere.

◄ The planet Jupiter is one of the most powerful magnets in the Solar System. It was first detected by 'synchrotron radiation' – the radiation from tiny electrons accelerating as they fall into a magnetic field.

- **Most of the planets** in the Solar System, including the Earth, have a magnetic field.
- **Planets have magnetic fields** because of the liquid iron in their cores. As the planets rotate, so the iron swirls, generating electric currents that create the magnetic field.
- **Jupiter's magnetic field** is 30 times stronger than that of the Earth, because Jupiter is huge and spins very quickly.
- **Neptune and Uranus** are unusual because, unlike other planets' magnetic fields, theirs are at right angles to their axis of rotation (the angle at which they spin).
- **Magnetism is linked** to electricity, and together they make up the force called electromagnetism.
- **Electromagnetism** is one of the four fundamental forces in the Universe, along with gravity and the two basic forces of the atomic nucleus.

Atmosphere

- **An atmosphere** is the gases held around a planet by its gravity.
- **Every planet in the Solar System** has an atmosphere.
- **Each atmosphere** is very different. Earth's atmosphere is the only one humans can breathe.
- **Atmospheres** are not fixed, but can change rapidly.

▼ *Earth's unique atmosphere shields us from the Sun's dangerous rays, as well as giving us oxygen and water.*

> ★ STAR FACT ★
> The oxygen in Earth's atmosphere was formed entirely by microscopic plants.

- **Moons** are generally too small and their gravity is too weak to hold on to an atmosphere. But some moons in the Solar System have one, including Saturn's moon Titan.
- **The primordial (earliest) atmospheres** came from the cloud of gas and dust surrounding the young Sun.
- **If Earth and the other rocky planets** had primordial atmospheres, they were stripped away by the solar wind (see solar eruptions).
- **Earth's atmosphere** was formed first from gases pouring out of volcanoes.
- **Jupiter's atmosphere** is partly primordial, but it has been altered by the Sun's radiation, and the planet's own internal heat and lightning storms.

Cosmic rays

- **Cosmic rays** are streams of high-energy particles that strike Earth's atmosphere.
- **The lowest-energy cosmic rays** come from the Sun, or are Galactic Cosmic Rays (GCRs) from outside the Solar System.
- **Medium-energy cosmic rays** come from sources within our own Milky Way, including powerful supernova explosions.
- **Collisions** between cosmic rays and the hydrogen gas clouds left by supernovae create a kind of radiation called synchrotron radiation, which can be picked up from places such as the Crab nebula by radio telescopes.
- **The highest-energy cosmic rays** may come from outside our galaxy.
- **About 85% of GCRs** are the nuclei of hydrogen atoms, stripped of their electron (see atoms).

◀ *Because Earth's magnetic field makes cosmic rays spiral into our atmosphere, it is not always easy to identify where they have come from. However, many are from the surface of the Sun.*

- **Most other GCRs** are helium and heavier nuclei, but there are also tiny positrons, electrons and neutrinos.
- **Neutrinos** are so small that they pass almost straight through the Earth without stopping.
- **The study of cosmic rays** provided scientists with most of their early knowledge about high-energy particles – every subatomic particle apart from electrons, protons and neutrons.
- **Most cosmic rays** are deflected (pushed aside) by the Earth's magnetic field or collide with particles in the atmosphere long before they reach the ground.

Jupiter

- **Jupiter** is the biggest planet in the Solar System – twice as heavy as all the other planets put together.

- **Jupiter has no surface** for a spacecraft to land on because it is made mostly from helium gas and hydrogen. The massive pull of Jupiter's gravity squeezes the hydrogen so hard that it is liquid.

- **Towards Jupiter's core**, immense pressure turns the hydrogen to solid metal.

- **The Ancient Greeks** originally named the planet Zeus, after the king of their gods. Jupiter was the Romans' name for Zeus.

- **Jupiter spins right round** in less than 10 hours, which means that the planet's surface is moving at nearly 50,000 km/h.

> **! NEWS FLASH !**
> The Galileo space probe reached Jupiter and its moons in the year 1995.

- **Jupiter's speedy spin makes** its middle bulge out. It also churns up the planet's metal core until it generates a hugely powerful magnetic field (see magnetism), ten times as strong as the Earth's.

- **Jupiter has a Great Red Spot** – a huge swirl of red clouds measuring more than 40,000 km across. The scientist Robert Hooke first noticed the spot in 1644.

- **Jupiter's four biggest moons** were first spotted by Galileo in the 17th century (see Jupiter's Galilean moons). Their names are Io, Europa, Callisto and Ganymede.

- **Jupiter also has 17 smaller moons** – Metis, Adastrea, Amalthea, Thebe, Leda, Himalia, Lysithea, Elkar, Ananke, Carme, Pasiphaë and Sinope and 5 recent discoveries.

- **Jupiter is so massive** that the pressure at its heart makes it glow very faintly with invisible infrared rays. Indeed, it glows as brightly as 4 million billion 100-watt light bulbs. But it is not quite big enough for nuclear reactions to start, and make it become a star.

Great Red Spot

◄ *Jupiter is a gigantic planet, 142,984 km across. Its orbit takes 11.86 years and varies between 740.9 and 815.7 million km from the Sun. Its surface is often rent by huge lightning flashes and thunderclaps, and temperatures here plunge to -150°C. Looking at Jupiter's surface, all you can see is a swirling mass of red, brown and yellow clouds of ammonia, including the Great Red Spot.*

Space probes

- **Space probes** are automatic, computer-controlled unmanned spacecraft sent out to explore space.
- **The first successful** planetary probe was the USA's *Mariner 2*, which flew past Venus in 1962.
- *Mariner 10* reached Mercury in 1974.
- *Vikings 1* and *2* landed on Mars in 1976.
- *Voyager 2* has flown over 6 billion km and is heading out of the Solar System after passing close to Jupiter (1979), Saturn (1980), Uranus (1986) and Neptune (1989).
- **Most probes** are 'fly-bys' which spend just a few days passing their target and beaming back data to Earth.
- **To save fuel** on journeys to distant planets, space probes may use a nearby planet's gravity to catapult them on their way. This is called a slingshot.

> **! NEWS FLASH !**
> NASA's Terrestrial Planet Finder (TPF) may set off to visit planets circling nearby stars in 2009.

- **In the next decade**, more than 50 space probes will be sent off to visit planets, asteroids and comets, as well as to observe the Moon and the Sun.
- **Space probes** will bring back samples from Mars, comets and asteroids early in the next few years.

▼ *Probes are equipped with a wealth of equipment for recording data and beaming it back to Earth.*

Hubble

▲ *One of Hubble's earliest achievements was to show that some 'nebulae' were really other galaxies.*

- **Edwin Hubble** (1889-1953) was an American who trained in law at Chicago and Oxford, and was also a great boxer before he turned to astronomy.
- **Until the early 20th century**, astronomers thought that our galaxy was all there was to the Universe.
- **In the 1920s Hubble** showed that the fuzzy patches of light once thought to be nebulae were in fact other galaxies far beyond the Milky Way.
- **In 1929 Hubble** measured the red shift of 18 galaxies, and showed that they were all moving away from us.
- **Red shift showed Hubble** that the further away a galaxy is, the faster it is moving.
- **The ratio of a galaxy's distance** to the speed it is moving away from us is now known as Hubble's Law.
- **Hubble's Law** showed that the Universe is getting bigger – and so must have started very small. This led to the idea of the Big Bang.
- **The figure given** by Hubble's law is Hubble's constant and is about 40 to 80 km/sec per megaparsec.
- **In the 1930s Hubble** showed that the Universe is isotropic (the same in all directions).
- **Hubble space telescope** is named after Edwin Hubble.

Meteors

▲ This crater in Arizona is one of the few large meteorite crater's visible on Earth. The Moon is covered in them.

- **Meteors** are space objects that crash into Earth's atmosphere. They may be stray asteroids, tiny meteoroids, or the grains of dust from the tails of dying comets.

- **Meteoroids** are the billions of tiny lumps of rocky material that hurtle around the solar system. Most are no bigger than a pea.

- **Most meteors** are very small and burn up as they enter the atmosphere.

- **Shooting stars** may look like stars shooting across the night sky, but they are actually meteors burning up as they hit Earth's atmosphere.

- **Meteor showers** are bursts of dozens of shooting stars which arrive as Earth hits the tail of a comet.

- **Although meteors are not stars**, meteor showers are named after the constellations they seem to come from.

- **The heaviest showers** are the Perseids (12 Aug), the Geminids (13 Dec) and the Quadrantids (3 Jan).

- **Meteorites** are larger meteors that penetrate right through Earth's atmosphere and reach the ground.

- **A large meteorite** could hit the Earth at any time.

> ★ STAR FACT ★
> The impact of a large meteorite may have chilled the Earth and wiped out the dinosaurs.

Pulsars

- **A pulsar** is a neutron star that spins rapidly, beaming out regular pulses of radio waves – rather like an invisible cosmic lighthouse.

- **The first pulsar** was detected by a Cambridge astronomer called Jocelyn Bell Burnell in 1967.

▶ The Crab nebula contains a pulsar also known as NP0532. It is the youngest pulsar yet discovered and it probably formed after the supernova explosion seen in the Crab nebula in AD 1054. It has a rotation period of 0.0331 seconds, but it is gradually slowing down.

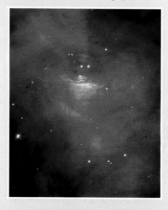

- **At first astronomers thought** the regular pulses might be signals from aliens, and pulsars were jokingly called LGMs (short for Little Green Men).

- **Most pulsars** send their radio pulse about once a second. The slowest pulse only every 4 seconds, and the fastest every 1.6 milliseconds.

- **The pulse rate** of a pulsar slows down as it gets older.

- **The Crab pulsar** slows by a millionth each day.

- **More than 650 pulsars** are now known, but there may be 100,000 active in our galaxy.

- **Pulsars probably result** from a supernova explosion – that is why most are found in the flat disc of the Milky Way, where supernovae occur.

- **Pulsars are not found** in the same place as supernovae because they form after the debris from the explosion has spread into space.

- **We know** they come from tiny neutron stars often less than 10 km across, because they pulse so fast.

Elements

- **Elements** are the basic chemicals of the Universe. There are no simpler substances, and they cannot be broken down into other substances.

- **Elements are formed** entirely of atoms that contain the same number of protons in their nuclei (see atoms). All hydrogen atoms have one proton, for instance.

- **More than 100 elements** are known.

- **The simplest and lightest elements** – hydrogen and helium – formed very early in the history of the Universe (see the Big Bang).

- **Other elements** formed as the nuclei of the atoms of the light elements joined in a process called nuclear fusion.

- **Nuclear fusion of element atoms** happens deep inside stars because of the pressure of their gravity.

> ★ STAR FACT ★
> Massive atoms like uranium and thorium are formed by the shock waves from supernovae.

- **Lighter elements** like oxygen and carbon formed first.

- **Helium nuclei** fused with oxygen and neon atoms to form atoms like silicon, magnesium and calcium.

- **Heavy atoms** like iron formed when massive supergiant stars neared the end of their life and collapsed, boosting the pressure of the gravity in their core hugely. Even now iron is forming inside dying supergiants.

▶ Nebulae like this one, Orion, contain many elements. Some (such as oxygen, silicon and carbon) formed in their stars, but their hydrogen and helium formed in deep space very long ago.

Kepler

▶ Despite almost losing his eyesight and the use of his hands through smallpox at the age of three, Johannes Kepler became an assistant to the great Danish astronomer Tycho Brahe, and took over his work when Brahe died.

- **Johannes Kepler** (1571-1630) was the German astronomer who discovered the basic rules about the way the planets move.

- **Kepler got his ideas** from studying Mars' movement.

- **Before Kepler's discoveries**, people thought that the planets moved in circles.

- **Kepler discovered** that the true shape of the planets' orbits is elliptical (oval). This is Kepler's first law.

- **Kepler's second law** is that the speed of a planet through space varies with its distance from the Sun.

- **A planet moves fastest** when its orbit brings it nearest to the Sun (called its perihelion). It moves slowest when it is furthest from the Sun (called its aphelion).

- **Kepler's third law** is that a planet's period – the time it takes to complete its yearly orbit of the Sun – depends on its distance from the Sun.

- **Kepler's third law states** that the square of a planet's period is proportional to the cube of its average distance from the Sun.

- **Kepler believed** that the planets made harmonious music as they moved – 'the music of the spheres'.

- **Kepler also wrote a book** about measuring how much wine there was in wine casks, which proved to be important for the mathematics of calculus.

Space shuttle

- **The space shuttle** is a reusable spacecraft, made up of a 37.2m-long orbiter, two big Solid Rocket Boosters (SRBs), three main engines and a tank.

- **The shuttle orbiter is launched** into space upright on the SRBs, which fall away to be collected for reuse. When the mission is over the orbiter lands like a glider.

- **The orbiter can only go** as high as a near-Earth orbit, some 300 km above the Earth.

- **The maximum crew** is eight, and a basic mission is seven days, during which the crew work in shirtsleeves.

- **Orbiter toilets** use flowing air to suck away waste.

- **The orbiter can carry** a 25,000kg-load in its cargo bay.

- **The first four orbiters** were named after old sailing ships – *Columbia, Challenger, Discovery* and *Atlantis*.

- **The three main engines** are used only for lift off. In space, the small Orbital Manoeuvring System (OMS) engines take over. The Reaction Control System (RCS) makes small adjustments to the orbiter's position.

- **The shuttle programme** was brought to a temporary halt in 1986, when the *Challenger* exploded shortly after launch, killing its crew of seven.

- **In 1994 the crew of *Discovery*** mended the Hubble space telescope in orbit.

▲ *The entire centre section of the orbiter is a cargo bay which can be opened in space so satellites can be placed in orbit.*

Moons

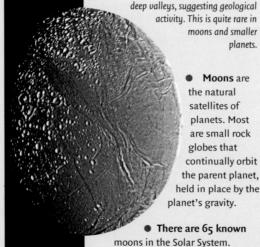

▼ *Saturn's moon Enceladus is marked by deep valleys, suggesting geological activity. This is quite rare in moons and smaller planets.*

- **Moons** are the natural satellites of planets. Most are small rock globes that continually orbit the parent planet, held in place by the planet's gravity.

- **There are 65 known** moons in the Solar System.

- **Every planet in the Solar System** has a moon, apart from Mercury and Venus, the nearest planets to the Sun.

- **New moons are frequently discovered**, as space probes such as the *Voyagers* reach distant planets.

- **Three moons** have atmospheres – Saturn's moon Titan, Jupiter's Io, and Neptune's Triton.

- **The largest moon** in the Solar System is Jupiter's moon Ganymede.

- **The second largest** is Saturn's moon Titan. This moon is rather like a small frozen Earth, with a rocky core beneath a cold, nitrogen atmosphere.

- **The smallest moons** are rocky lumps just a few kilometres across, rather like asteroids.

- **Saturn's moon Iapetus** is white on one side and black on the other.

- **Saturn's moon Enceladus** is only 500 km across, and glistens because it is covered in beads of ice.

Saturn

- **Saturn is the second biggest planet** in the Solar System – 815 times as big in volume as the Earth, and measuring 120,000 km around its equator.

- **Saturn takes 29 and a half years** to travel round the Sun, so Saturn's year is 29.46 Earth years. The planet's complete orbit is a journey of more than 4.5 billion km.

- **Winds ten times stronger than** a hurricane on Earth swirl around Saturn's equator, reaching up to 1,100 km/h – and they never let up, even for a moment.

- **Saturn is named after Saturnus**, the Ancient Roman god of seed-time and harvest. He was celebrated in the Roman's wild, Christmas-time festival of Saturnalia.

- **Saturn is not solid**, but is made almost entirely of gas – mostly liquid hydrogen and helium. Only in the planet's very small core is there any solid rock.

- **Because Saturn is so massive**, the pressure at its heart is enough to turn hydrogen solid. That is why there is a layer of metallic hydrogen around the planet's inner core of rock.

> ★ STAR FACT ★
> Saturn is so low in density that if you could find a bath big enough, you would be able to float the planet in the water.

- **Saturn is one of the fastest spinning** of all the planets. Despite its size, it rotates in just 11.5 hours – which means it turns round at over 10,000 km/h.

- **Saturn's surface appears** to be almost completely smooth, though *Voyager 1* and *2* did photograph a few small, swirling storms when they flew past.

- **Saturn has a very powerful magnetic field** (see magnetism) and sends out strong radio signals.

Saturn's rings are made of many millions of tiny, ice-coated rock fragments

◀ Saturn is the queen of the planets. Almost as big as Jupiter, and made largely of liquid hydrogen and helium, Saturn is stunningly beautiful, with its smooth, pale-butterscotch surface (clouds of ammonia) and its shimmering halo of rings. But it is a very secretive planet. Telescopes have never pierced its upper atmosphere, and data from the fly-bys of the Voyager probes focussed on its rings and moons. But the Cassini probe, launched in 1997, may change this when it eventually descends into Saturn's atmosphere.

Space stations

- **The first space station** was the Soviet *Salyut 1* launched in April 1971. Its low orbit meant it stayed up only five months.

- **The first US space station** was *Skylab*. Three crews spent 171 days in it in 1973-74.

- **The longest serving station** was the Soviet *Mir* – launched in 1986, it made more than 76,000 orbits of the Earth. The last crew left in late 1999.

- *Mir* **was built in stages.** It weighed 125 tonnes and had six docking ports and two living rooms, plus a bathroom and two small individual cabins.

- **There is neither an up nor a down** in a space station, but *Mir* had carpets on the 'floor', pictures on the 'wall' and lights on the 'ceiling'.

> **! NEWS FLASH !**
> The living space on the ISS will be bigger than the passenger space on two jumbo jets.

- **The giant International Space Station (ISS)** is being built in stages and should be complete in 2004.

- **The first crew** went on board the ISS in January 2000.

- **The ISS** will be 108 m long and 90 m wide, and weigh 450 tonnes.

- **In April 2001,** Dennis Tito became the first space tourist, ferried up to the ISS by the Russian Soyuz space shuttle.

▶ Mir *space station, photographed from the space shuttle Discovery in February 1995.*

Gravity

◀ *The Apollo astronauts' steps upon the Moon were the first human experience of another space object's gravity.*

- **Gravity** is the attraction, or pulling force, between all matter.

- **Gravity** is what holds everything on Earth on the ground and stops it flying off into space. It holds the Earth together, keeps the Moon orbiting the Earth, and the Earth and all the planets orbiting the Sun.

- **Gravity** makes stars burn by squeezing their matter together.

- **The force of gravity** is the same everywhere.

- **The force of gravity** depends on mass (the amount of matter in an object) and distance.

- **The more mass an object has**, and the closer it is to another object, the more strongly its gravity pulls.

- **Black holes** have the strongest gravitational pull in the entire Universe.

- **The basic laws of gravity** can be used for anything from detecting an invisible planet by studying the flickers in another star's light, to determining the flight of a space probe.

- **Einstein's theory of general relativity** shows that gravity not only pulls on matter, but also bends space and even time itself (see Einstein).

- **Orbits are the result** of a perfect balance between the force of gravity on an object (which pulls it inward towards whatever it is orbiting), and its forward momentum (which keeps it flying straight onwards).

Light-years

- **Distances in space** are so vast that the fastest thing in the Universe – light – is used to measure them.

- **The speed of light** is about 300,000 km per second.

- **A light-second** is the distance light travels in a second – 299 million metres.

- **A light-year** is the distance light travels in one year – 9.46 trillion km. Light-years are one of the standard distance measurements in astronomy.

- **It takes about 8 minutes** for light from the Sun to reach us on Earth.

- **Light takes 5.46 years** to reach us from the Sun's nearest star, Proxima Centauri. This means the star is 5.46 light-years away – more than 51 trillion km.

- **We see Proxima Centauri** as it was 5.46 years ago, because its light takes 5.46 years to reach us.

- **The star Deneb** is 1,800 light-years away, which means we see it as it was when the emperor Septimus Severius was ruling in Rome (AD 200).

▲ Distances in space are so vast that they are measured in light-years, the distance light travels in a year.

- **With powerful telescopes**, astronomers can see galaxies 2 billion light-years away. This means we see them as they were when the only life forms on Earth were bacteria.

- **Parsecs** may also be used to measure distances. They originally came from parallax shift measurements (see distances). A light-year is 0.3066 parsecs.

Rotation

▶ Rotating galaxies are just part of the spinning, moving Universe.

- **Rotation is the normal motion** (movement) of most space objects. Rotate means 'spin'.

- **Stars spin**, planets spin, moons spin and galaxies spin – even atoms spin.

- **Moons rotate** around planets, and planets rotate around stars.

- **The Earth rotates** once every 23.93 hours. This is called its rotation period.

- **We do not feel the Earth's rotation** – that it is hurtling around the Sun, while the Sun whizzes around the galaxy – because we are moving with it.

- **Things rotate because** they have kinetic (movement) energy. They cannot fly away because they are held in place by gravity, and the only place they can go is round.

- **The fastest rotating planet** is Saturn, which turns right around once every 10.23 hours.

- **The slowest rotating planet** is Venus, which takes 243.01 days to turn around.

- **The Sun takes 25.4 days** to rotate, but since the Earth is going around it too, it seems to take 27.27 days.

★ STAR FACT ★
The fastest spinning objects in the Universe are neutron stars – these can rotate 500 times in just one second!

Uranus

▼ Uranus is the third largest planet in the Solar System – 51,118 km across and with a mass 14.54 times that of the Earth's. The planet spins round once every 17.24 hours, but because it is lying almost on its side, this has almost no effect on the length of its day. Instead, this depends on where the planet is in its orbit of the Sun. Like Saturn, Uranus has rings, but they are much thinner and were only detected in 1977. They are made of the darkest material in the Solar System.

- **Uranus is the seventh planet** out from the Sun. Its orbit keeps it 1,784 million km away on average and takes 84 years to complete.

- **Uranus tilts so far on its side** that it seems to roll around the Sun like a gigantic bowling ball. The angle of its tilt is 98°, in fact, so its equator runs top to bottom. This tilt may be the result of a collision with a meteor or another planet a long time ago.

- **In summer on Uranus,** the Sun does not set for 20 years. In winter, darkness lasts for over 20 years. In autumn, the Sun rises and sets every 9 hours.

- **Uranus has over 20 moons,** all named after characters in William Shakespeare's plays. There are five large moons – Ariel, Umbriel, Titania, Oberon and Miranda. The ten smaller ones were discovered by the *Voyager 2* space probe in 1986.

- **Uranus's moon Miranda** is the weirdest moon of all. It seems to have been blasted apart, then put itself back together again!

- **Because Uranus is so far from the Sun,** it is very, very cold, with surface temperatures dropping to -210°C. Sunlight takes just 8 minutes to reach Earth, but 2.5 hours to reach Uranus.

- **Uranus's icy atmosphere** is made of hydrogen and helium. Winds whistle around the planet at over 2,000 km/h – ten times as fast as hurricanes on Earth.

- **Uranus's surface** is an ice-cold ocean of liquid methane (natural gas), thousands of kilometres deep, which gives the planet its beautiful colour. If you fell into this ocean even for a fraction of a second, you would freeze so hard that you would shatter like glass.

- **Uranus is only faintly visible** from Earth. It looks no bigger than a star through a telescope, and was not identified until 1781 (see Herschel).

- **Uranus was named** after Urania, the Ancient Greek goddess of astronomy.

The planet's surface of liquid methane gives it a stunning blue colour

Uranus has an atmosphere of hydrogen and helium gas

Uranus has its own, very faint set of rings

> ★ STAR FACT ★
> On Uranus in spring, the Sun sets every 9 hours – backwards!

Solar eruptions

- **Solar flares** are sudden eruptions on the Sun's surface. They flare up in just a few minutes, then take more than half an hour to die away again.

- **Solar flares reach temperatures** of 10 million °C and have the energy of a million atom bombs.

- **Solar flares not only send out** heat and radiation, but also streams of charged particles.

- **The solar wind** is the stream of charged particles that shoots out from the Sun in all directions at speeds of over a million km/h. It reaches the Earth in 21 hours, but also blows far throughout the Solar System.

- **Every second** the solar wind carries away over a million tonnes of charged particles from the Sun.

- **Earth is shielded** from the lethal effects of the solar wind by its magnetic field (see magnetism).

- **Solar prominences** are gigantic, flame-like tongues of hot hydrogen that sometimes spout out from the Sun.

- **Solar prominences** reach temperatures of 10,000°C.

- **Coronal mass ejections** are gigantic eruptions of charged particles from the Sun, creating gusts in the solar wind which set off magnetic storms on Earth.

- **Magnetic storms** are massive hails of charged particles that hit the Earth every few years or so, setting the atmosphere buzzing with electricity.

▼ Solar prominences can loop as far as 100,000 km out from the Sun's surface.

Jupiter's Galilean moons

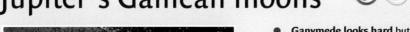

▲ Io's yellow glow comes from sulphur, which is spewed as far as 300 km upwards by the moon's volcanoes.

- **The Galilean moons** are the four biggest of Jupiter's 21 moons. They were discovered by Galileo, centuries before astronomers identified the other, smaller ones.

- **Ganymede is the biggest** of the Galilean moons – at 5,268 km across, it is larger than the planet Mercury.

- **Ganymede looks hard** but under its shell of solid ice is 900 km of slushy, half-melted ice and water.

- **Callisto is the second biggest**, at 4,806 km across.

- **Callisto is scarred** with craters from bombardments early in the Solar System's life.

- **Io is the third biggest**, at 3,642 km across.

- **Io's surface is a mass of volcanoes**, caused by it being stretched and squeezed by Jupiter's massive gravity.

- **The smallest** of the Galilean moons is Europa, at 3,138 km across.

- **Europa is covered in ice** and looks like a shiny, honey-coloured billiard ball from a distance – but a close-up view reveals countless cracks in its surface.

> ★ STAR FACT ★
> A crater called Valhalla on Callisto is so big it makes the moon look like a giant eyeball.

Tides

- **Ocean tides** are the twice daily rise and fall of the water level in the Earth's oceans.
- **Ocean tides on Earth are created** by the gravitational pull of the Moon and the Sun.
- **The Moon's pull** creates two bulges in the oceans – one beneath it and one on the opposite side of the Earth.
- **As the Earth spins**, the tidal bulges seem to move around the world, creating two high tides every day.
- **Spring tides** are very high tides that happen when the Sun and Moon are in line, and combine their pull.
- **Neap tides** are small tides that happen when the Sun and Moon are at right angles to the Earth and their pulls are weakened by working against one another.
- **The solid Earth has tides too,** but they are very slight and the Earth moves only about 0.5 m.
- **Tides are also any upheaval** created by the pull of gravity, as one space object orbits another.

- **Moons orbiting** large planets undergo huge tidal pulls. Jupiter's moon Io is stretched so much that its interior is heated enough to create volcanoes.
- **Whole galaxies** can be affected by tidal pulls, making them stretch this way and that as they are tugged by the gravitational pull of other, passing galaxies.

▼ As the Earth spins beneath the Moon, its oceans and seas are lifted by the Moon's gravity into tides.

Binary stars

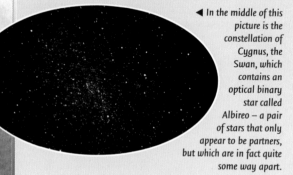

◀ In the middle of this picture is the constellation of Cygnus, the Swan, which contains an optical binary star called Albireo – a pair of stars that only appear to be partners, but which are in fact quite some way apart.

- **Our Sun is alone** in space, but most stars have one, two or more starry companions.
- **Binaries are double stars**, and there are various kinds.
- **True binary stars** are two stars held together by one another's gravity, which spend their lives whirling around together like a pair of dancers.

- **Optical binaries** are not really binaries at all. They are simply two stars that look as if they are together because they are in roughly the same line of sight from the Earth.
- **Eclipsing binaries** are true binary stars that spin round in exactly the same line of sight from Earth. This means they keep blocking out one another's light.
- **Spectroscopic binaries** are true binaries that spin so closely together that the only way we can tell there are two stars is by changes in colour.
- **The star Epsilon** in the constellation of Lyra is called the Double Double, because it is a pair of binaries.
- **Mizar, in the Great Bear,** was the first binary star to be discovered.
- **Mizar's companion Alcor** is an optical binary star.
- **Albireo in Cygnus** is an optical binary visible to the naked eye – one star looks gold, the other, blue.

Halley's comet

▲ *This photograph of Halley's comet was taken in 1986, when it last came close to the Earth.*

- **Halley's comet** is named after the British scientist Edmund Halley (1656-1742).
- **Halley predicted** that this particular comet would return in 1758, 16 years after his death. It was the first time a comet's arrival had been predicted.
- **Halley's comet** orbits the Sun every 76 years.

- **Its orbit** loops between Mercury and Venus, and stretches out beyond Neptune.
- **Halley's comet last** came in sight in 1986. Its next visit will be in 2062.
- **The Chinese** described a visit of Halley's comet as long ago as 240 BC.
- **When Halley's comet** was seen in AD 837, Chinese astronomers wrote that its head was as bright as Venus and its tail stretched right through the sky.
- **Harold, King of England,** saw the comet in 1066. When he was defeated by William the Conqueror a few months later, people took the comet's visit as an evil omen.
- **Halley's comet** was embroidered on the Bayeux tapestry, which shows Harold's defeat by William.

> ★ STAR FACT ★
> Halley's comet was seen in about 8 BC, so some say it was the Bible's Star of Bethlehem.

Asteroids

- **Asteroids** are lumps of rock that orbit the Sun. They are sometimes called the minor planets.
- **Most asteroids** are in the Asteroid belt, which lies between Mars and Jupiter.
- **Some distant asteroids** are made of ice and orbit the Sun beyond Neptune.
- **A few asteroids** come near the Earth. These are called Near Earth Objects (NEOs).
- **The first asteroid to be discovered** was Ceres in 1801. It was detected by Giuseppi Piazzi, one of the Celestial Police whose mission was to find a 'missing' planet.
- **Ceres** is the biggest asteroid – 940 km across, and 0.0002% the size of the Earth.

> ★ STAR FACT ★
> Every 50 million years, the Earth is hit by an asteroid measuring over 10 km across.

▼ *Most asteroids – more than half a million – orbit the Sun in the Asteroid belt, between Mars and Jupiter.*

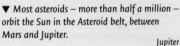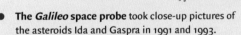

Jupiter

Asteroid belt

Mars

- **The *Galileo* space probe** took close-up pictures of the asteroids Ida and Gaspra in 1991 and 1993.
- **There are half a million or so** asteroids bigger than 1 km across. More than 200 asteroids are over 100 km across.
- **The Trojan asteroids** are groups of asteroids that follow the same orbit as Jupiter. Many are named after warriors in the Ancient Greek tales of the Trojan wars.

Solar changes

- **The Sun is about 5 billion years old** and half way through its life – as a medium-sized star it will probably live for around 10 billion years.

- **Over the next few billion years** the Sun will brighten and swell until it is twice as bright and 50% bigger.

- **In 5 billion years**, the Sun's hydrogen fuel will have

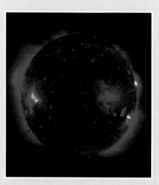

◀ The Sun seems to burn so steadily that we take for granted that it will be equally bright and warm all the time. In the short term, however, its brightness does seem to vary very slightly all the time, and over the next 5 billion years it will probably burn more and more ferociously.

burned out, and its core will start to shrink.

- **As its core shrinks**, the rest of the Sun will swell up with gases and its surface will become cooler and redder. It will be a red giant star.

- **The Earth will have been burned** to a cinder long before the Sun is big enough to swallow it up completely.

- **The Sun will end** as a white dwarf.

- **The Sun's brightness varies**, but it was unusually dim and had no sunspots between 1645 and 1715 – this period is called the Maunder minimum. The Earth suffered the Little Ice Age at this time.

- **More of the chemical carbon-14** is made on Earth when the Sun is more active. The carbon-14 is taken into trees, which means scientists can work out changes in solar activity in the past by measuring carbon-14 in old wood.

- **The SOHO space observatory** is stationed between the Earth and the Sun, monitoring the Sun to find out about changes in solar activity.

Star birth

▲ Stars are born in vast clouds of dust and gas, like this, an eagle nebula.

- **Stars are being born** and dying all over the Universe, and by looking at stars in different stages of their life, astronomers have worked out their life stories.

- **Medium-sized stars** last for about 10 billion years. Small stars may last for 200 billion years.

- **Big stars** have short, fierce lives of 10 million years.

- **Stars start life** in clouds of gas and dust called nebulae.

- **Inside nebulae**, gravity creates dark clumps called dark nebulae, each clump containing the seeds of a family of stars.

- **As gravity squeezes** the clumps in dark nebulae, they become hot.

- **Smaller clumps** never get very hot and eventually fizzle out. Even if they start burning, they lose surface gas and shrink to wizened, old white dwarf stars.

- **If a larger clump** reaches 10 million °C, hydrogen atoms in its core begin to join together in nuclear reactions, and the baby star starts to glow.

- **In a medium-sized star** like our Sun, the heat of burning hydrogen pushes gas out as fiercely as gravity pulls inwards, and the star becomes stable (steady).

- **Medium-sized stars** burn steadily until all of their hydrogen fuel is used up.

Neptune

▼ Neptune is the fourth largest planet. At 49,528 km across, it is slightly smaller than Uranus – but it is actually a little heavier. Like Uranus, its oceans of incredibly cold liquid methane make it a beautiful shiny blue, although Neptune's surface is a deeper blue than that of Uranus. Again like Uranus, Neptune has a thin layer of rings. But Neptune's are level, and not at right angles to the Sun. Neptune has a Great Dark Spot, like Jupiter's Great Red Spot, where storms whip up swirling clouds.

- **Neptune is the eighth** planet out from the Sun, varying in distance from 4,456 to 4,537 million km.

- **Neptune was discovered** in 1846 because two mathematicians, John Couch Adams in England and Urbain le Verrier in France, worked out that it must be there because of the effect of its gravity on the movement of Uranus.

- **Neptune is so far** from the Sun that its orbit lasts 164.79 Earth years. Indeed, it has not yet completed one orbit since it was discovered in 1846.

Great Dark Spot

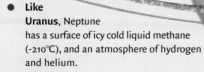

- **Like Uranus**, Neptune has a surface of icy cold liquid methane (-210°C), and an atmosphere of hydrogen and helium.

- **Unlike Uranus,** which is almost perfectly blue, Neptune has white clouds, created by heat inside the planet.

- **Neptune has the strongest winds** in the solar system, blowing at up to 700 m per second.

- **Neptune has eight moons**, each named after characters from Ancient Greek myths – Naiad, Thalassa, Despoina, Galatea, Larissa, Proteus, Triton and Nereid.

- **Neptune's moon Triton** looks like a green melon, while its icecaps of frozen nitrogen look like pink ice cream. It also has volcanoes that erupt fountains of ice.

- **Triton is the only moon** to orbit backwards.

▶ This photo of Neptune was taken by the Voyager 2 spacecraft in 1989. The Great Dark Spot, and the little white tail of clouds named Scooter by astronomers, are both clearly visible.

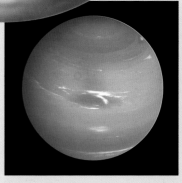

Atoms

- **Atoms are the building blocks** of the Universe, the invisibly small particles from which matter is made.

- **Atoms are so small** that you could fit a billion on the full stop at the end of this sentence.

- **Atoms** are the very smallest identifiable piece of a chemical element (see elements).

- **There are** as many different atoms as elements.

- **Atoms are mostly empty space** dotted with tiny sub-atomic particles (subatomic is 'smaller than an atom').

- **The core of an atom** is a nucleus made of a cluster of two kinds of subatomic particle – protons and neutrons.

- **Whizzing around the nucleus** are even tinier particles called electrons.

- **Electrons have** a negative electrical charge, and protons have a positive charge, so electrons are held to the nucleus by electrical attraction.

- **Under certain conditions** atoms can be split into over 200 kinds of short-lived subatomic particle. The particles of the nucleus are made from various even tinier particles called quarks.

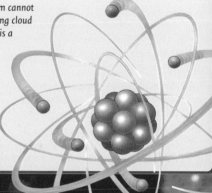

▶ This diagram cannot show the buzzing cloud of energy that is a real atom! Electrons (blue) whizz around the nucleus, made of protons (green) and neutrons (red).

> ★ STAR FACT ★
> Quarks came into existence in the very first few seconds of the Universe.

Observatories

- **Observatories** are special places where astronomers study space and, to give the best view of the night sky, most are built on mountain tops far from city lights.

- **One of the largest observatory complexes** is 4,200 m above sea level, in the crater of the extinct Hawaiian volcano, Mauna Kea.

- **In most observatories**, telescopes are housed in a dome-roofed building which turns around so they can keep aiming at the same stars while the Earth rotates.

▶ The Kitt Peak National Observatory in Arizona, USA.

- **The oldest existing observatory** is the Tower of the Winds in Athens, Greece, which dates from 100 BC.

- **In the imperial observatory** in Beijing, China, there are 500-year-old, bronze astronomical instruments.

- **One of the oldest** working observatories is London's Royal Greenwich Observatory, founded in 1675.

- **The highest observatory** on the Earth is 4,300 m above sea level, at Denver, Colorado, in the USA.

- **The lowest observatory** is 1.7 km below sea level, in Homestake Mine, Dakota, USA. Its 'telescope' is actually tanks of cleaning fluid which trap neutrinos from the Sun (see cosmic rays) .

- **The first photographs** of the stars were taken in 1840. Nowadays, most observatories rely on photographs rather than on the eyes of astronomers.

- **Observatory photographs are made** using sensors called Charge-Coupled Devices (CCDs) which give off an electrical signal when struck by light.

Voyagers 1 and 2

▲ Voyager 2 reached Neptune in 1989, revealing a wealth of new information about this distant planet.

- **The *Voyagers*** are a pair of unmanned US space probes, launched to explore the outer planets.

- ***Voyager 1*** was launched on 5 September 1977. It flew past Jupiter in March 1979 and Saturn in November 1980, then headed onwards on a curved path that will take it out of the Solar System altogether.

- ***Voyager 2*** travels more slowly. Although launched two weeks earlier than *Voyager 1*, it did not reach Jupiter until July 1979 and Saturn until August 1981.

- **The *Voyagers*** used the 'slingshot' of Jupiter's gravity (see space probes) to hurl them on towards Saturn.

- **While *Voyager 1* headed out** of the Solar System, *Voyager 2* flew past Uranus in January 1986.

- ***Voyager 2* also passed** Neptune on 24 August 1989. It took close-up photographs of the two planets.

- **The *Voyagers*** revealed volcanoes on Io, one of Jupiter's Galilean moons.

- ***Voyager 2*** found ten unknown moons around Uranus.

- ***Voyager 2*** found six unknown moons and three rings around Neptune.

> **! NEWS FLASH !**
> *Voyager 2* will beam back data until 2020 as it travels beyond the edges of the Solar System.

Space exploration

- **Space is explored** in two ways – by studying it from Earth using powerful telescopes, and by launching spacecraft to get a closer view.

- **Most space exploration** is by unmanned space probes.

- **The first pictures** of the far side of the Moon were sent back by the *Luna 3* space probe in October 1959.

- **Manned missions** have only reached as far as the Moon, but there may be a manned mission to Mars in 2005.

- **Apollo astronauts** took three days to reach the Moon.

- **No space probe** has ever come back from another planet.

- **Travel to the stars** would take hundreds of years, but one idea is that humans might go there inside gigantic spaceships made from hollowed-out asteroids.

- **Another idea is that spacecraft** on long voyages of exploration may be driven along by pulses of laser light.

- **The *Pioneer 10* and *11* probes** carry metal plaques with messages for aliens telling them about us.

▼ Most space exploration is by unmanned probes, guided by on-board computers and equipped with various devices which feed data back to Earth via radio signals.

> **! NEWS FLASH !**
> NASA may fund research on spacecraft that jump to the stars through wormholes (see black holes).

Pluto

- **When it was discovered in 1930**, Pluto became the ninth planet, but it was by far the smallest.

- **Since 2006**, Pluto has been classified as a dwarf planet by the International Astronomical Union (IAU).

- **This new ruling** was further strengthened by the discovery of more objects of similar size to Pluto in the outer Solar System.

- **Pluto is further out** than the main planets, orbiting between 4437 and 7376 million km from the Sun.

- **At this distance**, Pluto takes 248 years to travel once around the Sun, even at an average speed of 17,100 km/h. It spins around in 6.4 Earth days, so its day lasts nearly as long as an Earth week.

- **Its orbit is squashed** into an oval shape, less circular than the eight main planets, and it is also tilted. This brings Pluto closer to the Sun than Neptune for about 20 years in each orbit.

- **Unlike its gas giant neighbours**, Pluto is a tiny ball of rock covered by ice, with frozen methane on the surface.

- **When nearest to the Sun**, Pluto has a very thin atmosphere, but when it is further away, the atmosphere freezes into ice on the surface.

★ STAR FACT ★
Pluto was discovered on 18 February 1930 by American astronomer Clyde Tombaugh.

- **In 1978, American astronomer James Christy** discovered that Pluto had a large moon, which was named Charon. Then in 2005, two tiny moons, Nix and Hydra, were discovered.

- **Two other dwarf planets** have been named, Ceres and Eris. Ceres is the largest of the asteroids between Mars and Jupiter. Eris is slightly larger than Pluto.

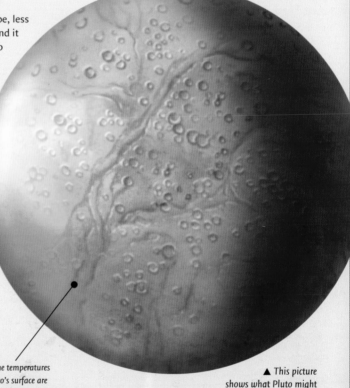

▼ Pluto is tiny in comparison to the Earth, which is why it was hard to find. Earth is five times bigger and 500 times as heavy. This illustration shows the relative sizes of the Earth and Pluto.

Daytime temperatures on Pluto's surface are -220°C or less, so the surface is thought to be coated in frozen methane.

▲ This picture shows what Pluto might look like. It is so small and far away that photographs from the Hubble space telescope show very little detail. Dark and light patches can be seen, but astronomers don't know what these indicate. However, a twinkling of starlight around the edge of Pluto shows that it must have some kind of atmosphere.

Einstein

▲ Einstein's theory of general relativity was proved right in 1919, when light rays from a distant star just grazing the Sun were measured during an eclipse and shown to be slightly bent.

- **The great scientist Albert Einstein** (1879-1955) is most famous for creating the two theories of relativity.

- **Special relativity** (1905) shows that all measurements are relative, including time and speed. In other words, time and speed depend on where you measure them.

- **The fastest thing in the Universe**, light, is the same speed everywhere and always passes at the same speed – no matter where you are or how fast you are going.

- **Special relativity** shows that as things travel faster, they seem to shrink in length and get heavier. Their time stretches too – that is, their clocks seem to run slower.

- **The theory of general relativity** (1915) includes the idea of special relativity, but also shows how gravity works.

- **General relativity** shows that gravity's pull is acceleration (speed) – gravity and acceleration are the same.

- **When things are falling** their acceleration cancels out gravity, which is why astronauts in orbit are weightless.

- **If gravity and acceleration** are the same, gravity must bend light rays simply by stretching space (and time).

- **Gravity works by bending space** (and time). 'Matter tells space how to bend; space tells matter how to move.'

- **General relativity** predicts that light rays from distant stars will be bent by the gravitational pull of stars they pass.

Space telescopes

- **Space telescopes** are launched as satellites so we can study the Universe without interference from Earth's atmosphere.

- **The first space telescope** was Copernicus, sent up in 1972.

- **The most famous** is the Hubble space telescope, launched from a space shuttle in 1990.

- **Different space telescopes** study all the different forms of radiation that make up the electromagnetic spectrum (see light).

- **The COBE satellite** picks up microwave radiation which may be left over from the Big Bang.

- **The IRAS satellite** studied infrared radiation from objects as small as space dust.

- **Space telescopes** that have studied ultraviolet rays from the stars include the International Ultraviolet Explorer (IUE), launched in 1978.

- **Helios** was one of many space telescopes studying the Sun.

- **X-rays** can only be picked up by space telescopes such as the Einstein, ROSAT and SXTE satellites.

- **Gamma rays** can only be picked up by space telescopes like the Compton Gamma-Ray Observatory.

▼ The Hubble space telescope's main mirror was faulty when it was launched, but a replacement was fitted by shuttle astronauts in 1994.

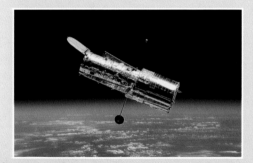

Radio telescopes

- **Radio telescopes** are telescopes that pick up radio waves instead of light waves.
- **Radio telescopes**, like reflecting telescopes (see telescopes), have a big dish to collect and focus data.
- **At the centre of its dish**, a radio telescope has an antenna which picks up radio signals.
- **Because radio waves** are much longer than light waves, radio telescope dishes are very big – often as much as 100 m across.
- **Instead of one big dish**, some radio telescopes use an array (collection) of small, linked dishes. The further apart the dishes are, the sharper the image.
- **The Very Long Baseline Array** (VLBA) is made of ten dishes scattered all the way across the USA.

◄ Many radio telescopes use an array of dishes linked by a process called interferometry.

- **Radio astronomy** led to the discovery of pulsars and background radiation from the Big Bang.
- **Radio galaxies** are very distant and only faintly visible (if at all), but they can be detected because they give out radio waves.
- **Radio astronomy** proved that the Milky Way is a disc-shaped galaxy with spiralling arms.

★ STAR FACT ★
At 305 m across, the Arecibo radio telescope in Puerto Rico is the largest dish telescope in the world.

Astronauts

▼ To cope with the demands of space missions and to help them deal with weightlessness, astronauts undergo tough physical training. They also spend long hours in simulators and jet aircraft.

- **The very first astronauts** were jet pilots.
- **Astronauts** must be extremely fit and also have very good eyesight.
- **The American** space agency NASA trains its astronauts at the Johnson Space Center near Houston, Texas.

- **The US space shuttle** carries three kinds of astronaut – pilots, mission specialists and payload specialists.
- **The pilot or commander's job** is to head the mission and control the spacecraft.
- **Mission specialists** are crew members who carry out specific jobs, such as running experiments or going on space walks.
- **Payload specialists** are not NASA astronauts, but scientists and other on-board guests.
- **Astronauts learn** SCUBA diving to help them deal with space walks.
- **During training**, astronauts experience simulated (imitation) weightlessness – first in a plunging jet aircraft, and then in a water tank. They are also exposed to very high and very low atmospheric pressure.
- **Weightlessness** makes astronauts grow several centimetres during a long mission.

Space catalogues

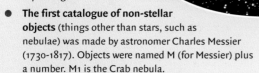

- **Astronomers list the stars** in each constellation according to their brightness, using the Greek alphabet (see constellations). So the brightest star in the constellation of Pegasus is Alpha Pegasi.

- **The first catalogue of non-stellar objects** (things other than stars, such as nebulae) was made by astronomer Charles Messier (1730-1817). Objects were named M (for Messier) plus a number. M1 is the Crab nebula.

- **Messier published a list** of 103 objects in 1781, and by 1908 the catalogue had grown to 15,000 entries.

- **Many of the objects** originally listed by Messier as nebulae are now known to be galaxies.

- **Today the standard list of non-stellar objects** is the

◀ With such an infinite number of stars, galaxies and nebulae in the night sky, astronomers need very detailed catalogues so they can locate each object reliably and check whether it has already been investigated.

New General Catalogue of nebulae and star clusters (NGC). First published in 1888, this soon ran to over 13,000 entries.

- **Many objects** are in both the Messier and the NGC and therefore have two numbers.

- **The Andromeda galaxy** is M31 and NGC224.

- **Radio sources** are listed in similar catalogues, such as Cambridge University's 3C catalogue.

- **The first quasar** to be discovered was 3c 48.

- **Many pulsars** are now listed according to their position by right ascension and declination (see celestial sphere).

Space travel

- **The first artificial satellite**, the Soviet *Sputnik 1*, was launched into space in 1957.

- **The first living creature** in space was the dog Laika on-board *Sputnik 2* in 1957. Sadly, she died when the spacecraft's oxygen supply ran out.

- **The first manned space flight** was made in April 1961 by the Soviet cosmonaut Yuri Gagarin, in *Vostok 1*.

- **The first controlled Moon landing** was made by the Soviet *Luna 9*, in February 1966.

- **In 1970, the Soviet** *Venera 7* was the first probe to touch down on another planet.

- **The Soviet robot vehicles**, the Lunokhods, were driven 47 km across the Moon in the early 1970s.

! NEWS FLASH !
The Lockheed Martin X33 was to make trips into space almost as easy as aeroplane flights, but the project has recently been cancelled.

- **The coming of the space shuttle** in 1981 made working in orbit much easier.

- **Some cosmonauts** have spent over 12 continuous months in space on-board the Mir space station.

- **Cosmonaut Valeri Poliakov** spent 437 days on-board the Mir space station.

▶ One problem facing a spacecraft returning to Earth is the heat produced by friction as it re-enters the Earth's atmosphere. Here you can see scorched, heatproof tiles on the underside of the shuttle.

Astronomy

- **Astronomy is the study of the night sky** – from the planets and moons to the stars and galaxies.

- **Astronomy** is the most ancient of all the sciences, dating back tens of thousands of years.

- **The Ancient Egyptians** used their knowledge of astronomy to work out their calendar and to align the pyramids.

- **The word astronomy** comes from the Ancient Greek words *astro* meaning 'star' and *nomia* meaning 'law'.

- **Astronomers** use telescopes to study objects far fainter and smaller than can be seen with the naked eye.

- **Space objects** give out other kinds of radiation besides light, and astronomers have special equipment to detect this (see radio and space telescopes).

- **Professional astronomers** usually study photographs and computer displays instead of staring through telescopes, because most faint space objects only show up on long-exposure photographs.

- **Astronomers can spot** new objects in the night sky by laying a current photograph over an old one and looking for differences.

- **Professional astronomy** involves sophisticated equipment, but amateurs with binoculars can still occasionally make some important discoveries.

▶ Most astronomers work in observatories far from city lights, where they can get a very clear view of the night sky.

Stars

▲ The few thousand stars visible to the naked eye are just a tiny fraction of the trillions in the Universe.

- **Stars are balls** of mainly hydrogen and helium gas.

- **Nuclear reactions** in the heart of stars, like those in atom bombs, generate heat and light.

- **The heart of a star** reaches 16 million°C. A grain of sand this hot would kill someone 150 km away.

- **The gas in stars** is in a special hot state called plasma, which is made of atoms stripped of electrons.

- **In the core of a star**, hydrogen nuclei fuse (join together) to form helium. This nuclear reaction is called a proton-proton chain.

- **Stars twinkle** because we see them through the wafting of the Earth's atmosphere.

- **Astronomers work out how big a star is** from its brightness and its temperature.

- **The size and brightness** of a star depends on its mass – that is, how much gas it is made of. Our Sun is a medium-sized star, and no star has more than 100 times the Sun's mass or less than 6-7% of its mass.

- **The coolest stars**, such as Arcturus and Antares, glow reddest. Hotter stars are yellow and white. The hottest are blue-white, like Rigel and Zeta Puppis.

- **The blue supergiant Zeta Puppis** has a surface temperature of 40,000°C, while Rigel's is 10,000°C.

The Sun

- **The Sun** is a medium-sized star measuring 1,392,000 km across – 100 times the diameter of the Earth.

- **The Sun weighs** 2,000 trillion trillion tonnes – about 300,000 times as much as the Earth – even though it is made almost entirely of hydrogen and helium, the lightest gases in the Universe.

- **The Sun's interior** is heated by nuclear reactions to temperatures of 15 million°C.

- **The visible surface layer of the Sun** is called the photosphere. This sea of boiling gas sends out the light and heat we see and feel on Earth.

- **Above the photosphere** is the chromosphere, a thin layer through which dart tongues of flame called spicules, making the chromosphere look like a flaming forest.

- **Above the chromosphere** is the Sun's halo-like corona.

- **The heat from the Sun's interior** erupts on the surface in patches called granules, and gigantic, flame-like tongues of hot gases called solar prominences (see solar eruptions).

- **The Sun gets hot** because it is so big that the pressure in its core is tremendous – enough to force the nuclei of hydrogen atoms to fuse (join together) to make helium atoms. This nuclear fusion reaction is like a gigantic atom bomb and it releases huge amounts of heat.

- **Halfway out from its centre** to its surface, the Sun is about as dense as water. Two-thirds of the way out, it is as dense as air.

- **The nuclear fusion reactions** in the Sun's core send out billions of light photons every minute (see light) – but they take 10 million years to reach its surface.

▶ *This artificially coloured photo was taken by a space satellite and shows the Sun's surface to be a turbulent mass of flames and tongues of hot gases – very different from the even, yellowish ball we see from Earth.*

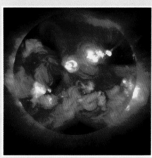

★ STAR FACT ★
The temperature of the Sun's surface is 6,000°C. Each centimetre burns with the brightness of 250,000 candles!

▶ *The Sun is not a simple ball of burning gases. It is made mostly of hydrogen and helium, but has many layers. It has a core, where most heat is made, then a number of layers building to the flaming chromosphere on its surface. Space observatories like SOHO (Solar and Heliospheric Observatory) have revealed a great deal about the Sun to astronomers.*

Nuclear energy

◄ The extraordinary power locked in the nucleus of atoms is shown when the explosion of an atom bomb releases some of the energy.

- **Nuclear energy** is the huge amount of energy that holds together the nucleus of every single atom.

- **Nuclear energy** fuels atom bombs and power stations – and every star in the Universe. It can be released either by fisson or fusion.

- **Nuclear fusion** is when nuclear energy is released by the joining together of nuclei – as inside stars, where they are squeezed together by gravity, and in hydrogen bombs.

- **Usually only tiny nuclei** such as those of hydrogen and helium fuse (join). Only under extreme pressure in huge, collapsing stars do big nuclei like iron fuse.

- **Nuclear fission** is when nuclear energy is released by the splitting of nuclei. This is the method used in most power stations and in atom bombs.

- **Nuclear fission** involves splitting big nuclei like Uranium-235 and plutonium.

- **When a nucleus splits**, it shoots out gamma rays, neutrons (see atoms) and intense heat.

- **In an atom bomb** the energy is released in one second.

- **In a power station**, control rods make sure nuclear reactions are slowed and energy released gradually.

> ★ STAR FACT ★
> The Hiroshima bomb released 84 trillion joules of energy. A supernova releases 125,000 trillion trillion times as much.

Supernova

- **A supernova** (plural supernovae) is the final, gigantic explosion of a supergiant star at the end of its life.

- **A supernova** lasts for just a week or so, but shines as bright as a galaxy of 100 billion ordinary stars.

- **Supernovae happen** when a supergiant star uses up its hydrogen and helium fuel and shrinks, boosting pressure in its core enough to fuse heavy elements such as iron (see nuclear energy).

- **When iron begins to fuse** in its core, a star collapses instantly – then rebounds in a mighty explosion.

- **Seen in 1987, supenova 1987A** was the first viewed with the naked eye since Kepler's 1604 sighting.

- **Supernova remnants** (leftovers) are the gigantic, cloudy shells of material swelling out from supernovae.

> ★ STAR FACT ★
> Many of the elements that make up your body were forged in supernovae.

- **A supernova** seen by Chinese astronomers in AD 184 was thought to be such a bad omen that it sparked off a palace revolution.

- **A dramatic supernova** was seen by Chinese astronomers in AD 1054 and left the Crab nebula.

- **Elements heavier** than iron were made in supernovae.

▼ Seeing a supernova is rare, but at any moment in time there is one happening somewhere in the Universe.

Red shift

- **When distant galaxies** are moving away from us, the very, very, fast light waves they give off are stretched out behind them – since each bit of the light wave is being sent from a little bit further away.

- **When the light waves** from distant galaxies are stretched out in this way, they look redder. This is called red shift.

- **Red shift** was first described by Czech mathematician Christian Doppler in 1842.

- **Edwin Hubble** showed that a galaxy's red shift is proportional to its distance. So the further away a galaxy is, the greater its red shift – and the faster it must be zooming away from us. This is Hubble's Law.

> ★ STAR FACT ★
> The most distant galaxies (quasars) have red shifts so big that they must be moving away from us at speeds approaching the speed of light!

▶ Massive red shifts reveal that the most distant objects in the Universe are flying away from us at absolutely astonishing speeds – often approaching the speed of light.

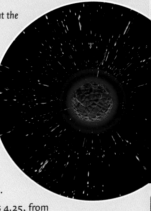

- **The increase of red shift** with distance proved that the Universe is growing bigger.

- **Only nearby galaxies** show no red shift at all.

- **The record red shift** is 4.25, from the quasar 8C 1435 + 63. It is 96% of the speed of light.

- **Red shift** can be caused by the expansion of the Universe, gravity or the effect of relativity (see Einstein).

- **Black holes** may create large red shifts.

Auroras

- **Auroras** are bright displays of shimmering light that appear at night over the North and South poles.

- **The Aurora Borealis** is the Northern Lights, the aurora that appears above the North Pole.

- **The Aurora Australis** is the Southern Lights, the aurora that appears above the South Pole.

▲ *The Northern Lights above the Arctic Circle are among nature's most beautiful sights. Shimmering, dancing curtains of colour – bright green rays flashing with red, and streamers of white – blaze into the darkness of the polar night.*

- **Auroras are caused** by streams of charged particles from the Sun known as the solar wind (see solar eruptions) crashing into the gases of the Earth's atmosphere.

- **Oxygen gas glows yellow-green** when it is hit low in the atmosphere, and orange higher up.

- **Nitrogen gas glows** bright red when hit normally, and bright blue when ionized.

- **Auroras form a halo of light** over the poles all the time, but they are usually too faint to see. They flare up brightly when extra bursts of energy reach the Earth's atmosphere from the Sun.

- **Auroras appear at the poles** and nowhere else in the world because there are deep cracks here in the Earth's magnetic field (see magnetism).

- **Auroras are more spectacular** when the solar wind is blowing strongly.

- **New York and Edinburgh** get an average of ten aurora displays every year.

The Moon

▼ Unlike the Earth's surface, which changes by the hour, the Moon's dusty, crater-pitted surface has remained much the same for billions of years. The only change happens when a meteorite smashes into it and creates a new crater.

▲ The Moon is the only other world that humans have ever set foot on. Because the Moon has no atmosphere or wind, the footprints planted in its dusty surface in 1969 by the Apollo astronauts are still there today, perfectly preserved.

● **Only the side of the Moon** lit by the Sun is bright enough to see. And because we see more of this side each month as the Moon orbits the Earth, and then less again, the Moon seems to change shape. These changes are called the Moon's phases.

● **During the first half of each monthly cycle**, the Moon waxes (grows) from a crescent-shaped new moon to a full moon. During the second half, it wanes (dwindles) back to a crescent-shaped old moon.

● **The Moon** is 384,400 km from the Earth and about 25% of Earth's size.

● **The Moon** orbits the Earth once every month, with each orbit taking 27.3 days. It spins round once on its axis every 720 hours.

● **The Moon** is the brightest object in the night sky, but it does not give out any light itself. It shines only because its light-coloured surface reflects sunlight.

● **A lunar month** is the time between one full moon and the next. This is slightly longer than the time the Moon takes to orbit the Earth because the Earth is also moving.

● **The Moon has no atmosphere** and its surface is simply white dust, pitted with craters created by meteorites smashing into it early in its history.

● **On the Moon's surface** are large, dark patches called seas – because that is what people once believed they were. They are, in fact, lava flows from ancient volcanoes.

● **One side of the Moon** is always turned away from us and is called its dark side. This is because the Moon spins round on its axis at exactly the same speed that it orbits the Earth.

> ★ **STAR FACT** ★
> The Moon's gravity is 17% of the Earth's, so astronauts in space suits can jump 4 m high!

Quasars

- **Quasars** are the most intense sources of light in the Universe. Although no bigger than the Solar System, they glow with the brightness of 100 galaxies.

- **Quasars are the most distant** known objects in the Universe. Even the nearest is billions of light-years away.

- **The most distant quasar** is on the very edges of the known Universe, 12 billion light-years away.

- **Some quasars** are so far away that we see them as they were when the Universe was still in its infancy – 20% of its current age.

- **Quasar** is short for Quasi-Stellar (star-like) Radio Object. This comes from the fact that the first quasars were detected by the strong radio signals they give out, and also because quasars are so small and bright that at first people thought they looked like stars.

- **Only one of the 200 quasars** now known actually beams out radio signals, so the term Quasi-Stellar Radio Object is in fact misleading!

- **The brightest** quasar is 3C 273, 2 billion light-years away.

- **Quasars** are at the heart of galaxies called 'active galaxies'.

- **Quasars** may get their energy from a black hole at their core, which draws in matter ferociously.

- **The black hole** in a quasar may pull in matter with the same mass as 100 million Suns.

▲ The Hubble space telescope's clear view of space has given the best-ever photographs of quasars. This is a picture of the quasar PKS2349, billions of light-years away.

Space walks

▲ An astronaut wearing an MMU can move completely independently in space.

- **The technical name** for going outside a spacecraft is Extra-Vehicular Activity (EVA).

- **In 1965** Soviet cosmonaut Alexei Leonov was the first person ever to walk in space.

- **The longest spells of EVA** were not floating about in space, but by Apollo astronauts walking on the Moon.

- **The first space walkers** were tied to their spacecraft by life-support cables.

- **Nowadays, most space walkers** use a Manned Manoeuvering Unit (MMU) – a huge, rocket-powered backpack that lets them move about freely.

- **In 1984**, US astronaut Bruce McCandless was the first person to use an MMU in space.

- **Damages to the *Mir* space station** and other satellites have been repaired by space-walking astronauts.

- **Russian and US astronauts** will perform more than 1,700 hours of space walks when building the International Space Station.

! NEWS FLASH !
Astronauts on space walks will be aided by a flying robot camera the size of a beach ball.

The night sky

- **The night sky** is brightened by the Moon and twinkling points of light.

- **Most lights** in the sky are stars. But moving, flashing lights may be satellites.

- **The brightest 'stars'** in the night sky are not actually stars at all, but the planets Jupiter, Venus, Mars and Mercury.

- **You can see** about 2,000 stars with the naked eye.

- **The pale band across** the middle of the sky is a side-on view of our own galaxy, the Milky Way.

◀ Look into the night sky and you can see about 2,000 stars twinkling above you (they twinkle because of the shimmering of heat in the Earth's atmosphere). With binoculars, you can see many more. Powerful telescopes reveal not just thousands of stars but millions. Even with the naked eye, though, some of the stars you see are trillions of kilometres away — and their light takes millions of years to reach us.

- **The pattern of stars** in the sky is fixed, but seems to rotate (turn) through the night sky as the Earth spins.

- **It takes 23 hours 56 minutes** for the star pattern to return to the same place in the sky.

- **As Earth orbits the Sun**, our view of the stars changes and the pattern starts in a different place each night.

- **Different patterns of stars** are seen in the northern hemisphere and the southern hemisphere.

> ★ STAR FACT ★
> You can see another galaxy besides the Milky Way with the naked eye – the Andromeda galaxy, over 2.2 million light-years away.

Water

- **Water is the only substance** on Earth which is commonly found as a solid, a liquid and a gas.

- **Over 70% of the Earth's surface** is covered in water.

- **Water is fundamental** (basic) to all life – 70% of our bodies is water.

- **Earth is the only planet** in the Solar System to have liquid water on its surface.

- **Neptune has a deep ocean** of ionized water beneath its icy surface of helium and hydrogen.

- **Dried-up river beds** show that Mars probably once had water on its surface. There is sometimes ice at the poles and may be water underground.

- **Jupiter's moon Europa** may have oceans of water beneath its icy surface, and it is a major target in the search for life in the Solar System.

- **In 1998** a space probe found signs of frozen water on the Moon, but they proved false.

- **Water is a compound** of the elements hydrogen and oxygen, with the chemical formula H_2O.

- **Water** is the only substance less dense (heavy) as a solid than as a liquid, which is why ice floats.

▼ There is a little water on the Moon, but Earth's blue colour shows it to be the real water planet of the solar system.

Galaxies

- **Galaxies are giant groups** of millions or even trillions of stars. Our own local galaxy is the Milky Way.

- **There may be 20 trillion** galaxies in the Universe.

- **Only three galaxies** are visible to the naked eye from Earth besides the Milky Way – the Large and Small Magellanic clouds, and the Andromeda galaxy.

- **Although galaxies are vast**, they are so far away that they look like fuzzy clouds. Only in 1916 did astronomers realize that they are huge star groups.

- **Spiral galaxies** are spinning, Catherine-wheel-like galaxies with a dense core and spiralling arms.

- **Barred spiral galaxies** have just two arms. These are linked across the galaxy's middle by a bar from which they trail like water from a spinning garden sprinkler.

> ★ STAR FACT ★
> Galaxies like the Small Magellanic Cloud may be the debris of mighty collisions between galaxies.

- **Elliptical galaxies** are vast, very old, egg-shaped galaxies, made up of as many as a trillion stars.

- **Irregular galaxies** are galaxies with no obvious shape. They may have formed from the debris of galaxies that crashed into each other.

- **Galaxies are often** found in groups called clusters. One cluster may have 30 or so galaxies in it.

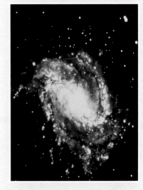

▲ Like our own Milky Way and the nearby Andromeda galaxy, many galaxies are spiral in shape, with a dense core of stars and long, whirling arms made up of millions of stars.

Radiation

- **Radiation** is energy shot out at high speed by atoms. There are two main forms – radioactivity and electromagnetic radiation.

- **Radiation either travels as waves** or as tiny particles called photons (see light).

- **Radioactivity** is when an atom decays (breaks down) and sends out deadly energy such as gamma rays.

- **Nuclear radiation** is the radiation from the radioactivity generated by atom bombs and power stations. In large doses, this can cause radiation sickness and death.

- **Electromagnetic radiation** is electric and magnetic fields (see magnetism) that move together in tiny bursts of waves or photons.

- **There are different kinds** of electromagnetic radiation, each one with a different wavelength.

- **Gamma rays** are a very short-wave, energetic and dangerous form of electromagnetic radiation.

- **Radio waves** are a long-wave, low-energy radiation.

- **In between these come** X-rays, ultraviolet rays, visible light, infrared rays and microwaves.

- **Together these forms of electromagnetic radiation** are called the electromagnetic spectrum. Visible light is the only part of the spectrum we can see with our eyes.

- **All electromagnetic rays** move at the speed of light – 300,000 km per second.

- **Everything we detect in space** is picked up by the radiation it gives out (see astronomy, the Big Bang and radio telescopes).

◄ The Sun throws out huge quantities of radiation of all kinds. Fortunately, our atmosphere protects us from the worst.

Mars landings

- **In the 1970s** the US *Vikings* 1 and 2 and the Soviet *Mars* 3 and 5 probes all reached the surface of Mars.

- **Mars 3** was the first probe to make a soft landing on Mars, on 2 December 1971, and sent back data for 20 seconds before being destroyed by a huge dust-storm.

- **Viking 1** sent back the first colour pictures from Mars, on 26 July 1976.

- **The aim of the Viking missions** was to find signs of life, but there were none. Even so, the *Viking* landers sent back plenty of information about the geology and atmosphere of Mars.

- **On 4 July 1997**, the US *Mars Pathfinder* probe arrived on Mars and at once began beaming back 'live' TV pictures from the planet's surface.

- **Mars Pathfinder** used air bags to cushion its landing on the planet's surface.

- **Two days after** the *Pathfinder* landed, it sent out a wheeled robot vehicle called the *Sojourner* to survey the surrounding area.

- **The Sojourner** showed a rock-strewn plain which looks as if it were once swept by floods.

- **Pathfinder and Sojourner** operated for 83 days and took more than 16,000 photos.

- **Missions to Mars** early in the 21st century will include the first return flight in 2010.

▶ The Mars Pathfinder mission provided many stunning images of the surface of the 'red planet', many taken by the Sojourner as it motored over the surface.

Telescopes

▶ This is the kind of reflecting telescope that many amateur astronomers use.

- **Optical telescopes** magnify distant objects by using lenses or mirrors to refract (bend) light rays so they focus (come together).

- **Other telescopes** detect radio waves (see radio telescopes), X-rays (see X-ray astronomy), or other kinds of electromagnetic radiation (see radiation).

- **Refracting telescopes** are optical telescopes that use lenses to refract the light rays.

- **Reflecting telescopes** are optical telescopes that refract light rays by reflecting them off curved mirrors.

- **Because the light rays** are folded, reflecting telescopes are shorter and fatter than refracting ones.

- **Most professional astronomers** do not gaze at the stars directly, but pick up what the telescope shows with light sensors called CCDs (see observatories).

- **Most early discoveries** in astronomy were made with refracting telescopes.

- **Modern observatories** use gigantic reflector dishes made up of hexagons of glass or coated metal.

- **Large telescope dishes** are continually monitored and tweaked by computers to make sure that the reflector's mirrored surface stays completely smooth.

> ★ STAR FACT ★
> Telescope dishes have to be made accurate to within 2 billionths of a millimetre.

Star charts

- **Plotting the positions** of the stars in the sky is a phenomenally complex business because there are a vast number of them and because they are at hugely different distances.

- **The first modern star charts** were the German Bonner Durchmusterung (BD) charts of 1859, which show the positions of 324,189 stars. The German word *durchmusterung* means 'scanning through'.

- **The AGK1 chart** of the German Astronomical was completed in 1912 and showed 454,000 stars.

- **The AGK charts** are now on version AGK3 and remain the standard star chart. They are compiled from photographs.

- **The measurements** of accurate places for huge numbers of stars depends on the careful determination of 1,535 stars in the Fundamental Catalog (FK3).

- **Photometric catalogues** map the stars by magnitude (see star brightness) and colour, as well as their position.

- **Photographic star atlases** do not actually plot the position of every star on paper, but include photos of them in place instead.

- **Three main atlases** are popular with astronomers – *Norton's Star Atlas*, which plots all stars visible to the naked eye; the *Tirion Sky Atlas*; and the photographic *Photographischer Stern-Atlas*.

- **Celestial coordinates** are the figures that plot a star's position on a ball-shaped graph (see celestial sphere). The altazimuth system of coordinates gives a star's position by its altitude (its angle in degrees from the horizon) and its azimuth (its angle in degrees clockwise around the horizon, starting from north). The ecliptic system does the same, using the ecliptic rather than the horizon as a starting point. The equatorial system depends on the celestial equator, and gives figures called right ascensions and declination, just like latitude and longitude on Earth.

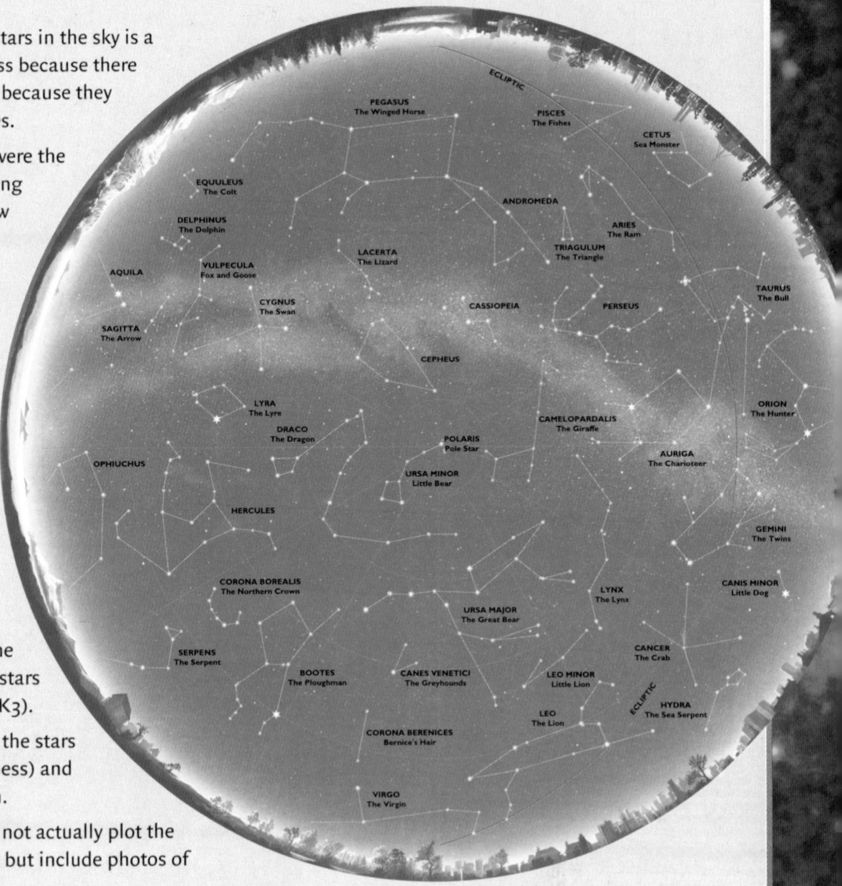

▲ The basic map of the sky shows the 88 constellations that are visible at some time during the year from each hemisphere (half) of the world. This picture shows the northern constellations visible in December.

★ STAR FACT ★
The star patterns we call constellations were the basis of the first star charts, dating back to the 2nd millennium BC. Even today astronomers divide the sky into 88 constellations, whose patterns are internationally recognized – even though the names of many constellations are the mythical ones given to them by the astronomers of Ancient Greece.

Planets

▲ Most of the eight planets in our Solar System have been known since ancient times, but in the last few years planets have been found orbiting other, faraway stars.

- **Planets** are globe-shaped space objects that orbit a star such as the Sun.

- **Planets begin life** at the same time as their star, from the leftover clouds of gas and dust.

- **Planets are never** more than 20% of the size of their star. If they were bigger, they would have become stars.

- **Some planets,** called terrestrial planets, have a surface of solid rock. Others, called gas planets, have a surface of liquid or airy gas.

  - **The Solar System** has eight planets. Pluto became the ninth, but in 2006 it was classified as a dwarf planet.

  - **Over 80 planets** have now been detected orbiting stars other than the Sun. These are called extra-solar planets.

- **Extra-solar planets** are too far away to see, but can be detected because they make their star wobble.

- **Most known extra-solar planets** are giants bigger than Jupiter and orbit rapidly as close to their stars as Mercury to the Sun.

- **Improved detection techniques** may reveal smaller planets orbiting further out which might support life.

- **The Kepler space telescope** was launched in 2009 to scan 100,000 stars for signs of Earth-sized planets.

Clusters

▲ Space looks like a formless collection of stars and clouds, but all matter tends to cluster together.

- **The Milky Way** belongs to a cluster of 30 galaxies called the Local Group, which is 7 million light-years across.

- **The Local Group** is 7 million light years across.

- **There are 3 giant spiral galaxies** in the Local Group, plus 15 ellipticals and 13 irregulars, such as the Large Magellanic Cloud.

★ STAR FACT ★
One film of superclusters makes up a vast structure called the Great Wall. It is the largest structure in the Universe – over 700 million light-years long, but just 30 million thick.

- **Beyond the Local Group** are many millions of similar star clusters.

- **The Virgo cluster** is 50 million light-years away and is made up of over 1,000 galaxies.

- **The Local Group plus millions** of other clusters make up a huge group called the Local Supercluster.

- **Other superclusters** are Hercules and Pegasus.

- **Superclusters** are separated by huge voids (empty space), which the superclusters surround like the film around a soap bubble.

- **The voids between superclusters** measure 350 to 400 million light-years across.

Variable stars

- **Variable stars** are stars that do not burn steadily like our Sun, but which flare up and down.

- **Pulsating variables** are stars that pulse almost as if they were breathing. They include the kinds of star known as Cepheid variables and RR Lyrae variables.

- **Cepheid variables** are big, bright stars that pulse with energy, flaring up regularly every 1 to 50 days.

▼ The constellation of Cygnus, containing a vanishing star.

- **Cepheid variables** are so predictable in brightness that they make good distance markers (see distances).

- **RR Lyrae variables** are yellow, supergiant stars near the end of their life, which flicker as their fuel runs down.

- **Mira-type variables** are similar to Mira in Cetus, the Whale, and vary regularly over months or years.

- **RV Tauri variables** are very unpredictable, flaring up and down over changing periods of time.

- **Eclipsing variables** are really eclipsing binaries (see binary stars). They seem to flare up and down, but in fact are simply one star getting in the way of the other.

- **The Demon Star** is Algol in Perseus. It seems to burn fiercely for 59 hours, become dim, then flare up again 10 hours later. It is really an eclipsing binary.

- **The vanishing star** is Chi in Cygnus, the Swan. It can be seen with the naked eye for a few months each year, but then becomes so dim that it cannot be seen, even with a powerful telescope.

Take off

- **The biggest problem** when launching a spacecraft is overcoming the pull of Earth's gravity.

- **To escape Earth's gravity**, a spacecraft must be launched at a particular velocity (speed and direction).

- **The mininum velocity** needed for a spacecraft to combat gravity and stay in orbit around the Earth is called the orbital velocity.

- **When a spacecraft** reaches 140% of the orbital velocity, it is going fast enough to break free of Earth's gravity. This is called the escape velocity.

- **The thrust (push)** that launches a spacecraft comes from powerful rockets called launch vehicles.

- **Launch vehicles** are divided into sections called stages, which fall away as their task is done.

★ STAR FACT ★
To stay in orbit 200 km up, a spacecraft has to fly at over 8 km per second.

- **The first stage** lifts everything off the ground, so its thrust must be greater than the weight of launch vehicle plus spacecraft. It falls away a few minutes after take off.

- **A second stage** is then needed to accelerate the spacecraft towards escape velocity.

- **After the two launch stages** fall away, the spacecraft's own, less powerful rocket motors start.

▶ A spacecraft cannot use wings to lift it off the ground, as wings only work in the lower atmosphere. Instead, launch rockets must develop a big enough thrust to power them straight upwards, overcoming gravity with a mighty blast of heat.

Saturn's rings

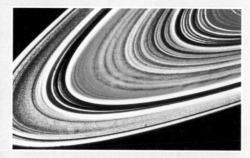

▲ *Saturn's rings are one of the wonders of the Solar System, and many people think they make it the most beautiful planet.*

- **Saturn's rings** are sets of thin rings of ice, dust and tiny rocks, which orbit the planet around its equator.

- **The rings shimmer** as their ice is caught by sunlight.

- **The rings** may be fragments of a moon that was torn apart by Saturn's gravity before it formed properly.

> ★ STAR FACT ★
> Saturn's rings measure over 270,000 km across, but are very thin – just 100 m or less.

- **Galileo was first** to see Saturn's rings, in 1610. But it was Dutch scientist Christian Huygens (1629-95) who first realized they were rings, in 1659.

- **There are two** main sets of rings – the A and the B rings.

- **The A and B rings** are separated by a gap called the Cassini division after Italian astronomer Jean Cassini (1625-1712), who spotted it in 1675.

- **A third large ring** called the C or *crepe* ring was spotted closer to the planet in 1850.

- **In the 1980s**, space probes revealed many other rings and 10,000 or more ringlets, some just 10 m wide.

- **The rings are** (in order out from the planet) D, C, B, Cassini division, A, F, G and E. The A ring has its own gap called the Encke division.

Neutron stars

- **Neutron stars** are incredibly small, super-dense stars made mainly of neutrons (see atoms), with a solid crust made of iron and similar elements.

- **Neutron stars** are just 20 km across on average, yet weigh as much as the Sun.

- **A tablespoon** of neutron star would weigh about 10 billion tonnes.

- **Neutron stars** form from the central core of a star that has died in a supernova explosion.

- **A star must be more than** 1.4 times as big as a medium-sized star like our Sun to

▶ *Neutron stars are tiny, super-dense stars that form in supernova explosions, as a star's core collapses within seconds under the huge force of its own immense gravity.*

produce a neutron star. This is the Chandrasekhar limit.

- **A star more than three times** as big as the Sun would collapse beyond a neutron star to form a black hole. This is called the Oppenheimer-Volkoff limit.

- **The first evidence** of neutron stars came when pulsars were discovered in the 1960s.

- **Some stars giving out X-rays**, such as Hercules X-1, may be neutron stars. The X-rays come from material from nearby stars squeezed on to their surfaces by their huge gravity.

- **Neutron stars** have very powerful magnetic fields (see magnetism), over 2,000 times stronger than Earth's, which stretch the atoms out into frizzy 'whiskers' on the star's surface.

Years

▶ Our years come from the time the Earth takes to go once round the Sun, so that the Sun appears at the same height in the sky again. But this journey actually takes not an exact number of days but 365 and a fraction. So the calendar gives a year as 365 days, and compensates with leap years and century years.

- **A calendar year is roughly the time** the Earth takes to travel once around the Sun – 365 days.

- **The Earth** actually takes 365.24219 days to orbit the Sun. This is called a solar year.

- **To compensate** for the missing 0.242 days, the western calendar adds an extra day in February every fourth (leap) year, but misses out three leap years every four centuries (century years).

- **Measured by the stars** not the Sun, Earth takes 365.25636 days to go round the Sun, because the Sun also moves a little relative to the stars. This is called the sidereal year.

- **Earth's perihelion** is the day its orbit brings it closest to the Sun, 3 January.

- **Earth's aphelion** is the day it is furthest from the Sun, 4 July.

- **The planet with the shortest year** is Mercury, which whizzes around the Sun in just 88 days.

- **The planet with the longest year** is Neptune, which takes 165 years to orbit the Sun.

- **The planet with the year** closest to Earth's in length is Venus, whose year lasts 225 days.

- **A year on Earth** is the time the Sun takes to return to the same height in the sky at noon.

Zodiac

◀ ▲ The zodiac signs are imaginary symbols ancient astronomers linked to star patterns, such as Aries and Taurus.

- **The zodiac** is the band of constellations the Sun appears to pass in front of during the year, as the Earth orbits the Sun. It lies along the ecliptic.

- **The ecliptic** is the plane (level) of the Earth's orbit around the Sun. The Moon and all planets lie in the same plane.

- **The Ancient Greeks** divided the zodiac into 12 parts, named after the constellation they saw in each part. These are the signs of the zodiac.

> ★ STAR FACT ★
> A 13th constellation, Ophiuchus, now lies within the zodiac; astrologers ignore it.

- **The 12 constellations of the zodiac** are Aries, Taurus, Gemini, Cancer, Leo, Virgo, Libra, Scorpio, Sagittarius, Capricorn, Aquarius and Pisces.

- **Astrologers** believe the movements of the planets and stars in the zodiac affect people's lives, but there is no physical connection.

- **For astrologers** all the constellations of the zodiac are equal in size. The ones used by astronomers are not.

- **The Earth has tilted** slightly since ancient times and the constellations no longer correspond to the zodiac.

- **The orbits of the Moon** and all the planets lie within the zodiac.

- **The dates that the Sun** seems to pass in front of each constellation no longer match the dates astrologers use.

Celestial sphere

- **Looking at the stars**, they seem to move across the night sky as though they were painted on the inside of a slowly turning, giant ball. This is the celestial sphere.

- **The northern tip** of the celestial sphere is called the North Celestial Pole.

- **The southern tip** is the South Celestial Pole.

- **The celestial sphere rotates** on an axis which runs between its two celestial poles.

- **There is an equator** around the middle of the celestial sphere, just like Earth's.

- **Stars are positioned** on the celestial sphere by their declination and their right ascension.

- **Declination** is like latitude. It is measured in degrees and shows a star's position between pole and equator.

- **Right ascension** is like longitude. It is measured in hours, minutes and seconds, and shows how far a star is from a marker called the First Point of Aries.

- **The Pole Star**, Polaris, lies very near the North Celestial Pole.

- **The zenith** is the point on the sphere directly above your head as you look at the night sky.

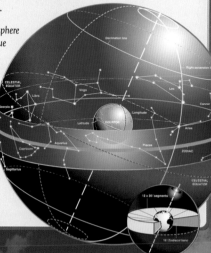

▶ *The celestial sphere is like a great blue ball dotted with stars, with the Earth in the middle. It is imaginary, but makes it easy to locate stars and constellations. The zodiac is shown on the inset.*

X-rays

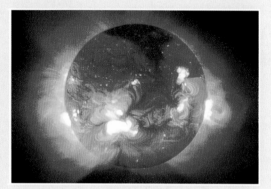

▲ *The Sun was the first X-ray source to be discovered.*

- **X-rays** are electromagnetic rays whose waves are shorter than ultraviolet rays and longer than gamma rays (see radiation).

- **X-rays in space** may be produced by very hot gases well over 1 million °C.

- **X-rays are also made** when electrons interact with a magnetic field in synchrotron radiation (see cosmic rays).

- **X-rays cannot get through** Earth's atmosphere, so astronomers can only detect them using space telescopes such as ROSAT.

- **X-ray sources** are stars and galaxies that give out X-rays.

- **The first and brightest X-ray source** found (apart from the Sun) was the star Scorpius X-1, in 1962. Now tens of thousands are known, although most are weak.

- **The remnants of supernovae** such as the Crab nebula are strong sources of X-rays.

- **The strongest sources of X-rays** in our galaxy are X-ray binaries like Scorpius X-1 and Cygnus X-1 (see binary stars). Some are thought to contain black holes.

- **X-ray binaries** pump out 1,000 times as much X-ray radiation as the Sun does.

- **X-ray galaxies** harbouring big black holes are powerful X-ray sources outside our galaxy.

Sunspots

- **Sunspots are dark spots** on the Sun's photosphere (surface), 2,000°C cooler than the rest of the surface.

- **The dark centre** of a sunspot is the umbra, the coolest bit of a sunspot. Around it is the lighter penumbra.

▼ *Infrared photographs reveal the dark sunspots that appear on the surface of the Sun.*

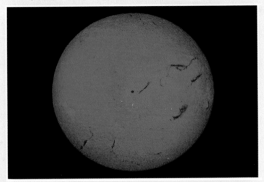

> ★ **STAR FACT** ★
> The SOHO satellite confirmed that sunspots move faster on the Sun's equator.

- **Sunspots appear in groups** which seem to move across the Sun over two weeks, as the Sun rotates.

- **Individual sunspots** last less than a day.

- **The number of sunspots** reaches a maximum every 11 years. This is called the solar or sunspot cycle.

- **The next sunspot maximum** will be in the year 2012.

- **Earth's weather** may be warmer and stormier when sunspots are at their maximum.

- **Long-term sunspot cycles** are 76 and 180 years, and are almost like the Sun breathing in and out.

- **Observations of the Sun** by satellites such as Nimbus-7 showed that less heat reaches the Earth from the Sun when sunspots are at a minimum.

The Big Bang

- **The Big Bang explosion** is how scientists think the Universe began some 15 billion years ago.

- **First there was a hot ball** tinier than an atom. This cooled to 10 billion billion °C as it grew to football size.

- **A split second later**, a super-force swelled the infant Universe a thousand billion billion billion times. Scientists call this inflation.

- **As it mushroomed out**, the Universe was flooded with energy and matter, and the super-force separated into basic forces such as electricity and gravity.

- **There were no atoms at first**, just tiny particles such as quarks in a dense soup a trillion trillion trillion trillion trillion times denser than water.

- **There was also antimatter**, the mirror image of matter. Antimatter and matter destroy each other when they meet, so they battled it out. Matter just won – but the Universe was left almost empty.

- **After 3 minutes**, quarks started to fuse (join) to

make the smallest atoms, hydrogen. Then hydrogen gas atoms fused to make helium gas atoms.

- **After 1 million years** the gases began to curdle into strands with dark holes between them.

- **After 300 million years**, the strands clumped into clouds, and then the clouds clumped together to form stars and galaxies.

- **The afterglow of the Big Bang** can still be detected as microwave background radiation coming from all over space (see below).

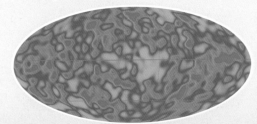

1000 THINGS
YOU SHOULD KNOW ABOUT

PLANET EARTH

KEY

 Planet Earth

 Weather and climate

 Volcanoes and earthquakes

 Continents

 Shaping the land

 Oceans

Air moisture

▲ Clouds are the visible, liquid part of the moisture in the air. They form when the water vapour in the air cools and condenses.

- **Up to 10 km** above the ground, the air is always moist because it contains an invisible gas called water vapour.

- **There is enough water vapour** in the air to flood the entire globe to a depth of 2.5 m.

- **Water vapour** enters the air when it evaporates from oceans, rivers and lakes.

- **Water vapour** leaves the air when it cools and condenses (turns to drops of water) to form clouds. Most clouds eventually turn to rain, and the water falls back to the ground. This is called precipitation.

- **Like a sponge,** the air soaks up evaporating water until it is saturated (full). It can only take in more water if it warms up and expands.

- **If saturated air cools,** it contracts and squeezes out the water vapour, forcing it to condense into drops of water. The point at which this happens is called the dew point.

- **Humidity** is the amount of water in the air.

- **Absolute humidity** is the weight of water in grams in a particular volume of air.

- **Relative humidity,** which is written as a percentage, is the amount of water in the air compared to the amount of water the air could hold when saturated.

The lithosphere

- **The lithosphere** is the upper, rigid layer of the Earth. It consists of the crust and the top of the mantle (see core and mantle). It is about 100 km thick.

- **The lithosphere** was discovered by 'seismology', which means listening to the pattern of vibrations from earthquakes.

- **Fast earthquake waves** show that the top of the mantle is as rigid as the crust, although chemically it is different.

- **Lithosphere** means 'ball of stone'.

- **The lithosphere** is broken into 20 or so slabs, called tectonic plates. The continents sit on top of these plates (see continental drift).

- **Temperatures** increase by 35°C for every 1,000 m you move down through the lithosphere.

- **Below the lithosphere,** in the Earth's mantle, is the hot, soft rock of the asthenosphere (see Earth's interior).

- **The boundary between the lithosphere** and the asthenosphere occurs at the point where temperatures climb above 1,300°C.

- **The lithosphere** is only a few kilometres thick under the middle of the oceans. Here, the mantle's temperature just below the surface is 1,300°C.

- **The lithosphere is thickest** – 120 km or so – under the continents.

◀ The hard rocky surface of the Earth is made up of the 20 or so strong rigid plates of the lithosphere.

Earthquake waves

- **Earthquake waves** are the vibrations sent out through the ground by earthquakes (see earthquakes). They are also called seismic waves.

- **There are two kinds** of deep earthquake wave: primary (P) waves and secondary (S) waves.

- **P waves** travel at 5 km per second and move by alternately squeezing and stretching rock.

- **S waves** travel at 3 km per second and move the ground up and down or from side to side.

- **There are two kinds** of surface wave: Love waves and Rayleigh waves.

- **Love, or Q, waves** shake the ground from side to side in a jerky movement that can often destroy very tall buildings.

- **Rayleigh, or R, waves** shake the ground up and down, often making it seem to roll.

- **In solid ground** earthquake waves travel too fast to be seen. However, they can turn loose sediments into a fluid–like material so that earthquake waves can be seen rippling across the ground like waves in the sea.

- **When waves ripple** across loose sediment they can uproot tall buildings.

▼ *Surface waves travel much slower than deep waves, but they are usually the ones that cause the most damage.*

Love waves

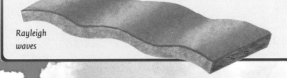
Rayleigh waves

Caves

- **Caves** are giant holes that run horizontally underground. Holes that plunge vertically are called potholes.

- **The most spectacular caves,** called caverns, are found in limestone. Acid rainwater trickles through cracks in the rock and wears away huge cavities.

- **The world's largest known** single cave is the Sarawak Chamber in Gunung Mulu in Sarawak, Malaysia.

- **The deepest** cave gallery yet found is the Pierre St Martin system, 800 m down in the French Pyrenees.

- **The longest** cave system is the Mammoth Cave in Kentucky, USA, which is 560 km long.

- **Many caverns** contain fantastic deposits called speleothems. They are made mainly from calcium carbonate deposited by water trickling through the cave.

- **Stalactites are icicle-like** speleothems that hang from cave ceilings. Stalagmites poke upwards from the floor.

- **The world's longest stalactite** is 6.2 m long. It is in the Poll an Ionain in County Clare, Ireland.

- **The world's tallest column** is the Flying Dragon Pillar in the Nine Dragons Cave, Guizhou, China.

▼ *Caverns can be subterranean palaces filled with glistening pillars.*

Africa

- **Africa is the world's second largest** continent. It stretches from the Mediterranean in the north to the Cape of Good Hope in the south. Area: 30,131,536 sq km.
- **Africa is the world's warmest** continent, lying almost entirely within the tropics or subtropics.
- **Temperatures in the Sahara** Desert are the highest on Earth, often soaring over 50°C.
- **The Sahara** in the north of Africa, and the Kalahari in the south, are the world's largest deserts. Most of the continent in between is savannah (grassland) and bush. In the west and centre are lush rainforests.
- **Much of Africa** consists of vast plains and plateaux, broken in places by mountains such as the Atlas range in the northwest and the Ruwenzori in the centre.

> ★ STAR FACT ★
> The River Nile is perhaps the second longest river in the world, measuring 6673 km long.

- **The Great Rift Valley** runs 7,200 km from the Red Sea. It is a huge gash in the Earth's surface opened up by the pulling apart of two giant tectonic plates.
- **Africa's largest lake** is Victoria, 69,484 sq km.
- **Africa's highest mountain** is Kilimanjaro, 5,895 m high.
- **The world's** biggest sand dune is 430 m high – Erg Tifernine in Algeria.

▶ Africa is a vast, warm, fairly flat continent covered in savannah, desert and tropical forest.

Ocean deeps

▲ Huge numbers of sea creatures live in the pelagic zone – the surface waters of the open ocean beyond the continental shelf.

- **The oceans** are over 2,000 m deep on average.
- **Along the edge** of the ocean is a ledge of land – the continental shelf. The average sea depth here is 130 m.
- **At the edge of the continental shelf** the sea-bed plunges thousands of metres steeply down the continental slope.

- **Underwater avalanches** roar down the continental slope at over 60 km/h. They carve out deep gashes called submarine canyons.
- **The gently** sloping foot of the continental slope is called the continental rise.
- **Beyond the continental rise** the ocean floor stretches out in a vast plain called the abyssal plain. It lies as deep as 5,000 m below the water's surface.
- **The abyssal plain** is covered in a thick slime called ooze. It is made partly from volcanic ash and meteor dust and partly from the remains of sea creatures.
- **The abyssal plain** is dotted with huge mountains, thousands of metres high, called seamounts.
- **Flat-topped seamounts** are called guyots. They may be volcanoes that once projected above the surface.
- **The deepest places** in the ocean floor are ocean trenches – made when tectonic plates are driven down into the mantle. The Mariana Trench is 10,863 m deep.

Earthquake damage

- **Many of the world's** major cities are located in earthquake zones, such as Los Angeles, Mexico City and Tokyo.

- **Severe earthquakes** can shake down buildings and rip up flyovers.

- **When freeways collapsed** in the 1989 San Francisco quake, some cars were crushed to just 0.5 m thick.

- **The 1906 earthquake** in San Francisco destroyed 400 km of railway track around the city.

- **Some of the worst** earthquake damage is caused by fire, often set off by the breaking of gas pipes and electrical cables.

- **In 1923** 200,000 died in the firestorm that engulfed Tokyo as an earthquake upset domestic charcoal stoves.

▲ *The complete collapse of overhead freeways is a major danger in severe earthquakes.*

- **In the Kobe** earthquake of 1995 and the San Francisco earthquake of 1989 some of the worst damage was to buildings built on landfill – loose material piled in to build up the land.

- **The earthquake** that killed the most people was probably the one that hit Shansi in China in 1556. It may have claimed 830,000 lives.

- **The most fatal** earthquake this century destroyed the city of Tangshan in China in 1976. It killed an estimated 255,000 people.

- **The worst earthquake** to hit Europe centred on Lisbon, Portugal, in 1755. It destroyed the city, killing 100,000 or more people. It probably measured 9.0 on the Richter scale (see earthquake measurement) and was felt in Paris.

Changing landscapes

- **The Moon's landscape** has barely changed over billions of years. The footprints left by Moon astronauts 30 years ago are still there, perfectly preserved in dust.

- **The Earth's surface** changes all the time. Most changes take millions of years. Sometimes the landscape is reshaped suddenly by an avalanche or a volcano.

- **The Earth's surface** is distorted and re-formed from below by the huge forces of the Earth's interior.

- **The Earth's surface** is moulded from above by weather, water, waves, ice, wind and other 'agents of erosion'.

- **Most landscapes,** except deserts, are moulded by running water, which explains why hills have rounded slopes. Dry landscapes are more angular, but even in deserts water often plays a major shaping role.

- **Mountain peaks** are jagged because it is so cold high up that the rocks are often shattered by frost.

- **An American scientist** W. M. Davis (1850–1935) thought landscapes are shaped by repeated 'cycles of erosion'.

- **Davis's cycles of erosion** have three stage: vigorous 'youth', steady 'maturity' and sluggish 'old age'.

- **Observation** has shown that erosion does not become more sluggish as time goes on, as Davis believed.

- **Many landscapes** have been shaped by forces no longer in operation, such as moving ice during past Ice Ages.

▼ *Rivers are one of the most powerful agents of erosion.*

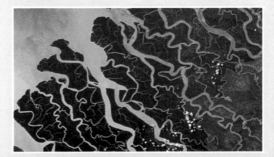

Continental drift

- **Continental drift** is the slow movement of the continents around the world.

- **About 220 million years ago** all the continents were joined together in one supercontinent, which geologists call Pangaea.

- **Pangaea** began to break up about 200 million years ago. The fragments slowly drifted apart to form the continents we know today.

- **South America** used to be joined to Africa. North America used to be joined to Europe.

- **The first hint** that the continents were once joined was the discovery by German explorer Alexander von Humboldt (1769–1859) that rocks in Brazil (South America) and the Congo (Africa) are very similar.

- **When German meteorologist** Alfred Wegener (1880–1930) first suggested the idea of continental drift in 1923, many scientists laughed. The chairman of the American Philosophical Society described the idea as 'Utter damned rot!'.

- **Strong evidence** of continental drift has come from similar ancient fossils found in separate continents, such as the *Glossopteris* fern found in both Australia and India; the *Diadectid* insect found in Europe and North America; and *Lystrosaurus*, a tropical reptile from 200 million years ago, found in Africa, India, China and Antarctica.

▶ It is hard to believe that the continents move, but they do. Over tens of millions of years they move huge distances. The drifting of the continents has changed the map of the world very, very slowly over the past 200 million years, and will continue to do so in the future.

> ★ STAR FACT ★
> New York is moving about 2.5 cm farther away from London every year.

- **Satellites** provide such incredibly accurate ways of measuring that they can actually measure the slow movement of the continents. The main method is satellite laser ranging (SLR), which involves bouncing a laser beam off a satellite from ground stations on each continent. Other methods include using the Global Positioning System (GPS) and Very Long Baseline Interferometry (VLBI).

- **Rates of continental drift** vary. India drifted north into Asia very quickly. South America is moving 20 cm farther from Africa every year. On average, continents move at about the same rate as a fingernail grows.

1. About 220 million years ago, all the continents were joined in the supercontinent of Pangaea. It was surrounded by a single giant ocean called Panthalassa, meaning 'all seas'.

2. By 200 million years ago Pangaea had split into two huge landmasses called Laurasia and Gondwanaland, separated by the Tethys Sea. About 135 million years ago these landmasses also began to divide.

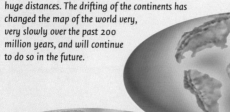

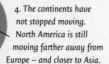

3. About 110 million years ago North and South America finally began to link up. Later, Australia and Antarctica separated. India broke off from Africa and drifted rapidly north into Asia. Europe and North America began to move apart about 60 million years ago, at about the same time that the dinosaurs died out.

4. The continents have not stopped moving. North America is still moving farther away from Europe – and closer to Asia.

Earthquake measurement

- **Earthquakes** are measured with a device called a seismograph.

- **The Richter scale** measures the magnitude (size) of an earthquake on a scale of 1 to 10 using a seismograph. Each step in the scale indicates a tenfold increase in the energy of the earthquake.

- **The Richter scale** was devised in the 1930s by an American geophysicist called Charles Richter (1900–1985).

- **The most powerful** earthquake ever recorded was an earthquake in Chile in 1960, which registered 9.5 on the Richter scale. The 1976 Tangshan earthquake registered 7.8.

- **Between 10 and 20** earthquakes each year reach 7 on the Richter scale.

- **The Modified Mercalli scale** assesses an earthquake's severity according to its effects on a scale of 1 to 12 in Roman numerals (I–XII).

▶ The Richter scale tells us how much energy an earthquake has – but the damage it does to somewhere depends on how far the place is from the centre.

- **The Mercalli scale** was devised by the Italian scientist Guiseppe Mercalli (1850–1914).

- **A Mercalli scale I** earthquake is one that is only detectable with special instruments.

- **A Mercalli scale XII** earthquake causes almost total destruction of cities and reshapes the landscape.

- **The Moment-magnitude** scale combines Richter readings with observations of rock movements.

Waterfalls

▲ The spectacular Iguacu Falls in Brazil are made up from 275 individual falls cascading 82 m into the gorge below.

- **Waterfalls** are places where a river plunges vertically.

- **Waterfalls** may form where the river flows over a band of hard rock, such as a volcanic sill. The river erodes the soft rock below but it has little effect on the hard band.

- **Waterfalls** can also form where a stream's course has

> ★ STAR FACT ★
> The world's highest falls are the Angel Falls in Venezuela, which plunge 979 m.

been suddenly broken, for example where it flows over a cliff into the sea, over a fault (see faults) or over a hanging valley (see glaciated landscapes).

- **Boulders often swirl** around at the foot of a waterfall, wearing out a deep pool called a plunge pool.

- **Angel Falls** are named after American pilot Jimmy Angel who flew over them in 1935.

- **Victoria Falls** in Zimbabwe are known locally as Mosi oa Tunya, which means the 'smoke that thunders'.

- **The roar** from Victoria Falls can be heard 40 km away.

- **Niagara Falls** on the US/Canadian border developed where the Niagara River flows out of Lake Erie.

- **Niagara Falls** has two falls: Horseshoe Falls, 54 m high, and American Falls, 55 m high.

Antarctica

- **Antarctica** is the ice-covered continent at the South Pole. It covers an area of 14 million square km and is larger than Australia.
- **It is the coldest place** on Earth. Even in summer, temperatures rarely climb over −25°C. On July 21, 1983, the air at the Vostok science station plunged to −89.2°C .
- **Antarctica** is one of the driest places on Earth, with barely any rain or snow. It is also very windy.
- **Until about 80 million years ago** Antarctica was joined to Australia.
- **Glaciers began to form** in Antarctica 38 million years ago, and grew rapidly from 13 million years ago. For the past five million years 98% of the continent has been covered in ice.

◀ Antarctica does not belong to any one nation. Under the Antarctic Treaty of 1959, 12 countries agreed to use it only for scientific research.

- **The Antarctic ice cap** contains 70% of the world's fresh water.
- **The ice cap** is thickest – up to 4,800 m deep – in deep sea basins dipping far below the surface. Here it is thick enough to bury the Alps.
- **Antarctica** is mountainous. Its highest point is the Vinson Massif, 5,140 m high, but there are many peaks over 4,000 m in the Transarctic Range.
- **The magnetic South Pole** – the pole to which a compass needle points – moves 8 km a year.
- **Fossils of tropical plants** and reptiles show that Antarctica was at one time in the tropics.

Formation of the Earth

- **The Earth formed** 4.57 billion years ago out of debris left over from the explosion of a giant star.
- **The Earth began to form** as star debris spun round the newly formed Sun and clumped into rocks called planetesimals.
- **Planetesimals** were pulled together by their own gravity to form planets such as Earth and Mars.

◀ When the Earth formed from a whirling cloud of stardust, the pieces rushed together with such force that the young planet turned into a fiery ball. It slowly cooled down, and the continents and oceans formed.

- **At first** the Earth was a seething mass of molten rock.
- **After 50 million years** a giant rock cannoned into the newborn Earth. The impact melted the rock into a hot splash, which cooled to become our Moon.
- **The shock of the impact** that formed the Moon made iron and nickel collapse towards the Earth's centre to form a hot, dense core. Radioactive disintegration of metal atoms in the core has kept the inside of the Earth hot ever since.
- **The molten rock** formed a thick mantle about 3,000 km thick around the metal core. The core's heat keeps the mantle warm and churning, like boiling porridge.
- **After about 100 million years** the surface of the mantle cooled and hardened to form a thin crust.
- **Steam and gases** billowing from volcanoes formed the Earth's first, poisonous atmosphere.
- **After 200 million years** the steam had condensed to water. It fell in huge rain showers to form the oceans.

Fog and mist

- **Like clouds,** mist is billions of tiny water droplets floating on the air. Fog forms near the ground.

- **Mist forms** when the air cools to the point where the water vapour it contains condenses to water.

- **Meteorologists** define fog as a mist that reduces visibility to less than 1 km.

- **There are four main kinds** of fog: radiation fog, advection fog, frontal fog and upslope fog.

- **Radiation fog** forms on cold, clear, calm nights. The ground loses heat that it absorbed during the day, and so cools the air above.

- **Advection fog** forms when warm, moist air flows over a cold surface. This cools the air so much that the moisture it contains condenses.

▲ Huge amounts of moisture transpire from the leaves of forest trees. It condenses on cool nights to form a thick morning mist.

> ★ STAR FACT ★
> Smog is a thick fog made when fog combines with polluted air.

- **Sea fog** is advection fog that forms as warm air flows out over cool coastal waters and lakes.

- **Frontal fog** forms along fronts (see weather fronts).

- **Upslope fog** forms when warm, moist air rises up a mountain and cools.

Earthquake prediction

◄ Modern earthquake prediction methods detect minute distortions of the ground that indicate the rock is under stress. Seismologists use the latest survey techniques, with precision instruments like this laser rangefinder.

- **One way to predict earthquakes** is to study past quakes.

- **If there has been no earthquake** in an earthquake zone for a while, there will be one soon. The longer it has been since the last quake, the bigger the next one will be.

- **Seismic gaps** are places in active earthquake zones where there has been no earthquake activity. This is where a big earthquake will probably occur.

- **Seismologists** make very accurate surveys with ground instruments and laser beams bounced off satellites (see earthquake measurement). They can spot tiny deformations of rock that show strain building up.

- **A linked network** of four laser-satellite stations called Keystone is set to track ground movements in Tokyo Bay, Japan, so that earthquakes can be predicted better.

- **The level of water** in the ground may indicate stress as the rock squeezes groundwater towards the surface. Chinese seismologists check water levels in wells.

- **Rising surface levels** of the underground gas radon may also show that the rock is being squeezed.

- **Other signs of strain** in the rock may be changes in the ground's electrical resistance or its magnetism.

- **Before an earthquake** dogs are said to howl, pandas moan, chickens flee their roosts, rats and mice scamper from their holes and fish thrash about in ponds .

- **Some people** claim to be sensitive to earthquakes.

Mineral resources

- **The Earth's surface** contains an enormous wealth of mineral resources, from clay for bricks to precious gems such as rubies and diamonds.
- **Fossil fuels** are oil, coal and natural gas.
- **Fossil fuels were made** from the remains of plant and animals that lived millions of years ago. The remains were changed into fuel by intense heat and pressure.
- **Coal** is made from plants that grew in huge warm swamps during the Carboniferous Period 300 million years ago.
- **Oil and natural gas** were made from the remains of tiny plants and animals that lived in warm seas.
- **Ores** are the minerals from which metals are extracted. Bauxite is the ore for aluminium; chalcopyrite for copper; galena for lead; hematite for iron; sphalerite for zinc.
- **Veins** are narrow pipes of rock that are rich in minerals such as gold and silver. They are made when hot liquids made from volcanic material underground seep upwards through cracks in the rock.

▶ *Bulk materials such as cement, gravel and clay are taken from the ground in huge quantities for building.*

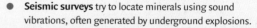

- **Mineral resources** can be located by studying rock strata, (layers), often by satellite and by taking rock samples.
- **Geophysical prospecting** is hunting for minerals using physics – looking for variations in the rock's electrical conductivity, magnetism, gravity or moisture content.
- **Seismic surveys** try to locate minerals using sound vibrations, often generated by underground explosions.

Deserts

▲ *Water erosion over millions of years has created these dramatic pillar-like mesas and buttes in Monument Valley in Utah, USA.*

- **Deserts are dry places** where it rarely rains. Many are hot, but one of the biggest deserts is Antarctica. Deserts cover about one-fifth of the Earth's land.
- **Hamada** is desert that is strewn with boulders. Reg is desert that is blanketed with gravel.
- **About one-fifth** of all deserts are seas of sand dunes. These are known as ergs in the Sahara.

- **The type of sand dune** depends on how much sand there is, and how changeable the wind is.
- **Barchans** are moving, crescent-shaped dunes that form in sparse sand where the wind direction is constant.
- **Seifs** are long dunes that form where sand is sparse and the wind comes from two or more directions.
- **Most streams** in deserts flow only occasionally, leaving dry stream beds called wadis or arroyos. These may suddenly fill with a flash flood after rain.
- **In cool, wet regions**, hills are covered in soil and rounded in shape. In deserts, hills are bare rock with cliff faces footed by straight slopes.
- **Mesas and buttes** are pillar-like plateaux that have been carved gradually by water in deserts.

> ★ STAR FACT ★
> In the western Sahara, two million dry years have created sand ridges over 300 m high.

Earthquakes

- **Earthquakes** are a shaking of the ground. Some are slight tremors that barely rock a cradle. Others are so violent they can tear down mountains and cities.

- **Small earthquakes** may be set off by landslides, volcanoes or even just heavy traffic. Big earthquakes are set off by the grinding together of the vast tectonic plates that make up the Earth's surface.

- **Tectonic plates** are sliding past each other all the time, but sometimes they stick. The rock bends and stretches for a while and then snaps. This makes the plates jolt, sending out the shock waves that cause the earthquake's effects to be felt far away.

- **Tectonic plates** typically slide 4 or 5 cm past each other in a year. In a slip that triggers a major quake they can slip more than 1 m in a few seconds.

- **In most quakes** a few minor tremors (foreshocks) are followed by an intense burst lasting just 1 or 2 minutes. A second series of minor tremors (aftershocks) occurs over the next few hours.

- **The starting point** of an earthquake below ground is called the hypocentre, or focus. The epicentre of an earthquake is the point on the surface directly above the hypocentre.

- **Earthquakes are strongest** at the epicentre and become gradually weaker farther away.

- **Certain regions** called earthquake zones are especially prone to earthquakes. Earthquake zones lie along the edges of tectonic plates.

- **A shallow earthquake** originates 0–70 km below the ground. These are the ones that do the most damage. An intermediate quake begins 70–300 km down. Deep quakes begin over 300 km down. The deepest ever recorded earthquake began over 720 km down.

> ★ STAR FACT ★
> The longest recorded earthquake, in Alaska on March 21, 1964, lasted just 4 minutes.

▶ During an earthquake, shock waves radiate in circles outwards and upwards from the focus of the earthquake. The damage caused is greatest at the epicentre, where the waves are strongest, but vibrations may be felt 400 km away.

As two tectonic plates jolt past each other, they send out shock waves.

Isoseismic lines show where the quake's intensity is equal.

Epicentre

The quake's intensity is reduced away from the epicentre.

Hypocentre where the quake begins

Climate

- **Climate is the typical weather** of a place over a long time.

- **Climates are warm** near the Equator, where the Sun climbs high in the sky.

- **Tropical climates** are warm climates in the tropical zones on either side of the Equator. Average temperatures of 27°C are typical.

- **The climate is cool** near the Poles, where the Sun never climbs high in the sky. Average temperatures of –30°C are typical.

- **Temperate climates** are mild climates in the temperate zones between the tropics and the polar regions. Summer temperatures may average 23°C. Winter temperatures may average 12°C.

◀ *The world climate map is very complex. This simplified map shows some of the main climate zones.*

Moist temperate
Tropical
Desert
Polar
Continental temperate
Mountain

- **A Mediterranean climate** is a temperate climate with warm summers and mild winters. It is typical of the Mediterranean, California, South Africa and South Australia.

- **A monsoon climate** is a climate with one very wet and one very dry season – typical of India and SE Asia.

- **An oceanic climate** is a wetter climate near oceans, with cooler summers and warmer winters.

- **A continental climate** is a drier climate in the centre of continents, with hot summers and cold winters.

- **Mountain climates** get colder and windier with height.

Weathering

- **Weathering** is the gradual breakdown of rocks when they are exposed to the air.

- **Weathering affects** surface rocks the most, but water trickling into the ground can weather rocks 200 m down.

- **The more extreme** the climate, the faster weathering takes place, whether the climate is very cold or very hot.

▼ *The desert heat means that both the chemical and the mechanical weathering of the rocks is intense.*

★ STAR FACT ★
At –22°C, ice can exert a pressure of 3,000 kg on an area of rock the size of a postage stamp.

- **In tropical Africa** the basal weathering front (the lowest limit of weathering underground) is often 60 m down.

- **Weathering** works chemically (through chemicals in rainwater), mechanically (through temperature changes) and organically (through plants and animals).

- **Chemical weathering** is when gases dissolve in rain to form weak acids that corrode rocks such as limestone.

- **The main form of mechanical weathering** is frost shattering – when water expands as it freezes in cracks in the rocks and so shatters the rock.

- **Thermoclastis** is when desert rocks crack as they get hot and expand in the day, then cool and contract at night.

- **Exfoliation** is when rocks crack in layers as a weight of rock or ice above them is removed.

Gems and crystals

- **Gems** are mineral crystals that are beautifully coloured or sparkling.

- **There are over 3,000 minerals** but only 130 are gemstones. Only about 50 of these are commonly used.

- **The rarest gems** are called precious gems and include diamonds, emeralds and rubies.

  - **Less rare gems** are known as semi-precious gems.

    - **Gems** are weighed in carats. A carat is one-fifth of a gram. A 50-carat sapphire is very large and very valuable.

      ◀ *Quartz is a very common mineral. Occasionally it forms beautiful purple amethyst. Minute traces of iron in the rock turn the quartz to amethyst.*

- **In the ancient world** gems were weighed with carob seeds. The word 'carat' comes from the Arabic for seed.

- **Gems** often form in gas bubbles called geodes in cooling magma. They can also form when hot magma packed with minerals seeps up through cracks in the rock to form a vein.

- **When magma** cools, minerals with the highest melting points crystallize first. Unusual minerals are left behind to crystallize last, forming rocks called pegmatites. These rocks are often rich in gems such as emeralds, garnets, topazes and tourmalines.

- **Some gems** with a high melting point and simple chemical composition form directly from magma, such as diamond, which is pure carbon, and rubies.

> ★ **STAR FACT** ★
> Diamonds are among the oldest mineral crystals, over 3,000 million years old.

Deep ocean currents

- **Ocean surface currents** (see ocean currents) affect only the top 100 m or so of the ocean. Deep currents involve the whole ocean.

- **Deep currents** are set in motion by differences in the density of sea water. They move only a few metres a day.

- **Most deep currents** are called thermohaline circulations because they depend on the water's temperature ('thermo') and salt content ('haline').

- **If sea water** is cold and salty, it is dense and sinks.

- **Typically, dense water** forms in the polar regions. Here the water is cold and weighed down by salt left behind when sea ice forms.

- **Dense polar water** sinks and spreads out towards the Equator deep below the surface.

- **Oceanographers** call dense water that sinks and starts deep ocean currents 'deep water'.

- **In the Northern Hemisphere** the main area for the formation of deep water is the North Atlantic.

- **Dense salty water** from the Mediterranean pours deep down very fast – 1 m per second – through the Straits of Gibraltar to add to the North Atlantic deep water.

- **There are three levels** in the ocean: the 'epilimnion' (the surface waters warmed by sunlight, up to 100–300 m down); the 'thermocline', where it becomes colder quickly with depth; and the 'hypolimnion', the bulk of deep, cold ocean water.

▼ *This satellite picture shows variations in ocean surface temperature.*

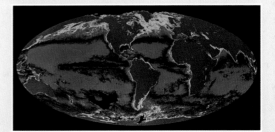

Glaciers

- **Glaciers** are rivers of slowly moving ice. They form in mountain regions when it is too cold for snow to melt. They flow down through valleys, creeping lower until they melt in the warm air lower down.

- **Glaciers** form when new snow, or névé, falls on top of old snow. The weight of the new snow compacts the old snow into denser snow called firn.

- **In firn snow**, all the air is squeezed out so it looks like white ice. As more snow falls, firn gets more compacted and turns into glacier ice that flows slowly downhill.

- **Nowadays** glaciers form only in high mountains and towards the North and South Poles. In the Ice Ages glaciers were widespread and left glaciated landscapes in many places that are now free of ice.

- **As glaciers** move downhill, they bend and stretch, opening up deep cracks called crevasses. Sometimes these occur where the glacier passes over a ridge of rock.

◄ The dense ice in glaciers is made from thousands of years of snow. As new snow fell, the old snow beneath it became squeezed more and more in a process called firnification.

- **The biggest crevasse** is often a crevasse called the bergschrund. It forms when the ice pulls away from the back wall of the hollow where the glacier starts.

- **Where the underside** of a glacier is warmish (about 0°C), it moves by gliding over a film of water that is made as pressure melts the glacier's base. It is called basal slip.

- **Where the underside** of a glacier is coldish (well below 0°C), it moves as if layers were slipping over each other like a pack of cards. This is called internal deformation.

- **Valley glaciers** are glaciers that flow in existing valleys.

- **Cirque glaciers** are small glaciers that flow from hollows high up. Alpine valley glaciers form when several cirque glaciers merge. Piedmont glaciers form where valley glaciers join as they emerge from the mountains.

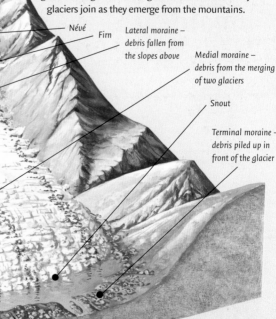

Névé

Firn

Lateral moraine – debris fallen from the slopes above

Medial moraine – debris from the merging of two glaciers

Snout

Terminal moraine – debris piled up in front of the glacier

Cirque

Crevasses

Step in rock floor

▲ Glaciers begin in small hollows in the mountain called cirques, or corries. They flow downhill, gathering huge piles of debris called moraine on the way.

Ocean currents

- **Ocean surface currents** are like giant rivers, often tens of kilometres wide, 100 m deep and flowing at 15 km/h.
- **The major currents** are split on either side of the Equator into giant rings called gyres.
- **In the Northern Hemisphere** the gyres flow round clockwise; in the south they flow anticlockwise.
- **Ocean currents** are driven by a combination of winds and the Earth's rotation.
- **Near the Equator** water is driven by easterly winds (see wind) to make westward-flowing equatorial currents.
- **When equatorial currents** reach continents, the Earth's rotation deflects them polewards as warm currents.
- **As warm currents flow** polewards, westerly winds drive them east back across the oceans. When the currents

> ★ STAR FACT ★
> The West Wind Drift around Antarctica moves 2,000 times as much water as the Amazon.

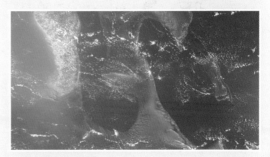

▲ Ocean currents start as wind blows across the water's surface.

reach the far side, they begin to flow towards the Equator along the west coasts of continents as cool currents.

- **The North Atlantic Drift** brings so much warm water from the Caribbean to SW England that it is warm enough to grow palm trees, yet it is as far north as Newfoundland.
- **By drying out the air** cool currents can create deserts, such as California's Baja and Chile's Atacama deserts.

Climate change

- **The world's climate** is changing all the time, getting warmer, colder, wetter or drier. There are many theories why this happens.
- **One way to see** how climate changed before weather records were kept is to look at the growth rings in old trees. Wide rings show the good growth of a warm summer.
- **Another way** of working out past climate is to look in ancient sediments for remains of plants and animals that only thrive in certain conditions.
- **One cause of climate change** may be shifts in the Earth's orientation to the Sun. These shifts are called Milankovitch cycles.
- **One Milankovitch cycle** is the way the Earth's axis wobbles round like a top every 21,000 years. Another is

◄ When more sunspots form on the Sun's surface, the weather on the Earth may be stormier.

the way its axis tilts like a rolling ship every 40,000 years. A third is the way its orbit gets more or less oval shaped every 96,000 years.

- **Climate** may also be affected by dark patches on the Sun called sunspots. These flare up and down every 11 years.
- **Sunspot activity** is linked to stormy weather on the Earth.
- **Climates may cool** when the air is filled with dust from volcanic eruptions or meteors hitting the Earth.
- **Climates** may get warmer when levels of certain gases in the air increase (see global warming).
- **Local climates** may change as continents drift around. Antarctica was once in the tropics, while the New York area once had a tropical desert climate.

Clouds

- **Clouds** are dense masses of water drops and ice crystals that are so tiny they float high in the air.

- **Cumulus clouds** are fluffy white clouds. They pile up as warm air rises and cools to the point where water vapour condenses.

- **Strong updraughts** create huge cumulonimbus, or thunder, clouds.

- **Stratus clouds** are vast shapeless clouds that form when a layer of air cools to

▲ *Cumulus clouds build up in fluffy piles as warm, moist air rises. Once it reaches about 2,000 m, the air cools enough for clouds to form.*

★ STAR FACT ★
Cumulonimbus thunder clouds are the tallest clouds, often over 10 km high.

the point where moisture condenses. They often bring long periods of light rain.

- **Cirrus clouds** are wispy clouds that form so high up they are made entirely of ice. Strong winds high up blow them into 'mares' tails.

- **Low clouds** lie below 2,000 m above the ground. They include stratus and stratocumulus clouds (the spread tops of cumulus clouds).

- **Middle clouds** often have the prefix 'alto' and lie from 2,000 m to 6,000 m up. They include rolls of altocumulus cloud, and thin sheets called altostratus.

- **High-level clouds** are ice clouds up to 11,000 m up. They include cirrus, cirrostratus and cirrocumulus.

- **Contrails** are trails of ice crystals left by jet aircraft.

Hot-spot volcanoes

- **About 5% of volcanoes** are not near the margins of tectonic plates. Instead they are over especially hot places in the Earth's interior called hot spots.

- **Hot spots** are created by mantle plumes – hot currents that rise all the way from the core through the mantle.

- **When mantle plumes** come up under the crust, they burn their way through to become hot-spot volcanoes.

- **Famous hot-spot volcanoes** include the Hawaiian island volcanoes and Réunion Island in the Indian Ocean.

- **Hot-spot volcanoes** ooze runny lava that spreads out to create shield volcanoes (see kinds of volcano).

- **Lava** from hot-spot volcanoes also creates plateaux, such as the Massif Central in France.

- **The geysers, hot springs and bubbling mud pots** of Yellowstone National Park, USA, indicate a hot spot below.

- **Yellowstone** has had three huge eruptions in the past two million years. The first produced over 2,000 times as much lava as the 1980 eruption of Mt St Helens.

- **Hot spots** stay in the same place while tectonic plates slide over the top of them. Each time the plate moves, the hot spot creates a new volcano.

- **The movement** of the Pacific plate over the Hawaiian hot spot has created a chain of old volcanoes 6,000 km long. It starts with the Meiji seamount under the sea north of Japan, and ends with the Hawaiian islands.

▼ *Hot spots pump out huge amounts of lava.*

Glaciated landscapes

- **Glaciers** move slowly but their sheer weight and size give them enormous power to shape the landscape.

- **Over tens of thousands of years** glaciers carve out winding valleys into huge, straight U-shaped troughs.

- **Glaciers** may truncate (slice off) tributary valleys to leave them 'hanging', with a cliff edge high above the main valley. Hill spurs (ends of hills) may also be truncated.

- **Cirques, or corries,** are armchair-shaped hollows carved

out where a glacier begins high up in the mountains.

- **Arêtes** are knife-edge ridges that are left between several cirques as the glaciers in them cut backwards.

- **Drift** is a blanket of debris deposited by glaciers. Glaciofluvial drift is left by the water made as the ice melts. Till is left by the ice itself.

- **Drumlins** are egg-shaped mounds of till. Eskers are snaking ridges of drift left by streams under the ice.

- **Moraine** is piles of debris left by glaciers.

- **Proglacial lakes** are lakes of glacial meltwater dammed up by moraine.

◄ After an Ice Age, glaciers leave behind a dramatically altered landscape of deep valleys and piles of debris.

Rocks

- **The oldest known rocks** are 3,900 million years old – they are the Acasta gneiss rocks from Canada.

- **There are three main kinds of rock:** igneous rock, sedimentary rock and metamorphic rock.

- **Igneous rocks** (igneous means 'fiery') are made when hot molten magma or lava cools and solidifies.

- **Volcanic rocks,** such as basalt, are igneous rocks that form from lava that has erupted from volcanoes.

- **Plutonic rocks** are igneous rocks made when magma solidifies underground, like granite.

- **Metamorphic rocks** are rocks formed when other rocks are changed by extreme heat and pressure, such as limestone which hot magma turns to marble.

- **Sedimentary rocks** are made from the slow hardening of sediments into layers, or strata.

- **Many sedimentary rocks,** like sandstone, are formed when sand, silt and other fragments of rocks are broken down by weathering and erosion.

- **Most sediments** form on the sea-bed. Sand is washed down onto the sea-bed by rivers.

- **Limestone and chalk** are sedimentary rocks made mainly from the remains of sea creatures.

▶ Rocks are continually recycled. Whether they form from volcanoes or sediments, all rocks are broken down into sand by weathering and erosion. The sand is deposited on sea-beds and river-beds where it hardens to form new rock. This process is the rock cycle.

Famous eruptions

- **One of the biggest eruptions** ever occurred 2.2 million years ago in Yellowstone, USA. It poured out enough magma to build half a dozen Mt Fujiyamas.

- **In 1645 BC** the Greek island of Thera erupted, destroying the Minoan city of Akroteri. It may be the origin of the Atlantis myth.

- **On August 24, AD79** the volcano Mt Vesuvius in Italy erupted. It buried the Roman town of Pompeii in ash.

- **The remains** of Pompeii were discovered in the 18th century, wonderfully preserved under metres of ash. They provide a remarkable snapshot of ancient Roman life.

- **The eruption** of the volcanic island of Krakatoa near Java in 1883 was heard a quarter of the way round the world.

- **In 1815** the eruption of Tambora in Indonesia was 60–80 times bigger than the 1980 eruption of Mt St Helens.

◀ *The eruption of Mt St Helens in Washington, USA on May 18, 1980 blew away the side of the mountain. It sent out a blast of gas that flattened trees for 30 km around.*

- **Ash from Tambora** filled the sky, making the summer of 1816 cool all around the world.

- **J. M. W. Turner's paintings** may have been inspired by fiery sunsets caused by dust from Tambora.

- **During the eruption of Mt Pelée** on Martinique on May 8, 1902, all but two of the 29,000 townspeople of nearby St Pierre were killed in a few minutes by a scorching flow of gas, ash and cinders.

- **The biggest eruption** in the past 50 years was that of Mt Pinatubo in the Philippines in April 1991.

Ice Ages

- **Ice Ages** are periods lasting millions of years when the Earth is so cold that the polar ice caps grow huge. There are various theories about why they occur (see climate change).

- **There have been four Ice Ages** in the last 1,000 million years, including one which lasted 100 million years.

▼ *California may have looked something like this 18,000 years ago when it was on the fringes of an ice sheet.*

- **The most recent Ice Age** – called the Pleistocene Ice Age – began about 2 million years ago.

- **In an Ice Age** the weather varies between cold spells called glacials and warm spells called interglacials.

- **There have been** 17 glacials and and interglacials in the last 1.6 million years of the Pleistocene Ice Age.

- **The last glacial,** called the Holocene glacial, peaked about 18,000 years ago and ended 10,000 years ago.

- **Ice covered 40% of the world** 18,000 years ago.

- **Glaciers spread** over much of Europe and North America 18,000 years ago. Ice caps grew in Tasmania and New Zealand.

- **About 18,000 years ago** there were glaciers in Hawaii.

> ★ STAR FACT ★
> Where Washington and London are today, the ice was 1.5 km thick 18,000 years ago.

Atmosphere

- **The atmosphere** is a blanket of gases about 1,000 km deep around the Earth. It can be divided into five layers: troposphere (the lowest), stratosphere, mesosphere, thermosphere and exosphere.

- **The atmosphere** is: 78% nitrogen, 21% oxygen, 1% argon and carbon dioxide with tiny traces of neon, krypton, zenon, helium, nitrous oxide, methane and carbon monoxide.

- **The atmosphere** was first created by the fumes pouring out from the volcanoes that covered the early Earth 4,000 million years ago. But it was changed as rocks and seawater absorbed carbon dioxide, and then algae in the sea built up oxygen levels over millions and millions of years.

- **The troposphere** is just 12 km thick yet it contains 75% of the weight of gases in the atmosphere. Temperatures drop with height from 18°C on average to about −60°C at the top, called the tropopause.

- **The stratosphere** contains little water. Unlike the troposphere, which is heated from below, it is heated from above as the ozone in it is heated by ultraviolet light from the Sun. Temperatures rise with height from −60°C to 10°C at the top, about 50 km up.

> ★ STAR FACT ★
> The stratosphere glows faintly at night because sodium from salty sea spray reacts chemically in the air.

- **The stratosphere** is completely clear and calm, which is why jet airliners try to fly in this layer.

- **The mesosphere** contains few gases but it is thick enough to slow down meteorites. They burn up as they hurtle into it, leaving fiery trails in the night sky. Temperatures drop from 10°C to −120°c 80 km up.

- **In the thermosphere** temperatures are very high, but there is so little gas that there is little real heat. Temperatures rise from −120°C to 2,000°C 700 km up.

- **The exosphere** is the highest level of the atmosphere where it fades into the nothingness of space.

▶ *The atmosphere is a sea of colourless, tasteless, odourless gases, mixed with moisture and fine dust particles. It is about 800 km deep but has no distinct edge, simply fading away into space. As you move up, each layer contains less and less gas. The topmost layers are very rarefied, which means that gas is very sparse.*

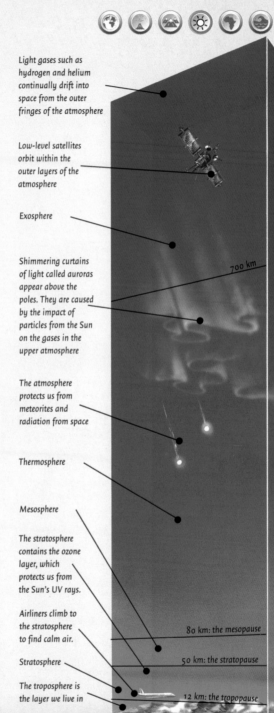

Light gases such as hydrogen and helium continually drift into space from the outer fringes of the atmosphere

Low-level satellites orbit within the outer layers of the atmosphere

Exosphere

Shimmering curtains of light called auroras appear above the poles. They are caused by the impact of particles from the Sun on the gases in the upper atmosphere

700 km

The atmosphere protects us from meteorites and radiation from space

Thermosphere

Mesosphere

The stratosphere contains the ozone layer, which protects us from the Sun's UV rays.

Airliners climb to the stratosphere to find calm air.

Stratosphere

The troposphere is the layer we live in

80 km: the mesopause

50 km: the stratopause

12 km: the tropopause

Waves

- **Waves in the sea** are formed when wind blows across the sea and whips the surface into ripples.
- **Water particles** are dragged a short way by the friction between air and water, which is known as wind stress.
- **If the wind continues to blow** long and strong enough in the same direction, moving particles may build up into a ridge of water. At first this is a ripple, then a wave.
- **Waves seem to move** but the water in them stays in the

> ★ STAR FACT ★
> A wave over 40 m high was recorded by the
> USS *Ramapo* in the Pacific in 1933.

same place, rolling around like rollers on a conveyor belt.

- **The size of a wave** depends on the strength of the wind and how far it blows over the water (the fetch).
- **If the fetch is short,** the waves may simply be a chaotic, choppy 'sea'. If the fetch is long, they may develop into a series of rolling waves called a swell.
- **One in 300,000 waves** is four times bigger than the rest.
- **The biggest waves** occur south of South Africa.
- **When waves** move into shallow water, the rolling of the water is impeded by the sea-bed. The water piles up, then spills over in a breaker.

◀ *When waves enter shallow water, the water in them piles up until eventually they spill over at the top and break.*

Ecosystems

- **An ecosystem** is a community of living things interacting with each other and their surroundings.

- **An ecosystem** can be anything from a piece of rotting wood to a huge swamp. In every ecosystem each organism depends on the others.

◀ *How vegetation may develop in a deciduous woodland. This process is called vegetation succession.*

- **When vegetation** colonizes an area, the first plants to grow there are small and simple, such as mosses and lichens. Grass and sedges appear next.
- **The simple plants** stabilize the soil so that bigger and more complex plants can move in. This is called vegetation succession.
- **Rainforest ecosystems** cover only 8% of the world's land, yet they include 40% of all the world's plant and animal species.
- **Farming has a huge effect** on natural ecosystems, reducing the number of species dramatically.
- **Green plants** are autotrophs, or producers, which means they make their own food (from sunlight).
- **Animals** are heterotrophs, or consumers, which means they get their food from other living things.
- **Primary consumers** are herbivores that eat plants.
- **Secondary consumers** are carnivores that eat herbivores or each other.

Asia

- **Asia is the world's largest continent**, stretching from Europe in the west to Japan in the east. It has an area of 44,680,718 sq km.

- **Asia has huge climate extremes,** from a cold polar climate in the north to a hot tropical one in the south.

- **Verkhoyansk** in Siberia has had temperatures as high as 37°C and as low as –68°C.

◀ *Asia is a vast continent of wide plains and dark forests in the north, separated from the tropical south by the Himalayas.*

> ★ STAR FACT ★
> Lake Baikal is the world's deepest lake – 1,743 m – and it holds 20% of the world's fresh water.

- **The Himalayas** are the highest mountains in the world, with 14 peaks over 8,000 m high. To the north are vast empty deserts, broad grasslands and huge coniferous forests. To the south are fertile plains and valleys and steamy tropical jungles.

- **Northern Asia** sits on one giant tectonic plate.

- **India** is on a separate plate that crashed into the north Asia plate 50 million years ago. It is piling up the Himalayas as it ploughs on northwards.

- **Asia's longest river** is China's Yangtze, 5,520 km long.

- **Asia's** highest mountain is the world's highest – Mt Everest, or Sagarmatha, in Nepal at 8,848 m.

- **The Caspian Sea** bewteen Azerbaijan and Kazakhstan is the world's largest lake, covering 378,400 sq km.

Cold

- **Winter weather is cold** because days are too short to give much heat. The Sun always rakes across the ground at a low angle, spreading out its warmth.

- **The coldest places** in the world are the North and South Poles. Here the Sun shines at a low angle even in summer, and winter nights last almost 24 hours.

- **The average temperature** at Polus Nedostupnosti (Pole of Cold) in Antarctica is –58°C.

- **The coldest temperature** ever recorded was –89.2°C at Vostok in Antarctica on July 21, 1983.

- **The interiors of the continents** can get very cold in winter because land loses heat rapidly.

- **When air cools** below freezing point (0°C), water vapour in the air may freeze without turning first to dew. It covers the ground with white crystals of ice or frost.

- **Fern frost** is feathery tails of ice that form on cold glass as dew drops freeze bit by bit.

- **Hoar frost** is spiky needles of frost that form when damp air blows over very cold surfaces and freezes onto them.

- **Rime** is a thick coating of ice that forms when drops of water in clouds and fogs stay liquid well below freezing point. The drops freeze hard when they touch a surface.

- **Black ice** forms when rain falls on a very cold road.

▼ *Rime is a thick coating of ice that forms when moisture cools well below 0°C before freezing onto surfaces.*

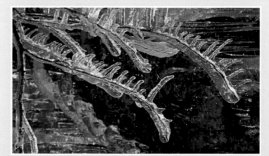

Converting plates

- **In many places** around the world, the tectonic plates that make up the Earth's crust, or outer layer, are slowly crunching together with enormous force.

- **The Atlantic** is getting wider, pushing the Americas further west. Yet the Earth is not getting any bigger because as the American plates crash into the Pacific plates, the thinner, denser ocean plates are driven down into the Earth's hot mantle and are destroyed.

- **The process** of driving an ocean plate down into the Earth's interior is called subduction.

- **Subduction** creates deep ocean trenches typically 6–7 km deep at the point of collision. One of these, the Mariana Trench, could drown Mt Everest with 2 km to spare on top.

> ★ **STAR FACT** ★
> Subduction creates a ring of volcanoes around the Pacific Ocean called the 'Ring of Fire'.

- **As an ocean plate** bends down into the Earth's mantle, it cracks. The movement of these cracks sets off earthquakes originating up to 700 km down. These earthquake zones are called Benioff–Wadati zones after Hugo Benioff, who discovered them in the 1950s.

- **As an ocean plate** slides down, it melts and makes blobs of magma. This magma floats up towards the surface, punching its way through to create a line of volcanoes along the edge of the continental plate.

▲ Volcanoes in subduction zones are usually highly explosive. This is because the magma becomes contaminated as it burns its way up through the continental crust.

- **If volcanoes in subduction zones** emerge in the sea, they form a curving line of volcanic islands called an island arc. Beyond this arc is the back-arc basin, an area of shallow sea that slowly fills up with sediments.

- **As a subducting plate sinks,** the continental plate scrapes sediments off the ocean plate and piles them in a great wedge. Between this wedge and the island arc there may be a fore-arc basin, which is a shallow sea that slowly fills with sediment.

- **Where two continental plates collide,** the plate splits into two layers: a lower layer of dense mantle rock and an upper layer of lighter crustal rock, which is too buoyant to be subducted. As the mantle rock goes down, the crustal rock peels off and crumples against the other to form fold mountains (see mountain ranges).

▼ This is a cross-section through the top 1,000 km or so of the Earth's surface. It shows a subduction zone, where an ocean plate is bent down beneath a continental plate.

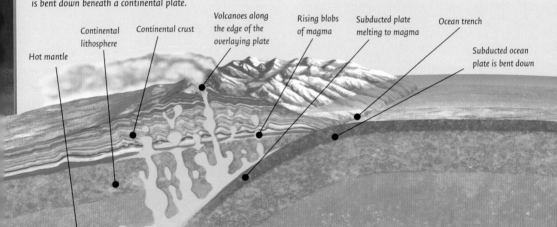

Continental lithosphere

Continental crust

Volcanoes along the edge of the overlaying plate

Rising blobs of magma

Subducted plate melting to magma

Ocean trench

Hot mantle

Subducted ocean plate is bent down

Great lakes

- **Most of the world's great lakes** lie in regions that were once glaciated. The glaciers carved out deep hollows in the rock in which water collected. The Great Lakes of the USA and Canada are partly glacial in origin.

- **In Minnesota, USA** 11,000 lakes were formed by glaciers.

- **The world's deepest lakes** are often formed by faults in the Earth's crust, such as Lake Baikal in Siberia (see Asia) and Lake Tanganyika in East Africa.

- **Most lakes** last only a few thousand years before they are filled in by silt or drained by changes in the landscape.

- **The world's oldest great lake** is Lake Baikal in Siberia, which is over 2 million years old.

- **The Great Lakes** include three of the world's five largest lakes: Superior, Huron and Michigan.

- **The world's largest lake** is the Caspian Sea (see Asia), which is a saltwater lake.

- **The world's highest great lake** is Titicaca in South America, which is 3,812 m above sea level.

- **The world's lowest great lake** is the Dead Sea between Israel and Jordan. It is 399 m below sea level and getting lower all the time.

- **The largest underground lake** in the world is Drauchen-hauchloch, which is inside a cave in Namibia.

▼ *Many of the world's great lakes were formed by glaciation, and will eventually disappear.*

Beaches

▲ *The little bays in this beach have been scooped out as waves strike the beach at an angle.*

- **Beaches** are sloping bands of sand, shingle or pebbles along the edge of a sea or lake.

- **Some beaches** are made entirely of broken coral or shells.

- **On a steep beach,** the backwash after each wave is strong. It washes material down the beach and so makes the beach gentler sloping.

★ STAR FACT ★
The world's largest pleasure beach is Virginia Beach, Virginia, USA, over 45 km long.

- **On a gently sloping beach,** each wave runs in powerfully and falls back gently. Material gets washed up the beach, making it steeper.

- **The slope of a beach** matches the waves, so the slope is often gentler in winter when the waves are stronger.

- **A storm beach** is a ridge of gravel and pebbles flung high above the normal high-tide mark during a storm.

- **At the top of each beach** a ridge, or berm, is often left at the high-tide mark.

- **Beach cusps** are tiny bays in the sand that are scooped out along the beach when waves strike it at an angle.

- **Many scientists** believe that beaches are only a temporary phenomenon caused by the changes in sea levels after the last Ice Age.

Seasons

- **Seasons** are periods of similar weather that occur at certain times of year.
- **Outside the tropics** there are four seasons each year. Each one lasts about three months.
- **The changes in the seasons** occur because the tilt of the Earth's axis is always the same as it circles the Sun.
- **When the Earth** is on one side of the Sun, the Northern Hemisphere (half of the world) is tilted towards the Sun. It is summer in the north of the world and winter in the south.
- **As the Earth moves** a quarter way round the Sun, the northern half begins to tilt away. This brings cooler autumn weather to the north and spring to the south.
- **When the Earth** moves another quarter round to the far side of the Sun,

▲ *In autumn, the leaves of deciduous trees change colour then drop off ready for winter. Nights grow cooler, and a mist will often develop by morning.*

the Northern Hemisphere is tilted away from the Sun. It is winter in the north of the world, and summer in the south.
- **As the Earth moves** three-quarters of the way round the Sun, the north begins to tilt towards the Sun again. This brings the warmer weather of spring to the north, and autumn to the south.
- **Around March 21** and September 21, the night is exactly 12 hours long all over the world. These times are called the vernal (spring) equinox and the autumnal equinox.
- **The day when** nights begin to get longer again is called the summer solstice. This is around June 21 in the north and December 21 in the south.
- **Many places** in the tropics have just two six-month seasons: wet and dry.

Global warming

- **Global warming** is the general increase in average temperatures around the world. This increase has been between 0.3°C and 0.8°C over the last hundred years.
- **Most scientists** now think that global warming is caused by human activities, which have resulted in an increase in the Earth's natural greenhouse effect.
- **The greenhouse effect** is the way that certain gases in

▼ *Could global warming make the Mediterranean look like this?*

the air – notably carbon dioxide – trap some of the Sun's warmth, like the panes of glass in a greenhouse.
- **The greenhouse effect** keeps the Earth pleasantly warm – but if it increases, the Earth may become hot.
- **Many experts** expect a 4°C rise in average temperatures over the next 100 years.
- **Humans** boost the greenhouse effect by burning fossil fuels, such as coal and oil, that produce carbon dioxide.
- **Emission of the greenhouse gas** methane from the world's cattle has added to global warming.
- **Global warming** is bringing stormier weather by trapping more energy inside the atmosphere.
- **Global warming** may melt much of the polar ice caps, flooding low-lying countries such as Bangladesh.

> **! NEWS FLASH !**
> Recent observations show global warming could be much worse than we thought.

Black smokers

- **Black smokers** are natural chimneys on the sea-bed. They billow black fumes of hot gases and water.

- **Black smokers** are technically known as hydrothermal vents. They are volcanic features.

- **Black smokers** form along mid-ocean ridges where the tectonic plates are moving apart.

- **Black smokers** begin when seawater seeps through

★ STAR FACT ★
Each drop of sea water in the world circulates through a smoker every ten million years.

cracks in the sea floor. The water is heated by volcanic magma, and it dissolves minerals from the rock.

- **Once the water is superheated,** it spews from the vents in scalding, mineral-rich black plumes.

- **The plume cools** rapidly in the cold sea, leaving behind thick deposits of sulphur, iron, zinc and copper in tall, chimney-like vents.

- **The tallest vents** are 50 m high.

- **Water jetting** from black smokers can reach 662°C.

- **Smokers** are home to a community of organisms that thrive in the scalding waters and toxic chemicals. The organisms include giant clams and tube worms.

◀ Black smokers were first discovered less than 30 years ago.

Australasia

- **Australasia** is a vast region that includes islands spread over much of the Pacific Ocean. The land area is 8,508,238 sq km, but the sea area is much, much bigger.

- **Australia** is the only country in the world which is a continent in its own right.

- **The largest island** is New Guinea, 787,878 sq km.

- **Fraser Island,** off Queensland, Australia, is the world's largest sand island with a sand dune 120 km long.

- **Australasia** is mostly tropical, with temperatures averaging 30°C in the north of Australia, and slightly lower on the islands where the ocean keeps the land cool.

- **New Zealand** is only a few thousand kilometres from the Antarctic Circle at its southern tip. As a result New Zealand has only mild summers and cold winters.

- **Australasia's highest peak** is Mt Wilhelm on Papua New Guinea, 4,300 m high.

- **The Great Barrier Reef** is the world's largest living thing, 2,027 km long. It is the only structure built by

animals, that is visible from space.

- **Australia** was the first modern continent to break off from Pangaea (see continental drift) about 200 million years ago, and so has developed its own unique wildlife.

- **Australia sits** on the Indian-Australian plate, which is moving very slowly north away from Antarctica. New Zealand sits astride the boundary (see converging plates) with the Pacific plate.

▶ Apart from the landmass of Australia, much of Australasia is open water.

Kinds of volcano

- **Each volcano and each eruption** are slightly different.
- **Shield volcanoes** are shaped like upturned shields. They form where lava is runny and spreads over a wide area.
- **Fissure volcanoes** are found where floods of lava pour out of a long crack in the ground.
- **Composite volcanoes** are cone shaped. They build up in layers from a succession of explosive eruptions.
- **Cinder cones** are built up from ash, with little lava.
- **Strombolian eruptions** are eruptions from sticky magma. They spit out sizzling clots of red-hot lava.
- **Vulcanian eruptions** are explosive eruptions from sticky magma. The magma clogs the volcano's vent between cannon-like blasts of ash clouds and thick lava flows.
- **Peléean eruptions** eject glowing clouds of ash and gas called *nuée ardente* (see famous eruptions).
- **Plinian eruptions** are the most explosive kind of eruption. They are named after Pliny who witnessed the eruption of Vesuvius in AD 79 (see famous eruptions).

- **In Plinian eruptions** boiling gases blast clouds of ash and volcanic fragments up into the stratosphere.

▼ *Fissure volcanoes shoot lava fountains in the air. This happens when gases in the lava boil suddenly as they reach the surface.*

Thunderstorms

◄ *Few places have more spectacular lightning displays than Nevada, USA. The energy in clouds piled up during hot afternoons is unleashed at night.*

- **Thunderstorms** begin when strong updraughts build up towering cumulonimbus clouds.
- **Water drops** and ice crystals in thunderclouds are buffeted together. They become charged with static electricity.
- **Negative charges** in a cloud sink; positive ones rise. Lightning is a rush of negative charge towards the positive.
- **Sheet lightning** is a flash within a cloud. Fork lightning flashes from a cloud to the ground.

- **Forked lightning** begins with a fast, dim flash from a cloud to the ground, called the leader stroke. It prepares the air for a huge, slower return stroke a split second later.
- **Thunder is the sound** of the shock wave as air expands when heated instantly to 25,000°C by the lightning.
- **Sound travels** more slowly than light, so we hear thunder 3 seconds later for every 1 km between us and the storm.
- **At any moment** there are 2,000 thunderstorms around the world, each generating the energy of a hydrogen bomb. Every second, 100 lightning bolts hit the ground.
- **A flash of lightning** is brighter than 10 million 100-watt light bulbs. For a split second it has more power than all the power stations in the USA put together. Lightning travels at up to 100,000 km per second down a path that is the width of a finger but up to 14 km long. Sheet lightning can be 140 km long.
- **Lightning** can fuse sand under the ground into hard root-like strands called fulgurites.

Coasts

- **Coastlines** are changing all the time as new waves roll in and out and tides rise and fall every six hours or so. Over longer periods coastlines are reshaped by the action of waves and the corrosion of salty water.

- **On exposed coasts** where waves strike the high rocks, they undercut the slope to create steep cliffs and headlands. Often waves can penetrate into the cliff to open up sea caves or blast through arches. When a sea arch collapses, it leaves behind tall pillars called stacks which may be worn away to stumps.

- **Waves work** on rocks in two ways. First, the rocks are pounded with a huge weight of water filled with stones. Second, the waves force air into cracks in the rocks with such force that the rocks split apart.

- **The erosive power** of waves is focused in a narrow band at wave height. So as waves wear away sea cliffs, they leave the rock below wave height untouched. As cliffs retreat, the waves slice away a broad shelf of rock called a wave-cut platform. Water left behind in dips when the tide falls forms rockpools.

- **On more sheltered coasts,** the sea may pile up sand into beaches (see beaches). The sand has been washed down by rivers or worn away from cliffs.

- **When waves hit** a beach at an angle, they fall straight back down the beach at a right angle. Any sand and shingle that the waves carry fall back slightly farther along the beach. In this way sand and shingle are moved along the beach in a zig-zag fashion. This is called longshore drift.

- **On beaches** prone to longshore drift, low fences called groynes are often built to stop the sand being washed away along the beach.

- **Longshore drift** can wash sand out across bays and estuaries to create sand bars called spits.

- **Bays** are broad indents in the coast with a headland on each side. Waves reach the headlands first, focusing their energy here. Material is worn away from the headlands and washed into the bay, forming a bay-head beach.

- **A cove is a small bay.** A bight is a huge bay, such as the Great Australian Bight. A gulf is a long narrow bight. The world's biggest bay is Hudson Bay, Canada, which has a shoreline 12,268 km long. The Bay of Bengal in India is larger in area.

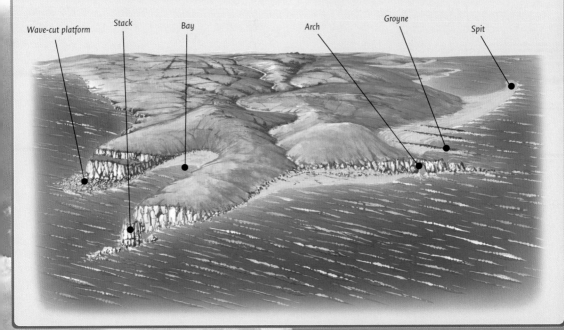

Wave-cut platform · Stack · Bay · Arch · Groyne · Spit

Europe

- **Europe** has an area of just 10,400,000 sq km. For for its size Europe has an immensely long coastline.
- **In the north** are the ancient glaciated mountains of Scandinavia and Scotland, which were once much, much higher.
- **Across the centre** are the lowlands of the North European Plain, stretching from the Urals in Russia to France in the west.
- **Much of southern Europe** has been piled up into young mountain ranges, as Africa drifts slowly north.
- **The highest point** in Europe is Mt Elbrus in the Russian Caucasus, 5,642 m high.

◀ Europe is a small continent but its peninsulas and inlets give it a long coast.

- **Northwest Europe** was once joined to Canada. The ancient Caledonian mountains of eastern Canada, Greenland, Scandinavia and Scotland were formed together as a single mountain chain 360–540 million years ago.
- **Mediterranean Europe** has a Mediterranean climate with warm summers and mild winters.
- **NW Europe** is often wet and windy. It has very mild winters because it is bathed by the warm North Atlantic Drift (see ocean currents).
- **The Russian islands** of Novaya Zimlya are far into the Arctic Circle and are icebound in winter.
- **The largest lake** is Ladoga in Russia, 18,389 sq km.

Floods

- **A flood** is when a river or the sea rises so much that it spills over the surrounding land.
- **River floods** may occur after a period of prolonged heavy rain or after snow melts in spring.

- **Small floods** are common; big floods are rare. So flood size is described in terms of frequency.
- **A 2-year flood** is a smallish flood that is likely to occur every two years. A 100-year

◀ Even when no one drowns, a flood can destroy homes and wash away soil from farmland, leaving it barren.

> ★ STAR FACT ★
> In 1887, one million people were killed when the Hwang Ho river in China flooded.

flood is a big flood that is likely to occur once a century.

- **A flash flood** occurs when a small stream changes to a raging torrent after heavy rain during a dry spell.
- **The 1993 flood** on the Mississippi–Missouri caused damage of $15,000 million and made 75,000 homeless, despite massive flood control works in the 1930s.
- **The Hwang Ho river** is called 'China's sorrow' because its floods are so devastating.
- **Not all floods** are bad. Before the Aswan Dam was built, Egyptian farmers relied on the yearly flooding of the River Nile to enrich the soil.
- **After the Netherlands** was badly flooded by a North Sea surge in 1953, the Dutch embarked on the Delta project, one of the biggest flood control schemes in history.

Core and mantle

- **The mantle** makes up the bulk of the Earth's interior. It reaches from about 10–90 km to 2,890 km down.

- **Temperatures** in the mantle climb steadily as you move through the mantle, reaching 3,000°C.

- **Mantle rock** is so warm that it churns slowly round like very, very thick treacle boiling on a stove. This movement is known as mantle convection currents.

▲ *Every now and then, mantle rock melts into floods of magma, which collects along the edges of tectonic plates. It then rises to the surface and erupts as a volcano.*

! NEWS FLASH !
Scientists have found 'anti-continents' on the CMB that match with continents on the surface.

- **Mantle rock moves** about 10,000 times more slowly than the hour hand on a kitchen clock. Cooler mantle rock takes about 200 million years to sink all the way to the core.

- **Near the surface,** mantle rock may melt into floods of magma. These may gush through the upper layers like oil that is being squeezed from a sponge.

- **The boundary** between the mantle and the core (see Earth's interior) is called the core–mantle boundary (CMB).

- **The CMB** is about 250 km thick. It is an even more dramatic change than between the ground and the air.

- **Temperatures jump by 1,500°C** at the CMB.

- **The difference** in density between the core and the mantle at the CMB is twice as great as the difference between air and rock.

The Arctic Ocean

- **Most of the Arctic Ocean** is permanently covered with a vast floating raft of sea ice.

- **Temperatures** are low all year round, averaging −30°C in winter and sometimes dropping to −70°C.

- **During the long winters,** which last more than four months, the Sun never rises above the horizon.

- **The Arctic** gets its name from *arctos*, the Greek word for 'bear', because the Great Bear constellation is above the North Pole.

- **There are three kinds of sea ice** in the Arctic: polar ice, pack ice and fast ice.

- **Polar ice** is the raft of ice that never melts through.

- **Polar ice** may be as thin as 2 m in places in summer, but in winter it is up to 50 m thick.

- **Pack ice** forms around the edge of the polar ice and only freezes completely in winter.

- **The ocean swell** breaks and crushes the pack ice into

▲ *The seal is one of the few creatures that can survive the bitter cold of the Arctic winter.*

chunky ice blocks and fantastic ice sculptures.

- **Fast ice** forms in winter between pack ice and the land around the Arctic Ocean. It gets its name because it is held fast to the shore. It cannot move up and down with the ocean as the pack ice does.

Diverging plates

▲ Unlike subduction zones, which create explosive volcanoes, diverging plates create volcanoes that ooze lava gently. For this to happen above the ocean surface is rare.

- **Deep down on the ocean floor**, some of the tectonic plates of the Earth's crust are slowly pushing apart. New molten rock wells up from the mantle into the gap between them and freezes onto their edges. As plates are destroyed at subduction zones (see converging plates), so new plate spreads the ocean floor wider.

- **The spreading of the ocean floor** centres on long ridges down the middle of some oceans, called mid-ocean ridges. Some of these ridges link up to make the world's longest mountain range, winding over 60,000 km beneath the oceans.

- **The Mid-Atlantic ridge** stretches through the Atlantic from North Pole to South Pole. The East Pacific Rise winds under the Pacific Ocean from Mexico to Antarctica.

- **Along the middle** of a mid-ocean ridge is a deep canyon. This is where molten rock from the mantle wells up through the sea-bed.

- **Mid-ocean ridges** are broken by the curve of the Earth's surface into short stepped sections. Each section is marked off by a long sideways crack called a transform fault. As the sea floor spreads out from a ridge, the sides of the fault rub together setting off earthquakes.

- **As molten rock wells** up from a ridge and freezes, its magnetic material sets in a certain way to line up with the Earth's magnetic field. Because the field reverses every now and then, bands of material set in alternate directions. This means that scientists can see how the sea floor has spread in the past.

- **Rates of sea floor spreading** vary from 1 cm to 20 cm a year. Slow-spreading ridges such as the Mid-Atlantic Ridge are much higher, with seamounts often topping the ridge. Fast-spreading ridges such as the East Pacific Rise are lower, and magma oozes from these just like fissure volcanoes on the surface (see kinds of volcano).

> ★ STAR FACT ★
> About 10 cubic km of new crust is created at the mid-ocean ridges every year.

- **Hot magma** bubbling up through a mid-ocean ridge emerges as hot lava. As it comes into contact with the cold seawater it freezes into blobs called pillow lava.

- **Mid-ocean ridges** may begin where a mantle plume (see hot-spot volcanoes) rises through the mantle and melts through the sea-bed. Plumes may also melt through continents to form Y-shaped cracks, which begin as rift valleys (see faults) and then widen into new oceans.

▼ This is a cross-section of the top 50 km or so of the Earth's surface. It shows where the sea floor is spreading away from the mid-ocean ridge.

Central canyon

Mid-ocean ridge

Magma erupts through the gap as lava solidifies into new sea floor

Ocean plate

Ridges are lower and older away from the centre

Transform fault

Mantle

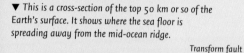

Rain

- **Rain falls** from clouds filled with large water drops and ice crystals. The thick clouds block out the sunlight.
- **The technical name** for rain is precipitation, which also includes snow, sleet and hail.
- **Drizzle** is 0.2–0.5 mm drops falling from nimbostratus clouds. Rain from nimbostratus is 1–2 mm drops. Drops from thunderclouds can be 5 mm. Snow is ice crystals. Sleet is a mix of rain or snow, or partly melted snow.
- **Rain starts** when water drops or ice crystals inside clouds grow too large for the air to support them.
- **Cloud drops grow** when moist air is swept upwards and cools, causing lots of drops to condense. This happens when pockets of warm, rising air form thunderclouds – at weather fronts or when air is forced up over hills.
- **In the tropics** raindrops grow in clouds by colliding with each other. In cool places, they also grow on ice crystals.
- **The world's rainiest place** is Mt Wai-'ale-'ale in Hawaii, where it rains 350 days a year.

- **The wettest place** is Tutunendo in Colombia, which gets 11,770 mm of rain every year. (London gets about 70 mm).
- **La Réunion in the Indian Ocean** received 1,870 mm of rain in one day in 1952.
- **Guadeloupe in the West Indies** received 38.1 mm of rain in one minute in 1970.

▼ Rain starts when moist air is lifted up dramatically. Water drops and ice crystals inside the cloud grow so big that it turns dark.

Great rivers

▲ All great rivers develop the same horseshoe-shaped meanders in their lower reaches (see river channels).

- **Measurements** of river lengths vary according to where the river is said to begin. So some people say that Africa's Nile is the world's longest river; others say that South America's Amazon is longer.
- **The source** of the Amazon was only discovered in 1971,

★ STAR FACT ★
The Amazon in flood could fill the world's biggest sports stadium with water in 13 seconds.

in snowbound lakes high in the Andes. It is named Laguna McIntyre after the American who found it.

- **If the full length** of the Amazon is counted, it is 6,750 km long compared with the Nile at 6,673 km.
- **The Amazon basin** covers more than 7 million sq km.
- **China's Yangtse** is the third longest river, at 6,300 km.
- **The world's longest tributary** is the Madeira flowing into the Amazon. At 3,380 km long it is the 18th longest river in the world.
- **The world's longest estuary** is that of the Ob' in Russia, which is up to 80 km wide and 885 km long.
- **The Ob'** is the biggest river to freeze solid in winter.
- **The shortest official river** is the North Fork Roe River in Montana, USA, which is just 17.7 m long.

Hills

- **One definition** of a hill is high ground up to 307 m high. Above that height it is a mountain.
- **Mountains are solid rock**; hills can be solid rock or piles of debris built up by glaciers or the wind.
- **Hills that are solid rock** are either very old, having been worn down from mountains over millions of years, or they are made from soft sediments that were low hills.
- **In moist climates** hills are often rounded by weathering and by water running over the land.
- **As solid rock is weathered**, the hill is covered in a layer of debris called regolith. This material either creeps slowly downhill or slumps suddenly in landslides.

▲ *The contours of hills in damp places have often been gently rounded over long periods by a combination of weathering and erosion by running water.*

- **Hills** often have a shallow S-shaped slope. Geologists call this kind of slope 'convexo-concave' because there is a short rounded convex section at the top, and a long dish-shaped concave slope lower down.
- **Hill slopes** may become gentler as they are worn away, because the top is worn away faster. This is called decline.
- **Some hill slopes** may stay equally steep, but are simply warn back. This is called retreat
- **Some hill slopes** may wear backwards, as gentler sections get longer and steeper sections get shorter. This is called replacement
- **Decline** may take place in damp places; retreat happens in dry places.

Snow

- **Snow** is crystals of ice. They fall from clouds in cold weather when the air is too cold to melt ice to rain.
- **Outside the tropics** most rain starts to fall as snow but melts on the way down.

- **More snow falls** in the northern USA than falls at the North Pole because it is too cold to snow at the North Pole.
- **The heaviest** snow falls when the

◄ *Fresh snow can contain up to 90% air, which is why snow can actually insulate the ground and keep it warm, protecting plants.*

air temperature is hovering around freezing.

- **Snow can be hard to forecast** because a rise in temperature of just 1°C or so can turn snow into rain.
- **All snow flakes** have six sides. They usually consist of crystals that are flat plates, but occasionally needles and columns are found.
- **W. A. Bentley** was an American farmer who photographed thousands of snowflakes through microscopes. He never found two identical flakes.
- **In February 1959** the Mt Shaska Ski Bowl in California had 4,800 mm of snow in just six days.
- **In March 1911** Tamarac in California was buried in 11,460 mm of snow. The Antarctic is buried in over 4,000 m of snow.
- **The snowline** is the lowest level on a mountain where snow remains throughout the summer. It is 5,000 m in the tropics, 2,700 m in the Alps, 600 m in Greenland and at sea level at the Poles.

Folds

- **Rocks usually form** in flat layers called strata. Tectonic plates can collide (see converging plates) with such force that they crumple up these strata.
- **Sometimes the folds** are just tiny wrinkles a few centimetres long. Sometimes they are gigantic, with hundreds of kilometres between crests (the highest points on a fold).

▼ *The main features of a fold.*

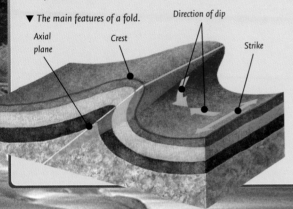

Axial plane

Crest

Direction of dip

Strike

★ STAR FACT ★
Most of the world's oil comes from reservoirs that are trapped in anticlines.

- **The shape of a fold** depends on the force that is squeezing it and on the resistance of the rock.
- **The slope of a fold** is called the dip. The direction of the dip is the direction in which it is sloping.
- **The strike of the fold** is at right angles to the dip. It is the horizontal alignment of the fold.
- **Some folds turn right over** on themselves to form upturned folds called nappes.
- **As nappes fold on top of other nappes,** the crumpled strata may pile up into mountains.
- **A downfold** is called a syncline; an upfolded arch of strata is called an anticline.
- **The axial plane** of a fold divides the fold into halves.

Biomes

- **A biome** is a community of plants and animals adapted to similar conditions in certain parts of the world.
- **Biomes** are also known as 'major life zones' or 'biogeographical regions'.
- **The soil** and animal life of a region are closely linked to its vegetation. Biomes are usually named after the dominant vegetation, e.g. grassland or coniferous forest.
- **Vegetation** is closely linked to climate, so biomes correspond to climate zones.
- **Major biome types** include: tundra, boreal (cold) coniferous forests, temperate deciduous forests, temperate grasslands, savannahs (tropical grasslands), tropical rainforests and deserts.
- **Most types of biome** are found across several different continents.
- **Species within a biome type** vary from continent to continent, but they share the same kind of vegetation.

- **Many plants and animals** have features that make them especially suited to a particular biome .
- **Polar bears** are adapted to life in the Arctic; cacti are well equipped to survive in the desert.
- **Biomes also exist in the sea,** for example coral reefs.

▼ *Extreme conditions, such as flooding in a swamp, can create different kinds of communities within the same biome.*

Sunshine

▲ *Without sunshine, the Earth would be cold, dark and dead.*

- **Half of the Earth** is exposed to the Sun at any time. Radiation from the Sun is the Earth's main source of energy, providing huge amounts of heat and light.
- **Solar** means anything to do with the Sun
- **About 41% of solar radiation** is light; 51% is long-wave radiation that our eyes cannot see, such as infrared light. The other 8% is short-wave radiation, such as UV rays.

- **Only 47%** of the solar radiation that strikes the Earth actually reaches the ground; the rest is soaked up or reflected by the atmosphere.
- **The air is not warmed** much by the Sun directly. Instead, it is warmed by heat reflected from the ground.
- **Solar radiation** reaching the ground is called insolation.
- **The amount of heat reaching** the ground depends on the angle of the Sun's rays. The lower the Sun in the sky, the more its rays are spread out and give off less heat.
- **Insolation is at a peak** in the tropics and during the summer. It is lowest near the Poles and in winter.
- **The tropics** receive almost two and a half times more heat per day than the Poles do.
- **Some surfaces** reflect the Sun's heat and warm the air better than others. The percentage they reflect is called the albedo. Snow and ice have an albedo of 85–95% and so they stay frozen even as they warm the air. Forests have an albedo of 12%, so they soak up a lot of the Sun's heat.

River channels

▶ *The river here is so wide and flat, and its bed so rough, that the water's flow is slowed by friction.*

- **A channel** is the long trough along which a river flows.
- **When a river's channel** winds or has a rough bed, friction slows the river down.
- **A river flows faster** through a narrow, deep channel than a wide, shallow one because there is less friction.
- **All river channels** tend to wind, and the nearer they are to sea level, the more they wind. They form remarkably regular horseshoe-shaped bends called meanders.

- **Meanders** seem to develop because of the way in which a river erodes and deposits sediments.
- **One key factor** in meanders is the ups and downs along the river called pools (deeps) and riffles (shallows).
- **The distance between pools and riffles,** and the size of meanders, are in close proportion to the river's width.
- **Another key factor** in meanders is the tendency of river water to flow not only straight downstream but also across the channel. Water spirals through the channel in a corkscrew fashion called helicoidal flow.
- **Helicoidal flow** makes water flow faster on the outside of bends, wearing away the bank. It flows more slowly on the inside, building up deposits called slip-off slopes.

> ★ STAR FACT ★
> Meanders can form almost complete loops with only a neck of land separating the ends.

Volcanoes

- **Volcanoes** are places where magma (red-hot liquid rock from the earth's interior) emerges through the crust and onto the surface.

- **The word 'volcano'** comes from Vulcano Island in the Mediterranean. Here Vulcan, the ancient Roman god of fire and blacksmith to the gods, was supposed to have forged his weapons in the fire beneath the mountain.

- **There are many types** of volcano (see kinds of volcano). The most distinctive are the cone-shaped composite volcanoes, which build up from alternating layers of ash and lava in successive eruptions.

- **Beneath a composite volcano** there is typically a large reservoir of magma called a magma chamber. Magma collects in the chamber before an eruption.

- **From the magma chamber** a narrow chimney, or vent, leads up to the surface. It passes through the cone of debris from previous eruptions.

- **When a volcano erupts,** the magma is driven forcefully up the vent by the gases within it. As the magma nears the surface, the pressure drops, allowing the gases dissolved in the magma to boil out. The expanding gases – mostly carbon dioxide and steam – push the molten rock upwards and out of the vent.

- **If the level of magma** in the magma chamber drops, the top of the volcano's cone may collapse into it, forming a giant crater called a caldera. *Caldera* is Spanish for 'boiling pot'. The world's largest caldera is Toba on Sumatra, Indonesia, which is 1,775 sq km.

- **When a volcano** with a caldera subsides, the whole cone may collapse into the old magma chamber. The caldera may fill with water to form a crater lake, such as Crater Lake in Oregon, USA.

- **All the magma** does not gush up the central vent. Some exits through branching side vents, often forming their own small 'parasitic' cones on the side of the main one.

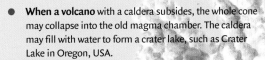

Volcanic bombs, or tephra, are fragments of the shattered volcanic plug flung out far and wide.

Before each eruption, the vent is clogged by old volcanic material from previous eruptions. The explosion blows the plug into tiny pieces of ash and cinder, and blasts them high into the air

Central vent

Side vent

Magma chamber where magma collects before an eruption

> **★ STAR FACT ★**
> At Urgüp, Turkey, volcanic ash has been blown into tall cones by gas fumes bubbling up. The cones have hardened like huge salt cellars. People have dug them out to make homes.

Air pollution

- **Air pollution** comes mainly from car, bus and truck exhausts, waste burners, factories, power stations and the burning of oil, coal and gas in homes.
- **Air pollution** can also come from farmers' crop sprays, farm animals, mining and volcanic eruptions.
- **Some pollutants,** such as soot and ash, are solid, but many more pollutants are gases.
- **Air pollution** can spread huge distances. Pesticides, for instance, have been discovered in Antarctica where they have never been used.
- **Most fuels** are chemicals called hydrocarbons. Any hydrocarbons that are left unburned in car exhausts, for example, can react in sunlight to form toxic ozone.
- **When exhaust gases** react in strong sunlight to form

> ★ STAR FACT ★
> Factories in the Chinese city of Benxi make so much smoke the city is invisible to satellites.

▲ *Factories pour out a range of fumes that pollute the air.*

   ozone, they may create a photochemical smog.

- **Air pollution** is probably a major cause of global warming (see global warming).
- **Air pollution** may destroy the ozone layer inside the Earth's atmosphere (see the ozone hole).
- **Breathing the air** in Mexico City is thought to be as harmful as smoking 40 cigarettes a day.

Hurricanes

- **Hurricanes** are powerful, whirling tropical storms. They are also called willy-willies, cyclones or typhoons.
- **Hurricanes develop** in late summer as clusters of thunderstorms build up over warm seas (at least 27°C).
- **As hurricanes grow,** they tighten into a spiral with a calm ring of low pressure called the 'eye' at the centre.
- **Hurricanes** move westwards at about 20 km/h. They strike east coasts, bringing torrential rain and winds gusting up to 360 km/h.
- **Officially** a hurricane is a storm with winds exceeding 119 km/h.
- **Hurricanes last,** on average, 3–14 days. They die out as they move towards the Poles into cooler air.

- **Each hurricane** is given a name in alphabetical order each year, from a list issued by the World Meteorological Organization. The first storm of the year might be, for instance, Hurricane Andrew.
- **The most fatal cyclone ever** was the one that struck Bangladesh in 1970. It killed 266,000 with the flood from the storm surge – the rapid rise in sea level created as winds drive ocean waters ashore.
- **A hurricane** generates the same energy every second as a small hydrogen bomb.
- **Each year** 35 tropical storms reach hurricane status in the Atlantic Ocean, and 85 around the world.

◀ *A satellite view of a hurricane approaching Florida, USA. Notice the yellow eye in the centre of the storm.*

Tsunamis

- **Tsunamis** are huge waves that begin when the sea floor is violently shaken by an earthquake, a landslide or a volcanic eruption.

- **In deep water** tsunamis travel almost unnoticeably below the surface. However, once they reach shallow coastal waters they rear up into waves 30 m or higher.

- **Tsunamis** are often mistakenly called 'tidal waves', but they are nothing to do with tides. The word *tsunami* (soon-army) is Japanese for 'harbour wave'.

- **Tsunamis** usually come in a series of a dozen or more – anything from five minutes to one hour apart.

- **Before a tsunami arrives**, the sea may recede dramatically, like water draining from a bath.

- **Tsunamis can travel** along the sea-

▶ Tsunamis may be generated underwater by an earthquake, then travel far along the seabed before emerging to swamp a coast.

bed as fast as a jet plane, at 700 km/h or more.

- **Tsunamis** arrive within 15 minutes from a local quake.

- **A tsunami** generated by an earthquake in Japan might swamp San Francisco, USA, 10 hours later .

- **The biggest tsunami** ever recorded was an 85-m high wave which struck Japan on April 24, 1771.

- **Tsunami warnings** are issued by the Pacific Tsunami Warning Centre in Honolulu.

A shift in the sea-bed sends out a pulse of water.

As the pulse moves into shallow water it rears into a giant wave.

The Indian Ocean

▲ Many of the Indian Ocean's islands have shining coral beaches.

- **The Indian Ocean** is the third largest ocean. It is about half the size of the Pacific and covers one-fifth of the world's ocean area. Area: 73,426,000 sq km.

- **The average depth** of the Indian Ocean is 3,890 m.

- **The deepest point** is the Java Trench off Java, in Indonesia, which is 7,450 m deep. It marks the line

where the Australian plate is being subducted (see converging plates) under the Eurasian plate.

- **The Indian Ocean** is 10,000 km across at its widest point, between Africa and Australia.

- **Scientists believe** that the Indian Ocean began to form about 200 million years ago when Australia broke away from Africa, followed by India.

- **The Indian Ocean** is getting 20 cm wider every year.

- **The Indian Ocean** is scattered with thousands of tropical islands such as the Seychelles and Maldives.

- **The Maldives** are so low lying that they may be swamped if global warming melts the polar ice.

- **Unlike in other oceans,** currents in the Indian Ocean change course twice a year. They are blown by monsoon winds towards Africa in winter, and then in the other direction towards India in summer.

- **The Persian Gulf** is the warmest sea in the world; the Red Sea is the saltiest.

Rivers

- **Rivers** are filled with water from rainfall running directly off the land, from melting snow or ice or from a spring bubbling out water that is soaked into the ground.

- **High up in mountains** near their source (start), rivers are usually small. They tumble over rocks through narrow valleys which they carved out over thousands of years.

- **All the rivers** in a certain area, called a catchment area, flow down to join each other, like branches on a tree. The branches are called tributaries. The bigger the river, the more tributaries it is likely to have.

- **As rivers flow downhill**, they are joined by tributaries and grow bigger. They often flow in smooth channels made not of big rocks but of fine debris washed down from higher up. River valleys are wider and gentler lower down, and the river may wind across the valley floor.

- **In its lower reaches** a river is often wide and deep. It winds back and forth in meanders (see river channels) across broad floodplains made of silt from higher up.

▲ *A river typically tumbles over boulders high up near its source.*

- **Rivers flow fast** over rapids in their upper reaches. On average, they flow as fast in the lower reaches where the channel is smoother because there is less turbulence.

- **Rivers wear away** their banks and beds, mainly by battering them with bits of gravel and sand and by the sheer force of the moving water.

- **Every river** carries sediment, which consists of large stones rolled along the river bed, sand bounced along the bed and fine silt that floats in the water.

- **The discharge of a river** is the amount of water flowing past a particular point each second (in cubic m per sec).

- **Rivers that flow** only after heavy rainstorms are 'intermittent'. Rivers that flow all year round are 'perennial' – they are kept going between rains by water flowing from underground.

▼ *Some of the ways in which a river changes as it flows from its source high up in the hills downwards to the sea.*

The neck of a meander may in time be worn through to leave an oxbow lake

In its lower reaches, a river winds broadly and smoothly across flat floodplains

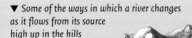

In its upper reaches, a river tumbles over rocks through steep valleys

In its middle reaches, a river winds through broad valleys

Over flat land, a river may split into branches

Tornadoes

- **Tornadoes,** or twisters, are long funnels of violently spiralling winds beneath thunderclouds.

- **Tornadoes** roar past in just a few minutes, but they can cause severe damage.

- **Wind speeds** inside tornadoes are difficult to measure, but they are believed to be over 400 km/h.

- **Tornadoes develop** beneath huge thunderclouds, called supercells, which develop along cold fronts.

- **England** has more tornadoes per square kilometre than any other country, but they are usually mild.

- **Tornado Alley** in Kansas, USA, has 1,000 tornadoes a year. Some of them are immensely powerful.

- **A tornado** may be rated on the Fujita scale, from F zero (gale tornado) to F6 (inconceivable tornado).

> ★ **STAR FACT** ★
> In 1879, a Kansas tornado tore up an iron
> bridge and sucked dry the river beneath it.

- **An F5 tornado** (incredible tornado) can lift a house and carry a bus hundreds of metres.

- **In 1990** a Kansas tornado lifted an 88-car train from the track and then dropped it in piles four cars high.

▶ *A tornado starts deep inside a thundercloud, where a column of strongly rising warm air is set spinning by high winds roaring through the cloud's top. As air is sucked into this column, or mesocyclone, it corkscrews down to the ground.*

Crust

▶ *The Horn of Africa and the Red Sea is one of the places where the Earth's thin oceanic crust is cracked and moving. It is gradually widening the Red Sea.*

- **The Earth's crust** is its hard outer shell.

- **The crust** is a thin layer of dense solid rock that floats on the mantle. It is made mainly of silicate minerals (minerals made of silicon and oxygen) such as quartz.

- **There are two kinds of crust:** oceanic and continental.

- **Oceanic crust** is the crust beneath the oceans. It is much thinner – just 7 km thick on average. It is also

young, with none being over 200 million years old.

- **Continental crust** is the crust beneath the continents. It is up to 80 km thick and mostly old.

- **Continental crust** is mostly crystalline 'basement' rock up to 3,800 million years old. Some geologists think at least half of this rock is over 2,500 million years old.

- **One cubic kilometre** of new continental crust is probably being created each year.

- **The 'basement' rock** has two main layers: an upper half of silica-rich rocks such as granite, schist and gneiss, and a lower half of volcanic rocks such as basalt which have less silica. Ocean crust is mostly basalt.

- **Continental crust** is created in the volcanic arcs above subduction zones (see converging plates). Molten rock from the subducted plate oozes to the surface over a period of a few hundred thousand years.

- **The boundary** between the crust and the mantle beneath it is called the Mohorovicic discontinuity.

Tectonic plates

- **The Earth's surface** is divided into thick slabs called tectonic plates. Each plate is a fragment of the Earth's rigid outer layer, or lithosphere (see the lithosphere).
- **There are 16 large plates** and several smaller ones.
- **The biggest plate** is the Pacific plate, which underlies the whole of the Pacific Ocean.
- **Tectonic plates** are moving all the time – by about 10 cm a year. Over hundreds of millions of years they move vast distances. Some have moved halfway round the globe.
- **The continents** are embedded within most of the plates and move with them.
- **The Pacific plate** is the only large plate with no part of a continent situated on it.
- **The movement** of tectonic plates accounts for many things, including the pattern of volcanic and earthquake activity around the world.

- **There are three kinds** of boundary between plates: convergent, divergent and transform.
- **Tectonic plates** are probably driven by convection currents of molten rock that circulate within the Earth's mantle (see core and mantle).
- **The lithosphere** was too thin for tectonic plates until 500 million years ago.

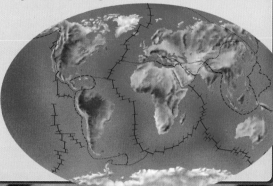

▶ This map shows some of the jagged boundaries between plates.

The ozone hole

▲ The loss of ozone was first spotted by scientists in the Antarctic.

- **Life on Earth** depends on the layer of ozone gas in the air (see atmosphere), which shields the Earth from the Sun's ultraviolet (UV) rays. Ozone molecules are made from three atoms of oxygen, not two like oxygen.
- **In 1982** scientists in Antarctica noticed a 50% loss of ozone over the Antarctic every spring. This finding was confirmed in 1985 by the *Nimbus-7* satellite.
- **The ozone hole** is a patch where the ozone layer becomes very thin.

! NEWS FLASH !
In 1996 an ozone hole appeared over the Arctic for the first time – and it is now getting bigger.

- **The ozone hole** appears over Antarctica every spring.
- **The ozone hole** is monitored all the time by the TOMS (Total Ozone Mapping Spectrometer) satellite.
- **The loss of ozone** is caused by manufactured gases, notably chlorofluorocarbons (CFCs), which drift up through the air and combine with the ozone.
- **CFCs** are used in many things, from refrigerators and aerosol sprays to forming the foam for fast-food cartons.
- **CFCs** were banned in 1996, but it may be at least 100 years before the ban takes effect. The hole is still growing.
- **UV rays** from the Sun come in three kinds: UVA, UVB and UVC. Both oxygen and ozone soak up UVA and UVC rays, but only ozone absorbs UVB. For every 1% loss of ozone, 1% more UVB rays reach the Earth's surface.

Minerals

- **Minerals** are the natural chemicals from which rocks are made.

- **All but a few minerals** are crystals.

- **Some rocks are made** from crystals of just one mineral; many are made from half a dozen or more minerals.

- **Most minerals** are combinations of two or more chemical elements. A few minerals, such as gold and copper, are made of just one element.

- **There are over 2,000** minerals, but around 30 of these are very common.

- **Most of the less common** minerals are present in rocks in minute traces. They may become concentrated in certain places by geological processes.

▲ *The rich range of colours in each layer is evidence of traces of different minerals within the rocks.*

- **Silicate minerals** are made when metals join with oxygen and silicon. There are more silicate minerals than all the other minerals together.

- **The most common** silicates are quartz and feldspar, the most common rock-forming minerals. They are major constituents in granite and other volcanic rocks.

- **Other common minerals** are oxides such as haematite and cuprite, sulphates such as gypsum and barite, sulphides such as galena and pyrite, and carbonates such as calcite and aragonite.

- **Some minerals** form as hot, molten rock from the Earth's interior, some from chemicals dissolved in liquids underground, and some are made by changes to other minerals.

The Pacific Ocean

- **The Pacific** is the world's largest ocean. It is twice as large as the Atlantic and covers over one third of the world, with an area of 181 million sq km.

- **It is over 24,000 km** across from Panama to the Malay Peninsula – more than halfway round the world.

- **The word 'pacific'** means calm. The ocean got its name from the 16th-century Portuguese explorer Magellan who was lucky enough to find gentle winds.

- **The Pacific is dotted** with thousands of islands. Some are the peaks of undersea volcanoes. Others are coral reefs sitting on top of the peaks.

- **The Pacific** has some of the greatest tides in the world (over 9 m off Korea). Its smallest tide (just 0.3 m) is on Midway Island in the middle of the Pacific.

- **On average,** the Pacific Ocean is 4,200 m deep.

- **Around the rim** there are deep ocean trenches including the world's deepest, the Mariana Trench.

- **A huge** undersea mountain range called the East Pacific Rise stretches from Antarctica up to Mexico.

- **The floor of the Pacific** is spreading along the East Pacific Rise at the rate of 12–16 cm per year.

- **The Pacific** has more seamounts (undersea mountains) than any other ocean.

▼ *The huge expanse of the Pacific means that waves breaking on the coast are often enormous – and popular with surfers.*

Volcanic eruptions

- **Volcanic eruptions** are produced by magma, the hot liquid rock under the Earth's surface. Magma is less dense than the rock above, and so it tries to bubble to the surface.

- **When magma** is runny, eruptions are 'effusive', which means they ooze lava gently all the time.

- **When magma** is sticky, eruptions are explosive. The magma clogs the volcano's vent until so much pressure builds up that

▲ There are about 60 major volcanic eruptions a year round the world, including two or three huge, violent eruptions.

> ★ STAR FACT ★
> Pressure of the magma below a volcano is 10 times greater than pressure on the surface.

the magma bursts out, like a popping champagne cork.

- **The explosion** shatters the plug of hard magma that blocks the volcano's vent, reducing it to ash and cinder.

- **Explosive eruptions** are driven by expanding bubbles of carbon dioxide gas and steam inside the magma.

- **An explosive eruption** blasts globs of hot magma, ash, cinder, gas and steam high up into the air.

- **Volcanoes** usually erupt again and again. The interval between eruptions, called the repose time, varies from a few minutes to thousands of years.

- **Magma near subduction zones** contains 10 times more gas, so the volcanic eruptions here are violent.

- **The gas inside magma** can expand hundreds of times in just a few seconds.

Mountain ranges

- **Great mountain ranges** such as the Andes in South America usually lie along the edges of continents.

- **Most mountain ranges** are made by the folding of rock layers (see folds) as tectonic plates move slowly together.

- **High ranges** are geologically young because they are soon worn down. The Himalayas are 25 million years old.

- **Many ranges** are still growing. The Himalayas grow a few centimetres each year as the Indian plate pushes into Asia.

- **Mountain** building is very slow because rocks flow like thick treacle. Rock is pushed up like the bow wave in front of a boat as one tectonic plate pushes into another.

- **Satellite techniques** show that the central peaks of the Andes and Himalayas are rising. The outer peaks are sinking as the rock flows slowly away from the 'bow wave'.

- **Mountain building** is very active during orogenic (mountain-forming) phases that last millions of years.

- **Different orogenic phases** occur in different places, for example the Caledonian, Hercynian and Alpine in Europe and the Huronian, Nevadian and Pasadenian in North America. The Caledonian was about 550 million years ago.

- **Mountain building** makes the Earth's crust especially thick under mountains, giving them very deep 'roots'.

- **As mountains** are worn down, their weight reduces and the 'roots' float upwards. This is called isostasy.

◀ Mountain ranges are thrown up by the crumpling of rock strata (layers) as the tectonic plates of the Earth's surface crunch together.

Weather fronts

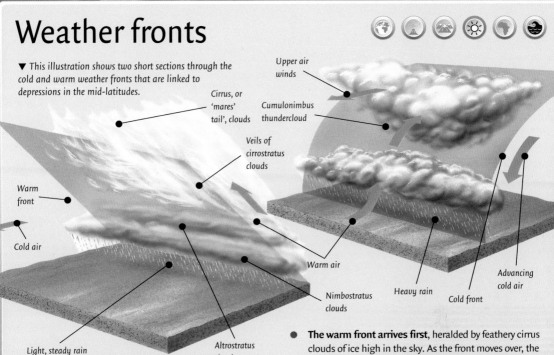

▼ This illustration shows two short sections through the cold and warm weather fronts that are linked to depressions in the mid-latitudes.

Upper air winds

Cirrus, or 'mares' tail', clouds

Cumulonimbus thundercloud

Veils of cirrostratus clouds

Warm front

Cold air

Warm air

Advancing cold air

Nimbostratus clouds

Heavy rain

Cold front

Light, steady rain

Altrostratus clouds

- **A weather front** is where a big mass of warm air meets a big mass of cold air.

- **At a warm front,** the mass of warm air is moving faster than the cold air. The warm air slowly rises over the cold air in a wedge. It slopes gently up to 1.5 km over 300 km.

- **At a cold front,** the mass of cold air is moving faster. It undercuts the warm air, forcing it to rise sharply and creating a steeply sloping front . The front climbs to 1.5 km over about 100 km.

- **In the mid-latitudes,** fronts are linked to vast spiralling weather systems called depressions, or lows. These are centred on a region of low pressure where warm, moist air rises. Winds spiral into the low – anticlockwise in the Northern Hemisphere, clockwise in the Southern.

- **Lows start** along the polar front, which stretches round the world. Here, cold air spreading out from the Poles meets warm, moist air moving up from the subtropics.

- **Lows develop** as a kink in the polar front. They then grow bigger as strong winds in the upper air drag them eastwards, bringing rain, snow and blustery winds. A wedge of warm air intrudes into the heart of the low, and the worst weather occurs along the edges of the wedge. One edge is a warm front, the other is a cold front.

- **The warm front arrives first**, heralded by feathery cirrus clouds of ice high in the sky. As the front moves over, the sky fills with slate-grey nimbostratus clouds that bring steady rain. As the warm front passes away, the weather becomes milder and skies may briefly clear.

- **After a few hours,** a build-up of thunderclouds and gusty winds warn that the cold front is on its way. When it arrives, the clouds unleash short, heavy showers, and sometimes thunderstorms or even tornadoes.

- **After the cold front passes,** the air grows colder and the sky clears, leaving just a few fluffy cumulus clouds.

- **Meteorologists** think that depressions are linked to strong winds, called jet streams, which circle the Earth high above the polar front. The depression may begin with Rossby waves, which are giant kinks in the jet stream up to 2,000 km long.

▶ Feathery cirrus clouds high up in the sky are a clear warning that a warm front is on its way, bringing steady rain. When there is a warm front, a cold front is likely to follow, bringing heavy rain, strong winds and perhaps even a thunderstorm.

The Southern Ocean

- **The Southern Ocean** is the world's fourth largest ocean. It stretches all the way round Antarctica, and has an area of 35,000,000 sq km.

- **It is the only ocean** that stretches all around the world.

- **In winter** over half the Southern Ocean is covered with ice and icebergs that break off the Antarctic ice sheet.

- **The East Wind Drift** is a current that flows anticlockwise around Antarctica close to the coast.

> ★ STAR FACT ★
> The circumpolar current could fill the Great Lakes in North America in just 48 hours.

- **Further out** from the coast of Antarctica, the Antarctic circumpolar current flows in the opposite direction – clockwise from west to east.

- **The circumpolar current** carries more water than any other current in the world.

- **The 'Roaring Forties'** is the band between 40° and 50° South latitude. Within this band strong westerly winds blow unobstructed around the world.

- **The waves in the 'Roaring Forties'** are the biggest in the world, sometimes higher than a ten-storey building.

- **Sea ice** forms in round pieces called pancake ice.

◀ *Many penguins such as the emperor, the world's largest penguin, live on the ice floes of the Southern Ocean.*

North America

- **North America** is the world's third largest continent. It has an area of 24,230,000 sq km.

- **North America** is a triangle, with its long side bounded by the icy Arctic Ocean and its short side by the tropical Caribbean Sea.

- **The north** of North America lies inside the Arctic Circle and is icebound for much of the year. Death Valley, in the southwestern desert in California and Nevada, is one of the hottest places on the Earth.

- **Mountain ranges** run down each side of North America – the ancient, worn-down Appalachians in the east and the younger, higher Rockies in the west.

- **In between** the mountains lie vast interior plains. These plains are based on very old rocks, the oldest of which are in the Canadian Shield in the north.

- **North America** is the oldest continent on the Earth. It has rocks that are almost 4,000 million years old.

- **The Grand Canyon** is one of the world's most spectacular gorges. It is 440 km long, and 1,800 m deep in places.

- **The longest river** in North America is the Mississippi–Missouri, at 6,019 km long.

- **The highest mountain** is Mt McKinley in Alaska, 6,194 m high.

- **The Great Lakes** contain one-fifth of the world's freshwater.

▶ *North America broke away from Europe about 100 million years ago. It is still moving 2.5 cm farther every year.*

Weather forecasting

- **Weather forecasting** relies partly on powerful computers, which analyse the Earth's atmosphere.

- **One kind of weather prediction** divides the air into parcels. These are stacked in columns above grid points spread throughout the world.

- **There are over one million** grid points, each with a stack of at least 30 parcels above it.

▶ This weather map shows isobars – lines of equal air pressure – over North America. It has been compiled from millions of observations.

- **Weather observatories** take millions of simultaneous measurements of weather conditions at regular intervals each day.

- **Every 3 hours** 10,000 land-based weather stations record conditions on the ground. Every 12 hours ballooons fitted with radiosondes go into the atmosphere to record conditions high up.

- **Satellites in the sky** give an overview of developing weather patterns.

- **Infrared satellite images** show temperatures on the Earth's surface.

- **Cloud motion winds** show the wind speed and wind direction from the way in which the clouds move.

- **Supercomputers** allow the weather to be predicted accurately 3 days in advance, and for up to 14 days in advance with some confidence.

- **Astrophysicist** Piers Corbyn has developed a forecasting system linked to variations in the Sun's activity.

River valleys

- **Rivers** carve out valleys as they wear away their channels.

- **High up in the mountains,** much of a river's energy goes into carving into the river bed. The valleys there are deep, with steep sides.

- **Farther down** towards the sea, more of a river's erosive energy goes into wearing away its banks. It carves out a broader valley as it winds back and forth.

- **Large meanders** normally develop only when a river is crossing broad plains in its lower reaches.

- **Incised meanders** are meanders carved into deep valleys. The meanders formed when the river was flowing across a low plain. The plain was lifted up and the river cut down into it, keeping its meanders.

- **The Grand Canyon** is made of incised meanders. They were created as the Colorado River cut into the Colorado Plateau after it was uplifted 17 million years ago.

- **The shape of a river valley** depends partly on the structure of the rocks over which it is flowing.

- **Some valleys** seem far too big for their river alone to have carved them. Such a river is 'underfit', or 'misfit'.

- **Many large valleys** with misfit rivers were carved out by glaciers or glacial meltwaters.

- **The world's rivers** wear the entire land surface down by an average of 8 cm every 1,000 years.

▼ Rivers carve out valleys over hundreds of thousands of years as they grind material along their beds.

Earth's interior

Continental crust (0–50 km)

Oceanic crust of cold hard rock (0–10 km)

Lithosphere, asthenosphere and mesosphere (0–400km)

▲ Hot material from the Earth's interior often bursts on to the surface from volcanoes.

Mantle of soft, hot rock where temperatures climb steadily to 4,500°C (10–2,890 km)

Outer core of liquid iron and nickel where temperatures climb to 6,000°C (2,890-5,150 km)

Inner core of solid iron and nickel where temperatures climb to 7,000°C (below 5,150 km)

▲ This illustration shows the main layers inside the Earth.

★ STAR FACT ★
The deepest drill into the Earth is on the Kola Peninsula in Arctic Russia. It has penetrated just 12 km into the crust.

- **The Earth's crust** (see crust) is a thin hard outer shell of rock which is a few dozen kilometres thick. Its thickness in relation to the Earth is about the same as the skin on an apple.

- **Under the crust,** there is a deep layer of hot soft rock called the mantle (see core and mantle).

- **The crust and upper mantle** can be divided into three layers according to their rigidity: the lithosphere, the asthenosphere and the mesosphere.

- **Beneath the mantle** is a core of hot iron and nickel. The outer core is so hot – climbing from 4,500°C to 6,000°C – that it is always molten. The inner core is even hotter (up to 7,000°C) but it stays solid because the pressure is 6,000 times greater than on the surface.

- **The inner core** contains 1.7% of the Earth's mass, the outer core 30.8%; the core–mantle boundary 3%; the lower mantle 49%; the upper mantle 15%; the ocean crust 0.099% and the continental crust 0.374%.

- **Satellite measurements** are so accurate they can detect slight lumps and dents in the Earth's surface. These indicate where gravity is stronger or weaker because of differences in rock density. Variations in gravity reveal things such as mantle plumes (see hot-spot volcanoes).

- **Our knowledge of the Earth's interior** comes mainly from studying how earthquake waves vibrate right through the Earth.

- **Analysis of how earthquake waves** are deflected reveals where different materials occur in the interior. S (secondary) waves pass only through the mantle. P (primary) waves pass through the core as well. P waves passing through the core are deflected, leaving a shadow zone where no waves reach the far side of the Earth.

- **The speed of earthquake waves** reveals how dense the rocky materials are. Cold, hard rock transmits waves more quickly than hot, soft rock.

High mountains

- **A few high mountains** are lone volcanoes, such as Africa's Kilimanjaro, which are built by many eruptions.
- **Some volcanic mountains** are in chains in volcanic arcs (see volcano zones), such as Japan's Fujiyama.
- **Most high mountains** are part of great mountain ranges stretching hundreds of kilometres.
- **Some mountain ranges** are huge slabs of rock called fault blocks (see faults). They were forced up by quakes.
- **The biggest mountain ranges,** such as the Himalayas and the Andes, are fold mountains.
- **The height of mountains** used to be measured from the ground, using levels and sighting devices to measure angles. Now mountains are measured more accurately using satellite techniques.
- **Satellite measurements** in 1999 raised the height of the world's highest peak, Mt Everest in Nepal in the Himalayas, from 8,848 m to 8,850 m.
- **All 14 of the world's peaks** over 8,000 m are in the Himalayas – in Nepal, China and Kashmir.
- **Temperatures drop 0.6°C** for every 100 m you climb, so mountain peaks are very cold and often covered in snow.
- **The air** is thinner on mountains, so the air pressure is lower. Climbers may need oxygen masks to breathe.

▼ *High peaks are jagged because massive folding fractures the rock and makes it very vulnerable to the sharp frosts high up.*

Limestone weathering

- **Streams and rainwater** absorb carbon dioxide gas from soil and air. It turns them into weak carbonic acid.
- **Carbonic acid** corrodes (wears away by dissolving) limestone in a process called carbonation.
- **When limestone rock** is close to the surface, carbonation can create spectacular scenery.
- **Corroded limestone scenery** is often called karst, because the best example of it is the Karst Plateau near Dalmatia, in Bosnia.
- **On the surface,** carbonation eats away along cracks to create pavements, with slabs called clints. The slabs are separated by deeply etched grooves called grykes.
- **Limestone rock** does not soak up water like a sponge. It has massive cracks called joints, and streams and rainwater trickle deep into the rock through these cracks.
- **Streams** drop down into limestone through swallow-holes, like bathwater down a plughole. Carbonation eats out such holes to form giant shafts called potholes.
- **Some potholes** are eaten out to create great funnel-shaped hollows called dolines, up to 100 m across.
- **Where water** streams out along horizontal cracks at the base of potholes, the rock may be etched out into caverns.
- **Caverns** may be eaten out so much that the roof collapses to form a gorge or a large hole called a polje.

◄ *Corrosion by underground streams in limestone can eat out huge caverns, often filled with spectacular stalactites (see caves).*

Icebergs

- **Icebergs** are big lumps of floating ice that calve, or break off, from the end of glaciers or polar ice caps. This often occurs when tides and waves move the ice up and down.

- **Calving of icebergs occurs** mostly during the summer when the warm conditions partially melt the ice.

- **Around 15,000 icebergs a year** calve in the Arctic.

- **Arctic icebergs** vary from car-sized ones called growlers to mansion-sized blocks. The biggest iceberg, 11 km long, was spotted off Baffin Island in 1882.

- **The Petterman and Jungersen** glaciers in northern Greenland form big table-shaped icebergs called ice islands. They are like the icebergs found in Antarctica.

- **Antarctic icebergs** are much, much bigger than Arctic ones. The biggest iceberg, which was 300 km long, was spotted in 1956 by the icebreaker USS *Glacier*.

- **Antarctic icebergs** last for ten years on average; Arctic icebergs last for about two years.

- **The ice** that makes Arctic icebergs is 3,000–6,000 years old.

- **Each year 375 or so icebergs** drift from Greenland into the shipping lanes off Newfoundland. They are a major hazard to shipping in that area.

- **The International Ice Patrol** was set up in 1914 to monitor icebergs after the great liner *Titanic* was sunk. The liner hit an iceberg off Newfoundland in 1912.

▼ *Icebergs are big chunks of floating ice that break off glaciers.*

The Atlantic Ocean

- **The Atlantic Ocean** is the world's second largest ocean, with an area of 82 million sq km. It covers about one-fifth of the world's surface.

- **At its widest point,** between Spain and Mexico, the Atlantic is 9,600 km across.

- **The Atlantic** was named by the ancient Romans after the Atlas Mountains of North Africa. The Atlas were at the limit of their known world.

- **There are very few islands** in the main part of the Atlantic Ocean. Most lie close to the continents.

- **On average,** the Atlantic is about 3,660 m deep.

- **The deepest point** in the Atlantic is the Puerto Rico Trench off Puerto Rico, which is 8,648 m deep.

- **The Mid-Atlantic Ridge** is a great undersea ridge which splits the sea-bed in half. Along this ridge, the Atlantic is growing wider by 2–4 cm every year.

- **Islands** in the mid-Atlantic are volcanoes that lie along the Mid-Atlantic Ridge, such as the Azores and Ascension Island.

- **The Sargasso Sea** is a huge area of water in the western Atlantic. It is famous for its floating seaweed.

- **The Atlantic** is a youngish ocean, about 150 million years old.

◄ *The damp, cool climate of the northern Atlantic frequently turns its waters steely grey.*

Wind

- **Wind is moving air.** Strong winds are fast-moving air; gentle breezes are air that moves slowly.

- **Air moves** because the Sun warms some places more than others, creating differences in air pressure.

- **Warmth makes** air expand and rise, lowering air pressure. Cold makes air heavier, raising pressure.

- **Winds blow** from areas of high pressure

▲ *The more of the Sun's energy there is in the air, the windier it is. This is why the strongest winds may blow in the warm tropics.*

to areas of low pressure, which are called lows.

- **The sharper the pressure difference,** or gradient, the stronger the winds blow.

- **In the Northern Hemisphere,** winds spiral in a clockwise direction out of highs, and anticlockwise into lows. In the Southern Hemisphere, the reverse is true.

- **A prevailing wind** is a wind that blows frequently from the same direction. Winds are named by the direction they blow from. A westerly wind blows from the west.

- **In the tropics** the prevailing winds are warm, dry trade winds. They blow from the northeast and the southeast towards the Equator.

- **In the mid-latitudes** the prevailing winds are warm, moist westerlies.

South America

- **South America** is the world's fourth largest continent. It has an area of 17,814,000 sq km.

- **The Andes Mountains,** which run over 4,500 km down the west side, are the world's longest mountain range.

- **The heart of South America** is the vast Amazon rain-forest around the Amazon River and its tributaries.

- **The southeast** is dominated by the huge grasslands of the Gran Chaco, the Pampas and Patagonia.

- **No other continent** reaches so far south. South America extends to within 1,000 km of the Antarctic Circle.

- **Three-quarters** of South America is in the tropics. In the high Andes are large zones of cool, temperate climate.

- **Quito, in Ecuador,** is called the 'Land of Eternal Spring' because its temperature never drops below 8°C at night, and never climbs above 22°C during the day.

- **The highest volcanic peak** is Aconcagua, 6,960 m high.

- **Eastern South America** was joined to western Africa until the Atlantic began to open up 90 million years ago.

▶ South America's triangular shape gives it the shortest coastline, for its size, of any of the continents.

- **The Andes** have been built up over the past 60 million years by the collision of the South American plate with both the Nazca plate under the Pacific Ocean and the Caribbean plate. The subduction of the Nazca plate has created the world's highest active volcanoes in the Andes.

Cold landscapes

▲ *Cold conditions have a dramatic effect on the landscape.*

- **'Periglacial'** used to describe conditions next to the ice in the Ice Ages. It now means similar conditions found today.
- **Periglacial conditions** are found on the tundra of northern Canada and Siberia and on nunataks, which are the hills that protrude above ice sheets and glaciers.
- **In periglacial areas** ice only melts in spring at the surface. Deep down under the ground it remains permanently frozen permafrost.

- **When the ground** above the permafrost melts, the soil twists into buckled layers called involutions.
- **When frozen soil melts** it becomes so fluid that it can creep easily down slopes, creating large tongues and terraces.
- **Frost heave** is the process when frost pushes stones to the surface as the ground freezes.
- **After frost heave,** large stones roll down leaving the fine stones on top. This creates intricate patterns on the ground.
- **On flat ground,** quilt-like patterns are called stone polygons. On slopes, they stretch into stone stripes.
- **Pingos** are mounds of soil with a core of ice. They are created when groundwater freezes beneath a lake.

> ★ **STAR FACT** ★
> In periglacial conditions temperatures never ever climb above freezing in winter.

Tides

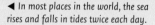

- **Tides are the way** in which the sea rises a little then falls back every 12 hours or so.
- **When the tide is flowing** it is rising. When the tide is ebbing it is falling.
- **Tides are caused** by the pull of gravity between the Earth, the Moon and the Sun.
- **The mutual pull** of the Moon's and the Earth's gravity stretches the Earth into an egg shape.
- **The solid Earth** is so rigid that it stretches only 20 cm.
- **Ocean waters** can flow freely over the Earth to create two tidal bulges (high tides) of water. One bulge is directly under the Moon, the other is on the far side of the Earth.
- **As the Earth rotates** every 24 hours the tidal bulges stay in the same place under the Moon. Each place on the ocean has high tide twice a day. The Moon is moving as

◄ *In most places in the world, the sea rises and falls in tides twice each day.*

well as the Earth, making high tides occur not once every 12 hours but once every 12 hours 25 minutes.

- **The continents** get in the way, making the tidal bulges slosh about in a complex way. As a result the timing and height of tides vary enormously. In the open ocean tides rise only 1 m or so, but in enclosed spaces such as the Bay of Fundy, in Nova Scotia, Canada they rise over 15 m.
- **The Sun is much farther away** than the Moon, but it is so big that its gravity has an effect on the tides.
- **The Moon and the Sun** line up at a Full and a New Moon, creating high spring tides twice a month. When the Moon and the Sun pull at right angles at a Half Moon, they cause neap tides which are lower than normal tides.

The Ages of the Earth

- **The Earth formed 4,570 million years ago (mya)** but the first animals with shells and bones appeared less than 600 mya. It is mainly with the help of their fossils that geologists have learned about the Earth's history since then. We know very little about the 4,000 million years before, known as Precambrian Time.

- **Just as days are divided** into hours and minutes, so geologists divide the Earth's history into time periods. The longest are eons, thousands of millions of years long. The shortest are chrons, a few thousand years along. In between come eras, periods, epochs and ages.

- **The years since Precambrian Time** are split into three eras: Palaeozoic, Mesozoic and Cenozoic.

- **Different plants and animals** lived at different times, so geologists can tell from the fossils in rocks how long ago the rocks formed. Using fossils, they have divided the Earth's history since Precambrian Time into 11 periods.

- **Layers of rock** form on top of each other, so the oldest rocks are usually at the bottom and the youngest at the top, unless they have been disturbed. The order of layers from top to bottom is known as the geological column.

- **By looking for certain fossils** geologists can tell if one layer of rock is older than another, and so place it within the geological column.

- **Fossils can only show** if a rock is older or younger than another; they cannot give a date in years. Also, many rocks such as igneous rocks contain no fossils. To give an absolute date, geologists may use radiocarbon dating.

- **Radiocarbon dating** allows the oldest rocks on Earth to be dated. After certain substances, such as uranium and rubidium, form in rocks, their atoms slowly break down into different atoms. As atoms break down they send out rays, or radioactivity. By assessing how many atoms in a rock have changed, geologists work out the rock's age.

- **Breaks in the sequence** of the geological column are called unconformities. They help to create a picture of the geological history of an area.

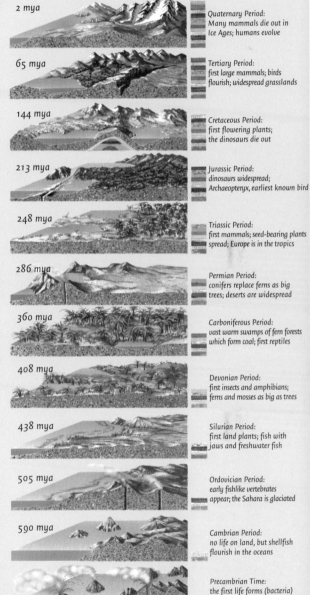

2 mya — Quaternary Period: Many mammals die out in Ice Ages; humans evolve

65 mya — Tertiary Period: first large mammals; birds flourish; widespread grasslands

144 mya — Cretaceous Period: first flowering plants; the dinosaurs die out

213 mya — Jurassic Period: dinosaurs widespread; Archaeopteryx, earliest known bird

248 mya — Triassic Period: first mammals; seed-bearing plants spread; Europe is in the tropics

286 mya — Permian Period: conifers replace ferns as big trees; deserts are widespread

360 mya — Carboniferous Period: vast warm swamps of fern forests which form coal; first reptiles

408 mya — Devonian Period: first insects and amphibians; ferns and mosses as big as trees

438 mya — Silurian Period: first land plants; fish with jaws and freshwater fish

505 mya — Ordovician Period: early fishlike vertebrates appear; the Sahara is glaciated

590 mya — Cambrian Period: no life on land, but shellfish flourish in the oceans

Precambrian Time: the first life forms (bacteria) appear, and give the air oxygen

Lava and ash

▲ *Runny lava flows in rivers of red-hot molten rock, but sticky lava from subduction zones creeps a few metres a day.*

- **When a volcano erupts** it sends out a variety of hot materials, including lava, tephra, ash and gases.

- **Lava is hot molten rock** from the Earth's interior. It is called magma while it is still underground.

- **Tephra** is material blasted into the air by an eruption. It includes pyroclasts (solid lava) and volcanic bombs.

- **Pyroclasts** are big chunks of volcanic rock that are thrown out by explosive volcanoes when the plug in the volcano's vent shatters. 'Pyroclast' means fire broken. Pyroclasts are usually 0.3 –1 m across.

- **Big eruptions** can blast pyroclasts weighing 1 tonne or more up into the air at the speed of a jet plane.

- **Cinders and lapilli** are small pyroclasts. Cinders are 6.4–30 cm in diameter; lapilli are 0.1–6.4 cm.

- **Volcanic bombs** are blobs of molten magma that cool and harden in flight.

- **Breadcrust bombs** are bombs that stretch into loaf shapes in flight; gases inside them create a 'crust'.

- **Around 90% of the material** ejected by explosive volcanoes is not lava, but tephra and ash.

> ★ **STAR FACT** ★
> Pumice rock is made from hardened lava froth
> – it is so full of air bubbles that it floats.

Fossils

1. A trilobite dies on the ocean floor long ago.

- **Fossils** are the remains of living things preserved for millions of years, usually in stone.

- **Most fossils** are the remains of living things such as bones, shells, eggs, leaves and seeds.

- **Trace fossils** are fossils of signs left behind by creatures, such as footprints and scratch marks.

- **Paleontologists** (scientists who study fossils) tell the age of a fossil from the rock layer in which it is found in. Also, they measure how the rock has changed radioactively since it was formed (radiocarbon dating).

- **The oldest fossils** are called stromatolites. They are fossils of big, pizza-like colonies of microscopic bacteria over 3,500 million years old.

2. The trilobite's soft parts eventually rot away.

3. The shell is slowly buried by mud.

4. Mineral-rich waters dissolve the shell.

5. New minerals fill the mould to form a fossil.

◄ When an animal dies, its soft parts rot away quickly. If its bones or shell are buried quickly in mud, they may turn to stone. When a shellfish such as this ancient trilobite dies and sinks to the sea-bed, its shell is buried. Over millions of years, water trickling through the mud may dissolve the shell, but minerals in the water fill its place to make a perfect cast.

- **The biggest fossils** are conyphytons, 2,000-million-year-old stromatolites over 100 m high.

- **Not all fossils** are stone. Mammoths have been preserved by being frozen in the permafrost (see cold landscapes) of Siberia.

- **Insects** have been preserved in amber, the solidified sap of ancient trees.

- **Certain widespread, short-lived fossils** are very useful for dating rock layers. These are known as index fossils.

- **Index fossils** include ancient shellfish such as trilobites, graptolites, crinoids, beleminites, ammonites and brachiopods.

Air pressure

- **Although air is light,** there is so much of it that air can exert huge pressure at ground level. Air pressure is the constant bombardment of billions of air molecules as they zoom about.

- **Air pushes** in all directions at ground level with a force of over 1 kg per sq cm – that is the equivalent of an elephant standing on a coffee table.

- **Air pressure varies** constantly from place to place and

- from time to time as the Sun's heat varies.

- **Air pressure** is measured with a device called a barometer in units called millibars (mb for short).

- **Normal air pressure** at sea level is 1,013 mb, but it can vary between 800 mb and 1,050 mb.

- **Air pressure** is shown on weather maps with lines called isobars, which join together places of equal pressure.

- **High-pressure zones** are called anticyclones; low-pressure zones are called cyclones, or depressions.

- **Barometers** help us to forecast weather because changes in air pressure are linked to changes in weather.

- **A fall in air pressure** warns that stormy weather is on its way, because depressions are linked to storms.

- **Steady high pressure** indicates clear weather, because sinking air in a high means that clouds cannot form.

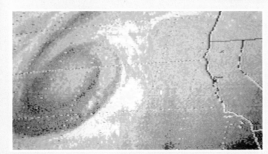

◀ In this satellite picture, a spiral of clouds indicates that stormy weather in a depression is heading for California, USA.

The Earth's chemistry

- **The bulk of the Earth** is made from iron, oxygen, magnesium and silicon.

- **More than 80 chemical elements** occur naturally in the Earth and its atmosphere.

- **The crust** is made mostly from oxygen and silicon, with aluminium, iron, calcium, magnesium, sodium, potassium, titanium and traces of 64 other elements.

- **The upper mantle** is iron and magnesium silicates; the lower is silicon and magnesium sulphides and oxides.

- **The core** is mostly iron, with a little nickel and traces of sulphur, carbon, oxygen and potassium.

- **Evidence for the Earth's chemistry** comes from analysing densities with the help of earthquake waves, and from studying stars, meteorites and other planets.

- **When the Earth** was still semi-molten, dense elements such as iron sank to form the core. Lighter elements such as oxygen floated up to form the crust.

- **Some heavy elements, such as uranium,** ended up in

- the crust because they easily make compounds with oxygen and silicon.

- **Large blobs of elements** that combine easily with sulphur, such as zinc and lead, spread through the mantle.

- **Elements that combine easily with iron,** such as gold and nickel, sank to the core.

▼ This diagram shows the percentages of the chemical elements that make up the Earth.

Magnesium 17%
Silicon 13%
Oxygen 28%
Nickel 2.7%
Sulphur 2.7%
Calcium 0.6%
Aluminium 0.4%
Others 0.6%
Iron 35%

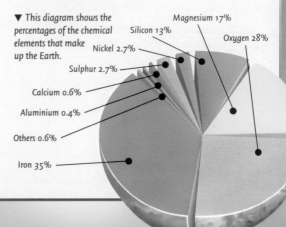

Volcano zones

▶ *One of many volcanoes in the Ring of Fire is Mt Rainier, in Washington State, USA.*

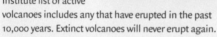

- **Worldwide** there are over 1,500 volcanoes; 500 of these are active. A volcano can have a lifespan of a million years and not erupt for several centuries.

- **Volcanoes** are said to be active if they have erupted recently. The official Smithsonian Institute list of active volcanoes includes any that have erupted in the past 10,000 years. Extinct volcanoes will never erupt again.

- **Volcanoes** occur either along the margins of tectonic plates, or over hot spots in the Earth's interior.

- **Some volcanoes** erupt where the plates are pulling apart, such as under the sea along mid-ocean ridges.

- **Some volcanoes** lie near subduction zones, forming either an arc of volcanic islands or a line of volcanoes on land, called a volcanic arc.

- **Subduction zone volcanoes** are explosive, because the magma gets contaminated and acidic as it burns up through the overlying plate. Acidic magma is sticky and gassy. It clogs up volcanic vents then blasts its way out.

- **Around the Pacific** there is a ring of explosive volcanoes called the Ring of Fire. It includes Mt Pinatubo in the Philippines, and Mt St Helens in Washington State, USA.

- **Away from subduction zones** magma is basaltic. It is runny and low in gas, so the volcanoes here gush lava.

- **Effusive volcanoes** pour out lava frequently but gently.

- **3D radar interferometry** from satellites may pick up the minutest swelling on every active volcano in the world. In this way it helps to predict eruptions.

Shape of the Earth

- **The study of the shape of the Earth** is called geodesy. In the past, geodesy depended on ground-based surveys. Today, satellites play a major role.

- **The Earth is not a perfect sphere**. It is a unique shape called a geoid, which means 'Earth shaped'.

- **The Earth spins** faster at the Equator than at the Poles, because the Equator is farther from the Earth's spinning axis.

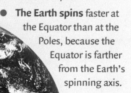

◀ *The ancient Greeks realized that the Earth is a globe. Satellite measurements show that it is not quite perfectly round.*

- **The extra speed** of the Earth at the Equator flings it out in a bulge, while it is flattened at the Poles.

- **Equatorial bulge** was predicted in 1687 by Isaac Newton.

- **The equatorial bulge** was confirmed 70 years after Newton – by French surveys in Peru by Charles de La Condamine, and in Lapland by Pierre de Maupertuis.

- **The Earth's diameter** at the Equator is 12,758 km. This is larger – by 43 km – than the vertical diameter from North Pole to South Pole.

- **The official measurement** of the Earth's radius at the Equator is 6,376,136 m, plus or minus 1 m.

- **The Lageos** (Laser Geodynamic) satellite launched in 1976 has measured gravitational differences with extreme precision. It has revealed bumps up to 100 m high, notably just south of India.

- **The Seasat** satellite confirmed the ocean surfaces are geoid. It took millions of measurements of the height of the ocean surface, accurate to within a few centimetres.

Seas

- **Seas** are small oceans, enclosed or partly enclosed by land.
- **Seas** are shallower than oceans and have no major currents flowing through them.
- **In the Mediterranean** and other seas, tides can set up a seiche – a standing wave that sloshes back and forth like a ripple running up and down a bath.
- **If the natural** wave cycle of a seiche is different from the ocean tides, the tides are cancelled out.

> ★ STAR FACT ★
> The Dead Sea is the lowest sea on Earth,
> 400 m below sea level.

- **If the natural** wave cycle of a seiche is similar to the ocean tides, the tides are magnified.
- **Scientists thought that** the Mediterranean was a dry desert six million years ago. They believed it was 3,000 m lower than it is today, and covered in salts.
- **Recent evidence** from microfossils suggests that the Mediterranean was never completely dry.
- **Warm seas such as the Mediterranean** lose much more water by evaporation than they gain from rivers. So a current of water flows in steadily from the ocean.
- **Warm seas** lose so much water by evaporation that they are usually much saltier than the open ocean.

◀ *Waves in enclosed seas tend to be much smaller than those in the open ocean, because there is less space for them to develop.*

Drought

- **A drought** is a long period when there is too little rain.
- **During a drought** the soil dries out, streams stop flowing, groundwater sinks and plants die.
- **Deserts** suffer from permanent drought. Many tropical places have a seasonal drought, with long dry seasons.
- **Droughts** are often accompanied by high temperatures, which increase water loss through evaporation.
- **Between 1931 and 1938** drought reduced the Great Plains of the USA to a dustbowl, as the soil dried out and turned to dust. Drought came again from 1950 to 1954.
- **Desertification** is the spread of desert conditions into surrounding grassland. It is caused either by climate changes or by pressure from human activities.
- **Drought**, combined with increased numbers of livestock and people, have put pressure on the Sahel, south of the Sahara in Africa, causing widespread desertification.
- **Drought** has brought repeated famine to the Sahel, especially the Sudan and Ethiopia.

- **Drought** in the Sahel may be partly triggered off by El Niño – a reversal of the ocean currents in the Pacific Ocean, off Peru, which happens every 2–7 years.
- **The Great Drought** of 1276–1299 destroyed the cities of the ancient Indian civilizations of southwest USA. It led to the cities being abandoned.

▶ *Drought bakes the soil so hard it shrinks and cracks. It will no longer absorb water even when rain comes.*

Faults

- **A fault** is a fracture in rock along which large blocks of rock have slipped past each other.

- **Faults usually occur** in fault zones, which are often along the boundaries between tectonic plates. Faults are typically caused by earthquakes.

- **Single earthquakes** rarely move blocks more than a few centimetres. Repeated small earthquakes can shift blocks hundreds of kilometres.

- **Compression faults** are faults caused by rocks being squeezed together, perhaps by converging plates.

- **Tension faults** are faults caused by rocks being pulled together, perhaps by diverging plates.

- **Normal, or dip-slip, faults** are tension faults where the rock fractures and slips straight down.

- **A wrench, or tear, fault** occurs when plates slide past each other and make blocks slip horizontally.

- **Large wrench faults,** such as the San Andreas in California, USA, are called transcurrent faults.

- **Rift valleys** are huge, trough-shaped valleys created by faulting, such as Africa's Great Rift Valley. The floor is a thrown-down block called a graben. Some geologists think they are caused by tension, others by compression.

- **Horst blocks** are blocks of rock thrown up between normal faults, often creating a high plateau.

▼ *Geologists who study faults describe the movement of a fault using the terms illustrated here.*

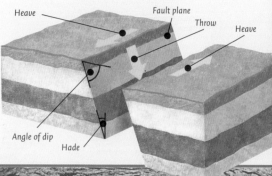

Heave

Fault plane

Throw

Heave

Angle of dip

Hade

Famous earthquakes

◄ *The San Fransisco earthquake was so strong that its effects were detected thousands of miles away. More than two thirds of its population were left homeless.*

- **In 1906** San Francisco in California, USA was shaken by an earthquake that lasted three minutes. The earthquake started fires that burned the city almost flat.

- **The palaces** of the Minoan people on Crete were destroyed by an earthquake in about 1750 BC.

- **The earliest documented earthquake** hit the ancient Greek town of Sparta in 464 BC, killing 20,000 people.

- **In AD 62** the musical debut of the Roman Emperor Nero in Naples was ended by an earthquake.

- **In July 1201** an earthquake rocked every city in the eastern Mediterranean. It may have killed well over one million people.

- **In 1556** an earthquake, which is thought to have been about 8.3 on the Richter scale, hit the province of Shansi in China (see earthquake damage).

- **The 1923** earthquake which devastated Tokyo and Yokohama (see earthquake damage) also made the sea-bed in nearby Sagami Bay drop over 400 m.

- **The 1755 Lisbon earthquake** (see earthquake damage) prompted the French writer Voltaire to write *Candide*, a book that inspired the French and American revolutions.

- **The Michoacán earthquake** of 1985 killed 35,000 in Mexico City 360 km away. Silts (fine soils) under the city amplified the ground movements 75 times.

- **The 1970 earthquake** in Peru shook 50 million cu m of rock and ice off the peak Huascaran. They roared down at 350 km/h and swept away the town of Yungay.

Swamps and marshes

- **Wetlands** are areas of land where the water level is mostly above the ground.

- **The main types** of wetland are bogs, fens, swamps and marshes.

- **Bogs and fens** occur in cold climates and contain plenty of partially rotted plant material called peat.

- **Marshes and swamps** are found in warm and cold places. They have more plants than bogs and fens.

- **Marshes** are in permanently wet places, such as shallow lakes and river deltas. Reeds and rushes grow in marshes.

- **Swamps** develop where the water level varies – often along the edges of rivers in the tropics where they are flooded, notably along the Amazon and Congo rivers. Trees such as mangroves grow in swamps.

- **Half the wetlands** in the USA were drained before most people appreciated their value. Almost half of Dismal Swamp in North Carolina has been drained.

▲ In the past, wetlands were seen simply as dead areas, ripe for draining. Now their value both for wildlife and for water control is beginning to be realized.

- **The Pripet Marshes** on the borders of Belorussia are the biggest in Europe, covering 270,000 sq km.

- **Wetlands act** like sponges and help to control floods.

- **Wetlands help** to top up supplies of groundwater.

Acid rain

- **All rain** is slightly acidic, but air pollution can turn rain into harmful acid rain.

- **Acid rain** forms when sunlight makes sulphur dioxide and nitrogen oxide combine with oxygen and moisture in the air.

- **Sulphur dioxide and nitrogen oxides** come from burning fossil fuels such as coal, oil and natural gas.

▲ Cuts in emissions are essential to reduce acid rain, but installing 'scrubbers' that soak up sulphur and nitrous oxide are expensive.

! NEWS FLASH !
Sulphur emissions from ships may double by 2010, counteracting cuts in power station emissions.

- **Acidity** is measured in terms of pH. The lower the pH, the more acid the rain is. Normal rain has a pH of 6.5. Acid rain has a pH of 5.7 or less.

- **A pH** of 2–3 has been recorded in many places in the eastern USA and central Europe.

- **Acid fog** is ten times more acid than acid rain.

- **Acid rain** washes aluminium from soil into lakes and streams, and so poisons fish. Limestone helps to neutralize the acid, but granite areas are vulnerable. Spring meltwaters are especially acid and damaging.

- **Acid rain** damages plants by removing nutrients from leaves and blocking the plants' uptake of nitrogen.

- **Acid rain has damaged** 20% of European trees; in Germany 60% of trees have been damaged.

1000 THINGS YOU SHOULD KNOW ABOUT

WILD ANIMALS

KEY

 Mammals

 Birds

 Reptiles and amphibians

 Sea creatures

 Insects, spiders and creepy crawlies

 How animals live

Monkeys

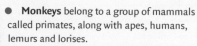

- **Monkeys** belong to a group of mammals called primates, along with apes, humans, lemurs and lorises.

- **Monkeys** live mostly in trees, and their hands have fingers and their feet have toes for gripping branches. Most monkeys also have tails.

- **There are about 150** species of monkey, and they live in tropical forests in Asia, Africa and the Americas.

- **New World monkeys** (from the Americas) live in trees and often have muscular tails that can grip like a hand. These tails are described as prehensile.

◀ *Baboons such as the Hamadryas (sacred) baboon are large, dog-like monkeys which are well adapted to living on the ground in African bush country.*

- **New World monkeys** include howler monkeys, spider monkeys, woolly monkeys and capuchins, as well as marmosets, and tamarins such as the golden lion tamarin, one of the world's most colourful mammals.

- **Old World monkeys** (from Africa and Asia) live on grasslands as well as in forests. They include baboons, colobus monkeys, langurs and macaques.

- **Old World monkeys** do not have a prehensile tail, but their thumbs and fingers can point together, like ours can, so they can grasp things well.

- **The proboscis monkey** gets its name from its huge nose (proboscis is another word for nose).

- **Most monkeys** eat anything from fruit to birds' eggs, but baboons may also catch and eat baby antelopes.

> ★ **STAR FACT** ★
> Howler monkeys can howl so loud that a pair
> of them can be heard over 3 km away.

Rays

- **Rays** are a huge group of over 300 species of fish, which includes skates, stingrays, electric rays, manta rays, eagle rays and guitar fish.

- **Many rays** have flat, almost diamond-shaped bodies, with pectoral fins elongated into broad wings. Guitar fish have longer, more shark-like bodies.

- **A ray's gills** are slot-like openings beneath its fins.

- **Rays have no bones.** Instead, like sharks, they are cartilaginous fish – their body framework is made of rubbery cartilage (you have this in your nose and ears).

- **Rays live mostly** on the ocean floor, feeding on seabed creatures such as oysters, clams and other shellfish.

- **Manta rays** live near the surface and feed on plankton.

- **The Atlantic manta ray** is the biggest ray, often over 7 m wide and 6 m long.

- **Stingrays** get their name from their whip-like tail with its poisonous barbs. A sting from a stingray can make humans very ill.

▲ *Manta rays often bask near the surface of the oceans, with the tips of their pectoral fins poking out of the water.*

- **Electric rays** are tropical rays able to give off a powerful electric charge to defend themselves against attackers.

- **The black torpedo ray** can put out a 220 volt shock – as much as a household electric socket.

Lizards

- **Lizards** are a group of 3,800 scaly-skinned reptiles, varying from a few centimetres long to the 3-m-long Komodo dragon.

- **Lizards cannot** control their own body heat, and so rely on sunshine for warmth. This is why they live in warm climates and bask in the sun for hours each day.

- **Lizards move** in many ways – running, scampering and slithering. Some can glide. Unlike mammals, their limbs stick out sideways rather than downwards.

- **Most lizards** lay eggs, although a few give birth to live young. But unlike birds or mammals, a mother lizard does not nurture (look after) her young.

- **Most lizards** are meat-eaters, feeding on insects and other small creatures.

> ★ STAR FACT ★
> The Basilisk lizard is also known as the Jesus Christ lizard because it can walk on water.

- **The glass lizard** has no legs. Its tail may break off and lie wriggling as a decoy if attacked. It can grow another tail later.

- **The Australian frilled lizard** has a ruff around its neck. To put off attackers, it can spread out its ruff to make itself look much bigger.

- **Horned lizards** can squirt a jet of blood from their eyes almost as far as 1 m to put off attackers.

- **The Komodo dragon** of Sumatra is the biggest lizard, weighing up to 150 kg. It can catch deer and pigs and swallow them whole.

▶ Lizards have four legs and a long tail. In most lizards, the back legs are much stronger than the front, and are used to drive the animal forwards in a kind of writhing motion.

Life on the seashore

- **Seashores** contain a huge variety of creatures which can adapt to the constant change from wet to dry as the tide rolls in and out.

- **Crabs, shellfish** and other creatures of rocky shores have tough shells to protect them from pounding waves and the sun's drying heat.

- **Anemones, starfish** and shellfish such as barnacles have powerful suckers for holding on to rocks.

- **Limpets** are the best rock clingers and can only be prised away if caught by surprise.

- **Anemones** may live on a hermit crab's shell, feeding on its leftovers but protecting it with their stinging tentacles.

▲ Crabs, lugworms, sandhoppers, shellfish and many other creatures live on seashores. Many birds come to feed on them.

- **Rock pools** are water left behind among the rocks as the tide goes out. They get very warm and salty.

- **Rock pool creatures** include shrimps, hermit crabs, anemones and fish such as blennies and gobies.

- **Sandy shores** are home to burrowing creatures such as crabs, razor clams, lugworms, sea cucumbers and burrowing anemones.

- **Sandhoppers** are tiny shelled creatures that live along the tide line, feeding on seaweed.

- **Beadlet anemones** look like blobs of jelly on rocks when the tide is out. But when the water returns, they open a ring of flower-like tentacles to feed.

Eagles and hawks

▲ *The bald eagle eats fish, snatching them from rivers.*

- **Eagles and hawks** are among 280 species of raptor (bird of prey). The group also includes kestrels, falcons, goshawks, buzzards and vultures.

- **Most birds of prey are hunters** that feed on other birds, fish and small mammals.

- **Most birds of prey** are strong fliers, with sharp eyes, powerful talons (claws) and a hooked beak.

- **Birds of prey lay** only a few eggs at a time. This makes them vulnerable to human egg collectors – one reason why many are endangered species.

- **Eagles** are the biggest of the hunting birds, with wing spans of up to 2.5 m. The harpy eagle of the Amazon catches monkeys and sloths.

- **The American bald eagle** is not really bald, but has white feathers on its head.

- **There are two kinds of hawks.** Accipiters, like the goshawk, catch their prey by lying in wait on perches. Buteos, like the kestrel, hover in the air.

- **Buzzards** are buteo hawks.

- **In the Middle Ages,** merlins and falcons were trained to fly from a falconer's wrist to catch birds and animals.

> ★ STAR FACT ★
> The peregrine falcon can reach speeds of
> 350 km/h when stooping (diving) on prey.

Frogs and toads

- **Frogs** and toads are amphibians – creatures that live both on land and in the water.

- **There are about 3,500 species** of frog and toad. Most live near water, but some live in trees and others live underground.

- **Frogs** are mostly smaller and better jumpers. Toads are bigger, with thicker, wartier skin which holds on to moisture and allows them to live on land longer.

- **Frogs and toads** are meat-eaters. They catch fast-moving insects by darting out their long, sticky tongues.

- **Frogs and toads begin life** as fish-like tadpoles, hatching in the water from huge clutches of eggs called spawn.

- **After 7 to 10 weeks,** tadpoles grow legs and lungs and develop into frogs ready to leave the water.

- **In midwife toads,** the male looks after the eggs, not

◄ *Frogs are superb jumpers, with long back legs to propel them into the air. Most also have suckers on their fingers to help them land securely on slippery surfaces.*

the female – winding strings of eggs around his back legs and carrying them about until they hatch.

- **The male Darwin's frog** swallows the eggs and keeps them in his throat until they hatch – and pop out of his mouth.

- **The goliath frog** of West Africa is the largest frog – at over 30 cm long. The biggest toad is the cane toad of Queensland, Australia – one weighed 2.6 kg and measured more than 25 cm in length.

- **The arrow-poison frogs** that live in the tropical rainforests of Central America get their name because natives tip their arrows with deadly poison from glands in the frogs' skin. Many arrow-poison frogs are very colourful, including some that are bright red.

Bats

- **Bats** are the only flying mammals. Their wings are made of leathery skin.

- **Most bats sleep** during the day, hanging upside down in caves, attics and other dark places. They come out at night to hunt.

- **Bats find things** in the dark by giving out a series of high-pitched clicks – the bats tell where they are and locate (find) prey from the echoes (sounds that bounce back to them). This is called echolocation.

- **Bats are not blind** – their eyesight is as good as that of most humans.

- **There are 900 species** of bat, living on all continents except Antarctica.

- **Most bats feed** on insects, but fruit bats feed on fruit.

- **Many tropical flowers** rely on fruit bats to spread their pollen.

- **Frog-eating bats** can tell edible frogs from poisonous ones by the frogs' mating calls.

▶ Bats spend their lives in darkness, finding their way with sounds so high-pitched only a young child can hear them.

- **The vampire bats** of tropical Latin America feed on blood, sucking it from animals such as cattle and horses. A colony of 100 vampire bats can drink blood from 25 cows or 14,000 chickens in one night.

- **False vampire bats** are bats that do not suck on blood, but feed on other small creatures such as bats and rats. The greater false vampire bat of Southeast Asia is one of the biggest of all bats.

Animal senses

- **Animals** sense the world in a variety of ways, including by sight, hearing, touch, smell and taste. Many animals have senses that humans do not have.

- **Sea creatures** rely on smell and taste, detecting tiny particles drifting in the water. For balance they often rely on simple balance organs called statocysts.

 Sharks have a better sense of smell than any other kind of fish. They can detect one part of animal blood in 100 million parts of water.

◀ The slow loris is nocturnal, and its enormous eyes help it jump safely through forests in the darkness.

- **For land animals**, sight is usually the most important sense. Hunting animals often have very sharp eyesight. Eagles, for instance, can see a rabbit moving from as far as 5 km away.

- **Owls** can hear sounds ten times softer than any human can.

- **Male gypsy moths** can smell a mate over 11 km away.

- **Pit vipers** have special sensory pits (holes) on their heads which can pinpoint heat. This lets them track warm-blooded prey such as mice in pitch darkness.

- **The forked tongues** of snakes and lizards are used to taste the air and detect prey.

- **Cats' eyes** absorb 50% more light than human eyes, so they can see very well in the dark.

★ STAR FACT ★
Many butterflies can smell with special sense organs in their feet.

Lions

- **Lions** (along with tigers) are the biggest members of the cat family, weighing up to 230 kg. Male lions may be 3 m long.

- **Lions used to live** through much of Europe and Asia. Now they are restricted to East and Southern Africa. Around 200 lions also live in the Gir forest in India.

- **Lions usually live** in grassland or scrub, in families called prides.

- **Lions are hunters** and they prey on antelopes, zebras and even young giraffes. The lionesses (females) do most of the hunting.

- **Male lions** are easily recognizable because of their huge manes. There are usually two to five adult males in each pride and they usually eat before the lionesses and cubs.

★ **STAR FACT** ★
A male lion can drag along a 300 kg zebra – it would take at least six men to do this.

The mane can be blonde, but gets darker with age

▲ To other lions, a male lion's shaggy mane makes him look even bigger and stronger, and protects him when fighting. A male lion is born without a mane. It starts growing when he is about two or three and is fully grown by the time he is five.

◄ Lion cubs live on milk at first, and eat their first meat after 50 days.

Cubs have very big paws for their size

▲ Female lions are called lionesses. They are slightly smaller than males but usually do most of the hunting, often in pairs. There are typically 4 to 12 adult lionesses in each pride, and each one mates with the male when she is about 3 years old.

- **Lions usually catch** something to eat every four days or so. They can eat up to 40 kg in a single meal. Afterwards they rest for 24 hours.

- **The lions in a pride** usually spend about 20 hours a day sleeping and resting, and they walk no farther than 10 km or so a day.

- **Lionesses catch their prey** not by speed, but by stealth and strength. They stalk their prey quietly, creeping close to the ground. Then, when it is about 15 m away, the lionesses make a sudden dash and pull the victim down with their strong forepaws.

- **Lionesses usually hunt** at dusk or dawn, but they have very good night vision, and so will often hunt in the dark.

- **Male lion cubs** are driven out of the pride when they are two years old. When a young male is fully grown, he has to fight an older male to join another pride.

Wading birds

- **Herons** are large wading birds that hunt for fish in shallow lakes and rivers. There are about 60 species.

- **When hunting**, a heron stands alone in the water, often on one leg, apparently asleep. Then it makes a lightning dart with its long beak to spear a fish or frog.

- **Herons** usually nest in colonies called heronries. They build loose stick-nests in trees.

- **Storks** are very large black-and-white water birds with long necks and legs. There are 17 species of stork.

- **The white stork** lives in Eurasia in the summer, and then migrates to Africa, India and southern China in the winter.

- **White storks** build twig-nests on roofs, and some people think they bring luck to the house they nest on.

- **Flamingoes** are large pink wading birds which live in huge colonies on tropical lakes.

- **Spoonbills and ibises** are wading birds whose bills are sensitive enough to let them feel their prey moving in the water.

- **There are 28 species** of spoonbill and ibis.

- **The spoonbill's name** comes from its spoon-shaped bill, which it swings through the water to scoop up fish.

◄ *Egrets are large wading birds that live in marshy areas, feeding on fish and insects.*

Beetles

- **At least 250,000** species of beetle have been identified. They live everywhere on Earth, apart from in the oceans.

- **Unlike other insects**, adult beetles have a pair of thick, hard, front wings called elytra. These form an armour-like casing over the beetle's body.

- **The goliath beetle** of Africa is the heaviest flying insect, weighing over 100 grams and growing to as much as 13 cm long.

- **Dung beetles** roll away the dung of grazing animals to lay their eggs on. Fresh dung from one elephant may contain 7,000 beetles – they will clear the dung away in little more than a day.

- **A click beetle** can jump 30 cm into the air.

> ★ STAR FACT ★
> The Arctic beetle can survive in temperatures below -60°C.

- **The bombardier beetle** shoots attackers with jets of burning chemicals from the tip of its abdomen.

- **The rove beetle** can zoom across water on a liquid given off by glands on its abdomen.

- **The leaf-eating beetle** can clamp on to leaves using the suction of a layer of oil.

- **Stag beetles** have huge jaws which look like a stag's antlers.

Elytra (hard front wings)

► *The jewel beetles of tropical South America get their name from the brilliant rainbow colours of their elytra (front wings).*

Surviving the winter

- **Some animals** cope with the cold and lack of food in winter by going into a kind of deep sleep called hibernation.

- **During hibernation**, an animal's body temperature drops and its heart rate and breathing slow, so it needs little energy to survive.

- **Small mammals** such as bats, squirrels, hamsters, hedgehogs and chipmunks hibernate. So do birds such as nighthawks and swifts.

- **Reptiles** such as lizards and snakes go into a state called torpor whenever it gets too cold. They wake up only when the temperature rises again.

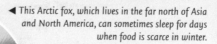

◀ This Arctic fox, which lives in the far north of Asia and North America, can sometimes sleep for days when food is scarce in winter.

- **Butterflies and other insects** go into a kind of suspended animation called diapause in winter.

- **The pika** (a small lagomorph) makes haystacks from grass in summer to provide food for the winter.

- **Beavers** collect branches in autumn and store them next to their lodges so they can feed on the bark during the winter.

- **Bears** go to sleep during winter, but not all scientists agree that they go into true hibernation.

- **Squirrels** bury dozens of stores of nuts in autumn to feed on during winter. They seem to have a remarkable memory, as they are able to find most of these stores when they need them.

> ★ STAR FACT ★
> Macaque monkeys in Japan keep warm in winter by bathing in hot volcanic springs.

Beavers

▶ In North America, beavers were once hunted so much that they were almost wiped out. They are now protected by law in some places.

- **Beavers are large rodents** (see rabbits and rats) with flat, paddle-like tails. They live in northern America and northern Eurasia.

- **Beavers live** in rivers, streams and lakes near woodlands and they are good swimmers, using their webbed feet as flippers and their tail as a rudder.

- **A beaver can swim underwater** for almost 1 km, holding its breath all the way.

- **Beavers can chop down** quite large trees with their incredibly strong front teeth, gnawing around the tree in a ring until it finally crashes down.

- **Beavers feed on** bark as well as tree roots and shrubs. They are especially fond of poplars and willows.

- **Beavers build dams** across streams from tree branches laid on to a base of mud and stones. Families of beavers often work together on a dam.

- **Beaver dams** are 5 to 30 m long on average, but they can be up to 300 m long.

- **Beavers repair** their dams year after year, and some beaver dams are thought to be centuries old.

- **In the lake** behind the dam, beavers build a shelter called a lodge to live in during winter. Most lodges are like mini-islands made of branches and mud, with only a few underwater tunnels as entrances.

- **Beaver lodges** keep a beaver family so warm that in cold weather steam can often be seen rising from the ventilation hole.

Jellyfish

- **Jellyfish** are sea creatures with bell-shaped, jelly-like bodies, and long stinging tentacles.
- **Biologists** call jellyfish medusa, after the mythical Greek goddess Medusa, who had wriggling snakes for hair.
- **Jellyfish** belong to a large group of sea creatures called cnidarians, which also includes corals and anemones.
- **Unlike anemones**, jellyfish float about freely, moving by squeezing water out from beneath their body. When a jellyfish stops squeezing, it slowly sinks.
- **A jellyfish's tentacles** are covered with stinging cells called nematocysts, which are used to catch fish and for protection. The stinging cells explode when touched, driving tiny poisonous threads into the victim.
- **Jellyfish vary in size** from a few millimetres to over 2 m.

> ★ STAR FACT ★
> The box jellyfish has one of the most deadly poisons. It can kill a human in 30 seconds.

- **The bell of one giant jellyfish** measured 2.29 m across. Its tentacles were over 36 m long.
- **The Portuguese man-of-war** is not a true jellyfish, but a collection of hundreds of tiny animals called polyps which live together under a gas-filled float.
- **The purple jellyfish** can be red, yellow or purple.

▼ Jellyfish are among the world's most ancient animals.

Otters

- **Otters** are small hunting mammals which are related to weasels. They are one of the 65 species of mustelid, along with stoats, skunks and badgers.
- **Otters live** close to water and are brilliant swimmers and divers.
- **Otters can close off** their nostrils and ears, allowing them to remain underwater for 4 or 5 minutes.

- **Otters are very playful creatures**, romping around on river banks and sliding down into the water.
- **Otters can use their paws** like hands, to play with things such as stones and shellfish.
- **Otters hunt fish**, mostly at night, but they also eat crayfish and crabs, clams and frogs.
- **Otters usually live** in burrows in riverbanks.
- **Sea otters** live on the shores of western North America.
- **Sea otters will float** on their backs for hours, eating or sleeping. Mother sea otters often carry their baby on their stomachs while floating like this.
- **Sea otters eat shellfish**. They will balance a rock on their stomach while floating on their back, and crack the shellfish by banging it on the rock.

◄ Sea otters float on their backs for hours in the seas off California and Alaska.

Farm animals

- **Cattle** are descended from a creature called the wild auroch, which was tamed 9,000 years ago. There are now over 200 breeds of domestic cow.

- **Female cows** reared for milk, butter and cheese production are called dairy cows. They give birth to one calf each year, and after it is born they provide milk twice a day.

- **A typical dairy cow** gives 16 litres of milk a day, or almost 6,000 litres a year.

- **Male cattle** are reared mainly for their meat, called beef. Beef breeds are usually heftier than dairy ones.

- **Sheep were first domesticated** over 10,000 years ago. There are now more than 700 million sheep in the world, and 800 different breeds.

◀ Female cattle are called cows, and males are called bulls. The young are calves. Female calves are also called heifers.

- **Hairy sheep** are kept for their milk and meat (lamb and mutton). Woolly sheep are kept for their wool.

- **Hens** lay one or two eggs a day – about 350 a year.

- **To keep hens laying**, their eggs must be taken from them every day. Otherwise the hens will try to nest so they can hatch them.

- **Turkeys** may have got their name from the mistaken idea that they came from Turkey.

> ★ STAR FACT ★
> When a cow chews the cud, the cud is food regurgitated from one of its four stomachs.

Colours and markings

▲ A zebra's stripes may seem to make it easy to see, but when it is moving they actually blur its outline and confuse predators.

- **Protective colouring** helps an animal hide from its enemies or warns them away.

- **Camouflage** is when an animal is coloured to blend in with its surroundings, making it hard to see.

- **Ground nesting birds** like the nightjar are mottled brown, making them hard to spot among fallen leaves.

- **The fur of wild pig and tapir babies** is striped and spotted to make them hard to see in the jungle light.

- **Squid** can change their colour to blend in with new surroundings.

- **Disruptive colouring** distorts an animal's body so that its real shape is disguised.

- **Bright colours** often warn predators that an animal is poisonous or tastes bad. For example, ladybirds are bright red and the cinnabar moth's caterpillars are black and yellow because they taste nasty.

- **Some creatures** mimic the colours of poisonous ones to warn predators off. Harmless hoverflies, for instance, look just like wasps.

- **Some animals** frighten off predators with colouring that makes them look much bigger. Peacock butterflies have big eyespots on their wings.

- **Courting animals**, especially male birds like the peacock, are often brightly coloured to attract mates.

Crocodiles and alligators

- **Crocodiles, alligators, caimans and gharials** are large reptiles that together form the group known as crocodilians. There are 14 species of crocodile, 7 alligators and caimans, and 1 gharial.

- **Crocodilian species** lived alongside the dinosaurs 200 million years ago, and they are the nearest we have to living dinosaurs today.

- **Crocodilians are hunters** that lie in wait for animals coming to drink at the water's edge. When crocodilians seize a victim they drag it into the water, stun it with a blow from their tail, then drown it.

- **Like all reptiles**, crocodilians get their energy from the Sun. Typically, they bask in the Sun on a sandbar or the river bank in the morning, then slip into the river at midday to cool off.

- **Crocodiles live** in tropical rivers and swamps. At over 5 m long, saltwater crocodiles are the world's largest reptiles – one grew to over 8 m long.

- **Crocodiles** are often said to cry after eating their victims. In fact only saltwater crocodiles cry, and they do it to get rid of salt, not because they are sorry.

- **Crocodiles have thinner snouts** than alligators, and a fourth tooth on the lower jaw which is visible when the crocodile's mouth is shut.

> ★ STAR FACT ★
> Crocodilians often swallow stones to help them stay underwater for long periods. Without this ballast, they might tip over.

▶ Crocodiles are huge reptiles with powerful bodies, scaly skin and great snapping jaws. When a crocodile opens its jaws, it reveals a flash of bright scarlet tongue and throat, as well as rows of very sharp teeth. The bright colour is thought to terrify potential victims.

The crocodile's eyes and nostrils are raised so it can see and breathe while floating under water

- **The female Nile crocodile** lays her eggs in nests which she digs in sandy river banks, afterwards covering the eggs in sand to keep them at a steady temperature. When the babies hatch they make loud piping calls. The mother then digs them out and carries them one by one in her mouth to the river.

- **Alligators** are found both in the Florida Everglades in the United States and in the Yangtze River in China.

▼ Crocodiles often lurk in rivers, with just their eyes and nostrils visible above the water.

A crocodile will often kill its victims with a swipe from its strong tail

The skin on its back has ridges formed by dozens of tiny bones called osteoderms

The skin on its belly is smooth and was once prized as a material for shoes and handbags

Bears

- **Although bears** are the largest meat-eating land animals, they also eat many other foods, including fruits, nuts and leaves.
- **The biggest bear** is the Alaskan brown bear, which grows to 2.7 m long and weighs up to 770 kg.
- **There are 7 species of bear**. Most live north of the equator. Only two live south of the equator – the spectacled bear of South America and the sun bear of Southeast Asia.
- **Bears do not hug** their prey to death, as is sometimes

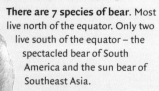

◀ *The polar bear has a white coat to camouflage it against the Arctic snow when it is hunting seals. Sometimes, only its black nose gives it away.*

thought. Instead, they kill their victims with a powerful cuff from their front paws, or with their teeth.

- **The grizzly bear** is actually a brown bear with white fur on its shoulders. Grizzly bears from Alaska are the biggest brown bears, along with kodiak bears.
- **Polar bears mainly eat** seals and they are the only truly carnivorous bears.
- **Polar bears catch seals** when the seals poke their heads up through breathing holes in the Arctic ice.
- **Polar bears often swim underwater** and come up under an ice floe to tip seals off. They may also chuck huge chunks of ice at seals to stun them.
- **The sun bear** of Southeast Asia is the smallest bear, and a very good climber.

Bees and wasps

▲ *Honey bees and bumble bees feed on pollen. They make honey from flower nectar to feed their young.*

- **Bees and wasps** are narrow-waisted insects (usually with hairy bodies). Many suck nectar from flowers.
- **There are 22,000 species of bee**. Some, like leaf-cutter bees, live alone. But most, like honey bees and bumble bees, live in vast colonies.

- **Honey bees** live in hives, either in hollow trees or in man-made beehive boxes. The inside of the hive is a honeycomb made up of hundreds of six-sided cells.
- **A honey bee colony** has a queen (the female bee that lays the eggs), tens of thousands of female worker bees, and a few hundred male drones.
- **Worker bees** collect nectar and pollen from flowers.
- **Each worker bee** makes ten trips a day and visits 1,000 flowers each trip. It takes 65,000 trips to 65 million flowers to make 1 kg of honey.
- **Honey bees** tell others where to find flowers, rich in pollen or nectar, by flying in a dance-like pattern.
- **Wasps** do not make honey, but feed on nectar and fruit juice. Many species have a nasty sting in their tail.
- **Paper wasps build** huge papier maché nests the size of footballs, containing 15,000 or more cells.
- **Paper wasps make** papier maché for their nest by chewing wood and mixing it with their spit.

Communication

- **Crows** use at least 300 different croaks to communicate with each other. But crows from one area cannot understand crows from another one.
- **When two howler monkey troops** meet, the males scream at each other until one troop gives way.
- **The male orang utan** burps to warn other males to keep away.
- **Dogs** communicate through barks, yelps, whines, growls and howls.
- **Many insects communicate** through the smell of chemicals called pheromones, which are released from special glands.

◀ Lone wolves often howl at dusk or in the night to signal their ownership of a particular territory and to warn off rival wolves.

- **Tropical tree ant species** use ten different pheromones, combining them with different movements to send 50 different kinds of message.
- **A gorilla** named Coco was trained so that she could use over 1,000 different signs to communicate, each sign meaning different words. She called her pet cat 'Soft good cat cat', and herself 'Fine animal gorilla'.
- **Female glow worms** communicate with males by making a series of flashes.
- **Many birds** are mimics and can imitate a whole variety of different sounds, including the human voice and machines like telephones. This is not communication, though, it is simply showing off.

> ★ STAR FACT ★
> Using sign language, Coco the gorilla took an IQ test and got a score of 95.

Parrots and budgerigars

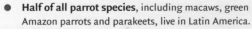

▲ The blue-and-yellow macaw of the Amazon rainforest has been trapped so much for the pet trade, it is now quite rare.

- **Parrots** are colourful birds with curved bills for eating fruits and seeds and for cracking nuts. They are very noisy birds and they live mostly in tropical rainforests.
- **Parrots** have feet with two toes pointing forwards and two backwards, allowing them to grip branches and hold food.
- **There are 330 or so parrot species** divided into three main groups – true parrots, cockatoos and lories.
- **Half of all parrot species**, including macaws, green Amazon parrots and parakeets, live in Latin America.
- **Australia and New Guinea** are home to parrots called cockatoos (which are white with feathered crests on their heads), as well as to lories and lorikeets.
- **The budgerigar** is a small parakeet from central Australia which is very popular as a pet.
- **The hanging parrots** of Southeast Asia get their name because they sleep upside down like bats.
- **The kea** of New Zealand is a parrot that eats meat as well as fruit. It was once wrongly thought to be a sheep killer.
- **Parrots** are well known for their mimicry of human voices. Some have a repertoire of 300 words or more.
- **An African grey parrot** called Alex was trained by scientist Irene Pepperberg to identify at least 50 different objects. Alex could ask for each of these objects in English – and also refuse them.

Ostriches and emus

▶ Ostriches live on the grasslands of Africa and nest in holes scooped out of the ground. The male scoops out the hole and leads several females to it to lay their eggs.

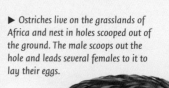

Bony crest

Two toes with very sharp toenails

★ **STAR FACT** ★
The biggest bird ever is now extinct – the flightless elephant bird of Madagascar was truly elephantine, growing up to 4.5 m tall (taller than two grown men).

◀ The cassowary lives in the forests of tropical Australia and New Guinea. It has a crest which it uses like a crash helmet as it charges through the undergrowth.

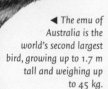

◀ The emu of Australia is the world's second largest bird, growing up to 1.7 m tall and weighing up to 45 kg.

- **Ratites are big, but flightless, birds** like the ostrich, emu, cassowary, rhea and kiwi. They are descended from an ancient group of birds, and have lost the ability to fly. Ratites always walk or run, only using their small wings for balance and for show.

- **The ostrich** is the biggest living bird, towering up to 2.75 m in height and weighing over 150 kg.

- **To escape a lion**, the ostrich can hurtle over the African savannah grasslands, where it lives, at speeds of 60 km/h – faster than a racehorse. Even when the ostrich tires, its strong legs can still deliver a massive kick.

- **Ostriches** have only two toes on each foot – unlike the rhea of South America which has three.

◀ Ostriches have soft downy plumage, but their head, neck and legs are almost bare.

- **The ostrich lays** the largest egg – almost as big as a football.

- **The kiwi of New Zealand** is the smallest ratite, no bigger than a chicken. It has fur-like feathers and is the only bird with nostrils at the tip of its bill, which it uses to sniff out worms and grubs.

- **The rare kakapo parrot** of New Zealand could fly once, but it lost the power of flight because it had no natural predators – until Europeans introduced dogs and cats to New Zealand.

- **The dodo** was a flightless bird that once lived on islands, such as Mauritius in the Indian Ocean. It was wiped out in the 17th century when its eggs were eaten by pigs and monkeys imported by Europeans.

- **The emu** of Australia is the best swimmer of any flightless bird. Ostriches can swim well, too.

Dogs and wolves

- **The dog family** is a large group of four-legged, long-nosed, meat-eating animals. It includes dogs, wolves, foxes, jackals and coyotes.

- **All kinds of dog** have long canine teeth for piercing and tearing their prey. (Canine means 'dog').

- **When hunting**, dogs rely mainly on their good sense of smell and acute hearing.

- **Wolves** are the largest wild dogs. They hunt together in packs to track down animals bigger than themselves, such as moose, deer, caribou and musk oxen.

- **A wolf pack** may have 7 to 20 wolves, led by the eldest male and female.

- **A wolf pack's territory** may be 1,000 square km or more. Wolves can travel vast distances when hunting.

- **Wolves once lived** all over Europe and North America, but are now rare in Europe and are found only in Asia and in remote areas of North America.

- **Foxes** are cunning hunters which prowl at night, alone or in pairs. Typical prey includes rats, mice and rabbits.

- **The red fox** has adapted to the growth of towns and cities and may often be seen at night raiding surburban rubbish bins and dumps.

- **The jackals** of Africa look like small wolves, but they hunt alone for small prey and only meet in packs to grab the leftovers from the kill of a lion.

▶ *Most wolves are grey wolves – either the timber wolf of cold forest regions, or the tundra wolf of the Arctic plains.*

Poisonous insects

- **Insects are small**, but many have nasty poisons to protect themselves.

- **Most poisonous insects** are brightly coloured – including many caterpillars, wasps and cardinal beetles – to warn off its potential enemies.

- **Ants, bees and wasps** have stings in their tails which they use to inject poison to defend themselves or paralyse prey.

- **Bee and wasp stings** have barbed ends to keep the sting in long enough to inject the poison. Honey bees cannot pull the barb out from human skins, and so tear themselves away and die.

- **Velvet ants** are not really ants at all, but wingless wasps with such a nasty sting that they are called 'cow killers'.

- **Ladybirds** make nasty chemicals in their knees.

- **When attacked**, swallowtail caterpillars whip out a smelly forked gland from a pocket behind their head and hit their attacker with it.

▲ *Wasps poison their victims with the sharp sting in their tail.*

- **The lubber grasshopper** is slow moving, but when attacked it oozes a foul smelling froth from its mouth and thorax.

- **It is not only insects** that are poisonous, but some spiders. The black widow spider is one of the deadliest spiders, with a bite that can kill a human. The funnel-web spider and many bird-eating spiders are also poisonous.

Penguins

- **There are 17 or 18 different species** of penguin, most of them living in huge colonies called rookeries along the coast of Antarctica and nearby islands.
- **Penguins** are superb swimmers, using their wings as flippers to push them through the water, and steering with their webbed feet.
- **Penguins have coats** waterproofed with oil and thick fat so they can survive in temperatures as low as -60°C.
- **The smallest** is the fairy penguin, at 40 cm high.
- **The emperor penguin** is the biggest swimming bird, at up to 1.2 m tall and weighing over 40 kg – twice the weight of any flying bird.
- **Emperor penguins** can dive briefly to depths of 250 m or more chasing fish, their main diet.

> ★ STAR FACT ★
> The male emperor penguin keeps the female's
> egg warm on his feet until it hatches.

▲ Penguins are sociable birds that live in large colonies.

- **Penguins** can leap high out of the water to land on an ice bank, but on land they can only waddle clumsily or toboggan along on their bellies.
- **Adélie penguins** waddle more than 320 km across the ice every year to reach their breeding ground.
- **When crossing the ice**, Adélie penguins steer by the sun. They lose their way when the sun goes down.

Iguanas

- **Iguanas** are large lizards that live around the Pacific and in the Americas.
- **Larger iguanas** are the only vegetarian lizards. Unlike other lizards, most eat fruit, flowers and leaves, rather than insects.
- **The common iguana** lives high up in trees, but lays its eggs in a hole in the ground.

- **Common iguanas** will jump 6 m or more out of the trees to the ground if they are disturbed.
- **The rhinoceros iguana** of the West Indies gets its name from the pointed scales on its snout.
- **The marine iguana** of the Galapagos Islands is the only lizard that spends much of its life in the sea.
- **Marine iguanas** keep their eggs warm ready for hatching in the mouth of volcanoes, risking death to put them there.
- **When in the water**, a marine iguana may dive for 15 minutes or more, pushing itself along with its tail.
- **Although marine iguanas** cannot breathe underwater, their heart rate slows so that they use less oxygen.
- **The chuckwalla** inflates its body with air to wedge itself in a rock crack if it is in danger.

◄ Before each dive into water, marine iguanas warm themselves in the sun to gain energy.

Crabs and lobsters

- **Crabs and lobsters** are part of an enormous group of creatures called crustaceans.
- **Most crabs and lobsters** have their own shell, but hermit crabs live inside the discarded shells of other creatures.
- **Crabs and lobsters are decapods**, which means they have ten legs – although the first pair are often strong pincers which are used to hold and tear food.
- **For spotting prey**, crabs and lobsters have two pairs of antennae on their heads and a pair of eyes on stalks.
- **One of a lobster's claws** usually has blunt knobs for crushing victims. The other has sharp teeth for cutting.
- **Male fiddler crabs** have one giant pincer which they waggle to attract a mate.
- **Robber crabs** have claws on their legs which they use to climb up trees to escape from predators.
- **The giant Japanese spider crab** can grow to measure 3 m across between the tips of its outstretched pincers.

- **When American spiny lobsters** migrate, they cling to each others' tails in a long line, marching for hundreds of kilometres along the seabed.
- **Sponge crabs** hide under sponges which they cut to fit. The sponge then grows at the same rate as the crab.

▼ Lobsters are dark green or blue when alive and only turn red when cooked.

Life in the desert

▲ Deserts like this are among the world's toughest environments for animals to survive.

- **In the Sahara desert**, a large antelope called the addax survives without waterholes because it gets all its water from its food.
- **Many small animals** cope with the desert heat by resting in burrows or sheltering under stones during the day. They come out to feed only at night.

- **Desert animals** include many insects, spiders, scorpions, lizards and snakes.
- **The dwarf puff adder** hides from the sun by burying itself in the sand until only its eyes show.
- **The fennec fox** and the antelope jack rabbit both lose heat through their ears. This way they keep cool.
- **The kangaroo rats** of California's Death Valley save water by eating their own droppings.
- **The Mojave squirrel** survives through long droughts by sleeping five or six days a week.
- **Swarms of desert locusts** can cover an area as big as 5,000 square kilometres.
- **Sand grouse** fly hundreds of kilometres every night to reach watering holes.

★ STAR FACT ★
The African fringe-toed lizard dances to keep cool, lifting each foot in turn off the hot sand.

Finding a mate

- **Humans** are among the few animals that mate at any time of year. Most animals come into heat (are ready to mate) only at certain times.
- **Spring** is a common mating time. The warmer weather and longer daylight hours triggers the production of sperm in males and eggs in females.
- **Some mammals**, such as bats, bears and deer, have only one mating time a year. Others, such as rabbits, have many.
- **Many large mammals** pair for a short time, but a few (including beavers and wolves) pair for life. Some animals (including lions and seals) have lots of mates.
- **To attract a mate**, many animals put on courtship displays such as special colours, songs and dances.

◀ *Prairie dogs live in families called coteries, each made up of a male and several females.*

- **The male capercaillies** (turkey-like birds) attract a mate with a loud display that can be heard for miles.
- **Great crested grebes** perform dramatic dances in the water and present water plants to one another.
- **Male bower birds** paint their nests blue with berry juice and line them with blue shells and flowers to attract a mate.
- **Male birds of paradise** flash their bright feathers while strutting and dancing to attract a mate.
- **The male tern** catches a fish as a gift for the female. The male dancefly brings a dead insect which the female eats while mating.

Life in tropical grasslands

- **Tropical grasslands** are home to vast herds of grazing animals such as antelope and buffalo – and to the lions, cheetahs and other big cats that prey on them.
- **There are few places to hide** on the grasslands, so most grassland animals are fast runners with long legs.

▼ *With their long necks, giraffes can feed on the high branches of the thorn trees that dot the savannah grasslands of Africa.*

> ★ STAR FACT ★
> Cheetahs are the fastest runners in the world, reaching 110 km/h in short bursts.

- **Pronghorns** can manage 67 km/h for 16 km.
- **There are more than 60 species** of antelope on the grasslands of Africa and southern Asia.
- **A century ago in South Africa**, herds of small antelopes called springboks could be as large as 10 million strong and hundreds of kilometres long.
- **The springbok** gets its name from its habit of springing 3 m straight up in the air.
- **Grazing animals** are divided into perissodactyls and artiodactyls, according to how many toes they have.
- **Perissodactyls** have an odd number of toes on each foot. They include horses, rhinos and tapirs.
- **Artiodactyls** have an even number. They include camels, deer, antelope, cattle and buffaloes.

Elephants

- **There are three kinds** of elephant – the African forest elephant, of central and west Africa, the African savanna elephant, of east and south Africa, and the Asian elephant, of India and Southeast Asia.

- **African elephants** are the largest land animals, growing as tall as 4 m and weighing more than 6,000 kg.

- **Asian elephants** are smaller than African elephants, with smaller ears and tusks. They also have one 'finger' on the tip of their trunk, while African elephants have two.

- **The scientific word** for an elephant's trunk is a proboscis. It is used like a hand to put food into the elephant's mouth, or to suck up water to squirt into its mouth or over its body to keep cool.

- **Elephants** are very intelligent animals, with the biggest brain of all land animals. They also have very good memories.

- **Female elephants,** called cows, live with their calves and younger bulls (males) in herds of 20 to 30 animals. Older bulls usually live alone.

- **Once a year**, bull elephants go into a state called musth (said 'must'), when male hormones make them very wild and dangerous.

- **Elephants** usually live for about 70 years.

- **When an elephant dies**, its companions seem to mourn and cry.

▼ In dry areas, herds may travel vast distances to find food, with the bigger elephants protecting the little ones between their legs.

★ STAR FACT ★
Elephants use their trunks like snorkels when crossing deep rivers.

▼ When the leader of the herd senses danger, she lifts her trunk and sniffs the air – then warns the others by using her trunk to give a loud blast called a trumpet. If an intruder comes too close, she will roll down her trunk, throw back her ears, lower her head and charge at up to 50 km/h.

Camels

- **Camels** are the biggest desert mammals and they have adapted in many ways to help them live in extremely dry conditions.

- **Dromedary camels** have one hump and live mainly in the Sahara desert and the Middle East. Bactrian camels live in central Asia and have two humps.

- **A camel's hump** is made of fat, but the camel's body can break the fat down into food and water when these are scarce.

- **Camels can go** many days or even months without water. But when water is available, they can drink over 200 litres in a day.

▶ The Dromedary camel has been the 'ship of the desert', transporting people and baggage, for thousands of years.

- **Camels sweat** very little, to save moisture. Instead, their body temperature rises by as much as 6°C when it is hot.

- **The camel's feet** have two joined toes to stop them sinking into soft sand (Dromedary camels) or soft snow (Bactrians).

- **The camel's nostrils** can close up completely to block out sand.

- **Camels have** a double row of eyelashes to protect their eyes from sand and sun.

- **The camel's stomach** is huge, with three different sections. Like cows, camels are ruminants – this means they partially digest food, then bring it back into their mouths to chew the cud.

★ STAR FACT ★
Camels have by far the worst smelling breath in the entire animal kingdom!

Eating food

▲ Bears are omnivores, eating fish and other meat, although they will eat berries, leaves and almost anything when hungry.

- **Herbivores** are animals that usually eat only plants.
- **Carnivores** are animals that eat animal flesh (meat).
- **Omnivores** eat plants and animals. Many primates such as monkeys, apes and humans are omnivorous.

- **Insectivores** eat insects. Some, such as bats, have teeth for breaking through insects' shells. Others, such as anteaters, have long, sticky tongues for licking up ants and termites, but few or no teeth.

- **Herbivores** such as cattle, elephants and horses either graze (eat grass) or browse (eat mainly leaves, bark and the buds of bushes and trees).

- **Herbivores** have tough, crowned teeth to cope with their hard plant food.

- **Carnivores** have pointed canine teeth for tearing meat.

- **Some carnivores**, such as hyenas, do not hunt and instead feed on carrion (the remains of dead animals).

- **Herbivores** eat for much of the time. However, because meat is very nourishing, carnivores eat only occasionally and tend to rest after each meal.

- **Every living thing** is part of a food chain, in which it feeds on the living thing before it in the chain and is in turn eaten by the living thing next to it in the chain.

Dolphins

- **Dolphins** are sea creatures that belong to the same family as whales – the cetaceans.

- **Dolphins are mammals**, not fish. They are warm-blooded, and mothers feed their young on milk.

- **There are two kinds** of dolphin – marine (sea) dolphins (32 species) and river dolphins (5 species).

- **Dolphins usually live** in groups of 20 to 100 animals.

- **Dolphins look after** each other. Often, they will support an injured companion on the surface.

- **Dolphins communicate** with high-pitched clicks called phonations. Some clicks are higher than any other animal noise and humans cannot hear them.

- **Dolphins use sound** to find things and can identify different objects even when blindfolded.

> ★ STAR FACT ★
> Dolphins have rescued drowning humans by pushing them to the surface.

▲ *Dolphins are among the most intelligent of the animals, along with humans and chimpanzees.*

- **Dolphins can be trained** to jump through hoops, toss balls, or 'walk' backwards through the water on their tails.

- **Bottle-nosed dolphins** get their name from their short beaks (which also make them look like they are smiling). They are friendly and often swim near boats.

Pheasants and peafowl

- **A game bird** is a bird that is hunted for sport.

- **Game birds** spend most of the time strutting along the ground looking for seeds. They fly only in emergencies.

- **There are 250 species** of game bird, including pheasants, grouse, partridges, quails, wild turkeys and peafowl.

- **Most of the 48 species** of pheasant originated in China and central Asia.

- **Many hen (female) game birds** have dull brown plumage that helps them to hide in their woodland and moorland homes.

- **Many cock (male) game birds** have very colourful plumage to attract mates.

- **In the breeding season**, cocks strut and puff up their plumage to attract a mate. They also draw attention to themselves by cackling, whistling and screaming.

- **Pheasant cocks** often fight each other violently to win a particular mating area.

- **The jungle fowl** of Southeast Asia is the wild ancestor of the domestic chicken.

- **Peacocks** were carried as treasure from India throughout the ancient world.

◀ *The peacock (the male peafowl) of India and Sri Lanka is the most spectacular of all pheasants. When courting the drab peahen, the peacock throws up his tail feathers to create a gigantic turquoise fan.*

Kangaroos and koalas

- **Kangaroos** are big Australian mammals that hop around on their hind (back) legs.

- **A kangaroo's tail** can be over 1.5 m long. It is used for balance when hopping, and to hold the kangaroo up when walking.

- **Red kangaroos** can hop at 55 km/h for short distances.

- **Red kangaroos** can leap 9 m forwards in one huge bound, and jump over fences that are 2 to 3 m high.

- **There are two kinds of kangaroo** – red kangaroos and grey kangaroos. Red kangaroos live in the dry grasslands of central Australia. Grey kangaroos live in the southeast, in woods and grassland.

- **Kangaroos are marsupials** – animals whose babies are born before they are ready to survive in the outside word and so live for a while protected in a pouch on their mother's belly.

▲ Koalas drink very little water, and their name comes from an Aboriginal word for 'no drink'.

- **Koalas** are Australian mammals that look like teddy bears, but which are no relation to any kind of bear.

- **Like kangaroos**, koalas are marsupials. A koala baby spends 6 months in its mother's pouch and another 6 months riding on her back.

- **Koalas** spend 18 hours a day sleeping. The rest of the time they feed on the leaves of eucalyptus trees.

- **Other Australian marsupials** include the wombat, and several kinds of wallaby (which look like small kangaroos) and bandicoots (which look like rats).

▼ When they are first born, kangaroos are naked and look like tiny jellybabies – just a few centimetres long, with two tiny arms. But straight away they have to haul themselves up through the fur on their mother's belly and into her pouch. Here the baby kangaroo (called a joey) lives and grows for 6 to 8 months, sucking on teats inside the pouch. Only when it is quite large and covered in fur will it pop out of the pouch to live by itself.

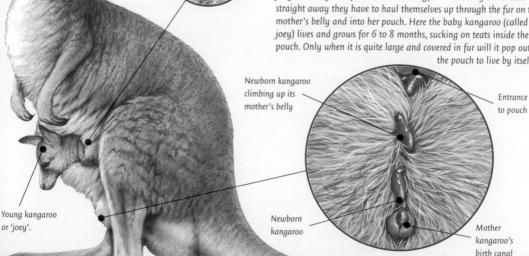

Inside the pouch, the baby sucks on its mother's teat

Young kangaroo or 'joey'.

Newborn kangaroo climbing up its mother's belly

Entrance to pouch

Newborn kangaroo

Mother kangaroo's birth canal

Migration

- **Migration** is when animals move from one place to another to avoid the cold or to find food and water.
- **Some migrations** are daily, some are seasonal, and some are permanent.
- **Starlings** migrate every day from the country to their roosts in the city.
- **Many birds, whales, seals and bats** migrate closer to the tropics in autumn to escape the winter cold.
- **One knot** (a kind of small bird) took just 8 days to fly 5,600 km, from Britain to West Africa.
- **Barheaded geese** migrate right over the top of the Himalayan mountains, flying as high as 8,000 m.
- **Migrating birds** are often brilliant navigators. Bristle-thighed curlews find their way from Alaska to tiny islands in the Pacific 9,000 km away.
- **Shearwaters**, sparrows and homing pigeons are able to fly home when released by scientists in strange places, thousands of kilometres away.

▶ In summer, moose spend most of the time alone. But in winter they gather and trample areas of snow (called yards) to help each other get at the grass beneath.

- **The Arctic tern** is the greatest migrator, flying 30,000 km from the Arctic to the Antarctic and back again each year.
- **Monarch butterflies** migrate 4,000 km every year, from North America to small clumps of trees in Mexico. Remarkably, the migrating butterflies have never made the journey before.

Eels

- **Eels** are long, slimy fish that look like snakes.
- **Baby eels** are called elvers.
- **Some eels** live in rivers, but most live in the sea, including moray eels and conger eels.
- **Moray eels** are huge and live in tropical waters, hunting fish, squid and cuttlefish.
- **Gulper eels** can live more than 7,500 m down in the Atlantic Ocean. Their mouths are huge to help them catch food in the dark, deep water – so big that they can swallow fish larger than themselves whole.
- **Every autumn**, some European common eels migrate over 7,000 km, from the Baltic Sea in Europe to the Sargasso Sea near the West Indies to lay their eggs.
- **Migrating eels** are thought to find their way partly

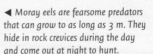

◀ Moray eels are fearsome predators that can grow to as long as 3 m. They hide in rock crevices during the day and come out at night to hunt.

by detecting weak electric currents created by the movement of the water.

- **When European eels** hatch in the Sargasso Sea they are carried northeast by the ocean current, developing as they go into tiny transparent eels called glass eels.
- **The electric eels** of South America can produce an electric shock of over 500 volts – enough to knock over an adult human.
- **Garden eels** live in colonies on the seabed, poking out from holes in the sand to catch food drifting by. Their colonies look like gardens of weird plants.

What are mammals?

- **Mammals** are animals with furry bodies, warm blood, and a unique habit of suckling their young on milk from the mother's teats.

- **Humans and most other mammals** keep their body temperatures at around 37°C, although the three-toed sloth's temperature varies from 24°C to more than 40°C.

- **Fur and fat** protect mammals from the cold. When they do get cold, they curl up, seek shelter or shiver.

- **All mammals** except monotremes (see strange mammals) give birth to live young.

- **Most mammals** are placental – their young are nourished inside the mother's womb through an organ called the placenta until they are fully developed.

- **Marsupials** are not placental. Their young develop mainly in the mother's pouch.

- **The time from mating to birth** is called the pregnancy or gestation period. In mammals, it varies from 20 days for some mice to 22 months for elephants.

▲ Pigs have 12 or so babies in a litter and 7 pairs of teats.

- **Marsupials** have short pregnancies – the opossum's is just 12 days.

- **Mammals** vary in size from the finger-sized Etruscan shrew to the 30 m-long blue whale.

- **One of the earliest mammals** was a tiny, shrew-like creature called megazostrodon that lived alongside the dinosaurs about 120 million years ago.

Ocean fish

◀ Flying fish beat their tails so fast they are able to 'fly' away from predators.

- **Nearly 75%** of all fish live in the seas and oceans.

- **The biggest, fastest swimming fish**, such as swordfish and marlin, live near the surface of the open ocean, far from land. They often migrate vast distances to spawn (lay their eggs) or find food.

- **Many smaller fish** live deeper down, including seabed-dwellers like eels and flatfish (such as plaice, turbot and flounders).

- **All flatfish** start life as normal-shaped fish, but as they grow older, one eye slowly slides around the head to join the other. The pattern of scales changes so that one side is the top, the other is the bottom.

- **Plaice** lie on the seabed on their left side, while turbot lie on their right side. Some flounders lie on their left and some on their right.

- **The upper side** of a flatfish is usually camouflaged to help it blend in with the sea floor.

- **In the temperate waters** of the Atlantic there are rich fishing grounds for fish such as herring.

- **The swordfish** can swim at up to 80 km/h. It uses its long spike to slash or stab squid.

- **The bluefin tuna** can grow to as long as 3 m and weigh more than 500 kg. It is also a fast swimmer – one crossed the Atlantic in 199 days.

> ★ STAR FACT ★
> Flying fish can glide over the sea for 400 m and soar up to 6 m above the waves.

Grasshoppers and crickets

- **Grasshoppers** are plant-eating insects related to crickets, locusts and katydids.
- **Grasshoppers** belong to two main families – short-horned, which includes locusts, and long-horned, which includes katydids and crickets.
- **Short-horned grasshoppers** have ears on the side of their body. Long-horned grasshoppers have ears in their knees.
- **Grasshoppers** have powerful back legs, which allow them to jump huge distances.
- **Some grasshoppers** can leap more than 3 m.
- **Grasshoppers** sing by rubbing their hind legs across their closed forewings.
- **A grasshopper's singing** is called stridulation.
- **Crickets** chirrup faster the warmer it is.
- **If you count** the number of chirrups a snowy tree cricket gives in 15 seconds, then add 40, you get the temperature in degrees Fahrenheit.

> ★ STAR FACT ★
> A frightened lubber grasshopper oozes a horrible smelling froth from its mouth.

▼ The spikes on the long-horned grasshopper's back legs are what make the chirruping sound as it rubs them against its forewings.

Life in the mountains

- **Mountains** are cold, windy places where only certain animals can survive – including agile hunters such as pumas and snow leopards, and nimble grazers such as mountain goats, yaks, ibex and chamois.
- **The world's highest-living** mammal is the yak, a type of wild cattle. It can survive over 6,000 m up in the Himalayas of Tibet.
- **Mountain goats** have hooves with sharp edges that dig into cracks in the rock, and hollow soles that act like suction pads.
- **In winter**, the mountain goat's pelage (coat) turns white, making it hard to spot against the snow.
- **The Himalayan snowcock** nests higher than almost any other bird, often above 4,000 m in the Himalayas.

▲ Sheep like these dall sheep are well equipped for life in the mountains, with their thick woolly coats and nimble feet.

- **The Alpine chough** has been seen flying at 8,200 m up on Everest.
- **Lammergeiers** are the vultures of the African and southern European mountains. They break bones, when feeding, by dropping them from a great height on to stones and then eating the marrow.
- **The Andean condor** of the South American Andes is a gigantic scavenger which can carry off deer and sheep. It is said to dive from the skies like a fighter plane (see also vultures).
- **The puma**, or mountain lion, can jump well over 5 m up on to a rock ledge – that is like you jumping into an upstairs window.
- **The snow leopard** of the Himalayan mountains is now one of the rarest of all the big cats, because it has been hunted almost to extinction for its beautiful fur coat.

Life in the oceans

▲ *Many kinds of fish and other sea creatures live in the sunlit zone near the surface of the oceans.*

- **Oceans** cover 70% of the Earth and they are the largest single animal habitat.
- **Scientists divide the ocean** into two main environments – the pelagic (which is the water itself), and the benthic (which is the seabed).
- **Most benthic animals** live in shallow waters around the continents. They include worms, clams, crabs and lobsters, as well as bottom-feeding fish.
- **Scientists call the sunny surface waters** the euphotic zone. This extends down 150 m and it is where billions of plankton (microscopic animals and plants) live.
- **Green plant plankton** (algae) of the oceans produce 30% of the world's vegetable matter each year.
- **Animal plankton** include shrimps and jellyfish.
- **The surface waters** are also home to squid, fish and mammals such as whales.
- **Below the surface zone**, down to about 2,000 m, is the twilit bathyal zone. Here there is too little light for plants to grow, but many hunting fish and squid live.
- **Below 2,000 m** is the dark abyssal zone, where only weird fish like gulper eels and anglerfish live (see strange sea creatures).
- **The Sargasso**, a vast area in the west Atlantic where seaweed grows thick, is a rich home to many sea creatures.

Corals and anemones

- **Sea anemones** are tiny, meat-eating animals that look a bit like flowers. They cling to rocks and catch tiny prey with their tentacles (see life on the seashore).
- **Coral reefs** are the undersea equivalent of rainforests, teeming with fish and other sea life. The reefs are built by tiny, sea-anemone-like animals called polyps.
- **Coral polyps** live all their lives in just one place, either fixed to a rock or to dead polyps.
- **When coral polyps die**, their cup-shaped skeletons become hard coral.
- **Coral reefs** are long ridges, and other shapes, made from billions of coral polyps and their skeletons.
- **Fringing reefs** are shallow coral reefs that stretch out from the seashore.

◀ *Sea anemones look like flowers with petals, but they are actually carnivorous animals with rings of tentacles.*

- **Barrier reefs** form a long, underwater wall a little way offshore.
- **The Great Barrier Reef** off eastern Australia is the longest reef in the world, stretching over 2,000 km. It can be seen from space (up to 200 km up) and is the only non-human, animal activity visible from space.
- **Coral atolls** are ring-shaped islands that formed from fringing reefs around an old volcano (which has long since sunk beneath the waves).
- **Coral reefs** take millions of years to form – the Great Barrier Reef is 18 million years old, for example. By drilling a core into ancient corals, and analysing the minerals and growth rate, scientists can read the history of the oceans back for millions of years.

Butterflies

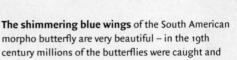

- **Butterflies** are insects with four large wings that feed either on the nectar of flowers or on fruit.

- **Together with moths**, butterflies make up the scientific order Lepidoptera – the word means 'scaly wings'. There are more than 165,000 species of Lepidoptera – 20,000 butterflies and 145,000 moths.

- **Many butterflies** are brightly coloured and fly by day. They have slim, hairless bodies and club-shaped antennae (feelers).

- **The biggest butterfly** is the Queen Alexandra's birdwing of New Guinea, with 25-cm-wide wings. The smallest is the Western pygmy blue.

- **Butterflies can only fly** if their wing muscles are warm. To warm up, they bask in the sun so their wings soak up energy like solar panels.

- **The monarch butterfly** is such a strong flier it can cross the Atlantic Ocean (see migration).

- **The shimmering blue wings** of the South American morpho butterfly are very beautiful – in the 19th century millions of the butterflies were caught and made into brooches.

- **Most female butterflies** live only a few days, so they have to mate and lay eggs quickly. Most males court them with elaborate flying displays.

- **Butterflies** taste with their tarsi (feet). Females 'stamp' on leaves to see if they are ripe enough for egg laying.

- **Every butterfly's caterpillar** has its own chosen food plants – different from the flowers the adult feeds on.

1. **Egg** – eggs are laid on plants that will provide food when the caterpillars hatch

2. **Larva** – when the caterpillar hatches, it begins eating and growing straight away

3. **Pupa** – butterfly caterpillars develop hard cases and hang from a stem or leaf

▲ Every species of butterfly has its own wing pattern, like a fingerprint – some drab like this, others brilliantly coloured.

◄ Few insects change as much as butterflies do during their lives. Butterflies start off as an egg, then hatch into a long, wiggly larva called a caterpillar, which eats leaves greedily and grows rapidly. When it is big enough, the caterpillar makes itself a case, which can be either a cocoon or a chrysalis. Inside, it metamorphoses (changes) into an adult, then breaks out, dries its new wings and flies away.

4. **Metamorphosis** – it takes a few days to a year for the pupa to turn into an adult

5. **Imago** – the adult's new wings are damp and crumpled, but soon dry in the sun

★ STAR FACT ★
Butterflies fly like no other insects, flapping their wings like birds.

Octopuses and squid

- **Octopuses and squid** belong to a family of molluscs called cephalopods.

- **Octopuses** are sea creatures with a round, soft, boneless body, three hearts and eight long arms called tentacles.

- **An octopus's tentacles** are covered with suckers that allow it to grip rocks and prey.

- **Octopuses** have two large eyes, similar to humans, and a beak-like mouth.

- **When in danger** an octopus may send out a cloud of inky black fluid. Sometimes the ink cloud is the same shape as the octopus and may fool a predator into chasing the cloud.

> ★ STAR FACT ★
> The 30-cm-long blue-ringed octopus's poison is so deadly that it kills more people than sharks.

- **Some octopuses can change colour** dramatically to startle a predator or blend in with its background.

- **The smallest octopus** is just 2.5 cm across. The biggest measures 6 m from tentacle tip to tentacle tip.

- **A squid** has eight arms and two tentacles and swims by forcing a jet of water out of its body.

- **Giant squid** in the Pacific can grow to 18 m or more long.

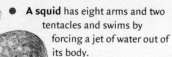

◄ Most of the hundreds of species of octopus live on the beds of shallow seas around the world. Octopuses are quite intelligent creatures.

Life on the grasslands

▲ Until they were wiped out by European settlers, vast herds of bison (buffalo) roamed the North American prairies.

- **Grasslands** form in temperate (moderate temperature) regions where there is too little rainfall for forests, but enough to allow grass to grow.

- **Temperate grasslands** include the prairies of North America, the pampas of South America, the veld of South Africa, and the vast steppes of Eurasia.

- **There is little cover** on grasslands, so many grassland animals have very good eyesight and large ears to detect predators from afar.

- **Some grassland animals escape** from predators by speed. These include jack rabbits, deer, pronghorn antelopes, wild asses and flightless birds like the emu.

- **Some animals**, such as mice and prairie dogs, escape by hiding underground in burrows.

- **Some birds hide** by building their nests in bushes. These include meadowlarks, quails and blackbirds.

- **The main predators** are dogs like the coyote and fox.

- **The North American prairies** have a small wild cat called the bobcat.

- **Prairie dogs** live in huge underground colonies called towns. One contained 400 million animals and covered over 60,000 square kilometres.

- **When they meet**, prairie dogs kiss each other to find out whether they are from the same group.

Seagulls and albatrosses

▲ *Seagulls catch small fish, steal eggs and young from other birds, scavenge on waste – and sometimes fly inland to find worms.*

- **Gulls are big sea birds** that live on coasts all around the world, nesting on cliffs, islands or beaches.

- **Gulls are related** to skuas and terns.

- **Skuas** have hooked claws and sharp bills, which they

★ **STAR FACT** ★
Herring gulls watch ducks diving for fish and then steal it when the ducks resurface.

use to attack other birds and force them to disgorge (throw up) their food – which the skua then eats.

- **Skuas are such good acrobats** that they can catch the disgorged meal of another bird in mid-air.

- **The great skua** often pounces on seagulls, drowns them, and then steals their chicks.

- **Wandering albatrosses** are the biggest of all sea birds, with white bodies and dark wings.

- **The wandering albatross** has the biggest wingspan of any bird – 3.7 m across.

- **An albatross** will often follow a ship for days without stopping to rest.

- **Wild albatrosses** may live for more than 50 years.

Giraffes

- **Giraffes** are the tallest mammals, growing to more than 5 m. Their height allows them to reach and eat the leaves, twigs and fruit at the tops of trees.

- **A giraffe's legs** are almost 2 m long.

- **A giraffe's neck** may be over 2 m long, but it only has seven bones – the same number as humans.

- **Giraffes live** in Africa, south of the Sahara, in bush country.

- **The giraffe's long tongue** is so tough that it can wrap around the thorns of a thorn tree to grab twigs.

- **When drinking**, a giraffe has to spread its forelegs wide or kneel down to reach the water. This position makes it very vulnerable to attack by lions.

▲ *Giraffes are the world's tallest animals – but they are five times as light as elephants.*

- **When giraffes walk**, they move the two legs on one side of their body, then the two on the other side. Their long legs mean that when it comes to running they can gallop along faster than the speediest racehorse.

- **A giraffe's coat** is patched in brown on cream, and each giraffe has its own unique pattern. The reticulated giraffes of East Africa have triangular patches, but the South African Cape giraffes have blotchy markings.

- **During breeding time**, rival males rub their necks together and swing them from side to side. This is called necking.

- **When first born**, a baby giraffe is very wobbly on its legs and so cannot stand up for at least its first half an hour.

Whales

- **Whales**, dolphins and porpoises are large mammals called cetaceans that live mostly in the seas and oceans. Dolphins and porpoises are small whales.

- **Like all mammals**, whales have lungs – this means they have to come to the surface to breathe every 10 minutes or so, although they can stay down for up to 40 minutes. A sperm whale can hold its breath for 2 hours.

- **Whales breathe** through blowholes on top of their head. When a whale breathes out, it spouts out water vapour and mucus. When it breathes in, it sucks in about 2,000 litres of air within about 2 seconds.

- **Like land mammals**, whales nurse their babies with their own milk. Whale milk is so rich that babies grow incredibly fast. Blue whale babies are over 7 m long when they are born and gain an extra 100 kg or so a day for about 7 months.

▲ Humpback whales live together in groups called pods and keep in touch with their own 'dialect' of noises.

- **Toothed whales**, such as the sperm whale and the orca or killer whale, have teeth and prey on large fish and seals. The six groups of toothed whale are sperm whales, beaked whales, belugas and narwhals, dolphins, porpoises, and river dolphins.

- **Baleen whales**, such as the humpback and blue, have a comb of thin plates called baleen in place of teeth. They feed by straining small, shrimp-like creatures called krill through their baleen. There are five baleen whale groups, including right whales, grey whales and rorquals. Rorquals have grooves on their throats and include humpback, minke and blue whales.

▶ Killer whales or orcas are one of the biggest deep-sea predators, growing to as long as 9 m and weighing up to 10 tonnes.
They feed on many types of fish, seals, penguins, squid, sea birds and sometimes even dolphins.

Dorsal fin

> ★ STAR FACT ★
> Male humpbacks make elaborate 'songs' lasting 20 minutes or more – perhaps to woo females.

- **The blue whale** is the largest creature that ever lived. Blue whales grow to be over 30 m long and weigh more than 150 tonnes. In summer, they eat over 4 tonnes of krill every day – that is 4 million krill.

- **Whales keep in touch** with sounds called phonations. Large baleen whales make sounds which are too low for humans to hear, but they can be heard by other whales at least 80 km away.

To swim, whales flap their fluke (tail) up and down

- **Most baleen whales** live alone or in small groups, but toothed whales – especially dolphins – often swim together in groups called pods or schools.

What are birds?

- **Not all birds** can fly, but they all have feathers.
- **Feathers** are light, but they are linked by hooks called barbs to make them strong enough for flight.
- **Wrens** have 1,000 feathers, while swans have 20,000.
- **Birds have four kinds** of wing feather – large primaries, smaller secondaries, coverts and contours.
- **Every kind of bird** has its own formation, pattern and colour of feathers, called its plumage.
- **Instead of teeth**, birds have a hard beak or bill.
- **Unlike humans**, birds do not give birth to babies. Instead they lay eggs, usually sitting on them to keep them warm until they hatch (see birds' nests and eggs).
- **Birds fly in two ways** – by gliding with their wings

▲ Most birds flap their wings to fly. Even birds that spend much of their time gliding have to flap their wings to take off and land.

held still, or by flapping their wings up and down.

- **Gliding is less effort** than flapping, and birds that stay in the air a long time tend to be superb gliders – including birds of prey, swifts, gulls and gannets.
- **Albatrosses and petrels** have long narrow wings that help them sail upwards on rising air currents.

> ★ STAR FACT ★
> Birds are probably descended from dinosaurs and took to the air about 150 million years ago.

Life in rivers and lakes

- **Rivers, lakes** and other freshwater habitats are home to all sorts of fish, including bream and trout.
- **Fast-flowing streams** are preferred by fish such as trout and grayling. Slow-flowing rivers and lakes are home to tench, rudd and carp.

▲ Upland lakes like these are home to many fish, including char, powan and bullhead. Fish such as brown trout swim in the streams that tumble down into the lake.

- **Some fish feed** on floating plant matter, while others take insects from the surface of the water.
- **Common bream and berbel** hunt on the riverbed, eating insect larvae, worms and molluscs.
- **Perch and pike** are predators of lakes and slow-flowing rivers.
- **Pike are the sharks** of the river – deadly hunters that lurk among weeds waiting for unwary fish, or even rats and birds. Pike can weigh as much as 30 kg.
- **Mammals of rivers and lakes** include voles, water rats and otters.
- **Birds of rivers and lakes** include birds that dive for fish (such as kingfishers), small wading birds (such as redshanks, avocets and curlews), large wading birds (such as herons, storks and flamingos), and waterfowl (such as ducks, swans and geese).
- **Insects** include dragonflies and water boatmen.
- **Amphibians** include frogs and newts.

Cobras and vipers

    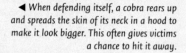

◀ *When defending itself, a cobra rears up and spreads the skin of its neck in a hood to make it look bigger. This often gives victims a chance to hit it away.*

- **Two kinds of poisonous snake** are dangerous to humans – vipers and elapids such as cobras and mambas.

- **Elapids** have their venom (poison) in short front fangs. A viper's fangs are so long that they usually have to be folded away.

- **The hamadryad cobra** of Southeast Asia is the world's largest poisonous snake, growing to over 5 m.

> ★ STAR FACT ★
> Fer-de-lance snakes have 60 to 80 babies, each of which is deadly poisonous.

- **In India, cobras kill** more than 7,000 people every year. The bite of a king cobra can kill an elephant in 4 hours. The marine cobra lives in the sea and its venom is 100 times more deadly.

- **Snake charmers** use the spectacled cobra, playing to it so that it follows the pipe as if about to strike – but the snake's fangs have been removed to make it safe.

- **A spitting cobra** squirts venom into its attacker's eyes, and is accurate at 2 m or more. The venom is not deadly, but it blinds the victim and is very painful.

- **The black mamba** of Africa can race along at 25 km/h with its head raised and its tongue flickering.

- **A viper's venom** kills its victims by making their blood clot. Viper venom has been used to treat haemophiliacs (people whose blood does not clot well).

- **The pit vipers** of the Americas hunt their warm-blooded victims using heat-sensitive pits on the side of their heads (see animal senses).

Horses

- **Horses** are big, four-legged, hooved animals, now bred mainly for human use.

- **Adult male horses** are stallions, females are mares, babies are foals, and young males are colts.

- **The only wild horses** are the Przewalski and the tarpan (possibly extinct) of central Asia.

- **The mustangs** (wild horses) of the USA are descended from tame horses.

▲ *All horses, wild and tame, may be descended from the prehistoric Merychippus (see evolution).*

- **Tame horses** are of three main kinds – light horses for riding (such as Morgans and Arabs), heavy horses for pulling ploughs and wagons (such as Pecherons and Suffolk punches), and ponies (such as Shetlands).

- **Most racehorses and hunting horses** are thoroughbred (pure) Arab horses descended from just three stallions that lived around 1700 – Darley Arabian, Godolphin Barb and Byerly Turk.

- **Lippizaners** are beautiful white horses, the best-known of which are trained to jump and dance at the Spanish Riding School in Vienna.

- **The shire horse** is probably the largest horse, bred after King Henry VIII had all horses under 1.5 m destroyed.

- **You can tell a horse's age** by counting its teeth – a 1-year-old has six pairs, a 5-year-old has twelve.

- **Quarter horses** are agile horses used by cowhands for cutting out (sorting cows from the herd). They got their name from running quarter-mile races.

Seals and sea lions

- **Seals, sea lions and walruses** are sea mammals that mainly live in water and are agile swimmers, but which waddle awkwardly when they come on land.
- **Most seals** eat fish, squid and shellfish. Crabeater seals eat mainly shrimps, not crabs.
- **Seals and sea lions** have ears, but only sea lions (which include fur seals) have ear flaps.

- **Only sea lions** can move their back flippers under their body when travelling about on land.
- **When seals come ashore** to breed, they live for weeks in vast colonies called rookeries.
- **Walruses** are bigger and bulkier than seals, and they have massive tusks and face whiskers.
- **When hunters kill seal pups** for their fur, or to keep numbers down, it is called culling.
- **Elephant seals** spend up to 8 months far out in the ocean, continuously diving, with each dive lasting 20 minutes or so.
- **There are freshwater seals** in Lake Baikal in Russia.

◀ *All seals and sea lions have fur. Only the walrus lacks a furry coat.*

Moths

- **Moths belong**, to the insect group Lepidoptera.
- **Most moths** have fat, hairy bodies, and feathery or thread-like antennae.
- **Many moths** fly at dusk or at night. By day, they rest on tree trunks and in leaves, where their colour makes them hard for predators such as birds to spot. However, there are also many brightly coloured day-flying moths.
- **Tiger moths** give out high-pitched clicks to warn that they taste bad and so escape being eaten.
- **The biggest moths** are the Hercules moth and the bent wing ghost moth of Asia, with wingspans of over 25 cm.
- **Night-flying** moths shiver their wings to warm them up for flight.
- **Hawk moths** are powerful fliers and migrate long distances. The oleander hawk moth flies from tropical Africa to far northern Europe in summer.
- **The caterpillars of small moths** live in seeds, fruit, stems and leaves, eating them from the inside.

- **The caterpillars of big moths** feed on leaves from the outside, chewing chunks out of them.
- **When threatened**, the caterpillar of the puss moth rears up and thrusts its whip-like tail forward and squirts a jet of formic acid from its head end.
- **Every caterpillar spins silk**, but the cloth silk comes from the caterpillar of the white *Bombyx mori* moth, known as the silkworm.

▶ Hawk moths have the longest proboscis (tongue) of all moths – as long as their bodies – for sucking nectar from narrow flowers. They often hover like hummingbirds when feeding.

Bird eggs and nests

> ★ STAR FACT ★
> Great auks' eggs are pointed at one end to
> stop them rolling off their cliff-edge nests.

- **All birds** begin life as eggs. Each species' egg is a slightly different colour.

- **The plover's egg** is pear-shaped. The owl's is round.

- **Hornbills** lay just one egg a year. Partridges lay up to 20 eggs. Hens and some ducks can lay around 350 a year.

- **Most birds build nests** to lay their eggs in – usually bowl-shaped and made from twigs, grass and leaves.

- **The biggest nest** is that of the Australian mallee fowl, which builds a mound of soil 5 m across, with egg-chambers filled with rotting vegetation to keep it warm.

- **The weaverbirds** of Africa and Asia are very sociable. Some work together to weave huge, hanging nests out of straw, with scores of chambers. Each chamber is for a pair of birds and has its own entrance.

- **Ovenbirds** of Central and South America get their name because their nests look like the clay ovens made by local people. Some ovenbirds' nests can be 3 m high.

- **Flamingos** nest on lakes, building mud nests that look like upturned sandcastles poking out of the water. They lay one or two eggs on top.

- **The great treeswift** lays its single egg in a nest the size of an eggcup.

▶ *After they lay their eggs, most birds sit on them to keep their eggs warm until they are ready to hatch. This is called incubating the eggs.*

Defence

- **Animals** have different ways of escaping predators – most mammals run away, while birds take to the air.

- **Some animals** use camouflage to hide (see colours and markings). Many small animals hide in burrows.

- **Turtles and tortoises** hide inside their hard shells.

▼ *Meerkats stand on their hind legs and give a shrill call to alert other meerkats to danger.*

> ★ STAR FACT ★
> The hognosed snake rolls over and plays dead
> to escape predators. It even smells dead.

- **Armadillos** curl up inside their bendy body armour.

- **The spiky-skinned** armadillo lizard of South Africa curls up and stuffs its tail in its mouth.

- **Hedgehogs**, porcupines and echidnas are protected by sharp quills (spines).

- **Skunks** and the stinkpot turtle give off foul smells.

- **Plovers** pretend to be injured to lure hunters away from their young.

- **Many animals defend themselves** by frightening their enemies. Some, such as peacock butterflies, flash big eye-markings. Others, such as porcupine fish and great horned owls, blow themselves up much bigger.

- **Other animals** send out warning signals. Kangaroo rats and rabbits thump their feet. Birds shriek.

Gorillas and other apes

- **Apes** are our closest relatives in the animal world. The great apes are gorillas, chimpanzees and the orang-utan. Gibbons are called lesser apes.

- **Like us**, apes have long arms, and fingers and toes for gripping. They are clever and can use sticks and stones as tools.

- **Gorillas** are the biggest of all the apes, weighing up to 225 kg and standing as tall as 2 m. But they are gentle vegetarians and eat leaves and shoots.

- **There are two gorilla species**, both from Africa – the western gorilla and eastern gorillas (including mountain gorillas).

- **Mountain gorillas** live in the mountains of Rwanda and Uganda. There are only about 650 of them.

- **When danger threatens a gorilla troop**, the leading adult male stands upright, pounds his hands against his chest, and bellows loudly.

- ◄ Gorillas climb trees only to sleep at night or to pull down branches to make a one-night nest on the ground. They usually walk on all fours.

- **Chimpanzees** are an ape species that live in the forests of central Africa.

- **Chimpanzees** are very clever and use tools more than any other animal apart from humans – they use leaves as sponges for soaking up water to drink, for example, and they crack nuts with stones.

- **Chimpanzees** communicate with each other through a huge range of grunts and screams. They also communicate by facial expressions and hand gestures, just as humans do. Experiments have shown that they can learn to respond to many words.

- **Only a few orang-utans** remain in the forests of Borneo and Sumatra. They get their name from a local word for 'old man of the woods'.

▶ Gorillas live in troops (groups) of a dozen or so. They travel through the forests searching for food led by a mature male, called a silverback because of the silver hairs on his back. Gorillas like to groom each other and cuddle when they rest in the afternoon.

An adult male has a crest of hair on his head

Gorillas have no hair on their face or chest, and their palms and soles are also bare

Baby gorillas are carried by their mother until they are 3 years old

Rhinos and hippos

- **Rhinoceroses** are big, tough-skinned animals of Africa and southern Asia.

- **African black and white** rhinos and the smaller Sumatran rhino have two horns in the middle of their heads. Indian and Javan rhinos have just one.

- **Powdered rhino horn** is believed by some to be a love potion, so thousands of rhinos have been slaughtered and most kinds are now endangered species.

- **Baluchitherium** lived 20 million years ago and was a type of rhino. At over 5 m tall, it was much bigger than any elephant.

◀ The African black rhino is almost extinct in the wild. Less than 3,000 are left on nature reserves. Some gamekeepers have tried cutting off their horns to make them less of a target for poachers.

- **Hippopotamuses** are big, grey, pig-like creatures that live in Africa. They have the biggest mouth of any land animal.

- **When a hippo yawns** its mouth gapes wide enough to swallow a sheep whole, but it only eats grass.

- **Hippos spend their days** wallowing in rivers and swamps, and only come out at night to feed.

- **A hippo's eyes**, ears and nose are all on the top of its head, and so remain above the water when the rest of its body is completely submerged.

- **The word hippopotamus** comes from the Ancient Greek words for horse (hippo) and river (potamos).

★ **STAR FACT** ★
The African white rhinoceros's horn can grow to over 1.5 m long.

Salmon

▲ Salmon returning to their spawning ground make mighty leaps up raging torrents. The journey can take months.

- **Salmon** are river and sea fish caught or farmed in huge quantities for food.

- **All salmon** are born in rivers and lakes far inland, then swim down river and out to sea.

- **Adult salmon** spend anything from 6 months to 7 years in the oceans, before returning to rivers and swimming upstream to spawn (lay their eggs).

- **Some salmon species**, including the chinook, spawn in North American rivers running into the North Pacific.

- **Cherry salmon** spawn in eastern Asian rivers, and amago salmon spawn in Japanese rivers.

- **Atlantic salmon** spawn in rivers in northern Europe and eastern Canada.

- **Amazingly, spawning salmon** return to the stream where they were born, up to 3,000 km inland. They may sense the chemical and mineral make-up of the water, helping them to recognise their own stream.

- **To reach their spawning grounds**, salmon have to swim upstream against strong currents, often leaping as high as 5 m to clear waterfalls.

- **When salmon** reach their spawning grounds, they mate. The female lays up to 20,000 eggs.

- **After spawning**, the weakened salmon head down river again, but few make it as far as the sea.

Turtles and tortoises

- **Turtles and tortoises** are reptiles that live inside hard, armoured shells. Together with terrapins, they make up a group called the chelonians.

- **Turtles** live in the sea, fresh water or on land, tortoises live on land, and terrapins live in streams and lakes.

- **The shield** on the back of a chelonian is called a carapace. Its flat belly armour is called a plastron.

- **Most turtles and tortoises** have no teeth, just jaws with very sharp edges, to eat plants and tiny animals.

- **Tortoises** live mostly in hot, dry regions and will hibernate in winter if brought to a cold country.

- **Turtles and tortoises** live to a great age. One giant tortoise found in 1766 in Mauritius lived 152 years.

- **The giant tortoise** grows to as long as 1.5 m.

- **The leatherback turtle** grows to as long as 2.5 m and weighs more than 800 kg.

- **Every three years**, green turtles gather together to swim thousands of kilometres to Ascension Island in the mid-Atlantic, where they lay their eggs ashore by moonlight at the highest tide. They bury the eggs in the sand, to be incubated by the heat of the sun.

▼ Tortoises are very slow moving and placid.

> ★ STAR FACT ★
> Giant tortoises were once kept on ships to
> provide fresh meat on long voyages.

Antelopes and deer

- **Antelopes and deer** are four-legged, hooved animals. Along with cows, hippos and pigs, they belong to the huge group called artiodactyls – animals with an even number of toes on each foot.

- **Antelopes and deer** chew the cud like cows – they chew food again, after first partially digesting it in a special stomach.

- **Most antelope species live** in herds in Africa. Many are very graceful, including the impala and Thompson's gazelle. Most are also fast runners.

- **The horns** on an antelope's head last its lifetime.

- **Deer have branching antlers** of bone (not horn) on their heads, which drop off and grow again each year.

- **Most deer species live** in woods and grasslands in mild regions such as northern Europe and North America.

- **The moose or elk** grows antlers more than 2 m wide.

- **Male deer** are called stags, young males are bucks, females are does and babies are fawns.

- **Usually only stags** have antlers. The only female deer to have them are caribou (or reindeer).

◄ Reindeer cope with harsh winters by finding lichen to eat under the snow – perhaps by smell.

> ★ STAR FACT ★
> Caribou can survive in the icy cold of
> Spitsbergen Island in the Arctic circle.

Evolution

▶ All life on Earth may have evolved almost 4 billion years ago from organisms like this archaebacteria. Archaebacteria thrive in extreme conditions such as those on the early Earth. This one came from under the Antarctic ice. Others thrive in scorching undersea volcanic vents.

> ★ **STAR FACT** ★
> Many, many more species of animal have come and gone than are alive today.

- **Charles Darwin's** *Theory of Evolution*, first published in 1859, showed how all species of plant and animal adapt and develop over millions of years. Only the fittest survive.

- **Darwin's theory** depended on the fact that no two living things are alike.

- **Some animals** start life with characteristics that give them a better chance of surviving to pass the characteristics on to their offspring.

- **Other animals' characteristics** mean that they are less likely to survive.

- **Over many generations** and thousands of years, better-adapted animals and plants survive and flourish, while others die out or find a new home.

- **Fossil discoveries** since Darwin's time have supported his theory, and lines of evolution can be traced for thousands of species.

- **Fossils** also show that evolution is not always as slow and steady as Darwin thought. Some scientists believe change comes in rapid bursts, separated by long slow periods when little changes.

Other scientists believe that bursts of rapid change interrupt periods of long steady change.

- **For the first 3 billion years** of Earth's history, the only life forms were microscopic, single-celled, marine (sea) organisms such as bacteria and amoeba. Sponges and jellyfish, the first multi-celled creatures, appeared by 700 million years ago (mya).

- **About 600 mya**, evolution speeded up dramatically in what is called the Precambrian explosion. Thousands of different organisms appeared within a very short space of time, including the first proper animals with bones and shells.

- **After the Precambrian**, life evolved rapidly. Fish developed, then insects and then, about 380 mya, amphibians – the first large creatures to crawl on land. About 340 mya, reptiles evolved – the first large creatures to live entirely on land.

- **Dinosaurs** developed from these early reptiles about 220 mya and dominated the Earth for 160 million years. Birds also evolved from the reptiles, and cynodonts (furry, mammal-like creatures).

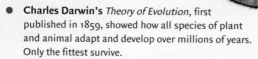

Hyracotherium

Mesohippus

Parahippus

Merychippus

Longer neck for grazing

Longer legs for running

Pliohippus

Equus

▶ The gradual evolution of the horse shows how creatures adapt to changing conditions over million years. One of the horse's earliest ancestors, Hyracotherium, appeared about 50 mya. It was a small woodland creature which browsed on leaves and was suited to the widespread woodlands of the time. So was mesohippus. But from then on, the woods began to disappear and grasslands became more widespread – and it paid to be bigger to run fast to escape predators. The modern horse, Equus, is the latest result of evolutionary adaptation.

What are insects?

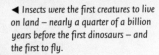

◀ Insects were the first creatures to live on land – nearly a quarter of a billion years before the first dinosaurs – and the first to fly.

- **Insects** may be tiny, but there are more of them than all the other animals put together – over 1 million known species.

- **They range** from tiny flies to huge beetles, and they are found everywhere there is land.

- **Insects** have six legs and a body divided into three sections – which is why they are called insects ('in sections'). The sections are the head, thorax (middle) and abdomen.

- **An insect's body** is encased in such a tough shell (its exoskeleton) that there is no need for bones.

- **Insects grow** by getting rid of their old exoskeleton and replacing it with a bigger one. This is called moulting.

- **Some insects change** dramatically as they grow. Butterflies, moths, and beetles undergo metamorphosis (see butterflies). Grasshoppers and mayflies begin as wingless nymphs, then gradually grow wings with each moult. Silverfish and springtails simply get bigger with each moult.

- **Insects' eyes** are called compound because they are made up of many lenses – from six (worker ants) to more than 30,000 (dragonflies).

- **Insects have** two antennae (feelers) on their heads.

- **Insects** do not have lungs. Instead, they breathe through holes in their sides called spiracles, linked to their body through tubes called tracheae.

- **The world's longest insect** is the giant stick insect of Indonesia, which can grow to 33 cm long.

Woodpeckers and toucans

- **Woodpeckers** are closely related to the colourful toucans and jacamars of tropical rainforests.

- **Woodpeckers**, toucans, barbets, jacamars and honeyguides all have two toes on each foot pointing forwards and two pointing backwards. Their toes help them cling to trees and branches.

- **Woodpeckers** use their powerful bills to bore into tree trunks to get at insects. They spear the insects with their incredibly long tongues.

- **Gila woodpeckers** escape the desert heat by nesting inside giant saguaro cacti (where it can be 30°C cooler).

- **Redhead woodpeckers** drill holes in trees and use them to store acorns for winter – wedging them in very tightly so that squirrels cannot steal them.

▲ The toucan's giant beak is full of air holes, so it is not heavy enough to overbalance the bird. Toucans eat mainly small fruit.

- **Woodpeckers** claim their territory not by singing, but by hammering their bills against trees.

- **Honeyguides** lead honey badgers to bees' nests. The badger gets the honey and the bird gets the beeswax.

- **When toucans sleep**, they turn their heads around and lay their bills down their backs.

> ★ STAR FACT ★
> At 23 cm, the toucan's bill is much longer than its body.

Rabbits and rats

▶ Rabbits and hares look like rodents. But they belong to another group of mammals called lagomorphs or "leaping shapes".

- **Mice and rats** belong to a group of 1,800 species of small mammals called rodents. The group also includes voles, lemmings, squirrels, beavers, porcupines and guinea pigs.

- **All rodents** have two pairs of razor-sharp front teeth for gnawing nuts and berries, and a set of ridged teeth in their cheeks for chewing.

- **A rodent's front teeth**, called incisors, grow all the time. Only gnawing keeps them the same length.

- **Rats and mice** are by far the most common rodents – they have adapted well to living alongside humans.

- **Brown and black rats** carry germs for diseases such as food poisoning, plague and typhus.

- **Hares** live above ground and escape enemies through sheer speed. Rabbits live in burrows underground.

- **Baby hares** are born above ground, covered in fur and with their eyes open. Rabbits are born naked and blind in burrows.

- **Rabbits breed quickly** – a female can have 20 babies every month during the breeding season, and her babies will have their own families after 6 months.

- **One single rabbit** could have more than 33 million offspring in just 3 years, if they all survived to breed.

- **A single mouse** can produce up to 34 young in one litter.

▶ Rats and mice have long thin tails, pointed noses, beady black eyes and four very sharp front teeth.

Ducks and geese

- **Ducks, geese and swans** are known as waterfowl, and they all live on or near freshwater.

- **Waterfowl** can float for hours and have webbed feet for paddling along. On water they are graceful, but on land they waddle awkwardly, since their legs are set far back under their body for swimming.

- **Ducks** have shorter necks and wings, and flatter bills than swans. Male ducks are called drakes, and females, ducks. Babies are called ducklings.

◀ Canada geese breed in the far north of Canada and Alaska, and migrate south to warmer regions in the autumn.

- **Diving ducks** (such as the pochard, tufted duck and the scoter) dive for food such as roots, shellfish and insects on the river bed.

- **Dabbling ducks** (such as the mallard, widgeon, gadwall and the teal) dabble – they sift water through their beaks for food.

- **Some dabblers** lap water at the surface. Others up-end – sticking their heads into the water to sift out water weeds and snails from muddy water.

- **Swans** are the largest waterfowl. They have long elegant necks and pure white plumage – apart from the black-neck swan of South America and the Australian black swan.

- **Baby swans** are called cygnets and are mottled grey.

- **Geese** mostly graze on grass. Unlike ducks, which quack and swans which hiss, geese honk.

- **Baby geese** are called goslings.

Coral reef fish

- **Many colourful fish species** live in warm seas around coral reefs. They are often very bright, which makes them instantly recognizable to their own kind.

- **Butterfly fish and angelfish** have colourful, slender, oval bodies and are popular as aquarium fish.

- **Male triggerfish** boost their colour to attract females.

- **Cuckoo wrasse** are all born female, but big females change sex when they are between 7 and 13 years old.

- **Cleaner fish** are the health clinics of the oceans. Larger fish such as groupers queue up for cleaner fish to go over them, nibbling away pests and dead skin.

- **The banded coral shrimp** cleans up pests in the same way as cleaner fish do, from fish such as moray eels.

- **The sabre-toothed blenny** looks so like a cleaner fish that

> ★ STAR FACT ★
> Cleaner fish will go to work inside
> a shark's mouth.

▲ *Coral reefs are home to many brilliantly coloured fish.*

it can nip in close to fish before it takes a bite out of them.

- **Cheilinus** is a carnivorous fish of coral reefs which changes colour to mimic harmless plant-eating fish, such as parrotfish and goatfish. It swims alongside them, camouflaged, until it is close to its prey.

Ants and termites

- **Ants** are a vast group of insects related to bees and wasps. Most ants have a tiny waist and are wingless.

- **Ants** are the main insects in tropical forests, living in colonies of anything from 20 to millions.

- **Ant colonies** are all female. Most species have one or several queens which lay the eggs. Hundreds of soldier ants guard the queen, while smaller workers build the nest and care for the young.

- **Males** only enter the nest to mate with young queens, then die.

- **Wood ants** squirt acid from their abdomen to kill enemies.

- **Army ants** march in huge swarms, eating small creatures they meet.

▲ *African termites use mud and saliva to build amazing nests more than 12 m high, housing over 5 million termites.*

- **Groups of army ants** cut any large prey they catch into pieces which they carry back to the nest. Army ants can carry 50 times their own weight.

- **Ants known as slavemakers** raid the nests of other ants and steal their young to raise as slaves.

- **Termite colonies** are even more complex than ant ones. They have a large king and queen who mate, as well as soldiers to guard them and workers to do all the work.

- **Termite nests** are mounds built like cities with many chambers – including a garden used for growing fungus. Many are air-conditioned with special chimneys.

Swifts and hummingbirds

- **Swifts and hummingbirds** are on the wing so much that their feet have become weak – which is why they are called *Apodiformes*, meaning 'footless ones'.

- **Swifts** are among the fastest flying birds. Spine-tailed swifts of eastern Asia have been recorded at 240 km/h.

- **Swifts use** their short, gaping bills to catch insects on the wing.

- **Swifts may fly** through the night without landing. They may even sleep on the wing. European swifts fly all the way to Africa and back without stopping.

- **When swifts land**, they cling to vertical surfaces such as walls, cliffs and trees.

- **Great dusky swifts** nest and roost behind waterfalls, and have to fly through the water to get in and out.

▲ Hummingbirds have long bills to suck nectar from flowers.

> ★ STAR FACT ★
> To hover, horned sungem hummingbirds beat their wings 90 times per second.

- **Hummingbirds** are about 325 species of tiny, bright, tropical birds which sip nectar from flowers.

- **Hummingbirds** are the most amazing aerial acrobats, hovering and twisting in front of flowers.

- **The bee hummingbird** is the world's smallest bird – including its long bill, it measures just 5 cm.

Lemurs and lorises

- **Lemurs** are small furry creatures with long tails and big eyes. They are primates, like monkeys and humans.

- **Lemurs** live only on the islands of Madagascar and Comoros, off the African east coast.

- **Most lemurs** are active at night and live in trees, but the ring-tailed lemur lives mostly on the ground and is active by day.

▲ Ring-tailed lemurs get their name from their black-ringed tail which they raise to show where they are.

- **Lemurs** eat fruit, leaves, insects and small birds.

- **The ring-tailed lemur** rubs its rear on trees to leave a scent trail for other lemurs to follow.

- **In the mating season**, ring-tailed lemurs have stink fights for females, rubbing their wrists and tails in stink glands under their arms and rear – then waving them at rivals to drive them off.

- **Lorises and pottos** are furry, big-eyed primates of the forests of Asia and Africa. All are brilliant climbers.

- **Bushbabies** are the acrobats of the loris family. They get their name because their cries sound like a human baby crying.

- **Bushbabies** are nocturnal animals and their big eyes help them see in the dark. Their hearing is so sensitive they have to block their ears to sleep during the day.

- **Tarsiers** of the Philippines are small, huge-eyed primates. They have very long fingers and can turn their heads halfway round to look backwards.

Pythons and boas

- **Constrictors** are snakes that squeeze their victims to death, rather than poisoning them. They include pythons, boas and anacondas.

- **A constrictor** does not crush its victim. Instead, it winds itself around, gradually tightening its coils until the victim suffocates.

- **Constrictors usually swallow** victims whole, then spend days digesting them. They have special jaws that allow their mouths to open very wide. A large meal can be seen as a lump moving down the body.

- **Pythons** are big snakes that live in Asia, Indonesia and Africa. In captivity, reticulated pythons grow to 9 m. Boas and anacondas are the big constrictors of South America.

- **Boas** capture their prey by lying in wait, hiding motionless under trees and waiting for victims to pass by. But like all snakes, they can go for many weeks without eating.

- **Like many snakes**, most constrictors begin life as eggs. Unusually for snakes, female pythons look after their eggs until they hatch by coiling around them. Even more unusually, Indian and green tree pythons actually keep their eggs warm by shivering.

- **Female boas** do not lay eggs, giving birth to live young.

- **Boas** have tiny remnants of back legs, called spurs, which males use to tickle females during mating.

- **Anacondas** spend much of their lives in swampy ground or shallow water, lying in wait for victims to come and drink. One anaconda was seen to swallow a 2-m-long caiman (a kind of crocodile).

- **When frightened**, the royal python of Africa coils itself into a tight ball, which is why it is sometimes called the ball python. Rubber boas do the same, but hide their heads and stick their tails out aggressively to fool attackers.

▲ Pythons are tropical snakes that live in moist forests in Asia and Africa. They are the world's biggest snakes, rivalled only by giant anacondas. Pythons are one long tube of muscle, well able to squeeze even big victims to death. They usually eat animals about the size of domestic cats, but occasionally they go for really big meals such as wild pigs and deer.

★ STAR FACT ★
A 4 to 5 m long African rock python was once seen to swallow an entire 60 kg impala (a kind of antelope) whole – horns and all.

Snails and slugs

- **Snails and slugs** are small, squidgy, slimy, soft-bodied crawling creatures. They belong to a huge group of animals called molluscs which have no skeleton. Squid and oysters are also molluscs.

- **Snails and slugs** are gastropods, a group that also includes whelks and winkles.

- **Gastropod** means 'stomach foot', because these animals seem to slide along on their stomachs.

- **Most gastropods** live in the sea. They include limpets which stick firmly to seashore rocks.

◀ Garden snails have a shell which they seal themselves into in dry weather, making a kind of trapdoor to save moisture. They have eyes on their horns.

- **Most land snails and slugs** ooze a trail of sticky slime to help them move along the ground.

- **Garden snails** are often hermaphrodites, which means they have both male and female sex organs.

- **The great grey slugs** of western Europe court by circling each other for over an hour on a branch, then launching themselves into the air to hang from a long trail of mucus. They then mate for 7 to 24 hours.

- **Among the largest gastropods** are the tropical tritons, whose 45–cm shells are sometimes used as warhorns. Conches are another big kind of gastropod.

- **Some cone snails** in the Pacific and Indian oceans have teeth that can inject a poison which can actually kill people.

> ★ STAR FACT ★
> Snails are a great delicacy in France, where they are called *escargot*.

Life in tropical rainforests

- **Tropical rainforests** are the richest and most diverse of all animal habitats.

- **Most animals** in tropical rainforests live in the canopy (treetops), and are either agile climbers or can fly.

- **Canopy animals** include flying creatures such as bats, birds and insects, and climbers such as monkeys, sloths, lizards and snakes.

▲ Year-round rainfall and warm temperatures make rainforests incredibly lush, with a rich variety of plant life.

- **Many rainforest creatures** can glide through the treetops – these include gliding geckos and other lizards, flying squirrels and even flying frogs.

- **Some tree frogs** live in the cups of rainwater held by plants growing high up in trees.

- **Antelopes, deer, hogs, tapir** and many different kinds of rodent (see rabbits and rats) roam the forest floor, hunting for seeds, roots, leaves and fruit.

- **Beside rivers** in South East Asian rainforests, there may be rhinoceroses, crocodiles and even elephants.

- **Millions of insect species** live in rainforests, including butterflies, moths, bees, termites and ants. There are also many spiders.

- **Rainforest butterflies and moths** are often big or vividly coloured, including the shimmering blue morpho of Brazil and the birdwing butterflies.

- **Rainforest birds** can be vividly coloured too, and include parrots, toucans and birds of paradise.

Sharks

- **Sharks** are the most fearsome predatory fish of the seas. There are 375 species, living mostly in warm seas.

- **Sharks** have a skeleton made of rubbery cartilage – most other kinds of fish have bony skeletons.

- **The world's biggest fish** is the whale shark, which can grow to well over 12 m long. Unlike other sharks, the whale shark and the basking shark (at 9 m long) mostly eat plankton and are completely harmless.

> ★ STAR FACT ★
> Great white sharks are the biggest meat-eating sharks, growing to over 7 m long.

- **A shark's main weapons** are its teeth – they are powerful enough to bite through plate steel.

- **Sharks** put so much strain on their teeth that they always have three or four spare rows of teeth in reserve.

- **Nurse sharks** grow a new set of teeth every 8 days.

- **Up to 20** people die from recorded shark attacks each year.

- **The killing machine** of the shark world is the great white shark, responsible for most attacks on humans.

- **Hammerhead sharks** can also be dangerous. They have T-shaped heads, with eyes and nostrils at the end of the T.

◀ *A shark's torpedo-shaped body makes it a very fast swimmer.*

Dinosaurs

- **Dinosaurs** were reptiles that dominated life on land from about 220 million to 65 million years ago, when all of them mysteriously became extinct.

- **Although modern reptiles** walk with bent legs splayed out, dinosaurs had straight legs under their bodies – this meant they could run fast or grow heavy.

- **Some dinosaurs** ran on two back legs, as birds do. Others had four sturdy legs like an elephant's.

- **Dinosaurs** are split into two groups according to their hipbones – saurischians had reptile-like hips and ornithischians had bird-like hips.

- **Saurischians** were either swift, two-legged predators called theropods, or hefty four-legged herbivores called sauropods.

- **Theropods** had acute eyesight, fearsome claws and sharp teeth. They included Tyrannosaurus rex, one of the biggest hunting animals to ever live on land – over 15 m long, 5 m tall and weighing more than 7 tonnes.

- **Sauropods** had massive bodies, long tails, and long, snake-like necks.

- **The sauropod Brachiosaurus** was over 23 m long, weighed 80 tonnes and towered 12 m into the air. It was one of the biggest creatures ever to live on land.

- **Most dinosaurs** are known from fossilized bones, but fossilized eggs, footprints and droppings have also been found. In 1913, mummified hadrosaur skin was found.

- **Some scientists** think the dinosaurs died out after a huge meteor struck the Earth off Mexico, throwing up a cloud that blocked the sun's light and heat.

▶ *Dinosaur means 'terrible lizard', and they came in all shapes and sizes. This is a plant-eating sauropod called Diplodocus.*

Pandas

▶ Giant pandas are big, chubby animals, usually weighing well over 100 kg. When they stand on their hind legs they are as tall as a man. But pandas have inefficient digestive systems and to sustain their huge bulk they have to eat more continuously than most other animals.

An extra thumb helps pandas hold the bamboo while they are chewing

Giant pandas eat only certain kinds of bamboo

- **Giant pandas** are large, black-and-white, furry mammals that live in the bamboo forests of western China and Tibet. Most pandas live between 1,500 and 3,000 m above sea level in the moist bamboo forests of western Szechuan and eastern Sikang.

- **Giant pandas are among the rarest species** of animal in the world. There are probably fewer than 1,000 left. The giant panda's habitat has been cut back by the loss of forests for wood and farmland.

- **One reason** that giant pandas are rare is because they feed only on the shoots of bamboos. Some bamboos flower once every century and then die, and it is many years before the seeds grow into new plants.

- **Giant pandas** spend most of their time sitting around on the ground eating, but they are surprisingly agile tree climbers.

- **Giant pandas spend 12 hours** a day feeding on bamboo shoots, because their digestive system is so ineffective that they have to eat more than 40 kg of bamboo a day.

- **To help it hold the bamboo**, the panda has an extra 'thumb' – it is not really a thumb, but a bone on the wrist which is covered by a fleshy pad.

- **The red panda** is a much smaller animal than the giant panda and it sleeps in trees, curled up like a cat.

- **Red pandas** look a little like raccoons and people once thought that pandas were related to raccoons, even though giant pandas look more like bears. DNA tests have shown that red pandas are close to raccoons, but that giant pandas are closer to bears.

- **In the wild**, giant pandas give birth to one or two cubs a year. The cubs are very tiny and the mother has to give up eating to look after them for the first 10 days or so. The cubs usually stay with their mother for nearly one year.

- **Attempts to breed** pandas in zoos have largely failed. Washington Zoo's giant panda Ling Ling, for instance, gave birth to several cubs in the 1970s and 1980s, but the cubs died very soon after birth.

▶ Giant pandas look like clowns with their black eye patches and ears. No one knows quite what the purpose of these eye patches is. When giant pandas were first introduced to Europe in 1869 by French priest Père Armand David, many people believed they were hoaxes.

! NEWS FLASH !
Chinese zoologists hope to clone giant pandas to save them for the future.

Flies

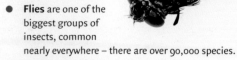

▶ Flies have only one pair of proper wings. The hind wings are small stumps called halteres which help a fly balance in flight.

- **Flies** are one of the biggest groups of insects, common nearly everywhere – there are over 90,000 species.
- **Unlike other insects**, flies have only one pair of proper wings.
- **Flies** include bluebottles, black flies, gnats, horseflies, midges, mosquitoes and tsetse flies.
- **A house fly** flies at over 7 km/h – equal to flying 350,000 times its own length in an hour. If a jumbo jet flew at the same speed relative to its length for an hour, it would get almost right around the world.
- **Alaskan flies** can stand being frozen at temperatures of -60°C and still survive.

- **Flies suck up** their food – typically sap from rotting plants and fruit. Houseflies often suck liquids from manure. Blowflies drink juices from rotting meat.
- **The larvae (young) of flies** are called maggots, and they are tiny, white, wriggling tube-shapes.
- **Flies resemble or mimic** many other kinds of insects. There are wasp-flies, drone-flies, ant-flies, moth-flies and beetle-flies.
- **Many species** of fly are carriers of dangerous diseases. When a fly bites or makes contact, it can infect people with some of the germs it carries – especially the flies that suck blood. Mosquitoes spread malaria, and tsetse flies spread sleeping sickness.

> ★ **STAR FACT** ★
> The buzzing of a fly is the sound of its wings beating. Midges beat their wings 1,000 times a second.

Sparrows and starlings

- **More than 70%** of all bird species – over 5,000 species altogether – are perching birds, or Passerines. They have feet with three toes pointing forwards and one backwards, to help them cling to a perch.
- **Perching birds** build neat, small, cup-shaped nests.
- **Perching birds sing** – this means that their call is not a single sound, but a sequence of musical notes.
- **Songbirds**, such as thrushes, warblers and nightingales, are perching birds with especially attractive songs.
- **Usually only male songbirds** sing – mainly in the mating season, to warn off rivals and attract females.
- **Sparrows** are small, plump birds, whose chirruping song is familiar almost everywhere.
- **Starlings** are very common perching birds which often gather in huge flocks, either to feed or to roost.
- **All the millions** of European starlings in North America are descended from 100 set free in New York's Central Park in the 1890s.

▲ Starlings often gather on overhead cables ready to migrate.

- **Many perching birds**, including mynahs, are talented mimics. The lyre bird of southeastern Australia can imitate car sirens and chainsaws, as well as other birds.
- **The red-billed quelea** of Africa is the world's most abundant bird. There are over 1.5 billion of them.

Spiders

- **Spiders** are small scurrying creatures which, unlike insects, have eight legs not six, and bodies with two parts not three.
- **Spiders** belong to a group of 70,000 creatures called arachnids, which also includes scorpions, mites and ticks.

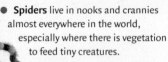

- **Spiders** live in nooks and crannies almost everywhere in the world, especially where there is vegetation to feed tiny creatures.
- **Spiders are hunters** and most of them feed mainly on insects. Despite their name, bird-eating spiders rarely eat birds, preferring lizards

▲ Like all arachnids, spiders have eight legs, plus two 'arms' called pedipalps and a pair of fangs called chelicerae. They also have eight simple eyes.

> ★ STAR FACT ★
> Female black widow spiders eat their mates after mating.

and small rodents such as mice.

- **Spiders have eight eyes**, but most have poor eyesight and hunt by feeling vibrations with their legs.
- **Many spiders** catch their prey by weaving silken nets called webs. Some webs are simple tubes in holes. Others, called orb webs, are elaborate and round. Spiders' webs are sticky to trap insects.
- **The Australian trapdoor** spider ambushes its prey from a burrow with a camouflaged entrance flap.
- **Most spiders** have a poisonous bite which they use to stun or kill their prey. Tarantulas and sun spiders crush their victims with their powerful jaws.
- **The bite of black widow**, redback and funnel-web spiders is so poisonous that it can kill humans.

Cockles and mussels

- **Cockles and mussels** belong to a group of molluscs called bivalves, which includes oysters, clams, scallops and razorshells.
- **Bivalve** means 'having two valves', and all these creatures have two halves to their shells, joined by a hinge that opens rather like that of a locket.
- **Most bivalves feed** by filtering food out from the water through a tube called a siphon.
- **Cockles** burrow in sand and mud on the seashore. Mussels cling to rocks and breakwaters between the high and low tide marks.
- **Oysters** and some other molluscs line their shells with a hard, shiny, silvery white substance called nacre.
- **When a lump of grit** gets into an oyster shell, it is gradually covered in a ball of nacre, making a pearl.

- **The best pearls** come from the Pinctada pearl oysters that live in the Pacific Ocean. The world's biggest pearl was 12 cm across and weighed 6.4 kg. It came from a giant clam.
- **Scallops** can swim away from danger by opening and shutting their shells rapidly to pump out water. But most bivalves escape danger by shutting themselves up inside their shells.
- **A giant clam** found on the Great Barrier Reef was over 1 m across and weighed more than 0.25 tonnes.
- **There are colonies** of giant clams living many thousands of metres down under the oceans, near hot volcanic vents.

◄ There are two main kinds of seashell – univalves like these (which are a single shell), and bivalves (which come in two, hinged halves).

Reptiles and amphibians

- **Reptiles** are scaly-skinned animals which live in many different habitats mainly in warm regions. They include crocodiles, lizards, snakes and tortoises.

- **Reptiles are cold-blooded**, but this does not mean that their blood is cold. A reptile's body cannot keep its blood warm, and it has to control its temperature by moving between hot and cool places.

- **Reptiles bask in the sun** to gain energy to hunt, and are often less active at cooler times of year.

- **A reptile's skin** looks slimy, but it is quite dry. It keeps in moisture so well that reptiles can survive in deserts. The skin often turns darker to absorb the sun's heat.

- **Although reptiles grow** most of their lives, their skin does not, so they slough (shed) it every now and then.

> ▶ Like all reptiles, crocodiles rely on basking in the sun to gain energy for hunting. At night, or when it is cold, they usually sleep.

- **Amphibians** are animals that live both on land and in water. They include frogs, toads, newts and salamanders.

- **Most reptiles** lay their eggs on land, but amphibians hatch out in water as tadpoles, from huge clutches of eggs called spawn.

- **Like fish**, tadpoles have gills to breathe in water, but they soon metamorphose (change), growing legs and lungs.

- **Amphibians** never stray far from water.

> ★ STAR FACT ★
> Reptiles were the first large creatures to live entirely on land, over 350 million years ago.

Pets

- **There are over 500 breeds** of domestic dog. All are descended from the wolves first tamed 12,000 years ago to help humans hunt. Dogs have kept some wolf-like traits such as guarding territory and hiding bones.

- **Many pet dogs** were originally working dogs. Collies were sheepdogs. Terriers, setters, pointers and retrievers all get their names from their roles as hunting dogs.

- **The heaviest dog breed** is the St Bernard, which weighs over 90 kg. The lightest is the miniature Yorkshire terrier, under 500 g.

- **Cocker spaniels** were named because they were used by hunters to flush out woodcocks in the 14th century.

- **Chihuahuas** were named after a place in Mexico – the Aztecs thought them sacred.

▲ Powerfully built, strong-jawed, pit bull terriers were first bred from bulldogs and terriers as fighting dogs, by miners in the 18th century.

- **The first domestic cats** were wild African bushcats tamed by the Ancient Egyptians to catch mice 3,500 years ago.

- **Like their wild ancestors**, domestic cats are deadly hunters – agile, with sharp eyes and claws – and often catch mice and birds.

- **Cats spend** a great deal of time sleeping, in short naps, but can be awake and ready for action in an instant.

- **Tabby cats** get their name from Attab in Baghdad (now in Iraq), where striped silk was made in the Middle Ages.

- **A female cat** is called a queen. A group of cats is called a clowder. A female dog is a bitch. A group of dogs is a kennel.

- **All pet golden hamsters** are descended from a single litter which was discovered in Syria in 1930.

Fleas and lice

- **Fleas and lice** are small wingless insects that live on birds and mammals, including humans. Dogs, cats and rats are especially prone to fleas.

- **Fleas and sucking lice** suck their host's blood.

- **Chewing lice** chew on their host's skin and hair or feathers. Chewing lice do not live on humans.

- **Fleas and lice** are often too small to see easily. But adult fleas grow to over 2 mm long.

- **A flea** can jump 30 cm in the air – the equivalent of a human leaping 200 m in the air.

- **The fleas** in flea circuses perform tricks such as jumping through hoops and pulling wagons.

- **Fleas spread** by jumping from one animal to another, to suck their blood.

> **★ STAR FACT ★**
> Fleas jump with a force of 140 g – over 20 times that required to launch a space rocket.

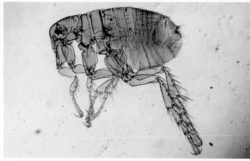

▲ A much-magnified flea with its powerful back legs for jumping.

- **When fleas lay their eggs**, they hatch as larvae and crawl off into the host's bedding, where they spin cocoons and emerge as adults 2 weeks later.

- **Head lice** gum their nits (eggs) to hair and spread from head to head through sharing of combs and hats.

Life in woodlands

- **Woodlands** in temperate zones between the tropics and the poles are home to many creatures.

- **Deciduous trees** lose their leaves in autumn. Evergreens keep theirs through cold winters.

- **In the leaf litter** under the trees live tiny creatures such as worms, millipedes, and ants and other insects.

▲ On a walk through a deciduous wood, you may be lucky enough to catch a glimpse of a shy young red deer as it crosses a clearing.

- **Spiders, shrews, salamanders and mice** feed on the small creatures in the leaf litter.

- **Some birds**, such as woodcocks, nest on the woodland floor and have mottled plumage to hide themselves.

- **Birds such as owls**, nuthatches, treecreepers, tits, woodpeckers and warblers live on and in trees, as well as insects such as beetles, moths and butterflies, and small mammals such as squirrels and raccoons.

- **Other small woodland mammals** include stoats, chipmunks, opossums, weasels, polecats, pinemartins and foxes.

- **Beavers, frogs, muskrats and otters** live near woodland streams.

- **The few large woodland mammals** include bears, deer, wolves and wild boar. Many of these have become rare because woods have been cleared away.

- **In winter**, many birds of deciduous woods migrate south, while small mammals like dormice hibernate.

Tigers

- **Tigers** are the largest of the big cats, with huge heads. The average male tiger's body grows to over 2 m long, plus a 1-m-long tail.

- **Tigers live** in the forests of Asia, Sumatra and Java, but as hunters kill them for their skin and farmers clear the forest for land, they are becoming very rare. They now live only on special reserves.

- **Tigers prey on large animals** such as deer, buffalo, antelopes and wild pigs. They hunt silently at night, stalking their prey, then making a sudden bound.

- **A tiger is fast and strong** but tires quickly, and it will give up if it fails to catch its prey the first time.

- **Adult tigers** usually live alone, and males try to keep other males out of their territory. But when two tigers meet, they may rub one another's head in greeting.

- **A male tiger's territory** often includes that of two or three females. But they only meet to mate.

- **Tigers mark** out their territory by scratching trees and urinating on them.

- **Usually, two to four cubs** are born at a time. The cubs are playful and boisterous, and are totally dependent on their mother for 2 to 3 years.

▲ When a tiger roars, the sound can be heard for 4 or 5 kilometres through the forest.

- **A tiger's stripes** make it instantly recognizable, but they make good camouflage in long grass and under trees. Each tiger has its own unique pattern of stripes.

- **White tigers** are rare. They have blue eyes, and their stripes are brown and white, not black and gold.

Most tigers have yellow eyes

In between the black stripes, the coat is amber or yellow

▼ Tigers are forest dwellers and can climb trees, but most of the time they like to lie around. On hot days, they will often lie in rivers to cool off and, unusually for a cat, they can swim quite well.

The fur on the throat, belly, and the insides of the legs is whitish

Male tigers usually have a ruff of hair around the face

Vultures

- **Vultures and condors** are the biggest birds of prey. They do not hunt, but feed on carrion (dead animals).

- **The palmnut vulture** is the only vegetarian bird of prey, and it feeds on oil nuts.

- **Many vultures are bald**, with no head feathers to mat with blood when digging into corpses.

- **The seven species** of New World vulture (those that live in the Americas) have a nostril hole right through their beak.

- **The Californian condor** is very rare. All the wild ones were captured in the mid 1980s, but some have since been bred in captivity and returned to the wild.

- **Vultures** are great fliers and spend hours soaring, scanning the ground for corpses with sharp eyes.

> ★ STAR FACT ★
> The Andean condor is the world's biggest
> flying bird, with a wingspan of 3 m or more.

▲ *A vulture closes in to feed on a dead animal.*

- **Condors** have such a sharp sense of smell that they can pinpoint a corpse under a thick forest canopy.

- **Vultures** have such weak bills that flesh must be rotten before they can eat it.

- **The lammergeier** is known as the bearded vulture because it has a beard of black bristles on its chin.

Strange sea creatures

- **Deep-sea anglerfish** live deep in the ocean where it is pitch black. They lure prey into their mouths using a special, fishing-rod-like fin spine with a light at its tip.

- **Anglerfish** cannot find each other easily in the dark, so when a male meets a female he stays with her until mating time.

- **Hatchet fish** have giant eyeballs that point upwards so they see prey from below as silhouettes against the surface.

- **Viperfish** shine in the dark, thousands of metres down, and look like a jet airliner at night, with rows of lights along their bodies.

◄ *If threatened, the dragon fish will try to stab its attacker with its poisonous spines.*

- **Siphonophores** are colonies of tiny creatures that live in the deep oceans. They string themselves together in lines 20 m long and glow – so they look like fairy lights.

- **The cirrate octopod** looks like a jelly because its skin is 95% water – the water cannot be crushed by the intense pressure of the deep oceans where it lives.

- **The weedy seadragon** of Australia is a seahorse, but it looks just like a piece of flapping seaweed.

- **The sleeper shark** lives in the freezing depths of the North Atlantic and Arctic Oceans. It is 6.5 m long, but very slow and sluggish.

- **Flashlight fish** have light organs made by billions of bacteria which shine like headlights. The fish can suddenly block off these lights and change direction in the dark to confuse predators.

- **In the Arab-Israeli War** of 1967 a shoal of flashlight fish was mistaken for enemy frogmen and blown right out of the water.

Baby animals

- **All baby mammals** except monotremes (see strange mammals) are born from their mother's body, but most other creatures hatch from eggs.

- **Most creatures** hatch long after their parents have disappeared. Birds and mammals, though, usually look after their young.

- **Most birds** feed their hungry nestlings until they are big enough to find food themselves.

- **Some small birds** may make 10,000 trips to the nest to feed their young.

- **Cuckoos** lay their egg in the nest of another, smaller bird. The foster

▶ *Lion cubs are looked after by several females until they are big enough to fend for themselves. Like many babies they have big paws, head and ears for their body.*

parents hatch it and look after it as it grows. It then pushes its smaller, foster brothers and sisters out of the nest.

- **Mammals nurse** their young (they feed them on the mother's milk). The nursing period varies. It tends to be just a few weeks in small animals like mice, but several years in large animals like elephants.

- **Many animals** play when they are young. Playing helps them develop strength and co-ordination, and practise tasks they will have to do for real when adults.

- **When they are young,** baby opossums cling all over their mother as she moves around.

- **Some baby animals**, including baby shrews and elephants, go around in a long line behind the mother, clinging to the tail of the brother or sister in front.

Chameleons

- **Chameleons** are 85 species of lizard, most of which live on the island of Madagascar and in mainland Africa.

- **The smallest chameleon**, the dwarf Brookesia, could balance on your little finger. The biggest, Oustalet's chameleon, is the size of a small cat.

- **A chameleon** can look forwards and backwards at the same time, as each of its amazing eyes can swivel in all directions independently of the other.

- **Chameleons** feed on insects and spiders, hunting them in trees by day.

- **A chameleon's tongue** is almost as long as its body, but is normally squashed up inside its mouth.

- **A chameleon shoots** out its tongue in a fraction of a second to trap its victim on a sticky pad at the tip.

- **The chameleon's tongue** is fired out from a special launching bone on its lower jaw.

- **Most lizards** can change colour, but chameleons are experts, changing quickly to all sorts of colours.

▲ *Most of a chameleon's bulging eyes are protected by skin.*

- **Chameleons change colour** when they are angry or frightened, too cold or too hot, or sick – but they change colour less often to match their surroundings.

- **The colour of the skin** is controlled by pigment cells called melanophores, which change colour as they change size.

Life in cold regions

▲ *Other animals are the only substantial food in the Arctic wastes, so polar bears have to be carnivorous.*

- **The world's coldest places** are at the Poles in the Arctic and Antarctic, and high up mountains.

- **Only small animals** such as ice worms and insects can stand the extreme polar cold all year round.

- **Insects** such as springtails can live in temperatures as low as -38°C in Antarctica, because their body

fluids contain substances that do not freeze easily.

- **Birds** such as penguins, snow petrels and skuas live in Antarctica. So do the leopard seals that eat penguins.

- **Polar seas** are home to whales, fish and shrimp-like krill.

- **Fish of cold seas** have body fluids that act like car anti-freeze to stop them freezing.

- **Mammals such as polar bears**, sea lions and walruses are so well insulated against the cold with their fur and fat that they can live on the Arctic ice much of the year.

- **Many animals** live on the icy tundra land in the far north of America and Asia. They include caribou, Arctic foxes and hares, and birds such as ptarmigans and snowy owls.

- **Arctic foxes and hares**, ermines and ptarmigans turn white in winter to camouflage them against the snow.

> ★ STAR FACT ★
> Ptarmigans can survive through the bitter
> Arctic winter by eating twigs.

Starfish and sea urchins

- **Despite their name** starfish are not fish, but belong instead to a group of small sea creatures called echinoderms.

- **Sea urchins** and sea cucumbers are also echinoderms.

- **Starfish** have star-shaped bodies and are predators that prey mostly on shellfish such as scallops and oysters. They have five, strong arms which they use to prise open their victim. The starfish inserts its stomach into its victim and sucks out its flesh.

- **Each arm** of a starfish has on the underside hundreds of tiny, tube-like 'feet'. Bigger tubes inside the starfish's body pump water in and out of the 'feet', flexing the arms and driving the starfish along.

- **Starfish** often drop some of their arms off to escape an enemy, but the arms grow again.

◀ *Starfish that live in cooler water tend to be brown or yellow, whereas many tropical starfish can be bright red or even blue.*

- **Sea urchins** are ball-shaped creatures. Their shell is covered with bristling spines, which can be poisonous and can grow up to 40 cm long in some species.

- **A sea urchin's spines** are used for protection. Urchins also have sucker-like feet for moving.

- **A sea urchin's mouth** is a hole with five teeth, on the underside of its body.

- **Sea cucumbers** have no shell, but a leathery skin and a covering of chalky plates called spicules.

- **When threatened**, a sea cucumber chucks out pieces of its gut as a decoy and swims away. It grows a new one later.

Dragonflies

- **Dragonflies** are big hunting insects with four large transparent wings, and a long slender body that may be a shimmering red, green or blue.

- **Dragonflies have** 30,000 separate lenses in each of their compound eyes, giving them the sharpest vision of any insect.

- **A dragonfly** can see something that is stationary from almost 2 m away, and something moving two to three times farther away.

- **As it swoops** in on its prey, a dragonfly pulls its legs forwards like a basket to scoop up its victim.

- **Dragonflies** often mate in mid-air, and the male may then stay hanging on to the female until she lays her eggs.

- **Dragonfly eggs** are laid in water or in the stem of a water plant, and hatch in 2 to 3 weeks.

- **Newly hatched dragonflies** are called nymphs and look like fatter, wingless adults.

- **Dragonfly nymphs** are ferocious hunters, often feeding on young fish and tadpoles.

- **Dragonfly nymphs** grow and moult over a many years, before they climb on to a reed or rock to emerge as an adult.

▶ *Dragonflies are big insects even today, but hundreds of millions of years ago, there were dragonflies with wings that were well over 70 cm across.*

> ★ STAR FACT ★
> Dragonflies can reach speeds of almost 100 km/h to escape from birds.

Owls

- **Owls** are nocturnal and hunt by night, unlike most other hunting birds.

- **There are two big families of owl** – barn owls and typical owls.

- **There are 135 species** of typical owl, including the great horned owl.

- **There are 12 species** of barn owl. The common barn owl is the most widespread – it is found on every continent but Antarctica.

◀ *An owl's big eyes face straight ahead to focus. However, owls cannot move their eyes so have to swivel their whole head to look to the side or the rear.*

- **Small owls** eat mostly insects. Bigger owls eat mice and shrews. Eagle owls can catch young deer.

- **In the country**, the tawny owl's diet is 90% small mammals, but many now live in towns where their diet is mainly small birds such as sparrows and starlings.

- **Owls have huge eyes** that allow them to see in almost pitch darkness.

- **An owl's hearing** is four times as sharp as a cat's.

- **An owl can pinpoint** sounds with astonishing accuracy from the slight difference in the sound levels it receives in each of its ears.

- **Most bird's eyes** look out to the sides, but an owl's look straight forward like a human's. This is probably why the owl has been a symbol of wisdom since ancient times.

- **The flight feathers** on an owl's wing muffle the sound of the bird's wingbeat so that it can swoop almost silently down on to its prey.

Turkeys and hens

- **Turkeys**, chickens, geese and ducks are all kinds of poultry – farm birds bred to provide meat, eggs and feathers.

- **Chickens** were first tamed 5,000 years ago, and there are now over 200 breeds, including bantams and Rhode Island reds.

- **Female chickens** and turkeys are called hens. Male chickens are called roosters or cockerels. Male turkeys are toms. Baby turkeys are poults.

- **To keep hens laying**, their eggs must be collected daily. If not, the hens will wait until they have a small

◀ *Roosters are renowned for their noisy cries every morning as the sun comes up. This harsh cry is called a crow.*

clutch of eggs, then try to sit on them to hatch them.

- **Battery hens** spend their lives in rows of boxes or cages called batteries inside buildings.

- **Free-range hens** are allowed to scratch outdoors for insects and seeds.

- **Chickens** raised only for eating are called broilers.

- **Turkeys** are a kind of pheasant. There are several species, but all are descended from the native wild turkey of North America, first tamed by Native Americans 1,000 years ago.

- **Male turkeys** have a loose fold of bare, floppy skin called a wattle hanging down from their head and neck.

> ★ STAR FACT ★
> All domestic chickens are descended from the wild red jungle fowl of India.

Strange mammals

- **The duck-billed platypus** and the echidnas live in Australia and are the only monotremes – mammals that lay eggs.

- **Duck-billed platypuses** are strange in other ways, too. They have a snout shaped like a duck's bill and webbed feet, which is why they are so happy in water.

▼ *The Tasmanian devil may be small, but it can be very fierce.*

- **Platypuses hatch** from eggs in a river-bank burrow.

- **Platypus babies** lick the milk that oozes out over the fur of their mother's belly.

- **Echidnas** are also known as spiny anteaters because they are covered in spines and eat ants.

- **After a female echidna** lays her single egg, she keeps it in a pouch on her body until it hatches.

- **The Tasmanian devil** is a small, fierce, Australian marsupial (see kangaroos and koalas). It hunts at night and eats almost any meat, dead or alive.

- **Tasmanian devils** stuff their victims into their mouth with their front feet.

- **The sugar glider** is a tiny, mouse-like jungle marsupial which can glide for 45 m between trees.

- **The aardvark** is a strange South African mammal with a long snout and huge claws. It can shovel as fast as a mechanical digger to make a home or find ants.

What is a fish?

- **Fish** are mostly slim, streamlined animals that live in water. Many are covered in tiny shiny plates called scales. Most have bony skeletons and a backbone.
- **There are well over 21,000 species** of fish, from the 8-mm-long pygmy goby to the 12-m-long whale shark.

▼ Angling (catching fish) is a popular pastime all around the world. The fish is hooked as it bites the lure or bait.

> ★ STAR FACT ★
> The drum fish makes a drumming sound with its swim bladder.

- **Fish** are cold-blooded.
- **Fish breathe** through gills – rows of feathery brushes inside each side of the fish's head.
- **To get oxygen,** fish gulp water in through their mouths and draw it over their gills.
- **Fish have fins** for swimming, not limbs.
- **Most fish** have a pectoral fin behind each gill and two pelvic fins below to the rear, a dorsal fin on top of their body, an anal fin beneath, and a caudal (tail) fin.
- **Fish let gas in** and out of their swim bladders to float at particular depths.
- **Some fish** communicate by making sounds with their swim bladder. Catfish use them like bagpipes.

Worms

- **Worms** are long, wriggling, tube-like animals. Annelids are worms such as the earthworm whose bodies are divided into segments.
- **There are 15,000 species** of annelid. Most live underground in tunnels, or in the sea.
- **The world's largest earthworm** is the giant earthworm of South Africa, which can grow to as long as 6.5 m.
- **Earthworms** spend their lives burrowing through soil. Soil goes in the mouth end, passes through the gut and comes out at the tail end.
- **An earthworm** is both male and female (called a hermaphrodite), and after two earthworms mate, both develop eggs.
- **Over half the annelid species** are marine (sea) bristleworms, such as ragworms and lugworms. They are named because they are covered in bristles, whch they use to paddle over the seabed or dig into the mud.
- **The sea mouse** is a bristleworm with furry hairs.

- **Flatworms** look like ribbons or as though an annelid worm has been ironed flat. Of the thousands of flatworm species, many live in the sea or in pond algae.
- **Flukes** are flatworms that live as parasites inside other animals. Diseases like bilharzia are caused by flukes.
- **Tapeworms** are parisitic flatworms that live inside their host's gut and eat their food.

▶ Plants would not grow half as well without earthworms to aerate the soil as they burrow in it, mix up the layers and make it more fertile with their droppings.

1000 THINGS
YOU SHOULD KNOW ABOUT

HUMAN
BODY

KEY

 Breathing and blood

 Skeleton and muscle

 Body control

 Food and water

 Growing and changing

 Health and disease

Airways

- **The upper airways** include the nose and the sinuses, the mouth and the pharynx (throat).

- **The lower airways** include the larynx (see vocal cords), the trachea (windpipe) and the airways of the lungs.

- **The sinuses** are air chambers within the bones of the skull that form the forehead and face. If mucus blocks them when you get a cold, your speech is affected.

- **The soft palate** is a flap of tissue at the back of the mouth, which is pressed upwards when you swallow to stop food getting into your nose.

- **Your throat** is the tube that runs down through your neck from the back of your nose and mouth.

- **Your throat branches** in two at the bottom. One branch, the oesophagus, takes food to the stomach. The other, the larynx, takes air to the lungs.

- **The epiglottis** is the flap that tilts down to block off the larynx to stop food entering it when you swallow.

- **The tonsils and the adenoids** are bunches of lymph nodes (see lymphatic system) that swell to help fight ear, nose and throat infections, especially in young children.

- **The adenoids** are at the back of the nose, and the tonsils are at the back of the upper throat.

- **If tonsils or adenoids** swell too much, they are sometimes taken out.

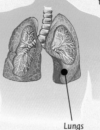

★ STAR FACT ★
Your throat is linked to your ears by tubes which open when you swallow to balance air pressure.

◄ *The lower airways include the larynx, the trachea (windpipe), and the bronchi which branch into the lungs.*

Lungs

Smell

▲ *Scents are closely linked to emotions in the brain, and perfume can be a powerful way of triggering feelings.*

- **Smells are scent molecules** which are carried in the air and breathed in through your nose. A particular smell may be noticeable even when just a single scent molecule is mixed in with millions of air molecules.

- **The human nose** can tell the difference between more than 10,000 different chemicals.

- **Dogs can pick up** smells that are 10,000 times fainter than the ones humans can detect.

- **Inside the nose**, scent molecules are picked up by a patch of cells called the olfactory epithelium.

- **Olfactory** means 'to do with the sense of smell'.

- **The olfactory epithelium** contains over 25 million receptor cells.

- **Each of the receptor cells** in the olfactory epithelium has up to 20 scent-detecting hairs called cilia.

- **When they are triggered** by scent molecules, the cilia send signals to a cluster of nerves called the olfactory bulb, which then sends messages to the part of the brain that recognizes smell.

- **The part of the brain** that deals with smell is closely linked to the parts that deal with memories and emotions. This may be why smells can evoke memories.

- **By the age of 20**, you will have lost 20% of your sense of smell. By 60, you will have lost 60% of it.

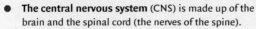
Central nervous system

- **The central nervous system** (CNS) is made up of the brain and the spinal cord (the nerves of the spine).

- **The CNS** contains billions of densely packed interneurons – nerve cells with very short connecting axons (see nerve cells).

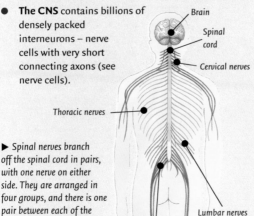

Brain

Spinal cord

Cervical nerves

Thoracic nerves

▶ *Spinal nerves branch off the spinal cord in pairs, with one nerve on either side. They are arranged in four groups, and there is one pair between each of the neighbouring 32 vertebrae.*

Lumbar nerves

Sacral nerves

- **The CNS is cushioned** from damage by a surrounding bath of cerebrospinal fluid.

- **There are 43 pairs** of nerves branching off the CNS.

- **The job of the nerves** is to send sense and movement signals to the brain.

- **Cranial nerves** are the 12 pairs of nerves that branch off the CNS in the head, branching out of the brain.

- **Spinal nerves** are the 31 pairs of nerves that branch off the spinal cord.

- **The spinal nerves** are made up of 8 cervical nerve pairs, 12 thoracic pairs, 5 lumbar, 5 sacral and 1 coccyx pair.

- **Many spinal nerves** join up just outside the spine in five spaghetti junctions called plexuses.

> ★ STAR FACT ★
> The CNS sends out messages to more than 640 muscles around the body.

Carbohydrates

- **Carbohydrates** in food are your body's main source of energy. They are plentiful in sweet things and in starchy food such as bread, cakes and potatoes (see diet).

- **Carbohydrates** are burned by the body to keep it warm and to provide energy for growth and muscle movement, as well as to maintain basic body processes.

- **Carbohydrates** are among the most common of all organic (life) substances. Plants, for instance, make carbohydrates when they take energy from sunlight.

- **Carbohydrates** include huge molecules made of long strings of sugars. Sucrose (the sugar in sugar lumps and caster sugar) is just one of these sugars.

- **Simple carbohydrates** such as glucose, fructose (the sweetness in fruit) and sucrose are sweet and soluble (they will dissolve in water).

- **Complex carbohydrates** (or polysaccharides) such as starch are made when the molecules of simple carbohydrates join together.

- **A third type of carbohydrate** is cellulose (see diet).

- **The carbohydrates** you eat are turned into glucose for your body to use at once, or stored in the liver as the complex sugar glycogen (body starch).

- **The average adult** needs 2,000 to 4,000 Calories a day.

- **A Calorie** is the heat needed to warm 1 litre of water by 1 °C.

▼ *Bread is especially rich in complex carbohydrates such as starch, as well as simpler ones such as glucose and sucrose. Both were made by the original cereal plant whose seeds were ground into flour.*

Veins

- **Veins** are pipes in the body for carrying blood.

- **Unlike arteries**, most veins carry 'used' blood back to the heart – the body cells have taken the oxygen they need from the blood, so it is low in oxygen.

- **When blood** is low in oxygen, it is a dark, purplish blue colour – unlike the bright red of the oxygenated blood carried by the arteries.

- **The only veins** that carry oxygenated blood are the four pulmonary veins, which carry blood from the lungs the short distance to the heart.

- **The two largest veins** in the body are the vena cavae that flow into the heart from above and below.

- **Inside most large veins** are flaps that act as valves to make sure that the blood only flows one way.

> ★ STAR FACT ★
> At any moment 75% of the body's blood
> is in veins.

- **The blood in veins** is not pumped as hard by the heart, so the blood pressure is lower than in arteries and vein walls do not need to be as strong.

- **Unlike arteries**, veins collapse when empty.

- **Blood is helped through** the veins by pressure placed on the vein walls by the surrounding muscles.

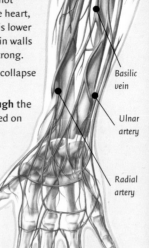

Basilic
vein

Ulnar
artery

Radial
artery

▶ This illustration of the lower arm shows the main veins (in blue) and the main arteries (in red).

Teeth

▼ Teeth have long roots that slot into sockets in the jawbones, but they sit in a fleshy ridge called the gums. In the centre of each tooth is a living pulp of blood and nerves. Around this is a layer of dentine, then on top of that a tough shield of enamel.

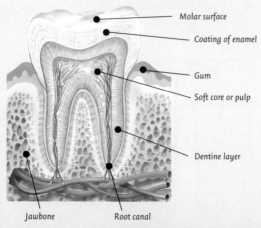

Molar surface

Coating of enamel

Gum

Soft core or pulp

Dentine layer

Jawbone   Root canal

- **Milk teeth** are the 20 teeth that start to appear when a baby is about six months old.

- **When you are six**, you start to grow your 32 adult teeth – 16 top in the top row and 16 in the bottom.

- **Molars** are the (usually) six pairs of big, strong teeth at the back of your mouth. They have flattish tops and are a good shape for grinding food.

- **The molars** in the four corners of your jaw are wisdom teeth. These grow last and sometimes never appear.

- **Premolars** are four pairs of teeth in front of the molars.

- **Incisors** are the four pairs of teeth at the front of your mouth. They have sharp edges for cutting food.

- **Canines** are the two pairs of big, pointed teeth behind the incisors. Their shape is good for tearing food.

- **The enamel** on teeth is the body's hardest substance.

- **Dentine** inside teeth is softer but still hard as bone.

- **Teeth** sit in sockets in the jawbones.

The thyroid gland

- **The thyroid** is a small gland about the size of two joined cherries. It is at the front of your neck, just below the larynx (see airways and vocal cords).
- **The thyroid** secretes (releases) three important hormones – tri-odothyronine (T3), thyroxine (T4) and calcitonin.
- **The thyroid hormones** affect how energetic you are by controlling your metabolic rate.
- **Your metabolic rate** is the rate at which your cells use glucose and other energy substances.

▶ The thyroid is part of your energy control system, telling your body cells to work faster or slower in order to keep you warm or to make your muscles work harder.

> ★ STAR FACT ★
> Everyone has a different metabolic rate. It goes up when you work hard or are afraid.

- **T3 and T4** control metabolic rate by circulating into the blood and stimulating cells to convert more glucose.
- **If the thyroid** sends out too little T3 and T4, you get cold and tired, your skin gets dry and you put on weight.
- **If the thyroid** sends out too much T3 and T4, you get nervous, sweaty and overactive, and you lose weight.
- **The amount of T3 and T4** sent out by the thyroid depends on how much thyroid-stimulating hormone is sent to it from the pituitary gland (see the brain).
- **If the levels of T3 and T4** in the blood drop, the pituitary gland sends out extra thyroid-stimulating hormone to tell the thyroid to produce more.

Water

- **Your body** is mainly made of water – over 60%.
- **You can survive weeks** without food, but no more than a few days without water.
- **You gain water** by drinking and eating, and as a by-product of cell activity.
- **You lose water** by sweating and breathing, and in your urine and faeces (see excretion).
- **The average person** takes in 2.2 litres of water a day – 1.4 litres in drink and 0.8 litres in food. Body cells add 0.3 litres, bringing the total water intake to 2.5 litres.
- **The average person** loses 1.5 litres of water every day in urine, 0.5 litres in sweat, 0.3 litres as vapour in the breath, and 0.2 litres in faeces.
- **The water balance** in the body is controlled mainly by the kidneys and adrenal glands.
- **The amount of water** the kidneys let out as urine depends on the amount of salt there is in the blood (see body salts).

▶ If you sweat a lot during heavy exercise, you need to make up for all the water you have lost by drinking. Your kidneys make sure that if you drink too much, you lose water as urine.

- **If you drink a lot**, the saltiness of the blood is diluted (watered down). To restore the balance, the kidneys let out a lot of water in the form of urine.
- **If you drink little** or sweat a lot, the blood becomes more salty, so the kidneys restore the balance by holding on to more water.

Diet

◀ *Garlic may give you fairly unpleasant breath and make your skin smell, but it is supposed to be good for the heart.*

- **Your diet** is what you eat. A good diet includes the correct amount of proteins, carbohydrates, fats, vitamins, minerals, fibre and water.

- **Most of the food** you eat is fuel for the body, provided mostly by carbohydrates and fats.

- **Carbohydrates** are foods made from kinds of sugar, such as glucose and starch. They are found in foods such as bread, rice, potatoes and sweet things.

- **Fats** are greasy foods that will not dissolve in water. Some, such as the fats in meat and cheese, are solid. Some, such as cooking oil, are liquid.

- **Fats are not** usually burned up straight away, but stored around your body until they are needed.

- **Proteins** are needed to build and repair cells, and they are made from chemicals called amino acids.

- **There are 20** different amino acids. Your body can make 11 of them. The other nine are called essential acids and they come from food.

- **Meat and fish** are very high in protein.

- **A correctly balanced vegetarian diet** can provide all the essential amino acids.

- **Fibre** or roughage is supplied by cellulose from plant cell walls. Your body cannot digest fibre, but needs it to keep the bowel muscles properly exercised.

▶ *Citrus fruits are a good source of vitamin C, which is vital for healthy teeth, gums and bones.*

Babies

◀ *Babies learn to walk when their leg muscles grow strong enough, after nine months or so.*

- **A baby's head** is three-quarters of the size it will be as an adult – and a quarter of its total body height.

- **The bones** of a baby's skeleton are fairly soft, to allow for growth. They harden over time.

- **Baby boys grow faster** than baby girls during the first seven months.

- **A baby** has a very developed sense of taste, with taste buds all over the inside of its mouth.

- **Babies have** a much stronger sense of smell than adults – perhaps to help them find their mother.

- **There are two gaps** called fontanelles between the bones of a baby's skull, where there is only membrane (a 'skin' of thin tissue), not bone. The gaps close and the bones join together by about 18 months.

- **A baby is born** with primitive reflexes (things it does automatically) such as grasping or sucking a finger.

- **A baby's body weight** will usually triple in its first year.

- **A baby seems to learn** to control its body in stages, starting first with its head, then moving on to its arms and legs.

> ★ STAR FACT ★
> A baby's brain is one of the fastest growing parts of its body.

The brain

- **The human brain** is made up of more than 100 billion nerve cells called neurons.

- **Each neuron** is connected to as many as 25,000 other neurons – so the brain has trillions and trillions of different pathways for nerve signals.

- **Girls' brains** weigh 2.5% of their body weight, on average, while boys' brains weigh 2%.

- **About 0.85 litres** of blood shoots through your brain every minute. The brain may be as little as 2% of your body weight, but it demands 15% of your blood supply.

- **An elephant's brain** weighs four times as much as the human brain. However, our brains are far bigger in relation to our bodies than those of most other animals.

- **The cerebral cortex** is the outside of the upper part of the brain, and if laid out flat, it would cover a bed.

- **The brain** is divided into two halves (hemisheres). Each controls the oposite side of the body.

- **Conscious thoughts and actions** happen in the cerebral cortex.

- **A human brain** has a cerebral cortex four times as big as a chimpanzee, about 20 times as big as a monkey's, and about 300 times as big as a rat's.

- **Unconscious, automatic activities** such as breathing, hunger, sleep and so on are controlled by structures such as the hypothalamus and the hippocampus in the middle of the brain.

- **The cerebellum** mainly controls body co-ordination and balance.

> **! NEWS FLASH !**
> Scientists can now grow human brain cells in a laboratory dish.

▼ Taking the top off the skull shows the brain to be a soggy, pinky-grey mass which looks rather like a giant walnut.

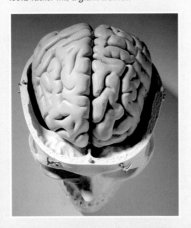

Hypothalamus controls body heat, water and hunger, and also wakes you up

Cerebrum – where you think and decide what to say and other clever things

Thalamus affects sensory levels, awareness and alertness

Limbic system affects body functions, emotions and smell

Pituitary gland controls hormones

Hippocampus, linked to moods, willpower, learning and memory

Amygdala, linked with moods and memories

Cerebellum controls co-ordination

Brain stem controls heartbeat and breathing

▲ In this illustration, the right hemisphere (half) of the cerebrum is shown in pink, surrounding the regions that control basic drives such as hunger, thirst and anger.

Tendons and ligaments

- **Tendons** are cords that tie a muscle to a bone or a muscle to another muscle.

- **Most tendons** are round, rope-like bundles of fibre. A few, such as the ones in the abdomen wall, are flat sheets called aponeuroses.

- **Tendon fibres are made** from a rubbery substance called collagen.

- **Your fingers are moved** mainly by muscles in the forearm, connected to the fingers by long tendons.

- **The Achilles tendon** pulls up your heel at the back.

- **Ligaments** are cords attached to bones on either side of a joint. They strengthen the joint.

- **Ligaments** also support various organs, including the liver, bladder and uterus (womb).

- **Women's breasts** are held in shape by bundles of ligaments.

- **Ligaments are made up** of bundles of tough collagen and a stretchy substance called elastin.

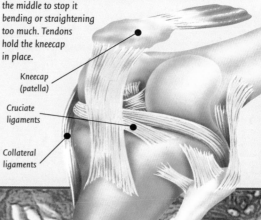

▶ Collateral (side) ligaments stop the knee wobbling from side to side. Cruciate (crossing) ligaments tie the knee across the middle to stop it bending or straightening too much. Tendons hold the kneecap in place.

Kneecap (patella)

Cruciate ligaments

Collateral ligaments

> ★ STAR FACT ★
> The Achilles tendon is named after the Greek hero Achilles whose only weakness was his heel.

Vaccination

- **Vaccination** helps to protect you against an infectious disease by exposing you to a mild or dead version of the germ in order to make your body build up protection, in the form of antibodies.

- **Vaccination** is also called immunization, because it builds up your resistance or immunity to a disease.

- **In passive immunization** you are injected with substances such as antibodies which have been exposed to the germ. This gives instant but short-term protection.

◀ Diseases such as diphtheria, rubella and whooping cough are now rare in many countries thanks to vaccination. The dangerous disease smallpox – once very common – has been wiped out.

- **In active immunization** you are given a killed or otherwise harmless version of the germ. Your body makes the antibodies itself for long-term protection.

- **Children in many countries** are given a series of vaccinations as they grow up, to protect them against diseases such as diphtheria, tetanus and polio.

- **There is a small risk** of a serious reaction against a vaccine. The measles vaccine carries a 1 in 87,000 chance of causing encephalitis (brain inflammation).

- **In cholera, typhoid, rabies and flu vaccines**, the germ in the vaccine is killed to make it harmless.

- **In measles, mumps, polio and rubella vaccines**, the germ is live attenuated – this means that its genes or other parts have been altered to make it harmless.

- **In diphtheria and tetanus vaccines**, the germ's toxins (poisons) are removed to make them harmless.

- **The hepatitis B vaccine** can be prepared by genetic engineering.

Thinking

- **Some scientists** claim that we humans are the only living things that are conscious – we alone are actually aware that we are thinking.

- **No one knows** how consciousness works – it is one of science's last great mysteries.

- **Most thoughts** seem to take place in the cerebrum (at the top of your brain), and different kinds of thought are linked to different areas, called association areas.

▲ *Modern scanning techniques have taught us a great deal about the human brain and brain processes by allowing us to see brains in action.*

- **Each half of the cerebrum** has four rounded ends called lobes: two at the front (frontal and temporal lobes) and two at the back (occipital and parietal lobes).

- **The frontal lobe** is linked to your personality and it is where you have your bright ideas.

- **The temporal lobe** is where you hear and understand what people say to you.

- **The occipital lobe** is where you work out what your eyes see.

- **The parietal lobe** is where you register touch, heat and cold, and pain.

- **The left half of the brain** (left hemisphere) controls the right side of the body. The right half (right hemisphere) controls the left side.

- **One half of the brain** is always dominant (in charge). Usually, the left brain is dominant, which is why 90% of people are right-handed.

Chromosomes

- **Chromosomes** are the microscopically tiny, twisted threads inside every cell that carry your body's life instructions in chemical form.

- **There are 46 chromosomes** in each of your body cells, divided into 23 pairs.

- **One of each chromosome pair** came from your mother and the other from your father

- **In a girl's 23 chromosome pairs**, each half exactly matches the other (the set from the mother is equivalent to the set from the father).

- **Boys** have 22 matching chromosome pairs, but the 23rd pair is made up of two odd chromosomes.

- **The 23rd chromosome pair** decides what sex you are, and the sex chromosomes are called X and Y.

- **Girls** have two X chromosomes, but boys have an X and a Y chromosome.

- **In every matching pair**, both chromosomes give your body life instructions for the same thing.

- **The chemical instructions** on each chromosome come in thousands of different units called genes.

- **Genes for the same feature** appear in the same locus (place) on each matching pair of chromosomes in every human body cell. Scientists one day hope to find out how the entire pattern, called the genome, works.

▼ *Girls turn out to be girls because they get an X – not a Y – chromosome from their father.*

Circulation

▶ Blood circulates continuously round and round your body through an intricate series of tubes called blood vessels. Bright red, oxygen-rich blood is pumped from the left side of the heart through vessels called arteries and arterioles. Purplish-blue, low-in-oxygen blood returns to the right of the heart through veins and venules.

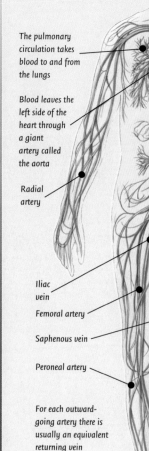

The brain receives more blood than any other part of the body

Blood returns to the heart through main veins called the vena cavae

The pulmonary circulation takes blood to and from the lungs

Blood leaves the left side of the heart through a giant artery called the aorta

Radial artery

Iliac vein

Femoral artery

Saphenous vein

Peroneal artery

For each outward-going artery there is usually an equivalent returning vein

- **Your circulation** is the system of tubes called blood vessels which carries blood out from your heart to all your body cells and back again.

- **Blood circulation** was discovered in 1628 by the English physician William Harvey (1578-1657), who built on the ideas of Matteo Colombo.

- **Each of the body's** 600 billion cells gets fresh blood once every few minutes or less.

- **On the way out** from the heart, blood is pumped through vessels called arteries and arterioles.

> ★ STAR FACT ★
> It takes less than 90 seconds on average for the blood to circulate through all of the body's 100,000 km of blood vessels!

- **On the way back** to the heart, blood flows through venules and veins.

- **Blood flows** from the arterioles to the venules through the tiniest tubes called capillaries.

- **The blood circulation** has two parts – the pulmonary and the systemic.

- **The pulmonary circulation** is the short section that carries blood which is low in oxygen from the right side of the heart to the lungs for 'refuelling'. It then returns oxygen-rich blood to the left side of the heart.

- **The systemic circulation** carries oxygen-rich blood from the left side of the heart all around the body, and returns blood which is low in oxygen to the right side of the heart.

- **Inside the blood**, oxygen is carried by the haemoglobin in red blood cells (see blood cells).

◀ Red blood cells can actually be brown in colour, but they turn bright scarlet when their haemoglobin is carrying oxygen. After the haemoglobin passes its oxygen to a cell, it fades to dull purple. So oxygen-rich blood from the heart is red, while oxygen-poor blood that is returning to the heart is a purplish-blue colour.

Birth

- **Babies are usually born** 38-42 weeks after the mother becomes pregnant.
- **Usually a few days** or weeks before a baby is born, it turns in the uterus (womb) so its head is pointing down towards the mother's birth canal (her cervix and vagina).
- **Birth begins** as the mother goes into labour – when the womb muscles begin a rhythm of contracting (tightening) and relaxing in order to push the baby out through the birth canal.
- **There are three stages** of labour. In the first, the womb muscles begin to squeeze, bursting the bag of fluid around the baby. This is called breaking the waters.
- **In the second stage** of labour, the baby is pushed out through the birth canal. Then the umbilical cord – its lifeline to its mother – is cut and the baby starts to breathe on its own.
- **In the third stage** of labour, the placenta is shed and comes out through the birth canal.

- **A premature baby** is one born before it is fully developed.
- **A miscarriage** is when the developing baby is 'born' before the 28th week of pregnancy and cannot survive.
- **A Caesarian section** is an operation that happens when a baby can't be born through the birth canal and emerges from the womb through a cut made in the mother's belly.

▼ A mother makes a special bond with her baby.

Diagnosis

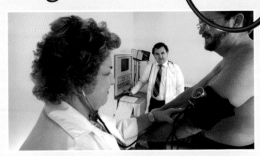

▲ To make a diagnosis, a doctor needs to carry out many different tests, such as taking the patient's blood pressure.

- **Diagnosis** is when a doctor works out what a patient is suffering from – the illness and perhaps its cause.
- **The history** is the patient's own account of their illness. This provides the doctor with a lot of clues.
- **The prognosis** is the doctor's assessment of how the illness will develop in future.

- **Symptoms** are the effects or signs of the illness.
- **After taking a history** the doctor may carry out a physical examination, looking at the patient's body for symptoms such as swelling and tenderness.
- **A stethoscope** is a set of ear tubes which allows the doctor to listen to body sounds such as breathing and the heart beating.
- **With certain symptoms**, a doctor may order special tests, such as laboratory tests of blood and urine samples. Devices such as ultrasounds and X-rays may also be used to take special pictures.
- **Doctors** nowadays may use computers to help them make a diagnosis.
- **Diagnosis** can take a few seconds or many months.

> **! NEWS FLASH !**
> In future, some illnesses may be diagnosed entirely by computer.

The cortex

- **A cortex** is the outer layer of any organ, such as the brain or the kidney.

- **The brain's cortex** is also known as the cerebral cortex. It is a layer of interconnected nerve cells around the outside of the brain, called 'grey matter'.

- **The cerebral cortex** is where many signals from the senses are registered in the brain.

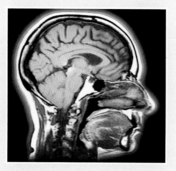

◀ The surface of the cortex is wrinkled into folds which are called gyri, with valleys in between them called sulci. The pattern of wrinkles can be seen clearly in this scan, which creates a slice through the brain.

- **The visual cortex** is around the lower back of the brain. It is the place where all the things you see are registered in the brain.

- **The somatosensory cortex** is a band running over the top of the brain like a headband. This where a touch on any part of the body is registered.

- **The motor cortex** is a band just in front of the sensory cortex. It sends out signals to body muscles to move.

- **The more nerve endings** there are in a particular part of the body, the more of the sensory cortex it occupies.

- **The lips and face** take up a huge proportion of the sensory cortex.

- **The hands** take up almost as much of the sensory cortex as the face.

> ★ STAR FACT ★
> Everyone has their own unique pattern of wrinkles on their cerebral cortex.

Bone

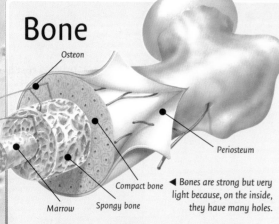

Osteon

Periosteum

Compact bone   ◀ Bones are strong but very light because, on the inside, they have many holes.

Marrow   Spongy bone

- **Bones are so strong** that they can cope with twice the squeezing pressure that granite can, or four times the stretching tension that concrete can, before breaking.

- **Weight for weight,** bone is at least five times as strong as steel.

- **Bones are so light** they only make up 14% of your body's total weight.

- **Bones get their rigidity** from hard deposits of minerals such as calcium and phosphate.

- **Bones get their flexibility** from tough, elastic, rope-like fibres of collagen.

- **The hard outside of bones** (called compact bone) is reinforced by strong rods called osteons.

- **The inside of bones** (called spongy bone) is a light honeycomb, made of thin struts or trabeculae, perfectly angled to take stress. The core of some bones is soft, jelly-like bone marrow.

- **Bones are living tissue** packed with cells called osteocytes. Each osteocyte, though, is housed in its own hole or lacuna.

- **In some parts of each bone,** there are special cells called osteoblasts which make new bone. In other parts, cells called osteoclasts break up old bone.

- **Bones grow** by getting longer near the end – at a region called the epiphyseal plate.

The spinal cord

- **The spinal cord** is the bundle of nerves running down the middle of the backbone.

- **The spinal cord** is the route for all nerve signals travelling between the brain and the body.

- **The spinal cord** can actually work independently of the brain, sending out responses to the muscles directly.

- **The outside** of the spinal cord is made of the long tails or axons of nerve cells and is called white matter; the inside is made of the main nerve bodies and is called grey matter.

- **Your spinal cord** is about 43 cm long and 1 cm thick; it stops growing when you are about five years old.

- **Damage to the spinal cord** can cause paralysis.

- **Injuries below the neck** can cause paraplegia – paralysis below the waist.

- **Injuries to the neck** can cause quadraplegia – paralysis below the neck.

- **Descending pathways** are groups of nerves that carry nerve signals down the spinal cord – typically signals from the brain for muscles to move.

- **Ascending pathways** are groups of nerves that carry nerve signals up the spinal cord – typically signals from the skin and internal body sensors going to the brain.

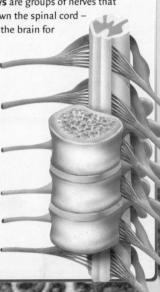

▶ The spinal cord is encased in a tunnel in the backbone at the back of each vertebra. Nerves branch off to the body in pairs either side.

Vitamins

- **Vitamins** are special substances the body needs to help maintain chemical processes inside cells.

- **Plants can make** their own vitamins, but humans must take most of their own from food.

- **A lack of any vitamin** in the diet can cause illness.

- **Before the 18th century,** sailors on long voyages used to suffer the disease scurvy, caused by a lack of vitamin C from fresh fruit in their diet.

- **There are at least 15 vitamins** known.

- **The first vitamins** discovered were given letter names like B. Later discoveries were given chemical names.

- **Some vitamins** such as A, D, E and K dissolve in fat and are found in animal fats and vegetable oils. They may be stored in the body for months.

- **Some vitamins** such as C and the Bs, dissolve in water and are found in green leaves, fruits and cereal grains. They are used daily.

★ STAR FACT ★
Lack of vitamin A ruins night vision, because it is needed for the working of the retina.

- **Vitamins D and K** are the only ones made in the body. Vitamin D is essential for bone growth in children. It is made by the skin when exposed to the sun – 15 minutes three times a week may be enough.

▶ This is a microscope photograph of a crystal of vitamin C, also known as ascorbic acid. This vitamin helps the body fight infections such as colds.

Disease

- **A disease** is something that upsets the normal working of any living thing. It can be acute (sudden, but short-lived), chronic (long-lasting), malignant (spreading) or benign (not spreading).

- **Some diseases** are classified by the body part they affect (such as heart disease), or by the body activity they affect (such as respiratory, or breathing, disease).

- **Heart disease** is the most common cause of death in the USA, Europe and Australia.

- **Some diseases** are classified by their cause. These include the diseases caused by the staphylococcus bacteria, such as pneumonia.

- **Diseases can be** either contagious (able to be passed on) or non-contagious.

- **Infectious diseases** are caused by germs such as

◀ This is a microscope photograph of a cancer cell.

bacteria and viruses (see germs). They include the common cold, polio, flu and measles. Their spread can be controlled by good sanitation and hygiene, and by vaccination programmes.

- **Non-infectious diseases** may be inherited or they may be caused by such things as eating harmful substances, poor nutrition or hygiene, getting old or being injured.

- **Endemic diseases** are diseases that occur in a particular area of the world, such as sleeping sickness in Africa.

- **Cancer** is a disease in which malignant cells multiply abnormally, creating growths called tumours.

- **Cancer kills** 6 million people a year around the world. The risk increases as you get older.

Blood groups

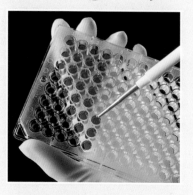

◀ Lives often depend on a patient receiving blood donated by someone else. But unless the blood belongs to a suitable group, the patient's body will react against it.

- **Most people's blood** belongs to one of four groups or types – A, O, B and AB.

- **Blood type O** is the most common.

- **Blood is also** either Rhesus positive (Rh+) or Rhesus negative (Rh-).

- **Around 85% of people** are Rh+. The remaining 15% are Rh-.

- **If your blood is Rh+** and your group is A, your blood group is said to be A positive. If your blood is Rh- and your group is O, you are O negative, and so on.

- **The Rhesus factors** got their name because they were first identified in Rhesus monkeys.

- **A transfusion** is when you are given blood from another person's body. Your body will only accept blood from certain groups which match with yours.

- **Blood transfusions** are given when someone has lost too much blood because of an injury or operation. It is also given to replace diseased blood.

> ★ STAR FACT ★
> A pregnant mother who is Rh- may develop damaging antibodies against the baby in her own womb if it is Rh+.

Digestion

- **Digestion** is the process by which your body breaks down the food you eat into substances that it can absorb (take in) and use.

- **Your digestive tract** is basically a long, winding tube called the alimentary canal (gut). It starts at your mouth and ends at your anus.

- **If you could lay** your gut out straight, it would be nearly six times as long as you are tall.

- **The food you eat** is softened in your mouth by chewing and by chemicals in your saliva (spit).

- **When you swallow**, food travels down your oesophagus (gullet) into your stomach. Your stomach is a muscular-walled bag which mashes the food into a pulp, helped by chemicals called gastric juices.

- **When empty**, your stomach holds barely 0.5 litres, but after a big meal it can stretch to more than 4 litres.

- **The half-digested food** that leaves your stomach is called chyme. It passes into your small intestine.

- **Your small intestine** is a 6 m long tube where chyme is broken down further, into molecules small enough to be absorbed through the intestine wall into the blood.

- **Food that cannot be** digested in your small intestine passes on into your large intestine. It is then pushed out through your anus as faeces when you go to the toilet (see excretion).

- **Digestive enzymes** play a vital part in breaking food down so it can be absorbed by the body.

▼ The food you eat is broken down into the nutrients your body needs as it passes down through your oesophagus into your stomach and your small intestine. Undigested food travels through your large intestine and leaves your body via your anus.

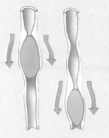

◀ Food is moved through your digestive system by the muscles of the gut wall contracting (tightening) and relaxing. This rippling movement is called peristalsis. Whenever food enters the gut, rings of muscle contract behind it, while muscles in front relax, easing the food slowly forward.

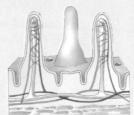

▶ The small intestine is lined with tiny, finger-like folds called villi. On the surface of each villi are even tinier, finger-like folds called microvilli. These folds give a huge area for absorbing food.

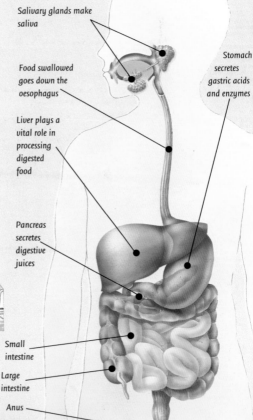

Salivary glands make saliva

Food swallowed goes down the oesophagus

Liver plays a vital role in processing digested food

Pancreas secretes digestive juices

Stomach secretes gastric acids and enzymes

Small intestine

Large intestine

Anus

★ STAR FACT ★
On average, food takes 24 hours to pass right the way through your alimentary canal and out the other end.

Joints

- **Body joints** are places where bones meet.
- **The skull** is not one bone, but 22 separate bones bound tightly together with fibres so that they can't move.
- **Most body joints** (apart from fixed joints like the skull's fibrous joints) let bones move, but different kinds of joint let them move in different ways.
- **Hinge joints**, such as the elbow, let the bones swing to and fro in two directions like door hinges do.
- **In ball-and-socket joints**, such as the hip, the rounded end of one bone sits in the cup-shaped socket of the other and can move in almost any direction.
- **Swivel joints** turn like a wheel on an axle. Your head can swivel to the left or to the right on your spine.

> ★ STAR FACT ★
> The knee joint can bend, straighten and (when slightly bent) rotate.

- **Saddle joints** such as those in the thumb have the bones interlocking like two saddles. These joints allow great mobility with considerable strength.
- **The relatively inflexible** joints between the spine's bones (vertebrae) are cushioned by pads of cartilage.
- **Flexible synovial joints** such as the hip-joint are lubricated with 'synovial fluid' and cushioned by cartilage

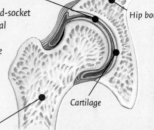

Synovial fluid

Hip bone

▶ The hip joint is a ball-and-socket joint which takes a great deal of wear and tear. When the cushioning layer of cartilage breaks down, it can be replaced with an artificial joint made of special plastics.

Cartilage

Thigh bone

Nerve cells

- **Nerves** are made of cells called neurons.
- **Neurons** are spider-shaped cells with a nucleus at the centre, lots of branching threads called dendrites, and a winding tail called an axon which can be up to 1 m long.
- **Axon terminals** on the axons of one neuron link to the dendrites or cell body of another neuron.
- **Neurons link up** like beads on a

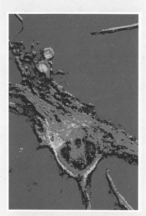

▲ Microscopically tiny nerve cells like this were first seen by being stained with silver nitrate by the Italian scientist Camillo Golgi in the late 19th century.

string to make your nervous system.

- **Most cells are** short-lived and are constantly being replaced by new ones. Some neurons, however, are never replaced after you are born.
- **Nerve signals** travel as electrical pulses, each pulse lasting about 0.001 seconds.
- **When nerves are resting** there are extra sodium ions with a positive electrical charge on the outside of the nerve cell, and extra negative ions inside.
- **When a nerve fires**, little gates open in the cell wall all along the nerve, and positive ions rush in to join the negative ions. This makes an electrical pulse.
- **Long-distance nerves** are insulated by a sheath of a fatty substance, myelin to keep the signal strong.
- **Myelinated (myelin-sheathed) nerves** shoot signals through at about 100 metres per second.
- **Ordinary nerves** send signals at about 1-2 metres per second.

The lungs

- **Your lungs** are a pair of soft, spongy bags inside your chest.

- **When you breathe** in, air rushes in through your nose or mouth, down your trachea (windpipe) and into the hundreds of branching airways in your lungs.

- **The two biggest airways** are called bronchi, and they both branch into smaller airways called bronchioles.

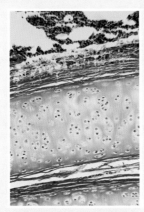

▲ Taken through a powerful microscope, this photo of a slice of lung tissue shows a blood vessel and the very thin walls of an alveolus next to it.

- **The surface of your airways** is protected by a slimy film of mucus, which gets thicker to protect the lungs when you have a cold.

- **At the end of each bronchiole** are bunches of minute air sacs called alveoli (singular alveolus).

- **Alveoli** are wrapped around with tiny blood vessels, and alveoli walls are just one cell thick – thin enough to let oxygen and carbon dioxide seep through them.

- **There are 300 million alveoli** in your lungs.

- **The huge surface area** of all these alveoli makes it possible for huge quantities of oxygen to seep through into the blood. Equally huge quantities of carbon dioxide can seep back into the airways for removal when you breathe out.

> ★ STAR FACT ★
> Opened out and laid flat, the alveoli would cover half a football field.

The liver

- **The liver** is your chemical processing centre.

- **The liver is your** body's biggest internal organ, and the word hepatic means 'to do with the liver'.

- **The liver's prime task** is handling all the nutrients and substances digested from the food you eat and sending them out to your body cells when needed.

- **The liver turns** carbohydrates into glucose, the main energy-giving chemical for body cells.

- **The liver keeps** the levels of glucose in the blood steady. It releases more when levels drop, and by storing it as glycogen, a type of starch, when levels rise.

- **The liver packs off** any excess food energy to be stored as fat around the body.

- **The liver breaks down** proteins and stores vitamins and minerals.

- **The liver produces bile**, the yellowish or greenish bitter liquid that helps dissolve fat as food is digested.

- **The liver clears the blood** of old red cells and harmful substances such as alcohol, and makes new plasma (see blood).

- **The liver's chemical processing units** are thousands of hexagonal-shaped units called lobules. These take in unprocessed blood on the outside and dispatch it through a collecting vein in the centre of each.

▶ The liver is a large organ situated to the right of the stomach.

Genes

- **Genes** are the body's chemical instructions for your entire life – for growing up, surviving, having children and, perhaps, even for dying.

- **Individual genes** are instructions to make particular proteins, the body's building-block molecules.

- **Small sets of genes** control features such as the colour of your hair or your eyes, or create a particular body process such as digesting fat from food.

- **Each of your body cells** (except egg and sperm cells) carries identical sets of genes. This is because all your cells were made by other cells splitting in two, starting with the original egg cell in your mother.

- **Your genes are a mixture** – half come from your mother and half from your father (see chromosomes). But none of your brothers or sisters will get the same mix, unless you are identical twins.

- **Genes make us unique** – making us tall or short, fair or dark, brilliant dancers or speakers, healthy or likely to get particular illnesses, and so on.

- **Genes are sections** of DNA – a microscopically tiny molecule inside each cell.

- **DNA** is shaped in a double helix with linking bars, like a twisted rope ladder.

> ★ **STAR FACT** ★
> There are more than 30,000 individual genes inside every single cell of your body.

- **The bars of DNA** are four special chemicals called bases – guanine, adenine, cytosine and thymine.

- **The bases in DNA** are set in groups of three called codons, and the order of the bases in each codon varies to provide a chemical code for the cell to make a particular amino acid. The cell puts together different amino acids to make different proteins.

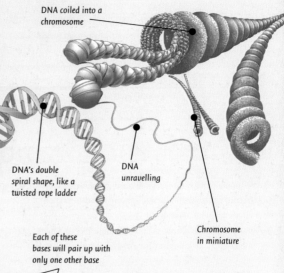

DNA coiled into a chromosome

'Rungs' made from four different chemical bases

DNA's double spiral shape, like a twisted rope ladder

DNA unravelling

The new copy, called RNA, is used to make the proteins

Chromosome in miniature

Each of these bases will pair up with only one other base

Strands of DNA dividing to make a template

◄ DNA (Deoxyribonucleic Acid) is the amazing tiny molecule inside every cell that carries all your genes in a chemical code – the genetic code. Most of the time it is coiled up inside the chromosomes, but when needed it unravels to reveal its double helix shape. Each of the four bases that make the rungs pairs with only one other: guanine with cytosine, and adenine with thymine. So the sequence of bases along one strand of the DNA is a perfect mirror image of the sequence on the other side. When the strand temporarily divides down the middle, each strand can be used like a template to make a copy. This is how instructions are issued.

Breathing

- **You breathe** because every single cell in your body needs a continuous supply of oxygen to burn glucose, the high-energy substance from digested food that cells get from blood.
- **Scientists** call breathing 'respiration'. Cellular respiration is the way that cells use oxygen to burn glucose.
- **The oxygen in air** is taken into your lungs, and then carried in your blood to your body cells.
- **Waste carbon dioxide** from your cells is returned by your blood to your lungs, to be breathed out.
- **On average** you breathe in about 15 times a minute. If you run hard, the rate soars to around 80 times a minute.
- **Newborn babies** breathe about 40 times a minute.
- **If you live to the age of 80**, you will have taken well over 600 million breaths.
- **A normal breath** takes in about 0.4 litres of air. A deep breath can take in ten times as much.

- **Your diaphragm** is a dome-shaped sheet of muscle between your chest and stomach, which works with your chest muscles to make you breathe in and out.
- **Scientists** call breathing in 'inhalation', and breathing out 'exhalation'.

▶ Air is sucked in through your nose and mouth as your diaphragm pulls your lungs down and your chest muscles pull your ribs up and out. Air is forced out again when the diaphragm arches up and the rib muscles relax to allow the ribs to tilt down.

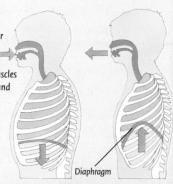

Diaphragm

Co-ordination

- **Co-ordination** means balanced or skilful movement.
- **To make you move**, your brain has to send signals out along nerves telling all the muscles involved exactly what to do.

◀ Ball skills demand incredible muscle co-ordination. The eyes follow the ball to tell the brain exactly where it is. At the same time, the brain also relies on a high-speed stream of sensory signals from the proprioceptor cells in order to tell it exactly where the leg is, and to keep the body perfectly balanced.

- **Co-ordination of the muscles** is handled by the cerebellum at the back of your brain (see the brain).
- **The cerebellum** is told what to do by the brain's motor cortex (see the cortex).
- **The cerebellum sends** its commands via the basal ganglia in the middle of the brain.
- **Proprioceptor** means 'one's own sensors', and proprioceptors are nerve cells that are sensitive to movement, pressure or stretching.
- **Proprioceptors are all over your body** – in muscles, tendons and joints – and they all send signals to your brain telling it the position or posture of every body part.
- **The hair cells** in the balance organs of your ear are also proprioceptors (see balance).

★ STAR FACT ★
Proprioceptors are what allow you to touch forefingers behind your back.

Mood

- **Mood is** your state of mind – whether you are happy or sad, angry or afraid, overjoyed or depressed.

- **Moods and emotions** seem to be strongly linked to the structures in the centre of the brain, where unconscious activities are controlled (see the brain).

- **Moods** have three elements – how you feel, what happens to your body, and what they make you do.

- **Some scientists** think the way you feel causes changes in the body – you are happy so you smile, for example.

- **Other scientists** think changes in the body alter the way you feel – smiling makes you happy.

- **Yet other scientists** think moods start automatically – before you even know it – when something triggers off a reaction in the thalamus in the centre of the brain.

- **The thalamus** then sends mood signals to the brain's cortex and you become aware of the mood.

- **The thalamus** also sets off automatic changes in the body through nerves and hormones.

- **Certain memories or experiences** are so strongly linked in your mind that they can trigger a certain mood.

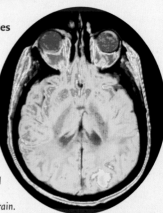

▶ *Scientists are only just beginning to discover how moods and emotions are linked to particular parts of the brain.*

> ★ **STAR FACT** ★
> In one experiment, people injected with adrenaline found rotten jokes much funnier!

Fats

- **Fats** are an important source of energy. Together with proteins and carbohydrates, they make up your body's three main components of foods.

- **While carbohydrates** are generally used for energy immediately, your body often stores fat to use for energy in times of shortage.

- **Weight for weight**, fats contain twice as much energy as carbohydrates.

- **Fats (or lipids)** are important organic (life) substances, found in almost every living thing. They are made from substances called fatty acids and glycerol.

- **Food fats** are greasy, vegetable or animal fats that will not dissolve in water.

- **Most vegetable fats** such as corn oil and olive oil are liquid, although some nut fats are solid.

◀ *Fats are either saturated or unsaturated. Cheese is a saturated fat, which means its fatty acids are saturated with as much hydrogen as they can hold. Saturated fats are linked to high levels of the substance cholesterol in the blood and may increase certain health risks such as heart attack.*

- **Most animal fats** as in meats, milk and cheese are solid. Milk is mainly water with some solid animal fats. Most solid fats melt when warmed.

- **Fats called triglycerides** are stored around the body as adipose tissue (body fat). These act as energy stores and also insulate the body against the cold.

- **Fats called phospholipids** are used to build body cells.

- **In your stomach**, bile from your liver and enzymes from your pancreas break fats down into fatty acids and glycerol. These are absorbed into your body's lymphatic system or enter the blood.

Capillaries

- **Capillaries** are the smallest of all your blood vessels, only visible under a microscope. They link the arterioles to the venules (see circulation).
- **Capillaries** were discovered by Marcello Malphigi in 1661.
- **There are 10 billion capillaries** in your body.
- **The largest capillary** is just 0.2 mm wide – thinner than a hair.

▲ The work done by an athlete's muscles generates a lot of heat – which the body tries to lose by opening up capillaries in the skin, turning the skin bright red.

- **Each capillary** is about 0.5 mm to 1 mm long.
- **Capillary walls** are just one cell thick, so it is easy for chemicals to pass through them.
- **It is through the capillary walls** that your blood passes oxygen, food and waste to and from each one of your body cells.
- **There are many more capillaries** in active tissues such as muscles, liver and kidneys than there are in tendons and ligaments.
- **Capillaries** carry more or less blood according to need. They let more blood reach the surface when you are warm. They let less blood reach the surface to save heat when you are cold.

> ★ STAR FACT ★
> The average capillary is 0.001 mm in diameter – just wide enough for red blood cells to pass through one at a time.

Germs

- **Germs** are microscopic organisms that enter your body and harm it in some way.
- **The scientific word** for 'germ' is 'pathogen'.
- **When germs** begin to multiply inside your body, you are suffering from an infectious disease.
- **An infection** that spreads throughout your body (flu or measles, for example) is called a systemic infection.
- **An infection** that affects only a small area (such as dirt in a cut) is called a localized infection.
- **It is often the reaction** of your body's immune system to the germ that makes you feel ill.
- **Bacteria** are single-celled organisms. They are found almost everywhere in huge numbers, and they multiply rapidly.

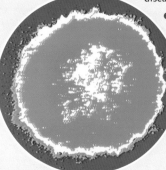

- **Most bacteria are harmless**, but there are three harmful groups – cocci are round cells, spirilla are coil-shaped, and bacilli are rod-shaped. These harmful bacteria cause diseases such as tetanus and typhoid.
- **Viruses** can only live and multiply by taking over other cells – they cannot survive on their own. They cause diseases such as colds, flu, mumps and AIDS.
- **Parasites** are animals such as tapeworms that may live in or on your body, feeding on it and making you ill.
- **Fungal spores** and tiny organisms called protozoa can also cause illness.

◄ The disease AIDS (Acquired Immune Deficiency Syndrome) is caused by a virus called HIV. This virus gets inside vital cells of the body's immune system and weakens its ability to fight against other infections.

Motor nerves

▲ *Motor nerves fire to make muscles move to hit the ball.*

- **Motor nerves** tell your muscles to move.

- **Each major muscle** has many motor nerve-endings that instruct it to contract (tighten).

- **Motor nerves cross over** from one side of your body to the other at the top of your spinal cord. This means that signals from the right side of your brain go to the left side of your body, and vice versa.

- **Each motor nerve** is paired to a proprioceptor on the muscle and its tendons (see co-ordination). This sends signals to the brain to say whether the muscle is tensed or relaxed.

- **If the strain** on a tendon increases, the proprioceptor sends a signal to the brain. The brain adjusts the motor signals to the muscle so it contracts more or less.

- **Motor nerve signals** originate in a part of the brain called the motor cortex (see the cortex).

- **All the motor nerves** (apart from those in the head) branch out from the spinal cord.

- **The gut** has no motor nerve-endings but plenty of sense endings, so you can feel it but cannot move it consciously.

- **The throat** has motor nerve-endings but few sense endings, so you can move it but not feel it.

- **Motor neuron disease** is a disease that attacks motor nerves within the central nervous system.

Glucose

- **Glucose** is the body's energy chemical, used as the fuel in all cell activity.

- **Glucose is a kind of sugar** made by plants as they take energy from sunlight. It is common in many fruits and fruit juices, along with fructose (see carbohydrates).

- **The body gets its glucose** from carbohydrates in food, broken down in stages in the intestine.

- **From the intestine**, glucose travels in the blood to the liver, where excess is stored in the form of glycogen.

- **For the body to work effectively**, levels of glucose in the blood (called blood sugar) must always be correct.

- **Blood sugar levels** are controlled by two hormones, glucagon and insulin, sent out by the pancreas.

- **When blood sugar is low**, the pancreas sends glucagon to the liver to tell it to change more glycogen to glucose.

- **When blood sugar is high**, the pancreas sends insulin to the liver to tell it to store more glucose as glycogen.

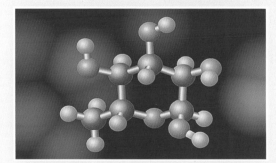

▲ *Glucose is built from 6 carbon, 12 hydrogen and 6 oxygen atoms.*

- **Inside cells**, glucose may be burned for energy, stored as glycogen, or used to make triglyceride fats (see fats).

> ★ STAR FACT ★
> Adrenaline and other hormones from the adrenals boost blood sugar levels.

The immune system

- **The immune system** is the complicated system of defences that your body uses to prevent or fight off attack from germs and other invaders.

- **Your body** has a variety of barriers, toxic chemicals and booby traps to stop germs entering it. The skin is a barrier that stops many germs getting in, as long as it is not broken.

- **Mucus is a thick, slimy fluid** that coats vulnerable internal parts of your body such as your stomach. It also acts as a lubricant (oil), making swallowing easier.

- **Mucus lines your airways** and lungs to protect them from smoke particles as well as from germs. Your airways may fill up with mucus when you have a cold, as your body tries to minimize the invasion of airborne germs.

> ★ STAR FACT ★
> Your vulnerable eyes are protected by tears which wash away germs. Tears also contain an enzyme called lysozome which kills bacteria.

- **Itching, sneezing, coughing and vomiting** are your body's ways of getting rid of unwelcome invaders. Small particles that get trapped in the mucus lining of your airways are wafted out by tiny hairs called cilia.

- **The body** has many specialized cells and chemicals which fight germs that get inside you.

- **Complement** is a mixture of liquid proteins in the blood which attacks bacteria.

- **Interferon** are proteins which help the body's cells to attack viruses and also stimulate killer cells (see lymphocytes).

- **Certain white blood cells** are cytotoxic, which means they are poisonous to invaders.

- **Phagocytes** are big white blood cells that swallow up invaders and then use an enzyme to dissolve them (see antibodies). They are drawn to the site of an infection whenever there is inflammation.

▶ HIV, the AIDS virus, attacks the body's immune cells and prevents them dealing with infections.

▼ The body's range of interior defences against infection is amazingly complex. The various kinds of white blood cells and the antibodies they make are particularly important.

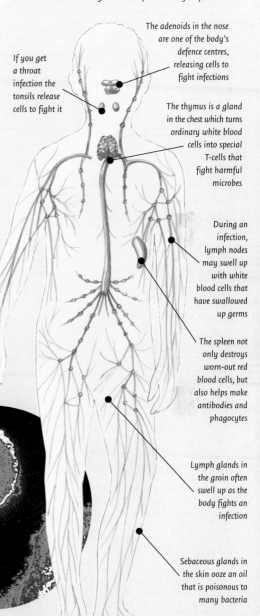

The adenoids in the nose are one of the body's defence centres, releasing cells to fight infections

If you get a throat infection the tonsils release cells to fight it

The thymus is a gland in the chest which turns ordinary white blood cells into special T-cells that fight harmful microbes

During an infection, lymph nodes may swell up with white blood cells that have swallowed up germs

The spleen not only destroys worn-out red blood cells, but also helps make antibodies and phagocytes

Lymph glands in the groin often swell up as the body fights an infection

Sebaceous glands in the skin ooze an oil that is poisonous to many bacteria

Heredity

- **Your heredity** is all the body characteristics you inherit from your parents, whether it is your mother's black hair or your father's knobbly knees.
- **Characteristics** are passed on by the genes carried on your chromosomes (see genes, chromosomes).
- **The basic laws** of heredity were discovered by the Austrian monk Gregor Mendel 150 years ago.
- **Your body characteristics** are a mix of two sets of instructions – one from your mother's chromosomes and the other from your father's.
- **Each characteristic** is the work of only one gene – either your mother's or your father's. This gene is said to be 'expressed'.
- **The gene that is not expressed** does not vanish. Instead, it stays dormant (asleep) in your chromosomes, possibly to pass on to your children.
- **A gene** that is always expressed is called the dominant gene.

- **A recessive gene** is one that loses out to a dominant gene and stays dormant.
- **A recessive gene** may be expressed when there is no competition – that is, when the genes from both of your parents are recessive.

▲ *The gene for blue eyes is recessive, but if a girl gets a blue-eye gene from both of her parents, she may have blue eyes.*

Fitness

- **Fitness** is about how much and what kind of physical activity you can do without getting tired or strained.
- **Fitness depends** on your strength, flexibility (bendiness) and endurance (staying power).
- **One key to fitness** is cardiovascular fitness – that is, how well

◀ *Skiing is one of the most demanding of all sports, and top skiers need to be extremely fit to cope with the extra strain on their bodies.*

your heart and lungs respond to the extra demands of exercise.
- **One measure of cardiovascular fitness** is how quickly your pulse rate returns to normal after exercise – the fitter you are, the quicker it returns.
- **Another measure of cardiovascular fitness** is how slowly your heart beats during exercise – the fitter you are, the slower it beats.
- **Being fit** improves your physical performance.
- **Being fit often** protects against illness.
- **Being fit can** slow down the effects of ageing.
- **Cardiovascular fitness** reduces the chances of getting heart disease.
- **Fitness tests** involve comparing such things as height, weight and body fat, and measuring blood pressure and pulse rate before and after exercise. Other tests may measure how you manage a standard exercise, such as running over a fixed distance.

Heartbeat

- **The heartbeat** is the regular squeezing of the heart muscle to pump blood around the body.
- **Four heart valves** make sure blood only moves one way.
- **The heartbeat** is a sequence called the cardiac cycle and it has two phases – systole and diastole.
- **Systole** is when the heart muscle contracts (tightens). Diastole is the resting phase between contractions.
- **Systole begins** when a wave of muscle contraction sweeps across the heart and squeezes blood from each of the atria into the two ventricles.
- **When the contraction** reaches the ventricles, they squeeze blood into the arteries.
- **In diastole**, the heart muscle relaxes and the atria fill with blood again.
- **Heart muscle** on its own would contract automatically.
- **Nerve signals** make the heart beat faster or slower.

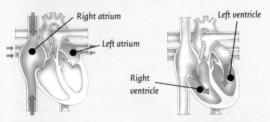 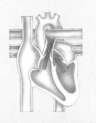 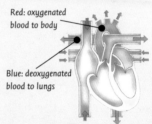

Right atrium

Left atrium

Left ventricle

Right ventricle

Red: oxygenated blood to body

Blue: deoxygenated blood to lungs

▲ Blood floods into the relaxed atria.

▲ The wave of contraction squeezes blood into ventricles.

▲ Blood is squeezed out the ventricles into the arteries.

▲ Blood starts to fill up the now relaxed atria again.

Blood

- **Blood** is the liquid that circulates around your body. It carries oxygen and food to body cells, and takes carbon dioxide and other waste away. It fights infection, keeps you warm, and distributes chemicals that control body processes.
- **Blood is made up of** red cells, white cells and platelets, all carried in a liquid called plasma.
- **Plasma** is 90% water, plus hundreds of other substances, including nutrients, hormones and special proteins for fighting infection.
- **Blood plasma** turns milky immediately after a meal high in fats.
- **Platelets** are tiny pieces of cell that make blood clots start to form to stop bleeding.
- **Blood clots also** involve a lacy, fibrous network made from a protein called fibrin. Fibrin is set in action by a

◄ Blood contains red cells and white cells, but is mainly a watery liquid called plasma.

sequence of chemicals called factors (factors I through to 8).

- **The amount of blood** in your body depends on your size. An adult who weighs 80 kg has about 5 litres of blood. A child who is half as heavy has half as much blood.
- **People who live high up mountains** have at least 20% more blood to carry more oxygen – this is because the higher you are, the less oxygen there is in the air.
- **If a blood donor** gives 0.5 litres of blood, the body replaces the plasma in a few hours, but it takes a few weeks to replace the red cells.

★ STAR FACT ★
Oxygen turns blood bright red when you bleed. In your veins it can be almost brown.

The heart

- **Your heart** is the size of your fist. It is inside the middle of your chest, slightly to the left.
- **The heart is a powerful pump** made almost entirely of muscle.
- **The heart contracts** (tightens) and relaxes automatically about 70 times a minute to pump blood out through your arteries.
- **The heart has two sides** separated by a muscle wall called the septum.
- **The right side** is smaller and weaker, and it pumps blood only to the lungs.
- **The stronger left side** pumps blood around the body.

- **Each side of the heart** has two chambers. There is an atrium (plural atria) at the top where blood accumulates (builds up) from the veins, and a ventricle below which contracts to pump blood out into the arteries.
- **Each of the heart's four chambers** ejects about 70 ml of blood with each beat.
- **There are two valves** in each side of the heart to make sure that blood flows only one way – a large one between the atrium and the ventricle, and a small one at the exit from the ventricle into the artery.
- **The coronary arteries** supply the heart. If they become clogged, the heart muscle may be short of blood and stop working. This is what happens in a heart attack.

> ★ STAR FACT ★
> During an average lifetime, the heart pumps
> 200 million litres of blood – enough to fill
> New York's Central Park to a depth of 15 m.

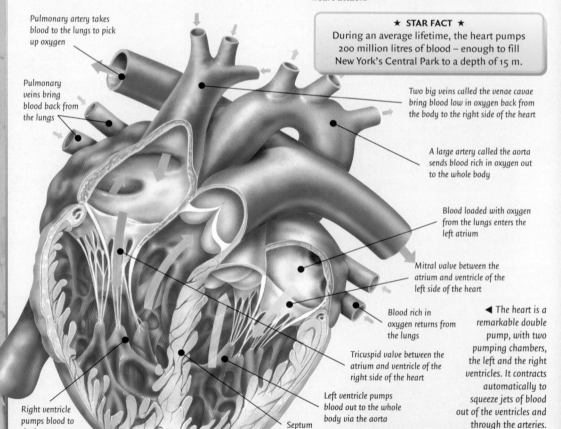

Pulmonary artery takes blood to the lungs to pick up oxygen

Pulmonary veins bring blood back from the lungs

Two big veins called the venae cavae bring blood low in oxygen back from the body to the right side of the heart

A large artery called the aorta sends blood rich in oxygen out to the whole body

Blood loaded with oxygen from the lungs enters the left atrium

Mitral valve between the atrium and ventricle of the left side of the heart

Blood rich in oxygen returns from the lungs

Tricuspid valve between the atrium and ventricle of the right side of the heart

Left ventricle pumps blood out to the whole body via the aorta

Right ventricle pumps blood to the lungs

Septum

◄ The heart is a remarkable double pump, with two pumping chambers, the left and the right ventricles. It contracts automatically to squeeze jets of blood out of the ventricles and through the arteries.

Pregnancy

- **Pregnancy** begins when a woman's ovum (egg cell) is fertilized by a man's sperm cell. Usually this happens after sexual intercourse, but it can begin in a laboratory.

- **When a woman becomes pregnant** her monthly menstrual periods stop. Tests on her urine show whether she is pregnant.

- **During pregnancy**, the fertilized egg divides again and again to grow rapidly – first to an embryo (the first eight weeks), and then to a foetus (from eight weeks until birth).

- **Unlike an embryo**, a foetus has grown legs and arms, as well as internal organs such as a heart.

- **Pregnancy lasts nine months**, and the time is divided into three trimesters (periods of about 12 weeks).

- **The foetus** lies cushioned in its mother's uterus (womb) in a bag of fluid called the amniotic sac.

- **The mother's blood** passes food and oxygen to the foetus via the placenta, or afterbirth.

- **The umbilical cord** runs between the foetus and the placenta, carrying blood between them.

- **During pregnancy** a woman gains 30% more blood, and her heart rate goes up.

- **During pregnancy** a woman's breasts grow and develop milk glands.

▼ *During pregnancy, a woman has ultrasound scans to check that the foetus is healthy and growing properly.*

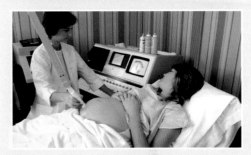

Muscle movement

◄ *A very high-powered electron microscope reveals purple myofibrils of myosin – each little more than 0.00001 mm wide. The orange is actin.*

- **Most muscles are long and thin** and they work by pulling themselves shorter, sometimes contracting by up to half their length.

- **Skeletal muscles**, which make you move, are made of cells which have not just one nucleus like other cells do, but many nuclei in a long fibre, called a myofibre.

- **Muscles are made** from hundreds or thousands of these fibres bound together like fibres in string.

- **Muscle fibres** are made from tiny strands called

> ★ STAR FACT ★
> If all the muscles in your body pulled together, they could lift a bus.

myofibrils, each marked with dark bands, giving the muscle its name of stripey or 'striated' muscle.

- **The stripes** in muscle are alternate bands of filaments of two substances: actin and myosin.

- **The actin and myosin** interlock, like teeth on a zip.

- **When a nerve signal** comes from the brain, chemical 'hooks' on the myosin twist and yank the actin filaments along, shortening the muscle.

- **The chemical hooks** on myosin are made from a stem called a cross-bridge and a head made of a chemical called adenosine triphosphate or ATP.

- **ATP is sensitive to calcium**, and the nerve signal from the brain that tells the muscle to contract does its work by releasing a flood of calcium to trigger the ATP.

Reflexes

- **Reflexes** are muscle movements that are automatic (they happen without you thinking about them).

- **Inborn reflexes** are reflexes you were born with, such as urinating or shivering when you are cold.

- **The knee-jerk** is an inborn reflex that makes your leg jerk up when the tendon below your knee is tapped.

- **Primitive reflexes** are reflexes that babies have for a few months after they are born.

- **One primitive reflex** is when you put something in a baby's hand and it automatically grips it.

- **Conditioned reflexes** are those you learn through habit, as certain pathways in the nervous system are used again and again.

- **Conditioned reflexes** help you do anything from holding a cup to playing football without thinking.

- **Reflex reactions** are what pull your hand from hot things before you have had time to think about it.

▲ Many sportsmen rely on lightning reflexes – actions too fast for the brain to even think about.

- **Reflex reactions** work by short-circuiting the brain. The alarm signal from your hand sets off motor signals in the spinal cord to move the hand.

- **A reflex arc** is the nerve circuit from sense to muscle via the spinal cord.

The kidneys

- **The kidneys** are a pair of bean-shaped organs inside the small of the back.

- **The kidneys** are the body's water control and blood-cleaning plants.

- **The kidneys** are high-speed filters that draw off water and important substances from the blood. They let unwanted water and waste substances go (see urine).

- **The kidneys filter** about 1.3 litres of blood a minute.

Nephrons

Ureter

◄ This cross-section diagram of a kidney shows blood entering through arteries (red) and leaving through veins (blue). Waste fluid drains away through the ureter (shown in yellow).

- **All the blood** flows through the kidneys every ten minutes, so blood is filtered 150 times a day.

- **The kidneys manage** to recycle every re-useable substance from the blood. It takes 85 litres of water and other blood substances from every 1,000 litres of blood, but only lets out 0.6 litres as urine.

- **The kidneys** save nearly all the amino acids and glucose from the blood and 70% of the salt.

- **Blood entering each kidney** is filtered through a million or more filtration units called nephrons.

- **Each nephron** is an incredibly intricate network of little pipes called convoluted tubules, wrapped around countless tiny capilliaries. Useful blood substances are filtered into the tubules, then re-absorbed back into the blood in the capilliaries.

- **Blood enters each nephron** through a cup called the Bowman's capsule via a bundle of capilliaries.

Puberty

- **Puberty** is the time of life when girls and boys mature sexually.
- **The age of puberty varies**, but on average it is between 11 and 13 years.
- **Puberty is started** by two hormones sent out by the pituitary gland (see the brain) – the follicle-stimulating hormone and the luteinizing hormone.
- **During puberty, a girl** will develop breasts and grow hair under her arms and around her genitals.
- **Inside her body**, a girl's ovaries grow ten times as big and release sex hormones (see reproduction – girls).
- **The sex hormones** oestrogen and progesterone spur the development of a girl's sexual organs and control her monthly menstrual cycle.

▲ In their early teens, girls go through puberty and begin to develop the sexual characteristics that will make them women.

> ★ STAR FACT ★
> By the time a boy is 15, his testicles can make 200 million new sperm a day.

- **A year or so after puberty begins**, a girl has her menarche (the first menstrual period). When her periods come regularly, she is able to have a baby.
- **For a boy during puberty**, his testes grow and hair sprouts on his face, under his arms and around his genitals.
- **Inside his body**, a boy's testes begin to make sperm.

The lymphatic system

    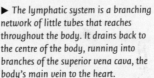

- **The lymphatic system** is your body's sewer, the network of pipes that drains waste from the cells.
- **The 'pipes' of the lymphatic system** are called lymphatics or lymph vessels.
- **The lymphatics** are filled by a watery liquid called lymph fluid which, along with bacteria and waste chemicals, drains from body tissues such as muscles.
- **The lymphatic system** has no pump to make it circulate. Instead, lymphatic fluid is circulated as a side effect of the heartbeat and muscle movement.
- **At places** in the lymphatic system there are tiny lumps called nodes. These are filters which trap germs that have got into the lymph fluid.
- **In the nodes**, armies of white blood cells called lymphocytes neutralize or destroy germs.
- **When you have** a cold or any other infection, the lymph nodes in your neck or groin, or under your arm, may swell, as lymphocytes fight germs.

▶ The lymphatic system is a branching network of little tubes that reaches throughout the body. It drains back to the centre of the body, running into branches of the superior vena cava, the body's main vein to the heart.

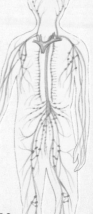

- **Lymph fluid** drains back into the blood via the body's main vein, the superior vena cava.
- **The lymphatic system** is not only the lymphatics and lymph nodes, but includes the spleen, the thymus, the tonsils and the adenoids (see the immune system).
- **On average**, at any time about 1 to 2 litres of lymph fluid circulate in the lymphatics and body tissues.

Reproduction – girls

- **A girl or woman's reproductive system** is where her body stores, releases and nurtures the egg cells (ova – singular, ovum) that create a new human life when joined with a male sperm cell.

- **All the egg cells** are stored from birth in the ovaries – two egg-shaped glands inside the pelvic region. Each egg is stored in a tiny sac called a follicle.

- **One egg cell** is released every monthly menstrual cycle by one of the ovaries.

- **A monthly menstrual cycle starts** when follicle-stimulating hormone (FSH) is sent by the pituitary gland in the brain to spur follicles to grow.

- **As follicles grow,** they release the sex hormone oestrogen. Oestrogen makes the lining of the uterus (womb) thicken.

- **When an egg is ripe,** it slides down a duct called a Fallopian tube.

- **If a woman** has sexual intercourse at this time, sperm from the man's penis may swim up her vagina, enter her womb and fertilize the egg in the Fallopian tube.

- **If the egg is fertilized,** the womb lining goes on thickening ready for pregnancy, and the egg begins to develop into an embryo.

- **If the egg is not fertilized,** it is shed with the womb lining in a flow of blood from the vagina. This shedding is called a menstrual period.

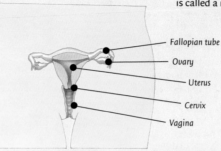

Fallopian tube
Ovary
Uterus
Cervix
Vagina

◄ This is a frontal view of the inside of a female reproductive system, showing the two ovaries and Fallopian tubes, which join to the uterus.

Lymphocytes

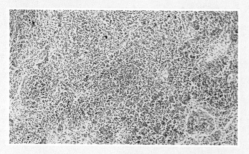

▲ A lymph node packed with lymphocytes fighting infection.

- **Lymphocytes** are white blood cells that play a role in the body's immune system, which targets invading germs.

- **There are two kinds of lymphocyte** – B lymphocytes (B-cells) and T lymphocytes (T-cells).

- **B-cells** develop into plasma cells that make antibodies to attack bacteria such as those which cause cholera, as well as some viruses (see antibodies).

- **T-cells** work against viruses and other micro-organisms that hide inside body cells. T-cells help identify and destroy these invaded cells or their products. They also attack certain bacteria.

- **There are two kinds of T-cell** – killers and helpers.

- **Helper T-cells** identify invaded cells and send out chemicals called lymphokines as an alarm, telling killer T-cells to multiply.

- **Invaded cells** give themselves away by abnormal proteins on their surface.

- **Killer T-cells** lock on to the cells identified by the helpers, then move in and destroy them.

- **Some B-cells,** called memory B-cells, stay for a long time, ready for a further attack by the same organism.

> ★ STAR FACT ★
> If you get flu, it is your T lymphocytes that come to the rescue and fight off the virus.

The ear

- **Pinnae** (singular, pinna) are the ear flaps you can see on the side of your head, and they are simply collecting funnels for sounds.

- **A little way inside your head**, sounds hit a thin, tight wall of skin, called the eardrum, making it vibrate.

- **When the eardrum vibrates**, it shakes three little bones called ossicles. These are the smallest bones in the body.

- **The three ossicle bones** are the malleus (hammer), the incus (anvil) and the stapes (stirrup).

> ★ STAR FACT ★
> If your hearing is normal, you can hear
> sounds as deep as 20 Hertz (Hz) – vibrations
> per second – and as high as 20,000 Hz.

- **When the ossicles vibrate**, they rattle a tiny membrane called the oval window, intensifying the vibration.

- **The oval window** is 30 times smaller than the eardrum.

- **Beyond the oval window** is the cochlea – a winding collection of three, liquid-filled tubes, which looks a bit like a snail shell.

- **In the middle tube** of the cochlea there is a flap which covers row upon row of tiny hairs. This is called the organ of Corti.

- **When sounds make** the eardrum vibrate, the ossicles tap on the oval window, making pressure waves shoot through the liquid in the cochlea and wash over the flap of the organ of Corti, waving it up and down.

- **When the organ of Corti waves**, it tugs on the tiny hairs under the flap. These send signals to the brain via the auditory nerve – and you hear a sound.

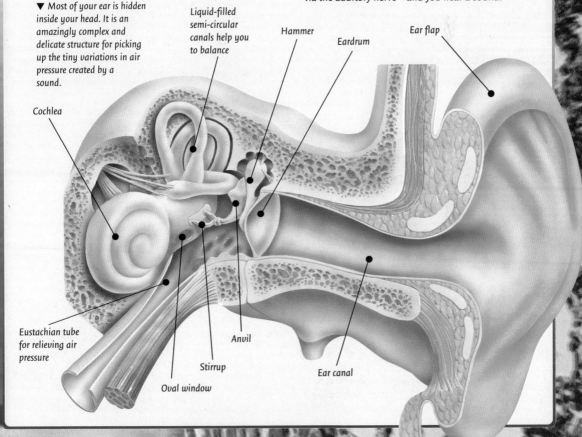

▼ Most of your ear is hidden inside your head. It is an amazingly complex and delicate structure for picking up the tiny variations in air pressure created by a sound.

Liquid-filled semi-circular canals help you to balance

Hammer

Eardrum

Ear flap

Cochlea

Eustachian tube for relieving air pressure

Anvil

Stirrup

Oval window

Ear canal

Excretion

- **Digestive excretion** is the way your body gets rid of food that it cannot digest.
- **Undigested food** is prepared for excretion in your large intestine or bowel.
- **The main part** of the large intestine is the colon, which is almost as long as you are tall.
- **The colon** converts the semi-liquid 'chyme' (see digestion) of undigested food into solid waste, by absorbing water.
- **The colon** soaks up 1.5 litres of water every day.
- **The colon walls** also absorb sodium and chlorine and get rid of bicarbonate and potassium.
- **Billions of bacteria** live inside the colon and help turn the chyme into faeces. These bacteria are

◀ To work well, your bowel needs plenty of roughage, the indigestible cellulose plant fibres found in food such as beans and wholemeal bread. Roughage keeps the muscles of the bowel properly exercised.

harmless as long as they do not spread to the rest of the body.

- **Bacteria in the colon** make vitamins K and B – as well as smelly gases such as methane and hydrogen sulphide.
- **The muscles of the colon** break the waste food down into segments ready for excretion.

> ★ STAR FACT ★
> About a third of all faeces is not old food but 'friendly' gut bacteria and intestinal lining.

Cartilage

- **Cartilage is a rubbery** substance used in various places around the body. You can feel cartilage in your ear flap if you move it back and forward.
- **Cartilage is made** from cells called chondrocytes embedded in a jelly-like ground substance with fibres of collagen, all wrapped in an envelope of tough fibres.
- **There are three types:** hyaline, fibrous and elastic.
- **Hyaline cartilage** is the most widespread in your body. It is almost clear, pearly white and quite stiff.
- **Hyaline cartilage** is used in many of the joints between bones to cushion them against impacts.
- **Fibrous cartilage** is really tough cartilage used in between the bones of the spine and in the knee.
- **Cartilage in the knee** makes two dish shapes called menisci between the thigh and shin bones. Footballers often damage these cartilages.
- **Elastic cartilage** is very flexible and used in your airways, nose and ears.

- **Cartilage grows** quicker than bone, and the skeletons of babies in the womb are mostly cartilage, which gradually ossifies (hardens to bone).
- **Osteoarthritis** is when joint cartilage breaks down, making movements painful.

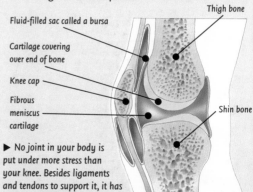

Fluid-filled sac called a bursa
Cartilage covering over end of bone
Knee cap
Fibrous meniscus cartilage
Thigh bone
Shin bone

▶ No joint in your body is put under more stress than your knee. Besides ligaments and tendons to support it, it has a thick cushion of cartilage.

Hormones

- **Hormones are** the body's chemical messengers, released from stores at times to trigger certain reactions in different parts of the body.

- **Most hormones** are endocrine hormones which are spread around your body in your bloodstream.

- **Each hormone** is a molecule with a certain shape that creates a certain effect on target cells.

- **Hormones are controlled** by feedback systems. This means they are only released when their store gets the right trigger – which may be a chemical in the blood or another hormone.

- **Major hormone sources** include: the thyroid gland; the pituitary glands; the adrenal glands; the pancreas; a woman's ovaries; a man's testes.

- **The pituitary** is the source of many important hormones, including growth hormones which spur growing.

- **Adrenalin** is released by the adrenals to ready your body for action.

▲ In hairy moments, adrenalin boosts your breathing and heartbeat, makes your eyes widen and your skin sweat.

- **Endorphins and enkephalins** block or relieve pain.

- **Oestrogen and progesterone** are female sex hormones that control a woman's monthly cycle.

- **Testosterone** is a male sex hormone which controls the workings of a man's sex organs.

Exercise

- **If you exercise hard,** your muscles burn energy 20 times as fast as normal, so they need much more oxygen and glucose (a kind of sugar) from the blood.

- **To boost oxygen,** your heart beats twice as fast and pumps twice as much blood, and your lungs take in ten times more air with each breath.

- **To boost glucose,** adrenalin triggers your liver to release its store of glucose.

▲ A sportsman such as a football player builds up his body's ability to supply oxygen to his muscles by regular aerobic training.

- **If oxygen delivery** to muscles lags, the muscles fill up with lactic acid, and can cause painful cramp.

- **The fitter you are,** the quicker your body returns to normal after exercise.

- **Aerobic exercise** is exercise that is long and hard enough for the oxygen supply to the muscles to rise enough to match the rapid burning of glucose.

- **Regular aerobic exercise** strengthens your heart and builds up your body's ability to supply extra oxygen through your lungs to your muscles.

- **Regular exercise** thickens and multiplies muscle fibres and strengthens tendons.

- **Regular exercise** can help reduce weight when it is combined with a controlled diet.

> ★ STAR FACT ★
> When you exercise hard, your body burns up energy 20 times as fast as normal.

The eye

- **Your eyes** are tough balls filled with a jelly-like substance called vitreous humour.

- **The cornea** is a thin, glassy dish across the front of your eye. It allows light rays through the eye's window, the pupil, and into the lens.

- **The iris** is the coloured muscular ring around the pupil. The iris narrows in bright light and widens when light is dim.

- **The lens** is just behind the pupil. It focuses the picture of the world on to the back of the eye.

- **The back of the eye** is lined with millions of light-sensitive cells. This lining is called the retina, and it registers the picture and sends signals to the brain via the optic nerve.

- **There are two kinds** of light-sensitive cell in the retina – rods and cones. Rods are very sensitive and work in even dim light, but they cannot detect colours. Cones respond to colour.

- **Some kinds of cone** are very sensitive to red light, some to green and some to blue. One theory says that the colours we see depend on how strongly they affect each of these three kinds of cone (see colour vision).

- **Each of your two eyes** gives you a slightly different view of the world. The brain combines these views to give an impression of depth and 3-D solidity.

- **Although each eye** gives a slightly different view of the world, we see things largely as just one eye sees it. This dominant eye is usually the right eye.

▼ This illustration shows your two eyeballs, with one cut away to reveal the cornea and lens (which projects the picture of the world) and the light-sensitive retina (which registers it).

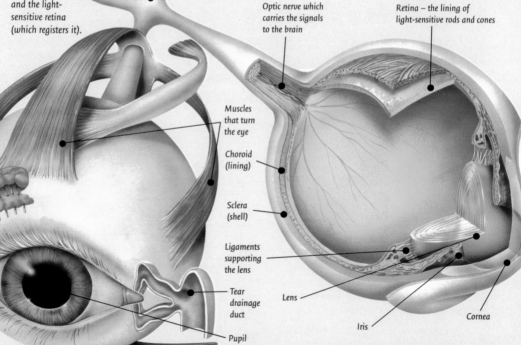

Optic chiasma in brain where signals from each eye cross over

Optic nerve which carries the signals to the brain

Retina – the lining of light-sensitive rods and cones

Muscles that turn the eye

Choroid (lining)

Sclera (shell)

Ligaments supporting the lens

Tear drainage duct

Lens

Iris

Cornea

Pupil

Osmosis and diffusion

▲ *Like these jellyfish, every living cell must maintain the correct balance of chemicals inside and outside of them.*

- **To survive**, every living cell must take in the chemicals it needs and let out the ones it does not through its thin membrane (casing). Cells do this in several ways, including osmosis, diffusion and active transport.

- **Osmosis** is when water moves to even the balance between a weak solution and a stronger one.

- **Diffusion** is when the substances that are dissolved in water or mixed in air move to even the balance.

- **Osmosis** happens when the molecules of a dissolved substance are too big to slip through the cell membrane – only the water can move.

- **Osmosis** is vital to many body processes, including the workings of the kidney and the nerves.

- **Urine** gets its water from the kidneys by osmosis.

- **In diffusion**, a substance such as oxygen moves in and out of cells, while the air or water it is mixed in stays put.

- **Diffusion** is vital to body processes such as cellular respiration (see breathing), when cells take in oxygen and push out waste carbon dioxide.

- **Active transport** is the way a cell uses protein-based 'pumps' or 'gates' in its membrane to draw in and hold substances that might otherwise diffuse out.

- **Active transport** uses energy and is how cells draw in most of their food such as glucose.

Reproduction – boys

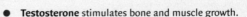

- **A boy or man's reproductive system** is where his body creates the sperm cells that combine with a female egg cell to create a new human life.

- **Sperm cells** look like microscopically tiny tadpoles. They are made in the testes, inside the scrotum.

- **The testes and scrotum** hang outside the body where it is cooler, because this improves sperm production.

- **At 15**, a boy's testes can make 200 million sperm a day.

- **Sperm leave** the testes via the epididymis – a thin, coiled tube, about 6 m long.

- **When the penis** is stimulated during sexual intercourse, sperm are driven into a tube called the vas deferens and mix with a liquid called seminal fluid to make semen.

- **Semen** shoots through the urethra (the tube inside the penis through which males urinate) and is ejaculated into the female's vagina.

- **The male sex hormone** testosterone is also made in the testes.

- **Testosterone** stimulates bone and muscle growth.

- **Testosterone** also stimulates the development of male characteristics such as facial hair and a deeper voice.

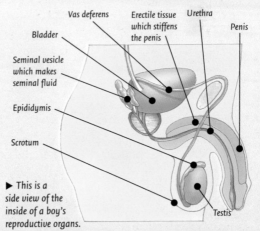

Vas deferens — Erectile tissue which stiffens the penis — Urethra — Penis

Bladder

Seminal vesicle which makes seminal fluid

Epididymis

Scrotum

Testis

▶ This is a side view of the inside of a boy's reproductive organs.

Ageing

▲ *Changes in health standards mean that more and more people than ever before are remaining fit in old age.*

- **Most people live** for between 60 and 100 years, although a few live even longer than this.

- **The longest officially confirmed age** is that of Frenchwoman Jeanne Calment, who died in 1997, aged 122 years and 164 days.

- **Life expectancy** is how long statistics suggest you are likely to live.

- **On average in Europe**, men can expect to live about 75 years and women about 80. However, because health is improving generally, people are living longer.

- **As adults grow older**, their bodies begin to deteriorate (fail). Senses such as hearing, sight and taste weaken.

- **Hair goes grey** as pigment (colour) cells stop working.

- **Muscles weaken** as fibres die.

- **Bones become more brittle** as they lose calcium. Cartilage shrinks between joints, causing stiffness.

- **Skin wrinkles** as the rubbery collagen fibres that support it sag. Exposure to sunlight speeds this up, which is why the face and hands get wrinkles first.

- **Circulation and breathing weaken.** Blood vessels may become stiff and clogged, forcing the heart to work harder and raising blood pressure.

Microscopes

- **Optical microscopes** use lenses and light to magnify things (make them look bigger). By combining two or more lenses, they can magnify specimens up to 2,000 times and reveal individual blood cells.

- **To magnify things more**, scientists use electron microscopes – microscopes that fire beams of tiny charged particles called electrons.

- **Electrons** have wavelengths 100,000 times smaller than light and so can give huge magnifications.

- **Scanning electron microscopes** (SEMs) are able to magnify things up to 100,000 times.

- **SEMs** show such things as the structures inside body cells.

- **Transmission electron microscopes** (TEMs) magnify even more than SEMs – up to 5 million times.

- **TEMs** can reveal the individual molecules in a cell.

- **SEM specimens** (things studied) must be coated in gold.

- **Optical microscope specimens** are thinly sliced and placed between two glass slides.

- **Microscopes help** to identify germs.

▼ *Microscopes reveal a lot about the body.*

Ribs

- **The ribs** are the thin, flattish bones that curve around your chest.

- **Together,** the rib bones, the backbone and the breastbone make up the rib cage.

- **The rib cage** protects vital organs such as heart, lungs, liver, kidneys and stomach.

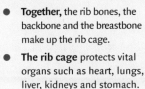

▶ The ribs provide a framework for the chest and form a protective cage around the heart, lungs and other organs.

True ribs

Sternum

False ribs

> ★ STAR FACT ★
> The bones of the ribs contain red marrow and are one of the body's major blood-cell factories.

- **You have 12 pairs** of ribs altogether.

- **Seven pairs** are true ribs. Each rib is attached to the breastbone and curves around to join one of the vertebrae that make up the backbone via a strip of costal cartilage.

- **There are three pairs** of false ribs. These are attached to vertebrae but are not linked to the breastbone. Instead, each rib is attached to the rib above it by cartilage.

- **There are two pairs** of floating ribs. These are attached only to the vertebrae of the backbone.

- **The gaps between** the ribs are called intercostal spaces, and they contain thin sheets of muscle which expand and relax the chest during breathing.

- **Flail chest** is when many ribs are broken (often in a car accident) and the lungs heave the chest in and out.

The pancreas

- **The pancreas** is a large, carrot-shaped gland which lies just below and behind your stomach.

- **The larger end** of the pancreas is on the right, tucking into the gut (see digestion). The tail end is on the left, just touching your spleen.

- **The pancreas** is made from a substance called exocrine tissue, embedded with hundreds of nests of hormone glands called the islets of Langerhans.

- **The exocrine tissue** secretes (releases) pancreatic enzymes such as amylase into the intestine to help digest food (see enzymes).

- **Amylase** breaks down carbohydrates into simple sugars such as maltose, lactose and sucrose.

- **The pancreatic enzymes** run into the intestine via a pipe called the pancreatic duct, which joins to the bile duct. This duct also carries bile (see the liver).

- **The pancreatic enzymes** only start working when they meet other kinds of enzyme in the intestine.

- **The pancreas** also secretes the body's own antacid, sodium bicarbonate, to settle an upset stomach.

- **The islets of Langerhans** secrete two important hormones – insulin and glucagon.

- **Insulin and glucagon** regulate blood sugar levels (see glucose).

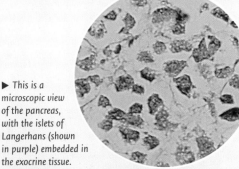

▶ This is a microscopic view of the pancreas, with the islets of Langerhans (shown in purple) embedded in the exocrine tissue.

Sensory nerves

- **Sensory nerves** are the nerves that carry information to your brain from sense receptors all over your body.

- **Each sense receptor** in the body is linked to the brain by a sensory nerve.

- **Most sensory nerves** feed their signals to the somatosensory cortex – the strip around the top of the brain where sensations are registered (see the cortex).

- **Massive bundles** of sensory nerve cells form the nerves that link major senses such as the eyes, ears and nose to the brain.

- **The eyes are linked to the brain** by the optic nerves.

- **The ears are linked to the brain** by the auditory nerves.

- **The nose is linked to the brain** by the olfactory tracts.

- **In the skin**, many sense receptors are simply 'free', exposed sensory nerve-endings.

- **The sciatic nerve** to each leg is the longest nerve in the body. Its name is from the Latin for 'pain in the thigh'.

▲ Some of our most pleasant feelings, such as being hugged or stroked, are sent to the brain by sensory nerves.

- **We can tell** how strong a sensation is by how fast the sensory nerve fires signals to the brain. But no matter how strong the sensation is, the nerve does not go on firing at the same rate and soon slows down.

Sex hormones

▲ A girl's sexual development depends on female sex hormones.

- **The sexual development** of girls and boys depends on the sex hormones (see reproduction).

- **Sex hormones** control the development of primary and secondary sexual characteristics, and regulate all sex-related processes such as sperm and egg production.

- **Primary sexual characteristics** are the development of the major sexual organs, such as the genitals.

- **Secondary sexual characteristics** are other differences between the sexes, such as men's beards.

- **There are three main types of sex hormones** – androgens, oestrogens and progesterones.

- **Androgens** are male hormones such as testosterone. They make a boy's body develop features such as a beard, deepen his voice and make his penis grow.

- **Oestrogen** is the female hormone made mainly in the ovaries. It not only makes a girl develop her sexual organs, but controls her monthly menstrual cycle.

- **Progesterone** is the female hormone that prepares a girl's uterus (womb) for pregnancy every month.

- **Some contraceptive pills** have oestrogen in them to prevent the ovaries releasing their egg cells.

> ★ STAR FACT ★
> Boys have female sex hormones and girls male sex hormones, but they usually have no effect.

Muscles

- **Muscles are special fibres** that contract (tighten) and relax to move parts of the body.

- **Voluntary muscles** are all the muscles you can control by will or thinking, such as your arm muscles.

- **Involuntary muscles** are the muscles you cannot control at will and that work automatically, such as the muscles that move food through your intestine.

- **Most voluntary muscles** cover the skeleton and are therefore called skeletal muscles. They are also called striated (striped) muscle because there are dark bands on the bundles of fibre that form them.

- **Most involuntary muscles** form sacs or tubes such as the intestine. They are called smooth muscle because they lack the bands or stripes of voluntary muscles.

- **Heart muscle** is a unique combination of skeletal and smooth muscle. It has its own built-in contraction rhythm of 70 beats a minute, and special muscle cells that work like nerve cells for transmitting the signals for waves of muscle contraction to sweep through the heart.

> **★ STAR FACT ★**
> Your body's smallest muscle is the stapedius, inside the ear – about as big as this l.

- **Most muscles are arranged in pairs**, because although muscles can shorten themselves, they cannot forcibly make themselves longer. So the flexor muscle that bends a joint is paired with an extensor muscle to straighten it out again.

- **With practice, most muscles** can be controlled individually, but they normally operate in combinations that are used to working together.

- **Your body's longest muscle** is the sartorius on the inner thigh.

- **Your body's widest muscle** is the external oblique which runs around the side of the upper body.

- **Your body's biggest muscle** is the gluteus maximus in your buttock (bottom).

> ▶ Under a microscope, you can see that muscles are made from bundles and bundles of tiny fibres.

▶ You have more than 640 skeletal muscles and they make up over 40% of your body's entire weight, covering your skeleton like a bulky blanket. The illustration here shows only the main surface muscles of the back, but your body has at least two layers, and sometimes three layers of muscle beneath its surface muscles. Most muscle is firmly anchored at both ends and attached to the bones either side of a joint, either directly or via tough fibres called tendons.

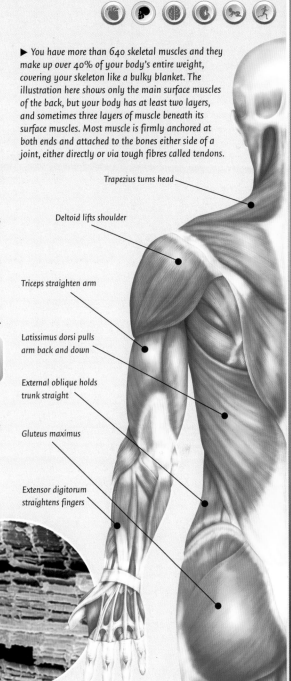

Trapezius turns head

Deltoid lifts shoulder

Triceps straighten arm

Latissimus dorsi pulls arm back and down

External oblique holds trunk straight

Gluteus maximus

Extensor digitorum straightens fingers

Anatomy

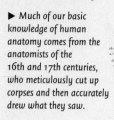

▶ Much of our basic knowledge of human anatomy comes from the anatomists of the 16th and 17th centuries, who meticulously cut up corpses and then accurately drew what they saw.

Fig. 1

- **Anatomy** is the study of the structure of the human body.

- **Comparative anatomy** compares the structure of our bodies to those of animals' bodies.

- **The first great anatomist** was the Ancient Roman physician, Galen (AD 129-199).

- **The first great book** of anatomy was written in 1543 by the Flemish scientist Andreas Vesalius (1514-1564). It is called *De Humani Corporis Fabrica* ('On the Fabric of the Human Body').

- **To describe the location** of body parts, anatomists divide the body into quarters.

- **The anatomical position** is the way the body is positioned to describe anatomical terms – upright, with the arms hanging down by the sides, and the eyes, palms and toes facing forwards.

- **The central coronal plane** divides the body into front and back halves. Coronal planes are any slice across the body from side to side, parallel to the central coronal plane.

- **The ventral or anterior** is the front half of the body.

- **The dorsal or posterior** is the back half of the body.

- **Every part of the body** has a Latin name, but anatomists use a simple English name if there is one.

Sleeping

- **When you are asleep,** your body functions go on as normal – even your brain goes on receiving sense signals. But your body may save energy and do routine repairs.

- **Lack of sleep** can be dangerous. A newborn baby needs 18 to 20 hours sleep a day. An adult needs 7 to 8.

- **Sleep is controlled** in the brain stem (see the brain). Dreaming is stimulated by signals fired from a part of the brain stem called the pons.

- **When you are awake,** there is little pattern to the electricity created by the firing of the brain's nerve cells. But as you sleep, more regular waves appear.

- **While you are asleep,** alpha waves sweep across the brain every 0.1 seconds. Theta waves are slower.

- **For the first 90 minutes** of sleep, your sleep gets deeper and the brain waves become stronger.

- **After about 90 minutes** of sleep, your brain suddenly starts to buzz with activity, yet you are hard to wake up.

- **After 90 minutes** of sleep, your eyes begin to flicker

▲ We all shut our eyes to sleep. Other marked changes to the body include the brain's activity pattern and slower heartbeat.

from side to side under their lids. This is called Rapid Eye Movement (REM) sleep.

- **REM sleep** is thought to show that you are dreaming.

- **While you sleep,** ordinary deeper sleep alternates with spells of REM lasting up to half an hour.

Body salts

- **Body salts** are not simply the salt (sodium chloride) some people sprinkle on food – they are an important group of chemicals which play a vital role in your body.

- **Examples of components** in body salts include potassium, sodium, chloride and manganese.

- **Body salts are important** in maintaining the balance of water in the body, and on the inside and the outside of body cells.

- **The body's thirst centre** is the hypothalamus (see the brain). It monitors salt levels in the blood and sends signals telling the kidneys to keep water or to let it go.

- **You gain salt** in the food you eat.

- **You can lose salt** if you sweat heavily. This can make muscles cramp, which is why people take salt tablets

▶ People who live in hot countries rely on salt in their food to make up for the loss made through sweating.

in the desert or drink a weak salt solution.

- **Too much salt** in food may result in high blood pressure.

- **When dissolved in water**, the chemical elements that salt is made from split into ions – atoms with either a positive or a negative electrical charge.

- **The balance** of water and salt inside and outside of body cells often depends on a balance of potassium ions entering the cell and sodium ions leaving it.

> ★ STAR FACT ★
> A saline drip is salt solution dripped via a tube into the arm of a patient who has lost blood.

Marrow

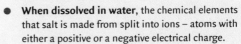

- **Marrow** is the soft tissue in the middle of some bones.

- **Bone marrow can be red** or yellow, depending on whether it has more blood tissue or fat tissue.

- **Red bone marrow** is the body's factory, where all blood cells apart from some white cells are made.

- **All bone marrow** is red when you are a baby, but as you grow older, more and more turns yellow.

- **In adults**, red marrow is only found in the ends of the limbs' long bones: the breastbone, backbone, ribs, shoulder blades, pelvis and the skull.

- **Yellow bone marrow** is a store for fat, but it may turn to red marrow when you are ill.

▶ Inside the tough casing of most bones is a soft, jelly-like core called the marrow, which can be either red or yellow. The red marrow of particular bones is the body's blood cell factory, making 5 million new cells a day.

- **All the different** kinds of blood cell start life in red marrow as one type of cell called a stem cell. Different blood cells develop as stem cells divide and re-divide.

- **Some stem cells** divide to form red blood cells and platelets.

- **Some stem cells** divide to form lymphoblasts. These divide in turn to form various different kinds of white cells – monocytes, granulocytes and lymphocytes.

- **The white cells** made in bone marrow play a key part in the body's immune system. This is why bone marrow transplants can help people with illnesses that affect their immune system.

The skeleton

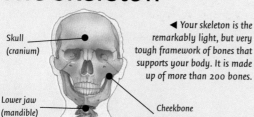

Skull
(cranium)

Lower jaw
(mandible)

Cheekbone
(zygomatic)

Collarbone
(clavicle)

Upper arm
(humerus)

Ribs

Backbone
(vertebrae)

Radius

Ulnar

Hip bone
(pelvis)

Sacrum

Thigh bone
(femur)

Kneecap
(patella)

Shinbone
(tibia)

Calf bone
(fibula)

◀ *Your skeleton is the remarkably light, but very tough framework of bones that supports your body. It is made up of more than 200 bones.*

- **Your skeleton** is a rigid framework of bones, which provides an anchor for your muscles, supports your skin and other organs, and protects vital organs.

- **An adult's skeleton has 206 bones** joined together by rubbery cartilage. Some people have extra vertebrae (the bones of the backbone, or spine).

- **A baby's skeleton has 300** or more bones, but some of these fuse (join) together as the baby grows older.

> ★ STAR FACT ★
> There are 26 bones in each of your feet – exactly the same number as in your hands.

- **The parts of an adult skeleton** that have fused into one bone include the skull and the pelvis (see the skull). The pelvis came from fusing the ilium bones, the ischium bones and the pubis. The ischium is the bone that you sit down on.

- **The skeleton** has two main parts – the axial skeleton and the appendicular skeleton.

- **The axial skeleton** is the 80 bones of the upper body. It includes the skull, the vertebrae of the backbone, the ribs and the breastbone. The arm and shoulder bones are suspended from it.

- **The appendicular skeleton** is the other 126 bones – the arm and shoulder bones, and the leg and hip bones. It includes the femur (thigh bone), the body's longest bone.

- **The word skeleton** comes from the Ancient Greek word for 'dry'.

- **Most women and girls** have smaller and lighter skeletons than men and boys. But in women and girls, the pelvis is much wider than in men and boys. This is because the opening has to be wide enough for a baby to get through when it is born.

◀ *A microscopic view of the inside of a bone shows just why the skeleton is so light and strong. Bone is actually full of holes, like a honeycomb. Its structure is provided by criss-crossing struts called trabeculae, each angled perfectly to cope with stresses and strains.*

Operations

- **A surgical operation** is when a doctor cuts into or opens up a patient's body to repair or remove a diseased or injured body part.

- **An anaesthetic** is a drug or gas that either sends a patient completely to sleep (a general anaesthetic), or numbs part of the body (a local anaesthetic).

- **Minor operations** are usually done with just a local anaesthetic.

- **Major operations** such as transplants are done under a general anaesthetic.

- **Major surgery** is performed by a team of people in a specially-equipped room called an operating theatre.

- **The surgical team** is headed by the surgeon. There is also an anaesthetist to make sure the patient stays asleep, as well as surgical assistants and nurses.

- **The operating theatre** must be kept very clean to prevent any infection getting into the patient's body during the operation.

▶ Many tricky operations are now performed using miniature cameras which help the surgeon see tiny details inside the body.

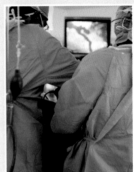

- **In microsurgery,** a microscope is used to help the surgeon work on very small body parts such as nerves or blood vessels.

- **In laser surgery,** the surgeon cuts with a laser beam instead of a scalpel. The laser seals blood vessels as it cuts, and it is used for delicate operations such as eye surgery.

- **An endoscope is** a tube-like instrument with a TV camera at one end. It can be inserted into the patient's body during an operation to look at body parts.

The arm

- **The arm is made** from three long bones, linked by a hinge joint at the elbow.

- **The two bones** of the lower arm are the radius and the ulnar.

- **The radius** supports the thumb side of the wrist.

- **The ulnar** supports the outside of the wrist.

- **The wrist** is one of the best places to test the pulse, since major arteries come nearer the surface here than at almost any other place in the body.

▶ Look at the inside of your wrist on a warm day and you may be able to see the radial artery beneath the skin.

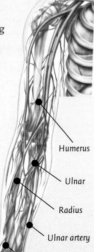

Humerus

Ulnar

Radius

Ulnar artery

Radial artery

- **The two major muscles** of the upper arm are the biceps (which bends the elbow) and the triceps (which straightens it).

- **The hand is made** from 26 bones, including the carpals (wrist bones), the metacarpals (hand bones) and the phalanges (finger bones).

- **There are no strong muscles** in the hand. When you grip firmly, most of the power comes from muscles in the lower arm, linked to the bones of the hand by long tendons.

- **The shoulder** is one of the weak points of the skeleton, since it is set in a very shallow socket. But it is supported by six major muscle groups, including the powerful deltoid (shoulder) muscle.

★ STAR FACT ★
The upper arm bone is called the humerus or, jokingly, the funny bone.

Antibodies

- **Antibodies** are tiny proteins that make germs vulnerable to attack by white blood cells called phagocytes (see the immune system).
- **Antibodies are produced** by white blood cells derived from B lymphocytes (see lymphocytes).
- **There are thousands** of different kinds of B-cell in the blood, each of which produces antibodies against a particular germ.
- **Normally, only a few B-cells** carry a particular antibody. But when an invading germ is detected, the correct B-cell multiplies rapidly to cause the release floods of antibodies.
- **Invaders** are identified when your body's immune system recognizes proteins on their surface as foreign. Any foreign protein is called an antigen.
- **Your body was armed** from birth with antibodies for

◄ Bacteria, viruses and many other micro-organisms have antigens which spur B-cells into action to produce antibodies as this artists impression shows.

germs it had never met. This is called innate immunity.

- **If your body comes across** a germ it has no antibodies for, it quickly makes some. It then leaves memory cells ready to be activated if the germ invades again. This is called acquired immunity.
- **Acquired immunity** means you only suffer once from some infections, such as chickenpox. This is also how vaccination works.
- **Allergies** are sensitive reactions that happen in your body when too many antibodies are produced, or when they are produced to attack harmless antigens.
- **Autoimmune diseases** are ones in which the body forms antibodies against its own tissue cells.

Blood cells

- **Your blood has two main kinds of cell** – red cells and white cells – plus pieces of cell called platelets (see blood).
- **Red cells** are button-shaped and they contain mainly red protein called haemoglobin.
- **Haemoglobin** is what allows red blood cells to ferry oxygen around your body.
- **Red cells** also contain enzymes which the body uses

> **! NEWS FLASH !**
> In the future, doctors may be able to make artificial red blood cells.

to make certain chemical processes happen (see enzymes).

- **White blood cells** are big cells called leucocytes and most types are involved in fighting infections.
- **Most white cells** contain tiny little grains and are called granulocytes.
- **Most granulocytes** are giant white cells called neutrophils. They are the blood's cleaners, and their task is to eat up invaders.
- **Eosinophils and basophils** are granulocytes that are involved in allergy or fighting disease. Some release antibodies that help fight infection (see antibodies).

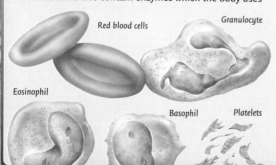

Red blood cells
Granulocyte
Eosinophil
Basophil
Platelets

◄ These are some of the most important kinds of cell in the blood – red cells, three kinds of white cells, and platelets.

Body systems

- **Your body systems** are interlinked – each has its own task, but they are all dependent on one another.

  - **The skeleton** supports the body, protects the major organs, and provides an anchor for the muscles.

    - **The skeletal muscles** are the ones that let you move. (Muscles are also involved in other systems.)

    - **The nervous system** is the brain and the nerves – the body's control and communications network.

  - **The digestive system** breaks down food into chemicals that the body can use.

◄ *The cardiovascular system is the heart and the blood circulation. It keeps the body cells supplied with food and oxygen, and defends them against germs.*

> ★ STAR FACT ★
> The reproductive system is the only system that can be removed without threatening life.

- **The immune system** is the body's defence against germs. It includes white blood cells, antibodies and the lymphatic system (which circulates lymph fluid and drains away cell waste).

- **The urinary system** controls the body's water balance, removing extra water as urine and getting rid of impurities in the blood. The excretory system gets rid of undigested food.

- **The respiratory system** takes air into the lungs to supply oxygen, and lets out waste carbon dioxide.

- **The reproductive system** is the smallest of all the systems. It is basically the sexual organs that enable people to have children. It is the only system that is different between men and women.

Transplants

- **More and more body parts** can now be replaced, either by transplants (parts taken from other people or animals) or by implants (artificial parts).

- **Common transplants** include – the kidney, the cornea of the eye, the heart, the lung, the liver and the pancreas.

- **Some transplant organs** (such as the heart, lungs and liver) are taken from someone who has died.

- **Other transplants** (such as kidneys) may be taken from living donors.

▶ *These are just some of the artificial implants now put in place – hip, knee, shoulder and elbow. Old people often need implants to replace joints that have deteriorated.*

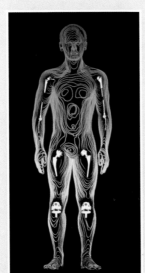

- **After the transplant organ** is taken from the donor, it is washed in an oxygenated liquid and cooled to preserve it.

- **One problem** with transplants is that the body's immune system identifies the transplant as foreign and attacks it. This is called rejection.

- **To cut down** the chance of rejection, patients may be given cyclosporin or other drugs to suppress their immune system.

- **Heart transplant** operations last 4 hours.

- **During a heart transplant**, the patient is connected to a heart-lung machine which takes over the heart's normal functions.

> ! NEWS FLASH !
> Surgeons think that in future they may be able to do head transplants.

Pulse

- **Your pulse** is the powerful high-pressure surge or wave that runs through your blood and vessels as the heart contracts strongly with each beat (see the heart).

- **You can feel your pulse** by pressing two fingertips on the inside of your wrist where the radial artery nears the surface (see the arm).

- **Other pulse points** include the carotid artery in the neck and the brachial artery inside the elbow.

- **Checking the pulse** is a good way of finding out how healthy someone is, which is why doctors do it.

- **Normal pulse rates** vary between 50 and 100 beats a minute. The average for a man is about 71, for a woman it is 80, and for children it is about 85.

- **Tachycardia** is the medical word for an abnormally fast heartbeat rate.

- **Someone who has tachycardia** when sitting down may have drunk too much coffee or tea, or taken drugs, or be suffering from anxiety or a fever, or have heart disease.

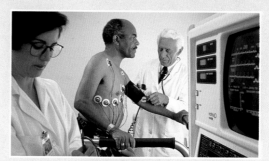

▲ By monitoring how much heart rate goes up and down during exercise, an ECG can show how healthy someone's heart is.

- **Bradycardia** is an abnormally slow heartbeat rate.

- **Arrhythmia** is any abnormality in a person's heart rate.

- **Anyone with a heart problem** may be connected to a machine called an electrocardiogram (ECG) to monitor (watch) their heartbeat.

Urine

- **Urine** is one of your body's ways of getting rid of waste (see water).

- **Your kidneys** produce urine, filtering it from your blood.

- **Urine runs from** each kidney down a long tube called the ureter, to a bag called the bladder.

- **Your bladder fills** up with urine over several hours. When it is full, you feel the need to urinate.

▲ Doctors can get clues to illnesses by testing what substances there are in urine. Diabetes, for instance, is shown up by the presence of glucose in the urine.

- **Urine is mostly water**, but there are substances dissolved in it. These include urea, various salts, creatinine, ammonia and blood wastes.

- **Urea** is a substance that is left after the breakdown of amino acids (see diet).

- **Urine gets its smell** from substances such as ammonia.

- **Urine gets its colour** from a yellowish blood waste called urochrome. Urochrome is left after proteins are broken down.

- **If you sweat a lot** – perhaps during a fever – your kidneys will let less water go and your urine will be stronger in colour.

★ STAR FACT ★
During your life, you will urinate 45,000 litres – enough to fill a small swimming pool!

Cells

- **Cells** are the basic building blocks of your body. Most are so tiny you would need 10,000 to cover a pinhead.

- **There are over 200 different kinds** of cell in your body, including nerve cells, skin cells, blood cells, bone cells, fat cells, muscle cells and many more.

- **A cell is basically** a little parcel of organic (life) chemicals with a thin membrane (casing) of protein and fat. The membrane holds the cell together, but lets nutrients in and waste out.

- **Inside the cell** is a liquid called cytoplasm, and floating in this are various minute structures called organelles.

- **At the centre** of the cell is the nucleus – this is the cell's control centre and it contains the amazing molecule DNA (see genes). DNA not only has all the instructions the cell needs to function, but also has the pattern for new human life.

> ★ STAR FACT ★
> There are 75 trillion cells in your body!

- **Each cell** is a dynamic chemical factory, and the cell's team of organelles is continually busy – ferrying chemicals to and fro, breaking up unwanted chemicals, and putting together new ones.

- **The biggest cells** in the body can be nerve cells. Although the main nucleus of nerve cells is microscopic, the tails of some cells can extend for a metre or more through the body, and be seen even without a microscope.

- **Among the smallest cells** in the body are red blood cells. These are just 0.0075 mm across and have no nucleus, since nearly their only task is ferrying oxygen.

- **Most body cells** live a very short time and are continually being replaced by new ones. The main exceptions are nerve cells – these are long-lived, but rarely replaced.

Mitochondria are the cell's power stations, turning chemical fuel supplied by the blood as glucose into energy packs of the chemical ATP (see muscle movement)

The endoplasmic reticulum is the cell's main chemical factory, where proteins are built under instruction from the nucleus

The ribosomes are the individual chemical assembly lines, where proteins are put together from basic chemicals called amino acids (see diet)

The nucleus is the cell's control centre, sending out instructions via a chemical called messenger RNA whenever a new chemical is needed

The lysosomes are the cell's dustbins, breaking up any unwanted material

The Golgi bodies are the cell's despatch centre, where chemicals are bagged up inside tiny membranes to send where they are needed

◀ *This illustration shows a typical cell, cutaway to show some of the different organelles (special parts of a cell) that keep it working properly. The instructions come from the nucleus in the cell's 'control centre', but every kind of organelle has its own task.*

Skin

- **Skin is your protective coat**, shielding your body from the weather and from infection, and helping to keep it at just the right temperature.

- **Skin is your largest sense receptor**, responding to touch, pressure, heat and cold (see touch).

- **Skin makes** vitamin D for your body from sunlight.

- **The epidermis** (the thin outer layer) is just dead cells.

- **The epidermis is made mainly** of a tough protein called keratin – the remains of skin cells that die off.

- **Below the epidermis** is a thick layer of living cells called the dermis, which contains the sweat glands.

- **Hair roots** have tiny muscles that pull the hair upright when you are cold, giving you goose bumps.

> ★ STAR FACT ★
> Even though its thickness averages just 2 mm, your skin gets an eighth of all your blood.

- **Skin is 6 mm thick** on the soles of your feet, and just 0.5 mm thick on your eyelids.

- **The epidermis** contains cells that make the dark pigment melanin – this gives dark-skinned people their colour and fair-skinned people a tan.

▶ This is a cross-section of skin, hugely magnified, showing its key components.

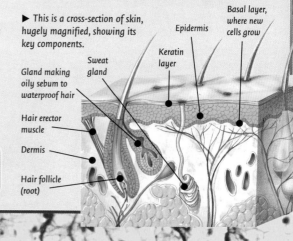

Gland making oily sebum to waterproof hair

Sweat gland

Keratin layer

Epidermis

Basal layer, where new cells grow

Hair erector muscle

Dermis

Hair follicle (root)

Temperature

▶ Sweating from the sweat glands (see right) in the skin keeps you cool – not only by letting warm water out of your body, but also because as the moisture evaporates it cools your skin.

- **The inside of your body** stays at a constant temperature of 37°C (98°F), rising a few degrees only when you are ill.

- **Your body creates heat** by burning food in its cells, especially the 'energy sugar' glucose.

- **Even when you are resting**, your body generates so much heat that you are comfortable only when the air is slightly cooler than you are.

- **When you are working hard**, your muscles can generate as much heat as a 2 kW heater.

- **Your body loses heat** as you breathe in cool air and breathe out warm air. Your body also loses heat by giving it off from your skin.

- **The body's temperature control** is the tiny hypothalamus in the brain.

- **Temperature sensors** in the skin, in the body's core, and in the blood by the hypothalamus tell the hypothalamus how hot or cold your body is.

- **If it is too hot**, the hypothalamus sends signals to your skin telling it to sweat more. Signals also tell blood vessels in the skin to widen – this increases the blood flow, increasing the heat loss from your blood.

- **If it is too cold**, the hypothalamus sends signals to the skin to cut back skin blood flow, as well as signals to tell the muscles to generate heat by shivering.

- **If it is too cold**, the hypothalamus may also stimulate the thyroid gland to send out hormones to make your cells burn energy faster and so make more heat.

Drugs

▲ Thousands of different drugs are today used to treat illness.

- **Antibiotic drugs** are used to treat bacterial infections such as tuberculosis (TB) or tetanus. They were once grown as moulds (fungi) but are now made artificially.

- **Penicillin** was the first antibiotic drug, discovered in a mould in 1928 by Alexander Fleming (1881-1955).

- **Analgesic drugs** such as aspirin relieve pain, mainly by stopping the body making prostaglandin, the chemical that sends pain signals to the brain.

- **Tranquillizers** are drugs that calm. Minor tranquillizers are drugs such as prozac, used to relieve anxiety.

- **Major tranquillizers** are used to treat mental illnesses such as schizophrenia.

- **Psychoactive drugs** are drugs that change your mood. Many, including heroin, are dangerous and illegal.

- **Stimulants** are drugs that boost the release of the nerve transmitter noradrenaline, making you more lively and awake. They include the caffeine in coffee.

- **Narcotics** are powerful painkillers such as morphine that mimic the body's own natural painkiller endorphin.

- **Depressants** are drugs such as alcohol which do not depress you, but instead slow down the nervous system.

> **! NEWS FLASH !**
> In future, more drugs may be made by animals with altered genes. Insulin is already made in the pancreas of pigs and oxen.

Synapses

- **Synapses** are the very tiny gaps between nerve cells.

- **When a nerve signal** goes from one nerve cell to another, it must be transmitted (sent) across the synapse by special chemicals called neurotransmitters.

- **Droplets of neurotransmitter** are released into the synapse whenever a nerve signal arrives.

- **As the droplets of neurotransmitter** lock on to the receiving nerve's receptors, they fire the signal onwards.

- **Each receptor site** on a nerve-ending only reacts to certain neurotransmitters. Others have no effect.

- **Sometimes** several signals must arrive before enough neurotransmitter is released to fire the receiving nerve.

- **More than 40 neurotransmitter chemicals** have been identified.

- **Dopamine** is a neurotransmitter that works in the parts of the brain that control movement and learning. Parkinson's disease may develop when the nerves that produce dopamine break down.

- **Serotonin** is a neurotransmitter that is linked to sleeping and waking up, and also to your mood.

- **Acetylcholine** is a neurotransmitter that may be involved in memory, and also in the nerves that control muscle movement.

▶ Nerve signals are transmitted across a synapse as chemical messengers called neurotransmitters. These lock on to receptors on the receiving nerve.

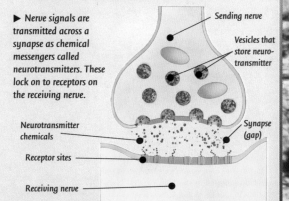

Sending nerve

Vesicles that store neuro-transmitter

Neurotransmitter chemicals

Receptor sites

Receiving nerve

Synapse (gap)

The nervous system

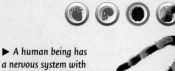

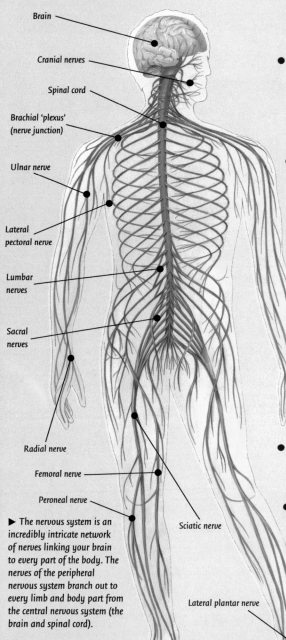

Brain

Cranial nerves

Spinal cord

Brachial 'plexus'
(nerve junction)

Ulnar nerve

Lateral
pectoral nerve

Lumbar
nerves

Sacral
nerves

Radial nerve

Femoral nerve

Peroneal nerve

Sciatic nerve

Lateral plantar nerve

▶ The nervous system is an
incredibly intricate network
of nerves linking your brain
to every part of the body. The
nerves of the peripheral
nervous system branch out to
every limb and body part from
the central nervous system (the
brain and spinal cord).

▶ A human being has
a nervous system with
about 60 billion nerve cells.
A spider has about 100,000.

● **The nervous system** is your
body's control and communication system, made up
of nerves and the brain. Nerves are your body's
hot-lines, carrying instant messages from the brain to
every organ and muscle – and sending back an
endless stream of data to the brain about what is
going on both inside and outside your body.

● **The central nervous system** (CNS) is the brain and
spinal cord (see central nervous system).

● **The peripheral nervous system** (PNS) is made up
of the nerves that branch out from the CNS to the rest
of the body.

● **The main branches of the PNS** are the 12 cranial
nerves in the head, and the 31 pairs of spinal nerves
that branch off the spinal cord.

● **The nerves of the PNS** are made up of long
bundles of nerve fibres, which in turn are made
from the long axons (tails) of nerve cells, bound
together like the wires in a telephone cable.

● **In many places**, sensory nerves (which carry
sense signals from the body to the brain) run
alongside motor nerves (which carry the brain's
commands telling muscles to move).

● **Some PNS nerves** are as wide as your
thumb. The longest is the sciatic, which runs
from the base of the spine to the knee.

● **The autonomic nervous system** (ANS) is the body's
third nervous system. It controls all internal body
processes such as breathing automatically, without
you even being aware of it.

● **The ANS** is split into two complementary
(balancing) parts – the sympathetic and the
parasympathetic. The sympathetic system speeds up
body processes when they need to be more active
such as when the body is exercising or under stress.
The parasympathetic slows them down.

★ STAR FACT ★
Millions of nerve signals enter your brain
every single second of your life.

Valves

- **Valves play** a crucial part in the circulation of your blood and lymph fluid (see the lymphatic system), ensuring that liquids flow only one way.

- **The heart has four valves** to make sure blood flows only one way through it.

- **On each side of the heart** there is a large valve between the atrium and the ventricle, and a smaller one where the arteries leave the ventricle.

- **The mitral valve** is the large valve on the left. The tricuspid is the large valve on the right.

- **The aortic valve** is the smaller valve on the left. The pulmonary is the smaller valve on the right.

- **Heart valves** can sometimes get blocked, making the heart work harder or leak. Both cause what a doctor using a stethoscope hears as a heart murmur.

- **The mitral** is the valve most likely to give problems, causing an illness called mitral stenosis.

- **A faulty heart valve** may be replaced with a valve

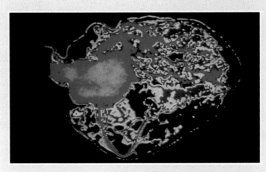

▲ Heart valve problems may arise if the blood supply to the heart is impaired – something that may show up on an angiogram like this.

from a human or pig heart, or a mechanical valve.

- **Valves in the arteries and veins** are simply flaps that open only when the blood is flowing one way.

- **The lymphatic system** also has its own small valves to ensure lymph is squeezed only one way.

The skull

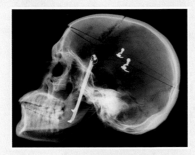

► An X-ray of the skull shows the cranial cavity which holds the brain. This is an old skull: the bright white bits are wires and clamps holding it together.

- **The skull** or cranium is the hard, bone case that protects your brain.

- **The skull looks** as though it is a single bone. In fact, it is made up of 22 separate bones, cemented together along rigid joints called sutures.

- **The dome on top** is called the cranial vault and it is made from eight curved pieces of bone fused (joined) together.

- **As well as the sinuses** of the nose (see airways), the

skull has four large cavities – the cranial cavity for the brain, the nasal cavity (the nose) and two orbits for the eyes.

- **There are holes in the skull** to allow blood vessels and nerves through, including the optic nerves to the eyes and the olfactory tracts to the nose.

- **The biggest hole** is in the base. It is called the foramen magnum, and the brain stem goes through it to meet the spinal cord.

- **In the 19th century**, people called phrenologists thought they could work out people's characters from little bumps on their skulls.

- **Archaeologists** can reconstruct faces from the past using computer analysis of ancient skulls.

> ★ STAR FACT ★
> A baby has soft spots called fontanelles in its skull because the bones join slowly over about 18 months.

Hair

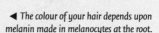

- **Humans are one of** very few land mammals to have almost bare skin. But even humans have soft, downy hair all over, with thicker hair in places.
- **Lanugo** is the very fine hair babies are covered in when they are inside the womb, from the fourth month of pregnancy onwards.
- **Vellus hair** is fine, downy hair that grows all over your body until you reach puberty.
- **Terminal hair** is the coarser hair on your head, as well as the hair that grows on men's chins and around an adult's genitals.
- **The colour of your hair** depends on how much there are of pigments called melanin and carotene in the hairs.
- **Hair is red or auburn** if it contains carotene.

◄ *The colour of your hair depends upon melanin made in melanocytes at the root.*

- **Black, brown and blonde hair** get their colour from black melanin.
- **Each hair** is rooted in a pit called the hair follicle. The hair is held in place by its club-shaped tip, the bulb.
- **Hair grows** as cells fill with a material called keratin and die, and pile up inside the follicle.
- **The average person** has 120,000 head hairs and each grows about 3 mm per week.

> ★ STAR FACT ★
> Hair in poor condition is said to be lifeless. In fact, all hair is lifeless since it is made of keratin, the material left by dead cells.

Balance

▲ *This gymnast's body is feeding her brain a continual stream of data about its position to help her stay perfectly balanced.*

- **To stay upright**, your body must send a continual stream of data about its position to your brain – and your brain must continually tell your body how to move to keep its balance.

- **Balance** is controlled in many parts of the brain including the cerebellum.
- **Your brain** finds out about your body position from many sources, including your eyes and the semicircular canals and other chambers in the inner ear.
- **Proprioceptors** are sense receptors in your skin, muscles and joints (see co-ordination).
- **The semicircular canals** are three, tiny, fluid-filled loops in your inner ear (see the ear).
- **Two chambers** called the utricle and saccule are linked to the semicircular canals.
- **When you move your head**, the fluid in the canals and cavities lags a little, pulling on hair detectors which tell your brain what is happening.
- **The canals** tell you whether you are nodding or shaking your head, and which way you are moving.
- **The utricle and saccule** tell you if you tilt your head or if its movement speeds up or slows down.

Colour vision

- **Seeing in colour** depends on eye cells called cones.
- **Cones do not** work well in low light, which is why things seem grey at dusk.
- **Some cones** are more sensitive to red light, some are more sensitive to green and some to blue.
- **The old trichromatic theory** said that you see colours by comparing the strength of the signals from each of the three kinds of cone – red, green and blue.

> ★ **STAR FACT** ★
> You have over 5 million colour-detecting cones in the retina of each eye.

- **Trichromatic theory** does not explain colours such as gold, silver and brown.
- **The opponent-process theory** said that you see colours in opposing pairs – blue and yellow, red and green.
- **In opponent-process theory,** lots of blue light is thought to cut your awareness of yellow, and vice versa. Lots of green cuts your awareness of red, and vice versa.
- **Now scientists** combine these theories and think that colour signals from the three kinds of cone are further processed in the brain in terms of the opposing pairs.
- **Ultraviolet light** is light waves too short for you to see, although some birds and insects can see it.

◀ *Seeing all the colours of the world around you depends on the colour-sensitive cone cells inside your eyes.*

Enzymes

- **Enzymes are** molecules – mostly protein – which alter the speed of chemical reactions in living things.
- **There are thousands of enzymes** in your body – it could not function without them.
- **Some enzymes** need an extra substance, called a coenzyme, to work. Many coenzymes are vitamins.
- **Most enzymes** have names ending in 'ase', such as lygase, protease and lipase.
- **Pacemaker enzymes** play a vital role in controlling your metabolism – the rate your body uses energy.
- **One of the most important enzyme groups** is that of the messenger RNAs, which are used as communicators by the nuclei of body cells (see cells).
- **Many enzymes** are essential for the digestion of food, including lipase, protease, amylase, and the peptidases. Many of these are made in the pancreas.
- **Lipase** is released mainly from the pancreas into the alimentary canal (gut) to help break down fat.

- **Amylase** breaks down starches such as those in bread and fruit into simple sugars (see carbohydrates). There is amylase in saliva and in the stomach.
- **In the gut**, the sugars maltose, sucrose and lactose are broken down by maltase, sucrase and lactase.

▼ *After you eat a meal, a complex series of enzymes gets to work, breaking the food down into the simple molecules that can be absorbed into your blood.*

Tissue and organs

- **Each of the many different kinds of cell** in your body combines to make substances called tissues.
- **As well as cells**, some tissues include other materials.
- **Connective tissues** are made from particular cells (such as fibroblasts), plus two other materials – long fibres of protein (such as collagen) and a matrix. Matrix is a material in which the cells and fibres are set like the currants in a bun.
- **Connective tissue** holds all the other kinds of tissue together in various ways. The adipose tissue that makes fat, tendons and cartilage is connective tissue.
- **Bone and blood** are both connective tissues.
- **Epithelial tissue** is good lining or covering material, making skin and other parts of the body.

> ★ STAR FACT ★
> All your body is made from tissue and tissue fluid (liquid that fills the space between cells).

▶ Lungs are largely made from special lung tissues (see right), but the mucous membrane that lines the airways is epithelial tissue.

- **Epithelial tissue** may combine three kinds of cell to make a thin waterproof layer – squamous (flat), cuboid (box-like) and columnar (pillar-like) cells.
- **Nerve tissue** is made mostly from neurons (nerve cells), plus the Schwann cells that coat them.
- **Organs** are made from combinations of tissues. The heart is made mostly of muscle tissue, but also includes epithelial and connective tissue.

Touch

▲ As we grow up, we gradually learn to identify more and more things instantly through touch.

- **Touch, or physical contact**, is just one of the sensations that are spread all over your body in your skin. The others include pressure, pain, hot and cold.
- **There are sense receptors** everywhere in your skin, but places like your face have more than your back.
- **There are 200,000 hot and cold receptors** in your skin, plus 500,000 touch and pressure receptors, and nearly 3 million pain receptors.
- **Free nerve-endings** are rather like the bare end of a wire. They respond to all five kinds of skin sensation and are almost everywhere in your skin.
- **There are specialized receptors** in certain places, each named after their discoverer.
- **Pacini's corpuscles** and Meissner's endings react instantly to sudden pressure.
- **Krause's bulbs**, Merkel's discs and Ruffini's endings respond to steady pressure.
- **Krause's bulbs** are also sensitive to cold.
- **Ruffini's endings** also react to changes in temperature.

> ★ STAR FACT ★
> Your brain knows just how hard you are touched from how fast nerve signals arrive.

The vocal cords

- **Speaking and singing** depend on the larynx (voice-box) in your neck (see airways).
- **The larynx** has bands of fibrous tissue called the vocal cords, which vibrate as you breathe air out over them.
- **When you are silent**, the vocal cords are relaxed and apart, and air passes between freely.
- **When you speak or sing**, the vocal cords tighten across the airway and vibrate to make sounds.
- **The tighter** the vocal cords are stretched, the higher-pitched sounds you make.
- **The basic sound** produced by the vocal cords is a simple 'aah'. But by changing the shape of your mouth, lips, and especially your tongue, you can change this simple sound into letters and words.
- **Babies' vocal cords** are just 6 mm long.
- **Women's vocal cords** are about 20 mm long.
- **Men's vocal cords** are about 30 mm long. Because men's cords are longer than women's, they vibrate more slowly and give men deeper voices.
- **Boys' vocal cords** are the same length as girls' until they are teenagers – when they grow longer, making a boy's voice 'break' and get deeper.

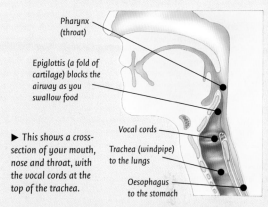

Pharynx (throat)

Epiglottis (a fold of cartilage) blocks the airway as you swallow food

Vocal cords

Trachea (windpipe) to the lungs

Oesophagus to the stomach

▶ This shows a cross-section of your mouth, nose and throat, with the vocal cords at the top of the trachea.

X-rays

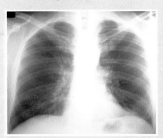

◀ An X-ray gives a clear picture of the inside of the chest, showing the ribs, the spine and the branching airways in the lung. Any lung problems and blockages show up as white shadows.

- **X-rays** are a form of electromagnetic radiation, as are radio waves, microwaves, visible light and ultraviolet. They all travel as waves, but have different wavelengths.
- **X-ray waves** are much shorter and more energetic than visible light waves. X-rays are invisible because their waves are too short for our eyes to see.
- **X-rays are made** when negatively charged particles called electrons are fired at a heavy plate made of the metal tungsten. The plate bounces back X-rays.
- **Even though they are invisible** to our eyes, X-rays register on photographic film.
- **X-rays are so energetic** that they pass through some body tissues like a light through a net curtain.
- **To make an X-ray photograph**, X-rays are shone through the body. The X-rays pass through some tissues and turn the film black, but are blocked by others, leaving white shadows on the film.
- **Each kind of tissue** lets X-rays through differently. Bones are dense and contain calcium, so they block X-rays and show up white on film. Skin, fat, muscle and blood let X-rays through and show up black on film.
- **X-ray radiation** is dangerous in high doses, so the beam is encased in lead, and the radiographer who takes the X-ray picture stands behind a screen.
- **X-rays are** very good at showing up bone defects. So if you break a bone, it will be probably be X-rayed.
- **X-rays also** reveal chest and heart problems.

Scans

- **Diagnostic imaging** means using all kinds of complex machinery to make pictures or images of the body to help diagnose and understand a problem.

- **Many imaging techniques** are called scans, because they involve scanning a beam around the patient.

- **CT scans** rotate an X-ray beam around the patient while moving him or her slowly forward. This gives a set of pictures showing different slices of the patient.

- **CT** stands for computerized tomography.

- **MRI scans** surround the patient with such a strong magnet that all the body's protons (tiny atomic particles) turn the same way. A radio pulse is then used to knock the protons in and out of line, sending out radio signals that the scanner picks up to give the picture.

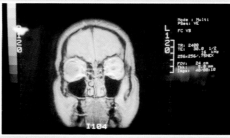

▲ *One of a series of CAT scans of the head and brain.*

- **MRI** stands for magnetic resonance imaging.

- **PET scans** involve injecting the patient with a mildly radioactive substance, which flows around with the blood and can be detected because it emits (gives out) particles called positrons.

- **PET** stands for positron emission tomography.

- **PET scans** are good for spotting heart stroke problems.

> ★ STAR FACT ★
> PET scans allow scientists to track blood through a live brain and see which areas are in action.

Backbone

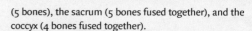

- **The backbone** (or spine) extends from the base of the skull down to the hips.

- **The backbone is not a single bone**, but a column of drum-shaped bones called vertebrae (singular, vertebra).

- **There are 33 vertebrae** altogether, although some of these fuse or join as the body grows.

- **Each vertebra** is linked to the next by facet joints, which are like tiny ball-and-socket joints.

- **The vertebrae are separated** by discs of rubbery material called cartilage. These cushion the bones when you run and jump.

- **The bones of the spine** are divided into five groups from top to bottom. These are the cervical (7 bones), the thoracic (12 bones), the lumbar

◄ *The backbone is not straight – instead, its 33 vertebrae curve into an S-shape.*

(5 bones), the sacrum (5 bones fused together), and the coccyx (4 bones fused together).

- **The cervical spine** is the vertebrae of the neck. The thoracic spine is the back of the chest, and each bone has a pair of ribs attached to it. The lumbar spine is the small of the back.

- **A normal spine** curves in an S-shape, with the cervical spine curving forwards, the thoracic section curving backwards, the lumbar forwards, and the sacrum backwards.

- **On the back** of each vertebra is a bridge called the spinal process. The bridges on each bone link together to form a tube which holds the spinal cord, the body's central bundle of nerves.

> ★ STAR FACT ★
> The story character the Hunchback of Notre Dame suffered from kyphosis – excessive curving of the spine.

Arteries

- **An artery** is a tube-like blood vessel that carries blood away from the heart.
- **Systemic arteries** deliver oxygenated blood around the body.
- **An arteriole** is a smaller branch off an artery.
- **Arterioles branch** into microscopic capillaries.
- **Blood flows through** arteries at up to 30 cm per second.
- **Arteries run alongside** most of the veins that return blood to the heart.
- **The walls of arteries** are muscular and can expand or relax to control the blood flow.
- **Arteries have** thicker, stronger walls than veins, and the pressure of the blood in them is a lot higher.
- **Over-thickening of the artery walls** may be one cause of hypertension (high blood pressure).
- **In old age** the artery walls can become very stiff. This hardening of the arteries, called arteriosclerosis, can cut blood flow to the brain.

> ★ STAR FACT ★
> Blood in arteries moves quickly in a pulsing way, while blood in a vein oozes slowly.

▶ This illustration shows how the main kinds of blood vessel in the body are connected. The artery (red) branches into tiny capillaries, which join up to supply the vein (blue).

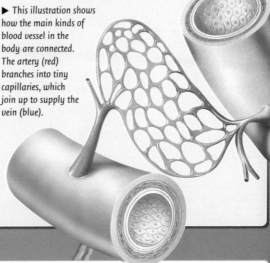

Memory

- **When you remember** something, your brain probably stores it by creating new nerve connections.
- **You have** three types of memory – sensory, short-term and long-term.
- **Sensory memory** is when you go on feeling a sensation for a moment after it stops.
- **Short-term memory** is when the brain stores things for a few seconds, like a phone number you remember long enough to dial.

▲ Learning to play the violin involves non-declarative memory – in which nerve pathways become reinforced by repeated use. This is why practising is so important.

- **Long-term memory** is memory that can last for months or maybe even your whole life.
- **Your brain** seems to have two ways of remembering things for the long term. Scientists call these declarative and non-declarative memories.
- **Non-declarative memories** are skills you teach yourself by practising, such as playing badminton or the flute. Repetition establishes nerve pathways.
- **Declarative memories** are either episodic or semantic. Each may be sent by the hippocampus region of the brain to the correct place in the cortex, the brain's wrinkly outer layer where you do most of your thinking.
- **Episodic memories** are memories of striking events in your life, such as breaking your leg or your first day at a new school. You not only recall facts, but sensations.
- **Semantic memories** are facts such as dates. The brain seems to store these in the left temporal lobe, at the front left–hand side of your brain.

1000
THINGS
YOU SHOULD KNOW ABOUT

SCIENCE

KEY

 Matter

 Chemicals and materials

 Electricity, magnetism and radiation

 The frontiers of science

 Technology

 Energy, force and motion

Computers

◀ Computers are developing so rapidly that models from the 1990s already look dated.

- **Part of a computer's** memory is microchips built in at the factory and known as ROM, or read-only memory. ROM carries the basic working instructions.

- **RAM** (random-access memory) consists of microchips that receive new data and instructions when needed.

- **Data can also** be stored as magnetic patterns on a removable disk, or on the laser-guided bumps on a CD (compact disk) or DVD (digital versatile disk).

- **At the heart** of every computer is a powerful microchip called the central processing unit, or CPU.

- **The CPU** works things out, within the guidelines set by the computer's ROM. It carries out programs by sending data to the right place in the RAM.

- **Computers** store information in bits (binary digits), either as 0 or 1.

- **The bits 0 and 1** are equivalent to the OFF and ON of electric current flow. Eight bits make a byte.

- **A kilobyte** is 1000 bytes; a megabyte (MB) is 1,000,000 bytes; a gigabyte (GB) is 1,000,000,000 bytes; a terabyte (TB) is 1,000,000,000,000 bytes.

- **A CD can hold** about 600 MB of data – about 375,000 pages of ordinary text.

> ★ STAR FACT ★
> The US Library of Congress's 70 million books could be stored in 25 TB of computer capacity.

Turning forces

- **Every force** acts in a straight line. Things move round because of a 'turning effect'.

- **A turning effect** is a force applied to an object that is fixed or pivots in another place, called the fulcrum.

- **In a door** the fulcrum is the hinge.

- **The size of a turning force** is known as the moment.

▲ Interlocking gear wheels are used in a huge range of machines, from cars to cameras. The wheels transmit movements and control their speed and size.

- **The farther from the fulcrum** that a force is applied, the bigger the moment is.

- **A lever** makes it much easier to move a load by making use of the moment (size of turning force).

- **A first-class lever,** such as pliers or scissors, has the fulcrum between the effort and the load; a second-class lever, such as a screwdriver or wheelbarrow, has the load between the effort and the fulcrum; a third-class lever, such as your lower arm or tweezers, has the effort between the load and the fulcrum.

- **Gears are sets of wheels** of different sizes that turn together. They make it easier to cycle uphill, or for a car to accelerate from a standstill, by spreading the effort over a greater distance.

- **The gear ratio** is the number of times that the driving wheel turns the driven wheel for one revolution of itself.

- **The larger the gear ratio** the more the turning force is increased, but the slower the driven wheel turns.

Archimedes

- **Archimedes** (c.287–212BC) was one of the first great scientists. He created the sciences of mechanics and hydrostatics.
- **Archimedes** was a Greek who lived in the city of Syracuse, Sicily. His relative, Hieron II, was king of Syracuse.
- **Archimedes' screw** is a pump supposedly invented by Archimedes. It scoops up water with a spiral device that turns inside a tube. It is still used in the Middle East.
- **To help defend** Syracuse against Roman attackers in 215BC, Archimedes invented many war machines. They included an awesome 'claw' – a giant grappling crane that could lift galleys from the water and sink them.
- **Archimedes** was killed by Roman soldiers when collaborators let the Romans into Syracuse in 212BC.
- **Archimedes** analysed levers mathematically. He showed that the load you can move with a particular effort is in exact proportion to its distance from the fulcrum.
- **Archimedes discovered** that things float because they are thrust upwards by the water.
- **Archimedes' principle** shows that the upthrust on a floating object is equal to the weight of the water that the object pushes out of the way.
- **Archimedes** realized he could work out the density, or specific gravity, of an object by comparing its weight to the weight of water it pushes out of a jar when submerged.
- **Archimedes** used specific gravity to prove a goldsmith had not made King Hieron's crown of pure gold.

▶ *Story says that Archimedes came up with the idea of measuring specific gravity while in the bath. He was so thrilled, he ran into the streets shouting 'Eureka!' (meaning 'I've got it').*

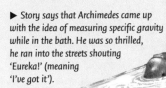

Magnetism

- **Magnetism** is the invisible force between materials such as iron and nickel. Magnetism attracts or repels.
- **A magnetic field** is the area around a magnet inside which its magnetic force can be detected.
- **An electric current** creates its own magnetic field.
- **A magnet** has two poles: a north pole and a south pole.
- **Like (similar) poles** (e.g. two north poles) repel each other; unlike poles attract each other.

> ★ **STAR FACT** ★
> One of the world's strongest magnets is at the Lawrence Berkeley National Laboratory, California, USA. Its field is 250,000 times stronger than the Earth's.

- **The Earth** has a magnetic field that is created by electric currents inside its iron core. The magnetic north pole is close to the geographic North Pole.
- **If left to swivel freely**, a magnet will turn so that its north pole points to the Earth's magnetic north pole.
- **The strength of a magnet** is measured in teslas. The Earth's magnetic field is 0.00005 teslas.
- **All magnetic materials** are made up of tiny groups of atoms called domains. Each one is like a mini-magnet with north and south poles.

◀ *The glowing skies above the poles are called auroras. They are created by the way the Earth's magnetic field channels electrically charged particles from the Sun down into the atmosphere.*

New materials

- **Synthetic materials** are man-made, such as plastics.

- **Many synthetic materials** are polymers. These are substances with long chains of organic molecules made up from lots of identical smaller molecules, monomers.

- **Some polymers** are natural, such as the plant fibre cellulose.

▲ Snowboards are made from composites such as Kevlar, which combine lightness with strength.

> **! NEWS FLASH !**
> New 'smart' materials might change their properties in response to conditions.

- **The first synthetic polymer** was Parkesine, invented by Alexander Parkes in 1862. The first successful synthetic polymer was celluloid, invented by John Hyatt in 1869 and soon used for photographic film.

- **Nylon** (a polymer) was the first fully synthetic fibre, created by Wallace Carothers of Du Pont in the 1930s.

- **PVC** is polyvinyl chloride, a synthetic polymer developed in the 1920s.

- **Composites** are new, strong, light materials created by combining a polymer with another material.

- **Carbon-reinforced plastic** consists of tough carbon fibres set within a polymer.

- **Kevlar** is a composite made by Du Pont in 1971. It is made of aramid (nylon-like) fibres set within a polymer.

Soaps

- **Some soaps** are natural; all detergents are synthetic.

- **All soaps and detergents** clean with a 'surfactant'.

- **Surfactants** are molecules that attach themselves to particles of dirt on dirty surfaces and lift them away.

- **Surfactants** work because one part of them is hydrophilic (attracted to water) and the other is hydrophobic (repelled by water).

- **The hydrophobic tail** of a surfactant digs its way into the dirt; the other tail is drawn into the water.

- **Soaps** increase water's ability to make things wet by reducing the surface tension of the water.

- **Soap** is made from animal fats or vegetable oil combined with chemicals called alkalis, such as sodium or potassium hydroxide.

- **Most soaps** include perfumes, colours and germicides (germ-killers) as well as a surfactant.

- **The Romans used** soap over 2000 years ago.

- **Detergents** were invented in 1916 by a German chemist called Fritz Gunther.

▼ Surfactant molecules in soap lift dirt off dirty surfaces.

The hydrophobic tail dips into the dirt

The hydrophilic tail is pulled by the water

The surfactant molecules in soap lift particles of dirt away

Musical sound

◀ In stringed instruments different notes – that is, different frequencies of vibrations – are achieved by varying the length of the strings.

- **Like all sounds,** musical sounds are made by something vibrating. However, the vibrations of music occur at very regular intervals.

- **The pitch** of a musical note depends on the frequency of the vibrations.

- **Sound frequency** is measured in hertz (Hz) – that is, cycles or waves per second.

> ★ STAR FACT ★
> A song can shatter glass if the pitch of a loud note coincides with the natural frequency of vibration of the glass.

- **Human ears** can hear sounds as low as about 20 Hz and up to around 20,000 Hz.

- **Middle C** on a piano measures 262 Hz. A piano has a frequency range from 27.5 to 4186 Hz.

- **The highest singing voice** can reach the E above a piano top note (4350 Hz); the lowest note is 20.6 Hz.

- **A soprano's voice** has a range from 262 to 1046 Hz; an alto from 196 to 698 Hz; a tenor from 147 to 466 Hz; a baritone from 110 to 392 Hz; a bass from 82.4 to 294 Hz.

- **Very few sounds** have only one pitch. Most have a fundamental (low) pitch and higher overtones.

- **The science of vibrating strings** was first worked out by Pythagoras 2500 years ago.

▶ In most brass and woodwind instruments, such as a tuba, different frequencies are achieved by varying the length of the air column inside.

Lasers

- **Laser light** is a bright artificial light. It creates an intense beam that can punch a hole in steel. A laser beam is so straight and narrow that it can hit a mirror on the Moon.

- **The name 'laser'** stands for light amplification by stimulated emission of radiation.

- **Laser light** is even brighter for its size than the Sun.

▲ The amazingly tight intense beam of a laser is used in a huge number of devices, from CD players to satellite guidance systems.

- **Laser light** is the only known 'coherent' source of light. This means the light waves are not only all the same wavelength (colour), but they are also perfectly in step.

- **Inside a laser** is a tube filled with gases, such as helium and neon, or a liquid or solid crystal such as ruby.

- **Lasers work** by bouncing photons (bursts of light) up and down the tube until they are all travelling together.

- **Lasing begins** when a spark excites atoms in the lasing material. The excited atoms emit photons. When the photons hit other atoms, they fire off photons too. Identical photons bounce backwards and forwards between mirrors at either end of the laser.

- **Gas lasers** such as argon lasers give a lower-powered beam. It is suitable for delicate work such as eye surgery.

- **Chemical lasers** use liquid hydrogen fluoride to make intense beams for weapons.

- **Some lasers** send out a continuous beam. Pulsed lasers send out a high-powered beam at regular intervals.

Aluminium

- **Aluminium** is by far the most common metal on the Earth's surface. It makes up 8% of the Earth's crust.

- **Aluminium** never occurs naturally in its pure form; in the ground it combines with other chemicals as minerals in ore rocks.

- **The major source** of aluminium is layers of soft ore called bauxite, which is mostly aluminium hydroxide.

- **Alum powders** made from aluminium compounds were used 5000 years ago for dyeing. Pure aluminium was first made in 1825 by Danish scientist Hans Oersted.

▲ *Although aluminium is common in the ground, it is worth recycling because extracting it from bauxite uses a lot of energy.*

- **Aluminium** production was the first industrial process to use hydroelectricity when a plant was set up on the river Rhine in 1887.

- **Aluminium is silver** in colour when freshly made, but it quickly

◄ Half of the soft drinks cans in the USA are made from recycled aluminium.

tarnishes to white in the air. It is very slow to corrode.

- **Aluminium** is one of the lightest of all metals.

- **Aluminium oxide** can crystallize into one of the hardest minerals, corundum, which is used to sharpen knives.

- **Aluminium** melts at 650°C and boils at 2450°C.

- **Each year 21 million tonnes** of aluminium are made, mostly from bauxite dug up in Brazil and New Guinea.

Stretching and pulling

▲ *The leverage of the bow string helps an archer to bend the elastic material of the bow so far that it has tremendous power as it snaps back into shape.*

- **Elasticity** is the ability of a solid material to return to its original shape after it has been misshapen.

- **A force** that misshapes material is called a stress.

- **All solids** are slightly elastic but some are very elastic, for example rubber, thin steel and young skin.

- **Solids** return to their original shape after the stress stops, as long as the stress is less than their 'elastic limit'.

- **Strain** is how much a solid is stretched or squeezed when under stress, namely how much longer it grows.

- **The amount** a solid stretches under a particular force – the ratio of stress to strain – is called the elastic modulus, or Young's modulus.

- **The greater the stress**, the greater the strain. This is called Hooke's law, after Robert Hooke (1635–1703).

- **Solids** with a low elastic modulus, like rubber, are stretchier than ones with a high modulus, such as steel.

- **Steel can be only stretched** by 1% before it reaches its elastic limit. If the steel is coiled into a spring, this 1% can allow a huge amount of stretching and squeezing.

> ★ STAR FACT ★
> Some types of rubber can be stretched 1000 times beyond its original length before it reaches its elastic limit.

Electrons

- **Electrons** are by far the smallest of the three main, stable parts of every atom; the other two parts are protons and neutrons (see atoms). In a normal atom there are the same number of electrons as protons.

- **Electrons** are 1836 times as small as protons and have a mass of just 9.109×10^{-31} kg. 10^{-31} means there are 30 zeros after the decimal point. So they weigh almost nothing.

- **Electrons were discovered** by English physicist Joseph John Thomson in 1897 as he studied the glow in a cathode-ray tube (see television). This was the first a anyone realized that the atom is not just one solid ball.

- **Electrons are** packets of energy. They can be thought of either as a tiny vibration or wave, or as a ball-like particle. They travel as waves and arrive as particles.

- **You can never be sure** just where an electron is. It is better to think of an electron circling the nucleus not as a planet circling the Sun but as a cloud wrapped around it. Electron clouds near the nucleus are round, but those farther out are other shapes, such as dumb-bells.

- **Electrons** have a negative electrical charge. This means they are attracted to positive electrical charges and pushed away by negative charges. 'Electron' comes from the Greek word for amber. Amber tingles electrically when rubbed.

- **Electrons cling** to the nucleus because protons have a positive charge equal to the electron's negative charge.

▶ *Each atom has a different number of electrons. Its chemical character depends on the number of electrons in its outer shell. Atoms with only one electron in their outer shell, such as lithium, sodium and potassium, have many properties in common. The electron shell structures for five common atoms are shown here.*

> ★ STAR FACT ★
> Electrons whizz round an atomic nucleus, zoom through an electric wire or spin on their own axis, either clockwise or anti-clockwise.

- **Electrons have so much energy** that they whizz round too fast to fall into the nucleus. Instead they circle the nucleus in shells (layers) at different distances, or energy levels, depending on how much energy they have. The more energetic an electron, the farther from the nucleus it is. There is room for only one other electron at each energy level, and it must be spinning in the opposite way. This is called Pauli's exclusion principle.

- **Electrons are** stacked around the nucleus in shells, like the layers of an onion. Each shell is labelled with a letter and can hold a particular number of electrons. Shell K can hold up to 2, L 8, M 18, N 32, O about 50, and P about 72.

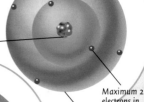

Hydrogen atom

Single electron

Nucleus with single proton

Nucleus with 6 protons

Carbon atom

Maximum 2 electrons in shell K

Shell L holds 4 electrons out of a possible 8. So carbon has four vacancies to form complex compounds with other elements.

Oxygen atom

Nucleus with 8 protons

Shell K holds a maximum of 2 electrons.

Shell L holds 6 electrons out of a possible 8. So oxygen has 2 'missing' electrons and is very reactive.

Chlorine atom

Nucleus with 17 protons

Sodium atom

Nucleus with 11 protons

Shell L holds a maximum of 8 electrons, so the next electron goes in shell M.

7 electrons out of 8 in shell M means that chlorine is drawn to atoms with a spare electron.

Single electron in shell M is easily drawn to other atoms.

Oxygen

▲ No animal can live for more than a minute or so without breathing in oxygen from the air to keep the body processes going.

- **Oxygen** is the second most plentiful element on Earth. Air is 20.94% oxygen.

- **Oxygen** is one of the most reactive elements. This is why oxygen in the Earth's crust is usually found joined with other chemicals in compounds.

- **Oxygen has an atomic number** of 8 and an atomic weight of 15.9994.

- **Oxygen molecules** in the air are made from two oxygen atoms; three oxygen atoms make the gas ozone.

- **Oxygen turns to a pale blue liquid** at −182.962°C. It freezes at −218.4°C.

- **Most life depends on oxygen** because it joins with other chemicals in living cells to give the energy needed for life processes. The process of using oxygen in living cells is called cellular respiration.

- **Liquid oxygen,** or LOX, is combined with fuels such as kerosene to provide rocket fuel.

- **Oxygen** was discovered independently by Carl Scheele and Joseph Priestley during the 1770s.

- **The name** 'oxygen' means acid-forming. It was given to the gas in 1779 by Antoine Lavoisier (see Lavoisier).

> ★ STAR FACT ★
> The oxygen in the air on which your life depends was produced mainly by algae.

Einstein

▶ Einstein's equation $E=mc^2$ revealed the energy in atoms that led to nuclear bombs and nuclear power.

- **Albert Einstein** (1879–1955) was the most famous scientist of the 20th century.

- **Einstein was half German** and half Swiss, but when Hitler came to power in 1933, Einstein made his home in the USA.

- **Einstein's fame** rests on his two theories of Relativity (see relativity).

- **His theory of Special Relativity** was published in 1905 while he worked in the Patent Office in Bern, Switzerland.

- **In 1905** Einstein also explained the photoelectric effect. From these ideas, photo cells were developed. These are the basis of TV cameras and many other devices.

- **Einstein completed his theory** of General Relativity in 1915.

- **Einstein** was not satisfied with his theory of General Relativity as it didn't include electromagnetism. He spent the last 25 years of his life trying to develop a 'Unified Field Theory' to include it.

- **Einstein** was once reported to have said that only 12 people in the world could understand his theory. He denied saying it.

- **On August 2, 1939** Einstein wrote a letter to US President Franklin Roosevelt in which he persuaded the president to launch the Manhattan Project to develop the nuclear bomb.

- **Einstein was married twice.** His first wife was Mileva Maric. His second wife Elsa was also his first cousin.

Atoms

- **Atoms are** the tiny bits, or particles, which build together to make every substance. An atom is the tiniest bit of any pure substance or chemical element.

- **You could fit** two billion atoms on the full stop after this sentence.

- **The number of atoms** in the Universe is about 10 followed by 80 zeros.

- **Atoms are mostly** empty space dotted with a few even tinier particles called subatomic particles.

- **In the centre** of each atom is a dense core, or nucleus, made from two kinds of particle: protons and neutrons. Protons have a positive electrical charge, and neutrons none. Both protons and neutrons are made from different combinations of quarks (see quarks).

- **If an atom** were the size of a sports arena, its nucleus

◄ *Inside every atom tiny electrons (blue) whizz around a dense nucleus built up from protons (red) and neutrons (green). The numbers of each particle vary from element to element.*

would be the size of a pea.

- **Around the nucleus** whizz even tinier, negatively-charged particles called electrons (see electrons).

- **Atoms can be split** but they are usually held together by three forces: the electrical attraction between positive protons and negative electrons, and the strong and weak 'nuclear' forces that hold the nucleus together.

- **Every element** is made from atoms with a certain number of protons in the nucleus. An iron atom has 26 protons, gold has 79. The number of protons is the atomic number.

- **Atoms with the same number** of protons but a different number of neutrons are called isotopes.

Microscopes

- **Microscopes** are devices for looking at things that are normally too small for the human eye to see.

- **Optical microscopes** use lenses to magnify the image by up to 2000 times.

- **In an optical microscope** an objective lens bends light rays apart to enlarge what you see; an eyepiece lens makes the big image visible.

- **Electron microscopes** magnify by firing electrons at an object. The electrons bounce off the object onto a screen, making them visible.

- **An electron microscope** can focus on something as small as 1 nanometre (one-billionth of a metre) and magnify it five million times.

- **Scanning Electron Microscopes** (SEMs) scan the surface of an object to magnify it by up to 100,000 times.

- **Transmission Electron Microscopes** shine electrons through thin slices of an object to magnify it millions of times.

- **Scanning Tunnelling Microscopes** are so powerful that they can reveal individual atoms.

- **The idea of electron microscopes** came from French physicist Louis de Broglie in 1924.

- **Scanning Acoustic Microscopes** use sound waves to see inside tiny opaque objects.

◄▼ *A Scanning Electron Microscope clearly reveals the tiny nerve fibres inside the human brain.*

Electromagnetic spectrum

- **The electromagnetic spectrum** is the complete range of radiation sent out by electrons (see light and atoms). It is given off in tiny packages of energy called photons, which can be either particles or waves (see moving light).

- **Electromagnetic waves** vary in length and frequency. The shorter the wave, the higher its frequency (and also its energy).

- **The longest waves** are over 100 kilometres long; the shortest are less than a billionth of a millimetre long.

- **All electromagnetic waves** travel at 300,000 kilometres per second, which is the speed of light.

- **Visible light** is just a small part of the spectrum.

- **Radio waves,** including microwaves and television waves, and infrared light, are made from waves that are too long for human eyes to see.

- **Long waves** are lower in energy than short waves. Long waves from space penetrate the Earth's atmosphere easily (but not solids, like short waves).

- **Ultraviolet light,** X-rays and gamma rays are made from waves that are too short for human eyes to see.

- **Short waves are very energetic.** But short waves from space are blocked out by Earth's atmosphere – which is fortunate because they are dangerous. X-rays and gamma rays penetrate some solids, and UV rays can damage living tissues, causing skin cancers.

> ★ STAR FACT ★
> Cosmic rays are not rays but streams of high-energy particles from space.

Gamma rays are dangerous high-energy rays with such short waves that they can penetrate solids. They are created in space and by nuclear bombs.

X-rays are longer waves than gamma rays but short enough to pass through most body tissues except bones, which show up white on medical X-ray photos.

The shortest ultraviolet rays in sunshine are dangerous, but longer ones give you a suntan in small doses. In large doses even long UV rays cause cancer.

Visible light varies in wavelength from violet (shortest) through all the colours of the rainbow to red (longest).

◀ *This illustration shows the range of radiation in the electromagnetic spectrum. The waves are shown emerging from the Sun because the Sun actually emits almost the full range of radiation. Fortunately, the atmosphere protects us from the dangerous ones.*

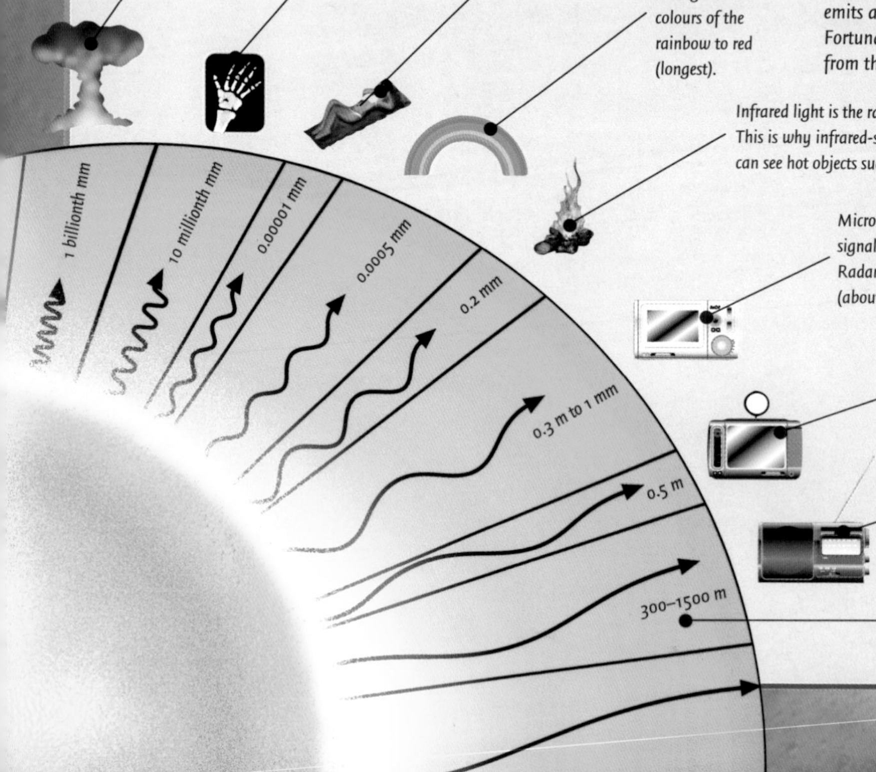

Infrared light is the radiation given out by hot objects. This is why infrared-sensitive 'thermal imaging' cameras can see hot objects such as people in pitch darkness.

Microwaves are used to beam telephone signals to satellites – and to cook food. Radars send out fairly short microwaves (about 1 cm long).

Television broadcasts use radio waves with waves about 0.5 m long.

Radio broadcasts use radio waves with waves from 300 m to 1500 m long.

Typical wavelength in metres or millimetres. Long waves are low frequency and low energy. Short waves are high frequency and high energy.

1 billionth mm

10 millionth mm

0.00001 mm

0.0005 mm

0.2 mm

0.3 m to 1 mm

0.5 m

300–1500 m

Chemical bonds

- **Chemical bonds** link together atoms to make molecules (see molecules).

- **Atoms can bond** in three main ways: ionic bonds, covalent bonds and metallic bonds.

- **In ionic bonds** electrons are transferred between atoms.

- **Ionic bonds** occur when atoms with just a few electrons in their outer shell give the electrons to atoms with just a few missing from their outer shell.

- **An atom** that loses an electron becomes positively charged; an atom that gains an electron becomes negatively charged so the two atoms are drawn together by the electrical attraction of opposites.

- **Sodium** loses an electron and chlorine gains one to form the ionic bond

◀ Each of the four hydrogen atoms in methane (CH_4) shares its electron with the central carbon atom to create strong covalent bonds.

▶ In this carbon dioxide molecule the carbon is held to two oxygen atoms by covalent bonds.

of sodium chloride (table salt) molecules.

- **In covalent bonding,** the atoms in a molecule share electrons.

- **Because they are negatively** charged, the shared electrons are drawn equally to the positive nucleus of both atoms involved. The atoms are held together by the attraction between each nucleus and the shared electrons.

- **In metallic bonds** huge numbers of atoms lose their electrons. They are held together in a lattice by the attraction between 'free' electrons and positive nuclei.

> ★ STAR FACT ★
> Seven elements, including hydrogen, are found in nature only as two atoms covalently bonded.

Pressure

▶ The worst storms, such as this hurricane seen from space, are caused when air from high-pressure areas rushes into low-pressure areas.

- **Pressure** is the force created by the assault of fast-moving molecules.

- **The pressure that keeps** a bicycle tyre inflated is the constant assault of huge numbers of air molecules on the inside of the tyre.

- **The water pressure that** crushes a submarine when it dives too deep is the assault of huge numbers of water molecules.

- **Pressure rises** as you go deeper in the ocean. This is because of an increasing weight of water – called hydrostatic pressure – pressing down from above.

- **The water pressure 10,000 m** below the surface is equivalent to seven elephants standing on a dinner plate.

- **The pressure of the air** on the outside of your body is balanced by the pressure of fluids inside. Without this internal pressure, air pressure would crush your body instantly.

- **Pressure** is measured as the force on a certain area.

- **The standard unit** of pressure is a pascal (Pa) or 1 newton per sq m (N/m^2).

- **High pressures:** the centre of the Earth may be 400 billion Pa; steel can withstand 40 million Pa; a shark bite can be 30 million Pa.

- **Low pressures:** the best laboratory vacuum is 1 trillionth Pa; the quietest sound is 200 millionths Pa. The pressure of sunlight may be 3 millionths Pa.

Machines

- **A machine** is a device that makes doing work easier by reducing the Effort needed to move something.

- **There are two forces** involved in every machine: the Load that the machine has to overcome, and the Effort used to move the Load.

- **The amount that a machine** reduces the Effort needed to move a Load is called the Mechanical Advantage. This tells you how effective a machine is.

- **Basic machines include** levers, gears, pulleys, screws, wedges and wheels. More elaborate machines, such as cranes, are built up from combinations of these basic machines.

- **Machines cut** the Effort needed to move a Load by spreading the Effort over a greater distance or time.

- **The distance** moved by the Effort you apply, divided

◄ Like many aspects of modern life, farming has become increasingly dependent on the use of machines.

by the distance moved by the Load, is called the Velocity Ratio (VR).

- **If the VR is greater** than 1, then the Effort moves farther than the Load. You need less Effort to move the Load, but you have to apply the Effort for longer.

- **The total amount** of Effort you use to move something is called Work. Work is the force you apply multiplied by the distance that the Load moves.

- **One of the earliest machines still used today** is a screwlike water-lifting device called a dalu, first used in Sumeria 5500 years ago.

- **One of the world's biggest machines** is the SMEC earthmover used in opencast mines in Australia. It weighs 180 tonnes and has wheels 3.5 m high.

Faraday

▲ Faraday drew huge crowds to his brilliant and entertaining Christmas lectures on science at the Royal Institution in London. These Christmas lectures at the Royal Institution are still a popular tradition today.

- **Michael Faraday** (1791–1867) was one of the greatest scientists of the 19th century.

- **Faraday was the son** of a poor blacksmith, born in the village of Newington in Surrey, England.

- **He started work as** an apprentice bookbinder but became assistant to the great scientist Humphry Davy after taking brilliant notes at one of Davy's lectures.

- **Faraday was said** to be Davy's greatest discovery.

- **Until 1830 Faraday** was mainly a chemist. In 1825 he discovered the important chemical benzene.

- **In 1821** Faraday showed that the magnetism created by an electric current would make a magnet move and so made a very simple version of an electric motor.

- **In 1831** Faraday showed that when a magnet moves close to an electric wire, it creates, or induces, an electric current in the wire. This was discovered at the same time by Joseph Henry in the USA.

- **Using** his discovery of electric induction, Faraday made the first dynamo to generate electricity and so opened the way to the modern age of electricity.

- **In the 1840s** Faraday suggested the idea of lines of magnetic force and electromagnetic fields. These ideas, which were later developed by James Clerk Maxwell, underpin much of modern science.

- **Faraday** was probably the greatest scientific experimenter of all time.

Electric currents

- **An electric charge** that does not move is called static electricity (see electricity). A charge may flow in a current providing there is an unbroken loop, or circuit.

- **A current only flows** through a good conductor such as copper, namely a material that transmits charge well.

- **A current only flows** if there is a driving force to push the charge. This force is called an electromotive force (emf).

- **The emf** is created by a battery or a generator.

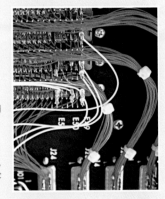

▶ For a current to flow, each of these wires must form a circuit.

> ★ STAR FACT ★
> The electrical resistance of dry skin is 500,000 ohms; wet skin's is just 1000 ohms.

- **Currents were once thought to** flow like water. In fact they move like a row of marbles knocking into each other.

- **In a good conductor** there are lots of free electrons that are unattached to atoms. These are the 'marbles'.

- **A current only flows** if there are more electrons at one point in the circuit. This difference, called the potential difference, is measured in volts.

- **The rate at which current** flows is measured in amps. It depends on the voltage and the resistance (how much the circuit obstructs the flow of current). Resistance is measured in ohms.

- **Batteries** give out Direct Current, a current that flows in one direction. Power stations send out Alternating Current , which swaps direction 50–60 times per second.

Plastics

- **Plastics are synthetic** (man-made) materials that can be easily shaped and moulded.

- **Most plastics are polymers** (see new materials). The structure of polymer molecules gives different plastics different properties.

- **Long chains of molecules** that slide over each other easily make flexible plastics such as polythene. Tangled chains make rigid plastics such as melamine.

- **Typically** plastics are made by joining carbon and hydrogen atoms. These form ethene molecules, which can be joined to make a plastic called polythene.

- **Many plastics** are made from liquids and gases that are extracted from crude oil.

- **Thermoplastics** are soft and easily moulded when warm but set solid when cool. They are used to make bottles and drainpipes and can be melted again.

- **Thermoset plastics,** which cannot be remelted once set, are used to make telephones and pan handles.

- **Blow moulding** involves using compressed air to push a tube of plastic into a mould.

- **Vacuum moulding** involves using a vacuum to suck a sheet of plastic into a mould.

- **Extrusion moulding** involves heating plastic pellets and forcing them out through a nozzle to give the right shape.

▼ Some plastics are light and soft and can be filled with air bubbles to make an ideal packing material.

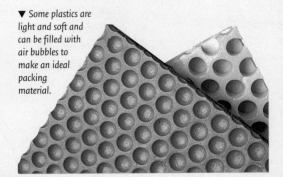

Chemical compounds

- **Compounds** are substances that are made when the atoms of two or more different elements join together.

- **The properties of a compound** are usually very different from those of the elements which it is made of.

- **Compounds** are different from mixtures because the elements are joined together chemically. They can only be separated by a chemical reaction.

- **Every molecule** of a compound is exactly the same combination of atoms.

- **The scientific name** of a compound is usually a combination of the elements involved, although it might have a different common name.

- **Table salt** is the chemical compound sodium chloride. Each molecule has one sodium and one chlorine atom.

- **The chemical formula** of a compound summarizes which atoms a molecule is made of. The chemical formula for water is H_2O because each water molecule has two hydrogen (H) atoms and one oxygen (O) atom.

- **There only 100 or so elements** but they can combine in different ways to form many millions of compounds.

- **The same combination of elements,** such as carbon and hydrogen, can form many different compounds.

- **Compounds** are either organic (see organic chemistry), which means they contain carbon atoms, or inorganic.

▼ The molecules of a compound are identical combinations of atoms.

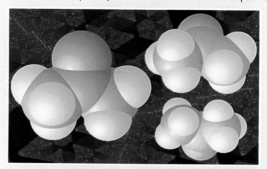

Halogens

▲ Chlorine salts are often added to the water in swimming pools to kill bacteria, giving the water a greenish-blue tinge.

- **Halogens** are the chemical elements fluorine, chlorine, bromine, iodine and astatine.

- **The word 'halogen'** means salt-forming. All halogens easily form salt compounds.

- **Many of the salts in the sea** are compounds of a halogen and a metal, such as sodium chloride and magnesium chloride.

- **The halogens** all have a strong, often nasty, smell.

- **Fluorine** is a pale yellow gas, chlorine a greenish gas, bromine a red liquid, and iodine a black solid.

- **Astatine** is an unstable element that survives by itself only briefly. It is usually made artificially.

- **The halogens** together form Group 17 of the Periodic Table, elements with 7 electrons in the outer shells.

- **Because halogens have** one electron missing, they form negative ions and are highly reactive.

- **The iodine and bromine** in a halogen lightbulb make it burn brighter and longer.

★ STAR FACT ★
Fluorides (fluorine compounds) are often
added to drinking water to prevent tooth decay.

Particle physics

- **Apart from the three** basic, stable particles of atoms – electrons, protons and neutrons – scientists have found over 200 rare or short-lived particles. Some were found in cosmic rays from space; some appear when atoms are smashed to bits in devices called particle accelerators.

- **Every particle** also has a mirror-image anti-particle. Although Antimatter may be rarer, it is every bit as real.

- **Cosmic rays** contain not only electrons, protons and neutrons, but short-lived particles such as muons and strange quarks. Muons flash into existence for 2.2 microseconds just before the cosmic rays reach the ground.

- **Smashing atoms** in particle accelerators creates short-lived high-energy particles such as taus and pions and three kinds of quark called charm, bottom and top.

- **Particles** are now grouped into a simple framework called the Standard Model. It divides them into elementary particles and composite particles to stop radiation leaks.

- **Elementary particles** are the basic particles which cannot be broken down in anything smaller. There are three groups: quarks, leptons and bosons. Leptons include electrons, muons, taus and neutrinos. Bosons are 'messenger' particles that link the others. They include photons and gluons which 'glue' quarks together.

- **Composite particles** are hadrons made of quarks glued together by gluons. They include protons, neutrons and 'hyperons' and 'resonances'.

> ★ STAR FACT ★
> When the Fermi particle accelerator is running 250,000 particle collisions occur every second.

- **To smash atoms** scientists use particle accelerators, which are giant machines set in tunnels. The accelerators use powerful magnets to accelerate particles through a tube at huge speeds, and then smash them together.

- **Huge detectors** pick up collisions between particles.

▼ A view of the particle accelerator tunnel at CERN in Switzerland.

Incredibly powerful electromagnets accelerate the particles.

Extra electromagnets keep the particles on track through the pipe.

The particles are split up and fed towards the detector from opposite directions so they collide head-on.

Some accelerators are ring-shaped so that the particles can whizz round again and again to build up speed.

New particles are fed in from a hot filament like a giant lightbulb filament.

The detectors that record the collisions are like giant electronic cameras. They can be three storeys high and weigh over 5000 tonnes.

The pipes are heavily insulated to stop particles escaping.

◄ The accelerators at Fermilab near Chicago, USA and CERN in Switzerland are underground tubes many kilometres long through which particles are accelerated to near the speed of light.

Forces

- **A force** is a push or a pull. It can make something start to move, slow down or speed up, change direction or change shape or size. The greater a force, the more effect it has.

- **The wind is a force.** Biting, twisting, stretching, lifting and many other actions are also forces. Every time something happens, a force is involved.

- **Force is measured** in newtons (N). One newton is the force needed to speed up a mass of one kilogram by one metre per second every second.

- **When something moves** there are usually several forces involved. When you throw a ball, the force of your throw hurls it forwards, the force of gravity pulls it down and the force of air resistance slows it down.

> ★ STAR FACT ★
> The thrust of *Saturn V*'s rocket engines was 33 million newtons.

- **The direction and speed** of movement depend on the combined effect of all the forces involved – this is called the resultant.

- **A force** has magnitude (size) and works in a particular direction.

- **A force can** be drawn on a diagram as an arrow called a vector (see vectors). The arrow's direction shows the force's direction. Its length shows the force's strength.

- **Four fundamental forces** operate throughout the Universe: gravity, electric and magnetic forces (together called electromagnetic force), and strong and weak nuclear forces (see nuclear energy).

- **A force field** is the area over which a force has an effect. The field is strongest closest to the source and gets weaker farther away.

◀ When a spacecraft lifts off, the force of the rocket has to overcome the forces of gravity and air resistance to power it upwards.

Electricity

- **Electricity** is the energy that makes everything from toasters to televisions work. It is also linked to magnetism. Together, as electromagnetism, they are one of the four fundamental forces holding the Universe together.

- **Electricity** is made by tiny bits of atoms called electrons. Electrons have an electrical charge which is a force that either pulls bits of atoms together or pushes them apart.

▼ Lightning is a dramatic display of natural electricity.

- **Some particles** (bit of atoms) have a negative electrical charge; others have a positive charge.

- **Particles** with the same charge push each other away. Particles with the opposite charge pull together.

- **Electrons** have a negative electrical charge.

- **There are the same number** of positive and negative particles in most atoms so the charges usually balance.

- **Electricity** is created when electrons move, building up negative charge in one place or carrying it along.

- **Static electricity** is when the negative charge stays in one place. Current electricity is when the charge moves.

- **Electric charge** is measured with an electroscope.

- **Materials** that let electrons (and electrical charge) move through them easily, such as copper, are called conductors. Materials that stop electrons passing through, such as rubber, are called insulators.

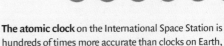

Time

▲ As the Sun moves through the sky we can clearly see the passing of time. Until 1967 the movement of the Sun was our most accurate way of measuring time.

- **No clock** keeps perfect time. For most of history clocks were set by the Sun and stars.

- **Since 1967** the world's time has been set by atomic clocks.

- **Atomic clocks** are accurate to 0.001 sec in 1000 years.

- **If a caesium atomic** clock ran for six million years it would not gain or lose a second.

- **The most** accurate clock is the American NIST-7 atomic clock.

- **The atomic clock** on the International Space Station is hundreds of times more accurate than clocks on Earth, because it is not affected by gravity.

- **Atomic clocks** work because caesium atoms vibrate exactly 9,192,631,770 times a second.

- **Some scientists** say that time is the fourth dimension – the other three are length, breadth and height. So time could theoretically run in any direction. Others say time only moves in one direction. Just as we cannot unburn a candle, so we cannot turn back time (see time travel).

- **Light takes** millions of years to reach us from distant galaxies, so we see them not as they are but as they were millions of years ago. Light takes a little while to reach us even from nearby things.

- **Einstein's theory of General Relativity** shows that time actually runs slower nearer strong gravitational fields such as stars. This does not mean that the clock is running slower but that time itself is running slower.

Chemical reactions

- **A candle burning,** a nail rusting, a cake cooking – all involve chemical reactions.

- **A chemical reaction** is when two or more elements or compounds meet and interact to form new compounds or separate out some of the elements.

- **The chemicals** in a chemical reaction are called the reactants. The results are called the products.

- **The products** contain the same atoms as the reactants but in different combinations.

- **The products** have the same total mass as the reactants.

- **Some reactions** are reversible – the products can be changed back to the original reactants. Others, such as making toast, are irreversible.

- **Effervescence** is a reaction in which gas bubbles form in a liquid, turning it fizzy.

- **A catalyst** is a substance that speeds up or enables a chemical reaction to happen, but slows down or remains unchanged at the end.

- **Nearly all reactions** involve energy. Some involve light or electricity. Most involve heat. Reactions that give out heat are called exothermic. Those that draw in heat are called endothermic.

- **Oxidation** is a reaction in which oxygen combines with a substance. Burning is oxidation; as the fuel burns it combines with oxygen in the air. Reduction is a reaction in which a substance loses oxygen.

▶ Burning is an oxidation reaction. Carbon in the trees combines with oxygen in the air to form carbon dioxide.

The Periodic Table

- **The Periodic Table** is a chart of all the 100-plus different chemical elements (see elements).

- **The Periodic Table** was devised by Russian chemist Dmitri Mendeleyev (1834–1907) in 1869. Mendeleyev realized that each element is part of a complete set, and so he predicted the existence of three then unknown elements – gallium, scandium and germanium.

- **The Periodic Table** arranges all the elements according to their Atomic Number, which is the number of protons in their atoms (see atoms). The table lists the elements in order of Atomic Number, starting with hydrogen at 1.

- **Atoms** usually have the same number of electrons (see electrons) as protons. So the Atomic Number also indicates the normal number of electrons an atom has.

- **Atomic mass** is the average weight of an atom of an element and corresponds to the average number of protons and neutrons in the nucleus. The number of neutrons varies in a small number of atoms, called isotopes, so the atomic mass is never a round number.

- **The columns** in the Periodic Table are called Groups. The rows are called Periods.

- **The number** of layers, or shells, of electrons in the atoms of an element increases one by one down each Group. So all the elements in each Period have the same number of electron shells.

- **The number of electrons** in the atom's outer shell goes up one by one across each Period.

- **Each Group** is made up of elements with a certain number of electrons in their outer shell. This is what largely determines the element's character. All the elements in each Group have similar properties. Many of the Groups have a name as well as a number, as below.

- **Each Period** starts on the left with a highly reactive alkali metal of Group 1, such as sodium. Each atom of elements in Group 1 has a single electron in its outer shell. Each Period ends on the right with a stable 'noble' gas of Group 18, such as argon. These elements have the full number of electrons in their outer shell and so they do not react.

▼ The Periodic Table arranges all the chemical elements in columns and rows according to their atomic number, showing clearly how they are related.

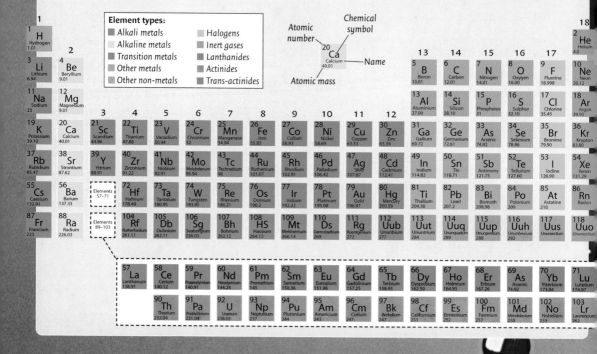

Crystals

- **Crystals** are particular kinds of solids that are made from a regular arrangement, or lattice, of atoms. Most rocks and metals are crystals, so are snowflakes and salt.

- **Most crystals** have regular, geometrical shapes with smooth faces and sharp corners.

- **Most crystals** grow in dense masses, as in metals. Some crystals grow separately, like grains of sugar.

- **Some crystals** are shiny and clear to look at. Crystals got their name from the chunks of quartz that the ancient Greeks called *krystallos*. They believed the chunks were unmeltable ice.

- **Crystals** form by a process called crystallization. As liquid evaporates or molten solids cool, the chemicals dissolved in them solidify.

▶ *Crystals such as these grow naturally as minerals are deposited from hot mineral-rich liquids underground.*

- **Crystals** grow as more atoms attach themselves to the lattice, just as icicles grow as water freezes onto them.

- **The smallest crystals** are microscopically small. Occasionally crystals of a mineral such as beryl may grow to the size of telegraph poles.

- **A liquid crystal** is a crystal that can flow like a liquid but has a regular pattern of atoms.

- **A liquid crystal** may change colour or go dark when the alignment of its atoms is disrupted by electricity or heat. Liquid crystal displays (LCDs) use a tiny electric current to make crystals affect light.

- **X-ray crystallography** uses X-rays to study the structure of atoms in a crystal. This is how we know the structure of many important life substances such as DNA.

Friction

- **Friction** is the force that acts between two things rubbing together. It stops them sliding past each other.

- **The friction** that stops things starting to slide is called static friction. The friction that slows down sliding surfaces is called dynamic friction.

- **The harder** two surfaces are pressed together, the greater the force that is needed to overcome friction.

- **The coefficient of friction (CF)** is the ratio of the friction to the weight of the sliding object.

- **Metal sliding on metal** has a CF of 0.74; ice sliding on ice has a CF of 0.1. This means it is over seven times harder to make metal slide on metal than ice on ice.

- **Friction often makes things hot.** As the sliding object is slowed down, much of the energy of its momentum is turned into heat.

- **Fluid friction** is the friction between moving fluids or between a fluid and a solid. It is what makes thick fluids viscous (less runny).

- **Oil reduces friction** by creating a film that keeps the solid surfaces apart.

- **Brakes use dynamic friction** to slow things down.

- **Drag is friction** between air and an object. It slows a fast car, or any aircraft moving through the air.

▼ *Waxed skis on snow have a CF of just 0.14, allowing cross-country skiers to slide along the ground very easily.*

Lavoisier

- **Antoine Laurent Lavoisier** (1743–1794) was a brilliant French scientist who is regarded as the founder of modern chemistry.

- **He was elected** to the French Royal Academy of Sciences at just 25 for an essay on street lighting. A year later, he worked on the first geological map of France.

- **Lavoisier earned his living** for a long while as a 'tax farmer', which meant he worked for a private company collecting taxes.

- **In 1771** he married 14-year-old Marie Paulze, who later became his illustrator and collaborator in the laboratory.

- **Lavoisier** was the first person to realize that air is essentially a mixture of two gases: oxygen and nitrogen.

- **Lavoisier discovered** that water is a compound of hydrogen and oxygen.

◄ *Lavoisier showed the importance of precision weighing in the laboratory.*

- **Lavoisier** showed that the popular phlogiston theory of burning was wrong and that burning involves oxygen instead.

- **Lavoisier** gave the first working list of chemical elements in his famous book *Elementary Treatise of Chemistry* (1789).

- **From 1776** Lavoisier headed research at the Royal Arsenal in Paris, developing gunpowder manufacture.

- **Lavoisier ran schemes** for public education, fair taxation, old-age insurance and other welfare schemes. But his good deeds did not save him. When Lavoisier had a wall built round Paris to reduce smuggling, revolutionary leader Marat accused him of imprisoning Paris's air. His past as a tax farmer was remembered and Lavoisier was guillotined in 1794.

Electromagnetism

▲ *Wind turbines generate electricity by using the wind to turn their blades. These drive magnets around inside coils of electric wire.*

- **Electromagnetism** is the combined effect of electricity and magnetism.

- **Every electric current** creates its own magnetic field.

- **Maxwell's screw rule** says that the magnetic field runs the same way a screw turns if you screw it in the direction of the electric current – clockwise.

- **An electromagnet** is a strong magnet that is only magnetic when an electric current passes through it. It is made by wrapping a coil of wire, called a solenoid, around a core of iron.

- **Electromagnets** are used in everything from ticket machines and telephones to loudspeakers.

- **Magnetic levitation** trains use strong electromagnets to carry the train on a cushion of magnetic repulsion.

- **When an electric wire** is moved across a magnetic field, an electric current is created, or induced, in the wire. This is the basis of every kind of electricity generation.

- **Fleming's right-hand rule** says that if you hold your right thumb, first and middle fingers at 90° to each other, your middle finger shows the direction of the induced current – if your thumb points in the direction the wire moves and your first finger points out the magnetic field.

- **Electromagnets** can be switched on and off, unlike permanent magnets.

- **Around every** electric or magnetic object is an area, or electromagnetic field, where its force is effective.

Heat

- **Heat is the energy** of moving molecules. The faster molecules move, the hotter it is.
- **When you hold your hand** over a heater the warmth is the assault of billions of fast-moving molecules of air.
- **Heat** is the combined energy of all the moving molecules; temperature is how fast they are moving.
- **The coldest temperature possible** is absolute zero, or −273.15°C, when molecules stop moving.
- **When you heat a substance** its temperature rises because heat makes its molecules move faster.
- **The same amount** of heat raises the temperature of different substances by different amounts.
- **Specific heat** is the energy needed, in joules, to heat a substance by 1°C.

> ★ STAR FACT ★
> Heat makes the molecules of a solid vibrate;
> it makes gas molecules zoom about.

- **Argon gas** gets hotter quicker than oxygen. The shape of oxygen molecules means they absorb some energy not by moving faster but by spinning faster.
- **Heat always spreads out** from its source. It heats up its surroundings while cooling down itself.

◀ Fire changes the energy in fuel into heat energy. Heat makes the molecules rush about.

Iron and steel

- **Iron** is the most common element in the world. It makes up 35% of the Earth, but most of it is in the Earth's core.
- **Iron is never found** in its pure form in the Earth's crust. Instead it is found in iron ores, which must be heated in a blast furnace to extract the iron.
- **The chemical symbol** for iron is Fe from *ferrum*, the Latin word for iron. Iron compounds are called either ferrous or ferric.

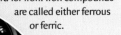

- **Iron has** an atomic number of 26 and an atomic weight of 55.85.

◀ A solid-state laser can cut through carbon steel like butter even though steel is incredibly tough.

- **Iron melts** at 1535°C and boils at 3000°C. It conducts heat and electricity quite well and dissolves in water very slowly. Iron is easily magnetized. It loses its magnetism easily but steel can be permanently magnetic.
- **Iron** combines easily with oxygen to form iron oxide, especially in the presence of moisture. This is rusting.
- **Cast iron** is iron with 2–4% carbon and 1–3% silicon. It is suitable for pouring into sand moulds. Wrought iron is almost pure iron with carbon removed to make it easy to bend and shape for railings and gates.
- **Iron is made into steel** by adding traces of carbon for making cars, railway lines, knives and much more. Alloy steels are made by adding traces of metals such as tungsten (for tools) and chromium (for ball bearings).
- **60% of steel** is made by the basic oxygen process in which oxygen is blasted over molten iron to burn out impurities.
- **Special alloy steels** such as chromium steels can be made from scrap iron (which is low in impurities) in an electric arc furnace.

Fibre optics

- **Fibre optic cables** are bundles of transparent glass threads that transmit messages by light.
- **The light is transmitted** in coded pulses.
- **A thin layer of glass,** called cladding, surrounds each fibre and stops light from escaping.
- **The cladding** reflects all the light back into the fibre so that it bends round with the fibre. This is called total internal reflection.
- **Single-mode fibres** are very narrow and the light bounces very little from side to side. These fibres are suitable for long-distance transmissions.
- **Aiming light** into the narrow core of a single-mode fibre needs the precision of a laser beam.
- **Multi-mode fibres** are wider than single-mode fibres. They accept LED (light-emitting diodes) light, so they are cheaper but they are unsuitable for long distances.
- **The largest cables** can carry hundreds of thousands of phone calls or hundreds of television channels.

▲ *A bundle of optical fibres glows with transmitted light.*

- **Underwater fibre optic** cables transmit signals under the Atlantic and Pacific Oceans.
- **Optical fibres** have medical uses, such as in endoscopes. These are flexible tubes with a lens on the end, which are inserted into the body to look inside it. Optical fibres are used to measure blood temperature and pressure.

Metals

▼ *Metals are very tough but can be easily shaped. They are used for an enormous variety of things, from chains to cars.*

- **75% of all known elements** are metals.
- **Most metals** ring when hit. A typical metal is hard but malleable, which means it can be hammered into sheets.
- **Metals** are usually shiny. They conduct both heat and electricity well.
- **Metals** do not form separate molecules. Instead atoms of metal knit together with metallic bonds (see chemical bonds) to form lattice structures.
- **The electron shells of all metals** are less than half-full. In a chemical reaction metals give up their electrons to a non-metal.
- **Most metals** occur naturally in the ground only in rocks called ores.
- **Gold, copper,** mercury, platinum, silver and a few other rare metals occur naturally in their pure form.
- **Mercury** is the only metal that is liquid at normal temperatures. It melts at −38.87°C.
- **A few atoms** of the new metal ununquadium (atomic number 114) were made in January 1999.

> ★ **STAR FACT** ★
> At 3410°C, tungsten has the highest melting point of any metal.

Radioactivity

- **Radioactivity** is when a certain kind of atom disintegrates spontaneously and sends out little bursts of radiation from its nucleus (centre).

- **Isotopes** are slightly different versions of an atom, with either more or less neutrons (see atoms). With stable elements, such as carbon, only certain isotopes called radio-isotopes are radioactive.

- **Some large atoms**, such as radium and uranium, are so unstable that all their isotopes are radio-isotopes.

- **Radioactive isotopes** emit three kinds of radiation: alpha, beta and gamma rays.

- **When the nucleus** of an atom emits alpha or beta rays it changes and becomes the atom of a different element. This is called radioactive decay.

- **Alpha rays** are streams of alpha particles. These are made from two protons and two neutrons – basically the nucleus of a helium atom. They travel only a few centimetres and can be stopped by a sheet of paper.

- **Beta rays** are beta particles. Beta particles are electrons (or their opposite, positrons) emitted as a neutron decays into a proton. They can travel up to 1 m and can penetrate aluminium foil.

▶ The radioisotope carbon-14 is present in all living things, but when they die it begins to steadily decay radioactively. By measuring how much carbon-14 is left relative to carbon-12 isotopes, which don't decay, scientists can tell exactly when a living thing died, including wood and bone.

- **Gamma rays** are an energetic, short-wave form of electromagnetic radiation (see electromagnetic spectrum). They penetrate most materials but lead.

- **The half-life** of a radioactive substance is the time it takes for its radioactivity to drop by half. This is much easier to assess than the time for the radioactivity to disappear altogether.

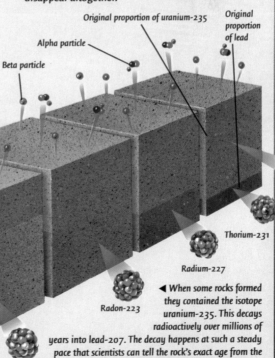

Original proportion of uranium-235

Original proportion of lead

Alpha particle

Beta particle

Thorium-231

Radium-227

◀ When some rocks formed they contained the isotope uranium-235. This decays radioactively over millions of years into lead-207. The decay happens at such a steady pace that scientists can tell the rock's exact age from the proportion of uranium-235 left compared to lead-207. The higher proportion of lead-207, the older the rock.

Radon-223

Polonium-219

Lead-207

Light and atoms

- **Light comes** from atoms. They give out light when they gain energy – by absorbing light or other electromagnetic waves or when hit by other particles.

- **Atoms** are normally in a 'ground' state. Their electrons circle close to the nucleus where their energy is at its lowest ebb.

- **An atom emits light** when 'excited' by taking in energy. Excitement boosts an electron's energy so it jumps further from the nucleus.

- **An atom** only stays excited a fraction of second before the electron drops back in towards the nucleus.

- **As an electron** drops back, it releases energy it gained as a packet of electromagnetic radiation called a photon.

- **Electrons** drop towards the nucleus in steps, like a ball bouncing down stairs.

◀ Spectroscopy is used to analyse the colour of light from distant stars and galaxies. It allows scientists to identify what the stars are made of.

- **Since each step** the electron drops in has a particular energy level, so the energy of the photon depends precisely on how big the steps are. Big steps send out higher-energy short-wave photons like X-rays.

- **The colour of light** an atom sends out depends on the size of the steps its electrons jump down.

- **Each kind of atom** has its own range of electron energy steps, so each sends out particular colours of light. The range of colours each kind of atom sends out is called its emission spectrum. For gases, this acts like a colour signature to identify in a process called spectroscopy.

- **Just as an atom** only emits certain colours, so it can only absorb certain colours. This is its absorption spectrum.

Quantum physics

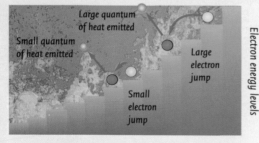

Small quantum of heat emitted

Large quantum of heat emitted

Large electron jump

Small electron jump

Electron energy levels

▲ Quantum physics shows how radiation from a hot object is emitted in little chunks called quanta.

- **By the 1890s** most scientists thought light moves in waves.

- **Max Planck** (1858–1947) realized that the range of radiation given out by a hot object is not quite what scientists would calculate it to be if radiation is waves.

- **Planck realized** that the radiation from a hot object could be explained if the radiation came in chunks, or quanta.

- **Quanta** are very, very small. When lots of quanta are

emitted together they appear to be like smooth waves.

- **In 1905** Einstein showed that quanta explain the photoelectric effect.

- **In 1913** Niels Bohr showed how the arrangement of electrons in energy levels around an atom (see electrons) could be thought of in a quantum way too.

- **In the 1920s** Erwin Schrödinger and Werner Heisenberg developed Bohr's idea into quantum physics, a new branch of physics for particles on the scale of atoms.

- **Quantum physics** explains how electrons emit radiation (see above). It shows that an electron is both a particle and a wave, depending on how you look at it. It seems to work for all four fundamental forces (see forces) except gravity.

- **The development** of the technologies that gave us lasers and transistors came from quantum physics.

- **Quantum physics** predicts some strange things on the scale of atoms, such as particles appearing from nowhere and electrons seeming to know where each other are.

Floating and sinking

- **Things float** because they are less dense than water, which is why you can lift quite a heavy person in a swimming pool. This loss of weight is called buoyancy.

- **Buoyancy** is created by the upward push, or upthrust, of the water.

- **When an object** is immersed in water, its weight pushes it down. At the same time the water pushes it

▼ The liner Titanic was said to be unsinkable. However, as soon as an iceberg breached her hull and let in water to replace the air, she sank like a stone.

- back up with a force equal to the weight of water displaced (pushed out of the way). This is called Archimedes' principle (see Archimedes).

- **An object sinks** until its weight is exactly equal to the upthrust of the water, at which point it floats.

- **Things that are less dense** than water float; those that are more dense sink.

- **Steel ships** float because although steel is denser than water, their hulls are full of air. They sink until enough water is displaced to match the weight of steel and air in the hull.

- **Oil floats** on water because it is less dense.

- **Ships float** at different heights according to how heavily laden they are and how dense the water is.

- **Ships float higher** in sea water than in fresh water because salt makes the sea water more dense.

- **Ships float higher** in dense cold seas than in warm tropical ones. They float higher in the winter months.

Electronics

- **Electronics** are the basis of many modern technologies, from hi-fi systems to missile control systems.

- **Electronics** are systems that control things by automatically switching tiny electrical circuits on and off.

- **Transistors** are electronic switches. They are made of materials called semiconductors that change their ability to conduct electricity.

- **Electronic systems work** by linking many transistors together so that each controls the way the others work.

- **Diodes** are transistors with two connectors. They control an electric current by switching it on or off.

- **Triodes** are transistors with three connectors that amplify the electric current (make it bigger) or reduce it.

- **A silicon chip** is thousands of transistors linked by thin

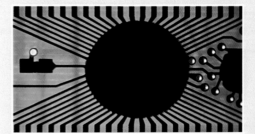

▲ Microprocessors contain millions of transistors in a package that is no bigger than a human fingernail.

metal strips in an integrated circuit, on a single crystal of the semiconductor silicon.

- **The electronic areas** of a chip are those treated with traces of chemicals such as boron and phosphorus, which alter the conductivity of silicon.

- **Microprocessors** are complete Central Processing Units (see computers) on a single silicon chip.

> ★ STAR FACT ★
> Some microprocessors can now handle billions of bits of data every second.

Telecommunications

- **Telecommunications** is the almost instantaneous transmission of sounds, words, pictures, data and information by electronic means.

- **Every communication system** needs three things: a transmitter, a communications link and a receiver.

- **Transmitters** can be telephones or computers with modems (see the internet). They change the words, pictures, data or sounds into an electrical signal and send it. Similar receivers pick up the signal and change it back into the right form.

- **Communications links** carry the signal from the transmitter to the receiver in two main ways. Some give a direct link through telephone lines and other cables. Some are carried on radio waves through the air, via satellite or microwave links.

- **Telephone lines** used to be mainly electric cables which carried the signal as pulses of electricity. More and more are now fibre optics (see fibre optics) which carry the signal as coded pulses of light.

▼ *This illustration shows some of the many ways in which telecommunications are carried. At present, TV, radio and phone links are all carried separately, but increasingly they will all be carried the same way. They will be split up only when they arrive at their destination.*

- **Communications satellites** are satellites orbiting the Earth in space. Telephone calls are beamed up on radio waves to the satellite, which beams them back down to the right part of the world.

- **Microwave links** use very short radio waves to transmit telephone and other signals direct from one dish to another in a straight line across Earth's surface.

- **Mobile phones** or cellular phones transmit and receive phone calls directly via radio waves. The calls are picked up and sent on from a local aerial.

- **The information superhighway** is the network of high-speed links that might be achieved by combining telephone systems, cable TV and computer networks. TV programmes, films, data, direct video links and the Internet could all enter the home in this way.

> ★ STAR FACT ★
> Calls across the ocean go one way by satellite and the other by undersea cable to avoid delays.

TV and radio signals are either broadcast as pulses of radio waves, sent direct via cables or bounced off satellites.

Computer data are translated by a modem into signals that can be carried on phone lines.

Signals from individual transmitters are sent on from a telephone exchange or a service provider.

More and more communications are beamed off satellites in space.

Communications that travel via satellites are beamed up from antenna dishes on the ground.

Telephones can link in to the phone network by a direct cable link. Mobile phones link through the air to local relay towers by radio waves.

Splitting the atom

► You cannot actually see sub-atomic particles, but after collisions they leave tracks behind them, like these particle tracks in smoke. Photographs of these tracks tell scientists a great deal.

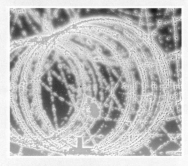

- **In the 1890s** scientists thought that atoms were solid like billiard balls and completely unbreakable.

- **In 1897** J. J. Thomson discovered that atoms contained even smaller particles, which he called electrons (see electrons).

- **In 1900** scientists thought atoms were like plum puddings with electrons like currants on the outside.

- **In 1909** Ernest Rutherford was firing alpha particles (see radioactivity) at a sheet of gold foil. Most went straight through, but 1 in 8000 particles bounced back!

- **Rutherford concluded** that the atom was mostly empty space (which the alpha particles passed straight through) but had a tiny, dense nucleus at its centre.

- **In 1919** Rutherford split the nucleus of a nitrogen atom with alpha particles. Small atoms could be split.

- **In 1932** James Chadwick found the nucleus contained two kinds of particle: protons and neutrons.

- **In 1933** Italian Enrico Fermi bombarded the big atoms of uranium with neutrons. Fermi thought the new atoms that formed had simply gained the neutrons.

- **In 1939** German scientists Hahn and Strassman repeated Fermi's experiment and found smaller atoms of barium.

- **Austrian Lise Meitner** realized that Hahn and Strassman had split uranium atoms. This discovery opened the way to releasing nuclear energy by fission.

Heat movement

- **Heat moves** in three different ways: conduction, convection and radiation.

- **Conduction** involves heat spreading from hot areas to cold areas by direct contact. It works a bit like a relay race. Energetic, rapidly moving or vibrating molecules cannon into their neighbours and set them moving.

- **Good conducting materials** such as metals feel cool to the touch because they carry heat away from your fingers quickly. The best conductors of heat are the metals silver, copper and gold, in that order.

- **Materials** that conduct heat slowly are called insulators. They help keep things warm by reducing heat loss. Wood is one of the best insulators. Water is also surprisingly effective as an insulator, which is why some divers and surfers often wear wetsuits.

- **Radiation** is the spread of heat as heat rays, that is, invisible waves of infrared radiation.

◄ Hot-air balloons work because hot air is lighter and rises through cold air.

- **Radiation** spreads heat without direct contact.

- **Convection** is when warm air rises through cool air, like a hot-air balloon.

- **Warm air rises** because warmth makes the air expand. As it expands the air becomes less dense and lighter than the cool air around it.

- **Convection currents** are circulation patterns set up as warm air (or a liquid) rises. Around the column of rising warmth, cool air continually sinks to replace it at the bottom. So the whole air turns over like a non-stop fountain.

★ STAR FACT ★
Convection currents in the air bring rain; convection currents in the Earth's interior move continents.

Light sources

▲ Gas mixtures in neon lights glow different colours. Pure neon glows red.

◄ Electrical resistance makes the thin filament in a bulb glow.

- **Our main sources of natural light** are the Sun and the stars. The hot gases on their surface glow fiercely.

- **The brightness** of a light source is measured in candelas (cd); 1 candela is about as bright as a small candle.

- **For 0.1 millisecond** an atom bomb flashes out 2000 billion candelas for every square metre (m²).

- **The Sun's surface** pumps out 23 billion candela per m². Laser lights are even brighter, but very small.

- **The light falling** on a surface is measured in lux. 1 lux is how brightly lit something is by a light of 1 candela 1 m away. You need 500 lux to read by.

- **Electric lightbulbs** are incandescent, which means that their light comes from a thin tungsten wire, or filament, that glows when heated by an electric current.

- **Lightbulbs** are filled with an inert (unreactive) gas, such as argon, to save the filament from burning out.

- **Electric lights** were invented independently in 1878 by Englishman Sir Joseph Swan and Americans Thomas Alva Edison and Hiram Maxim.

- **Fluorescent lights** have a glass tube coated on the inside with powders called phosphors. When electricity excites the gases in the tube to send out invisible UV rays, the rays hit the phosphors and make them glow, or fluoresce.

- **In neon lights,** a huge electric current makes the gas inside a tube electrically charged and so it glows.

Weight and mass

- **Mass** is the amount of matter in an object.

- **Weight** is not the same as mass. Scientists say weight is the force of gravity pulling on an object. Weight varies with the mass of the object and the strength of gravity.

- **Objects weigh more** at sea level, which is nearer the centre of the Earth, than up a mountain.

- **A person on the Moon** weighs one sixth of their weight on Earth because the Moon's gravity is one sixth of the Earth's gravity.

- **Weight varies** with gravity but mass is always the same, so scientists use mass when talking about how heavy something is.

▶ Brass is used for weights as it is reasonably dense and and does not corrode.

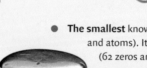

- **The smallest** known mass is that of a photon (see light and atoms). Its mass is 5.3 times 10^{-63} (62 zeros and a 1 after the decimal point) kg.

- **The mass of the Earth** is 6×10^{24} (six trillion trillion) kg. The mass of the Universe may be 10^{51} (10 followed by 50 zeros) kg.

- **Density is** the amount of mass in a certain space. It is measured in grams per cubic centimetre (g/cm³).

- **The lightest** solids are silica aerogels made for space science, with a density of 0.005 g/cm³. The lightest gas is hydrogen, at 0.00008989 g/cm³. The density of air is 0.00128 g/cm³.

- **The densest** solid is osmium at 22.59 g/cm³. Lead is 11.37 g/cm³. A neutron star has an incredible density of about one billion trillion g/cm³.

The Curies

- **Pierre and Marie Curie** were the husband and wife scientists who discovered the nature of radioactivity. In 1903 they won a Nobel Prize for their work .

- **Marie Curie** (1867–1934) was born Marya Sklodowska in Poland. She went to Paris in 1891 to study physics.

- **Pierre Curie** (1859–1906) was a French lecturer in physics who discovered the piezoelectric effect in crystals. His discovery led to the development of devices from quartz watches to microphones.

- **The Curies** met in 1894 while Marie was a student at the Sorbonne. They married in 1895.

- **In 1896** Antoine Becquerel found that uranium salts emitted a mysterious radiation that affected photographic paper in the same way as light.

- **In 1898** the Curies found the intensity of radiation was in exact proportion to the amount of uranium – so it must be coming from the uranium atoms.

- **The Curies called** atomic radiation 'radioactivity'.

- **In July 1898** the Curies discovered a new radioactive element. Marie called it polonium after her native Poland.

- **In December** the Curies found radium – an element even more radioactive than uranium.

- **In 1906** Pierre was killed by a tram. Marie died later from the effects of her exposure to radioactive materials, the dangers of which were unknown at that time.

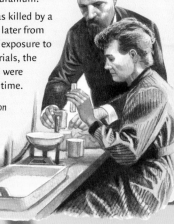

▶ The Curies' combination of brilliant insight with exact, patient work led to their historic breakthrough in discovering radioactivity.

Hydrogen

▲ Hydrogen's combination with oxygen in water makes it one of the most important elements on the Earth.

- **Hydrogen** is the lightest of all gases and elements. A large swimming pool of hydrogen would weigh just 1 kg.

- **Hydrogen** atoms have just one proton and one electron.

- **Hydrogen** is the first element in the Periodic Table. It has an Atomic Number of 1 and an atomic mass of 1.00794.

- **One in every 6000** hydrogen atoms has a neutron as well as a proton in its nucleus, making it twice as heavy. This atom is called deuterium.

- **Rare** hydrogen atoms have two neutrons as well as the proton, making them three times as heavy. These are called tritium.

- **Hydrogen** is the most common substance in the Universe, making up over 90% of the Universe's weight.

- **Hydrogen** was the first element to form after the Universe began. It was billions of years before another element formed.

- **Most hydrogen** on Earth occurs in combination with other elements, such as oxygen in water. Pure hydrogen occurs naturally in a few places, such as small underground pockets and as tiny traces in the air.

- **Hydrogen** is one of the most reactive gases. It bursts easily and often explosively into flames.

- **Under extreme pressure** hydrogen becomes a metal – the most electrically conductive metal of all.

Quarks

- **Quarks** are one of the three tiniest basic, or elementary, particles from which every substance is made.

- **Quarks** are too small for their size to be measured, but their mass can. The biggest quark, called a top quark, is as heavy as an atom of gold. The smallest, called an up quark, is 35,000 times lighter.

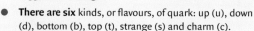

6 kinds of lepton   6 kinds of quark   3 kinds of bosons

▲ These are the main kinds of elementary particle – quarks, leptons and bosons. Hadrons are combinations of two or three quarks.

Hadrons

Baryons   Mesons

- **There are six** kinds, or flavours, of quark: up (u), down (d), bottom (b), top (t), strange (s) and charm (c).

- **Down, bottom and strange** quarks carry one third of the negative charge of electrons; up, top and charm ones carry two-thirds of the positive charge of protons.

- **Quarks never exist** separately but in combination with one or two other quarks. Combinations of two or three quarks are called hadrons.

- **Three-quark hadrons** are called baryons and include protons and neutrons. Rare two-quark hadrons are mesons.

- **A proton** is made from two up quarks (two lots of +2/3 of a charge) and one down quark (−1/3) and has a positive charge of 1.

- **A neutron** is made from two down quarks (two lots of −1/3 of a charge) and an up quark (+2/3). The charges cancel each other out, giving a neutron no charge.

- **The theory of quarks** was first proposed by Murray Gell-Mann and Georg Zweig in 1964.

- **Quarks** are named after a famous passage in James Joyce's book *Ulysses*: 'Three quarks for Muster Mark!'

Air

- **The air** is a mixture of gases, dust and moisture.

- **The gas nitrogen** makes up 78.08% of the air. Nitrogen is largely unreactive, but it sometimes reacts with oxygen to form oxides of nitrogen.

- **Nitrogen** is continually recycled by the bacteria that consume plant and animal waste.

- **Oxygen** makes up 20.94% of the air. Animals breathe

> ★ STAR FACT ★
> Air is a unique mixture that exists on Earth and nowhere else in the solar system.

in oxygen. Plants give it out as they take their energy from sunlight in photosynthesis.

- **Carbon dioxide** makes up 0.03% of the air. Carbon dioxide is continually recycled as it is breathed out by animals and taken in by plants in photosynthesis.

- **The air contains** other, inert (unreactive) gases: 0.93% is argon; 0.0018% is neon; 0.0005% is helium.

- **There are tiny traces** of krypton and xenon which are also inert.

- **Ozone makes up** 0.00006% of the air. It is created when sunlight breaks up oxygen.

- **Hydrogen makes up** 0.00005% of the air. This gas is continually drifting off into space.

Relativity

- **Einstein** (see Einstein) was the creator of two theories of relativity which have revolutionized scientists' way of thinking about the Universe: the special theory of relativity (1905) and the general theory (1915).

- **Time is relative** because it depends where you measure it from (see time). Distances and speed are relative too. If you are in a car and another car whizzes past you, for instance, the slower you are travelling, the faster the other car seems to be moving.

- **Einstein showed** in his special theory of relativity that you cannot even measure your speed relative to a beam of light, which is the fastest thing in the Universe. This is because light always passes you at the same speed, no matter where you are or how fast you are going.

> ★ STAR FACT ★
> When astronauts went to the Moon, their clock lost a few seconds. The clock was not faulty, but time actually ran slower in the speeding spacecraft.

- **Einstein** realized that if light always travels at the same speed, there are some strange effects when you are moving very fast (see below).

- **If a rocket** passing you zoomed up to near the speed of light, you would see it shrink.

- **If a rocket** passing you zoomed up to near the speed of light, you'd see the clocks on the rocket running more slowly as time stretched out. If the rocket reached the speed of light, the clocks would stop altogether.

- **If a rocket** accelerates towards the speed of light, its mass increases dramatically. This is because its momentum is its mass multiplied by its speed. As it still has the same momentum , it must be gaining mass.

- **Einstein's general relativity theory** brought in gravity. It showed that gravity works basically by bending space–time. From this theory scientists predicted black holes (see Hawking) and wormholes (see time travel).

- **In 1919** an eclipse of the Sun allowed Arthur Eddington to observe how the Sun bends light rays, proving Einstein's theory of General Relativity.

▼ In normal everyday life, the effects of relativity are so tiny that you can ignore them. However, in a spacecraft travelling very fast they may become quite significant.

▲ In a spacecraft travelling almost at the speed of light, time runs slower. So astronauts going on a long, very fast journey into space come back a little younger than if they had stayed on the Earth.

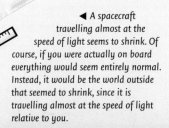

◄ A spacecraft travelling almost at the speed of light seems to shrink. Of course, if you were actually on board everything would seem entirely normal. Instead, it would be the world outside that seemed to shrink, since it is travelling almost at the speed of light relative to you.

◄ In a spacecraft travelling almost at the speed of light, everything becomes a little heavier. Many scientists believe an object will never be able to accelerate to the speed of light because the faster it goes the heavier it gets. Even in a fast-moving lift, things become very marginally heavier.

Hawking

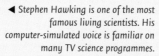

◀ *Stephen Hawking is one of the most famous living scientists. His computer-simulated voice is familiar on many TV science programmes.*

- **Stephen Hawking** (b.1942) is a British physicist who is famous for his ideas on space and time.

- **Hawking was born** in Oxford, England and studied at Cambridge University, where he is now a professor.

- **Hawking suffers** from the paralysing nerve disease called amyotrophic lateral sclerosis. He cannot move any more than a few hand and face muscles, but he gets around very well in an electric wheelchair.

- **Hawking cannot speak,** but he communicates effectively with a computer-simulated voice.

- **Hawking's** book *A Brief History of Time* (1988) outlines his ideas on space, time and the history of the Universe since the Big Bang. It was one of the best-selling science books of the 20th century.

- **Hawking's contributions** to the study of gravity are considered to be the most important since Einstein's.

- **More than anyone else,** Hawking has developed the idea of black holes – points in space where gravity becomes so extreme that it even sucks in light.

- **Hawking developed** the idea of a singularity, which is an incredibly small point in a black hole where all physical laws break down.

- **Hawking's work** provides a strong theoretical base for the idea that the Universe began with a Big Bang, starting with a singularity and exploding outwards.

- **Hawking** is trying to find a quantum theory of gravity (see quantum physics) to link in with the three other basic forces (electromagnetism and nuclear forces).

Oil

- **Oils** are liquids that do not dissolve in water and burn easily.

- **Oils are usually made** from chains of carbon and hydrogen atoms.

- **There are three main kinds of oil:** essential, fixed and mineral oils.

- **Essential oils** are thin, perfumed oils from plants. They are used in flavouring and aromatherapy.

▲ *Oil from underground and undersea sediments provides over half the world's energy needs.*

> ★ STAR FACT ★
> Petroleum is used to make products from aspirins and toothpaste to CDs, as well as petrol.

- **Fixed oils** are made by plants and animals from fatty acids. They include fish oils and nut and seed oils.

- **Mineral oils** come from petroleum formed underground over millions of years from the remains of sea organisms.

- **Petroleum,** or crude oil, is made mainly of hydrocarbons – compounds of hydrogen and carbon, such as methane.

- **Hydrocarbons** in petroleum are mixed with oxygen, sulphur, nitrogen and other elements.

- **Petroleum** is separated by distillation into various substances such as aviation fuel, petrol or gasoline paraffin. As oil is heated in a distillation column, a mixture of gases evaporates. Each gas cools and condenses at different heights to a liquid, or fraction, which is then drawn off.

Scanners

- **Scanners** are electronic devices that move backwards and forwards in lines in order to build up a picture.
- **Image scanners** are used to convert pictures and other material into a digital form for computers to read.
- **A photoelectric cell** in the scanner measures the amount of light reflected from each part of the picture and converts it into a digital code.
- **Various complex scanners** are used in medicine to build up pictures of the inside of the body. They include CT scanners, PET scanners and MRI scanners.
- **CT stands** for computerized tomography. An X-ray beam rotates around the patient and is picked up by detectors on the far side to build up a 3-D picture.
- **PET** stands for Positron Emission Tomography. The scanner picks up positrons (positively charged electrons) sent out by radioactive substances injected into the blood.
- **PET scans** can show a living brain in action.
- **MRI** stands for Magnetic Resonance Imaging.

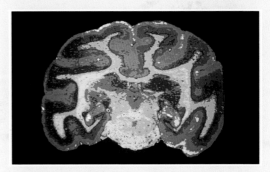

▲ *This PET scan shows a monkey's brain from above.*

- **An MRI scan** works like CT scans but it uses magnetism, not X-rays. The patient is surrounded by such powerful magnets that all the body's protons (see atoms) line up.
- **The MRI scan begins** as a radio pulse that knocks the protons briefly out of alignment. The scanner detects radio signals sent out by the protons as they snap back into line.

Vectors

- **For scientists,** vectors are things that have both a particular size and a particular direction.
- **Forces** such as gravity, muscles or the wind are vector quantities.
- **Acceleration** is a vector quantity.
- **Scalar quantities** are things which have a particular size but have no particular direction.
- **Speed, density and mass** are all scalar quantities.
- **Velocity** is speed in a particular direction, so it is a vector quantity.
- **A vector** can be drawn on a diagram with an arrow that is proportional in length to its size, pointing in the right direction.
- **Several vectors** may affect something at the same time. As you sit on a chair, gravity pulls you downwards while the chair pushes you up, so you stay still. But if someone pushes the chair from behind, you may tip over. The combined effect of all the forces involved is called the resultant.
- **When several vectors** affect the same thing, they may act at different angles. You can work out their combined effect – the resultant – by drawing geometric diagrams with the vectors.
- **The parallelogram of forces** is a simple geometric diagram for working out the resultant from two forces. A vector arrow is drawn for each force from the same point. A parallel arrow is then drawn from the end of each arrow to make a parallelogram. The resultant is the simple diagonal of the parallelogram.

◄ *As a gymnast pauses in mid-routine, she unconsciously combines the forces acting on her to keep her in balance. These forces, such as her weight and forward momentum, are all vectors and could be worked out geometrically on paper.*

Genetic engineering

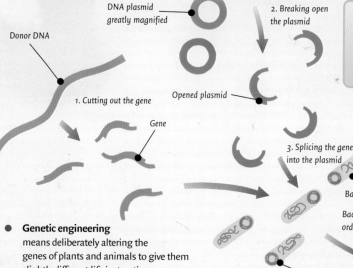

DNA plasmid
greatly magnified

Donor DNA

2. Breaking open
the plasmid

1. Cutting out the gene

Opened plasmid

Gene

3. Splicing the gene
into the plasmid

Bacteria

Bacteria's
ordinary DNA

Altered DNA plasmid
less magnified

! NEWS FLASH !
In late 1999, scientists worked out
the first complete gene sequence
for a multi-celled organism –
allowing them to create a new
organism articially.

◀ This illustration shows the steps in gene
splicing: 1. The bit of the donor DNA carrying
the right gene is snipped out using
restriction enzymes. 2. A special ring of
DNA called a plasmid is then broken
open. 3. The new gene is spliced into
the plasmid, which is sealed up with
DNA ligase and introduced into
bacteria. 4. The bacteria
then reproduce.

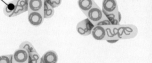

4. Bacteria with altered
DNA multiplying

- **Genetic engineering**
  means deliberately altering the
  genes of plants and animals to give them
  slightly different life instructions.

- **Genes** are found in every living cell on special
  molecules called DNA (deoxyribonucleic acid).
  Engineering genes means changing the DNA.

- **Scientists alter genes** by snipping them from the DNA
  of one organism and inserting them into the DNA of
  another. This is called gene splicing. The altered DNA is
  called recombinant DNA.

- **Genes are cut** from DNA using biological scissors called
  restriction enzymes. They are spliced into DNA using
  biological glue called DNA ligase.

- **Once a cell** has its new DNA, every time the cell
  reproduces the new cells will have the same altered DNA.

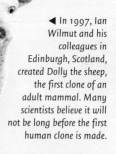

◀ In 1997, Ian
Wilmut and his
colleagues in
Edinburgh, Scotland,
created Dolly the sheep,
the first clone of an
adult mammal. Many
scientists believe it will
not be long before the first
human clone is made.

- **By splicing new genes** into the DNA of bacteria,
  scientists can turn them into factories for making
  valuable natural chemicals. One protein made like this is
  interferon, a natural body chemical which protects
  humans against certain viruses. Enzymes for detergents
  and melanin for suntan lotion can be made like this too.

- **Scientists are now** finding ways of genetically modifying
  food crops. Crops may be engineered, for instance, to
  make them resistant to pests or frost. The first GM food
  was the 'Flavr Savr' tomato, which was introduced by the
  US biotechnology company Calgene in 1994.

- **Gene therapy** means altering the genes to cure diseases
  that are inherited from parents or caused by faulty genes.

- **Cloning** means creating an organism with exactly the
  same genes as another. Normally, new life grows from
  sex cells – cells from both parents – in which genes are
  mixed. Cloning takes DNA from any body cell and uses it
  to grow a new life. Since the new life has the same genes
  as the donor of the DNA, it is a perfect living replica.

Mixing colours

- **White light** such as sunlight contains all the colours of the rainbow: red, orange, yellow, green, blue, indigo and violet – and all the colours in between.

- **There are three basic,** or primary colours of light – red, green and blue. They can be mixed in various proportions to make any other colour.

- **The primary colours** of light are called additive primaries, because they are added together to make different colours.

- **Each additive primary** is one third of the full spectrum of white light, so adding all three together makes white.

- **When two additive primaries** are added together they make a third colour, called a subtractive primary.

- **The three subtractive primaries are:** magenta (red plus blue), cyan (blue plus green) and yellow (green plus red).

◄ *These circles are the primary colours of light: red, green and blue. Where they overlap, you see the three subtractive primaries: magenta, cyan and yellow.*

They too can be mixed in various proportions to make other colours.

- **Coloured surfaces** such as painted walls and pictures get their colour from the light falling on them. They soak up some colours of white light and reflect the rest. The colour you see is the colour reflected.

- **With reflected colours,** each subtractive primary soaks up one third of the spectrum of white light and reflects two-thirds of it. Mixing two subtractive primaries soaks up two-thirds of the spectrum. Mixing all three subtractive primaries soaks up all the spectrum, making black.

- **Two subtractive primaries** mixed make an additive primary.

- **Cyan and magenta** make blue; yellow and cyan make green; yellow and magenta make red.

Velocity and acceleration

- **Velocity** is speed in a particular direction.

- **Uniform velocity** is when the velocity stays the same. It can be worked out simply by dividing the distance travelled (d) by the time (t): $v = d/t$.

- **Acceleration** is a change in velocity.

- **Positive acceleration** is getting faster; negative acceleration, or deceleration, is getting slower.

- **Acceleration** is typically given in metres per second per second (m/s²). In each second a velocity gets faster by so many metres per second per second.

- **A rifle bullet** accelerates down the barrel at 3000 m/s². A fast car accelerates at 6 m/s².

- **When an object falls,** the Earth's gravity makes it accelerate at 9.81 m/s². This is called g.

- **Acceleration** is often described in gs.

- **In a rocket taking off** at 1 g, the acceleration has little effect. But at 3 g, it is impossible to move your

arms and legs; at 4.5 g you black out in five seconds.

- **A high-speed lift** goes up at 0.2 g. An plane takes off at 0.5 g. A car brakes at up to 0.7 g. In a crash, you may survive a momentary deceleration of up to 100 g, but the effects are likely to be severe.

▶ *For a brief moment as they come away from the start, sprinters accelerate faster than a Ferrari car.*

Organic chemistry

- **Organic chemistry** is the study of compounds that contain carbon atoms.
- **Over 90%** of all chemical compounds are organic.
- **Organic chemicals** are the basis of most life processes.
- **Scientists once thought** carbon compounds could only be made by living things. However, in 1828 Friedrich Wöhler made the compound urea in his laboratory.
- **By far the largest** group of carbon compounds are the hydrocarbons (see Oil).
- **Aliphatic organic compounds** are formed from long or branching chains of carbon atoms. They include ethane, propane and paraffin, and the alkenes from which many polymers are made (see oil compounds).
- **Cyclic organic compounds** are formed from closed rings of carbon atoms.
- **Aromatics** are made from a ring of six atoms (mostly carbon), with hydrogen atoms attached. They get their name from the strong aroma (smell) of benzene.

- **Benzene** is the most important aromatic. Friedrich von Stradonitz discovered its six-carbon structure in 1865, after dreaming about a snake biting its own tail.
- **Isomers** are compounds with the same atoms but different properties. Butane and 2-methyl propane in bottled gas are isomers.

▼ *All living things are made basically of carbon compounds.*

Colour

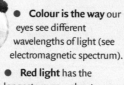

- **Colour is the way** our eyes see different wavelengths of light (see electromagnetic spectrum).
- **Red light** has the longest waves – about 700 nanometres, or nm (billionths of a metre).
- **Violet light** has the shortest waves – about 400 nm.
- **Light that is a mixture** of every colour, such as sunlight and the light from torches and ordinary lightbulbs, is called white light (see mixing colours).

◄ *The macaw gets its brilliant colours because pigment molecules in its feathers soak up certain wavelengths of light and reflect others, including reds, yellows and blues, very strongly.*

- **Things are different colours** because molecules in their surface reflect and absorb certain wavelengths of light.
- **Deep-blue printers inks** and bright-red blood are vividly coloured because both have molecules shaped like four-petalled flowers, with a metal atom at the centre.
- **Iridescence** is the shimmering rainbow colours you see flashing every now and then on a peacock's feathers, a fly's wings, oil on the water's surface or a CD.
- **Iridescence** can be caused by the way a surface breaks the light into colours like a prism does (see spectrum).
- **Iridescence** can be also caused by interference when an object has a thin, transparent surface layer. Light waves reflected from the top surface are slightly out of step with waves reflected from the inner surface, and they interfere.

★ **STAR FACT** ★
As a light source gets hotter, so its colour changes from red to yellow to white to blue.

Motion

- **Every movement** in the Universe seems to be governed by physical laws devised by people such as Isaac Newton and Albert Einstein.

- **Newton's first law of motion** says that an object accelerates, slows down or changes direction only when a force is applied.

- **Newton's second law of motion** says that the acceleration depends on how heavy the object is, and on how hard it is being pushed or pulled.

- **The greater the force** acting on an object, the more it will accelerate.

- **The heavier an object is** – the greater its mass – the less it will be accelerated by a particular force.

- **Newton's third law of motion** says that when a force pushes or acts one way, an equal force pushes in the opposite direction.

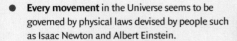

◀ To start moving, a skater uses the force of his muscles to push against the ground. As he or she pushes, the ground pushes back with equal force.

- **Newton's third law of motion** is summarized as follows: 'To every action, there is an equal and opposite reaction'.

- **Newton's third law** applies everywhere, but you can see it in effect in a rocket in space. In space there is nothing for the rocket to push on. The rocket is propelled by the action and reaction between the hot gases pushed out by its engine and the rocket itself.

- **You cannot always see** the reaction. When you bounce a ball on the ground, it looks as if only the ball bounces, but the Earth recoils too. The Earth's mass is so great compared to the ball's that the recoil is tiny.

- **Einstein's theory** of relativity modifies Newton's second law of motion under certain circumstances.

Molecules

- **A molecule** is two or more atoms bonded together. It is normally the smallest bit of a substance that exists independently.

- **Hydrogen atoms** exist only in pairs, or joined with atoms of other elements. A linked pair of hydrogen atoms is a hydrogen molecule.

- **Molecule atoms** are held together by chemical bonds.

- **The shape of a molecule** depends on the arrangement of

> ★ STAR FACT ★
> If the DNA molecule in every human body cell were as thick as a hair, it would be 8 km long.

bonds that hold its atoms together.

- **Ammonia molecules** are pyramid shaped; some protein molecules are long spirals.

- **Compounds** only exist as molecules. If the atoms in the molecule of a compound were separated, the compound would cease to exist.

- **Chemical formulas** show the atoms in a molecule.

- **The formula for ammonia**, a choking gas, is NH_3, because an ammonia molecule is made from one nitrogen atom and three hydrogen atoms.

- **The mass of a molecule** is called the molecular mass. It is worked out by adding the mass of all the atoms in it.

◀ A crystal such as this is built from billions of identical molecules.

Space

- **A flat or plane surface** has just two dimensions at right angles to each other: length and width.

- **Any point** on a flat surface can be pinpointed exactly with just two figures: one showing how far along it is and the other how far across.

- **There are three** dimensions of space at right angles to each other: length, width and height.

- **A box** can be described completely with just one figure for each dimension.

- **A point in space** can be pinpointed with three figures: one shows how far along it is, one how far

▶ *An eclipse of the Sun in 1919 showed Einstein's suggestion that gravity can bend light is true. In bending light, gravity is also bending space–time.*

- across it is and a third how high up or down it is.

- **If something is moving,** three dimensions are not enough to locate it. You need a fourth dimension – time – to describe where the object is at a particular time.

- **In the early 1900s,** mathematician Hermann Minkowski realized that for Einstein's relativity theory you had to think of the Universe in terms of four dimensions, including time.

  - **Four-dimensional** space is now called space–time.

  - **Einstein's** theory of general relativity shows that space–time is actually curved.

  - **After Minkowski's ideas,** mathematicians began to develop special geometry to describe four or even more dimensions.

Elements

- **Elements** are the basic chemicals of the Universe. Each one is made from one kind of atom, with a certain number of sub-atomic particles and its own unique character.

- **More than 115** elements have so far been identified.

- **Each element** is listed in the periodic table.

- **At least 20** of the most recently identified elements were created entirely by scientists and do not exist naturally.

> **! NEWS FLASH !**
> Scientists have made three atoms of a new element, 118 or ununoctium, which is probably a colourless gas.

- **All the most recently discovered elements** have very large, heavy atoms.

- **The lightest atom** is hydrogen.

- **The heaviest naturally occuring** element is osmium.

- **When different elements combine** they make chemical compounds (see chemical compounds).

- **New elements** get temporary names from their atomic number (see the Periodic Table). So the new element with atomic number 116 is called ununhexium. *Un* is the Latin word for one; *hex* is Latin for six.

◀ *Very few elements occur naturally by themselves. Most occur in combination with others in compounds. Gold is one of the few elements found as a pure 'native' element.*

Light

▶ This straw is not a light source, so we see it by reflected light. As the light rays reflected from the straw leave the water, they are bent, or refracted, as they emerge from the water and speed up. So the straw looks broken even though it remains intact.

- **Light is a form of energy.** It is one of the forms of energy sent out by atoms when they become excited.

- **Light is just one** of the forms of electromagnetic radiation (see electromagnetic spectrum). It is the only form that we can see.

- **Although we are surrounded** by light during the day, very few things give out light. The Sun and other stars and electric lights are light sources, but we see most things only because they reflect light. If something does not send out or reflect light, we cannot see it.

- **Light beams** are made of billions of tiny packets of energy called photons (see moving light). Together, these photons behave like waves on a pond. But the waves are tiny – 2000 would fit across a pinhead.

- **Light travels** in straight lines. The direction can be changed when light bounces off something or passes through it, but it is always straight. The straight path of light is called a ray.

- **When the path of a light ray** is blocked altogether, it forms a shadow. Most shadows have two regions: the umbra and penumbra. The umbra is the dark part where light rays are blocked altogether. The penumbra is the lighter rim where some rays reach.

- **When light rays** hit something, they bounce off, are soaked up or pass through. Anything that lets light through, such as glass, is transparent. If it mixes the light on the way through, such as frosted glass, it is translucent. If it stops light altogether, it is opaque.

- **When light strikes a surface**, some or all of it is reflected. Most surfaces scatter light in all directions, and all you see is the surface. But mirrors and other shiny surfaces reflect light in exactly the same pattern in which it arrived, so you see a mirror image.

- **When light passes** into transparent things such as water, rays are bent, or refracted. This happens because light travels more slowly in glass or water, and the rays swing round like the wheels of a car running onto sand.

▶ Glass lenses are shaped to refract light rays in particular ways. Concave lenses are dish-shaped lenses – thin in the middle and fat at the edges. As light rays pass through a concave lens they are bent outwards, so they spread out. The result is that when you see an object through a concave lens, it looks smaller than it really is.

▶ Convex lenses bulge outwards. They are fatter in the middle and thin around the edges. As light rays pass through a convex lens they are bent inwards, so they come together, or converge. When you see an object through a convex lens, it looks magnified. The point where the converging light rays meet is called the focus.

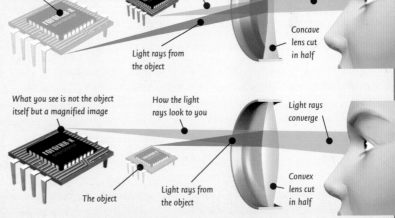

What you see is not the object itself but a reduced image

How the light rays look to you

Light rays spread out

The object

Concave lens cut in half

Light rays from the object

What you see is not the object itself but a magnified image

How the light rays look to you

Light rays converge

Convex lens cut in half

The object

Light rays from the object

Television

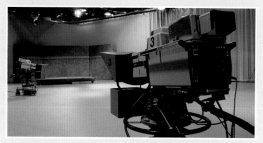
▲ *TV cameras convert a scene into an electrical signal.*

- **Television relies** on the photoelectric effect – the emission of electrons by a substance when struck by photons of light. Light-sensitive photocells in cameras work like this.

- **TV cameras** have three sets of tubes with photocells (reacting to red, green and blue light) to convert the picture into electrical signals.

- **The sound signal** from microphones is added, and a 'sync pulse' is put in to keep both kinds of signal in time.

- **The combined signal** is turned into radio waves (see electromagnetic spectrum) and broadcast.

- **An aerial** picks up the signal and feeds it to your television set.

- **Most TV sets** are based on glass tubes shaped like giant lightbulbs, called cathode-ray tubes. The narrow end contains a cathode, which is a negative electrical terminal. The wide end is the TV screen.

- **The cathode** fires a non-stop stream of electrons (see electrons) at the inside of the TV screen.

- **Wherever electrons** hit the screen, the screen glows as its coating of phosphors heats up.

- **To build up the picture** the electron beam scans quickly back and forth across the screen, making it glow in certain places. This happens so quickly that it looks as if the whole screen is glowing.

- **Colour TVs** have three electron guns: one to make red phosphors glow, another for green and a third for blue.

Huygens

- **Christiaan Huygens** (1629–1695) was, after Isaac Newton, the greatest scientist of the 1600s.

- **Huygens** was born to a wealthy Dutch family in The Hague, in Holland.

- **He studied law** at the University of Leiden and the College of Orange in Breda before turning to science.

- **He worked** with his brother Constanijn to grind lenses for very powerful telescopes.

- **With his powerful telescope,** Huygens discovered in 1655 that what astronomers had thought were Saturn's 'arms' were actually rings. He made his discovery known to people in code.

- **Huygens discovered** Titan, one of Saturn's moons.

◀ *Christiaan Huygens was the leading figure of the Golden Age of Dutch science in the 17th century, making contributions in many fields.*

- **Huygens** built the first accurate pendulum clock.

- **Responding to Newton's theory** that light was 'corpuscles', Huygens developed the theory that light is waves (see moving light) in 1678.

- **Huygens** described light as vibrations spreading through a material called ether, which is literally everywhere and is made of tiny particles. The idea of ether was finally abandoned in the late 19th century, but not the idea of light waves.

- **Huygens' wave idea** enabled him to explain refraction (see light) simply. It also enabled him to predict correctly that light would travel more slowly in glass than in air.

Engines

- **Engines are devices** that convert fuel into movement.
- **Most engines** work by burning the fuel to make gases that expand rapidly as they get hot.
- **Engines** that burn fuel to generate power are called heat engines. The burning is called combustion.
- **An internal combustion** engine, as used in a car, a jet or a rocket, burns its fuel on the inside.

▶ The Thrust car used a jet engine to give it the acceleration it needed for its attempt on the world land speed record.

- **In engines** such as those in cars and diesel trains, the hot gases swell inside a chamber (the combustion chamber) and push against a piston or turbine.
- **An external combustion** engine burns its fuel on the outside in a separate boiler that makes hot steam to drive a piston or turbine. Steam engines on trains and boats work in this way.
- **Engines with pistons** that go back and forth inside cylinders are called reciprocating engines.
- **In jets and rockets,** hot gases swell and push against the engine as they shoot out of the back.
- **In four-stroke engines,** such as those in most cars, the pistons go up and down four times for each time they are thrust down by the hot gases.
- **In two-stroke engines,** such as those on small motorcycles and lawnmowers, the piston is pushed by burning gases every time it goes down.

Solutions

- **Tap water** is rarely pure water; it usually contains invisible traces of other substances. This makes it a solution.
- **A solution** is a liquid that has a solid dissolved within it.
- **When a solid dissolves,** its molecules separate and mix completely with the molecules of the liquid.
- **The liquid** in a solution is called the solvent.
- **The solid** dissolved in a solution is the solute.
- **The more of a solid that dissolves,** the stronger the solution becomes until at last it is saturated and no more will dissolve. There is literally no more room in the liquid.
- **If a saturated** solution is heated the liquid expands, making room for more solute to dissolve.

▶ There are at least 30 common solutes in sea water. They include simple salt (sodium chloride) and magnesium chloride, but most are in very tiny amounts.

- **If a saturated** solution cools or is left to evaporate there is less room for solute, so the solute is precipitated (comes out of the solution).

- **Precipitated solute** molecules often link together to form solid crystals.

> ★ STAR FACT ★
> Ancient alchemists searched for a universal solvent in which all substances would dissolve.

Nuclear power

- **Nuclear power** is based on the huge amounts of energy that bind together the nucleus of every atom in the Universe. It is an incredibly concentrated form of energy.

- **Nuclear energy** is released by splitting the nuclei of atoms in a process called nuclear fission (see nuclear energy). One day scientists hope to release energy by nuclear fusion – by fusing nuclei together as in the Sun.

- **Most nuclear reactors** use uranium-235. These are special atoms, or isotopes, of uranium with 235 protons and neutrons in their nucleus rather than the normal 238.

- **The fuel** usually consists of tiny pellets of uranium dioxide in thin tubes, separated by sheets called spacers.

- **Three kilograms of uranium fuel** provide enough energy for a city of one million people for one day.

- **The earliest reactors,** called N-reactors, were designed to make plutonium for bombs. Magnox reactors make both plutonium and electricity.

- **Pressurized water reactors** (PWRs), originally used in submarines, are now the most common kind. They are built in factories, unlike Advanced Gas Reactors (AGRs).

- **Fast-breeder reactors** actually create more fuel than they burn, but the new fuel is highly radioactive.

- **Every stage of the nuclear process** creates dangerous radioactive waste. The radioactivity may take 80,000 years to fade. All but the most radioactive liquid waste is pumped out to sea. Gaseous waste is vented into the air. Solid waste is mostly stockpiled underground. Scientists debate fiercely about what to do with radioactive waste.

> ★ STAR FACT ★
> One kilogram of deuterium (a kind of hydrogen) can give the same amount of energy as three million kilograms of coal.

▼ Like coal- and oil-fired power stations, nuclear power stations use steam to drive turbines to generate electricity. The difference is that nuclear power stations obtain the heat by splitting uranium atoms, not by burning coal or oil. When the atom is split, it sends out gamma rays, neutrons and immense heat. In a nuclear bomb this happens in a split second. In a nuclear power plant, control rods soak up some of the neutrons and slow the process down.

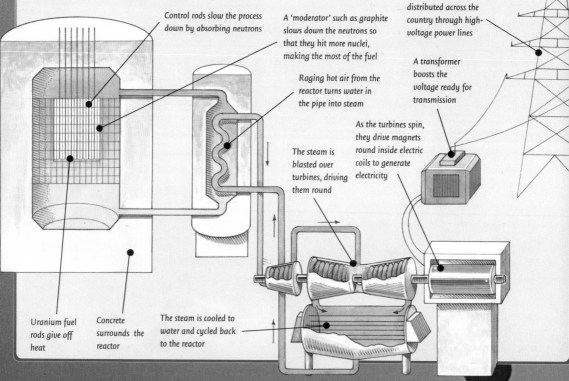

Control rods slow the process down by absorbing neutrons

A 'moderator' such as graphite slows down the neutrons so that they hit more nuclei, making the most of the fuel

The electricity is distributed across the country through high-voltage power lines

Raging hot air from the reactor turns water in the pipe into steam

A transformer boosts the voltage ready for transmission

As the turbines spin, they drive magnets round inside electric coils to generate electricity

The steam is blasted over turbines, driving them round

Uranium fuel rods give off heat

Concrete surrounds the reactor

The steam is cooled to water and cycled back to the reactor

Moving particles

- **The atoms and molecules** from which every substance is made are always moving.
- **The speed** at which they move depends on temperature.
- **Heat gives atoms and molecules** extra energy, making them move faster.
- **In 1827** Scottish botanist Robert Brown saw through a microscope that pollen grains in water were constantly dancing. They are buffeted by moving molecules that are too small to be seen. The effect is called Brownian motion.
- **In a gas,** the atoms and molecules are so far apart that they zoom about freely in all directions.
- **Smells spread** quickly because the smell molecules move about very quickly.

◀ As liquids boil, atoms and molecules move more and more energetically until some break away and turn to gas. This is evaporation.

- **In a liquid,** molecules are closely packed and move like dancers in a nightclub. If molecules stopped moving in liquids we would all die, because this movement is what moves materials in and out of human cells.
- **In a solid**, atoms and molecules are bound together and vibrate on the spot.
- **Air and water pressure** is simply bombardment by billions of moving molecules.
- **At −273.15°C,** absolute zero, the movement of atoms and molecules slows down to a complete standstill.

Inertia and momentum

- **Everything that is standing still** has inertia, which means that it will not move unless forced to.
- **Everything that moves** has momentum – it will not slow down, speed up or change direction unless forced to.
- **There is no real difference** between inertia and momentum, because everything in the universe is moving. Things only appear to be still because they are not moving relative to something else.
- **An object's momentum** is its mass times its velocity.
- **Something heavy** or fast has a lot of momentum, so a large force is needed to slow it down or speed it up.
- **A ball moves** when you kick it because when a moving object strikes another, its momentum is transferred. This is the law of conservation of momentum.
- **Angular momentum** is the momentum of something spinning. It depends on its speed and the size of the circle.
- **When a spinning skater** draws his arms close to his body, the circle he is making is smaller yet his angular momentum must be the same. So he spins faster.
- **For the same reason a satellite** orbiting close to the Earth travels faster than one orbiting farther out.
- **A spinning top stays** upright because its angular momentum is greater than the pull of gravity.

▼ The lead shot that athletes throw when they put the shot has a large mass. It takes a lot of muscle power to overcome its inertia.

The Internet

- **The Internet** is a vast network linking millions of computers around the world.

- **The Internet began** in the 1960s when the US Army developed a network called ARPAnet to link computers.

- **To access the Internet** a computer's output is translated into a form that can be sent by phone lines with a modem (short for modulator/demodulator).

- **Computers** access the Internet via a local phone to a large computer called the Internet Service Provider (ISP).

- **Each ISP** is connected to a giant computer called a main hub. There are about 100 linked main hubs worldwide.

- **Some links between** hubs are made via phone lines; some are made via satellite.

- **Links between** hubs are called fast-track connections.

> ! NEWS FLASH !
> Very soon, people will be able to access the
> Internet via mobile phones.

▶ *The Internet links computers instantly around the world.*

- **The World Wide Web** is a way of finding your way to the data in sites on all the computers linked to the Internet. The Web makes hyperlinks (fast links) to sites with the word you select.

- **The World Wide Web** was invented in 1989 by Tim Berners-Lee of the CERN laboratories in Switzerland.

Temperature

- **Temperature** is how hot or cold something is. The best-known temperature scales are Celsius and Fahrenheit.

- **The Celsius (C) scale** is part of the metric system of measurements and is used everywhere except in the USA. It is named after Swedish astronomer Anders Celsius, who developed it in 1742.

- **Celsius is also** known as centigrade because water boils at 100°C. *Cent* is the Latin prefix for 100. Water freezes at 0°C.

- **On the Fahrenheit (F) scale** water boils at 212°F. It freezes at 32°F.

- **To convert Celsius** to Fahrenheit, divide by 5, multiply by 9 and add 32.

- **To convert Fahrenheit** to Celsius, subtract 32, divide by 9 and multiply by 5.

◀ *A digital thermometer measures temperature with a thermistor, which is a probe whose electrical resistance varies with the heat.*

- **The Kelvin (K) scale** used by scientists is like the Celsius scale, but it begins at −273.15°C. So 0°C is 273.15K.

- **Cold:** absolute zero is −273.15°C. Helium turns liquid at −269°C. Oxygen turns liquid at −183°C. Gasoline freezes at −150°C. The lowest air temperature ever recorded on Earth is −89.2°C.

- **Hot:** the highest shade temperature recorded on Earth is 58°C. A log fire burns at around 800°C. Molten magma is about 1200°C. Tungsten melts at 3410°C. The surface of the Sun is around 6000°C. The centre of the Earth is over 7000°C. A lightning flash reaches 30,000°C. The centre of a hydrogen bomb reaches 4 million°C.

- **The blood temperature** of the human body is normally 37°C. A skin temperature above 40°C is very hot, and below 31°C is very cold. Hands feel cold below 20°C and go numb below 12°C. Anything above 45°C that touches your skin hurts, although people have walked on hot coals at 800°C. The knee can tolerate 47°C for 30 seconds.

Newton

- **Sir Isaac Newton** was one of the greatest scientists. His book *The Mathematical Principles of Natural Philosophy* is the most influential science book ever written.

- **Newton was born** on December 25, 1642 in Woolsthorpe in Lincoln, England. As a boy, he often made mechanical devices such as model windmills and water clocks.

- **With his theory of gravity** Newton discovered how the Universe is held together.

- **Newton** said that his theory of gravity was inspired by seeing an apple fall from a tree.

- **Newton invented** an entirely new branch of mathematics called calculus. Independently, Leibniz also invented it.

- **Newton** discovered that sunlight is a mixture of all colours (see spectrum).

- **The interference patterns** from reflected surfaces such as a CD or pool of oil are called Newton's rings (see colour).

- **Newton** spent much of his life studying astrology and alchemy.

- **Newton never married** and at times was almost a recluse. Shortly before he died in 1727 he said: 'I seem to have been only like a boy playing on the seashore, and diverting myself in now and then finding a smoother pebble or prettier shell than ordinary, whilst the great ocean of truth lay all undiscovered before me.'

- **Newton** was a Member of Parliament, president of the Royal Society and master of the Royal Mint, where he found a way to make coins more accurately.

▶ *Newton invented a kind of telescope that is now standard for astronomers.*

Moving light

- **Light is the fastest thing** in the Universe.

- **The speed of light** is 299,792,458 metres per second.

- **Scientists remember** light's speed from the number of letters in each word of this sentence: 'We guarantee certainty, clearly referring to this light mnemonic'.

- **Isaac Newton** suggested in 1666 that light is made up of streams of tiny particles, or corpuscles.

- **The Dutch scientist** Christiaan Huygens (1629–1695)

> ★ STAR FACT ★
> On a sunny day one thousand billion photons fall on a pinhead every second.

said in 1678: no, light is waves or vibrations instead.

- **In 1804 Thomas Young** showed that light is waves in a famous experiment with two narrow slits in a light beam. Light coming through each slit creates bands of shadow that must be caused by waves interfering with each other.

- **James Clerk Maxwell** suggested in the 1860s that light is electromagnetic waves.

- **Albert Einstein** showed with the photoelectric effect that light must also be particles called photons.

- **Light sometimes** looks like photons, sometimes like waves. Weirdly, in a way scientists can't explain, a single photon can interfere with itself in Young's slit experiment.

◀ *The shimmering colours on a CD are caused by interfering light waves – different wavelengths cancel out their peaks and troughs.*

Holograms

- **Holograms** are three-dimensional photographic images made with laser lights.

- **The idea of holograms** was suggested by Hungarian-born British physicist Dennis Gabor in 1947. The idea could not be tried until laser light became available.

- **The first holograms** were made by Emmett Leith and Juris Upatnieks in Michigan, USA in 1963 and by Yuri Denisyuk in the Soviet Union.

- **To make a hologram,** the beam from a laser light is split in two. One part of the beam is reflected off the subject onto a photographic plate. The other, called the reference beam, shines directly onto the plate.

- **The interference** between light waves in the reflected beam and light waves in the reference beam creates the hologram in complex microscopic stripes on the plate.

- **Some holograms** only show up when laser light is shone through them.

- **Some holograms** work in ordinary light, such as those

▲ *Holograms seem to hover strangely in space.*

used in credit cards to stop counterfeiting.

- **Holograms** are used to detect defects in engines and aeroplanes, and forgeries in paintings by comparing two holograms made under slightly different conditions.

- **Huge amounts of digital data** can be stored in holograms in a crystal.

- **In 1993** 10,000 pages of data were stored in a lithium nobate crystal measuring just 1 cm across.

Sound measurement

▲ *Heavy traffic is about 90 decibels, but it can rise higher.*

- **The loudness of a sound** is usually measured in units called decibels (dB).

- **One decibel** is one tenth of a bel, the unit of sound named after Scots-born inventor Alexander Graham Bell.

- **Decibels** were originally used to measure sound intensity. Now they are used to compare electronic power output and voltages too.

- **Every 10 points up** on the decibel scale means that a sound has increased by ten times.

- **1 dB** is the smallest change the human ear can hear.

- **The quietest sound** that people can hear is 10 dB.

- **Quiet sounds:** a rustle of leaves or a quiet whisper is 10 dB. A quiet conversation is 30–40 dB. Loud conversation is about 60 dB. A city street is about 70 dB.

- **Loud sounds:** thunder is about 100 dB. The loudest scream ever recorded was 128.4 dB. A jet taking off is 110–140 dB. The loudest sound ever made by human technology (an atom bomb) was 210 dB.

- **The amount of energy** in a sound is measured in watts per square metre (W/m^2). Zero dB is one thousand billionths of $1\ W/m^2$.

> ★ STAR FACT ★
> Sounds over 130 dB are painful; sounds over 90–100 dB for long periods cause deafness.

Electric power

- **Most electricity is generated in power stations** by magnets that spin between coils of wire to induce an electric current (see electric circuits).

- **The magnets** are turned by turbines, which are either turned by steam heated by burning coal, oil or gas, or by nuclear fuel, or turned by wind or water.

- **The stronger the magnet**, the faster it turns and the more coils there are, so the bigger the voltage created.

- **Simple dynamos** generate a direct current (DC) that always flows in the same direction.

- **The generators** in power stations are alternators that give an alternating current (AC) which continually swaps direction. In an alternator, as the magnets spin they pass the wires going up on one side and down on the other.

- **The system of power transmission** that takes electricity into homes was developed by Croatian-born US engineer Nikola Tesla at Niagara, USA in the 1880s.

- **Electricity from power stations** is distributed around a country in a network of cables known as the grid.

- **Power station** generators push out 25,000 volts or more. This voltage is too much to use in people's homes, but not enough to transmit over long distances.

- **To transmit** electricity over long distances, the voltage is boosted to 400,000 volts by step-up transformers. It is fed through high-voltage cables. Near its destination the electricity's voltage is reduced by step-down transformers at substations for distribution to homes, shops, offices and factories.

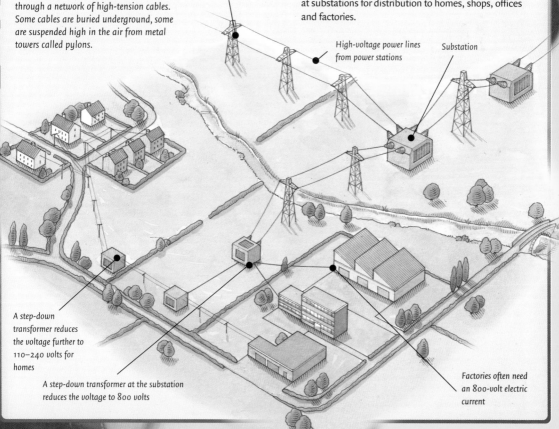

▼ Electricity is brought to our homes through a network of high-tension cables. Some cables are buried underground, some are suspended high in the air from metal towers called pylons.

Pylon

High-voltage power lines from power stations

Substation

A step-down transformer reduces the voltage further to 110–240 volts for homes

A step-down transformer at the substation reduces the voltage to 800 volts

Factories often need an 800-volt electric current

Copper

▲ The high conductivity of copper makes it a perfect material for the core of electrical cables.

- **Copper** was one of the first metals used by humans over 10,000 years ago.
- **Copper** is one of the few metals that occur naturally in a pure form.
- **Most of the copper** that we use today comes from ores such as cuprite and chalcopyrite.

- **The world's biggest deposits** of pure copper are in volcanic lavas in the Andes Mountains in Chile.
- **Copper has** the atomic number 29, an atomic mass of 63.546 and melts at 1083°C.
- **Copper is** by far the best low-cost conductor of electricity, so it is widely used for electrical cables.
- **Copper is also** a good conductor of heat, which is why it is used to make the bases of saucepans.
- **Copper is so ductile** (easily stretched) that a copper rod as thick as a finger can be stretched out thinner than a human hair.
- **After being in the air** for some time, copper gets a thin green coating of copper carbonate called verdigris. 'Verdigris' means green of Greece.

> ★ STAR FACT ★
> Copper is mixed with tin to make bronze, the an alloys dating back more than 5000 years.

Energy

- **Energy is the ability** to make things happen or, as scientists say, do work.
- **Energy comes in many forms,** from the chemical energy locked in sugar to the mechanical energy in a speeding train.
- **Energy does its work** either by transfer or conversion.

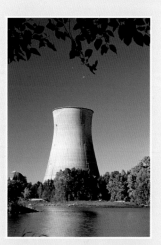

▲ Power stations do not create energy. They simply convert it into a convenient form for us to use – electricity.

- **Energy transfer** is the movement of energy from one place to another, such as heat rising above a fire or a ball being thrown.
- **Energy conversion** is when energy changes from one form to another – as when wind turbines generate electric power, for instance.
- **Energy is never lost nor gained;** it simply moves or changes. The total amount of energy in the Universe has stayed the same since the dawn of time.
- **Energy and mass** are actually the same thing. They are like flip sides of a coin and are interchangeable.
- **Potential energy** is energy stored up ready for action – as in a squeezed spring or a stretched piece of elastic.
- **Kinetic energy** is energy that something has because it is moving, such as a rolling ball or a falling stone.
- **Kinetic energy** increases in proportion with the velocity of an object squared. So a car has four times more kinetic energy at 40 km/h than at 20 km/h.

Thermodynamics

- **Energy cannot be destroyed** but it can be burned up. Every time energy is used, some turns into heat. This is why you feel hot after running.

- **Energy that turns into heat** may not be lost. It dissipates (spreads out thinly in all directions) and is hard to use again.

◀ Waste gases produced from this chemial plant are burnt off and released into the atmosphere as unwanted heat.

- **Every time energy is used,** some free energy (energy available to make things happen) gets lost as heat.

- **Scientists use** the word 'entropy' to describe how much energy has become unusable. The less free energy there is, the greater the entropy.

- **The word 'entropy'** was invented by the German physicist Rudolf Clausius in 1865.

- **Clausius showed** that everything really happens because energy moves from areas of high energy to areas of low energy, from hot areas to cold areas.

- **Energy goes on flowing** from high to low until there is no difference to make anything happen. This is an equilibrium state. Entropy is the maximum.

- **Clausius summed this idea up** in the 1860s with two laws of thermodynamics.

- **The first law of thermodynamics** says the total energy in the Universe was fixed forever at the beginning of time.

- **The second law of thermodynamics** says that heat cannot by itself pass from a colder object or place to a warmer one.

Sound

- **Most sounds** you hear, from the whisper of the wind to the roar of a jet, are simply moving air. When any sound is made it makes the air vibrate, and these vibrations carry the sound to your ears.

- **The vibrations** that carry sound through the air are called sound waves.

- **Sound waves** move by alternately squeezing air molecules together and then stretching them apart.

- **The parts of the air** that are squeezed are called condensations; the parts of the air that are stretched are called rarefactions.

- **Sound waves** travel faster through liquids and solids than through air because the molecules are more closely packed together in liquids and solids.

- **In a vacuum** such as space there is complete silence because there are no molecules to carry the sound.

- **Sound travels** at about 344 m per second in air at 20°C.

- **Sound travels** faster in warm air, reaching 386 metres per second at 100°C.

- **Sound travels** at 1500 metres per second in water and about 6000 metres per second in steel.

- **Sound travels a million times** slower than light, which is why you hear thunder after you see a flash of lightning, even though they both happen at the same time.

▶ When you sing, talk or shout, you are actually vibrating the vocal cords in your throat. These set up sound waves in the air you push up from your lungs.

Time travel

- **Einstein showed** that time runs at different speeds in different places – and is just another dimension. Ever since, some scientists have wondered whether we could travel through time to the past or the future (see time).

- **Einstein said** you cannot move through time because you would have to travel faster than light. If you travelled as fast as light, time would stop and you would not exist.

- **A famous argument** against time travel is about killing your grandparents. What if you travelled back in time before your parents were born and killed your grandparents? Then neither your parents nor you could have been born. So who killed your grandparents?

- **In the 1930s** American mathematician Kurt Gödel found time travel might be possible by bending space–time.

- **Scientists have come up** with all kinds of weird ideas for bending space–time, including amazing gravity machines. The most powerful benders of space–time are black holes in space.

- **Stephen Hawking** said you cannot use black holes for time travel because everything that goes into a black hole shrinks to a singularity (see Hawking). Others say you might dodge the singularity and emerge safely somewhere else in the Universe through a reverse black hole called a white hole.

- **US astronomer Carl Sagan** thought small black hole–white hole tunnels might exist without a singularity. There might be tunnels such as these linking different parts of the Universe, like a wormhole in an apple.

- **The mathematics** says that a wormhole would snap shut as soon as you stepped into it. However, it might be possible to hold it open with an anti-gravity machine based on a quantum effect called the Casimir effect.

- **Stephen Hawking** says wormholes are so unstable that they would break up before you could use them to time travel. Martin Visser says you might use them for faster than light (FTL) travel, but not for time travel.

▼ If wormholes exist, they are thought to be very, very tiny – smaller than an atom. So how could they be used for time travel? Some scientists think you may be able to use an incredibly powerful electric field to enlarge them and hold them open long enough to make a tunnel through space–time.

2000

The wormhole time machine depends on blowing a wormhole up large enough and holding it open long enough for you to slip through.

Although it's hard to imagine, space–time is not space with stars like this at all. It is a four-dimensional space and travelling through space–time means travelling through time as well as space.

The far end of a wormhole is the opposite of a black hole – a white hole. It pushes things out, not sucks them in.

1500

If you could create a wormhole time machine, just where and when would the other end be?

! NEWS FLASH !
A new theory called the Many Worlds Theory suggests that at any moment there are many different possible futures – and all of these futures actually happen.

Sound recording

▲ In a recording studio, the sound is recorded either on computer or on big master tapes.

- **Sound is recorded** by using a microphone to turn the vibrations of sound into a varying electrical current.

- **Sound recording** in the past was analogue, which means that the electrical current varies continually exactly as the sound vibrations do.

- **Most sound recording** today is digital, which means that sound vibrations are broken into tiny electrical chunks.

- **To make a digital recording** a device called an analogue-to-digital converter divides the vibrations into 44,100 segments for each second of sound.

- **Each digital segment** is turned into a digital code of ON or OFF electrical pulses.

- **With analogue sound,** each time the signal is passed on to the next stage, distortion and noise are added. With digital sound no noise is added, but the original recording is not a perfect replica of the sound.

- **On a CD (compact disc)** the pattern of electrical pulses is burned by laser as a pattern of pits on the disc surface.

- **During playback,** a laser beam is reflected from the tiny pits on a CD to re-create the electrical signal.

- **DVDs** work like CDs. They can store huge amounts of data on both sides, but most can only be recorded on once.

- **Minidiscs** (MDs) use magneto-optical recording to allow you to record on the disc up to one million times. A laser burns the data into a magnetic pattern on the disc.

Glass

- **Glass** is made mainly from ordinary sand (made of silica), from soda ash (sodium carbonate) and from limestone (calcium carbonate).

- **Glass** can be made from silica alone. However, silica has a very high melting point (1700°C), so soda ash is added to lower its melting point.

- **Adding a lot of soda ash** makes glass too soluble in water, so limestone is added to reduce its solubility.

- **To make sheets of glass,** 6% lime and 4% magnesia (magnesium oxide) are added to the basic mix.

- **To make glass for bottles,** 2% alumina (aluminium oxide) is added to the basic mix.

- **Very cheap glass** is green because it contains small impurities of iron.

> ★ STAR FACT ★
> The person who controls the fires and loads the glass into the furnace is called a teaser.

▲ Glass is one of the most versatile of all materials – transparent, easily moulded and resistant to the weather. This is why it is used in modern buildings such as this extension to the Louvre in Paris.

- **Metallic oxides** are added to make different colours.

- **Unlike most solids,** glass is not made of crystals and does not have the same rigid structure. It is an amorphous solid.

- **When glass is very hot** it flows slowly like a thick liquid.

Radiation

- **Radiation** is an atom's way of getting rid of its excess energy.

- **There are two main kinds** of radiation: electromagnetic and particulate.

- **Electromagnetic radiation** is pure energy. It comes from electrons (see electrons).

- **Particulate radiation** is tiny bits of matter thrown out by the nuclei of atoms.

▲ *Exposure to radiation can cause illnesses ranging from nausea to cancer and death. So radioactive materials must be safely guarded.*

- **Particulate** radiation comes mainly from radioactive substances (see radioactivity) such as radium, uranium and other heavy elements as they break down.

- **Radiation is measured** in curies and becquerels (radiation released), röntgens (victim's exposure), rads and grays (dose absorbed), rems and sieverts (amount of radiation in the body).

- **Bacteria can stand** a radiation dose 10,000 times greater than the dose that would kill a human being.

- **The Chernobyl nuclear accident** released 50 million curies of radiation. A 20-kilotonne nuclear bomb releases 10,000 times more radiation.

- **The natural radioactivity** of a brazil nut is about six becquerels (0.000000014 curies), which means six atoms in the nut break up every second.

- **The natural background** radiation you receive over a year is about 100 times what you receive from a single chest X-ray.

Water

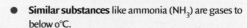

- **Water is the only substance** that is solid, liquid and gas at normal temperatures. It melts at 0°C and boils at 100°C.

- **Water is at its densest** at 4°C.

- **Ice is much less dense** than water, which is why ice forms on the surface of ponds and why icebergs float.

- **Water is one of the few substances** that expands as it freezes, which is why pipes burst during cold weather.

- **Water has a unique capacity** for making mild solutions with other substances.

- **Water is a compound** made of two hydrogen atoms and one oxygen atom. It has the chemical formula H_2O.

- **A water molecule** is shaped like a flattened V, with the two hydrogen atoms on each tip.

- **A water molecule** is said to be polar because the oxygen end is more negatively charged electrically.

◄ *A water molecule has two hydrogen atoms and one oxygen atom in a shallow V-shape.*

- **Similar substances** like ammonia (NH_3) are gases to below 0°C.

- **Water stays liquid** until 100°C because pairs of its polar molecules make strong bonds, as the positively charged end of one molecule is drawn to the negatively charged end of another.

▼ *Water is found in liquid form, such as rivers, and as a gas in the atmosphere.*

Carbon

- **Pure carbon** occurs in four forms: diamond, graphite, amorphous carbon and fullerenes.

- **Fullerenes** are made mostly artificially, but all four forms of carbon can be made artificially.

- **Diamond** is the world's hardest natural substance.

- **Natural diamonds** were formed deep in the Earth billions of years ago. They were formed by huge pressures as the Earth's crust moved, and then brought nearer the surface by volcanic activity.

- **Graphite** is the soft black carbon used in pencils. It is soft because it is made from sheets of atoms that slide over each other.

- **Amorphous carbon** is the black soot left behind when candles and other objects burn.

▶ The extraordinary hardness of diamonds comes from the incredibly strong tetrahedron (pyramid shape) that carbon atoms form.

- **Fullerenes** are big molecules made of 60 or more carbon atoms linked together in a tight cylinder or ball. The first was made in 1985.

- **Fullerenes** are named after the architect Buckminster Fuller who designed a geodesic (Earth-shaped) dome.

- **Carbon forms** over one million compounds that are the basis of organic chemistry. It does not react chemically at room temperature. Carbon has the chemical formula C and the atomic number 6. Neither diamond nor graphite melts at normal pressures.

Echoes and acoustics

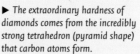

▶ Sydney Opera House in Australia is famous for its stunning design, but some orchestras have complained about its acoustics.

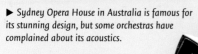

- **An echo** is the reflection of a sound. You hear it a little while after the sound is made.

- **You can only hear** an echo if it comes back more than 0.1 seconds after the original sound.

- **Sound travels** 34 metres in 0.1 seconds, so you only hear echoes from surfaces at least 17 metres away.

- **Smooth hard surfaces** give the best echoes because they break up the sound waves the least.

- **Acoustics** is the study of how sounds are created, transmitted and received.

- **The acoustics** of a space is how sound is heard and how it echoes around that space, whether it is a room or a large concert hall.

- **When concert halls** are designed, the idea is not to eliminate echoes altogether but to use them effectively.

- **A hall with too much echo** sounds harsh and unclear, as echoing sounds interfere with new sounds.

- **A hall without echoes** sounds muffled and lifeless.

- **Even in the best** concert halls, the music can be heard fading after the orchestra stops playing. This delay is called the reverberation time. Concert halls typically have a reverberation time of two seconds. A cathedral may reverberate for up to eight seconds, giving a more mellow, but less clear, sound.

Acids and alkalis

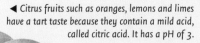

◄ Citrus fruits such as oranges, lemons and limes have a tart taste because they contain a mild acid, called citric acid. It has a pH of 3.

● **Mild acids,** such as acetic acid in vinegar, taste sour .

● **Strong acids,** such as sulphuric acid, are highly corrosive. They dissolve metals.

● **Acids** are solutions that are made when certain substances containing hydrogen dissolve in water.

● **Hydrogen atoms** have a single electron. When acid-making substances dissolve in water, the hydrogen atoms lose their electron and become positively charged

ions. Ions are atoms that have gained or lost electrons.

● **The strength of an acid** depends on how many hydrogen ions form.

● **The opposite of an acid** is a base. Weak bases such as baking powder taste bitter and feel soapy. Strong bases such as caustic soda are corrosive.

● **A base that dissolves** in water is called an alkali. Alkalis contain negatively charged ions – typically ions of hydrogen and oxygen, called hydroxide ions.

● **When you add an acid** to an alkali, both are neutralized. The acid and alkali react together forming water and a salt.

● **Chemists** use indicators such as litmus paper to test for acidity. Acids turn litmus paper red. Alkalis turn it blue. The strength of an acid may be measured on the pH scale. The strong acid (laboratory hydrochloric) has a pH of 1. The strongest alkali has a pH of 14. Pure water has a pH of about 7 and is neutral – neither acid nor alkali.

> ★ STAR FACT ★
> Hydrochloric acid in the stomach (with a pH of between 1 and 2) is essential for digestion.

Solids, liquids and gases

● **Most substances** can exist in three states– solid, liquid or gas. These are the states of matter.

● **Substances** change from one state to another at particular temperatures and pressures.

● **As temperature rises,** solids melt to become liquids. As it rises further, liquids evaporate to become gases.

● **The temperature** at which a solid melts is its melting point.

● **The maximum temperature** a liquid can reach before turning to gas is called its boiling point.

● **Every solid has strength** and a definite shape as its molecules are firmly bonded in a rigid structure.

▲ Ice melts to water as heat makes its molecules vibrate faster and faster until the bonds between them eventually break.

● **A liquid has a fixed volume** and flows and takes up the shape of any solid container into which it is poured.

● **A liquid flows** because although bonds hold molecules together, they are loose enough to move over each other, rather like dry sand.

● **A gas** such as air does not have any shape, strength or fixed volume. Its molecules move too quickly for any bonds to hold them together.

● **When a gas cools,** its molecules slow down until bonds form between them to create drops of liquid. This process is called condensation.

Nitrogen

- **Nitrogen** is a colourless, tasteless, odourless, inert (unreactive) gas, yet it is vital to life.

- **Nitrogen is** 78.08% of the air.

- **Nitrogen** turns liquid at −196°C and freezes at −210°C.

- **Liquid nitrogen** is so cold that it can freeze organic substances so quickly they suffer little damage.

- **Food such as cheesecakes** and raspberries are

◀ On average 100 kg of nitrate fertilizer are used on every hectare of farmland in the world to replace nitrogen taken from the soil by crops.

preserved by being sprayed with liquid nitrogen.

- **Compounds of nitrogen** and oxygen are called nitrates.

- **Nitrogen and oxygen** compounds are an essential ingredient of the proteins and nucleic acids from which all living cells are made.

- **Lightning makes** 250,000 tonnes of nitric acid a day. It joins nitrogen and oxygen in the air to make nitrogen oxide.

- **On a long sea dive,** the extra pressure in a diver's lungs makes extra nitrogen dissolve in the blood. If the diver surfaces too quickly the nitrogen forms bubbles, giving 'the bends' which can be painful or even fatal.

> **! NEWS FLASH !**
> When they die, some people have their bodies frozen with liquid nitrogen in the hope that medical science will one day bring them back to life.

Nuclear energy

- **The energy** that binds the nucleus of an atom together is enormous, as Albert Einstein showed.

- **By releasing the energy** from the nuclei of millions of atoms, nuclear power stations and bombs can generate a huge amount of power.

- **Nuclear fusion** is when nuclear energy is released by fusing together small atoms such as deuterium (a kind of hydrogen).

- **Nuclear fusion** is the reaction that keeps stars glowing and gives hydrogen bombs their terrifying power.

- **Nuclear fission** releases energy by splitting the large nuclei of atoms such as uranium and plutonium.

- **To split atomic nuclei** for nuclear fission, neutrons are fired into the nuclear fuel.

- **As neutrons crash** into atoms and split their nuclei, they split off more neutrons. These neutrons bombard other nuclei, splitting off more neutrons that bombard more nuclei. This is called a chain reaction.

- **An atom bomb,** or A-bomb, is one of the two main kinds of nuclear weapon. It works by an explosive, unrestrained fission of uranium-235 or plutonium-239.

- **A hydrogen bomb (H-bomb)** or thermonuclear weapon uses a conventional explosion to fuse the nuclei of deuterium atoms in a gigantic nuclear explosion.

- **The H-bomb** that exploded at Novaya Zemlya in 1961 released 10,000 times more energy than the bombs dropped on Hiroshima, in Japan, in 1945.

Neutron

Nucleus of
Uranium atom

▶ **Nuclear** fission involves firing a neutron (blue ball) into the nucleus of a uranium or plutonium atom. When the nucleus splits, it fires out more neutrons that split more nuclei, setting off a chain reaction.

Split nucleus

More neutrons

Spectrum

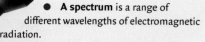

▶ When the beam from a torch passes through a prism it fans out into a rainbow of colours.

- **A spectrum** is a range of different wavelengths of electromagnetic radiation.

- **The white light of sunlight** can be broken up into its spectrum of colours with a triangular block of glass called a prism. The prism is set in a dark room and lit by a shaft of sunlight or similar white light.

- **The prism refracts (bends)** short wavelengths of light more than longer wavelengths, so the light fans out in bands ranging from violet to red.

- **The order of colours** in a spectrum is always the same: red, orange, yellow, green, blue, indigo, violet.

> ★ **STAR FACT** ★
> Spectral analysis can reveal what anything from a distant galaxy to a drug is made of.

- **Scientists** remember the order of the colours with the first letter of each word in this ancient phrase: 'Richard Of York Gained Battles in Vain'.

- **Infrared** is red light made of waves that are too long for human eyes to see.

- **Ultraviolet** is violet light made of waves that are too short for our eyes to see.

- **Spectroscopy**, or spectral analysis, is the study of the spectrum created when a solid, liquid or gas glows.

- **Every substance** produces its own unique spectrum, so spectroscopy helps to identify substances.

Energy conversion

- **Energy is measured** in joules (J). One joule is the energy involved in moving a force of 1 newton over 1 metre.

- **A kilojoule (kJ)** is 1000 joules.

- **A calorie** was the old measure of energy, but is now used only for food: 1 calorie is 4.187 J; 1 Cal is 1000 calories.

- **For scientists,** 'work' is the transfer of energy. When you move an object, you do work. The work done is the amount of energy (in joules) gained by the object.

- **For scientists, 'power'** is the work rate, or the rate at which energy is changed from one form to another.

- **The power of a machine** is the amount of work it does divided by the length of time it takes to do it.

- **The power of a car's engine** is the force with which the engine turns multiplied by the speed at which it turns.

- **A transducer** is a device for turning an electrical signal into a non-electrical signal (such as sound) or vice versa. A loudspeaker is a transducer.

- **The energy in the Big Bang** was 10^{68} joules. The world's coal reserves are 2×10^{23} joules; a thunderstorm has 10^{11} joules of energy; a large egg has 400,000 joules.

- **When sleeping** you use 60 Cals an hour and 80 Cals when sitting. Running uses 600 Cals. Three hours of reading or watching TV uses 240 Cals. Seven hours' hard work uses about 1000 Cals – or about 10 eggs' worth.

◀ A hydroelectric power station is a device that converts the energy of moving water into electrical energy.

Calcium

- **Calcium** is a soft, silvery white metal. It does not occur naturally in pure form.
- **Calcium** is the fifth most abundant element on Earth.
- **Calcium** is one of six alkaline-earth metals.
- **Most calcium compounds** are white solids called limes. They include chalk, porcelain, enamel on teeth, cement, seashells, the limescale on taps and much more.
- **The word 'lime'** comes from the Latin word for slime.
- **Quicklime** is calcium oxide. It is called 'quick' (Old English for living) because when water drips on it, it twists and swells as if it is alive.
- **Slaked lime** is calcium hydroxide. It may be called 'slaked' because it slakes (quenches) a plant's thirst for lime in acid soils.
- **Calcium has** an atomic number of 20. It has a melting point of 839°C and a boiling point of 1484°C.
- **Limelight** was the bright light used by theatres in the

▲ *Calcium is one of the basic building materials of living things. It is one of the crucial ingredients in shell and bone, which is why they are typically white.*

days before electricity. It was made by applying a mix of oxygen and hydrogen to pellets of calcium.

- **Calcium adds rigidity** to bones and teeth and helps to control muscles. Your body gets it from milk and cheese.

Oil compounds

◀ *This is a propane molecule. The carbon atoms are purple, the hydrogen atoms are grey.*

- **Alkanes or paraffins** are a family of hydrocarbons in which the number of hydrogen atoms is two more than twice the number of carbon atoms.
- **Lighter alkanes** are gases like methane, propane and butane (used in camping stoves). All make good fuels.
- **Candles** contain a mixture of alkanes.
- **Alkenes or olefins** are a family of hydrocarbons in which there are twice as many hydrogen atoms as carbon atoms.
- **The simplest alkene** is ethene, also called ethylene (C_2H_4), which is used to make polythene and other plastics such as PVC.
- **Green bananas and tomatoes** are often ripened rapidly in ripening rooms filled with ethene.
- **Ethene** is the basis of many paint strippers.
- **Ethene** can be used to make ethanol – the alcohol in drinks.

▲ *In an oil refinery, crude oil is broken down into an enormous range of different hydrocarbons.*

- **Hydrocarbons** are compounds made only of carbon and hydrogen atoms. Most oil products are hydrocarbons.
- **The simplest hydrocarbon** is methane, the main gas in natural gas (and flatulence from cows!). Methane molecules are one carbon atom and four hydrogen atoms.

1000 THINGS YOU SHOULD KNOW ABOUT

BUILDINGS &
TRANSPORT

KEY

 Cars

 Trains

 Planes

 Buildings

 Great monuments

 Boats

Cathedrals

- **Cathedrals** are the churches of Christian bishops.
- **The word cathedral** comes from the Greek word for 'seat', *kathedra*.
- **Cathedrals** are typically built in the shape of a cross. The entrance of the cathedral is at the west end.
- **The long end** of the cross is the nave.

▲ Paris's famous Notre Dame dates from 1163, but was remodelled in the 1840s by Viollet-le-Duc.

The short end, containing the altar and choir stalls, is called the apse. The arms of the cross are called transepts.

- **Canterbury and a few other cathedrals** were built as early as the 6th-century AD. Most European cathedrals were built between 1000 and 1500.
- **Medieval cathedrals** were often built in the 'gothic' style with soaring, pointed arches, tall spires and huge pointed arch windows.
- **Many gothic cathedrals** have beautiful stained-glass windows. Chartres Cathedral in France has 176.
- **The modern Crystal Cathedral** in California is star-shaped and made of glass for TV broadcasts.
- **The world's tallest** cathedral spire is in Ulm, Germany, which is 160.9 m tall.
- **The world's smallest** cathedral is Christ Church in Highlandville, Missouri, USA which is just 4.2 by 5.2 m and holds only 18 people.

The first railways

- **Railways** were invented long before steam power.
- **The Diolkos** was a 6 km long railway that transported boats across the Corinth isthmus in Greece in the 6th-century BC. Trucks pushed by slaves ran in grooves in a limestone track.
- **The Diolkos** ran for over 1300 years until AD 900.
- **Railways** were revived in Europe in the 14th century with wooden trackrails to guide horse and hand carts taking ore out of mines.
- **In the 1700s,** English ironmakers began to make rails of iron. First the rail was wood covered in iron. Then the whole rail was made of iron. Iron wheels with 'flanges' (lips) ran inside the track.

▶ The Stephensons' 'Rocket' was the most famous early locomotive, winning the first locomotive speed trials at Rainhill in England in 1829.

- **In 1804** Cornish engineer Richard Trevithick built the first successful steam railway locomotive.
- **Trevithick's** engine pulled a train of five wagons with 9 tonnes of iron and 70 men along 15 km of track at the Pendarren ironworks in Wales.
- **On 27 September 1825** George and Robert Stephenson opened the world's first steam passenger railway, the Stockton and Darlington in England.
- **The gauge (trackwidth)** used for the Stockton and Darlington was 1.44 m, the same length as axles on horse-wagons. This became the standard gauge in the USA and much of Europe.
- **The English-built 'Stourbridge Lion'** was the first full-size steam locomotive to run in the USA. It ran on wooden track in Pennsylvania in 1829.

Controlling a plane

- **A plane** is controlled in the air by moving hinged flaps on its wings and tail.
- **Changing pitch** is when the plane goes nose-up or nose-down to dive or climb.
- **Rolling** is when the plane rolls to one side, dipping one wing or the other.
- **Yawing** is when the plane steers to the left or right like a car.
- **Pitch** is controlled by raising or lowering hinged flaps on the rear wings called elevators.
- **To pitch up** in a small or simple plane, the pilot pulls back on the control column to raise the elevators.
- **Rolling** is controlled by large hinged flaps on the wings called ailerons.

◄ In old-fashioned planes, the pilot controlled the flaps manually by moving a control stick linked to the flaps by cables. In modern planes, the flaps are controlled automatically via electric wires (fly-by-wire) or laser beams (fly-by-light). The flight deck of this plane from 30 years ago has lots of dials to help the pilot. Modern planes have 'glass cockpits', which means they have computer screens.

- **To roll left,** the pilot pushes the control column to the left, which raises the aileron on the left wing and lowers it on the right.
- **Yawing** is controlled by the vertical hinged flap on the tail called the rudder.
- **To yaw left,** the pilot pushes the foot-operated rudder bar forward with his left foot, to swing the rudder left.

Trucks

- **Trucks or lorries** can weigh 40 tonnes or more – maybe as much as 50 cars.
- **Cars** are powered by petrol engines; trucks are typically powered by diesel engines.
- **Cars** typically have five forward gears; trucks often have as many as 16.
- **Cars** typically have four wheels. Trucks often have 12 or 16 to help spread the load.
- **Many trucks** have the same basic cab and chassis (the framework supporting the body). Different bodies are fitted on to the chassis to suit the load.
- **Some trucks** are in two parts, hinged at the join. These are called articulated trucks.
- **The cab and engine** of an articulated truck is called the tractor unit. The load is carried in the trailer.
- **In Australia** one tractor may pull several trailers in a 'road-train' along the long, straight desert roads.

▲ This 14-wheel tanker is articulated, and the tank and tractor unit can be separated.

- **The longest truck** is the Arctic Snow Train, first made for the US army. This is 174 m long and has 54 wheels.
- **Large trucks** are sometimes called 'juggernauts'. Juggernaut was a form of the Hindu god Vishnu who rode a huge chariot, supposed by Europeans to crush people beneath its wheels.

Mosques

- **The word 'mosque'** comes from the Arabic *masjid*, which means a place of kneeling.

- **Mosques** are places where Muslims worship. Muslims can worship anywhere clean. So a mosque can be just a stick in the sand to mark out a space for praying or even just a mat. But many mosques are beautiful buildings.

- **Cathedral or Friday** mosques are large

▲ *Typically minarets on mosques have onion-shaped roofs.*

mosques big enough to hold all the adult Muslims in the area.

- **Typically** mosques have a courtyard surrounded by four walls called iwans. There is often a fountain or fuawara at the centre for ceremonial washing.

- **The mihrab** is a decorative niche on the inner wall closest to the city of Mecca that muslims face when praying.

- **The mimbar** is the stone or wooden pulpit where the Imam leads the people in prayer.

- **Most mosques** have two to six tall pointed towers which are called minarets.

- **On each minaret** is a balcony from which muezzin (criers) call the faithful to prayer five times a day.

- **Minarets** may have been inspired by the Pharos, the famous lighthouse at Alexandria in Egypt.

- **There are** no paintings or statues in mosques, only abstract patterns, often made of tiles.

Motorbikes

▲ *Many enthusiasts still ride motorbikes like this from the 1930s when motorcycling was in its heyday.*

- **The first petrol engine** motorbike was built by Gottlieb Daimler in Germany in 1885.

- **Most small motorbikes** have a two-stroke petrol engine, typically air-cooled and quite noisy.

- **Most larger motorbikes** have four-stroke petrol engines, typically water-cooled.

- **On most bikes** the engine drives the rear wheel via a chain; on some the drive is via a shaft.

- **A trail bike** is a bike with a high mounted frame and chunky tyres, designed to be ridden over rough tracks.

- **Motorbikes** with engines smaller than 50cc may be called mopeds, because in the past they had pedals as well as an engine.

- **The biggest motorbikes** have engines of around 1200cc.

- **The most famous** motorbike race in the world is the Isle of Man TT, or Tourist Trophy.

- **In Speedway,** bikes with no brakes or gears are raced round dirt tracks.

> ★ STAR FACT ★
> The first motorbike was steam powered, and built by the Michaux brothers in 1868.

Building of the railways

- **On the 15th September 1830** the world's first major passenger railway opened between Liverpool and Manchester.

- **At the opening** of the Liverpool and Manchester railway, government minister William Huskisson was the first railway casualty, killed by the locomotive.

- **In 1831** the Best Friend started a regular train service between Charleston and Hamburg, South Carolina in the USA.

- **By 1835** there were over 1600 km of railway in the USA.

- **In Britain** railway building became a mania in the 1840s.

- **Hundreds of acts** of parliament gave railway companies the powers to carve their way through cities

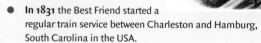

◄ The new railways often meant demolishing huge strips through cities to lay track into stations.

and the countryside .

- **By the late 1840s** Great Western Railway trains were able to average well over 100 km/h all the way from London to Exeter via Bristol, completing the 300 odd km journey in under 4 hours.

- **On 10th May 1869** railways from either side of the United States met at Promontory, Utah, giving North America the first transcontinental railway.

- **The British** built 40,000 km of railways in India in the 1880s and 90s.

- **Vast armies of men** worked on building the railways – 45,000 on the London and Southampton railway alone.

Early boats

- **The Aborigines** arrived by boat in Australia at least 50,000 years ago, as cave paintings show.

- **The oldest remains** of boats are 8000 or so years old, like the 4 m canoe found at Pesse in Holland.

- **Many early canoes** were simply hollowed out logs, called dugouts.

- **The islands of the Pacific** were probably colonized by dugouts, stabilized by attaching an outrigger (an extra float on the side) or adding extra hulls.

- **Lighter canoes** could be made by stretching animal skins over a light frame of bent wood.

- **4000 years ago,** Ancient Egyptians were making ships over 30 m long by interlocking planks of wood and lashing them together with tough grass rope.

- **By 1000 BC,** Phoenician traders were sailing into the Atlantic in ships made of planks of Cedar trees.

▲◄ Outriggers (above) were used to colonize the Pacific tens of thousands of years ago. But many early boats like the Welsh coracle (left) were made by stretching animal skins over a wooden frame.

- **All early boats** were driven by hand – using either a pole pushed along the bottom, or a paddle.

- **Sails** were first used 7000 years ago in Mesopotamia on reed trading boats.

- **The first known picture** of a sail is 5500 years old and comes from Egypt.

Castles

- **Castles** were the fortress homes of powerful men such as kings and dukes in the Middle Ages. The castle acted as a stronghold for commanding the country around it. They were also barracks for troops, prisons, armouries and centres of local government.

- **The first castles,** in the 11th century, had a high earth mound called a motte, topped by a wooden tower. Around this was an enclosure called a bailey, protected by a fence of wooden stakes and a ditch.

- **From the 12th century** the tower was built of stone and called a keep or donjon. This was the last refuge in an attack. Soon the wooden fences were replaced by thick stone walls and strong towers.

- **Walls and towers** were topped by battlements – low walls with gaps for defenders to fire weapons from.

- **Castles evolved** from a simple square tower to elaborate rings of fortifications. The entrance or gatehouse was equipped with booby traps.

- **From the 13th century** the ditch around the castle was often dug deep, filled with water and called a moat. This stopped enemies from sapping (digging under the walls).

- **Many castles** in England and Wales were first built by the Norman conquerors in the 11th century, including Windsor Castle which dates from 1070.

- **In early castles** there was just a single great hall. Later castles had extra small rooms for the lord and lady, such as the solar, which had windows.

- **The gong farmer** was the man who had to clean out the pit at the bottom of the garderobe (toilet shute).

- **An attack on a castle** was called a siege and could last many months, or even years.

▼ *This shows some of the main features of a medieval castle. Very few castles had all of these features. Innovations were constantly being added over the centuries as attackers came up with better ways of breaching the defences and defenders found ways to hold them at bay.*

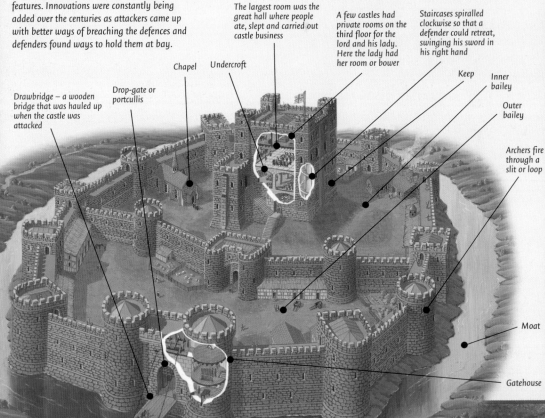

The largest room was the great hall where people ate, slept and carried out castle business

A few castles had private rooms on the third floor for the lord and his lady. Here the lady had her room or bower

Staircases spiralled clockwise so that a defender could retreat, swinging his sword in his right hand

Chapel   *Undercroft*

Keep   *Inner bailey*

Drop-gate or portcullis

Outer bailey

Drawbridge – a wooden bridge that was hauled up when the castle was attacked

Archers fire through a slit or loop

Moat

Gatehouse

Galleons

◀ In this replica of a ship from around 1600, the tall stern castle where the captain lived is clearly visible.

- **Galleons** were huge sailing ships that were built from the mid 1500s onwards.
- **Galleons** had tall structures called castles at either end.
- **The front castle** was called the forecastle or fo'c'sle (said folk-sel).
- **The rear castle** was called the stern castle and it housed elaborate living quarters for the officers.

The crew lived in crowded rows below deck.

- **The stern of the ship** was often ornately carved and painted in gold and bright colours.
- **A galleon** had three tall masts – the foremast, the mainmast and the mizzenmast at the rear.
- **Galleons** were both warships and trading boats and carried vast numbers of cannon and troops.
- **In the 1500s,** enormous Spanish galleons crossed the Atlantic carrying gold from the Americas to Spain.
- **When the Spanish Armada** of galleons was sent to attack England in 1588, they were outfought by the smaller but faster and lighter English ships, despite their heavy armament.

> ★ STAR FACT ★
> The biggest Spanish galleons weighed well over 1000 tonnes.

The Colosseum

- **The Colosseum** was a huge stone sports arena built in Ancient Rome.
- **It was 189 m long,** 156 m wide, and 52 m high.
- **It held** up to 73,000 spectators who entered through 80 entrances. Each spectator had a ticket corresponding to one of the 76 arcades.
- **The sports** included fights between gladiators with swords, nets and other weapons who fought to the death, or fought against lions and other wild beasts.
- **Counterweighted** doors allowed 64 wild beasts to be released from their cages simultaneously.
- **It took just eight years** – from around AD 70 to AD 78 – to build the Colosseum.
- **To build it** the Romans brought almost a quarter of a million tonnes of stone by barge from quarries 20 km outside Rome.
- **During construction**, a cart carrying a tonne of stone would have left the riverside wharves every seven

▲ The Colosseum in Rome was one of the greatest buildings of the ancient world.

minutes on the 1.5 km journey to the site.

- **A huge awning** called a velarium, supported by 240 masts, protected the arena from bad weather.
- **Its opening was celebrated** by spectacular games lasting 100 days.

Tractors

- **Tractors** are motor vehicles used mostly on farms for pulling or pushing machines such as ploughs.

- **Tractors** are also used in factories, by the army, for logging and for clearing snow.

- **Steam-powered tractors** called 'traction engines' were introduced in 1834 by Walter Hancock.

- **Traction-engines** could pull up to 40 ploughs at once via long chains, but they were too cumbersome to be practical in hilly country.

- **Petrol-powered tractors** were introduced in the 1890s but they were not powerful enough for most farm work.

- **The first all-purpose** farm tractors appeared in the 1920s and soon began to replace horses and oxen.

> ★ STAR FACT ★
> There are now well over 16 million tractors around the world.

▲ Modern tractors can be adapted to operate all kinds of devices, including this haybailer, via the power take-off.

- **Ploughs and other equipment** are drawn along via the drawbar on the back of the tractor.

- **The power take-off** or PTO allows the tractor's engine to power equipment such as potato diggers.

- **25% of all tractors** are in the USA.

The Age of Sail

- **East Indiamen** were ships that carried ivory, silks and spices to Europe from India, China and the East Indies.

- **By 1800** Indiamen could carry 1000 tonnes of cargo.

- **Packet ships** were ships that provided a regular service across the Atlantic between Europe and the USA – no matter whether they had a full load or not.

- **The first packet service** began in 1818 with the Black Ball Line from Liverpool to New York. Red Star and Swallowtail followed.

◀ The tea clippers of the mid-1800s were the pinnacle of sailing ship technology, able to carry thousands of tonnes of tea at speeds of 20 knots or more.

- **Clippers** were the big, fast sailing ships that 'clipped off' time as they raced to get cargoes of tea from China and India back first to markets in Europe and the USA.

- **Clippers** had slender hulls, tall masts and up to 35 sails.

- **Clippers could reach** speeds of 30 knots (55 km/h). Many could sail from New York, round South America, to San Francisco in under 100 days.

- **In 1866** the clippers *Taeping*, *Serica* and *Ariel* raced 25,700 km from Foochow in China to London in 99 days.

- **Canadian Donald Mckay** of Boston, Massachusetts, was the greatest clipper builder. His ship the *Great Republic* of 1853 was the biggest sailing ship of its time, over 100 m long and able to carry 4000 tonnes of cargo.

- **A famous clipper,** the *Cutty Sark*, built in 1869 is preserved at Greenwich, London. Its name is Scottish for 'short shirt' and comes from the witch in Robert Burns's poem *Tam O'Shanter*.

Parachutes, hang-gliders

- **Leonardo da Vinci** drew a design for a parachute around 1500.
- **The first human parachute drop** was made by Jacques Garnerin from a balloon over Paris in 1797.
- **Folding parachutes** were used first in the USA in 1880.
- **Early parachutes** were made of canvas, then silk. Modern parachutes are made of nylon, stitched in panels to limit tears to a small area.
- **Until recently** parachutes were shaped like umbrellas; now most are 'parafoils' – wing-shaped.
- **Drogues** are parachutes thrown out by jet planes and high-speed cars to slow them down.
- **German Otto Lilienthal** flew his own canvas and wood hang-gliders in the 1890s.
- **Modern hang-gliding** began with the fabric delta

◀ *Parachutes really came into their own with the massive parachute drops of troops into battle during World War 2.*

(triangular) wing design developed by the American Francis Rogallo in the 1940s.

- **Today's hang-gliders** are made by stretching nylon over a very light and strong nylon and kevlar frame. They combine long aeroplane-like wings and a double skin of fabric to achieve very long flights.
- **The first hang-gliders** achieved a glide ratio of 1:2.5 – that is, they travelled only 2.5 m forward for every 1 m that they dropped. Today's hang-gliders give glide ratios of 1:14 or better.

Skyscrapers

- **The first skyscrapers** were built in Chicago and New York in the 1880s.
- **A crucial step** in the development of skyscrapers was the invention of the fast safety lift by US engineer Elisha Otis (1811-61) in 1857.
- **The Home Insurance Building** in Chicago, built in 1885, was one of the first skyscrapers.
- **In buildings** over 40-storeys high, the weight of the building is less important in terms of strength than the wind load (the force of the wind against the building).
- **The Empire State Building,** built in New York in 1931, was for decades the world's tallest building at 381 m.
- **The tallest building** in America is the 442 m-high Sears Tower in Chicago, built in 1974.

▶ *New York's Manhattan has more skyscrapers than anywhere else in the world.*

- **The world's tallest building** is the 452 m Petronas twin towers in Kuala Lumpur, Malaysia.
- **If the Grollo Tower** is built in Melbourne Australia it will be 560 m high.
- **An early concept** design has been presented for a Tokyo building measuring 4000 m!

> **! NEWS FLASH !**
> The Landmark Tower in Kowloon, Hong Kong, could be 574 m high.

St Sophia

- **Saint or Hagia Sophia** was built as an ancient Christian cathedral in Istanbul in Turkey (Roman 'Byzantium').

- **Hagia Sophia** is Greek for 'holy wisdom'.

- **St Sophia** was built between AD 532 and 537 , when Istanbul was called Constantinople.

- **The great Byzantine** emperor Justinian I ordered the building of St Sophia after a fire destroyed an earlier church on the site.

- **St Sophia** was designed by the brilliant Byzantine architects Anthemius of Tralles and Isidorus of Miletus.

- **The main structure** is a framework of arches and vaults (high arched ceilings).

- **The dome** is 31 m across and 56 m high. It is supported by four triangular brick pillars called pendentives.

- **St Sophia is decorated** with marble veneers and mosaics of Mary, Christ, angels and bishops.

- **In 1453** the Ottoman Turks took the city and converted St Sophia to a mosque. They plastered over the mosaics and added four minarets on the outside.

- **In 1935** St Sophia was converted into a museum and the mosaics were uncovered.

▼ *Istanbul's St Sophia is one of the world's oldest cathedrals and one of the most remarkable pieces of ancient architecture.*

Viking longships

- **Viking longships** were the long narrow boats built by the Viking warriors of Scandinavia around AD 1000.

- **A virtually** intact ship was found in 1880 at Gokstad near Oseberg in Norway. A king was buried inside it.

- **Longships** were very fast, light and seaworthy.

▲ *The Gokstad ship dates from c. AD 900.*

They carried the Viking explorer Leif Ericsson all the way across the Atlantic to North America.

- **In 1893** a replica of the Gokstad ship sailed across the Atlantic in 28 days.

- **Some Viking longships** were up to 30 m long and 17 m across and could carry 200 warriors.

- **At sea** longships relied on a single square sail made up from strips of woollen cloth; on rivers and in calm they used oar-power, with 20-30 rowers on each side.

- **Their ships' shallow build** allowed the Vikings to make raids far up shallow rivers.

- **The prow curved** up to a carved dragon head.

- **Longships** were for carrying warriors on raids, but the Vikings also built wider, deeper 'knorrs' for trade and small rowing boats called 'faerings'.

- **The Viking** ships were very stable because they had a keel, a wooden board about 17 m long and 45 cm deep, along the bottom of the boat.

Diesel trains

- **The diesel engine** was invented by Rudolf Diesel in 1892 and experiments with diesel locomotives started soon after. The first great success was the *Flying Hamburger* which ran from Berlin to Hamburg in the 1930s at speeds of 125 km/h. Diesel took over from steam in the 1950s and 1960s.

- **Diesel locomotives** are really electric locomotives that carry their own power plant. The wheels are driven by an electric motor which is supplied with electricity by the locomotive's diesel engine.

- **The power output of a diesel** engine is limited, so high-speed trains are electric – but diesels can supply their own electricity so need no trackside cables.

- **There are two other kinds** of diesel apart from diesel-electrics: diesel-hydraulic and diesel-mechanical.

- **In diesel-hydraulics,** the power from the diesel engine is connected to the wheels via a torque converter, which is a turbine driven round by fluid.

- **In diesel-mechanicals,** the power is transmitted from the diesel engine to the wheels via gears and shafts. This only works for small locomotives.

- **Diesel locomotives** may be made up from one or more separate units. An A unit holds the driver's cab and leads the train. A B unit simply holds an engine.

- **A typical diesel** for fast, heavy trains or for trains going over mountains may consist of one A unit and six B units.

- **The usual maximum** power output from a single diesel locomotive is about 3500–4000 horsepower. In Russia, several 3000-horsepower units are joined together to make 12,000-horsepower locomotives.

▼ This is a typical British diesel-electric locomotive from the 1960s. It has a cab at both ends so that it can be operated in either direction. This is one of the older generation of diesel-electrics that use DC (Direct Current) generators. DC generators give a current that flows in only one direction. Most newer engines take advantage of electronic devices called rectifiers to use the current from an AC (Alternating Current) generator. An AC generator gives a current that swaps direction many times a second. The rectifiers convert this into a direct current. AC generators are far more powerful and efficient.

Diesel engine in which diesel fuel is squeezed inside cylinders until it bursts into flame. The expansion of the fuel as it burns provides the engine's power

Fuel tank carrying diesel fuel. Because a diesel train carries its fuel on board, it is entirely independent, unlike electric locomotives

Cooling fan

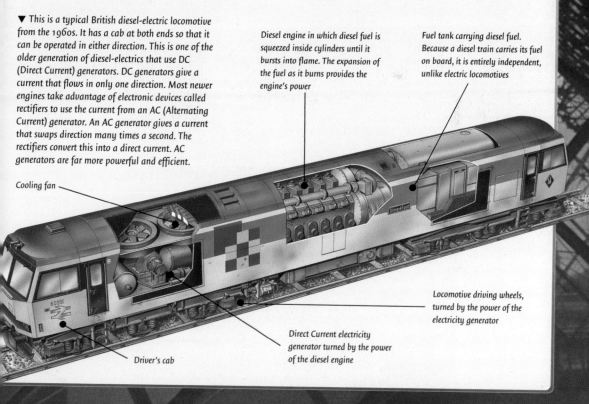

Locomotive driving wheels, turned by the power of the electricity generator

Direct Current electricity generator turned by the power of the diesel engine

Driver's cab

Supersonic planes

▶ The Soviet Tupolev Tu-144 of 1968 was the very first supersonic jetliner, but the Anglo-French Concorde of 1969 is the only one that is still flying.

> **! NEWS FLASH !**
> Spaceplanes of the near future may reach speeds of Mach 15.

- **Supersonic planes** travel faster than the speed of sound.
- **The speed of sound** is about 1220 km/h at sea level at 15°C.
- **Sound travels** slower higher up, so the speed of sound is about 1060 km/h at 12,000 m.
- **Supersonic** plane speeds are given in Mach numbers. These are the speed of the plane divided by the speed of sound at the plane's altitude.
- **A plane flying** at 1500 km/h at 12,000 m, where the speed of sound is 1060 km/h, is at Mach 1.46.
- **A plane flying** at supersonic speeds builds up shock waves in front and behind because it keeps catching up and compressing the sound waves in front of it.
- **The double shock waves** create a sharp crack called a sonic boom that is heard on the ground. Two booms can often be heard a second or two apart.
- **In 1947** Chuck Yeager of the USAF made the first supersonic flight in the Bell X-1 rocket plane. The X-15 rocket plane later reached speeds faster than Mach 6. Speeds faster than Mach 5 are called hypersonic.
- **The first jet plane** to fly supersonic was the F-100 Super Sabre fighter of 1953. The first supersonic bomber was the USAF's Convair B-58 Hustler of 1956.

Famous castles

▲ Eilean Donan in Scotland was used in the film 'Braveheart'.

- **The Arab Gormaz Castle** in the Castile region of Spain is Western Europe's biggest and oldest castle. It was started in AD 956 by Caliph Al-Hakam II. It is 1 km round and over 400 m across.
- **Bran Castle** in Romania was built in 1212 by Teutonic (German) knights. In the 1450s, it was one of the castles of Vlad the Impaler, the original Count Dracula.
- **Windsor Castle** in England has been one of the main homes of English kings and queens since the 1100s.
- **Malbork Castle** near Gdansk in Poland is the biggest medieval castle, built by the Teutonic knights in 1309.
- **Germany's Neuschwanstein** castle was started in 1869 by 'Mad' King Ludwig II. Its name means 'new swan castle' after Swan Knight in Wagner's opera *Lohengrin*.
- **Neuschwanstein** is the model for the castle in Walt Disney's cartoon film *Sleeping Beauty*.
- **15th century Blarney Castle** in Ireland is home to the famous 'Blarney stone'. Kissing the stone is said to give people the 'gift of the gab' (fast and fluent talk).
- **Tintagel Castle** in Cornwall is where legend says the mythical King Arthur was conceived.
- **Colditz Castle** in Germany was a notorious prison camp in World War 2.
- **Carcassone** in southern France is a whole town fortified by Catholics c.1220 against those of the Cathar religion.

Golden Gate Bridge

- **The Golden Gate Bridge** spans the entrance to San Francisco Bay in California, USA.
- **The Golden Gate Bridge** is one of the world's largest suspension bridges.
- **The total length** of the bridge is 2737 m.

◀ San Francisco's Golden Gate Bridge is one of the most beautiful – and busiest – bridges in the world.

> **! NEWS FLASH !**
> The tower's foundations are being reinforced to withstand earthquakes.

- **The towers** at either end are 340 m high. The suspended span between the towers is 1280 m, one of the longest in the world.
- **The roadway is** 67 m above the water, although this varies according to the tide
- **The Golden Gate Bridge** was designed by Joseph Baerman Strauss and built for $35 million, a third of the original cost estimate.
- **The bridge** was opened to traffic on 27 May 1937.
- **The bridge** carries two six-lane highways and pedestrian paths.
- **Unusually,** the bridge is double-deck, carrying traffic one way on the upper deck and the other way on the lower deck.

Junks

- **Junks** are wooden sailing boats that have been used in China and the Far East for thousands of years.
- **Typical junks** have a broad flat bow (front).
- **Typical junks** have a broad, high stern castle (rear).
- **Junks have lugsails**. These are triangular sails arranged almost in line with the boat, allowing the boat to sail almost into the wind – unlike the square sails of early European boats which only worked with the wind behind.
- **The Chinese** are believed to have invented lugsails.
- **By the 1400s,** the Chinese were building junks 150 m long and almost 100 m wide – much bigger than any sailing ship yet built in Europe.
- **In 1405** the Chinese admiral Cheng Ho led a fleet of exploration through the Indian Ocean. His fleet consisted of 62 large junks and 255 small junks. Each of the large junks was gigantic compared with Columbus's *Santa Maria*. The biggest junk was over

1500 tonnes – the *Santa Maria* was only 98 tonnes.

- **Between 1790 and 1810,** traders in the South Seas were terrorized by vast fleets of pirate junks, led by the female pirate Cheng I Sao.
- **Nowadays** most junks are motorized.
- **Junks** are often moored permanently as homes.

▶ Most sailing junks have two or three masts. Some have more. The sails are made from cotton and supported by bamboo struts.

Fighters of World War II

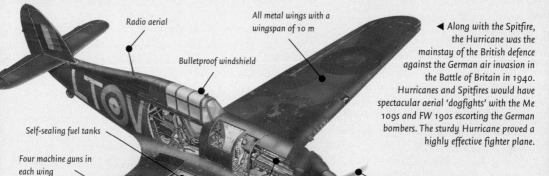

Radio aerial

All metal wings with a
wingspan of 10 m

Bulletproof windshield

Self-sealing fuel tanks

Four machine guns in
each wing

One 20 mm cannon
in each wing

1030 hp Rolls-Royce
Merlin engine capable of
powering the plane to over
520 km/h

Three-blade propeller

◀ Along with the Spitfire,
the Hurricane was the
mainstay of the British defence
against the German air invasion in
the Battle of Britain in 1940.
Hurricanes and Spitfires would have
spectacular aerial 'dogfights' with the Me
109s and FW 190s escorting the German
bombers. The sturdy Hurricane proved a
highly effective fighter plane.

> ★ STAR FACT ★
> The 'Night Witches' were a crack
> Soviet squadron of female fighter
> pilots who flew night raids on the
> Germans in the Caucasus Mountains.

▲ In the dogfights of the Battle of Britain, the Spitfire's 650 km/h
top speed and amazing agility proved decisive.

- **World War II** fighter planes were sleek monoplanes
  (single-winged aircraft) very different from the biplanes
  of World War I. Many were developed from racing
  machines of the 1920s and 1930s.

- **The most famous** British plane was the Supermarine
  Spitfire. This was developed from the S.6B seaplane which
  won the coveted Schneider trophy in the late 1920s.

- **The most famous American** fighter was the North
  American P-51 Mustang, which could reach speeds of
  over 700 km/h and had a range of 1700 km. It was
  widely used as an escort for bombers.

- **In the Pacific** US planes like the Grumman Wildcat and
  Hellcat fought against the fast and highly
  manoeuvrable Japanese Mitsubishi A6M 'Zero'.

- **The most famous German** fighter was the fast, agile
  Messerschmitt Bf 109. This was the plane flown by
  German ace Erich Hartmann, who shot down 352 enemy
  planes. Over 33,000 Me 109s were made during the war.

- **Me 109s** were nicknamed by model. The Bf109E was the
  Emil. The Bf109G was the Gustav.

- **The German Focke-Wulf 190** was the first German
  fighter to have a BMW radial engine.

- **The most famous Soviet** fighter was the MiG LaGG-3
  Interceptor, flown by Soviet air ace Ivan Kozhedub who
  shot down 62 German planes.

- **The British Hawker Hurricane** was more old-
  fashioned, slower and less famous than the Spitfire,
  but its reliability made it highly effective. Hurricanes
  actually destroyed more enemy aircraft than Spitfires.

The Benz

- **Karl Benz (1844-1929)** and his wife Berta were the German creators of the first successful petrol-driven car in 1885.

- **At the age of 16,** before the first petrol-powered cart was built, Karl Benz dreamed of 'a unit that could supplant the steam engine'.

- **Karl and Berta Benz** began developing their car in the 1870s, while trying to earn money from a tin-making business. By 1880, they were so penniless they could barely afford to eat everyday.

- **Their first car** was a small tricycle, but had a water-cooled four-stroke engine with electric ignition.

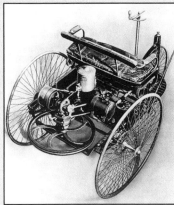

▶ *The Benz tricycle was the world's first successful petrol-driven car.*

- **Karl Benz** tested the car round the streets of their home town of Mannheim after dark to avoid scaring people.

- **Berta Benz** recharged the car's battery after each trip by pedalling a dynamo attached to her sewing machine.

- **Berta Benz** secretly made the first long, 100 km journey in the car, without Karl knowing. On the journey to her home in Pforzheim, she had to clear the fuel-line with a hairpin and use her garters to cure an electrical short.

- **The Benz** caused a stir when shown at the Paris World Fair in 1889.

- **Backed by F. von Fischer** and Julian Ganss, Benz began making his cars for sale in 1889 – the first cars ever made for sale.

- **By 1900** Benz was making over 600 cars a year.

Stonehenge

- **Stonehenge** is an ancient stone monument in southern England made from circles of huge rough-cut stones.

- **The main circle of stones** or 'sarsens' is a ring of 30 huge upright stones, joined at the top by 30 lintels. Many of these sarsens have now fallen or been looted.

- **Inside the sarsen ring** are five 'doorways' called trilithons, each made with three gigantic stones, weighing up to 40 tonnes each.

- **In between** are rings of smaller bluestones.

- **The bluestones** come from the Preseli Hills in Wales, 240 km away. Archeologists puzzle over how they were carried here.

▶ *Experiments have shown a team of 150 people could haul the stones upright, but dragging them to the site on greased wooden sleds must have been a huge undertaking.*

- **At the centre** is a single tall stone, called the Heel Stone.

- **Stonehenge was built** in three phases between 2950 BC and 1600 BC, starting with just a huge earth ring.

- **Archaeologists** believe it was a gathering place and a site for religious ceremonies for Bronze Age people.

- **Newman, Thom and Hawkins** have shown the layout of the stones ties in with astronomical events.

- **At sunrise on midsummer's day** (the solstice), the sun shines directly along the avenue to the Heel Stone.

Warplanes

◀ Pilots flying modern jets fly at supersonic speeds aided by laser-guided weapons, night-vision goggles and other high-tech equipment.

- **The 870 km/h** German Messerschmitt Me 262 was the first jet fighter. It had straight wings like propeller planes.
- **The Lockheed Shooting Star** was the first successful US jet fighter.
- **The Korean War** of the 1950s saw the first major combat between jet fighters. Most now had swept-back wings, like the Russian MiG-15 and the US F-86 Sabre.
- **In 1954** Boeing introduced the B-52 Superfortress, still the USAF's main bomber because of its huge bomb-carrying capacity.

- **In the 1950s** aircraft began flying close to the ground to avoid detection by radar. On modern planes like the Lockheed F-111 a computer radar system flies the plane automatically at a steady height over hills and valleys.
- **The Hawker Harrier** of 1968 was the only successful 'jump jet' with swivelling jets for vertical take-off (VTOL).
- **Airborne Early Warning** systems (AEWs) detect low-flying aircraft. To evade them, the Americans began developing 'stealth' systems like RCS and RAM.
- **RCS** or Radar Cross Section means altering the plane's shape to make it less obvious to radar. RAM (Radar Absorbent Material) is a coating that doesn't reflect radar.
- **In 1988** the US unveiled its first 'stealth' bomber, the B-2, codenamed Have Blue. The F117 stealth fighter followed.
- **The 2500 km/h Russian Sukhoi S-37** Berkut ('golden eagle') of 1997 uses Forward Swept Wings (FSW) for maximum agility, rather than stealth technology.

Gears

▲ Gears are used in a huge range of machines, from watches to motorbikes, for transmitting movement from one shaft to another.

- **Gears** are pairs of toothed wheels that interlock and so transmit power from one shaft to another.
- **The first gears** were wooden, with wooden teeth. By the 6th century AD, wooden gears of all kinds were used in windmills, watermills and winches.

- **Metal gears** appeared in 87 BC and were later used for clocks. Today, all gears are metal and made on a 'gear-hobbing' machine.
- **Simple gears** are wheels with straight cut teeth.
- **Helical gears** have slanting rather than straight teeth, and run smoother. The gears in cars are helical.
- **Bevel or mitre gears** are cone-shaped, allowing shafts to interlock at right angles.
- **In worm gears** one big helical gear interlocks with a long spiral gear on a shaft at right angles.
- **Planetary gears** have a number of gear wheels called spurs or planets that rotate around a central 'sun' gear.
- **In a planetary gear** the planet and sun gear all rotate within a ring called an annulus.

★ STAR FACT ★
Automatic gearboxes in cars use planetary or epicyclic gears.

Arches

- **Before arches,** door openings were just two uprights spanned by a straight piece of wood or stone called a lintel.

- **Arches** replace a straight lintel with a curve. Curved arches can take more weight than a lintel, because downwards weight makes a lintel snap in the middle.

- **The Romans** were the first to use round arches, so round arches are called Roman or Romanesque arches.

- **Roman arches** were built from blocks of stone called voussoirs. They were built up from each side on a semi-circular wooden frame (later removed). A central wedge or keystone is slotted in at the top to hold them together.

- **The posts** supporting arches are called piers. The top of each post is called a springer.

◀ The famous Arc de Triomphe in Paris was commissioned by Napoleon in 1806 in the style of the triumphal arches built in Ancient Rome to celebrate great victories.

- **Pointed arches** were first used in Arab mosques like the Dome of the Rock in the 7th century.

- **Pointed arches** were brought to Europe from the Middle East by Crusader knights in the 1100s and put in churches to become part of the gothic style.

- **Horseshoe arches** are used in islamic buildings all round the world.

- **The sides** of an ogee arch are S-shaped. Tudor arches are flattened ogees.

- **The world's biggest free-standing arch** is the Gateway to the West arch in St Louis, Missouri, USA. Completed in 1965, this arch is 192 m high and 192 m across.

Record breaking trains

- **The fastest steam train** ever was by Gresley-designed steam engine *Mallard* pulling seven coaches on 3 July 1938, (see steam locomotives). It travelled at 201 km/h.

- **The most powerful** steam loco was the US Virginian Railway's No.700. It pulled with a force of over 90,000 kg.

- **The heaviest trains** ever pulled by a single locomotive were 250-truck trains that ran on the Erie Railroad in the USA from 1914 to 1929. They weighed over 15,000 tonnes.

- **The longest train** was a 7.3 km 660-truck train that ran from Saldanha to Sishen in South Africa on 26 Aug 1989.

- **The longest passenger train** was a 1732 m 70-coach train from Ghent to Ostend in Belgium on 27 April 1991.

- **The fastest diesel train** was 248 km/h by a British Rail Intercity 125 between Darlington and York on 1 November 1987.

- **The fastest scheduled service** is the Hiroshima-Kokura

bullet train in Japan which covers 192 km in 44 minutes at an average 261.8 km/h.

- **The TGV** from Lille to Roissy in France covers 203 km in 48 mins at an average 254.3 km/h.

- **The fastest train speed ever** was 515.3 km/h by the TGV between Courtalain and Tours, France 18 May 1990.

- **The fastest speed on rail** was 9851 km/h by a rocket sled on White Sands Missile Range, New Mexico in Oct 1982.

▼ TGV Atlantiques often hit 300 km/h on the French part of the Eurostar run from Paris to London.

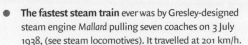

Supercars

▲ *The Porsche 911 is one of the classic supercars, first introduced in 1964, but still looking sleek many years later.*

- **The Mercedes Benz 300SL** of 1952 was one of the first supercars of the post-war years, famous for its stylish flip-up 'Gullwing' doors.

- **The Jaguar E-type** was the star car of the early 1960s with incredibly sleek lines and 250 km/h performance.

- **The Ford Mustang** was one of the first young and lively 'pony' cars, introduced in 1964.

- **The Aston Martin DB6** was the classic supercar of the late 1960s, driven by film spy James Bond.

- **The Porsche 911 turbo** was the fastest accelerating production car for almost 20 years after its launch in 1975, scorching from 0 to 100 km/h in 5.4 seconds.

- **The Lamborghini** Countach was the fastest supercar of the 1970s and 1980s, with a top speed of 295 km/h.

- **The McLaren F1** can accelerate from 0-160 km/h in less time than it takes to read this sentence.

- **The McLaren F1** can go from 0 to 160 km/h and back to 0 again in under 20 seconds.

- **A tuned version** of the Chevrolet Corvette, the Callaway SledgeHammer, can hit over 400 km/h.

> ★ **STAR FACT** ★
> The Ford GT-90 has a top speed of 378 km/h and zooms from 0-100 kmh in 3.2 seconds.

A sailor's life

- **Sailors** used to be called 'tars' after the tarpaulins used for making sails. Tarpaulin is canvas and tar.

- **A sailor's duties** included climbing masts, rigging sails, taking turns on watch and swabbing (cleaning) decks.

- **The eight-hour** watches were timed with an hour glass.

- **Storing food** on ships in the days before canning was a problem. Sailors survived on biscuits and dried meat.

- **Hard tack** was hard biscuits that kept for years – but often became infested with maggots. The maggots were picked out before the biscuit was eaten.

- **Every sailor** had a daily ration of water of just over a litre since all water had to be carried on board.

- **Sailors** often made clothes from spare materials such as sail canvas.

- **Sailors who offended** against discipline might be flogged with a 'cat-o'-nine-tails' – a whip with nine lengths of knotted cord.

- **Sailors slept** in any corner they could find, often next to the cannon or in the darkness below decks.

- **Sailors' lavatories** on old ships were simply holes overhanging the sea called 'jardines', from the French for garden.

▼ *The introduction of the hammock in the 18th century made sleeping much less uncomfortable for sailors.*

Theatres

▶ There were several Wooden O theatres like this in Elizabethan London in the late 16th century – including the famous Globe where Shakespeare first staged his plays.

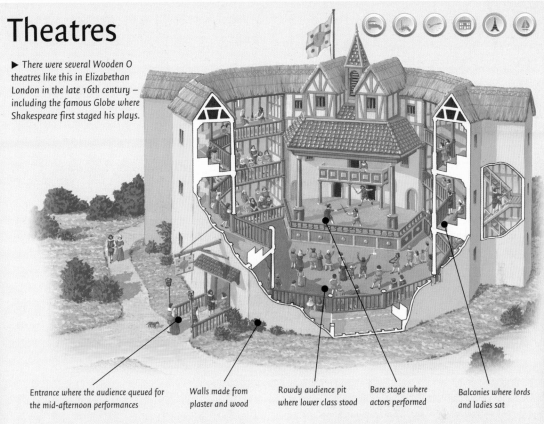

Entrance where the audience queued for the mid-afternoon performances

Walls made from plaster and wood

Rowdy audience pit where lower class stood

Bare stage where actors performed

Balconies where lords and ladies sat

- **In the days of Ancient Greece and Rome** thousands of people went to see dramas in huge, stone-built open-air theatres like sport arenas.

- **The Wooden Os** which appeared in England around 1570 were the first real theatres since Roman times. They were round wooden buildings with the stage and audience arena in the middle, open to the sky.

- **The 17th century** was the 'Golden Age' of drama in Spain, and people crammed into open courtyard theatres called corrales to see plays by great writers, such as Caldéron de la Barca and Lope de Vega.

- **In the 17th century** theatre moved indoors for the first time. Performances were by candlelight in large halls with rows of balconies round the edge.

- **In early theatres** the actors mostly performed on a bare stage. Towards the end of the 18th century, cutout boards with realistic scenes painted on them were slid in from the wings (the sides of the stage).

- **In the early 19th century** theatres grew much bigger to cater for the populations of the new industrial cities, often holding thousands. Huge stages were illuminated by 'limelight' – brightly burning pellets of calcium.

- **Most of the grand old theatres** we can visit today date from the mid 19th century.

- **The big theatres** of the early 19th century had huge backstage areas with lots of room for 'flying in' scenery, and also spring loaded trapdoors and other ingenious mechanisms for creating giant special effects, like exploding volcanoes and runaway trains.

- **Towards the end of the 19th century** dedicated amateurs, fed up with special effects, performed in smaller spaces, such as clubs, barns and private houses. These developed into intimate 'studio' theatres where actors could stage subtle, realistic plays.

- **Many modern theatres** are equipped with very bright, computer-controlled lighting, sound systems and motorized stage machinery.

Submarines

- **The first workable submarine** was a rowing boat covered with waterproofed skins, built by Dutch scientist Cornelius Van Drebbel in 1620.
- **In 1776** David Bushnell's one-man sub USS Turtle attacked British ships in America's War of Independence.
- **Petrol engines** and electric batteries were combined to make the first successful subs in the 1890s.
- **Powerful,** less fumy diesel engines took over from 1908.
- **In 1954** the US launched the *Nautilus*, the first nuclear power sub. Now all subs are nuclear-powered.
- **U-boats** were German subs that attack Allied convoys of ships in World War I and II.
- **In a modern sub** a strong hull of steel or titanium stops it from being crushed by the pressure of water.

> ★ STAR FACT ★
> The tower on top of a submarine is called the sail or conning tower.

▶ To gain weight for a dive, submarines fill their 'ballast' tanks with water. To surface, they empty the tanks.

- **Most subs** are designed for war and have missiles called torpedoes to fire at enemy ships.
- **Attack** subs have guided missiles for attacking ships. Ballistic subs have missiles with nuclear warheads for firing at targets on land. The Russian navy has subs that can strike targets 8000 km away.

Model T Ford

- **In 1905** most cars were 'coach-built' which meant they were individually built by hand. This made them the costly toys of the rich only.
- **The dream of Detroit farmboy** Henry Ford was to make 'a motor car for the great multitude – a car so low in price that no man making a good fortune will be unable to own one.'

◀ The tough, cheap and reliable Model T – the first mass-produced car – put America on the road for the first time and earned the affection of two generations of American families.

- **Ford's solution** was to make a car, which he called the Model T, by the same mass production techniques also used to make guns at the time.
- **Mass production** meant using huge teams of men, each adding a small part to the car as it moved along the production line.
- **Body-panels** for the Model T were stamped out by machines, not hammered by hand as with earlier cars.
- **In 1908** when Ford launched the Model T, fewer than 200,000 people in the USA owned cars.
- **In 1913** 250,000 people owned Model Ts alone.
- **By 1930** 15 million Model Ts had been sold.
- **One of the keys to the T** was standardizations. Ford said early Ts were available in 'any colour they like so long as it's black.' Later models came in other colours.
- **The T's fragile-looking chassis** earned it the nickname 'Tin Lizzie', but it was made of tough vanadium steel.

Bridges of wood and stone

- **The first bridges** were probably logs and vines slung across rivers to help people across.

- **The oldest known bridge** was an arch bridge built in Babylon about 2200 BC.

- **Clapper bridges** are ancient bridges in which large stone slabs rest on piers (supports) of stone.

- **There are clapper bridges** in both Devon in England and Fujian in China.

- **The first brick bridges** were built by the Romans – like the Alcántara bridge over the Tagus River in Spain which was built around AD 100.

- **Long bridges** could be made with a series of arches linked together. Each arch is called a span.

- **Roman arches** were semi-circular, so each span was short; Chinese arches were flatter so they could span greater distances.

- **The Anji bridge** at Zhao Xian in China was built in AD 610 and it is still in use today.

▲ The Ponte Vecchio in Florence, built in 1345, is one of the oldest flattened arch bridges in Europe.

- **Flattened arched bridges** were first built in Europe in the 14th century. Now they are the norm.

- **London Bridge** was dismantled and reconstructed stone by stone in Arizona as a tourist attraction in 1971.

Autogiros and microlights

- **In the 1400s** many European children played with flying toys kept aloft by whirling blades.

- **The autogiro** was invented by the Spanish inventor Juan de la Cierva in 1923.

- **An autogiro** is lifted, not by wings, but by turning rotor blades.

- **A helicopter uses** a powerful motor to turn the rotors; an autogiro's rotors are turned round by the pressure of air as the plane flies forward.

- **The autogiro** is pulled forward by propeller blades on the front like an ordinary small plane.

- **The autogiro** can fly at up to 225 km/h, but cannot hover like a helicopter.

- **In the USA and Australia** microlights are called ultralights. They are small, very light aircraft.

- **The first microlight** was a hang-glider with a chainsaw motor, built by American hang-glider pioneer Bill Bennett in 1973.

- **Some microlights** have flexible fabric wings like hang-gliders.

- **Some microlights** have fixed wings with control flaps to steer them in flight.

◄ For a while in the 1930s, many people believed autogiros would be the Model T Fords of the air – aircraft for everyone.

Helicopters

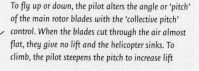

Without a tail rotor, the helicopter would spin round the opposite way to the main rotors. This is called torque reaction. The tail rotor also acts as a rudder to swing the tail left or right

To fly up or down, the pilot alters the angle or 'pitch' of the main rotor blades with the 'collective pitch' control. When the blades cut through the air almost flat, they give no lift and the helicopter sinks. To climb, the pilot steepens the pitch to increase lift

Tail rotor drive shaft

To fly forwards or back, or for a banked turn, the pilot tilts the whole rotor with the 'cyclic pitch' control

The angle of the blades is changed via rods linked to a sliding collar round the rotor shaft, called the swashplate

Rockets

▶ A helicopter's rotor blades are really long, thin wings. The engine whirls them round so that they cut through the air and provide lift just like conventional wings (see taking off). But they are also like huge propellers, hauling the helicopter up just as a propeller pulls a plane.

Engine

Stabilizers

- **Toy helicopters** have been around for centuries, and those made by air pioneer Sir George Cayley in the early 19th century are the most famous.

- **On 13 November 1907** a primitive helicopter with two sets of rotors lifted French mechanic Paul Cornu off the ground for 20 seconds.

- **The problem** with pioneer helicopters was control. The key was to vary the pitch of the rotor blades.

- **In 1937** German designer Heinrich Focke built an aircraft with two huge variable pitch rotors instead of wings and achieved a controlled hover. Months later, German Anton Flettner built the first true helicopter.

- **Focke and Flettner's** machines had two rotors turning in opposite directions to prevent torque reaction. In 1939, Russian born American Igor Sikorsky solved the problem by adding a tail rotor.

- **The Jesus nut** that holds the main rotor to the shaft got its name because pilots said, "Oh Jesus, if that nut comes off...".

- **The biggest helicopter** was the Russian Mil Mi-12 Homer of 1968 which could lift 40,204 kg up to 2255 m.

- **The fastest helicopter** is the Westland Lynx, which flew at 402 km/h on 6 August 1986.

- **The Boeing/Sikorsky RAH-66** Comanche unveiled in 1999 is the first helicopter using stealth technology (see warplanes). It is made of carbon-fibre and other composite materials, and the rotor hub is hidden.

▲ The Vietnam war saw the rise of heavily armed helicopter gunships designed to hit targets such as tanks.

! NEWS FLASH !
The Bell Quad Tiltrotor has wings like a plane for fast flying. The propellers on the end of each wing tilt up in 20 seconds for vertical lift off. It could evacuate 100 people from danger in minutes.

Dams

▲ The gates of the Thames Barrier in London are designed to shut in times of very high tides to stop seawater flooding the city.

- **The earliest known dam** is a 15 m high brick dam on the Nile River at Kosheish in Egypt, built around 2900 BC.
- **Two Ancient Roman** brick dams, at Proserpina and Cornalbo in Southwest Spain, are still in use today.
- **In China** a stone dam was built on the Gukow in 240 BC.
- **Masonry dams** today are usually built of concrete blocks as gravity dams, arch dams or buttress dams.

- **Gravity dams** are very thick dams relying entirely on a huge weight of concrete to hold the water. They are very strong, but costly to build.
- **Arch dams** are built in narrow canyons and curve upstream. Buttress dams are thin dams strengthened by supports called buttresses on the downstream side.
- **Embankment dams** or fill dams are simple dams built from piles of earth, stones, gravel or clay.
- **The Aswan dam** on the Nile in Egypt has created Lake Nasser – one of the world's biggest artificial lakes.
- **The world's highest dams** are fill dams in Tajikistan – the Rogun (335 m) and Nurek (300 m). The highest gravity dam is the 285 m Grand Dixence in Switzerland. The highest arch dam is the 272 m Inguri in Georgia.

> ★ STAR FACT ★
> The world's biggest dam is the 255 m high, 112 million cu metre Kambaratinsk Dam in Russia.

Warships

- **21st-century navies** have five main classes of surface warship in descending size order: aircraft carriers, landing craft, cruisers, destroyers and frigates.
- **The biggest** warships are 332.9 m-long US aircraft carriers Nimitz, Dwight D. Eisenhower, Carl Vinson, Abraham Lincoln, John C. Stennis, George Washington and Harry S. Truman.
- **In World War II** cruisers had big guns and often acted independently; destroyers protected the main fleet; and frigates protected slower ships against submarines.
- **The distinction between** classes is now blurred. Cruisers are rare, and many small warships carry helicopters or even VTOL planes (see warplanes).

▶ A destroyer armed with a rotating gun for fleet escort.

- **The Russian** Moskva class are a cross between cruisers and aircraft carriers with rear flight decks for helicopters.
- **The British** Invincible class are small aircraft carriers able to carry six Harrier jump jets and twelve helicopters.
- **Warships** have largely replaced guns with missiles.
- **Warships** have both short-range missiles to fire against missiles and long-range supersonic missiles to fire against ships up to 500 km away.
- **The US Ticonderoga** ships are small cruisers built in the 1970s. They are powered by gas-turbine engines and armed with Tomahawk nuclear or conventional missiles.
- **The nuclear-powered** Russian Kirov class begun in 1973 are among the few big cruisers, over 22,000 tonnes.

Steam locomotives

- **Steam locomotives** get their power by burning coal in a firebox. This heats up water in a boiler, making steam. The steam drives a piston to and fro and the piston turns the wheels via connecting rods and cranks.
- **It takes about three hours** for the crew to get up enough steam to get a locomotive moving.
- **Coal and water** are often stored in a wagon called a tender, towed behind the locomotive.
- **A tender** holds 10 tonnes coal and 30,000 litres water.
- **Loco classes** are described by their wheel layout.
- **A 4-6-2** has four small leading 'bogie' wheels, six big driving wheels and two small trailing wheels. The small bogie wheels carry much of the weight.
- **The greatest 19th-century** loco designer was James Nasmyth.
- **In the American Civil War** (1861-65) *The General* was recaptured by Confederates after a chase in another loco.
- **The Flying Scotsman** was a famous loco designed by Sir Nigel Gresley (1876-1941). It pulled trains non-stop 630 km from London to Edinburgh in under six hours.

▼ *An American locomotive of the 1890s.*

> ★ STAR FACT ★
> The first loco to hit 100 mph (160 km/h) was the City of Truro in 1895.

Dhows

- **Dhows** are wooden Arab boats that have been used in the Mediterranean and Indian Ocean for thousands of years.
- **Most dhows** are now made of teak (or Glass Reinforced Plastic). In the past, mango wood was common.
- **In the past** dhows were made, not by nailing planks of

▼ *Dhows like this are still built today in Lamu in Africa, much as they were 1000 or more years ago.*

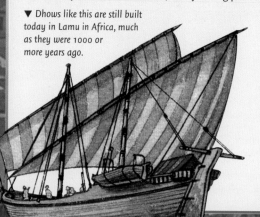

wood together, but by sewing them with coconut fibre.
- **Dhow builders** rarely work from plans. They judge entirely by eye and experience.
- **Dhows traditionally** had lateen sails – triangular sails in line with the boat. This allows them to sail almost into the wind.
- **Although many dhows** are now motorized, they usually have a tall mast for unloading.
- **There are several kinds** of dhow, including the shu'ai, the boum, the sambuq, the jelbut and the ghanjah.
- **The jelbut** is thought to get its name from the English 'jolly boat' – the little boats visiting British East Indiamen sent ashore. Jelbuts were often used for pearl fishing. Racing jelbuts have a tree-trunk-like bowsprit almost as long as the hull to carry extra sails.
- **Sambuqs and ghanjahs** are thought to get their square sterns from 17th-century Portuguese galleons.
- **Boums** can be up to 400 tonnes and 50 m long.

Towns and cities

▲ The city of Florence is one of the most beautiful in the world. Many buildings dating from the time when European towns began to flourish in the 15th century – especially in Italy.

- **The first cities** may date from the time when hunters and gatherers settled down to farm 10,000 years ago.
- **The city of Jericho** has been settled for over 10,000 years.
- **One of the oldest** known cities is Catal Hüyük in Anatolia in Turkey, dating from earlier than 6000 BC.
- **The first Chinese cities** developed around 1600 BC.
- **The cities of Ancient Greece** and Rome were often carefully laid out, with major public buildings. The first known town planner was the Ancient Greek Hippodamus, who planned the city of Miletus.
- **In the 1200s** Paris was by far the biggest city in Europe with a population of 150,000.
- **In the 1200s** 320,000 people lived in Hangzhou in China; Guangzhou (Canton) was home to 250,000.
- **In the 1400s** towns like Genoa, Bruges and Antwerp grew as trading centres. Medieval towns were rarely planned.
- **In the 1800s** huge industrial cities based on factories grew rapidly. Chicago's population jumped from 4000 in 1840 to 1 million in 1890.
- **The fastest growing** cities are places like Sao Paulo in Brazil where many poor people live in quickly erected shanty towns. The world's biggest city is Mexico City.

Luxury cars

- **The first Rolls-Royce** was made by Charles Rolls and Henry Royce. It was known as the 'best car in the world'.
- **The Rolls-Royce Silver Ghost** got its name for its ghost-like quietness and shiny aluminium body.
- **Today** each Rolls-Royce takes three months to build.
- **The winged girl** statuette on the bonnet of a Rolls-Royce is called 'Spirit of Ecstasy' and dates from 1911.
- **In the 1930s** Ettore Bugatti set out to build the best car ever with the Bugatti Royale. Only six were built, and they are now the world's most valuable cars.
- **The name Royale** comes from the King of Spain, Alfonso XIII, who was to buy the first model.
- **In 1925** drinksmaker André Dubonnet had a special version of the Hispano-Suiza H6B built with a body made entirely of tulipwood.
- **In the 1930s** American carmakers like Cord, Auburn and Packard made magnificent cars that Hollywood stars posed beside and Chicago gangsters drove.

- **Every 1934** Auburn speedster was sold with a plaque certifying it had been driven at over 100 mph (160 km/h) by racing driver Ab Jenkins.
- **The Mercedes in** Mercedes-Benz was the name of the daughter of Emil Jellinek, who sold the cars in the USA.

▶ Bentley is one of the great names in luxury cars. But founder Owen Bentley believed in racing as advertisement. The Bentley name gained lasting fame with success in the Le Mans 24-hour races of the 1920s. Seen here is a 1950s rally entry.

Towers

- **Romans, Byzantines** and medieval Europeans built towers in city walls and beside gates to give platforms for raining missiles on enemies.

- **Early churches** had square towers as landmarks to be seen from afar. From the 1100s, European cathedrals had towers called steeples, topped by a pointed spire.

- **Spires began** as pyramids on a tower, but got taller and were tapered to blend into the tower to make a steeple.

- **In the 17th and 18th centuries** church spires became simple and elegant, as in Park Street Church, Boston, USA.

- **The tallest unsupported tower** is Toronto's 553 m-high CN tower.

- **The tallest** tower supported by cables is the 629 m TV broadcast tower near Fargo and Blanchard in the USA.

- **The Tower of Babel** was a legendary tower built in ancient Babylon in the Near East. The Bible says God didn't want this high tower built, so he made the builders speak different languages to confuse them.

- **The Pharos** was a 135 m lighthouse built around 283 BC to guide ships into the harbour at Alexandria in Egypt.

- **The Tower of Winds,** or Horologium, was built in Athens around 100 BC to hold a sundial, weather vane and water clock.

- **Big Ben** is the bell in St Stephen's Tower in London's Houses of Parliament. The tower once had a cell where 'rioters' like suffragette Emmeline Pankhurst were held.

◀ *The Leaning Tower of Pisa in Italy is a 55 m high belltower or 'campanile'. Building began in 1173, and it started to lean as workers built the third storey. It is now 4.4 m out of true.*

The first houses

- **It was once thought** that all prehistoric humans lived in caves, but most caves were for religious rituals. The earliest houses were made of materials like wood, leaves, grass and mud – so traces have long since vanished.

- **Stone Age people** probably lived in round huts, with walls of wooden posts and thatches of reed.

- **In Britain** post holes and hearths have been found dating back 10,000 years in places like London's Hampstead Heath and Broom Hill in Hampshire.

- **Early mudbrick** houses dating from at least 9500 years ago are found in Anatolia in the Middle East.

- **Low walls** of big stones were the base for thatched roofs 6500 years ago at places like Carn Brea in Cornwall.

- **Two-storey houses** in Mohenjo Daro in Pakistan from 5000 years ago were built from sun-dried mud bricks and had courtyards, doors, windows and bathrooms.

- **Big Ancient Egyptian** houses had three main areas – a reception room for business, a hall in the centre for guests and private quarters at the back for family.

- **Tomb models** show what Egyptian homes were like.

- **Big Roman country houses** were called villas; a town house was called a domus.

- **Villas** had tiled roofs, verandahs, central heating, marbled floors, lavishly decorated walls and much more.

◀ *Some home-building styles have changed little in thousands of years. These houses are in French Polynesia.*

Record breaking cars

- **The first car speed record** was achieved by an electric Jentaud car in 1898 at Acheres near Paris. Driven by the Comte de Chasseloup-Laubat, the car hit 63.14 km/h. Camille Jenatzy vied with de Chasseloup-Laubat for the record, raising it to 105.85 km/h in his car *Jamais Contente* in 1899.

- **Daytona Beach** in Florida became a venue for speed trials in 1903. Alexander Winton reached 111 km/h in one of his Bullet cars.

- **The biggest engine** ever to be raced in a Grand Prix was the 19,891cc V4 of American Walter Christie, which he entered in the 1907 French Grand Prix. Later the Christie was the first front-wheel drive car to win a major race – a 400 km race on Daytona Beach.

- **The record** for the outer circuit at Brooklands in England was set in 1935 by John Cobb in a Napier-Railton at 1 min 0.41 sec (230.84 km/h) and never beaten.

- In **1911** the governing body for the land speed record said that cars had to make two runs in opposite directions over a 1 km course to get the record.

- In **1924** Sir Malcolm Campbell broke the Land Speed Record for the first of many times in a Sunbeam at 235.17 km/h. In 1925 he hit 150 mph (242 km/h) for the first time. But his most famous record-breaking runs were in the 1930s in his own *Bluebirds*.

- In **1947** John Cobb drove with tremendous skill to reach 634.27 km/h in his Railton-Mobil. This stood as the record for 17 years.

- In **1964** the rules were changed to allow jet and rocket-propelled cars to challenge for the Land Speed Record. The next year Craig Breedlove drove his three-wheeler jet *Spirit of America* to over 500 mph (846.78 km/h).

- In **1970** Gary Gabelich set the record over 1000 km/h with his rocket-powered *Blue Flame*. This record wasn't beaten until Richard Noble roared to 1019.37 km/h in his Rolls-Royce jet-powered *Thrust 2* in 1983.

▶ Donald Campbell took on the record-breaking mantle of his father –and the Bluebird name for his car. On 17 July 1964, Campbell's Bluebird hit a world record 690.909 km/h on the salt flats at Lake Eyre in South Australia. At one moment he hit over 716 km/h – faster than any wheel-driven car has ever been.

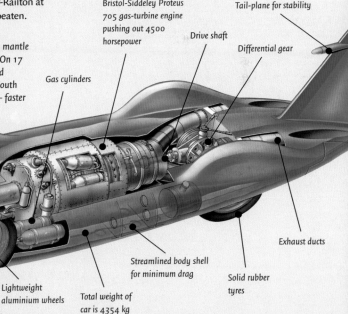

Bristol-Siddeley Proteus 705 gas-turbine engine pushing out 4500 horsepower

Tail-plane for stability

Drive shaft

Differential gear

Gas cylinders

Air intake

Tiny windscreen providing driver's only view

Driver's cockpit

Lightweight aluminium wheels

Total weight of car is 4354 kg

Streamlined body shell for minimum drag

Solid rubber tyres

Exhaust ducts

Ocean liners

▲ *One of the great transatlantic liners of the 1930s, the 'Queen Mary' (sister-ship of the 'Queen Elizabeth') is now a hotel at Long Beach California.*

- **The great age** of ocean liners lasted from the early 1900s to the 1950s.
- **Ocean liners** were huge boats, often with luxurious cabins, bars, games rooms and swimming pools.
- **The main route** was across the Atlantic. From 1833 liners competed for the Blue Riband title for fastest crossing.
- **Great Blue Riband** contenders included Brunel's Great Western in the 1830s, the Mauretania which held it from 1907 to 1929, and the French Normandie of the 1930s.
- **The last** ocean liner to hold the Blue Riband was the United States in the 1960s.
- **The famous Cunard line** was set up by Nova Scotia Quaker Samuel Cunard with George Burns and David MacIver in 1839.
- **The *Titanic*** was the largest ship ever built at 46,329 tonnes when launched in 1912 – but it sank on its maiden (first) voyage.
- **The sinking** of the liner Lusitania by a German submarine on 7 May 1915 with the loss of 1198 lives spurred the US to join the war against Germany.
- **The *Queen Elizabeth*** launched in 1938 was the largest passenger ship ever built – 314 m long and 83,673 tonnes. It burned and sank during refitting in Hong Kong in 1972.
- **Future liners** may be based on FastShip technology, with a very broad flat hull for high-speed stability.

The Tower of London

- **The Tower of London** is the oldest stone castle in London, started by William the Conqueror after his conquest of England in 1066. The Crown Jewels are kept here.
- **The oldest part of the tower** is the great square keep called the White Tower which dates from 1078.
- **The Tower** later gained two surrounding 'curtain' walls, like other castles.
- **The inner curtain** wall has 13 towers, including the Bloody Tower, Beauchamp Tower and Wakefield Tower.
- **Traitors' Gate** is an arch beside the River Thames. It gets its name from the time when high-ranking traitors were ferried here by boat to

▶ *The Tower of London is the most famous medieval castle in the UK.*

be imprisoned in the Tower. They entered this way.
- **Many people** have been imprisoned here like Princess (later Queen) Elizabeth and her mother Anne Boleyn (though not at the same time) in the 1500s.
- **Little Ease** is a dark 3.3 square metre cell where prisoners could neither stand up nor lie down.
- **Many prisoners were** beheaded, including Sir Thomas More and Sir Walter Raleigh.
- **In 1483** Edward V and his young brother were thought to have been murdered here. Bones which could have been theirs were later found under stairs.
- **Yeoman Warders** are the Tower's special guards. They are nicknamed beefeaters. The name may have come from a fondness for roast beef or the French word *buffetier*.

Greek and Roman building

▲ ▶ *The most famous Greek temple is the Parthenon in Athens, built c.450 BC.*

- **Ancient Greek and Roman** architecture are together known as Classical architecture.
- **The key features** of Classical buildings are solid, elegantly plain geometric shapes including pillars, arches and friezes.

- **The main Greek** building was the temple with its triangular roof of pale stone on rows of tall columns.
- **Greek temples** were designed in mathematical ratios.
- **Roman architect** Vitruvius described three orders (styles) of columns: Doric, Ionic and Corinthian.
- **Each order** has its own character: Doric serious and strong, Ionic graceful and Corinthian rich and festive.
- **The Parthenon** is a Doric temple built by architects Ictinus and Callicrates guided by the sculptor Phidias.
- **Roman buildings** used many arches and vaults (ceilings made from arches joined together).

- **The ruined Baths of Caracalla** in Rome (AD 217) has huge and graceful vaults.
- **Classical** architecture has inspired many imitations over the centuries, including the Palladian style of the 1600s.

Peoples' cars

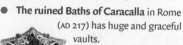

- **The first car** for ordinary people was Ford's Model T. Ford built their ten millionth car in 1924 and their 50 millionth in 1959.
- **The USA** began making more than one million cars a year in 1916, of which over a third were Model Ts. No other country made a million cars a year until the UK in 1954.
- **Ford US** introduced weekly payment plans for new cars in 1923. The Nazis later borrowed the idea for the VW Beetle.
- **The Model A Ford** sold one million within 14 months of its launch in December 1927. The Ford Escort of 1980 sold a million in just 11 months.
- **The French Citroën 2CV** was designed to carry 'a farmer in a top hat across a ploughed field without breaking the eggs on the seat beside him'.
- **The VW Beetle** was the brain child of the Nazi dictator Adolf Hitler who wanted a cheap car for all Germans. It was created in 1938 by Ferdinand Porsche.
- **The war interrupted** VW Beetle production before it

had barely begun, but it was resumed after the war.
- **The ten millionth** VW Beetle was built in 1965. Over 22 million have now been sold.
- **The Soviet built Lada,** based on a design by Fiat, was one of the cheapest cars ever built.
- **The first British car** to sell a million was the Morris Minor, between 1949 and 1962.

▼ *The 1959 Mini, designed by Alec Issigonis set a trend in small car design, with the engine mounted across the car driving the front wheels.*

Bridges

▲ London's Tower Bridge was opened in 1894. It has a strong steel frame clothed in stone to support the two opening halves.

- **Rope suspension** bridges have been used for thousands of years. One of the first to use iron chains was the Lan Jin Bridge at Yunnan in China, built AD 65.

- **The first** all-iron bridge was at Coalbrookdale, England. It was designed by Thomas Pritchard and built in 1779 by Abraham Darby.

- **In the early 1800s** Thomas Telford began building superb iron bridges such as Craigellachie over the Spey in Scotland (1814). He built Europe's first iron chain suspension bridge over the Menai Straits in Wales in 1826.

- **Stephenson's** Britannia railway bridge of 1850, also over the Menai Straits, was the first hollow box girder bridge.

▶ Most bridges are now built of concrete and steel. Shown here are some of the main kinds. The longest are normally suspension bridges, usually carrying roads, but Hong Kong's 1377 m-long Tsing Ma (1998) takes both road and rail.

★ STAR FACT ★
The Akashi-Kaikyo Bridge (1998), Japan, is the world's longest suspension bridge with a main span of 1991 m and two side spans of 960 m.

- **John Roebling's** Cincinnati suspension bridge was the world's longest bridge when built in 1866 at 322 m. Like all suspension bridges today, it was held up by iron wires, not chains. It was the prototype for his Brooklyn Bridge.

- **The Forth Railway Bridge** in Scotland was the world's first big cantilevered bridge. At 520 m it was also the world's longest bridge when it was built in 1890.

- **In 1940** the Tacoma suspension bridge in Washington USA, was blown down by a moderate wind just months after its completion. The disaster forced engineers to make suspension bridges aerodynamic.

- **Aerodynamic design** played a major part in the design of Turkey's Bosphorus Bridge (1973) and England's Humber Bridge (1983), for a while the longest bridge at 1410 m.

- **In the 1970s** Japanese engineers began to build a bridge that by 2000 gave Japan nine of the world's 20 longest bridges.

In cable-stayed bridges, the bridge hangs directly from steel cables

In suspension bridges the bridge hangs on steel wires on a cable suspended between tall towers. They are light so can be very long

In cantilevered bridges, each half of the bridge is balanced on a support

Arch bridges are one of the oldest kinds and make very strong bridges

Bascule or lifting bridges like London's Tower Bridge swing up in the middle to allow tall ships through

Steel or concrete beam bridges are carried on piers. The beam may be a hollow steel girder through which cars and trains can run

The Statue of Liberty

- **New York's Statue of Liberty** stands on Liberty island off the tip of Manhattan.

- **The statue** was dedicated on 28 Oct 1886 by President Cleveland.

- **It was paid** for by the French people to celebrate their friendship with the USA.

- **Sculptor** Frédéric-Auguste Bartholdi began work on the statue in Paris in 1875.

◀ New York's famous Statue of Liberty, before it was restored in 1986 and the flame covered in gold leaf.

- **It was built** from 452 copper sheets hammered into shape by hand and mounted on four huge steel supports designed by Eiffel and Viollet-le-Duc.

- **The 225-tonne statue** was shipped to New York in 1885.

- **A pedestal** designed by Richard Hunt and paid for by 121,000 Americans brought it to a total height of 93 m.

- **The statue's** full name is *Liberty Enlightening the World*. The seven spikes in the crown stand for liberty's light shining on the world's seven seas and continents. The tablet in her left arm is America's Declaration of Independence.

- **Emma Lazarus's sonnet** *The New Colossus* on the pedestal ends: "Give me your tired poor, your huddled masses of your teeming shore. Send these, the homeless, tempest-tossed to me. I lift my lamp beside the golden door!"

> ★ STAR FACT ★
> The Statue of Liberty's crown houses an observation deck for up to 20 people.

Buses and coaches

- **Horse-drawn stage coaches** were the first regular public coach services between two or more points or 'stages'. They were first used in London in the 1630s.

- **Stage coaches** reached their heyday in the early 1800s when new tarred roads made travel faster. Coaches went from London to Edinburgh in 40 hours.

- **Bus is short** for 'omnibus' which in Latin means 'for all'. The word first came into use in Paris in the 1820s for big coaches carrying lots of people on local journeys.

- **In 1830** Goldsworthy Gurney put a steam engine in a coach to make the first powered bus. It ran four times a day between Cheltenham and Gloucester in England.

- **In the 1850s** British government laws restricted steam road vehicles, so big new cities developed horse buses.

- **In 1895** a petrol-engined bus was built in Germany.

- **In 1904** the London General Omnibus Co. ran the first petrol-engined bus services. They were double-decked.

- **1905:** the first motor buses ran on New York's 5th Avenue.

▲ Like most early buses, this one from the early 1920s was built by adding a coach body to a lorry base.

- **1928:** the first transcontinental bus service crossed the USA.

- **From the 1950s** articulated buses were used in European cities. A trailer joined to the bus carries extra passengers.

St Basil's cathedral

- **The cathedral of** St Basil the Blessed in Moscow's Red Square was built from 1554 to 1560.

- **St Basil's** is made up of ten tower churches, the biggest of which is 46 m tall.

- **It began with** eight little wooden churches – each built between 1552 and 1554 after a major Russian victory against the Tartars of Kazan in central Asia.

- **After the final victory**, Ivan the Terrible ordered stone churches to be built in place of the wooden ones.

- **Legend says** each of the onion-shaped domes represents the turban of a defeated Tartar lord.

▲ With its ten famous colourful towers, St Basil's in Moscow one of the most beautiful Christian cathedrals in the world.

- **St Basil's** was designed by two Russians, Posnik and Barma, who may have been one person.

- **Legend says** the Italian builder was blinded afterwards so he could build nothing like it again.

- **Originally** it was known as the Cathedral of the Intercession, but in 1588 a tenth church was added in honour of St Basil and it was known afterwards as St Basil's.

- **St Basil** was the jester (comedian) to a Moscow lord of the time.

- **In 1955**, restorers found the secret of the cathedral's construction embedded in the brickwork – wooden models used as silhouettes to guide the builders.

Hydrofoils

- **Hydrofoils** are boats with hulls that lift up above the water when travelling at high speeds.

- **The hydrofoils** are wings attached to the hull by struts that move underwater like aeroplane wings and lift the boat up.

- **Because only the foils** dip in the water, hydrofoils avoid water resistance, so can travel faster with less power.

- **Surface-piercing hydrofoils** are used in calm inland waters and skim across the surface.

▼ By lifting themselves out of the water and almost flying across the surface, hydrofoils achieve very high speeds.

> ★ STAR FACT ★
> The biggest hydrofoil, built in Seattle, is the 64 m long, 92 km/h *Plainview* navy transport.

- **Full-submerged hydrofoils** dip deep into the water for stability in seagoing boats.

- **The foils** are usually in two sets, bow and stern.

- **The bow and stern foils** are in one of three arrangements. 'Canard' means the stern foil is bigger. 'Airplane' means the bow foil is bigger. 'Tandem' means they are both the same size.

- **The first successful hydrofoil** was built by Italian Enrico Forlanini in 1906.

- **In 1918** Alexander Graham Bell, inventor of the telephone, built a hydrofoil that set a world water speed record at 61.6 knots (114 km/h). The record was not beaten until the American Fresh 1, another hydrofoil, set a new record of 84 knots (155 km/h) in 1963.

Balloons

- **Balloons** are bags filled with a light gas or hot air – both so light that the balloon floats in the air.
- **Balloons** designed to carry people into the air are of two types: hot-air balloons and gas balloons filled with hydrogen or helium.
- **Hot-air balloons** have a burner that continually fills the balloon with warm air to keep it afloat.
- **To carry two people** a hot-air balloon must have a bag of about 1700 cubic metres in volume.
- **Balloons** are normally launched at dusk or dawn when the air is quite calm.
- **As the air in the bag cools**, the balloon gradually sinks. To maintain height, the balloonist lights the burner to add warm air again.
- **To descend quickly** the balloonist pulls a cord to let air out through a vent in the top of the bag.
- **The first flight** in a hot air balloon was made in Paris on 15 October 1783 by French scientist Jean de Rozier in a

▶ Hot air ballooning has become a popular sport since Ed Yost, Tracy Barnes and other Americans began to make the bags from polyester in the 1960s.

balloon made by the Montgolfier brothers.

- **The first hydrogen gas balloon flight** was made in Paris on 1 December 1783.
- **On 20 March 1999** Swiss Bertran Piccard and British Brian Jones made the first round-the-world hot air balloon flight.

Record breaking flights

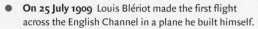

- **On 25 July 1909** Louis Blériot made the first flight across the English Channel in a plane he built himself.
- **In May 1919** Capt A.C. Read and his crew made the first flight across the Atlantic in a Curtiss flying boat.
- **On 14-15 June 1919** John Alcock and Arthur Brown made the first non-stop flight across the Atlantic in an open cockpit Vickers Vimy biplane.

◀ Blériot being greeted near Dover after completing his flight across the English channel.

> ★ STAR FACT ★
> In December 1986, *Voyager*, piloted by Rutan and Yeager, flew non-stop round the world in 9 days.

- **In November 1921** brothers Keith and Ross Smith made the first flight from England to Australia.
- **On 4 May 1924** Frenchman Étienne Oehmichen flew his helicopter in a 1 km circle.
- **In 1927** Frenchman Louis Breguet made the first flight across the South Atlantic.
- **On 21 May 1927** American Charles Lindbergh made the first solo flight across the Atlantic in the *Spirit of St Louis*.
- **In July 1933** Wiley Post made the first solo round-the-world flight.
- **The story of Post's epic** flight was told in the book *Round the World in Eight Days*.

St Paul's cathedral

- **The current St Paul's** cathedral in London is the fifth church on the site.

- **On the same site** in Roman times, there was a temple dedicated to Diana.

- **The first St Paul's** was built of wood in AD 604 by St Ethelbert, King of Kent.

- **The Norman cathedral** was started around 1090 by Maurice, chaplain to William the Conqueror.

- **The Norman cathedral** called 'Old St Paul's' had the highest spire ever built, but it was struck down by lightning in 1561.

- **The first public lottery** was held in Old St Paul's in 1569 to raise money for repairs. The churchyard was famous for its booksellers, like Wynkyn de Worde in the 1400s.

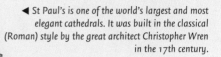

◄ St Paul's is one of the world's largest and most elegant cathedrals. It was built in the classical (Roman) style by the great architect Christopher Wren in the 17th century.

- **Old St Paul's** burned to the ground in the Great Fire of London in 1666.

- **The new St Paul's** was designed by Sir Christopher Wren, who designed many other London buildings. Wren thought the 111 m-high dome he wanted to be seen from the outside was too lofty for the inside. So inside the outer dome, he built another 20 m lower. Work began in 1675 and was completed in 1711.

- **If you whisper** inside the dome's famous 'whispering gallery' you can be heard on the far side 35 m away.

- **Among the famous tombs** in the crypt of St Paul's are those of Admiral Nelson and the Duke of Wellington.

Boat building

◄ Building boats in wood is a tremendously skilled craft that dates back many thousands of years.

- **For much of history** ships were built and designed by shipwrights.

- **Shipwrights** worked from experience and rarely drew plans. But in the 17th and 18th centuries, they often made models.

- **Nowadays** ships are designed by 'naval architects' and built by shipbuilders.

> ★ **STAR FACT** ★
> A futtock is one of the big bent timber ribs of a boat near the stern.

- **Wooden ships** were put together on a building berth. Timbers and planks were cut and shaped around, then fitted together on the berth to form the ship's hull.

- **First the long spine** or keel of the boat was laid down. Thick wooden ribs were added to make a strong frame.

- **In the Middle Ages** in the Mediterranean, wooden ships were carvel-built. This means the planks were fitted together edge to edge onto the ribs.

- **In the Middle Ages** in northern Europe, wooden ships were clinker-built. This means the planks overlapped, as in Viking ships.

- **Ships** are launched down a slope called a slipway.

- **After launching** a ship has just the bare bones of a hull and main structures. It is finished in a fitting-out basin.

Hovercraft

- **A hovercraft** or air cushion vehicle floats on a layer of compressed air just above the ground. It is also called a ground-effect machine. The air means there is very little friction between the craft and the ground.

- **A hovercraft** has one or more big fans that suck air into the craft, then blow it down underneath. The air is trapped underneath by a flexible rubber skirt.

- **The idea began with** Sir John Thornycroft in the 1870s. He thought drag on a ship's hull could be reduced if an indent in the hull allowed it to ride on a cushion of air. But for decades no-one could work out how to contain the air.

- **In the 1950s** Christopher Cockerell cracked the problem by pumping air down around the edge of a curtain-like skirt. The air itself then sealed the cushion of air inside the curtain.

- **In 1959** the world's first practical hovercraft, the SRN1 was built, using Cockerell's system. It crossed the English Channel on the 50th anniversary of Blériot's first flight across the channel.

- **In the late 1960s** the US Army and navy began using hovercraft in the Vietnam war for patrol and rescue missions because of their ability to go over land, water and swampy ground equally easily. The Russian and US armies are still the biggest users of hovercraft.

- **In 1968** big hovercraft able to carry scores of cars and lorries were introduced as ferries across the English Channel, but elsewhere they have not lived up to expectations. The biggest cross-Channel hovercraft was the 56 m-long SRN4 MkIII which carried 418 passengers and 60 cars at speeds over 120 km/h.

- **In the late 1950s** French engineer Jean Bertin developed a train called a tracked air cushion vehicle or TACV. This is basically a hovercraft on rails. Trains like this could swish between cities almost silently at speeds of 500 km/h.

- **On 25 January 1980** a 100-tonne US Navy hovercraft, the SES 100-B, reached a record speed of 170 km/h – faster than any warship has ever travelled.

> ! NEWS FLASH !
> Hospitals can use special hoverbeds to support badly burned patients on air.

▼ *Hovercraft vary in speed, size and power, but they are used essentially for one of two purposes – as ferries across short stretches of water, like this one, or by the army and navy. In smaller hovercraft, the fan that forces the air into the cushion is often the same one that drives the craft forward. In bigger ones like this, there are separate driving propellers mounted on the back, working in much the same way as aircraft propellers to drive the craft along.*

Rubberized bag skirt, holding the air cushion in

Flight deck

Powerful gas turbine for the lifting fan

Passenger compartment in which people travel as they would on an aeroplane. There is no deck as on a conventional boat

Double propellers for driving the hovercraft forwards or backwards at speeds of up to 120 km/h

Rudders to steer the craft. These become more effective the faster the hovercraft is travelling

Chinese building

- **China** developed its own distinctive style of building over 3000 years ago.
- **Traditionally, large Chinese buildings** were made of wood on a stone base.
- **A distinctive feature** is a large tiled overhanging roof, ending in a graceful upturn. The tiles were glazed blue, green or yellow.
- **The roof** is supported not by the walls but by wooden columns, often carved and painted red and gold.
- **Walls were thin** and simply gave privacy and warmth.
- **Chinese temples** were large wooden halls with elaborate roof beams in the ceiling.
- **Pagodas** are tall tapering towers often linked to Buddhist temples. They have from 3 to 15 storeys.

> ★ STAR FACT ★
> Chinese pagodas have eight sides and an uneven number of storeys.

▲ The Forbidden City in Beijing dates mostly from the Ming era from 1368-1644. Only the emperor's household could enter it.

- **In China, pagodas** were believed to bring happiness to the surrounding community. They were made of wood, bricks, tiles or even porcelain and decorated with ivory.
- **Pagodas**, originally from India, developed from Buddhist burial mounds called stupas.

Canoes

- **The first canoes** were scooped out logs.
- **A skin canoe** was made by stretching animal skins over a bent wood frame.
- **A skin canoe** dating from around 4500 BC was found on the Baltic island of Fünen.

◀ ▼ The materials may be different, but today's bright fibreglass canoes are based on the same principles as the ancient bark canoes of native Americans.

- **Some skin canoes** are round like the paracil and the Welsh coracle.
- **Some skin canoes** are long and thin like the Irish curach and the Inuit kayak.
- **Kayaks** have a watertight cover made from sealskin to keep out water in rough conditions.
- **The ancient quffa** of Iraq is a large canoe made of basketwork sealed with tar and dates back to 4000 BC.
- **Native Americans** made canoes from bark. The Algonquins used paper birch, the Iroquois elm.
- **Bark canoes** were the basis for today's sport canoes of fibreglass, plastic and aluminium.
- **Unlike ordinary boats,** canoes are often so light that they can easily be carried overland to avoid waterfalls or to move from one river to another.

Electric trains

- **The first practical** electric trains date from 1879, but they only became widespread in the 1920s.

- **Electric locos** pick up electric current either from a third 'live' rail or from overhead cables.

- **To pick up** power from overhead cables, locos need a spring-loaded frame or pantograph to conduct electricity to the transformer.

- **Electric trains** are clean and powerful, and can also travel faster than other trains.

- **Older systems** mostly used Direct Current (DC) motors, operating at 1500–3000 volts for overhead cables and 700 volts for live rails.

- **High-speed trains** like France's TGV and Japan's Shinkansen use 'three-phase' Alternating Current (AC) motors operating at 25,000 volts.

◀ *Japan's Shinkansen 'bullet train' was the first of the modern high speed electric trains, regularly operating at speeds of over 400 km/h.*

- **The Paris-London Eurostar** works on 25,000 volt AC overhead cables in France, and 750 volt live rails after it comes out of the Channel Tunnel in England.

- **Magnetic levitation** or maglev trains do not have wheels but glide along supported by electromagnets.

- **In electrodynamic maglevs**, the train rides on repulsing magnets. In electromagnetic maglevs, they hang from attracting magnets.

- **Maglevs** are used now only for short, low-speed trains, but they may one day be the fastest of all. High-speed maglev developments now use 'superconducting' electromagnets which are costly to make. But a new idea is to use long strings of ordinary permanent magnets.

Stations

- **London Bridge** station is the oldest big city terminal, first built from wood in 1836, then of brick in the 1840s.

- **In the 19th century** railway companies competed to make the grandest, most palatial railway stations.

- **The Gare d'Orsay** in Paris was an incredibly luxurious station built in 1900 in what is called the *Beaux Arts* (beautiful arts) style. It is now a museum and gallery.

- **When first built** in 1890, Sirkeci in Istanbul – terminal of the Orient Express – glittered like an oriental palace.

- **Bombay's Victoria** – now Chhatrapati Sivaji – was built in 1888 over a shrine to Mumba Devi, named after the patron goddess of original inhabitants of Bombay.

- **Grand Central Station** in New York cost a staggering 43 million dollars to build in 1914.

- **Liverpool Street Station** in London was built in 1874 on the site of the 13th century Bedlam hospital for lunatics.

- **London's St Pancras** is a stunning Gothic building designed by George Gilbert Scott. It was built 1863-72.

- **Chicago's** North Western is a monument to the Jazz Age in the city, dating from 1911.

- **In April 1917** Lenin returned to Russia and announced the start of the Russian revolution at St Petersburg's famous Finland Railway station.

▼ *The great hall at Grand Central Station in New York is one of the most spectacular railway halls in the world.*

Submersibles

- **Submersibles** are small underwater craft. Some are designed for very deep descents for ocean research. Others are designed for exploring wrecks.

- **One early submersible** was a strong metal ball or bathysphere, lowered by cables from a ship.

- **The bathysphere** was built by Americans William Beebe and Otis Barton who went down 900 m in it off Bermuda on 11 June 1931. The possibility of the cable snapping meant the bathysphere was very dangerous.

- **The bathyscaphe** was a diving craft that could be controlled underwater, unlike the bathysphere. Its strong steel hull meant it could descend 4000 m or more.

- **The first bathyscaphe**, the FNRS 2, was developed by Swiss scientist August Piccard between 1946 and 1948. An improved version, the FNRS 3, descended 4000 m off Senegal on 15 February 1954. The FNRS 3 was further improved to make the record-breaking *Trieste*.

- **In the 1960s** the Woods Hole Oceanographic Institute in the USA began to develop a smaller, more manoeuvrable submersible, called *Alvin*. *Alvin* is one of the most famous of all submersibles, making thousands of dives to reveal a huge amount about the ocean depths.

- **ROVs** or Remote Operated Vehicles are small robot submersibles. ROVs are controlled from a ship with video cameras and computer virtual reality systems. ROVs can stay down for days while experts are called in to view results. Using the ROV Argo-Jason, Robert Ballard found the wreck of the liner *Titanic* in 1985.

- ***Deep Flight*** is a revolutionary submersible with wings that can fly underwater like an aeroplane, turning, diving, banking and rolling.

- **A new breed** of small submersibles, like the *Sea Star* and *Deep Rover*, cost about the same as a big car and are designed for sports as well as research.

▶ This is one of the first of the huge range of submersibles that began to appear in the 1960s and 70s. They are now much smaller, neater and more manoeuvrable, but still work in much the same way.

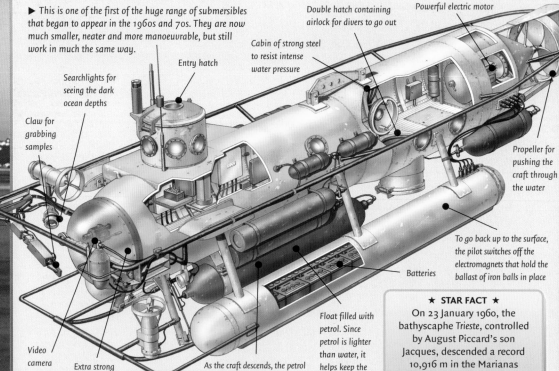

Double hatch containing airlock for divers to go out

Powerful electric motor

Cabin of strong steel to resist intense water pressure

Entry hatch

Searchlights for seeing the dark ocean depths

Claw for grabbing samples

Propeller for pushing the craft through the water

To go back up to the surface, the pilot switches off the electromagnets that hold the ballast of iron balls in place

Batteries

Video camera

Extra strong perspex dome

As the craft descends, the petrol is compressed and gives less buoyancy, speeding the descent

Float filled with petrol. Since petrol is lighter than water, it helps keep the craft afloat

★ STAR FACT ★
On 23 January 1960, the bathyscaphe *Trieste*, controlled by August Piccard's son Jacques, descended a record 10,916 m in the Marianas Trench in the Pacific.

Airports

- **The world's first airport** was built at Croydon near London in 1928. Many early airports, like Berlin's, were social centres attracting thousands of visitors.

- **Before airports,** flying boats would land on water. So airports like New York's La Guardia were set close to water to take flying boats.

- **Over 50 airports** around the world now handle over 10 million passengers a year. 25 of these are in the USA.

- **Six airports** handle over 30 million passengers, including Chicago's O'Hare and Hong Kong's Chep Lap Kok.

- **The world's largest** airport is King Abdul Aziz in Saudi Arabia. It covers 22,464 hectares. The USA's biggest is Dallas. Europe's biggest is Paris's Charles de Gaulle.

- **Hong Kong's** Chep Lap Kok airport, opened in 1998, is one of the world's most modern.

- **Kansai** airport in Japan is built entirely on an artificial island in Osaka Bay so that it can operate 24-hours a day, without disturbing people with noise.

▲ In the 1970s, Boeing 747 jumbo jets needed 4 km runways to take-off, but better performance means they now need less distance.

- **In early airports** terminals for each flight were set in a line as at Kansas and Munich. But as flights increased, this layout meant passengers had a long way to walk.

- **Terminals in the 1970s** were set in extending piers like Amsterdam's Schiphol, or satellites like Los Angeles.

- **New airport terminals** like London's Stansted are set apart and linked by electric cars called 'people-movers'.

Trams and cable cars

- **Trams** are buses that run on rails laid through city streets. They are called streetcars in the USA.

- **Early trams** in the 1830s were pulled by horses. By the 1870s, horse-drawn trams were used in many cities.

- **In 1834** Thomas Davenport, a blacksmith from Vermont, USA built a battery-powered electric tram.

- **In 1860** an American called George Train set up battery-powered electric tram systems in London.

- **In 1873** Andrew Hallidie introduced cable cars in San Francisco. The cars were hauled by a cable running in a slot in the street. A powerhouse pulled the cable at around 14 km/h. Similar systems were built in many cities in the 1880s but were soon replaced by electric trams.

- **In 1888** Frank Sprague demonstrated a tram run from electric overhead cables in Richmond in the USA.

- **In most US trams,** electric current was picked up via a long pole with a small wheel called a shoe that slid along the cable. The pick-up was called a trolley.

Many European trams, however, picked up current via a collapsible frame called a pantograph.

- **In the early 1900s,** electric tram systems were set up in most world cities.

  - **In the 1930s** most cities, except in eastern Europe and Russia, replaced trams with buses.

  - **In the 1990s** some cities, like Manchester in England, built new tramways, because they are fume-free.

◄ The original Hallidie cable car system dating from 1873 still runs in San Francisco.

The Wright brothers

- **The Wright brothers,** Orville and Wilbur, built the world's first successful plane, the *Flyer.*

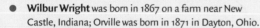

◄ One of the five who witnessed the flight took this picture. But apart from a report in 'Popular Science' the Wrights' success was little known about for five years.

- **On 17 December 1903** the Wright brothers made the first powered, long and controlled airplane flight at Kitty Hawk, USA.

- **Wilbur Wright** was born in 1867 on a farm near New Castle, Indiana; Orville was born in 1871 in Dayton, Ohio.

- **The Wright brothers** began as bicycle makers but became keen on flying after hearing about the death of pioneer glider Otto Lilienthal in 1896.

- **From 1899 to 1903** they worked at Kitty Hawk methodically improving their design and flying skill.

- **Many early planes** took off but lacked control. The key to the Wrights' success was stopping the plane rolling, using wires to 'warp' (twist) the wings to lift one side or the other.

- **The *Flyer*'s** wing warp meant it could not only fly level but make balanced, banked turns (like a bicycle cornering).

- **For the first flight** Orville was at the controls.

- **The historic first flight** lasted 12 seconds, in which the *Flyer* travelled 37 m and landed safely.

- **On 5 October 1905** the Wrights flew 38.9 km in 38 mins.

Bicycles

▲ Bicycles are the cheapest, most reliable form of transport ever, and in the 1920s many tradesmen adapted them for use.

- **The first bicycle** was the 'draisienne' of 1818 of Baron de Drais. The rider scooted his feet on the ground to move.

- **In 1839** Scots blacksmith Kirkpatrick Macmillan invented the first bicycle with pedals and brakes.

- **On Macmillan's 'velocipede'** pedals were linked by rods to cranks on the back wheel. These turned the wheel slowly.

- **In 1861** French father and son Pierre and Ernest Michaux stuck the pedals directly on the front wheel to make the first successful bicycle, nicknamed 'boneshaker'.

- **In 1870** James Starley improved the boneshaker with the Ordinary. A huge front wheel gave high speed with little pedalling.

- **In 1874** H. J. Lawson made the first chain-driven bicycle. This was called a 'safety bicycle' because it was safer than the tall Ordinary.

- **In 1885** Starley's nephew John made the Rover Safety bicycle. Air-filled tyres were added in 1890, and the modern bicycle was born.

- **By 1895** four million Americans were riding bicycles.

- **Today** 50 million people in the USA cycle regularly.

- **More people** in China cycle today than the rest of the world put together.

Great voyages

▶ In 1580, Sir Francis Drake became the first Englishman to sail round the world. En route, he visited what is now California.

- **In 330 BC** the Greek sailor Pytheas sailed out into the Atlantic through the Straits of Gibraltar and found his way to 'Thule' (Britain).

- **Around AD 1000** the Viking Leif Ericsson was the first European to cross the Atlantic to North America.

- **In 1405** Chinese admiral Cheng Ho began a series of seven epic voyages around the Indian Ocean in a huge fleet of junks.

- **In 1492** Genoese Christopher Columbus crossed the Atlantic from Cadiz in Spain and discovered the New World. His ship was the *Santa Maria*.

> ★ STAR FACT ★
> In 1522, Ferdinand Magellan's ship *Victoria* completed the first round-the-world voyage.

- **From 1499–1504** Italian Amerigo Vespucci sailed the Atlantic and realized South America was a continent. America is named after him.

- **In 1492** Italian John Cabot crossed the North Atlantic from Bristol in England and found Canada.

- **In 1498** Portuguese Vasco da Gama was the first European to reach India by sea, sailing all round Africa.

- **In 1642** Dutchman Abel Tasman sailed to what is now Australia and New Zealand. The island of Tasmania is named after him.

- **From 1768–79** James Cook explored the South Pacific in his ship the *Endeavour* and landed at Botany Bay.

▶ Like many 15th century explorers, Columbus sailed a 'carrack' with 'lateen' sails for sailing close in to the wind.

Ancient palaces

- **The word palace** comes from the Palatine Hill in Rome, where the emperors of Rome had their palaces.

- **The earliest known** palaces are those built in Thebes in Ancient Egypt by King Thutmose III in the 15th century BC.

- **Egyptian palaces** had a rectangular wall enclosing a maze of small rooms and a courtyard – a pattern later followed by many Asian palaces.

- **The Babylonians** and Persians introduced grand halls in their palaces at Susa and elsewhere.

- **Minoan palaces** on Crete introduced extra storeys.

- **Roman palaces** were the grandest of the ancient world.

- **The Sacred Palace** of Byzantium (now Istanbul) was biggest of all, covering 334,000 square metres.

- **Palaces** in China and Japan, like Beijing's Forbidden City, often had a high wall surrounding small houses for the ruler and his officials.

- **Ancient palaces in the Americas** like the Mayan palace at Uxmal dating from AD 900, are usually simpler.

- **Potala palace** stands high above Lhasa in Tibet. Potala means 'high heavenly realm'. The original, built by King Srong-brtsan-sgam-po in the 7th century was destroyed by the Chinese c.1600. The Dalai Lama rebuilt it in 1645.

◀ The 12th-century Khmer emperors of Cambodia built magnificent palaces in their capital of Angkor, now overgrown by jungle. But most magnificent of all was the temple, Angkor Wat.

Docks and ports

- **Some ports** like Hong Kong and Rio, are based on natural harbours; others are constructed artificially.

- **The Phoenicians** built artificial harbours at Tyre and Sidon in the Lebanon in the 13th-century.

- **The Romans** invented waterproof concrete to build the quays and breakwaters at their port of Ostia.

- **Roman and other ancient ports** had animal and human powered cranes. Saxon London and Viking Dublin had well-built wooden wharves.

- **Traditionally,** big boats would anchor in mid stream and barges called lighters would take the cargo ashore.

- **In the 18th-century** the first enclosed deep water docks were built at London and Liverpool. Here big ships could moor and unload directly onto the wharves.

> ★ STAR FACT ★
> The world's busiest ports are Rotterdam, Singapore and Hong Kong.

- **In the 20th century,** ports specializing in particular cargoes, such as oil terminals, grew.

- **Since the 1950s** there has been a huge growth in container ports. Containers are big standardized metal crates that can be loaded on and off quickly.

- **The world's main container ports** are Hong Kong, Singapore, Rotterdam, Hamburg and New York.

▲ The port of Balstad in Norway, a perfect natural harbour.

Modern architecture

▶ The old and new in Hong Kong: the ultra modern Hong Kong-Shanghai bank dwarfs a 19th-century classical building.

- **In the 1920s** many architects rejected old styles to experiment with simple shapes in materials like glass, steel and concrete.

- **The International Style** was pioneered by architect Le Corbusier who built houses in smooth geometric shapes like boxes.

- **The Bauhaus** school in Germany believed buildings should look like the job they were meant to do.

- **Walter Gropius** and Mies van de Rohe took Bauhaus ideas to the US and developed sleek, glass-walled, steel-framed skyscrapers like New York's Seagram Building.

- **American Frank Lloyd Wright** (1869-1959) was famous both for his low, prairie-style bungalows 'growing' from their site and his airy and elegant geometric buildings.

- **In the 1950s** architects like Kenzo Tange of Japan reacted against the 'blandness' of the International Style, introducing a rough concrete look called Brutalism.

- **In the 1960s** many critics reacted against the damage done by modern architecture to historic cities.

- **Post-modernists** were united in rejecting modern architecture, often reviving historical styles. American Robert Venturi added traditional decoration.

- **Richard Rogers'** Pompadou centre in Paris (1977) was a humorous joke on the Bauhaus idea, exposing the 'bones' of the building.

- **With shiny metal** and varied shapes the Guggenheim gallery in Bilbao in Spain is a new masterpiece.

Pyramids

- **Pyramids** are huge ancient monuments with a square base and triangular sides coming together in a point at the top. Remarkably, they are found not only in Egypt, but also in Greece, Cyprus, Italy, India, Thailand, Mexico, South America and various Pacific islands.

- **The earliest tombs** of the pharaohs were mud chambers called mastabas. But c.2686 BC, the wise man Imhotep had a pyramid-shaped tomb built for Zoser at Saqqara. This rose in steps and so is called the Step Pyramid.

- **In 2600BC** the Egyptians filled in the steps on a pyramid with stones to make the first smooth pyramid at Medum.

- **The ruins of 80 pyramids** stand near the Nile in Egypt, built over 1000 years. Each has an elaborate system of hidden passageways and chambers to stop robbers getting at the tomb of the pharaoh inside.

- **The largest pyramid** is the Great Pyramid at Giza, built for the Pharaoh Khufu c.2551-2472 BC. This was once 147 m high, but is now 140 m, since some upper stones have been lost. Khufu is known as Cheops in Greek.

> ★ STAR FACT ★
> The Great Pyramid at Giza was made of 2.3 million 2.5 tonne blocks of limestone.

▶ *The strange half lion, half pharaoh statue called the Sphinx stands near the pyramid of pharaoh Khafre at Giza.*

- **Later,** the Egyptians abandoned pyramids and cut tombs into rock, as in the Valley of Kings at Thebes. The tomb of Tutankhamun was one of these.

- **The Moche Indians** of Peru built large brick pyramids, including the Pyramid of the Sun near Trujillo.

- **Another Pyramid of the Sun** is on the site of the ancient Aztec capital of Teotihuacan, 50 km from Mexico City. Built around 2000 years ago it is exactly the same size (230 m square) as the Great Pyramid at Giza.

- **The American pyramids** were not tombs like those in Egypt, but temples, so they have no hidden chambers inside. They are built not from blocks of cut stone but from millions of basketloads of volcanic ash and gravel.

▶ *No-one knows just how the Egyptians managed to build such huge structures as the pyramids. It is thought that over 100,000 people worked on each big pyramid. Each big block was probably cut from the quarry, dragged on rollers to the River Nile and carried on barge to the building site. The stones were then dragged into place up earth ramps.*

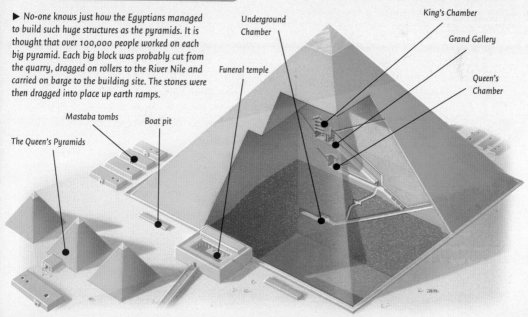

Underground Chamber

King's Chamber

Grand Gallery

Funeral temple

Queen's Chamber

Mastaba tombs

Boat pit

The Queen's Pyramids

Moving on snow

▲ Cutters are still used in the north eastern USA as a charming way of getting around in the winter snows.

- **Vehicles** designed to move on snow are supported on flat boards called runners, skids or skis. These slide over snow easily and spread the vehicle's weight over a larger area.

- **Sleds or sleighs** drawn by horses or dogs may have been the first vehicles ever used by humans.

- **Cutters** are light, graceful horse-drawn sleighs first introduced in the USA about 1800.

- **Troikas** are Russian sleighs (or carriages) drawn by three horses. The middle horse is supposed to trot while the outer horses gallop in particular ways.

- **Native Americans** had toboggans made of poles tied with leather thongs.

- **Snowmobiles** are vehicles with two skis at the front and a motor-driven track roll at the back. Racing snowmobiles can reach over 160 km/h.

- **Snowmobiles** are steered by handlebars that control the skis and by the shifting of the driver's weight.

- **The first propeller-driven** snowmobile was built in the 1920s. Tracked snowmobiles were developed in 1959 by Canadian Joseph Bombardier.

- **In the 1960s**, carved wooden skis dating back 8000 years were found in a bog at Vis near the Urals in Russia.

- **The earliest skates** were made from small bones.

Rescue boats

- **Several designs** for 'unsinkable' lifeboats were tried in 18th-century France and England.

- **After many drowned** when the ship *Adventure* went down in 1789, a competition for a lifeboat was set up.

- **The competition winner** was Newcastle boatbuilder Henry Greathead. His boat the *Original* would right itself when capsized and still float even when nearly filled with water.

- **The first land-based** powered lifeboat was steam powered and launched in 1890.

- **Around 1907** diesel-power lifeboats were introduced. Without the need for oars, most

of the boat could be covered in and so made even more unsinkable.

- **Modern land-based lifeboats** are either steel-hulled or made of a double-skin of timber.

- **The hull** usually contains a large number of sealed air containers so it is almost impossible for the boat to sink.

- **Some lifeboats** are afloat all the time. Others are kept ashore in a lifeboat house ready for emergencies.

- **Lifeboats** kept ashore are launched down a slipway into the sea or wheeled into the sea on a cradle until they float.

- **As leisure sailing** and bathing has increased, so there has been an increase in the number of inshore rescue boats. These are small rubber or fibreglass boats, kept afloat by an inflatable tube of toughened rubber.

► This is a typical inflatable inshore rescue boat. Boats like these are bonded together by heat and glue, and are incredibly tough.

Famous trains

- **Pullman coaches** became a byword for luxury in the USA in the 1860s.
- **After a trip to the USA,** young Belgian George Nagelmackers set up the Wagon-Lits company to do in Europe as Pullman had in the USA.
- **The most famous** Wagon-Lits was the luxurious *Orient-Express* from Paris to Istanbul, which started in 1883.
- **Among the many famous** travellers on the *Orient Express* were the female spy Mata Hari, the fictional spy James Bond and 40s film star Marlene Dietrich.
- **Another famous** Wagon-Lits train is the Trans-Siberian express, set up in 1898.
- **The Trans-Siberian** takes eight days to go right across Russia and Siberia from Moscow to Vladivostok.

▲ The Orient Express gained the glamour of intrigue as well as luxury after Agatha Christie wrote 'Murder on the Orient Express'.

> ★ STAR FACT ★
> At 9438 km, the Trans-Siberian Express is the world's longest train journey.

- **The *Flying Scotsman*** was famed for its fast, non-stop runs from London to Edinburgh in the 1920s.
- **The *Golden Arrow*** ran from London to Paris.
- **The *Indian Pacific*** in Australia runs on the world's longest straight track, 478 km across the Nullarbor Plain.

Sailing and tacking

- **Sailing ships** can sail into the wind because the wind does not so much push the sail as suck it.
- **The sail** is always angled so that the wind blows across it, allowing it to act like the wing of an aircraft.
- **As the wind blows** over the curve of the sail, it speeds up and its pressure drops in front of the sail. The extra pressure of the other side drives the boat forward.
- **The sail** works as long as the wind is blowing straight across it, so to go in a particular direction, the sailor simply changes the angle of the sail.
- **The boat's keel,** or centreboard, stops it slipping sideways.

▲ With their sails in line with the hull, these yachts are sailing close to the wind.

- **The boat can sail** with the wind behind it, to the side of it or even slightly ahead of it.
- **To sail directly** or nearly directly into the wind, a boat has to 'tack'. This means zig-zagging to and fro across the path of the wind so wind is always blowing across the sails.
- **At the end** of each tack, the sail 'comes about' (changes course). The tiller (steering arm) is turned to point the boat on the new course and the sail is allowed to 'gybe' (swing over to the other side).
- **'Sailing close to the wind'** is sailing nearly into the wind.
- **'Running with the wind'** is sailing with a fast wind behind.

Airships

Rigid envelope shell

Envelope filled with helium

▼ This is a cutaway of one of the new breed of small airships made from lightweight materials and filled with safe, non-flammable helium gas.

Airbags or 'ballonets' inside the helium-filled envelope. As the airship climbs, air pressure drops and the helium expands, pushing air out of the ballonets. As the airship drops again, the helium contracts and air is let into the ballonets again

Valve to let air in and out of the ballonets

Gondola where pilot sits

Landing wheel

Propeller powered by a motor car engine

Elevator flaps to help climbing or diving

Rudder to steer the airship to the left or right

● **By the mid-1800s** ballooning was a popular activity, but balloons have to float where the wind takes them. So in 1852, French engineer Henri Giffard made a cigar-shaped balloon filled with the very light gas hydrogen. He powered it with a steam-driven propeller and added a rudder to make it more 'dirigible' or steerable.

● **In 1884** two French inventors, Charles Renard and Arthur Krebs, built the first really dirigible balloon, *La France*. This was powered by an electric motor.

● **In 1897** Austrian David Schwartz gave a powered, cigar-shaped balloon a rigid frame to create the first airship.

● **In 1900** Count Ferdinand von Zeppelin built the first of his huge airships, the 128 m long LZ-1.

● **In 1909** Zeppelin helped set up the wold's first airline, DELAG, flying 148 m long airships, carrying 10,000 passengers in their first four years.

● **In World War 1** Germany used Zeppelin airships to scout enemy positions and make the first aerial bombing raids.

● **By the 1920s** vast airships were carrying people to and fro across the Atlantic in the style of a luxury ocean-liner. The *Graf Zeppelin* flew at 130 km/h. In its gondola, 60 or more passengers sat in comfortable lounges, walked to cocktail bars or listened to bands playing.

● **On 6 May 1937** disaster struck the giant 245 m-long airship *Hindenburg* as it docked at Lakehurst, New Jersey. The hydrogen in its balloon caught fire and exploded, killing 35 people. The day of the airship was over. Hydrogen was just too dangerous.

● **In recent years** there has been a revival of airships for advertising, filled with safer helium gas. Most are non-rigid, but Airship Industries Skyship is semi-rigid and made from modern light material like carbon-fibre.

★ STAR FACT ★
Fighter planes could take-off from and land on the 1930s airship *Akron* in mid-air.

Underground railways

- **Underground railways** are also called subways, metros or even just tubes.
- **There are three kinds:** open-cut; cut and cover and tube.
- **Open-cut subways** are built by digging rectangular ditches in streets, like much of New York's subway.
- **Cut-and-cover subways** are when an open-cut subway is covered again with a road or pavement.
- **Tubes** are deep, round tunnels created by boring through the ground, like most of London's lines.
- **The world's first underground** was the cut-and-cover Metropolitan Line in London, opened on 10 January 1863, using steam engines.
- **In 1890** the world's first electric tube trains ran on London's first deep tube, the City and South London.
- **After 1900** American Charles Yerkes, builder of the Chicago Loop railway, helped give London the world's most extensive tube network with 225 km of deep tubes.
- **Moscow's Metro** grand stations were built in the 1930s

▲ London was the first city in the world to have an underground system. Much of it is now in deep tube tunnels.

with marble, stained glass, statues and chandeliers.
- **New York City** has the world's largest subway network, but unlike London's most of it is quite shallow. The first line opened on 27 October 1904.

The Eiffel Tower

- **The Eiffel Tower** in Paris was 312.2 m high when it was first built. An antenna brings it up to 318.7 m. There are 1665 steps up to the top.
- **On a clear day** you can see 80 km in all directions from the top. It is often sunny at the top when the weather in the Paris streets is cloudy.
- **It was made** from 18,038 pieces of iron, held together by 2,500,000 rivets.
- **It was built in 1889** for the exhibition celebrating the 100th anniversary of the French Revolution.
- **Gustave Eiffel** (1832-1923) was the most successful engineer of the day, building not only the Eiffel Tower but New York's Statue of Liberty too.

▲ Paris's Eiffel Tower is one of the world's most famous landmarks.

- **The Eiffel Tower** was designed by Maurice Koechlin and Emile Nougier who calculated the effects of wind and gravity with amazing precision.
- **The Tower** was intended to show what could be done with cast iron.
- **During building work** Parisian artists, such as the composer Gounod and poet Maupassant, protested against its ugliness. But when completed it was an instant success with ordinary people.
- **Eiffel** was responsible for financing the construction of the tower, which cost more than $1 million.
- **When Paris was occupied** by the Nazis during the war, the lifts 'mysteriously' stopped working. They restarted the day Paris was liberated.

Missiles

> ★ STAR FACT ★
> American Tomahawk cruise missiles could be aimed through goalposts at both ends of a football field 500 km away.

Explosive warhead

Solid rocket fuel

▶ *90% of the weight of a ballistic missile is the rocket propellant needed to reach its distant target.*

- **In AD1232** the Chinese defended the city of K'ai-feng against the Mongols with gunpowder rockets.

- **In the early 1800s** British army officer William Congreve developed metal rockets carrying explosives.

- **In World War 2** the Germans developed the first guided missiles – missiles steered to their target in flight.

- **The most frightening** German guided missiles were the V-1 flying bombs or 'doodlebugs' and the V-2 supersonic rockets. The V-2 flew at 5300 km/h.

- **Ballistic missiles** arch through the air like a thrown ball. Rockets propel them on the upward trajectory (path). They then coast down on their target. Cruise missiles are propelled by jet on a low flat path all the way.

- **In the 1950s** the USA and Soviet Union competed to develop long-range ICBMs (Intercontinental Ballistic Missiles) usually armed with nuclear warheads.

- **In the 1960s,** antiballistic missiles were developed to shoot down missiles.

- **Some ICBMs** have a range of over 5000 km. Short range missiles (SRBMs) like Pershings reach up to 500 km.

- **SAMS** (surface-to-air missiles) like Redeye are fired from the ground at aircraft. Some can be fired by a soldier with a backpack. AAMs (air-to-air missiles) like Sidewinders are fired from planes against other planes.

Ancient America

- **The largest buildings** in Ancient America were Mayan pyramids, like the Tomb of Pakal in Mexico.

- **Teotihuacan** in Mexico is one of the best preserved ancient cities in the world, with its magnificent pyramids, palaces, temples, courts and homes.

- **At its height** around 2000 years ago, Teotihuacan was the world's biggest city with 100,000 people.

- **Hopewell Indians** of Newark, Ohio built earthwork tombs in AD250 to rival Egypt's pyramids in size.

> ★ STAR FACT ★
> The Incas of Peru built 25,000 km of stone-paved roads between 1450 and 1532.

- **Aztecs** built the Great Temple pyramid in their ancient capital of Tenochtitlan (now Mexico City) from 1325-1500. Human sacrifices were made at the top.

- **The Mesa Verde** is a famous 'pueblos' (stone village) of the Anasazi in New Mexico, abandoned around 1100 AD.

- **In the Chaco Canyon** the Anasazi built 650 km of mysterious roads to nowhere.

- **Nazca Lines** are huge outlines of birds, monkeys and other things up to 100 m across, drawn by Nazca people in the desert in S. Peru. They date from c. 100BC to AD700.

- **The Nazca Lines** are only clearly seen from the air. They may have been part of a giant astronomical calendar.

◀ *The 1500 year-old pyramids of the Maya were once overgrown by jungle, but most have now been restored.*

Palaces

- **The palaces** of Europe owe much to the vast palaces of the caliphs of the Near East, built in 7th and 8th centuries, with their cool courtyards and rich decoration.

- **The Topkapi Palace** in Istanbul was the sumptuous home of the Ottoman sultans for over 400 years until it was made into a museum in 1924, after the sultans' fall.

- **Venice's Doge's Palace** (mainly 1400s) shows oriental touches bought from the east by Venetian merchants.

- **The elegant Pitti Palace** in Florence was designed by the brilliant architect Brunelleschi for the merchant Luca Pitti in 1440. It was taken over by the Medici family in 1550.

- **Hampton Court Palace** southwest of London was begun in 1514 by King Henry VIII's favourite Cardinal Wolsey – but when Wolsey fell from favour, the King took it over.

- **The Escorial** in Madrid is a massive granite palace built 1563-84 by Phillip II to celebrate victories over the French.

- **Many 18th-century princes** built their own Versailles – lavish palaces like Dresden and Potsdam in Germany,

▲ London's Buckingham Palace is the home of the Queen of Britain.

Vienna's Schönbrunn and St Petersburg's Winter Palace.

- **Buckingham House** was built in 1702-5 for the Duke of Buckingham but remodelled as a palace in 1825.

- **Inspired by English gardens** Peter the Great made Russia's oldest garden, the Summer Garden in St Petersburg in 1710. He built the Summer Palace in it.

- **Catherine the Great** had the St Petersburg's Winter Palace built by architect Bartolomeo Rastrelli in 1762.

First steamships

- **In 1783** French nobleman Marquis Claude de Jouffroy d'Abbans built a massive steam boat that churned up the Saone River near Lyon in France for 15 minutes before the pounding engines shook it to bits.

- **In 1787** American John Fitch made the first successful steamship with an engine driving a series of paddles.

- **In 1790** Fitch started the world's first steam service on the Delaware River.

- **In 1802** Scot William Symington built a tug, the *Charlotte Dundas*, able to tow two 70-tonne barges.

- **In 1807** American Robert Fulton made the first steam passenger boats, running 240 km up the Hudson River from New York.

- **In 1819** the New York-built ship *Savannah* made the first steam-assisted crossing of the Atlantic.

- **In 1833** Canadian ship *Royal William* made the first mainly steam-powered Atlantic crossing in two days.

- **In 1843** British engineer Isembard Kingdom Brunel launched the first all-iron hull steamship, the *Great Britain*.

- **In 1858** Brunel launched *Great Eastern*, the biggest ship of the 19th century, 211 m long and weighing 30,000 tonnes.

- **Early steamships** had paddles, but in 1835 Swede John Ericsson invented a screw propeller. In 1845 a screw-driven boat won a tug-of-war with a paddle steamer.

◀ Warships like this, HMS *Theseus*, were built in the 1880s.

Taking off

- **An aircraft's wings** or 'foils' are lifted by the air flowing above and beneath them as they slice through the air.
- **Because the top** of the wing is curved, air pushed over the wing speeds up and stretches out. The stretching of the air reduces its pressure.
- **Underneath the wing** air slows down and bunches up, so air pressure here rises.
- **The wing gains 'lift'** as the wing is sucked from above and pushed from below.

> ★ **STAR FACT** ★
> Slots on the wing's leading edge smooth airflow to increase the safe angle of attack.

- **The amount of lift** depends on the angle of the wing – called the angle of attack – and its shape, and also how fast it is moving through the air.
- **Aircraft** get extra lift for climbing by increasing their speed through the air and by dropping the tail so that the main wings cut through the air at a steeper angle.
- **If the angle of attack** becomes too steep, the air flow breaks up and the wing loses lift. This is called a stall.
- **Planes** take off when air is moving fast enough over the wing to provide enough lift.
- **Airliners** have 'high-lift' slots and flaps on the wings to give extra lift for slow take-off and landing speeds.

◀ *The high-lift flaps are down to give extra lift on a climb.*

The Taj Mahal

- **The Taj Mahal** (said *tarj m'harl*) in Agra in India is perhaps the most beautiful tomb in the world.
- **Mughal Indian** ruler Shah Jehan ordered it to be built in honour of his favourite wife Mumtaz Mahal, who died giving birth to their 14th child.
- **Mumtaz** died in 1629, and the Taj was built over 22 years from 1632 to 1653.
- **The Taj** is set at the north end of a formal Persian garden with water courses and rows of cypress trees.
- **It is made of white** marble and sits on a platform of sandstone.
- **Inside** behind an octagonal screen of alabaster marble tracery lie the jewel-inlaid

- cenotaphs (tombs) of Mumtaz and Shah Jehan. The Shah was placed there when he died and his tomb is the only asymmetrical feature in the Taj.
- **20,000 workers** worked in marble and sandstone, silver, gold, carnelian, jasper, moonstone, jade, lapis lazuli and coral to enhance the Taj's beauty.
- **At each corner** of the platform is a slender minaret 40.5 m tall.
- **In the centre** is a dome 21.3 m across and 36.6 m high.
- **The main architect** was Iranian Isa Khan, but the decorations were said to be by Austin of Bordeaux and Veroneo of Venice.

◀ *So perfect are the Taj's proportions that it was said to have been designed by giants and finished by jewellers.*

Jet engines

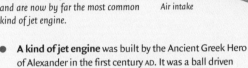

Front fan to create 'cold' bypass stream

The engine casing is made of carbon-fibre and plastic honeycomb for lightness. Inside is an outer bypass duct for the 'cold-stream' of air from the front fan. An inner duct takes the 'hot stream' through the compressor, combustion chamber and turbine to create the exhaust.

▶ All but the very fastest warplanes are powered by turbofan jet engines, like this Russian MiG. Turbofans first came into widespread use in the 1970s and are now by far the most common kind of jet engine.

Air intake

Exhaust where a hot jet of air roars out

- **A kind of jet engine** was built by the Ancient Greek Hero of Alexander in the first century AD. It was a ball driven round by jets of steam escaping from two nozzles.

- **The first jet engines** were built at the same time in the 1930s by Pabst von Ohain in Germany and Frank Whittle in Britain – though neither knew of the other's work.

> ★ STAR FACT ★
> In a typical turbojet, exhaust gases roar from the engine at over 1600 km/h.

- **Ohain's engine** was put in the Heinkel HE-178 which first flew on 27 August 1939; Whittle's was put in the Gloster E28 of 1941. The first American experimental jet was the Bell XP-59 Aircomet of 1942.

- **Jets** work by pushing a jet of air out the back. This hits the air so fast that the reaction thrusts the plane forward like a deflating balloon.

- **Jet engines** are also called gas turbines because they burn fuel gas to spin the blades of a turbine non-stop.

- **Turbojets** are the original form of jet engine. Air is scooped in at the front and squeezed by spinning 'compressor' blades. Fuel sprayed into the squeezed air in the middle of the engine burns, making the mixture expand dramatically. The expanding air not only pushes round turbines which drive the compressor, but also sends out a high-speed jet of hot air to propel the plane. This high-speed jet is noisy but good for ultra-fast warplanes and the supersonic Concorde.

- **Turboprops** are turbojets that use most of their power to turn a propeller rather than force out a hot air jet.

- **Turbofans** are used by most airliners because they are

quieter and cheaper to run. In these, extra turbines turn a huge fan at the front. Air driven by this fan bypasses the engine core and gives a huge extra boost at low speeds.

- **Ramjets** or 'flying stovepipes' are the simplest type of jet engine, used only on missiles. They dispense with both compressor and turbine blades and simply rely on the speed of the jet through the air to ram air in through the intake into the engine.

▶ Like nearly all warplanes today, 'stealth' aircraft are jet-propelled. But the afterburner stream of hot gases from the jets provides a 'signature' that can show up all too clearly on some detection equipment. So stealth aircraft are designed to 'supercruise' – that is, fly at supersonic speeds without much afterburn.

Yachts and catamarans

▲ *Catamarans with twin hulls and outriggers (extra floats) are all developed from traditional Polynesian outriggers.*

- **The word yacht** comes from the 17th-century Dutch word *jacht*, which meant 'ship for chasing'.

- **English yachting** began in 1662 when King Charles II raced his brother James from Greenwich for a £100 bet in a small pleasure boat given to him by the Dutch.

- **In 1898** Joshua Slocum sailed single-handed round the world in the 11.3 m *Spray*, proving the seaworthiness of small craft.

- **From the 1920s** the same aerodynamic principles applied to hulls were used for sails and rigging.

- **Most racing yachts** are now built from aluminium and light, strong composites such as carbon-fibre.

- **In the 1960s** twin-hulled catamarans became popular since they pierce waves well yet are wide and stable.

- **In 1983** Australian Ben Lexcen became the first non-American to win the famous America's Cup race.

- **The key to Lexcen's** success was revolutionary winglets on the keel to improve stability.

- **Sails on some yachts** are now computer controlled to keep them at exactly the right angle.

> **! NEWS FLASH !**
> America's Cup yachts have winglets on their
> rudder and keels for extra stability.

Powerboats

- **Powerboating** began in 1863 when Frenchman Jean Lenoir installed a petrol engine in a small boat.

- **The first major race** was in 1903 across the English Channel. The Gold Cup of the American Power Boat Association (APBA) started on the Hudson in 1904.

- **About 1910** motor makers like Evinrude introduced detachable 'outboard' motors that clamp to the stern. Inboard motors have the engine built into the hull.

- **In the 1920s** racing boats adopted 'planing hulls' for skimming across the water at high speeds, rather than traditional deep v-shaped 'displacement' hulls.

▼ *Powerboat racing has become hugely competitive like motor racing, and Formula 1 boats roar round at speeds over 200 km/h.*

After World War II hulls were made more and more, not from wood, but metals and fibreglass.

- **Most powerboats** are driven, not by a propeller screw, but a high-speed jet of water.

- **In 1994** American Tom Gentry set the offshore Class 1 record of 253.35 km/h in Skater powerboats.

- **In 1996** Gentry's *Gentry Eagle* crossed the Atlantic in 2 days 14 hours 7 mins. In 1997, the *Destriero* made it in 2 days 6 hours 34 minutes.

- **The official water speed** record is 511.11 km/h by Kenneth Warby in his hydroplane *Spirit of Australia* on Blowering Lake, New South Wales on 8 October 1978.

- **Jet skis** are like motorboats that skim across the water on a ski. They were developed by the American Clayton Jacobsen back in the 1960s.

- **The jet ski** speed record is 69 km/h by French D. Condemine in 1994 on a Yahama.

Biplanes

- **Most early planes** were biplanes (double-wingers) or even triplanes (triple-wingers).

- **Monoplanes** (single-wingers) like Blériot's (see record breaking flights) were fast and won many early races – because they did not drag on the air like multi-wings.

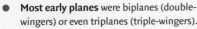

◀ *The biplanes of World War I were slow but highly manoeuvrable. Pilots were able to show tremendous flying skill in the first aerial 'dog fights' between planes.*

- **Accidents** by overstressed competition monoplanes made it look as if they were dangerous. Single wings were weak, it seemed, because they had to be very long to give a similar lifting area to multi-wings.

- **In 1912** the French and British banned monoplanes, so all World War I fighter planes were multi-wingers.

- **Biplane wings** were strong because struts and wires linked the small, light wings to combine their strength.

- **Famous World War I** fighters included the British Sopwith Camel and Bristol Fighter.

- **The Fokker triplane** flown by German air ace Baron von Richtofen (the Red Baron) was said to be 'fearsome to look at and climbs like a lift'.

- **With their network** of struts and wires, biplanes were affectionately known as 'string bags'.

- **In the years** after World War I, huge biplane airliners were built including the Handley Page Heracles of the 1930s.

- **By the late 1920s** planes could be built strongly all in metal. So to cut drag and boost speed, designers went back to monoplanes with planes like the Supermarine S6B. Soon biplanes seemed old-fashioned.

The Palace of Versailles

▲ *Versailles is perhaps the most expensive palace ever built.*

- **Versailles**, in France, is a magnificent palace built for Louis XIV. Work began in 1661 and carried on for a century.

- **When complete** Versailles was 500 m long, had over 1300 major rooms and could accommodate 5000 people.

- **The first architect** was Louis le Vau but Jules Hardouin-Mansart took over in 1676, adding the second storey.

- **The interior** was conceived by Charles le Brun. His Hall of Mirrors is a long hall lined with mirrors. A masterly painted ceiling shows Louis XIV's achievements.

- **Throughout Versailles** high ceilings and great doors are emblazoned in gold with the mark of the sun god, Apollo – and of King Louis, known as the Sun King.

- **The huge gardens** of tree-lined terraces and ponds were landscaped by Andre le Notre with 1400 fountains, 400 new pieces of sculpture and four million tulips.

- **The fountains** appear 'magically' still to show the power of the king over nature.

- **The palace** had a famous state-of-the-art theatre designed by Jacques-Ange Gabriel in 1769.

- **During the French Revolution** on 6 October 1789, mobs invaded the palace and wrecked its interiors. Restoration began in 1837 and has continued ever since.

- **The avenues of Washington DC** were laid out in imitation of Versailles by a French architect.

Trains of the future

▲ *Many cities now have short monorails, but they seem unlikely to get much bigger because of the disruption building would cause.*

- **Monorails** are single beam tracks raised over city streets.
- **The first monorail** was built in Wuppertal in Germany as long ago as 1901 and monorails have been seen as trains of the future ever since.
- **Monorails** of the future may be air-cushion trains or maglev, as at Birmingham airport.

- **A maglev** is proposed in Japan to take passengers the 515 km from Tokyo to Osaka in under 60 minutes. Germany is planning a system called Transrapid.
- **PRT** or Personalized Rapid Transport is automatic cars on monorails. AGT (Automated Guideway Transit) is the same for coaches, as in Detroit, or London's DLR.
- **300 km/h plus** High Speed Train (HST) systems like the French TGV are being built in many places, such as from Moscow to St Petersburg.
- **In 2004** the 320 km/h Tampa-Miami Florida Overland Express opens. The same year a 4500 km 300 km/h line may open from Melbourne to Darwin, Australia.
- **Most HSTs** run on special straight tracks. Tilting trains lean into bends to give high speeds on winding old tracks.
- **Tilting trains** include the 300 km/h Italian Fiat Pendolini and the Swedish X2000.
- **From 2000** the 240 km/h tilting train *The American Flyer* – Washington to Baltimore – is the USA's fastest train.

Rockets

> **· STAR FACT ·**
> The *Saturn V* rocket that launched the Apollo mission to the Moon is the most powerful rocket ever built.

- **Rockets** work by burning fuel. As fuel burns and swells out behind, the swelling pushes the rocket forward.
- **Solid-fuel rockets** are the oldest of all engines, used by the Chinese a thousand years ago.
- **Solid-fuel engines** are basically rods of solid, rubbery

◀ *Only powerful rockets can give the thrust to overcome gravity and launch spacecraft into space. They fall away in stages once the spacecraft is travelling fast enough.*

fuel with a tube down the middle. When the fuel is set alight it burns out through the fuel until all is used.

- **Solid fuel** rockets are usually only used for model rockets and small booster rockets. But the Space Shuttle has two solid rocket boosters (SRBs) as well as three main liquid fuel engines.
- **Most powerful launch rockets** use liquid fuel. The Shuttle uses hydrogen. Other fuels include kerosene.
- **Liquid fuel** only burns with oxygen, so rockets must also carry an oxidizer (a substance that gives oxygen) such as liquid oxygen (LOX) or nitrogen tetroxide.
- **Future rocket drives** include nuclear thermal engines that use a nuclear reactor to heat the gas blasted out.
- **NASA's Deep Space-1** project is based on xenon ion engines which thrust, not hot gases out the back, but electrically charged particles called ions.
- **Solar thermal engines** of the future would collect the Sun's rays with a large mirror to heat gases.

Navigation

- **Early sailors** found their way by staying near land, looking for 'landmarks' on shore. Away from land they steered by stars, so had only a vague idea of direction in the day.

- **After 1100** European sailors used a magnetic compass needle to find North.

- **A compass** only gives you a direction to steer; it does not tell you where you are.

- **The astrolabe** was used from c.1350. This measured the angle of stars above the horizon, or the Sun at noon giving an idea of latitude (how far north or south of the equator).

- **From the 1500s** the cross-staff gave a more accurate measure of latitude at night from the angle between the Pole Star and the horizon.

- **From the mid-1700s** until the 1950s, sailors measured latitude with a mirror sextant. This had two mirrors. It gave the angle of a star (or the Sun) when

◀ *A navigational instrument for measuring latitude from the angle of certain stars.*

one mirror was adjusted until the star was at horizon height in the other.

- **For centuries** the way to find longitude – how far east or west – was by dead reckoning. This meant trailing a knotted rope in the water to calculate speed, and so estimate how far you had come.

- **You can find longitude** by comparing the Sun's height with its height at the same time at a longitude you know. But early pendulum clocks did not work well enough aboard ship to give the correct time.

- **The longitude problem** was solved when John Harrison made a very accurate spring-driven clock or chronometer.

- **Ships** can now find their position with pinpoint accuracy using the Global Positioning System or GPS. This works by electronically comparing signals from a ring of satellites.

Sydney Opera House

▲ *Standing by the water's edge in Sydney Harbour, Sydney Opera House is one of the world's most distinctive buildings.*

- **Sydney Opera House** in Sydney, opened in October 1973, is one of Australia's best known landmarks.

- **The design** by Danish architect Jorn Utzon was agreed in January after a competition involving 233 entries, but it took 14 years to build.

- **The radical sail-like** roofs were said to have been inspired by sea shells.

- **The original design** was so unusual that it proved impossible to build structurally, so Utzon altered the shape of the roofs to base them on sections of a ball.

- **The altered design** meant the roofs could be made from pre-cast concrete slabs.

- **The roofs** were made from 2194 pre-cast concrete slabs, weighing up to 15 tonnes each.

- **The slabs** are tied together with 350 km of tensioned steel cable and covered with 1 million Swedish tiles.

- **In the mouths of the roofs** are 6225 sq m of French glass in double layers, one tinted topaz-colour.

- **Inside** there were originally four theatres – the Concert Hall, the Opera Theatre, the Drama Theatre and the Playhouse.

- **A new theatre, The Studio,** was added in March 1999 for small cast plays and films.

Bombers of World War II

- **In the 1930s** Boeing built the B-17 'Flying Fortress', with gun turrets to battle its way through to targets even by day.

- **The 1929** Curtis F8C Helldiver was the first 'dive-bomber' – designed to drop its bombs at the end of a long dive on targets like aircraft carriers. German 'Stuka' dive-bombers gained a fearsome name in the German invasions of 1939.

- **The twin-engined** Heinkel 111, Dornier D017 and Junkers Ju88 were the main German bombers in the *Blitzkrieg* (literally 'lightning war') raids of the Battle of Britain.

- **In December 1939** the heavy loss of British Wellingtons showed that lightly armed bombers could not sustain daylight raids, so the British switched to night raids.

- **Blind bombing** radar systems like the Hs2, and flare trails left by advance 'Pathfinder' missions, improved accuracy on night raids.

◄ *The British Avro Lancaster could carry 6000 kg of bombs on low altitude raids.*

- **The ultra-light** De Havilland Mosquito was fast enough to fly daylight raids.

- **The Russian Ilyushin Il-2** or Stormovik was so good at bombing tanks Stalin said it was 'as necessary to the Red Army as air or bread.'

- **The dambusters** were the Lancasters of 617 squadron of 1943 that attacked German dams with 'bouncing bombs'. These were round bombs designed by Barnes Wallis that bounced over the water surface towards the target dams.

- **Kamikaze** (Japanese for 'divine wind') were fighters loaded with bombs and gasoline which their pilots aimed in suicide dives at enemy ships.

- **The biggest bomber** was the Boeing B-29 Superfortress which could fly over 10,000 m up. In 1945, B-29s dropped the atomic bombs on Hiroshima and Nagasaki in Japan.

Early cars

- **In 1890** Frenchman Emile Levassor made the first real car, with an engine at the front. He laughed, saying, *C'est brutal, mais ca marche* ('It's rough, but it goes'.)

- **The Duryea** brothers made the first successful American car in 1893.

- **Early accidents** made cars seem dangerous. Until 1896 in Britain and 1901 in New York cars had to be preceded by a man on foot waving a red flag.

- **In 1895** the French Panhard-Levassor company made the first covered 'saloon' car.

- **In 1898** Renault drove the wheels with a shaft not a chain.

- **The Oldsmobile** Curved Dash of 1900 was the first car to sell in thousands.

- **On early cars** speed was controlled by moving a small ignition advance lever backwards or forwards.

- **Dirt roads,** oil spray and noise meant early motorists needed protective clothing such as goggles and earmuffs.

- **The first cars** had wooden or wire spoked wheels. Pressed steel wheels like today's came in after 1945.

- **In 1906** an American steam-driven car, the Stanley Steamer, broke the land speed record at over 205 kmh.

◄ *By 1904, many cars were starting to have the familiar layout of cars today – engine at the front, driver on one side, steering wheel, petrol tank at the back, a shaft to drive the wheels and so on.*

Canals

- **In 1470 BC** the Egyptian Pharaoh Sesostris had the first Suez Canal built, linking the Mediterranean and Red Sea.

- **The Grand Canal** in China is the world's longest man-made waterway, running 1747 km west of Beijing.

- **The origins** of the Grand Canal date to the 4th century BC, but it was rebuilt in 607 AD.

- **The late 1700s and early 1800s** saw many canals built for the factories of the Industrial Revolution, like James Brindley's Bridgwater Canal in Lancashire, England.

- **Clinton's Folly** is the Erie Canal linking Lake Erie to the Hudson in the USA, pushed through by governor De Witt Clinton in 1825.

- **The current Suez Canal** was built by Ferdinand de Lesseps (1859-1869). It is the world's longest big-ship canal, 161.9 km long.

- **The Panama Canal** links the Atlantic and Pacific Oceans 82 km across Central America, and cutting the sea journey from New York to San Francisco by 14,400 km.

▲ Amsterdam's canals were dug in the city's heyday in the 1600s.

- **The Panama Canal** takes over 400 million tonnes of shipping a year – more than any other canal.

- **The world's busiest canal** is Germany's Kiel which takes 45,000 ships a year from the North Sea to the Baltic.

- **In Russia** one of the world's longest canal systems links the Black Sea to the Arctic Ocean via the Volga River.

Airliners

- **The Boeing 247** of 1933 was the world's first modern airliner, with smooth monoplane wings, streamlined metal body and retractable landing wheels.

- **The Douglas DC-3** of 1936 could carry 21 passengers smoothly at 320 km/h and was the first popular airliner.

- **In 1952** the world's first jet airliner, the De Havilland Comet 1 came into service.

- **The Comet** more than halved international flight times but several tragic accidents led to its grounding in 1954.

! NEWS FLASH !
Spaceplanes like Lockheed-Martin's *Venture Star* may make space trips routine flights.

- **The age of jet** air travel really began with the American Boeing 707 and Douglas DC-8 of the late 1950s.

- **The Boeing 747** jumbo jet of 1970 – the first 'wide-bodied jet' – had over 400 seats, making air travel cheap.

- **Four-engined jets** like the 747 can fly 10,000 km non-stop at speeds of 1000 km/h. Two and three-engine jets like the DC-10 make shorter flights.

- **Supersonic airliners** able to travel at over 2000 km/h like the Anglo-French Concorde and Russian Tupolev Tu-144 have proved too heavy on fuel and too noisy.

- **The 555-seat Airbus** A380 is the first full-length double-deck airliner.

▶ The four-engined Boeing 747 flies at 10-13,000 m – well above most storms – and can fly non-stop from New York to Tokyo.

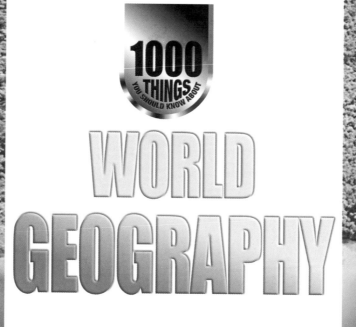

1000
THINGS
YOU SHOULD KNOW ABOUT

WORLD
GEOGRAPHY

KEY

 Asia

 The Americas

 Europe

 Africa and Australasia

 People

 Places

The Alps

▲ *The pointed summit of the Matterhorn is the third highest peak of the Alps.*

- **The Alps** are Europe's largest mountain range, 1050 km long, up to 250 km wide and covering 210,000 sq km.

- **The highest Alpine peak** is Mont Blanc (4807 m) on the France-Italy border.

- **Famous peaks** include the Matterhorn (4478 m) and Monte Rosa (4634 m) on the Swiss-Italian border.

> ★ STAR FACT ★
> The highest village in the Swiss Alps is Juf which lies at a height of 2126 m.

- **The Alps began to form** about 65 million years ago when the African crustal plate shifted into Europe.

- **The Alps are the source** of many of Europe's major rivers such as the Rhone, Po and Rhine.

- **Warm, dry winds** called föhns blow down leeward slopes, melting snow and starting avalanches.

- **The high Alpine pastures** are famous for their summer grazing for dairy cows. In winter, the cows come down into the valleys. This is called transhumance.

- **The Alps** are being worn away by human activity. In valleys, cities and factories are growing, while skiing wears away the slopes at the tops of the mountains.

- **The Alps** have Europe's highest vineyards, 1500 m up.

Thailand and Myanmar

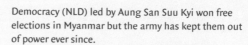

▶ *Many canals thread through Bangkok and provide a way for poor people to bring goods to sell.*

- **Thailand:** Capital: Bangkok. Population: 60.8 million. Currency: Baht. Language: Thai.

- **Myanmar:** Capital: Rangoon. Population: 49.4 million. Currency: Kyat. Language: Burmese.

- **In 1990** the National League for Democracy (NLD) led by Aung San Suu Kyi won free elections in Myanmar but the army has kept them out of power ever since.

- **Growing opium poppies** to make the painkiller morphine and the drug heroin is one of the few ways the people of north Myanmar can make money.

- **The world's best rubies** come from Mogok in Myanmar.

- **Thailand's capital** is called Bangkok by foreigners but its real name has over 60 syllables. Many locals call it Krung Thep which are the first two syllables.

- **Most people in Thailand** and Myanmar still live in the countryside growing rice to eat.

- **Most people** live on fertile plains and deltas – around the Irrawaddy River in Myanmar and the Chao Phraya in Thailand.

- **Millions** of tourists come to Thailand each year to visit the country's beaches, and the attractions of the city of Bangkok.

Greece

- **Capital:** Athens. Area: 131,957 sq km. Currency: euro. Language: Greek.
- **Physical features:** Highest mountain: Mt Olympus (2,917 m).
- **Population:** 10.6 million. Population density: 80/sq km. Life expectancy: men 76.0 years; women 81.3 years.
- **Wealth:** GDP: $130.6 billion. GDP per head: $12,320.
- **Exports:** Clothes, olive oil, petroleum products, fruit and tobacco.
- **Farming:** Greece is so mountainous that less than a third can be

▼ Greece is one of the most mountainous countries in Europe.

cultivated, but a fifth of all workers work on the land, many raising sheep or growing olives or vines for wine.

- **Greece** is the world's third largest grower of olives after Spain and Italy.
- **Greek salad** includes olives and feta cheese from goats milk. In some small villages, bakers allow villagers to cook their food in their *fuorno* oven.
- **More than 11 million** visitors come to Greece each year – some to see the relics of Ancient Greece, but most to soak up the sun.
- **Athens** is the ancient capital of Greece, dominated by the Acropolis with its famous Parthenon temple ruins. Athens is also a modern city, with pollution caused by heavy traffic.

World trade

- **International trade** is the buying and selling of goods and services between different countries.
- **International trade** has increased so much people talk of the 'globalization' of the world economy. This means that goods are sold around the world.
- **The balance of world trade** is tipped in favour of the world's richest countries and companies.
- **Just 200 huge multinational** companies control much of world trade.
- **Just five countries** – the USA, Germany, Japan, France and the UK – control almost half world trade.
- **The 30 richest countries** control 82% of world trade.
- **The 49 poorest countries** control just 2% of world trade.
- **Some countries** rely mainly on just one export. 95% of Nigeria's export earnings come from oil; 75% of Botswana's come from diamonds.

- **Some countries** such as the USA want 'free trade' – that is, no restrictions on trade; other less powerful nations want tariffs (taxes on foreign goods) and quotas (agreed quantities) to protect their home industries.
- **The World Trade Organization** was founded on Jan 1, 1995 to police world trade, and to push for free trade.

▼ This diagram shows the proportions of each kind of good traded around the world.

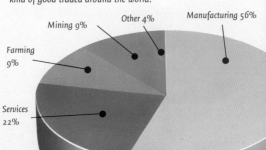

Mining 9%

Other 4%

Manufacturing 56%

Farming 9%

Services 22%

Peoples of northern Asia

- **86% of Russians** are descended from a group of people called Slavs who first lived in eastern Europe 5,000 years ago.
- **East Slavs** are the Great Russians (or Russians), the Ukrainians and the Belarusians (or White Russians).
- **West Slavs** are eastern Europeans such as Czechs, Poles and Slovaks.
- **South Slavs** are

▲ The Kazakhs were famous for their horseriding skills.

- people such as Croats, Serbs and Slovenes.
- **Slavs speak** Slavic or Slavonic languages such as Russian, Polish or Czech.
- **In the old Soviet Union** there were over 100 ethnic groups. 70% were Slavs. Many of the rest were Turkic people such as Uzbeks, Kazakhs and Turkmen. Many of these peoples now have their own nations.
- **Slavic** people are mainly Christian; Turkic people are mainly Islamic.
- **Many Turkic peoples** such as the Kazakhs have a nomadic tradition that is fast vanishing.
- **The Mongols** were a people whose empire under the great Khans once spread far south into China and far west across Asia.
- **The Tatars** are 4.6 million Turkic people who now live mainly in the Tatar Republic in the Russian Federation.

Romania and Bulgaria

- **Romania:** Capital: Bucharest. Population: 22.5 million. Currency: Leu. Language: Romanian.
- **Bulgaria:** Capital: Sofia. Population: 8.3 million. Currency: Lev. Language: Bulgarian.
- **Romania** gets its name from the Romans who occupied it almost 2,000 years ago.

- **Transylvania** is a beautiful, wooded, mountain area of Romania, once home to the 15th-century tyrant Vlad the Impaler, the original Dracula.
- **Like Bulgaria,** Romania was communist until 1989 when the people overthrew President Ceausescu.
  - **Ceausescu's** attempts to develop industry forced people off the lands into towns. Many orphans were left as families broke up.
  - **Romania** is a major wine grower.
  - **Romania** is home not only to native Romanians but 400,000 Roma (gypsies).
  - **The Valley of Roses** is a valley near Kazanluk in Bulgaria full of fields of damask roses.
  - **Bulgarian women pick** damask rose blossoms to get the oil to make 'attar of roses', used for perfumes.

◄ Damask rose blossoms in Bulgaria's Valley of Roses are picked early mornings in May and June, before the sun dries out the petals.

DR Congo

     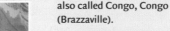

- **Capital:** Kinshasa. Area: 2,344,856 sq km. Currency: Congolese franc. Official language: French.
- **Physical features:** Highest mountain: Mont Ngaliema (5109 m). Longest river: Congo (4667 km).
- **Population:** 51.8 million. Population density: 22/sq km. Life expectancy: men 49 years; women 52 years.
- **Wealth:** GDP: $5 billion. GDP per head: $110.
- **Exports:** Copper, diamonds, coffee, cobalt, petroleum.
- **DR Congo** is called Democratic Republic of Congo to distinguish it from a neighbouring country

▲ Congo lies on the Equator. Over a third of it is thick equatorial rainforest.

also called Congo, Congo (Brazzaville).

- **Once called the** Belgian Congo DR Congo then became the Congolese Republic, then Zaire. Since 1997 it has been the Democratic Republic of Congo.
- **Congo** is one of the world's leading copper producers. There is a vast copper mine in Shaba.
- **Congo is** the world's leading industrial diamonds producer.
- **The Congo River** is the world's ninth longest river, and carries more water than any river but the Amazon.

Southern USA

- **The south central states** such as Texas, Oklahoma and New Mexico produce a lot of oil and gas.
- **Texas** produces more oil than any other state apart from Alaska.
- **One of the world's** largest oil companies, was founded on Texan oil.
- **Texas** is known as the Lone Star state.

> ★ STAR FACT ★
> The first integrated circuit was invented in 1958 in Dallas

- **Louisiana** is known as the Sugar state because it grows so much sugar.
- **Oil wealth and aerospace** have attracted high-tech industries to Texan cities like Dallas, Houston and San Antonio.
- **Cotton** is grown on the Mississippi plains, while tobacco is important in the Carolinas and Virginia.
- **In the mid 1800s** the southern states grew 80% of the world's cotton, largely using black slave labour.
- **Florida** is famous for Disneyworld, the Cape Canaveral space centre and the Everglades, a vast area of steamy tropical swamp infested by alligators.

◄ Texas's wealth came with the discovery of oil in 1901. Now aerospace and high-tech industries are thriving in this sunny state.

Zimbabwe

▶ Victoria Falls on the Zambezi is one of the world's biggest waterfalls. Its roar can be heard 40 km away.

- **Capital:** Harare. Area: 390,759 sq km. Currency: Zimbabwe dollar. Official language: English.

- **Physical features:** Highest mountain: Mt Inyangani (2592 m). Longest river: Zambezi (3540 km).

- **Population:** 12.4 million. Population density: 30/sq km. Life expectancy: men 39 years; women 40 years.

- **Wealth:** GDP: $6.3 billion. GDP per head: $520.

- **Exports:** Tobacco, ferrochrome, textiles and clothing, nickel.

- **Zimbabwe** was once the British colony of Rhodesia but was granted independence in 1980.

- **The name Zimbabwe** came from the huge ancient stone palace of Great Zimbabwe (which means 'house of stone').

- **Zimbabwe** is a fertile farming country, growing lots of tobacco, cotton and other crops. Much of the land still remains in the hands of white farmers, but the government plans to change this situation.

- **Zimbabwe** is the most industrial African nation after S. Africa, making steel, cement, cars, machines, textiles and much more. Harare is the biggest industrial centre.

- **98% of Zimbabweans** are black. The Shona people are the biggest group, then come the Ndebele (or Matabele). The Shona speak a language called Shona, the Ndebele speak Matabele.

Chinese food

- **The staple foods** in China are rice and wheat with corn, millet and sorghum. In the south, the people eat more rice. In the north, they eat more wheat, as bread or noodles.

- **Vegetables** such as cabbage, bean and bamboo shoots are popular. So too is *tofu* (soya bean curd).

- **Favourite meats** in China are pork and poultry, but the Chinese also eat a lot of eggs, fish and shellfish.

- **A Chinese breakfast** may be rice and vegetables or rice porridge and chicken noodle soup or sweet pastries.

- **A Chinese lunch** may include egg rolls or meat or prawn dumplings called *dim sum*.

◀ A favourite snack in China is fried savoury dumplings.

- **A Chinese main meal** may be stir-fried vegetables with bits of meat or seafood in a stock, with rice or noodles.

- **China has** a long tradition of fine cooking, but styles vary. Cantonese cooking in the south has lots of fish, crabs and prawn. Huaiyang has steamed dishes. Sichuann is spicy. Beijing cooking in the north is the most sophisticated, famous for its Peking duck (cripsy roast duck).

- **The Chinese** often cook their food by stir-frying (stirring while hot frying) in big round pans called woks. They eat the food from bowls with chopsticks and small china spoons, not with knives and forks.

- **Chinese** drink tea without milk, typically made from jasmine leaves, oolong (green tea) or chrysanthemum.

★ STAR FACT ★
The Chinese were drinking tea at least 4,000 years ago.

Russia

In eastern Siberia, milk is sold in frozen blocks with a wooden handle

Vladivostok is the terminus of the 9438 km Trans-Siberian Railway, the world's longest railway

Lake Baikal is the world's oldest and deepest lake

▶ Russia stretches 10,000 km – almost a third of the way around the world – from the open steppes south of Moscow to the chilly pine forests of the Kamchatka in the east.

- **Capital:** Moscow. Area: 17,075,400 sq km. Currency: Rouble. Language: Russian.

- **Physical features:** Highest mountain: Mt Elbrus (5642m). Longest river: Yenisey-Angara (5540 km).

- **Population:** 147.7 million. Population density: 9/sq km. Life expectancy: men 60.7 years; women 72.9 years.

- **Wealth:** GDP: $330 billion. GDP per head: $2270. Exports: fuels and lubricants, metals, machinery, transport equipment.

- **Russia** or the Russian Federation is the country created by the Russians after the break up of the Soviet Union in 1991. It includes republics such as Chechnya, Osetiya, Kalmykiya, Tatarstan, Mordoviya and Bashkortostan. Many of these republics, such as Chechnya, are waiting to be independent.

▼ *The Ural mountains run from north to south forming a natural boundary between Russia and Siberia, Europe and Asia.*

- **Russia is** the biggest country in the world, almost twice as big as the next country, Canada. It stretches from the subtropical south to the Arctic north, where it has the longest Arctic coastline of any country.

- **Russia has huge** mineral resources and is among the world's leading producers of oil, natural gas, coal, asbestos, manganese, silver, tin and zinc. It also has giant forests for timber in the east in Siberia.

- **Russia** has some of the biggest factories in the world around Moscow, producing everything from high-tech goods to iron and steel and trucks. Yet in the far north and east, people still live as they have done for many thousands of years, herding reindeer or hunting.

- **After the USSR broke up**, Russia and its people were plunged into crisis. Encouraged by western nations, Russian presidents – first Boris Yeltsin, then Vladimir Putin – have tried to establish a free market economy in place of the old communist one.

> ★ STAR FACT ★
> In Yakutsk in Siberia, winter temperatures can plunge to -69°C while summers can soar to 39°C – more extreme than anywhere else. Oymyakon is the world's coldest village. It once had temperatures of -72°C.

New Zealand

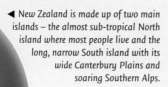

◀ New Zealand is made up of two main islands – the almost sub-tropical North island where most people live and the long, narrow South island with its wide Canterbury Plains and soaring Southern Alps.

- **Capital:** Wellington. Area: 270,534 sq km. Currency: NZ dollar. Language: English.

- **Physical features:** Highest mountain: Mt Cook (3754 m). Longest river: Waikato (425 km).

- **Population:** 3.8 million. Population density: 14/sq km. Life expectancy: men 74.3 years; women 79.9 years.

- **Wealth:** GDP: $74.7 billion. GDP per head: $19,660.

- **Exports:** Meat, milk, butter, cheese, wool, fish, fruit.

- **New Zealand** was one of the last places to be inhabited by humans and remains a clean, beautiful land, with rolling farmland, thick forests and towering mountains.

- **New Zealand** is mainly a farming country, with 64% of the land devoted to crops and pasture for sheep and cattle. 60% of New Zealand's exports are farm produce.

- **Fast-flowing** rivers provide 61% of New Zealand's power through hydroelectric plants. Geothermal energy from hot springs provides some of the rest. Nuclear power is banned.

- **The first** inhabitants of New Zealand were the Maoris, who came about AD900 and now form 14.2% of the population. The remaining 85.8% are mostly descended from British and Irish settlers who came in the 19th and 20th centuries.

> ★ STAR FACT ★
> There are 45 million sheep in New Zealand – 12 sheep to every person!

Yellowstone Park

- **Yellowstone** is the oldest and best-known national park in the USA. It was established by Act of Congress on March 1, 1872.

- **It is one of the world's largest** parks covering 8987 sq km of rugged mountains and spectacular deep valleys.

- **It is situated** across Wyoming, Montana and Idaho.

- **Yellowstone** is famous for its lakes and rivers such Yellowstone Lake and Snake River.

- **Most of Yellowstone** is forested in lodgepole pines, along with other conifers, cottonwoods and aspens. It also has a wealth of wild flowers.

▼ Yellowstone sits on top of a volcanic hot spot which gives it its famous geysers and hot springs – and may make it the site of the biggest eruption of all time.

- **Yellowstone's** wild animals include bison, elk, bighorn sheep, moose, grizzly bears and wolves.

- **Yellowstone** has the world's greatest concentration of geothermal features including 10,000 hot springs and 300 geysers, as well as steam vents, mud cauldrons, fumaroles and paint pots.

- **The most famous geyser** is Old Faithful, which spouts every hour or so. The biggest is the 115 m Steamboat.

- **One of the biggest** volcanic eruptions ever occured in Yellowstone Park two million years ago. Enough lava poured out in one go to build six Mt Fujiyamas.

- **There are signs** that Yellowstone may soon erupt as a 'supervolcano' – an eruption on an unimaginable scale.

International organizations

◀ The Red Cross was set up by Swiss Jean Dunant in the 19th century after he witnessed the bloody slaughter at the battle of Solferino in Italy. It now plays a vital role in helping suffering people everywhere.

- **International organizations** are of three main types: those set up by governments, like the UN; multinationals; and human rights and welfare organizations like the Red Cross and Amnesty International.

- **The United Nations** or UN was formed after World War II to maintain world peace and security. It now has over 190 member nations.

- **UN headquarters** are in New York City. The name was coined by US President Roosevelt in 1941.

- **All UN members** meet in the General Assembly. It has five permanent members (Russia, USA, China, France and UK) and ten chosen every two years.

- **The UN** has agencies responsible for certain areas such as children (UNICEF), food and farming (FAO), health (WHO), science (UNESCO) and nuclear energy (IAEA).

- **Multinationals** or TNCs (transnational corporations) are huge companies that work in many countries.

- **TNCs** like Coca-Cola and Kodak are well known; others like cigarette-makers Philip Morris are less known.

- **Some TNCs** take in more money than most countries. Just 500 TNCs control 70% of all the world's trade.

- **90% of world** grain is handled by six big US TNCs. Cargill and Continental alone control half the world's grain.

- **Amnesty International** was founded in 1961 to campaign for those imprisoned for religious and political beliefs.

Italy

- **Capital:** Rome. Area 301,277 sq km. Currency: euro. Language: Italian.

- **Physical features:** Highest mountain: Monte Bianco di Courmayeur (4760 m). Longest river: Po (652 km).

- **Population:** 57.3 million. Population density: 190/sq km. Life expectancy: men 75.4 years; women 82.1.

- **Wealth:** GDP: $1240 billion. GDP per head: $21,650.

- **Exports:** Wine, machinery, cars and trucks, footwear, clothes, olive oil, textiles, mineral products.

- **Italy** is a narrow, mountainous country. The north is cool and moist, with big industrial cities. Tuscany and Umbria have rich farmland and ancient cities famous for their art treasures. The south is hot, dusty and often poor.

- **Vines and olives** are grown widely and Italy is one of the world's main producers of both wine and olive oil.

- **Italy is one of the biggest** industrial nations. Industry is concentrated in the north in cities like Turin and Milan.

▲ The ancient city of Venice is set on 117 islands in a lagoon. Instead of streets, there are 177 canals, plied by boats called gondolas.

- **Italians** like to dress in style and the fashion trade is big business. Italian fashion labels like Armani, Versace, Valentino, Moschino and Gucci are now world famous.

- **Italy is full of beautiful** historic towns like Florence, Padua and Mantua, many dating from the Renaissance.

Rich and poor

▶▼ Expensive cars and fine foods are often seen as status symbols for the wealthy.

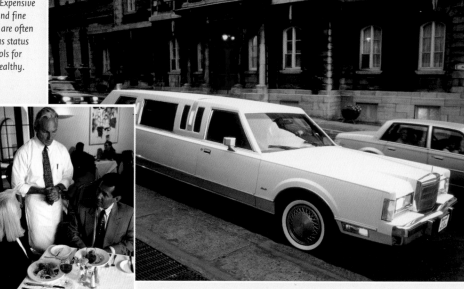

> ★ STAR FACT ★
> About half a billion people are starving or don't get enough to eat.

- **The world's richest country** is the USA, with a GDP of $8650 billion ($31,330 per head). But Luxembourg has an even higher GDP per head – $45,320.

- **The world's poorest country** by GDP per head is Sierra Leone. Each person has, on average, $130, but many are even poorer.

- **The world's richest countries** with less than a quarter of the world's population take three-quarters of its wealth.

- **Most of the world's rich countries** are in the Northern Hemisphere. Most poor countries are in the South. So people talk of the North-South divide.

- **One billion people** around the world live in 'absolute poverty'. This means they have no real homes. In cities, they sleep rough or live in shacks. They rarely have enough to eat or drink.

- **In the 1970s** richer countries encouraged poorer countries like Mexico and Brazil to borrow money to build new dams and industrial works.

- **By 1999** poor countries were paying $12 in debt interest for every $1 rich countries were donating in aid.

- **Famine** has become a common problem in the poorer parts of the world. One reason is that so much farmland is used for growing crops for export – raising the cost of food, and restricting the land available for growing food for local people.

- **250,000** children die a week from a poor diet. 250,000 die a month from diarrhoea, because of a lack of clean water.

◀ Since 1960, the divide between North and South has grown wider leaving many in abject poverty.

Israel

- **Capital:** Jerusalem. Area: 20,770 sq km. Currency: New Shekel. Languages: Hebrew, Arabic.
- **Physical features:** Highest mountain: Mt Meron (1208 m). Longest river: River Jordan (325 km).
- **Population:** 6.1 million. Population density: 299/sq km. Life expectancy: men 75 years; women 79.9 years.
- **Wealth:** GDP: $107.2 billion. GDP per head: $17,570.
- **Exports:** Diamonds, chemicals and chemical products, fruit and vegetables, machinery.
- **Israel** was founded in 1948 as a home for Jews who have since come here from all over the world.
- **The city of Jericho** may be the oldest in the world, dating back more than 10,000 years.

- **Some people** in rural areas work on kibbutzim – collective farms where work and profits are shared.
- **Israel is famous** for its Jaffa oranges, named after Jaffa, the old name for a town close to Tel Aviv. They are grown on the Plain of Sharon.

> ★ STAR FACT ★
> Jerusalem is sacred for three major religions: Judaism, Islam and Christianity.

Rome

- **Rome** is the capital of Italy, and its biggest city, with a population of almost three million.
- **Rome's Vatican** is the home of the Pope.
- **The Vatican** is the smallest independent country in the world covering just 0.4 sq km.
- **Rome is known** as the Eternal City because of its importance within the Roman Empire.
- **Ancient Rome ruled** much of Europe and the lands around the Mediterranean for hundreds of years as the capital of the Roman Empire.
- **Ancient Rome** was famously built on seven hills – the Aventine, Caelian, Capitoline, Esquiline, Palatine, Quirinal and Viminal.
- **Rome has** one of the richest collections of art treasures and historic buildings in the world. The Trevi is one of many beautiful fountains.
- **There are many Ancient Roman** relics in Rome including the Colosseum arena and the Pantheon.

▲ St Peter's Church is located in the Vatican city in Rome.

- **The Vatican's** Sistine Chapel has a ceiling painted brilliantly by Michelangelo and frescoes (wall paintings) by Botticelli, Ghirlandaio and Perugino.
- **Rome is** now a major centre for film-making, publishing and tourism.

Peoples of Africa

- **Africa has been** inhabited longer than any other continent. The earliest human fossils were found here.

- **In the north** in countries such as Algeria, Morocco and Egypt, people are mainly Arabic.

- **The Berber people** were the first people to live in northwest Africa, with a culture dating back to at least 2400BC. Their culture survives in remote villages in the Atlas mountains of Algeria and Morocco.

- **Tuaregs** are camel-herding nomads who live in the Sahara desert, but much of their traditional grazing land has been taken over by permanent farms.

- **South of the Sahara** most people are black Africans.

◄ Zulus are Bantu-speaking people who live in South Africa. They have a proud warrior tradition.

- **There are more than 3000** ethnic groups of black Africans.

- **Over 1,000** different languages are spoken in Africa.

- **Most people** in southern Africa speak English or one of 100 Bantu languages such as Zulu or Swahili.

- **Many people** in rural southern Africa live in round houses.

- **Africa was ruled** by the Europeans as colonies. By the early 20th century the country was divided into nations. Many small groups became dominated by tribes and cultures perhaps hostile to their own.

Turkey and Cyprus

- **Turkey:** Capital: Ankara. Population: 65.7 million. Currency: Turkish Lira. Language: Turkish.

- **Cyprus:** Capital: Nicosia. Population: 757,000. Currency: Cyprus pound. Languages: Greek and Turkish.

- **Turkey lies** partly in Europe, partly in Asia.The two continents are separated by a narrow sea called the Bosphorus.

◄ A hubble-bubble is a special pipe popular in Turkey. Sucking on the long pipe draws the smoke bubbling through water.

- **Turkey is a republic** with a mix of Islamic and Western traditions.

- **Istanbul** is one of the world's great historic capital cities. As Byzantium, it was capital of the Byzantine Empire for 1,000 years. Then it was Constantinople, the capital of the great Ottoman Empire for 500 years, until 1923.

- **Street cafés** are popular with Turkish men, who come to drink thick, dark, sweet Turkish coffee, smoke pipes called hubble-bubbles and play backgammon.

- **An estimated 25 million Kurds** live on the borders of Turkey, Iran, Iraq and Syria and have no country of their own.

- **31% Turkish people** live in the country growing wheat, cotton, tobacco, sugar beet, fruit and tea.

- **Turkey's national motto** is Yurtta sulh, Cihand sulh ('Peace at home, peace in the world').

- **Turkish food** is famous for its shish kebabs – cubes of meat and vegetables barbecued on a skewer.

Venezuela & neighbours

▲ Venezuela and its neighbours lie along the northern coast of South America, along the edge of the tropical waters of the Caribbean.

- **Venezuela:** Capital: Caracas. Population: 24.2 million. Currency: Bolivar. Language: Spanish.
- **Colombia:** Capital: Bogota. Population: 42.3 million. Currency: Colombian peso. Language: Spanish.

- **Guyana:** Capital: Georgetown. Population: 875,000. Currency: Guyana dollar. Official language: English.
- **Suriname:** Capital: Paramaribo. Population: 452,000. Currency: Suriname guilder. Language: Dutch.
- **French Guiana:** Capital: Cayenne. Population: 173,000. Currency: euro. Language: French.
  - **The discovery of oil** in Venezuela's Lake Maracaibo in 1917 turned it from one of South America's poorest countries to one of its richest.
  - **The Venezuelan city** of Merida has the world's highest cable car (altitude 4764m).
  - **The world's highest waterfall** is the Angel Falls in Venezuela, plunging 979 m.
  - **The Yanomami** are a native people who survive in remote forest regions of Venezuela and live by hunting with spears and gathering roots and fruit.
- **Kourou** in French Guiana is the launch site for European spacecraft such as the Ariane.

New York

> ★ STAR FACT ★
> New York is the USA's largest port and the finance centre of the world.

- **New York City** is the largest city in the USA and one of the largest in the world, with a population of 8 million.
- **Over 21 million people** live in the New York metropolitan area.
- **New York has five** boroughs: Manhattan, Brooklyn, the Bronx, Queens and Staten Island.
- **Manhattan** is the oldest part of the city, and is home to many attractions, including Central Park, Greenwich Village, the Rockefeller Center and Wall Street.
- **The 381 m high** Empire State Building, on Fifth Avenue, is one of the world's tallest and most famous buildings.
- **New York's most famous** statue is the Statue of Liberty, erected in 1886 at the entrance to New York harbour.
- **Dutch settler** Peter Minuit is said to have bought

Manhattan island from the Iroquois Indians for trinkets with a value of $24.

- **New York** began in 1614 with the Dutch settlement of Fort Orange. It was renamed New York in 1664.
- **New York's famous** finance centre Wall Street is named after a protective wall built by Dutch colonists in 1653.

▼ The skyscrapers of Manhattan give New York one of the most famous skylines in the world.

Population

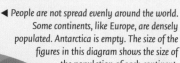

- **The world's population** climbed above 6 billion in 1999.

- **Over a quarter** of a million babies are born every day around the world.

- **World population** is growing at a rate of about 1.22% per year.

- **At the current rate** world population will hit 7.5 billion by 2020.

- **Between 1950** and 1990, the world's population doubled from about 2.5 billion to 5 billion, adding 2.5 billion people in 40 years.

- **The 1990s** added a billion people. The next decade will add 800 million. This adds 1.8 billion in 20 years.

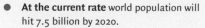

Asia: 60.7%

Oceania: 0.5%

Africa: 12.7%

Europe: 12.4 %

Antarctica: 0%

South America: 8.5%

North America: 5.2%

◄ *People are not spread evenly around the world. Some continents, like Europe, are densely populated. Antarctica is empty. The size of the figures in this diagram shows the size of the population of each continent. The size of the segment the figure is standing on shows the area of the continent.*

- **Asia has** about 60% of the world's population. China alone has 1.3 billion people and India has 1 billion.

- **The number of babies** born to each woman varies from 1.11 in Bulgaria to 7.11 in Somalia.

- **Latvia** has 100 women to every 86 men; Qatar has 184 men to every 100 women.

- **In the developed world** people are living longer. In Andorra people expect to live 83 years on average. In Mozambique, people only expect to live 36.5 years.

Berlin

- **Berlin** is Germany's capital and largest city, with a population of about 3.4 million.

- **Berlin** was originally capital of Prussia, which expanded to become Germany in the 1800s.

- **The city** was wrecked by Allied bombs in World War II.

- **After the War** Berlin was left inside the new communist East Germany and split into East and West by a high wall.

> ★ STAR FACT ★
> Almost every Berliner has a fragment of the Wall, torn down in 1989.

- **East Berlin** was the capital of East Germany; the West German capital moved to Bonn.

- **In 1989** the East German government collapsed and the Berlin Wall was torn down. East and West Germany were united in 1990 and Berlin was made capital again.

- **The Brandenburg Gate** is a huge stone arch built in 1791. It now marks the boundary between east and west.

- **Kurfurstendamm** is a famous shopping avenue. The Hansa quarter was designed by architects in the 1950s.

- **Since reunification** many spectacular new buildings have been built in Berlin including the refurbished Reichstag designed by Norman Foster.

◄ *When Germany was reunited, the old Reichstag became home of the German parliament again. It has now been given a major facelift.*

The USA

The Great Lakes hold a fifth of the world's fresh water

Seattle

Rocky Mountains

Cascade Range

Coast Ranges

Lake Superior

NEW ENGLAND

Lake Michigan

Detroit

Chicago

New York

Great Basin

WASHINGTON DC

San Francisco

CALIFORNIA

Grand Canyon

Appalachian Mountains

Los Angeles

Atlanta

The Pilgrim Fathers of the famous ship the **Mayflower** landed at Plymouth, Massachusetts in 1620

Houston

New Orleans

FLORIDA

Miami

Disney World in Orlando, Florida, is one of the world's biggest theme parks

► The United States is the richest and most powerful country in the world. Nearly 280 million people live here, and it covers a vast area of North America, from the freezing wastes of Alaska to the hot and steamy Everglades (marshes) of Florida.

Where it flows into the Gulf of Mexico, North America's longest river the Mississippi creates a huge delta

- **Capital:** Washington DC. Area: 9,529,063 sq km. Currency: US dollar. Language: English.

- **Physical features:** Highest mountain: Mt McKinley (6194 m). Longest river: the Mississippi-Missouri-Red Rock (6020 km).

- **Population:** 281.4 million. Population density: 29/sq km. Life expectancy: men 73.4 years; women 80.1 years.

- **Wealth:** GDP: $8650 billion. GDP per head: $30,725.

- **Exports:** Road vehicles, chemicals, aircraft, generators, machinery, office equipment, scientific instruments.

- **Native Americans lived** in North America for 10,000 years before the Europeans arrived in the 16th century and gradually drove westwards, brushing the Native Americans aside. In 1788, English colonists founded the United States of America, now the world's oldest democratic republic, with a famous constitution (set of laws).

- **The USA** is the world's fourth largest in area, third largest in population, and has the largest GDP.

- **In the 1950s and 60s** Americans earned more money, ate more food, used more energy and drove more cars than anyone else in the world.

> ★ STAR FACT ★
> One in two Americans owns a computer – more than any other country in the world.

- **Now the USA** is the world's prime consumer of energy, oil, copper, lead, zinc, aluminium, corn, coffee and cocoa. It is also prime producer of aluminium and corn, and one of the top five producers of energy, oil, copper, lead, zinc, wheat and sugar.

▼ Through the films made in Hollywood, California, most of the world has become familiar with the American 'dream' of success.

Moscow and St Petersburg

▲ St Petersburg is an elegant city with many beautiful houses and palaces such as the famous Hermitage museum.

> ★ STAR FACT ★
> Leningrad was dubbed 'Hero City' for its desperate defence against the Nazis from 1941-44.

- **Moscow's biggest shop** is Detsky Mir (Children's World).
- **Moscow's historic centre** is Red Square and the Kremlin, the walled city-within-a-city.
- **In the past** Moscow had wooden buildings and was often burnt down, most famously by Napoleon's troops in 1812.
- **Moscow is snow-covered** from November to April each year, but snow-ploughs keep all the main roads clear.
- **St Petersburg** is Russia's second largest city.
- **St Petersburg** was founded in 1703 by Tsar Peter the Great to be his capital instead of Moscow.
- **After the 1917 Russian Revolution**, communists called Petersburg (then called Petrograd) Leningrad and made Moscow capital. St Petersburg regained its name in 1991.

- **Moscow** is the largest city in the Russian Federation and capital of Russia.
- **Moscow** is Russia's main industrial centre, with huge textile and car-making plants, like the Likhachyov works.

India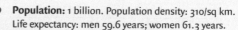

- **Capital:** New Delhi. Area: 3,287,263 sq km. Currency: Indian rupee. Languages: Hindi and English.
- **Physical features:** Highest mountain: K2 (8607 m). Longest river: Ganges (2510 km).

▼ Hindu women in India traditionally wear beautifully coloured wraps or saris made of fine cloth such as silk.

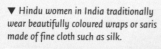

- **Population:** 1 billion. Population density: 310/sq km. Life expectancy: men 59.6 years; women 61.3 years.
- **Wealth:** GDP: $473.4 billion. GDP per head: $464.
- **Exports:** Gems, jewellery, clothes, cotton, fish, rice, textiles, engineering goods.
  - **India has heavy** monsoon rains for six months of the year and dry weather for the rest.
  - **India is the world's** largest democracy.
  - **Two-thirds** of India's population grow their own food, mainly rice and wheat.
  - **India's wheat production** has doubled since the Green Revolution of the 1960s when high-yield hybrids were introduced – but much wheat is sold abroad, pushing prices too high for many poor Indians.
- **India is the world's** 12th biggest industrial nation. Textiles remain important, but there is a growing emphasis on heavy industry, including iron and steel, vehicles, machine tools and pharmaceuticals.

Brazil

- **Capital:** Brasilia. Area: 8,547,404 sq km. Currency: Real. Language: Portuguese.

- **Physical features:** Highest mountain: Neblina (3014 m). Longest river: Amazon (6448 km).

- **Population:** 169.2 million. Population density: 19/sq km. Life expectancy: men 63.7 years; women 71.7 years.

- **Wealth:** GDP: $990 billion. GDP per head: $5845.

- **Exports:** Iron ore, coffee, timber, sugar, transport equipmet.

- **Brazil has one of** the biggest national debts of any country in the world – not far short of $200 billion.

◄ Brazil is the world's fifth largest country, but most people live on the eastern edge. Much of the central area is cerrado (grass wilderness) or thick Amazon rainforest.

- **Brazil** is the world's biggest coffee grower. Soya, sugarcane, cotton, oranges, bananas and cocoa are also major crops.

- **The city of São Paulo** has grown faster than any other big city in the world and now 17.8 million people live there. Housing shortages in cities such as Rio de Janeiro and São Paulo mean 25 million Brazilians live in rickety sheds in sprawling shanty towns called favelas.

- **Brazilians are soccer-mad** and have won the World Cup more times than any other country.

- **The Amazon basin** contains the world's largest area of virgin rainforest – but an area almost the size of Ireland is being cleared each year for short-term cattle ranching.

North European food

- **Fish and bread** play a major role in the traditional Scandinavian diet.

- **Gravadlax** is a Swedish form of smoked salmon, usually served with pepper, dill and mustard sauce.

- **Smörgåsbord** is a Swedish speciality. It is a huge spread of bread and cold foods, including fish such as herring and salmon, and also cheeses.

- **Smörgåsbord** gets its name from the Swedish smörgås, meaning bread and bord, meaning table.

- **Every region in Germany** has its own range of foods, but things like wurst (sausages), pretzels and sauerkraut (pickled cabbage) are widely popular.

- **The German national drink** is beer, and every October a huge beer festival is held in Munich.

- **England is well known** for its hearty stews and winter roasts, especially roast beef. But the most popular food for those eating out is Indian.

- **An English speciality** is fish (deep-fried in batter) and chips (fried slices of potato).

- **Vienna** in Austria is renowned for its coffee houses where the Viennese sit and eat Kaffee und Kuchen (coffee and cakes).

- **Poland is famous** for its rye bread and thick beet.

▼ The seas around Northern Europe were once teeming with fish and fish still plays a major role in the diet of people here.

Japan

- **Capital:** Tokyo. Area: 377,835 sq km. Currency: Yen. Language: Japanese.

- **Physical features:** Highest mountain: Mt Fujiyama (3776 m). Longest river: the Shinano-gawa (367 km).

- **Population:** 127 million. Population density: 337/sq km. Life expectancy: Men 77.6 years; women 84.2 years.

- **Wealth:** GDP: $4555 billion. GDP per head: $35,830.

- **Exports:** Electronic goods, steel, cars, ships, chemicals, textiles, machinery.

- **Japan** is very mountainous, so the big cities where nine out of ten people live are crowded into the coastal plains. 40 million people are crammed into Tokyo and its suburbs alone, making it the biggest urban centre in the world. Tokyo and the nearby cities have tall skyscrapers to make the most of the limited space available – but also with deep foundations, because Japan is prone to earthquakes.

- **Japan** is famous for its electronic goods – including walkmans and games consoles. It also makes huge amounts of steel, half the world's ships and more cars than any other country.

The Seikan Tunnel links Hokkaido to Honshu under the stormy Tsugaru Straits

The Hida, Japan's highest mountains, are also known as the Japanese Alps

◄ Japan is made up of four large islands – Hokkaido, Honshu, Shikoku and Kyushu – and nearly 4,000 smaller ones, stretching over almost 2400 km of the western Pacific Ocean. 75% of Japanese people live on Honshu, the largest island. But the most densely populated is Kyushu. After some gigantic engineering projects in the late 20th century, Kyushu, Honshu, Shikoku and other islands are now all linked by bridges and tunnels. The massive Seto Ohashi bridge links several islands. The bridge from Honshu to Shikoku at Akashi-Kaikyo has the world's longest single span – 2 km. Hokkaido and Honshu are linked by the Seikan tunnel, the world's longest undersea tunnel, 53.85 km long.

- **All but 14%** of the land is too steep for farming, but millions of little square rice fields are packed on to the coastal plains and on hillside terraces.

- **Most Japanese live** a very modern way of life. But traditions still survive and there are many ancient Buddhist and Shinto shrines.

▼ The beautiful, snow-capped Mt Fujiyama is the most famous of Japan's 1500 volcanoes and is sacred to the Shinto religion.

★ STAR FACT ★
Japan has one of the world's largest fishing fleets which hauls in over 5 million metric tonnes of fish a year.

Sapporo

HOKKAIDO

Tsugaru Strait

Sea of Japan

HONSHU

Hida Mountains

● TOKYO

Yokohama

Chūgoku Mountains

Kyoto

Kobe ● Osaka

Hiroshima

Inland Sea

SHIKOKU

Mt Fujiyama

Pacific Ocean

KYUSHU

Nagasaki ●

Australian landmarks

- **Australia's most famous landmark** is Uluru or Ayers Rock, the biggest monolith (single block of stone) in the world, 348 m high and 9 km around.
- **Uluru** is the tip of a huge bed of coarse sand laid down in an inland sea some 600 million years ago.
- **Lake Eyre** is Australia's lowest point, 15 m below sea level. It is also Australia's biggest lake by far, but it is normally dry and fills only once every 50 years or so.
- **Nullarbor plain** is a vast, dry plain in southern Australia. Its name comes from the Latin *nulla arbor* ('no tree').
- **Shark Bay** is famous for its sharks and dolphins.
- **Shark Bay** is also famous for its stromatolites, the world's oldest fossils, dating back 3.5 billion years. These are pizza-like mats made by colonies of blue-green algae.

> ★ STAR FACT ★
> The Great Barrier Reef is the world's largest
> structure made by living things.

▲ *Uluru is sacred to the Aboriginals. On its surface and in its caves are paintings made long ago by Aboriginal artists.*

- **The Murray-Darling River** is Australia's longest river (2739 km long).
- **The Great Barrier Reef** is a coral reef off the coast of Queensland in northwest Australia.
- **The Great Barrier Reef** is the world's biggest coral reef, over 2000 km long.

Ukraine and Belarus

- **Ukraine:** Capital: Kiev. Population: 50.8 million. Currency: Hryvnya. Language: Ukrainian.
- **Belarus:** Capital: Minsk. Population: 10 million. Currency: Belarusian rouble. Language: Belarusian.
- **Ukraine** is Europe's largest country (except for Russia), covering over 603,700 sq km.
- **Ukraine** is famous for its vast plains or *steppes*. The fertile black soils have made it 'the breadbasket of Europe', growing huge amounts of wheat and barley.
- **During the Soviet era** Soviet policies forced Ukrainians to speak Russian and adopt Russian culture, but the Ukrainian identity has been found again since they gained independence in 1991.

▶ *Ukraine and Belarus are flat countries that form the western margin of Russia, north of the Black Sea.*

- **In the Soviet era** over a quarter of Ukraine's industrial output was arms. Now Ukraine is trying to use these factories to make other products.
- **In 1986** a terrible accident occurred at the Chernobyl nuclear power plant north of Kiev. A reactor exploded spreading radioactovity over a wide area.
- **Nuclear energy** still provides 44% of Ukraine's power, but many Ukrainians are firmly against it.
- **Belarus** (known as Byelorussia under the USSR) is a flat country, covered in many places by thick forests and marshes. The Pripet Marshes are the largest in Europe covering 27,000 sq km.
- **Belarus** is known for making heavy-duty trucks, tractors and bicycles among other things. The forests provide products such as furniture, matches and paper.

Peoples of Australia

- **The Aborigines** make up 1.8% of Australia's population today, but they were the first inhabitants.

- **The word aborigine** comes from the Latin *ab origine*, which means 'from the start'.

- **Aborigine cave paintings** and tools have been found in Australia dating back to at least 45,000 years ago.

- **Aborigines** prefer to be called Kooris.

- **British and Irish people** began to settle in Australia about 200 years ago. They now form the majority of the population, along with other white Europeans.

- **Many of the earliest** settlers in Australia were convicts, transported from Britain for minor crimes.

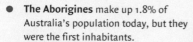

◄ *The Kooris or Aborigines of Australia spread right across the Pacific many thousands of years ago and were probably the first inhabitants of America as well.*

- **Many Australians** have ancestral roots in the British Isles.

- **British and Irish settlers** drove the Aborigines from their land and 60% now live in cities.

- **After hard campaigning** some Aboriginal sacred sites are being returned to them, with their original names. Ayers Rock is now known as Uluru. A famous trial in 1992 returned to Aborigine Eddy Mabo land on Murray Island first occupied by his ancestors before the Europeans arrived.

- **Many recent immigrants** to Australia are from Southeast Asia, Serbia, Croatia and Greece.

Kazakhstan & neighbours

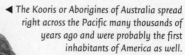

- **Kazakhstan:** Capital: Astana. Population: 16.9 million. Currency: Tenge. Language: Kazakh.

- **Uzbekistan:** Capital: Tashkent. Population: 25 million. Currency: Som. Language: Uzbek.

- **Turkmenistan:** Capital: Ashgabat. Population: 4.5 million. Currency: Manat. Language: Turkmen.

- **Some of the people** in this part of the world are still nomads, moving from place to place in search of new pastures for their herds.

- **Uzbekistan** has become wealthy from natural gas

◄ *The break-up of the Soviet Union left the countries around the Caspian Sea a legacy of some of the world's worst pollution. But they have a wealth of minerals and a venerable history.*

> ★ **STAR FACT** ★
> Kazakhstan has huge iron and coal reserves and the world's largest chrome mine.

and also from cotton, which they call 'white gold'.

- **The Baykonur Cosmodrome** in Kazakhstan is where the Russians launch most of their spacecraft.

- **The Soviet Union** forced nomads in Kalmykia by the Caspian Sea to boost sheep production beyond what the fragile steppe grass could handle. This created 1.4 million acres of desert.

- **The Aral Sea** on the Kazakh/Uzbek border was once the world's fourth largest lake. But irrigating farmland has cut the supply of water from the Amu Darya River and the Aral Sea is now shrinking rapidly.

- **The Caspian Sea** once had the sturgeon fish giving the most highly prized beluga caviar, but pollution has decimated the fish population.

East Africa

▲ *Tanzania is famous for safaris in the Serengeti park where lions, elephants, giraffes and many other animals are seen.*

- **Tanzania:** Legislative capital: Dodoma. Population: 33.7 million. Currency: Shilling. Languages: English, Swahili.

- **Rwanda:** Capital: Kigali. Population: 7.7 million. Currency: Franc. Languages: French, Kinyarwanda.

- **Burundi:** Capital: Bujumbura. Population: 7 million. Currency: Franc. Languages: French, Kirundi.

- **Uganda:** Capital: Kampala. Population: 22.2 million. Currency: Shilling. Languages: Swahili, English.

- **Malawi:** Capital: Lilongwe. Population: 10.9 million. Currency: Kwacha. Languages: Chichewa, English.

- **A fifth of Malawi** is taken up by Lake Nyasa, one of the world's largest, deepest lakes. .

- **The countries** of East Africa are the least urbanized in the world with 9 out of 10 living in the countryside.

- **In 1993 and 1994** Rwanda and Burundi were ravaged by one of the worst genocides in African history as tribal war flared between the Tutsi and Hutu peoples.

- **Lake Victoria** on the Tanzania and Uganda border covers 69,484 sq km, one of the world's largest lakes.

- **Tanzania's** main crops include maize, bananas andrice.

The Gran Chaco

- **The Gran Chaco** is a vast area of tropical grassland in Argentina, Paraguay and Bolivia.

- **It covers** an area of over 720,00 sq km, an area as large as northwest Europe.

- **It is home** to scattered native Indian groups such as the Guaycurú, Lengua, Mataco, Zamuco and Tupi-Guarani people.

- **The word Chaco** comes from the Quechua Indian word for 'Hunting Land' because it is rich in wildlife. *Gran* is Spanish for 'big'.

- **The major activities** on the Chaco are cattle grazing and cotton growing.

- **In the east** huge factories have been built to process tannin from the trees for leather production.

> ★ STAR FACT ★
> The sediments under the Gran Chaco are well over 3,000 m deep in places.

- **In places** grass can grow up to 3 m tall, higher than a rider on horseback.

- **The Chaco** is home to many wild animals, including pumas, tapir, rheas and giant armadillos.

- **The Chaco** is the last refuge of the South American maned or red wolf.

▶ *The jaguar is the Chaco's biggest hunting animal, and the biggest cat in the Americas. Yet unlike other big cats, it never roars. It just makes a strange cry rather like a loud sneeze.*

Poland and neighbours

▲ *Poland and its neighbours cluster around the Baltic Sea.*

- **Poland:** Capital: Warsaw. Population: 38.6 million. Currency: Zloty. Language: Polish.
- **Lithuania:** Capital: Vilnius. Population: 3.7 million. Currency: Litas. Language: Lithuanian.
- **Latvia:** Capital: Riga. Population: 2.4 million. Currency: Lats. Language: Latvian.

- **Estonia:** Capital: Tallinn. Population: 1.4 million. Currency: Kroon. Language: Estonian.
- **Poland** was led away from communism by trade union leader Lech Walesa, who became the first president democratically elected of Poland for 72 years.
- **The name Poland** comes from the Slavic word *polane* which means plain, and much of Poland is flat plains.
- **The shipyards at Gdansk** on the Baltic make Poland the world's fifth largest builder of merchant ships.
- **Krakow** has many historic buildings but the nearby Nowa Huta steelworks make it very polluted.
- **The Traditional way of life** in Latvia, Lithuania and Estonia suffered badly in the Soviet era. They are now rebuilding their identity.
- **Latvian** is one of the oldest European languages, related to the ancient Indian language Sanskrit.

West Coast USA

- **The western USA** is mountainous, with peaks in the Rockies, Cascades and Sierra Nevada soaring over 4,000 m.
- **Seattle** is the home of computer software giant Microsoft, and Boeing, the world's biggest aircraft maker.
- **Seattle** is the home of the Starbucks café chain – made famous by the TV series Frasier.

◀ *Sunset Boulevard in LA is a 32 km long road. Its Sunset Strip section is popular with film stars.*

- **Los Angeles** (LA) sprawls over a larger area than any other city in the world and has endless kilometres of freeways.
- **Film-makers** came to the LA suburb of Hollywood in 1908 because of California's sunshine. It has been the world's greatest film-making centre ever since.
- **The San Andreas fault** is the boundary between two huge continental plates. As it moves it gives west coast cities earthquakes. The worst may be yet to come.
- **San Francisco's** Golden Gate is named after the 1849 rush when prospectors came in thousands to look for gold.
- **California is** known as the 'Sunshine State'.
- **California's** San Joaquin valley is one of the world's major wine-growing regions.

> ★ STAR FACT ★
> Silicon Valley near San Francisco has the world's greatest concentration of electronics firms.

World religions

- **Christianity** is the world's largest religion, with 1.9 billion followers worldwide. Christians believe in a saviour, Jesus Christ, a Jew who lived in Palestine 2,000 years ago. Christ, they believe, was the Son of God. When crucified to death (nailed to a wooden cross), he rose from the dead to join God in heaven.

- **Islam** is the world's second largest religion with 1.3 billion believers. It was founded in Arabia in the 7th century by Mohammed, who Muslims believe was the last, greatest prophet sent by *Allah* (Arabic for God). The word *Islam* means 'act of resignation' and Muslims believe they must obey God totally and live by the holy book *The Koran*.

- **Hinduism** is almost 4,000 years old. Hindus worship many gods, but all believe in *dharma*, the right way to live. Like Buddhists, Hindus believe we all have past lives. By following the *dharma*, we may reach the perfect state of *Moksha* and so need never be born again.

- **Christianity** is split into three branches: Catholics whose leader is the Pope in Rome; Protestants; and the Eastern Orthodox church. Islam is split into Sunnis

and Shi'ites. Shi'ites are the majority in Iraq and Iran.

- **Buddhism** is the religion of 350 million SE Asians. It is based on the teachings of Prince Siddhartha Gautama, the Buddha, who lived in NE India from 563 to 483BC.

- **Judaism** is the religion of Jews. They were the first to believe in a single god, who they called *Yahweh*, over 4,000 years ago. There are over 10 million Jews living outside Israel and 4.4 million living in Israel.

- **Most of the world's** major religions except for Hinduism are monotheistic – that is, they believe in just one God.

- **Three million Muslims** visit their holy city of Mecca in Saudi Arabia every year on pilgrimage.

- **Jains** of India will not take any form of life. They eat neither meat nor fish, nor, usually, eggs. Jain priests often sweep paths in front of them as they go to avoid stepping on insects.

> ★ STAR FACT ★
> The Hindu holy text, the *Bhagaavadgita*, contains almost 100,000 couplets. It is 7 times the length of the Iliad and Odyssey combined.

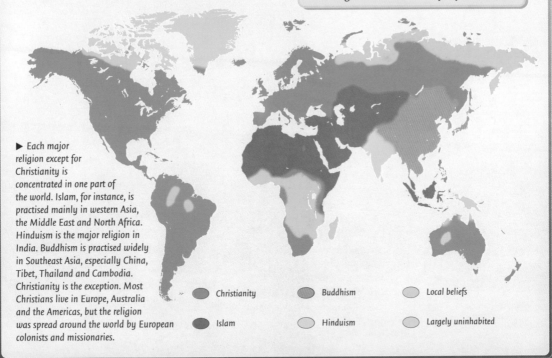

▶ Each major religion except for Christianity is concentrated in one part of the world. Islam, for instance, is practised mainly in western Asia, the Middle East and North Africa. Hinduism is the major religion in India. Buddhism is practised widely in Southeast Asia, especially China, Tibet, Thailand and Cambodia. Christianity is the exception. Most Christians live in Europe, Australia and the Americas, but the religion was spread around the world by European colonists and missionaries.

- Christianity
- Islam
- Buddhism
- Hinduism
- Local beliefs
- Largely uninhabited

Peoples of the Middle East

- **People have farmed** in the Middle East longer than anywhere else in the world.

- **The Middle East** was the site of the first cities and ancient civilizations such as those of Sumer and Babylon.

- **Most people** in the Middle East are Arabs.

- **Arabic is spoken** in all Middle East countries except for Iran where Farsi (Persian) is spoken, Turkey where most speak Turkish and Israel where most speak Hebrew.

- **Most people** in the Middle East are Muslims, but Lebanon has many Christians and Israel is mostly Jewish.

- **Many of the Arab** countries of the Middle East – except Israel – are

▲ *Many people in the Middle East wear traditional Arab head coverings.*

dominated by Islamic traditions.

- **Islamic countries** of the Middle East are often ruled by kings and emirs, sultans and sheikhs who have absolute power. Yemen, Turkey and Israel are all republics.

- **The Jews of Israel** are locked in a conflict with the Arab people the roots of which which date back to the 1920s.

- **The people of the United Arab Emirates** (UAE) are among the richest in the world, with a yearly income of over $25,000 each.

- **The people of Yemen** are among the poorest in the world, with a yearly income of just $325 each.

Central America

- **Central American countries** are: Mexico, Guatemala, Belize, Honduras, El Salvador, Nicaragua, Costa Rica and Panama.

- **Mexico:** Capital: Mexico City. Population: 97 million. Currency: Peso. Language: Spanish.

- **Mexico City** is the world's second largest city after Tokyo, with a population of 18.4 million.

▼ *The Panama Canal cuts right across Central America to link the Atlantic and Pacific Oceans and save ships huge journeys.*

- **Most Central American** countries were torn apart by revolution and civil war in the 1900s, but are now quiet.

- **Mexico owes** in foreign debt almost $167 billion and pays over $37 billion a year back to other countries.

- **Much land** is used for 'cash crops' (crops that can be sold abroad for cash) like coffee rather than for food.

- **Many Central Americans** work the land, growing food for themselves or labouring on plantations.

- **Maize** (corn) has been grown in Mexico for 7,000 years to make things such as tortillas (cornflour pancakes).

- **Bananas** are the most important export in Central American countries, forming a third of Honduras's entire exports. While bananas are grown on lowlands, coffee beans are important exports for highland regions, especially in Nicaragua, Guatemala, Costa Rica and El Salvador.

- **Most of Mexico's people** are mestizos, descendants of both Spanish settlers and American Indians.

Georgia & its neighbours

◄ Georgia, Armenia and Azerbaijan lie in a band between the Black Sea and the Caspian Sea. Georgia and Armenia are mountainous. Azerbaijan contains flat plains.

● **Georgia:** Capital: Tbilisi. Population: 5.4 million. Currency: Lari. Language: Georgian.

● **Armenia:** Capital: Yerevan. Population: 3.7 million. Currency: Dram. Language: Armenian.

● **Azerbaijan:** Capital: Baku. Population: 8 million. Currency: Manat. Language: Azeri.

● **Georgia, Azerbaijan and Armenia** were once part of the Imperial Russia.

● **In Georgia more people** live to be 100 years old than anywhere else in the world except Japan.

● **Georgia's capital Tbilisi** is said to be one of the world's oldest cities.

● **The oil** under the Caspian Sea off Azerbaijan once helped Russia produce half the world's oil. Villages on floating platforms house oilworkers.

● **New oil strikes** suggest there is 200 billion barrels of oil under the Caspian Sea – as much as Iran and Iraq combined.

● **Oil has made** some people around the Caspian Sea rich, while others have remained desperately poor.

● **A 1520 km** pipeline from Kazakhstan's huge Tengiz field to Russia's Black Sea port of Novorossiysk has been opened.

South Africa

◄ Nelson Mandela was the hero of the struggle against apartheid in South Africa. In 1994 he became the country's first president elected by all the people.

● **Capitals:** Pretoria and Cape Town. Area: 1,219,080 sq km. Currency: Rand. Languages: 11 official languages including Zulu, Xhosa, English and Afrikaans.

● **Physical features:** Highest mountain: Injasuti (3408 m). Longest river: the Orange (2092 km).

● **Population:** 43.7 million. Population density: 36/sq km. Life expectancy: men 47.3 years; women 49.7 years.

> ★ STAR FACT ★
> In the 1900s, almost half the world's gold came from South Africa.

● **Wealth:** GDP: $150.3 billion. GDP per head: $3440.

● **Exports:** Gold, diamonds, pearls, metals, metal products, machinery, citrus fruit, wine.

● **Until 1991** people of different races in South Africa were separated by law. This was called apartheid.

● **Apartheid** meant many black people were forced to live in specially built townships such as Soweto. Townships are far from cities and workplaces, so workers must commute for hours each on crowded buses.

● **South Africa** has two capital cities. The administration is in Pretoria and parliament is in Cape Town.

● **The Kruger National Park** supports the greatest variety of wildlife species on the African continent.

Germany

Hamburg is Germany's biggest port

North Sea

Hamburg

Baltic Sea

Germany's northwest is known as Lower Saxony

North German Plain

BERLIN

RUHR • Dortmund

• Düsseldorf

• Cologne

• Bonn

Dresden

When trees began to die from acid rain in the famous Black Forest, many Germans became committed to the Green cause. The country now has strong environment protection laws

• Frankfurt

• Stuttgart

BAVARIA

Black Forest

• Munich

Zugspitze

Alps

Germany's longest river, the Danube rises in the Black Forest in Germany. It empties into the Black Sea

▲ Neuschwanstein, built for 'Mad' King Ludwig II of Bavaria in the 1870s, is the most famous of the many castles in Bavaria and Germany's Rhineland.

▶ The flatter northern part of Germany is a mixture of heath, marsh and rich farmland, where cereals such as rye are widely grown. The south is mountainous, with powerful rivers flowing through deep, wooded valleys.

- **Capital:** Berlin. Area: 356,973 sq km. Currency: euro. Language: German.

- **Physical features:** Highest mountain: Zugspitze (2962 m). Longest river: Danube (2850 km).

- **Population:** 82.7 million. Population density: 231/sq km. Life expectancy: men 74 years; women 80.3 years.

- **Wealth:** GDP: $2257 billion. GDP per head: $27,300.

- **Exports:** Machinery, vehicles, chemicals, iron, steel, textiles, food, wine.

- **Germany** is the world's third biggest industrial nation after the USA and Japan, famous for its precision engineering and quality products, such as tools and machine tools.

- **Germany's smoky industrial** heartland was the Ruhr valley, where dozens of coal mines fed huge steelworks. Many mines and steelworks have now closed and many

people have moved south to places like Stuttgart and Munich to escape unemployment and dirty air. But the Ruhr remains important to industry.

- **Germany is** the world's third biggest car-maker after the USA and Japan. It is well known for its upmarket cars such as Mercedes, BMW and Audi.

- **German farms** are often small, family-run affairs. Yet the country can grow almost all its own food – growing huge quantities of cereal and sugar beet, and raising large numbers of cows and pigs.

North Africa

- **Morocco:** Capital: Rabat. Population: 29 million. Currency: Dirham. Language: Arabic.
- **Algeria:** Capital: Algiers. Population: 31.6 million. Currency: Algerian dinar. Language: Arabic.
- **Tunisia:** Capital: Tunis. Population: 9.8 million. Currency: Tunisian dinar. Language: Arabic.
- **Libya:** Capitals: Tripoli and Surt. Population: 6.4 million. Currency: Libyan dinar. Language: Arabic.
- **Much of** the world's phosphate supply comes from Morocco and Tunisia.
- **Algeria and Libya** both have large reserves of oil and gas.
- **People in Morocco,** Tunisia and Algeria eat a lot of couscous. Couscous is made from wheat which is pounded into hard grains of semolina, then steamed until soft. The couscous is then served with stewed lamb or vegetables.
- **The Moroccan** custom is to eat using the right hand rather than knives and forks.
- **The historic cities** of Fez and Marrakesh in Morocco are famous for their colourful souks or markets, where thousands of tourists each year come to haggle over beautiful hand-woven carpets, leather goods and jewellery.

> ★ STAR FACT ★
> Libya is building the 3870 km Great Manmade River, the world's longest water pipe, to irrigate 800sq km of land.

▶ The coastal areas of northwest Africa have warm, Mediterranean climates and farmers grow things like olives and citrus fruits.

Pacific food

- **Most places** around the Pacific are near the sea, so fish plays an important part in diets.
- **In Japan** fish is often eaten raw in thin slices called sashimi, or cooked with vegetables in batter as a dish called tempura, often served with soy sauce.
- **At home** most Japanese eat traditional foods including rice and noodles, as well as fish, tofu and vegetables or eggs.
- **When out,** many Japanese people eat American-style foods from fast food restaurants.
- **The Japanese** eat only half as much rice now as they did in 1960, as younger people prefer bread and doughnuts.
- **Younger Japanese** people have a diet richer in protein and fat than their parents', so grow 8–10 cm taller.
- **Pacific islanders** traditionally ate fish like bonito and tuna and native plants like breadfruit, coconuts, sweet potatoes and taro. They made flour from sago palm pith.
- **Many islanders** now eat mainly canned Western food and suffer malnutrition.
- **Filippino** food is a mix of Chinese, Malay, American and Spanish. *Adobo* is chicken or pork in soy sauce.
- **Some Australians** now often eat 'fusion' food which blends Asian with European cooking styles.

▶ Lightly grilled or barbecued giant prawns and other seafood play a major role in Pacific food.

London

▲ London's Houses of Parliament and its tower with its bell Big Ben were built in 1858 after a fire destroyed an earlier building.

- **London** is the capital of the United Kingdom and its largest city by far, with a population of about 7.2 million.

- **People have settled** here for thousands of years, but the city of London began with the Roman city of Londinium.

- **Throughout the 19th century** London was the world's biggest city, with a million people, and the hub of the world's largest empire, the British Empire.

- **London** is based on two ancient cities: the City of London, which developed from the Roman and Saxon towns, and Westminster, which developed around the palaces of English kings around 1,000 years ago.

- **London** has 500,000 factory workers, but most people work in services, such as publishing and other media. London is one of the world's major finance centres.

- **Eight million tourists** come to London each year.

- **London's tallest building** is 244 m Canary Wharf tower.

- **The London Eye** is the biggest wheel in the world, giving people a bird's eye view over London.

- **London's oldest large buildings** are the Tower of London and Westminster Abbey, both 1,000 years old. The Tower of London was built for William the Conqueror.

> ★ STAR FACT ★
> 700,000 people work in banking and finance
> – more than in any other city in the world.

Iraq and Iran

- **Iran:** Capital: Tehran. Population: 76.4 million. Currency: Iranian rial. Language: Persian (Farsi).

- **Iraq:** Capital: Baghdad. Population: 23.1 million. Currency: Iraqi dinar. Language: Arabic.

- **Iran is the largest** non-Arabic country in the Middle East.

- **Iran was once** called Persia, and was the centre of an empire ruled by the Shah that dates back thousands of years. The last Shah was overthrown in 1979.

- **Iran is an Islamic** country, and the strong views of religious leader Ayatollah Khomeini (who died in 1989) played a key role in the revolution in 1979, which brought him to power.

▶ Iraq and Iran are mostly hot, dry countries, but Iran is much more mountainous, ringed by the Zagros and Elburz mountains.

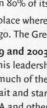

- **Iran is famous for its carpets,** often called Persian carpets. They are Iran's second largest export, after oil. Oil brings Iran 80% of its export earnings.

- **Iraq** was the place where civilization probably began 7,000 years ago. The Greeks called it Mesopotamia.

- **Between 1979 and 2003,** Iraq was ruled by Saddam Hussein and his leadership brought the country into conflict with much of the world – especially when he invaded Kuwait and started the Gulf War in 1991 when the USA and other nations retaliated.

- **Only about** a sixth of Iraq is suitable for farming and so it has to import much of its food, but it is one of the world's major oil producers.

- **United Nations** sanctions applied after the Gulf War still restrict trade with Iraq.

West Africa

- **West African countries** are: Cape Verde, Liberia, Equatorial Guinea, Niger, Mauritania, Mali, Burkina Faso, Senegal, Gambia, Guinea Bissau, Liberia, Guinea, Ivory Coast, Ghana, Sierra Leone, Togo, Benin and São Tomé and Príncipe. All have populations under 10 million except for Ghana, Ivory Coast and Mali.

- **Ghana:** Capital: Accra. Population: 18.4 million. Currency: Cedi. Language: English.

- **Ivory Coast:** Capital: Yamoussoukro. Population: 15.1 million. Currency: CFA franc. Language: French.

- **Mali:** Capital: Bamako. Population: 12.6 million. Currency: CFA franc. Language: French.

▲ Ivory Coast alone grows 40% of the world's cocoa beans. Here beans are drying in the sun.

- **West Africa** grows over half the world's cocoa beans.

- **Yams** are a vital part of the diet of people in West Africa, often providing breakfast, dinner and tea.

- **West Africa** is rich in gold and diamonds, which once sustained ancient Mali and its capital of Timbuktu.

- **Ghana and Guinea** are rich in bauxite (aluminium ore).

- **Ghana** was called Gold Coast by Europeans because of the gold used by the Ashanti peoples there.

- **Ghana** is still poor, but many of its young people are the best educated in Africa.

Peoples of North America

- **82%** of the population of North America are white descendants of immigrants from Europe.

- **Among the smaller groups** 13% are black, 3% are Asian and 1% are American Indians.

- **Hispanics** are descended from a mix of white, black and American Indian people from Spanish-speaking countries of Latin America such as Mexico, Puerto Rico and Cuba. 12% of the US population is Hispanic.

- **92%** of the population of the USA was born there. Many new immigrants are Hispanic.

- **The original peoples** of North America were the American Indians who were living here for thousands of years before Europeans arrived.

▲ The original peoples of North America were the Indians, but they have been overwhelmed by European settlers.

- **The native people** of America were called Indians by the explorer Christopher Columbus, but they have no collective name for themselves. Most American Indians prefer to be identified by tribe.

- **There are about** 540 tribes in the USA. The largest are the Cherokee, Navajo, Chippewa, Sioux and Choctaw.

- **Most black Americans** are descendants of Africans brought here as slaves from 1600 to 1860.

- **Most European** immigrants before 1820 were from Britain, so the main language is English.

- **Spanish** is spoken by many Americans and French is spoken by 24% of Canadians.

The Amazon

- **The Amazon River** in South America is the world's second longest river (6448 km), and carries far more water than any other river.

- **The Amazon basin** – the area drained by the Amazon and its tributaries – covers over 7 million sq km and contains the world's largest tropical rainforest.

- **Temperatures** in the Amazon rainforest stay about 27°C all year round.

- **The Amazon rainforest** contains more species of plant and animal than anywhere else in the world.

- **The Amazon is home** to over 60,000 different plants, 1550 kinds of bird, and 3000 species of fish in its rivers.

- **Manaus** in the Amazon basin has a population of over a million and a famous 19th century opera house.

> ★ STAR FACT ★
> The Amazon basin is home to more than 2 million different kinds of insect.

▲ In its upper reaches in the Andes, the Amazon tumbles over 5000 m in the first 1000 km.

- **Since the 1960s** the Brazilian government has been building highways and airports in the forest.

- **10%** of the forest has been lost for ever as trees are cut for wood, or to clear the way for gold-mining and ranching.

- **Forest** can sometimes regrow, but has far fewer species.

Egypt and neighbours

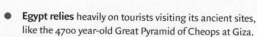

- **Egypt:** Capital: Cairo. Population: 68.1 million. Currency: Egyptian pound. Language: Arabic.

- **Ethiopia:** Capital: Addis Ababa. Population: 66.2 million. Currency: birr. Language: Amharic, Oromo.

- **Sudan:** Capital: Khartoum. Population: 29.8 million. Currency: Sudanese dinar. Language: Arabic.

- **Egypt relies** heavily on tourists visiting its ancient sites, like the 4700 year-old Great Pyramid of Cheops at Giza.

- **99% of Egyptians** live by the River Nile which provides water for farming, industry and drinking. A vast reservoir, Lake Nasser, was created when the Nile was dammed by the Aswan High Dam.

- **Cairo** has a population of 11.6 million and is growing so rapidly there are major housing and traffic problems.

- **Lots of cotton** is grown in Egypt and the Sudan.

- **Sudan is the largest** country in Africa.

- **In the 1980s and 1990s** the people of Ethiopia, Sudan and Somalia suffered dreadful famine. Many people here are still very poor and without enough to eat.

- **Grasslands south of the Sahara** are dotted with acacia thorn trees which ooze a liquid called gum arabic when their bark is cut. This was used in medicine and inks.

◀ Camels have provided desert transport in Egypt for thousands of years. The pyramids of the pharaohs are in the background.

Australia

- **Capital:** Canberra. Area: 7,682,300 sq km. Currency: Australian dollar. Language: English.

- **Physical features:** Highest mountain: Mt Kosciuszko (2230 m). Longest river: Murray-Darling (3750 km).

- **Population:** 18.8 million. Population density: 2/sq km. Life expectancy: men 76.8 years; women 82.2 years.

- **Wealth:** GDP: $428.7 billion. GDP per head: $22,755.

- **Exports:** Ores and minerals, coal, oil, machinery, gold, diamonds, meat, textiles, cereals.

- **Australia** enjoyed its own goldrush when gold was discovered there in 1851.

- **Most of Australia** is so dry only 6% is good for growing crops, although the country sells a lot of wheat.

But huge areas are used for rearing cattle and sheep, many raised on vast farms called 'stations'. Australia is also famous for its wines.

- **Australia has huge amounts** of iron, aluminium, zinc, gold and silver. The Mount Goldsworthy mine in Western Australia alone is thought to have 15 billion tonnes of iron ore. Cannington in Queensland is the world's largest silver mine.

- **Australia's climate** encourages outdoor activities like surfing. Thousands head for Bondi Beach near Sydney on Christmas Day for a party or to surf. Australia is also the world's top cricketing nation.

Darwin

Arnhem Land

Gulf of Carpentaria

Great Barrier Reef

Kimberley Plateau

Great Sandy Desert

QUEENSLAND

Alice Springs

Great Artesian Basin

Lake Eyre

Brisbane

WESTERN AUSTRALIA

Flinders Ranges

Perth

Great Australian Bight

The railtrack across Nullabor Plain is the world's longest straight track

Adelaide

Mt Kosciusko

CANBERRA

Sydney

Melbourne

Bass Strait

TASMANIA

Hobart

The Great Dividing Range divides the moist coastal plain from the dry outback

▲ Australia is the world's smallest continent but sixth biggest country. Much of it is dry and thinly populated. Most people live in the southeast or along the coast.

★ **STAR FACT** ★
Australia's 115 million sheep produce more than a quarter of the world's wool.

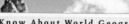

Grand Canyon

- **The Grand Canyon** in Arizona in the southwest USA is one of the most spectacular gorges in the world.

- **The Grand Canyon** is about 466 km long and and varies in width from less than 1 km to over 30 km.

- **In places** the Grand Canyon is so narrow that motorcycle stunt riders have leaped right across from one side to the other.

- **The Grand Canyon** is about 1600 m deep, with almost sheer cliff sides in some places.

- **Temperatures** in the bottom of the Canyon can be as much as 14°C hotter than they are at the top, and the bottom of the Canyon gets only 180 mm of rain per year compared to 660 mm at the top.

▲ The shadows cast by the evening sun reveal the layer upon layer of rock in the steep sides of the Grand Canyon.

- **The Grand Canyon** was cut by the Colorado River over millions of years as the whole Colorado Plateau was rising bit by bit. The bends in the river's course were shaped when it still flowed over the flat plateau on top, then the river kept its shape as it cut down through the rising plateau.

- **As the Colorado** cut down, it revealed layers of limestone, sandstone, shale and other rocks in the cliffs.

- **The Colorado** is one of the major US rivers, 2334 km long.

- **The Hoover Dam** across the Colorado is one of the world's highest concrete dams, 221 m high.

- **The Hoover Dam** creates 185 km long Lake Mead, North America's biggest artificial lake.

Peru and neighbours

- **Peru:** Capital: Lima. Area: 1,285,216 sq km. Currency: Nuevo Sol. Languages: Spanish and Quechua.

- **Physical features:** Highest mountain: Huascaran (6768 m). Longest river: Amazon (6448 km).

- **Population:** 25.7 million. Population density: 20/sq km. Life expectancy: men 65.6 years; women 69.1 years.

- **Wealth:** GDP: $70.2 billion. GDP per head: $2730.

- **Exports:** Fish products, gold, copper, zinc, iron, oil, coffee, llama and alpaca wool, cotton.

- **Peru** is the third largest country in South America. The coastal plain is desert, but Peru's biggest city Lima is here. Inland are the towering Andes mountains, where rivers have cut deep gorges.

- **Peru** was the home of the Inca Empire conquered by the Spaniard Francisco Pizarro in the 1520s. Now it has a larger Indian population than any other South American nation.

- **Peru** is a leading producer of copper, lead, silver and zinc, and a major fishing nation. But most people are poor, especially in the mountains. In the 1990s guerillas called *Sendero Luminoso* (Shining Path) and *Tupac Amaru* sparked off violent troubles.

- **Ecuador:** Capital: Quito. Population: 12.7 million. Currency: US dollar. Language: Spanish.

- **Bolivia:** Capital: La Paz. Population: 8.3 million. Currency: boliviano Language: Spanish.

▶ The llama was for centuries the main source of meat and wool and the main means of transport for people in Peru.

Kenya

- **Capital:** Nairobi. Area: 582,646 sq km. Currency: Kenyan shilling. Languages: Swahili and English.

- **Physical features:** Highest mountain: Mt Kenya (5199 m). Longest river: Tana (708 km).

- **Population:** 30.3 million (est). Population density: 52/sq km. Life expectancy: men 47.3 years; women 48.1 years.

- **Wealth:** GDP: $11.5 billion. GDP per head: $380.

- **Exports:** Tea, coffee, fruit, flowers, vegetables, petroleum products.

- **Remains of early human ancestors** found by Lake Turkana show people have lived in Kenya for millions of years.

- **Much of Kenya** is a vast, dry, grassland plain, home to spectacular wildlife such as lions, giraffes and elephants. They attract thousands of tourists each year.

- **Most Kenyans** live on small farm settlements, raising crops and livestock for themselves, but there are big cash crop plantations for tea, coffee, vegetables and flowers.

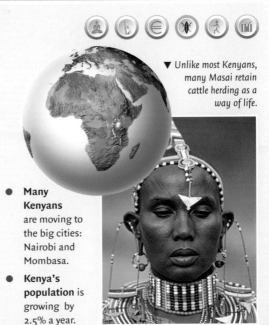

▼ Unlike most Kenyans, many Masai retain cattle herding as a way of life.

- **Many Kenyans** are moving to the big cities: Nairobi and Mombasa.

- **Kenya's population** is growing by 2.5% a year.

Health and education

- **Progress** in medical science, better diet and improved hygiene have made the world a healthier place for many.

- **How long** people are likely to live is called life expectancy. In 1950, the world average was just 40 years. Now it is over 63 years.

- **Life expectancy** is usually high in richer countries. The Andorrans live on average for 83.5 years; the Japanese live for 80.8 years.

- **Life expectancy** is much lower in poor countries. People in Zambia live just 37.3 years; people in Mozambique live 36.5 years.

- **Vaccination programmes** have reduced the effects of some major diseases. The terrible disease smallpox was thought to be wiped out in 1977.

- **Some diseases** are on the increase in poorer parts of the world. AIDS (Acquired Immune Deficiency Syndrome) is now killing huge numbers of Africans.

- **In some parts** of the world, disease, lack of food and water and poor healthcare mean that one child in every four dies before reaching the age of five in poor countries like Afghanistan and Sierra Leone.

- **In the USA and Europe** less than one child in a hundred dies before the age of five.

- **In wealthier** countries such as Italy and Switzerland, there is on average one doctor for every 350 people.

- **In most poor African** countries, there is just one doctor for every 50,000 people.

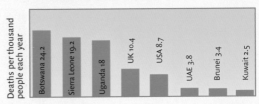

Deaths per thousand people each year

Botswana 24.2 | Sierra Leone 19.2 | Uganda 18 | UK 10.4 | USA 8.7 | UAE 3.8 | Brunei 3.4 | Kuwait 2.5

▲ Death rates per thousand people vary from over 20 in many African countries to under 3 in many Arab countries of the Gulf.

France

- **Capital:** Paris. Area: 543,965 sq km. Currency: euro. Language: French.

- **Physical features:** Highest mountain: Mont Blanc (4810 m). Longest river: Loire (1020 km).

- **Population:** 58.7 million. Population density:108/sq km. Life expectancy: men 74.9 years; women 83.6 years.

- **Wealth:** GDP: $1407 billion. GDP per head: $24,330.

- **Exports:** Agricultural products, chemicals, machinery, vehicles, pharmaceuticals.

- **France** is the biggest food producer in Europe, apart from Russia. In the north and west, wheat, sugar beet and many other crops are grown and dairy cattle are raised. In the warmer, drier south of France grapes and other fruit are grown.

▶ France is famous both for its beef cattle, like this Charolais, and its dairy cows, which give cheeses including the delicious soft cheeses Brie and Camembert.

- **France has limited** coal and oil reserves, but nuclear power gives France 75% of its energy.

- **France** is the biggest country in western Europe. Much is still rural, with ancient farmhouses and villages looking as if they have changed little in centuries. But French cities like Lyon and Marseille are famous for their sophisticated culture. They are also the centres of so much industry that France is the world's fifth largest industrial nation after the USA, Japan, Germany and UK.

- **The French** are traditionally famous for their *haute cuisine* (fine cooking) using the best ingredients, and creating fantastic table displays. Later, plainer styles developed and a lighter style of cooking called *nouvelle cuisine* (new cooking) has developed to suit today's tastes.

▶ France is a large and enormously varied country. In the centre are the rugged hills and volcanic peaks of the Massif Central. To the south is the warm sunny Mediterraean coast. The low, rolling countryside of the north and west is cooler. The highest mountains are the Alps in the southeast and the Pyrenees in the southwest, along the border with Spain.

Antarctica

- **Antarctica** is the fifth largest continent, larger than Europe and Australia, but 98% of it is under ice.
- **The Antarctic population** is made up mostly of scientists, pilots and other specialists there to do research in the unique polar environment.
- **About 3000 people** live in Antarctica in the summer, but less than 500 stay all through the bitter winter.
- **The biggest community** in Antarctica is McMurdo which is home to up to 1200 people in summer and has cafés, a cinema, a church and a nuclear power station.
- **People and supplies** reach McMurdo either on ice-breaker ships that smash through the sea ice, or by air.

- **McMurdo settlement** was built around the hut the British polar explorer Captain Scott put up on his 1902 expedition to the South Pole.
- **The Amundsen–Scott** base is located directly underneath the South Pole.
- **Antarctica** has a few valuable mineral resources including copper and chrome ores.
- **There is coal** beneath the Transarctic Mountains, and oil under the Ross Sea.
- **Under the Antarctic Treaty** of 1961, 27 countries agreed a ban on mining to keep the Antarctic unspoiled. They allow only scientific research.

◀ *Emperor penguins are among the few large creatures that can survive the bitter Antarctic winter. They breed on the ice cap itself.*

Industry

▲ *Nearly every country in the world is becoming more and more industrialized. New industries include services like banking rather than traditional manufacturing.*

- **Primary industries** are based on collecting natural resources. They include farming, forestry, fishing, mining and quarrying.
- **Things made** by primary industries are called primary products or raw materials.

- **Primary industries** dominate the economies of poorer countries. Copper is 80% of Zambia's exports.
- **Primary products** are much less important in developed countries. Primary products earn 2% of Japan's GDP.
- **Secondary industry** is taking raw materials and turning them into products from knives and forks to jumbo jets. This is manufacturing and processing.
- **Tertiary industries** are the service industries that provide a service, such as banking or tourism, not a product.
- **Tertiary industry** has grown enormously in the most developed countries, while manufacturing has shrunk.
- **'Postindustrialization'** means developing service industries in place of factories.
- **Tertiary industries** include internet businesses.

> ★ STAR FACT ★
> More than 70% of the UK's income now comes from tertiary industry.

The Middle East

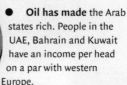

- **Saudi Arabia:** Capital: Riyadh. Population: 21.7 million. Currency: Rial. Language: Arabic.

- **Yemen:** Capital: Sana. Population: 18.1 million. Currency: Riyal. Language: Arabic.

- **Kuwait:** Capital: Kuwait City. Pop: 2.3 m. Curr: dinar. Language: Arabic.

- **United Arab Emirates (UAE):** Capital: Abu Dhabi. Population: 2.4 million. Currency: Dirham. Language: Arabic.

- **Population:** Oman: 2.7 million. Bahrain: 620,000. Qatar: 590,000.

- **Much of the Middle East** is desert. Rub'al Khali in Saudi Arabia lives up to its name, 'Empty Quarter'. Nomads called Bedouins have herded sheep and goats here for thousands of years. Now most Bedouins live in houses.

- **Oil has made** the Arab states rich. People in the UAE, Bahrain and Kuwait have an income per head on a par with western Europe.

- **Saudi Arabia** is the world's leading exporter of oil and second only to Russia as oil producer. It has 25% of the world's known oil reserves.

- **Yemen** is one of the world's poorest countries.

- **The oil-rich states** along the Gulf are short of water. Most comes from wells, but now they are building desalination plants which remove salt so they can use water from the sea.

◀ *Civilization began in the Middle East, but the climate dried and turned much of it to desert.*

The Russian steppes

- **The steppes** are a vast expanse of temperate grassland, stretching right across Asia.

- **'Steppes'** is a word meaning lowland.

- **The Western Steppe** extends 4000 km from the grassy plains of the Ukraine through Russia and Kazakhstan to the Altai mountains on the Mongolian border.

- **The steppes** extend 300-800 km from north to south.

> ★ STAR FACT ★
> The steppes extend 8000 km across Eurasia, a fifth of the way round the world.

- **The Eastern Steppe** extends 2500 km from the Altai across Mongolia to Manchuria in north China.

- **The Eastern Steppe** is higher and colder than the Western Steppe and the difference between winter and summer is as extreme as anywhere on Earth.

- **Nomadic herders** have lived on the steppes for over 6000 years.

- **It was on the steppes** near the Black and Caspian Seas that people probably first rode horses 5000 years ago.

- **The openness** of the steppes meant that travel by horse was easy long before roads were built.

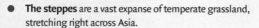

◀ *The steppes have supported nomadic herding people for thousands of years, but their way of life is rapidly dying out.*

American food

▲ The American hamburger has been spread around the world by fast-food chains. The American people eat 45,000 hamburgers every minute!

- **Many American** foods were brought from Europe by immigrants.
- **Hamburgers** were brought to the USA by German immigrants in the 1880s, but are now the most famous American food.
- **Frankfurters** came from Frankfurt in Germany (though this is disputed by people from Coburg, now in Bavaria). They became known in the USA as 'hot dogs' by the early 1890s.

- **The pizza** came from Naples in Italy, but the first pizzeria opened in New York in 1895. Pizzas caught on after 1945.
- **The bagel** originated in Poland early in the 17th century where it was known as beygls. It was taken to New York by Jewish immigrants and is often eaten filled with smoked salmon and cream cheese.
- **Self-service** cafeterias began in the 1849 San Francisco Gold Rush.
- **The world's first** fast-food restaurant may have been the White Castle which opened in Wichita, Kansas in 1921.
- **The world's biggest** fast-food chain is McDonalds which has over 29,000 branches worldwide.
- **Pies** have been popular in the US since colonial times, and apple pie is the symbol of American home cooking.
- **American home cooking** includes beef steaks, chicken and ham with potatoes plus a salad. But Americans eat out often – not only fast-food such as hamburgers and French fries, but Chinese, Italian and Mexican dishes.

Southern Africa

- **Mozambique:** Capital: Maputo. Population: 19.6 million. Currency: Metical. Language: Portuguese.
- **Angola:** Capital: Luanda. Population: 12.8 million. Currency: Kwanza. Language: Portuguese.
- **Zambia:** Capital: Lusaka. Pop: 9.9 million. Currency: Kwacha. Language: English.
- **Population:** Namibia: 1.7 million. Botswana: 1.6 million. Swaziland: 985,000.
- **Large areas** of southern African countries are too dry to farm intensively. Most people grow crops such as maize or raise cattle to feed themselves.
- **In Mozambique** plantations grow crops like tea and coffee for export, but most people who work on them are poor.
- **In 2000** much of Mozambique was devastated by huge floods from the Zambezi and Limpopo Rivers.

- **Zambia is the** world's fourth largest copper producer and relies on copper for 80% of its export earnings.
- **Namibia is the** world's second largest lead producer.
- **Namibia** has the world's biggest uranium mine and an estimated three billion carats of diamond deposits.

▼ The Namib and Kalahari deserts cover much of Namibia and Botswana with sand and dust. Even beyond the deserts, vegetation is sparse and the living poor – except in the mines.

Tokyo

- **Tokyo** is the world's biggest city. With the port of Yokohama and the cities of Chiba and Kawasaki, it makes an urban area that is home to 27.3 million people.
- **Tokyo** is Japan's capital and leading industrial and financial centre.
- **Tokyo's stock exchange** is one of the world's three giants, along with London and New York.
- **Tokyo** was originally called Edo when it first developed as a military centre for the Shoguns. It was named Tokyo in 1868 when it became imperial capital.
- **14,000 people** live in every square kilometre of Tokyo – twice as many as in the same area in New York.
- **Some hotels** in Tokyo have stacks of sleeping cubicles little bigger than a large refrigerator.

> ★ STAR FACT ★
> Tokyo probably has more neon signs than any other city in the world.

▲ Tokyo is perhaps the busiest, most crowded city in the world.

- **During rush hours** *osiyas* (pushers) cram people on to commuter trains crowded with 10 million travellers a day.
- **Traffic police** wear breathing apparatus to cope with traffic fumes.
- **Tokyo mixes** the latest western-style technology and culture with traditional Japanese ways.

Canada

- **Capital:** Ottawa. Area: 9,970,610 sq km. Currency: Canadian dollar. Languages: English, French.
- **Physical features:** Highest mountain: Mt Logan (5951 m). Longest river: the Mackenzie, linked to the Peace by the Great Slave Lake (4241 km).
- **Population:** 30.7 million. Population density: 3/sq km. Life expectancy: men 76.2 years; women 81.9 years.

- **Wealth:** GDP: $683.6 billion. GDP per head: $22,280.
- **Exports:** Vehicles and parts, machinery, petroleum, aluminium, timber, wood pulp, wheat.
  - **Canada** is the world's second largest country.
  - **Three-quarters** of Canada's small population live within 100 km of the southern border with the USA; the rest of the country is rugged and only thinly inhabited.
  - **Only 5%** of Canada is farmed, but this is a big area. The Prairie provinces – Saskatchewan, Alberta and Manitoba – grow a lot of wheat and raise many cattle.
  - **Canada** has 10% of the world's forest and is the world's largest exporter of wood products and paper.
- **The Inuit people** of the far north in the Arctic were given their own homeland of Nunavut in 1999.

◄ The completion of the Canadian Pacific railroad right across Canada in 1886 was one of the great engineering feats of the 1800s.

Energy

- **Humans** now use well over 100 times as much energy as they did 200 years ago, and the amount is rising.

- **Europe, North America and Japan** use 70% of the world's energy with just a quarter of the people.

- **Fossil fuels** are coal, oil and natural gas – fuels made from organic remains buried and fossilized over millions of years. Fossil fuels provide 90% of the world's energy.

- **Fossil fuel** pollutes the atmosphere as it burns, causing health problems, acid rain and also global warming.

- **Fossil fuel** is non-renewable. This means it can't be used again once burned. At today's rates, the world's coal and oil will be burned in 70 years and natural gas in 220 years.

- **Renewable energy** like running water, waves, wind and sunlight will not run out. Nuclear energy is non-renewable, but uses far less fuel than fossil fuel.

▼ *The pie diagram in the centre shows how much of the world's energy is provided by different sources. The top layer shows proportions ten years ago. The bottom layer shows proportions now. See how biomass energy use has risen.*

- **Alternative energy** is energy from sources other than fossil fuels and nuclear power. It should be renewable and clean.

- **Major alternative energy** sources are waves, geothermal, tides, wind and hydro-electric power.

Food for living
Home
Industry
Transport

◀▼ *Each person in developed countries uses 10 times as much energy as each person in less developed countries.*

Energy use in developed countries   Energy use in less developed countries

- **The Sun** provides the Earth with about the same as 500 trillion barrels of oil in energy a year – 1,000 times as much as the world's oil reserves. Yet little is used. Solar panels provide just 0.01% of human energy needs.

> ★ STAR FACT ★
> The average American uses 340 times as much energy as the average Ethiopian.

Oil is our most important energy source, now providing almost 40% of the world's energy needs. The biggest reserves are in the Middle East and Central Asia.

Coal still provides almost 23% of the world's energy needs. Two-thirds of the world's reserves are in China, Russia and the USA. India and Australia are major producers too.

Wood and dried animal dung – called biomass – provide the main fuel for half the world's population. In some poorer countries, it provides 90% of all fuel.

Natural gas provides over 22% of world energy needs, and the proportion is rising. The biggest reserves are in Russia, the USA and Canada.

Hydrolectric power (HEP) uses fast-flowing rivers or water flowing through a dam to generate electricity. HEP supplies 7% of world energy needs.

Nuclear power now provides about 5% of the world's energy needs. The major producers are France, the USA and Russia.

Geothermal power uses heat from deep inside the Earth – either to heat water or make steam to generate electricity. Experts think geothermal use will go up.

Windpower, wavepower and solar energy produce barely 5% of the world's energy needs. The proportion is going up, but only very, very slowly.

Peoples of southern Asia

▶ *Thai people are descended from peoples who migrated from China between the 11th and 12th centuries.*

- **There is a huge** variety of people living in southern Asia from India to the Philippines.

- **India** has hundreds of different ethnic groups speaking 30 languages and 1652 dialects.

- **Indonesia** also has many different ethnic groups and over 400 different languages and dialects.

- **In Cambodia,** Vietnam, Thailand, Myanmar and Sri Lanka, people are mostly Buddhists.

- **In Indonesia**, Malaysia, Pakistan and Bangladesh, people are mostly Muslim.

- **In India,** 81% of people are Hindus.

- **The word Hindu** comes from the Indus river where Dravidian people created one of the world's great ancient civilizations 4,500 years ago.

- **By Hindu tradition** people are born into social classes called castes. Members of each caste can only do certain jobs, wear certain clothes and eat certain food.

- **Most Indians** are descended from both the Dravidians and from the Aryans who invaded and pushed the Dravidians into the south about 3,500 years ago.

- **The people of East Timor** in Indonesia are mainly Christian. Before they became independent they were under the oppressive rule of the Indonesian military government.

Afghanistan & neighbours

- **Afghanistan:** Capital: Kabul. Population: 25.6 million. Currency: Afghani. Language: Pashto, Dari.

- **Tajikistan:** Capital: Dushanbe. Population: 6.4 million. Currency: Tajik rouble. Language: Tajik.

- **Kyrgyzstan:** Capital: Bishkek. Population: 4.5 million. Currency: Som. Language: Kyrgyz.

- **Nepal:** Capital: Kathmandu. Population: 24.4 million. Currency: Nepalese rupee. Language: Nepali.

- **These four** countries plus Tibet contain most of the world's highest mountains, including Everest (8863 m) and Kanchenjunga (8598 m) in Nepal and Garmo in Tajikistan (7495 m).

- **The blue** gemstone lapis lazuli has been mined at Sar-e-Sang in Afghanistan for over 6000 years.

- **Kyrgyzstan** has been independent from the USSR since 1991, but 16% of the people are Russian or half-Russian. Only a few still live in the traditional kyrgyz tents or 'yurts'.

- **Tajikistan** is still mostly rural and farmers in the deep valleys grow cotton and melons.

- **Afghanistan** was wracked by war for 17 years until the fiercely Muslim Taliban came to power in the late 1996. Their regime was overthrown in 2001.

▼ *The Himalayas, highlighted on these maps, are the world's highest mountains.*

Hungary and neighbours

▲ Hungary is one of the world's leading producers of sunflower oil, and in summer vast areas of its Great Plain turn yellow with sunflower blooms.

- **Hungary:** Capital: Budapest. Population: 10 million. Currency: Forint. Language: Hungarian.
- **Czech Republic:** Capital: Prague. Population: 10.2 million. Currency: Koruna. Language: Czech.

- **Slovakia:** Capital: Bratislava. Population: 5.3 million. Currency: Koruna. Language: Slovak.
- **Slovenia:** Capital: Ljubljana. Population: 2 million. Currency: Tolar. Language: Slovenian.
- **Until 1990** all of these countries were under Soviet rule except Slovenia. It was part of Yugoslavia.
- **Since 1990**, the historic city of Prague has become a popular destination, especially with the young, and many recording artists have worked in studios here.
- **The Czech Republic** is famous for Pilsen beer brewed in the town of Plzen with hops grown locally.
- **Hungary's** national dish is *goulash*. This is a rich stew made from meat, onion and potatoes, spiced with paprika (red pepper) and served with black rye bread.
- **Slovakian people** were largely rural, with a strong tradition of folk music, dancing and dress. Now over half the population has moved into industrial towns.
- **Vienna's white** Lippizaner horses are bred in Slovenia.

Hong Kong

> **! NEWS FLASH !**
> The proposed Landmark tower in Kowloon could be 576 m tall.

- **Hong Kong** is a Special Adinistrative Region on the coast of China. It comprises a peninsula and 237 islands.
- **Hong Kong** was administered by the British from 1842 until July 1 1997.
- **6.8 million** people are crowded into Hong Kong, mostly in the cities of Kowloon and Hong Kong itself.
- **Hong Kong** is one of the world's most bustling, dynamic, overcrowded cities. It makes huge amounts of textiles, clothing and other goods and is also one of the world's major financial and trading centres.
- **All but 3%** of Hong Kong people are Chinese, but many speak English as well as Chinese.
- **Hong Kong** is one of the world's three biggest ports, along with Rotterdam and Singapore.

- **Hong Kong** is the world's biggest container port.
- **Hong Kong's Chep Lap Kok** airport, opened in 1998, is one of the world's most modern airports.
- **The Hong Kong-Shanghai Bank** tower is one of the world's most spectacular modern office blocks.

▼ Hong Kong is quite mountainous, so people are crowded on to a small area of land, often in huge, high-rise apartment blocks.

China

> ★ **STAR FACT** ★
> A baby is born in China every two seconds,
> and someone dies every two and a half.

- **Capital:** Beijing. Area: 9,573,998 sq km. Currency: Yuan. Language: Guoyo (Mandarin).

- **Physical features:** Highest mountain: Qomolanjma Feng (Mt Everest, 8863 m). Longest river: Chang Jiang (Yangtze) (6300 km).

- **Population:** 1276.3 million. Population density: 133/sq km. Life expectancy: men 68.1 years; women 71.1 years.

- **Wealth:** GDP: $1392 billion. GDP per head: $1000.

- **Exports:** Electrical machinery, textiles and clothing, footwear, toys and games, iron and steel, crude oil, coal, tobacco.

- **China** is the world's third largest country, stretching from the soaring Himalayas in the west to the great plains of the Huang (Yellow) and Chang Jiang (Yangtze) rivers in the east where most people live.

- **China** is the most highly populated country in the world. In 1979, it was growing so rapidly the government made it illegal for couples to have more than one child. In the countryside, people disliked the law because extra children were needed to work the fields. In towns, the law worked better, but single children were often spoiled and so called 'Little Emperors'.

- **68%** of China's people still live and work on the land, growing rice and other crops to feed themselves. But as China opens up to western trade, so industry is growing in cities like Guangzhou (Canton) and more and more country people are going to work there.

- **China** became communist in 1949, and the nationalist government fled to the island of Taiwan. Taiwan now has a thriving economy and makes more computer parts – especially microchips – than anywhere else in the world.

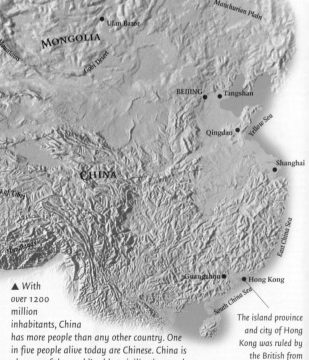

▲ With over 1200 million inhabitants, China has more people than any other country. One in five people alive today are Chinese. China is also one of the world's oldest civilizations and Chinese cities date back at least 4200 years. People were farming here long before the pharaohs came to power in Egypt.

The island province and city of Hong Kong was ruled by the British from 1842 onwards. It was returned to Chinese rule in 1997

▲ Rice is grown all over China in flooded fields called paddies.

Netherlands and Belgium

- **Netherlands:** Capitals: The Hague and Amsterdam. Population: 15.9 million. Currency: euro. Language: Dutch.

- **Belgium:** Capital: Brussels. Population: 10.2 million. Currency: euro. Languages: Flemish, French.

- **Belgium and the Netherlands** along with Luxembourg are often called the Low Countries because they are quite flat. The Netherlands' highest hill is just 321 m.

- **A quarter of the Netherlands** (also known as Holland) is polders – land once covered by the sea, but now protected by banks called dykes and pumped dry.

- **The Netherlands** exports more cheese than any other country in the world. Edam and Gouda are famous.

- **The Netherlands** is famous for its vast fields of tulips.

> ★ STAR FACT ★
> The Netherlands is the world's biggest trader in cut flowers.

- **Rotterdam** at the mouth of the Rhine is one of the world's biggest ports, handling a million tonnes of goods each day.

- **Brussels** is the seat of the European Union Commission and Council.

- **The Belgian** city of Antwerp is the diamond-cutting centre of the world.

▶ Holland is famous for its windmills. These are not for grinding flour but for working the pumps that keep the flat land dry.

Peoples of South America

- **South America** has a population of a little over 345 million people.

- **Before its conquest** by the Spanish and Portuguese in the 16th century, South America was home to many native peoples.

- **There are native villages** in the Andes with only one race, and a few native tribes in the Amazon rainforest who have had little contact with the outside world.

- **The main population groups now** are American Indians, whites, blacks (whose ancestors were brought as slaves) and people of mixed race.

▶ In the Amazon, small tribes like the Matses still survive as they have done for thousands of years.

- **Most people** in Latin America are mixed race.

- **The largest mixed race** groups are mestizos (people with both American Indian and white ancestors) and mulattoes (people with black and white ancestors).

- **Mestizos** are the majority in countries such as Paraguay and Venezuela. Mulattoes are the majority in Brazil.

- **The Europeans** who came to South America were mostly Spanish and Portuguese, so nearly two-thirds of South Americans speak Spanish.

- **Many American Indians** speak their own languages.

- **Quechua** is a native language, which Peru has made its official language along with Spanish.

Midwest USA

- **Huge amounts** of wheat and maize are grown on the damper eastern side of the vast rolling plains.

- **Millions** of beef cattle are raised on ranches in the drier west.

- **The weather is often extreme** here with scorching summer days and winter blizzards.

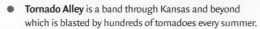

◄ The midwest is North America's agricultural heartland, raising millions of cattle and growing vast areas of yellow corn.

- **Detroit** on the Great Lakes is the centre of the US car and truck industry. Ford, Chrysler and General Motors all have their headquarters here.

- **Tornado Alley** is a band through Kansas and beyond which is blasted by hundreds of tornadoes every summer.

- **Heavy farming** in the 1930s let dry winds strip away soil leaving just dust over a vast area called the Dust Bowl. Irrigation and windbreaks have lessened the problem.

- **Millions of buffalo (bison)** roamed the Great Plains 200 years ago. Now just 50,000 live on reserves.

- **Detroit** is sometimes known as Motown (short for 'motor town') and was famous in the 1960s for its black soul 'Motown' music.

- **Many Italians** have emigrated to the USA and most US cities have an Italian area. Chicago's Italians invented their own deep, soft version of the pizza.

- **Chicago,** known as 'The Windy City', is the USA's third largest city, home to over nine million people.

Ireland

- **Capital:** Dublin. Area: 70,285 sq km. Currency: euro. Languages: Irish and English. Over two-thirds of Ireland is in the Republic of Ireland. The rest is Northern Ireland, which is part of the UK.

- **Physical features:** Highest mountain: Carrauntoohil (1041 m). Longest river: Shannon (372 km).

- **Population (Republic):** 3.7 million. Population density: 53/sq km. Life expectancy: men 73.8 years; women 79.4 years.

- **Wealth (Republic):** GDP: $99.8 billion. GDP per head: $26,880.

◄ Right out on the northwest of Europe in the Atlantic, Ireland is a mild, moist place. Damp mists and frequent showers keep grass lush and green, earning the island the name 'The Emerald Isle'.

- **Exports:** Machinery, transport equipment, chemicals.

- **Peat** is one of Ireland's few natural energy resources. Peat is the compressed rotten remains of plants found in peat bogs. Once dried it can be burned as fuel.

- **Ireland** is famous for its pubs, folk music and hospitality. Large numbers of Irish are returning home because of its booming economy and labour shortages.

- **Ireland,** and Dublin in particular, have been thriving in recent years – partly because of the success of high-tech electronics and computer industries.

- **Entertainment** is big business in Ireland. Many films – both American and Irish – are made in Ireland, and pop, rock and folk music are huge money earners.

> ★ STAR FACT ★
> Ireland has enjoyed the fastest growing economy in Europe since the mid 1990s.

North and South Korea

- **North Korea:** Capital: Pyongyang. Population: 22.2 million. Currency: Won. Language: Korean.
- **South Korea:** Capital: Seoul. Population: 46.1 million. Currency: Won. Language: Korean.
- **Korea** split into the communist North and capitalist South in 1948.
- **A bitter war** between North and South involving the USA ended with a treaty in 1953.
- **North and South Korea** both still have large armies. South Korea's has over half a million soldiers.
- **After the war** money from US banks helped the South, for a time, to become the world's fastest growing economy.
- **Huge factories** run by companies called chaebol

churned out everything from computers to Hyundai and Daewoo cars.

- **South Korean shipyards** build one in six of the world's ships. Only Japan builds more.
- **Since 1997** North Korea has suffered food shortages after two years of floods followed by drought.
- **In 1997-98** the uncovering of massive government dishonesty made many South Korean businesses bankrupt. New President Kim Dae Jung has led a recovery.

◀ *The Korean company of Daewoo not only makes cars, but ships, computers, TVs, videos and much more besides.*

Central Africa

- **Equatorial Guinea:** Capital: Malabo. Population: 450,000. Currency: CFA franc. Languages: Fang, Spanish.
- **Gabon:** Capital: Libreville. Population: 1.2 million. Currency: CFA franc. Language: French.
- **Congo (Brazzaville):** Capital: Brazzaville. Pop: 3 million. Currency: CFA franc. Languages: Monokutuba, French.
- **Cameroon:** Capital: Yaoundé. Population: 15.1 million. Currency: CFA Franc. Languages: Fang, French, English.
- **Central African Republic (CAR):** Capital: Bangui. Population: 3.6 million. Currency: CFA Franc. Languages: Sango, French.
- **French and English** are official languages, but most people speak their own African language.
- **Most Gabonese** are farmers, but Gabon is rich in oil, iron and manganese and famous for its ebony and mahogany.
- **70% of people** in Cameroon are farmers, growing crops such as cassava, corn, millet, yams and sweet potatoes. Most of Cameroon's roads are dust roads.

- **Congo (Brazzaville)** is so called to distinguish it from neighbouring DR Congo. It is one of the world's poorest countries. It is thickly forested and many people travel by dugout canoes. Many raise bananas or grow crops to feed themselves.
- **The CAR and Equatorial Guinea** are among the least developed countries in Africa.

▶ *Cameroon, Gabon, CAR, Congo and Equatorial Guinea lie near the Equator, and are often thickly wooded with rainforest.*

Nigeria and neighbours

- **Nigeria:** Capital: Abuja. Population: 128.8 million. Currency: Naira. Languages: include English Creole, Hausa, Yoruba, English.
- **Niger:** Capital: Niamey. Population: 10.8 million. Currency: CFA franc. Languages: Hausa, French.
- **Chad:** Capital: N'Djamena. Population: 7.3 million. Currency: CFA franc. Languages: Arabic and French.
- **Most people** in the north of Nigeria, and in Niger and Chad live by growing food for themselves.
- **The amount of rainfall** increases dramatically from north to south, and the vegetation changes from rainforest to dry grassland to desert in marked bands.
- **In the dry north** people grow mainly millet; in the moist south, they grow rice and roots such as cassava and yam.
- **Oil makes up 95%** of Nigeria's exports.
- **The money from oil** has made Nigeria among the most heavily urbanized and populous countries in Africa, especially around its main city Lagos.

- **Nigeria** is home to over 250 different peoples.
- **Nigeria** became a democracy again in 1998 after years of bitter civil war and military dictatorship, but tensions remain.

▼ *The position of Nigeria, Niger and Chad on the southern fringes of the Sahara desert makes them prone to drought as climate change and overgrazing push the desert further south.*

Argentina

▼ *'Gaucho' means orphan, but the tough gauchos are Argentina's heroes.*

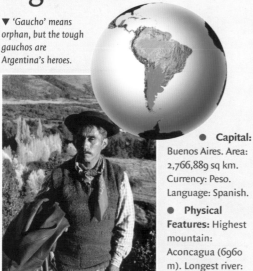

- **Capital:** Buenos Aires. Area: 2,766,889 sq km. Currency: Peso. Language: Spanish.
- **Physical Features:** Highest mountain: Aconcagua (6960 m). Longest river: Paraná (4880 km).

- **Population:** 37 million. Population density: 13/sq km. Life expectancy: men 69.7 years; women 76.8 years.
- **Wealth:** GDP: $367 billion. GDP per head: $9900.
- **Exports:** Wheat, maize, meat, hides, wool, tannin, linseed oil, peanuts, processed foods, minerals.
- **The Argentinian landscape** is dominated by the pampas, the vast flat grasslands which stretch all the way to the high Andes mountains in the west.
- **Most of Argentina's** exports are pampas products – wheat, corn, meat, hides and wool.
- **Cattle** on the pampas – 49 million of them – are herded by Argentina's famous cowboys, the gauchos.
- **Argentina** is the most educated country in South America, with a third of students going to university.

> ★ STAR FACT ★
> Argentineans eat more meat than any other nation in the world.

The United Kingdom

- **Capital:** London. Area: 244,088 sq km. Currency: Pound. Language: English.

- **Physical features:** Highest mountain: Ben Nevis (1343 m). Longest river: Severn (354 km).

- **Population:** 59.7 million. Population density: 245/sq km. Life expectancy: men 74.5 years; women 79.8 years.

- **Wealth:** GDP: $1450 billion. GDP per head: $24,280.

- **Exports:** Manufactured goods such as chemicals and electronics, financial services, music and publishing.

- **The British Isles** are 4,000 islands with 20,000 km of coast. There are two large islands: Great Britain and Ireland. The United Kingdom (UK) is four countries joined politically – England, Scotland, Wales and N. Ireland.

- **England** is intensively farmed, especially in the south where wheat, barley, rape, sugar beet and vegetables are grown. In the moister west and north of England, especially, and Scotland and Wales, cattle and sheep are reared.

- **The Industrial Revolution** began in the UK. In the 1800s, heavy industries such as steelmaking and engineering grew in northern coalfield cities like Manchester and Leeds. Now coal's importance as an energy source has dwindled, and some smaller northern towns are finding it difficult to survive. But southern England is thriving on light industries and services.

- **London** is one of the world's great financial centres. Over 500 international banks are crammed into a small area of the city called the Square Mile. Here billions of dollars' worth of money deals are done every day.

▲ The Millennium Dome was erected by the River Thames in east London to celebrate the year 2000.

◀ England is the biggest and most densely populated of the countries of the UK – a lush land of rolling hills, rich farmland and big cities. Wales is a land of hills and sheep farms, except for the south where industry is important and coal was once mined in huge amounts. Much of Scotland is wild moors and valleys, and most people live in the central lowlands around the cities of Glasgow and Edinburgh. A third of Northern Ireland's population lives in Belfast.

SCOTLAND
Ben Nevis
Grampian Mountains
Atlantic Ocean
EDINBURGH
Glasgow
Southern Uplands
North Sea
N. IRELAND
BELFAST
Irish Sea
Manchester
Liverpool
IRELAND
DUBLIN
Cumbrian Mts
Cork
St George's Channel
WALES
Birmingham
ENGLAND
CARDIFF
Bristol
LONDON
Dover
English Channel
Plymouth

★ **STAR FACT** ★
Over 60% of the UK's workforce now work in financial and service industries.

The Near East

- **Syria:** Capital: Damascus. Population: 16.1 million. Currency: Syrian pound. Language: Arabic.
- **Jordan:** Capital: Amman. Population: 5.2 million. Currency: Jordan dinar. Language: Arabic.
- **Lebanon:** Capital: Beirut. Population: 3.3 million. Currency: Lebanese pound. Language: Arabic.
- **Damascus** was a major trading centre 4000 years ago.
- **Syria** is at the western end of the belt of rich farmland known as the fertile crescent, which was the cradle of the earliest civilizations, along the banks of the Tigris and Euphrates rivers.
- **Most Syrian farmers** still work on small plots growing cotton and wheat. But 40% of Syrians now work in services.
- **Around 70% of Jordan's** income is from services like tourism and banking.

- **The people of Syria,** Jordan and Lebanon are mostly Arabs. 86% of Syrians and 96% of Jordanians are Muslims, but 35% of Lebanese are Christians.
- **In 1948** Palestine was split between Israel, Jordan and Egypt. Palestinian Arabs' desire for their own country has caused conflict with Israelis.
- **In 1996** Israeli troops withdrew from the Gaza strip region, and Palestinians elected their own local administration.

Indian food

- **Most Indians** live on very plain diets – based on staples such as rice in the east and south, *chapatis* (flat wheat bread) in the north and northwest, and *bajra* (millet bread) in the Maharashtra region.
- **The staple foods** are supplemented by *dal* (lentil porridge), vegetables and yoghurt.
- **Chillis and other spices** such as coriander, cumin, ginger and turmeric add flavour.
- **Chicken and mutton** are costly and eaten occasionally. Hindus will not eat beef and Muslims will not eat pork.
- **Many Indian meals** are cooked in *ghee* (liquid butter). Ghee is made by heating butter to boil off water, then allowing it to cool and separate. Ghee is scooped off the top.

- **Although many Indians** have simple diets, India has an ancient and varied tradition of fine cooking.
- **Curries are** dishes made with a sauce including the basic Indian spices – turmeric, cumin, coriander and red pepper. The word curry comes from the Tamil *kari*, or sauce.
  - **The basis of a curry** is a *masala*, a mix of spices, often blended with water or vinegar to make a paste.
  - **Southern Indian** vegetable curries are seasoned with hot blends like *sambar podi*.
  - **Classic northern Indian** Mughal dishes are often lamb, or chicken based, and seasoned with milder *garam masala*.

◄ An Indian meal is rarely served on a single plate. Instead, it comes in different dishes, which diners dip into.

Paris

▲ Les Halles was the main market for Paris from the 12th century, but in the 1970s was transformed into a modern shopping centre.

- **Paris** is the capital of France and its largest city with a population of over nine million.

- **Paris** is France's main business and financial centre. The Paris region is also a major manufacturing region, notably for cars.

- **Paris is famed** for luxuries like perfume and fashion.

- **Paris is known** for restaurants like La Marée, cafés like Deux Magots and nightclubs like the Moulin Rouge.

- **Paris monuments** include the Arc de Triomphe, Eiffel Tower, Notre Dame cathedral and the Beauborg Centre.

- **Paris gets its name** from a Celtic tribe called the Parisii who lived there 2000 years ago.

- **The Roman general** Julius Caesar said the Parisii were 'clever, inventive and given to quarrelling among themselves'. Some say this is true of Parisians today.

- **Paris was redeveloped** in the 1850s and 60s by Baron Haussman on the orders of Emperor Napoleon III.

- **Haussman** gave Paris broad, tree-lined streets called boulevards, and grand, grey, seven-storey houses.

> ★ **STAR FACT** ★
> Well over half of France's business deals are done in Paris.

Balkan peninsula

- **The Balkan peninsula** is a mountainous region in SE Europe between the Adriatic and Aegean Seas.

- **The Balkans** include several different nations, some of which were under either the Austro-Hungarian or Turkish Empires until 1918.

- **In 1945 Yugoslavia** became six republics in a federal Communist state. This ended in 1991.

- **Bosnia-Herzegovina,** Croatia, Macedonia, Slovenia and Kosovo broke away from Yugoslavia in the 1990s amid much bitter conflict. Serbia and Montenegro formed a smaller Yugoslavia in 1992 but are now independant countries.

- **Serbia:** Capital: Belgrade. Population: 7.4 million. Currency: Serbian Dinar. Language: Serb, Hungarian.

- **Montenegro:** Capital: Podgorica. Population: 0.6 million. Currency: Euro. Language: Serb, Albanian.

- **Croatia:** Capital: Zagreb. Population: 4.5 million. Currency: Kuna. Language: Croat.

- **Bosnia-Herzegovina:** Capital: Sarajevo. Pop: 4.3 m. Currency: Bosnian dinar. Languages: Serb, Croat.

- **Albania:** Capital: Tirana. Population: 3.5 million. Currency: New lek. Language: Albanian.

- **Macedonia:** Capital: Skopje. Pop: 2.2 m. Curr: Dinar. Languages: Macedonian, Albanian.

▼ This bridge at Mostar in Bosnia-Herzegovina was a casualty of the wars of the 1990s.

Agriculture

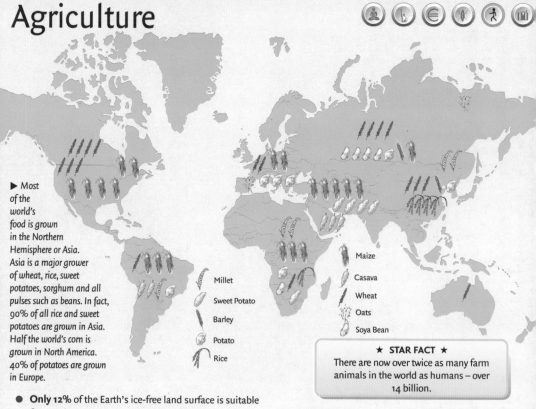

▶ Most of the world's food is grown in the Northern Hemisphere or Asia. Asia is a major grower of wheat, rice, sweet potatoes, sorghum and all pulses such as beans. In fact, 90% of all rice and sweet potatoes are grown in Asia. Half the world's corn is grown in North America. 40% of potatoes are grown in Europe.

Millet
Sweet Potato
Barley
Potato
Rice

Maize
Casava
Wheat
Oats
Soya Bean

★ STAR FACT ★
There are now over twice as many farm animals in the world as humans – over 14 billion.

● **Only 12%** of the Earth's ice-free land surface is suitable for growing crops – that is, about 13 billion hectares. The rest is either too wet, too dry, too cold or too steep. Or the soil is too shallow or poor in nutrients.

● **A much higher** proportion of Europe has fertile soil (36%) than any other continent. About 31% is cultivated.

● **In North America** 22% of the land is fertile but only 13% is cultivated, partly because much fertile land is lost under concrete. Surprisingly, 16% of Africa is potentially fertile, yet only 6% is cultivated.

● **Southern Asia** is so crowded that even though less than 20% of the land is fertile, over 24% is cultivated.

● **Dairy farms** produce milk, butter and cheese from cows in green pastures in fairly moist parts of the world.

● **Mixed farming** involves both crops and livestock as in the USA's Corn Belt, where farmers grow corn to feed pigs and cattle. Many European farms are mixed, too.

● **Mediterranean farming** is in areas with mild, moist winters and warm, dry summers – like California, parts of South Africa and the Mediterranean. Here winter crops include wheat, barley and broccoli. Summer crops include peaches, citrus fruits, grapes and olives.

● **Shifting cultivation** involves growing crops like corn, rice, manioc, yams and millet in one place for a short while, then moving on before the soil loses goodness.

● **Shifting cultivation** is practised in the forests of Latin America, in Africa and parts of Southeast Asia.

◀ In places farming is now a highly mechanized industry, but in SE Asia many farmers work the land as they have for thousands of years.

The West Indies

▶ Famous Jamaica rum is made from cane sugar, still the West Indies' major crop despite the rise of beet sugar.

- **Cuba:** Capital: Havana. Population: 11.2 million. Currency: Cuban peso. Language: Spanish.

- **Jamaica:** Capital: Kingston. Population: 2.6 million. Currency: Jamaican dollar. Language: English.

- **The four largest islands** in the West Indies are Cuba, Hispaniola, Jamaica and Puerto Rico. Hispaniola is split into two countries: Haiti and the Dominican Republic.

- **The islands** are mostly in a long curve stretching from Cuba to Trinidad. The Greater Antilles are the islands of the western end. The Lesser Antilles are the eastern end.

- **The original inhabitants** of the West Indies were Carib and Arawak peoples. Most died soon after the Spanish arrived in the 1500s from disease and abuse.

- **Today most West Indians** are descended from Africans brought here as slaves to work on the sugar plantations.

- **The slaves** were freed in the mid-1800s, but most people here are still poor and work for low wages.

- **In Haiti** only one person in 250 has a car; fewer than 1 in 10 has a phone.

- **Many people** work the land on sugar, banana or coffee plantations, and also farm a plot to grow their own food.

- **Many tourists** come for the warm weather and clear blue seas.

Vietnam and neighbours

- **Vietnam:** Capital: Hanoi. Population: 80.5 million. Currency: dong. Language: Vietnamese.

- **Laos:** Capital: Vientiane. Population: 5.6 million. Currency: kip. Language: Lao.

- **Cambodia:** Capital: Phnom Penh. Population: 12.5 million. Currency: riel. Language: Khmer.

- **Indonesia:** Capital: Jakarta. Population: 212.6 million. Currency: rupiah. Main language: Bahasa Indonesia.

◀ Warm and damp, Southeast Asia is a fertile region where Buddhist and Hindu kings once built giant temples in the forests, but many people today are desperately poor.

- **Laos, Vietnam and Cambodia** were once French colonies and the end of French rule in the 1950s led to years of suffering and war.

- **Both Laos and Vietnam** are one-party communist states, although their governments are elected by popular vote. In Cambodia, the king was reinstated in 1993.

- **Many people** in Laos and Vietnam are poor and live by growing rice. Laos is the world's poorest country.

- **In Indonesia,** an elected president has replaced dictator General Suharto but the military still have great power.

- **Spread over 13,700 islands,** Indonesia is one of the world's most densely populated countries. Jakarta is home to 12.4 million, and is heavily industrialized. In the country hillside terraces ensure every inch is used for rice.

- **Indonesian rainforest** is being rapidly destroyed by loggers. In 1997, parts of the country were engulfed by smoke from fires started by loggers.

Malaysia and Singapore

- **Malaysia:** Capitals: Kuala Lumpur and Putrajaya. Pop: 22.3 million. Curr: Malaysian dollar (ringgit). Language: Bahasa Malaysia.

- **Singapore:** Capital: Singapore. Population: 4 million. Currency: Singapore dollar. Languages: English, Mandarin, Malay and Tamil.

- **Malaysia** is split into sections: peninsular Malaysia and Sarawak and Sabah on the island of Borneo.

- **In the 1980s** Malaysia was a farming country relying on rubber for exports.

- **Malaysia** is still the world's top rubber producer.

- **Cheap, skilled labour** and oil have turned Malaysia into one of the world's most rapidly developing economies.

- **A plan called 2020 Vision** aims to have Malaysia fully developed by the year 2020.

- **Singapore** may be the world's busiest port. Huge

▲ *Singapore is one of the busiest and most prosperous cities in Asia.*

ships tie up here every 3 minutes.

- **Singapore** is also one of Asia's most successful trading and manufacturing centres.

- **Singapore** has a state-of-the-art transport system, kept immaculately clean by strict laws governing litter.

Peoples of Europe

◀ *In East Europe, many people, like these Romanians, have their own traditional dress.*

- **About 730 million** people live in Europe – about 12% of the world's population.

- **Europe** is one of the most densely populated continents averaging 70 people per square kilometre.

- **Most Europeans** are descended from tribes who migrated into Europe more than 1500 years ago.

- **Most British people** are descended from a mix of Celts, Angles, Saxons, Danes and others. Most French people are descended from Gauls and Franks. Most Eastern Europeans are Slavic (see peoples of Northern Asia).

- **North Europeans** such as Scandinavians often have fair skin and blonde hair. South Europeans such as Italians often have olive skin and dark hair.

- **Most European countries** have a mix of people from all parts of the world, including former European colonies in Africa and Asia.

- **Most Europeans** are Christians.

- **Most Europeans** speak an Indo-European language, such as English, French or Russian.

- **Languages** like French, Spanish and Italian are romance languages that come from Latin, language of the Romans.

- **Basque people** in Spain speak a language related to no other language. Hungarians, Finns and Estonians speak a Uralic-Altaic language like those of Turkey and Mongolia.

Chile

- **Capitals:** Santiago and Valparaiso. Area: 756,626 sq km. Currency: Chilean peso. Language: Spanish.

- **Physical features:** Highest mountain: Ojos del Solado (6895 m). Longest river: Bio-Bio (380 km).

- **Population:** 15.2 million. Population density: 20/sq km. Life expectancy: men 72.4 years; women 78.4 years.

- **Wealth:** GDP: $95 billion. GDP per head: $6240.

- **Exports:** Copper, manufactured goods, fresh fruit.

- **Chile** is one of the world's most volcanically active countries, with 75 volcanoes. Chile also has eight of the world's highest active volcanoes, including Guallatiri and San Pedro which are both active.

- **Chile is a major** wine producer.

- **The copper mine** at Chuquicamata is the world's biggest man-made hole, 3 km wide and 750 m deep. The El Teniente copper mine is the world's deepest.

- **Chile is the** world's largest copper producer.

- **The Mapuche Indians** live in the forest area around Temuco in southern Chile and those who preserve their traditional way of life live in round straw houses.

▶ Chile is very long and narrow – 4270 km long and less than 180 km wide.

Spain and Portugal

- **Spain:** Capital: Madrid. Area: 505,990 sq km. Currency: euro. Language: Spanish.

- **Physical features:** Highest mountain: Pico de Tiede (3718 m). Longest river: Tagus (1007 km).

- **Population:** 39.5 million. Population density: 71/sq km. Life expectancy: men 74.7 years; women 81.6 years.

- **Wealth:** GDP: $592.5 billion. GDP per head: $14,990.

- **Exports:** Cars, machinery, wine, fruit, steel, textiles, chemicals.

- **Much of the centre of Spain** is too hot and dry for some crops, but perfect for olives, sunflowers and for grapes, oranges and other fruit. Spain is one of the world's leading fruit-growers.

- **Spain is one of the leading** carmakers in Europe, with huge plants in Valencia and Saragossa. It also makes a lot of iron and steel. Toledo in the south was once famous for its fine sword steel.

- **Portugal:** Capital: Lisbon. Population: 9.8 million. Currency: euro. Language: Portuguese.

- **Portugal** once had a large empire including large parts of Latin America and Africa. Yet it is fairly underdeveloped. Most people still live in the countryside, growing wheat, rice, almonds, olives and maize. Portugal is famous for its 'port', a drink made by adding brandy to wine.

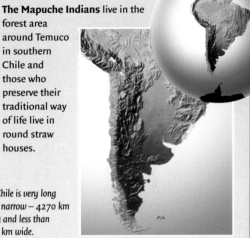

◀ Spain and Portugal are isolated from the rest of Europe by the Pyrenees on their own peninsula, called Iberia. Mainland Europe's most westerly point, Cabo da Roca, is in Portugal.

> ★ STAR FACT ★
> Every summer, 63 million sunseekers come to Spain's cities, beaches and islands.

Scandinavia

▲ *Norway's mountainous coast has been gouged into deep fjords by glaciers.*

- **Denmark:** Capital: Copenhagen. Population: 5.3 million. Currency: Danish krone. Language: Danish.
- **Finland:** Capital: Helsinki. Population: 5.2 million. Currency: euro. Languages: Finnish and Swedish.
- **Scandinavia** has among the iciest, most northerly inhabited countries in the world. Yet they enjoy a high standard of living and welfare provision.
  - **Norway's fishing boats** land 2.4 million tonnes of fish a year – more than those of any other European country except Russia.
    - **Sweden is known** for its high-quality engineering, including its cars such as Volvos and aircraft-makers such as Saab.
    - **Finland and Sweden** are known for their glass and ceramic work.
- **Norway:** Capital: Oslo. Population: 4.5 million. Currency: Norwegian krone. Language: Norwegian.
- **Sweden:** Capital: Stockholm. Population: 8.9 million. Currency: Swedish krona. Language: Swedish.
- **Sweden's capital Stockholm** is built on 14 islands in an archipelago comprising thousands of islands.
- **Danish farms** are famous for butter and bacon.

Political systems

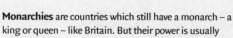

▶ *Bill Clinton was President of the USA from 1992–2000.*

- **Democracies** are countries with governments elected every few years by popular vote.
- **Most democracies** have a constitution, a written set of laws saying how a government must be run.
- **Democracies** like France are republics. This means the head of state is an elected president. In some republics like the USA, the president is in charge; in others, the president is a figurehead and the country is run by a chancellor or prime minister.

- **Monarchies** are countries which still have a monarch – a king or queen – like Britain. But their power is usually limited and the country is run by an elected government.
- **In autocracies** a single person or small group of people hold all the power, as in China and North Korea.
- **Most governments** are split into the legislature who make or amend laws, the executive who put them into effect and the judiciary who see they are applied fairly.
- **Most countries** are capitalist, which means most things – capital – are owned by individuals or small groups.
- **A few countries** like Cuba are communist, which means everything is owned by the community, or rather the state.
- **Socialists** believe the government should ensure everyone has equal rights, a fair share of money, and good health, education and housing.
- **Fascists** believe in rigid discipline and that they and their country are superior to others, like Hitler's Germany in the 1930s. There is no openly fascist country at present.

The Pacific Islands

- **Scattered** around the Pacific are countless islands – approximately 25,000. Some are little more than rocks; some are thousands of square kilometres.

- **The Pacific Islands** are in three main groups: Melanesia, Micronesia and Polynesia.

- **Melanesia** includes New Guinea, the Solomons, New Caledonia, Vanuatu and Fiji.

- **Melanesia** means 'black islands' and gets its name from the dark skin of many of the islanders here.

- **Micronesia** is 2,000 islands to the north of Melanesia, including Guam and the Marshall Islands.

- **Micronesia** means 'tiny islands'.

- **Polynesia** is a vast group of islands 8000 km across. It includes Tahiti, Samoa, Tonga, Kiribati and Easter Island.

- **Polynesia** means 'many islands'.

- **Some of the islands** in the Pacific are either extinct volcanoes, or coral islands built around a volcanic peak. Atolls are coral rings left as the volcano sinks.

- **Most Pacific islanders** live in small farming or fishing villages as they have for thousands of years, but western influences are changing the island way of life rapidly.

◀ Like many Pacific islands, Fiji seems like a paradise.

Mexico

- **Capital:** Mexico City. Area: 1,958,201 sq km. Currency: Mexican peso. Language: Spanish.

- **Physical features:** Highest mountain: Volcán Citlaltépetl (5610 m). Longest river: Rio Bravo (3035 km).

- **Population:** 97 mill. Population density: 50/sq km. Life expectancy: men 69.7 years; women 75.7 years.

- **Wealth:** GDP: $469.5 billion. GDP per head: $4840.

- **Exports:** Petroleum, vehicles, machinery, cotton, coffee, fertilizers, minerals.

- **Mexico** is quite mountainous and only 13% of the land is suitable for farming, but the soil that develops on lava poured out by Mexico's many volcanoes is very fertile. Where there is enough rain, there are big plantations for tobacco, coffee, cane, cocoa, cotton and rubber.

- **Over half Mexico's** export earnings come from manufactured goods – notably cars.

- **Mexico has** a rapidly growing population. The birth rate is high and half the population is under 25.

- **Most of Mexico's people** are mestizos – descended from both American Indians and Europeans. But there are still 29 million American Indians.

- **Mexico City** is one of the world's biggest, busiest, dirtiest cities. The urban area has a population of over 18.4 million – and it is growing rapidly as more people move in from the country to find jobs.

◀ Mexico lies immediately south of the USA, between the Gulf of Mexico and the Pacific.

Gulf of California

Pacific Ocean

Gulf of Mexico

Yucatán Peninsular

Mexico City

Gulf of Tehuantapec

Mediterranean food

- **Mediterranean food** depends on ingredients grown in the warm Mediterranean climate. It tends to be lighter than north European food, including salads, flat bread and fish rather than sauces and stews.

  - **Olive oil** is used for dressing salads and frying food.

  - **Major styles** of Mediterranean food include Italian, Greek, Turkish, Spanish and North African.

  ◀ *Spaghetti Bolognese – spaghetti pasta with meat and tomato sauce – is the centrepiece of a typical Italian meal.*

- **Italian meals** often include pasta, which is made from durum wheat flour and served with a sauce.

- **Popular forms of pasta** include spaghetti ('little strings'), vermicelli ('little worms'), fusilli ('spindles') and tube-shaped macaroni.

- **In north Italy** ribbon pastas served with cream sauces are popular. In the south, macaroni served with tomato-based sauces are more popular.

- **Pizzas** are popular snacks, especially in the south.

- **Greek food** includes meats – especially lamb – and fish cooked in olive oil.

- **Greek salad** includes olives, cucumber, tomatoes, herbs and feta cheese (soft goat's cheese).

- **Spanish food** often includes seafood such as *calamares* (squid). *Paella* includes seafoods and chicken combined with rice and cooked in saffron. *Gazpacho* is a cold tomato soup. *Tapas* are small snacks, originating in southern Spain.

Pakistan and Bangladesh

- **Pakistan:** Capital: Islamabad. Population: 156 million. Currency: Pakistan rupee. Language: Urdu.

- **Bangladesh:** Capital: Dhaka. Population: 128.3 million. Currency: taka. Language: Bengali.

- **The Punjab** region is where many Pakistanis live. It gets its name – which means 'five waters' – from five tributaries of the River Indus: the Jhelum, Chenab, Ravi, Sutlej and Beus. These rivers water the Punjab's plains and make it fertile. All the same, large areas of the Punjab are dry and rely on one of the world's biggest irrigation networks.

- **Pakistan's major exports** include textiles, cement, leather and machine tools.

▶ *Pakistan and Bangladesh were once one nation, East and West Pakistan, but East Pakistan broke away in 1971 to become Bangladesh.*

- **Buses, lorries and rickshaws** in Pakistan are decorated with colourful patterns, pictures of film stars and religious themes. Many people think that the better the vehicle looks, the more careful the driver will be.

- **Pakistan's capital** is the brand new city of Islamabad, built in the 1960s, but its biggest city and industrial centre is the port of Karachi.

- **While people in India** are mainly Hindu, in Pakistan and Bangladesh they are mainly Muslim.

  - **Jute is a reed** that thrives in Bangladesh's warm, moist climate. It is used for making rope, sacking and carpet backing.

  - **Over 70 big jute mills** make jute Bangladesh's most important export.

  - **Most of Bangladesh** is low-lying and prone to flooding. Floods have devastated Bangladesh several times in the past 40 years.

Switzerland and Austria

- **Switzerland:** Capital: Berne. Population: 7.4 million. Currency: Franc. Languages: German, French, Italian.
- **Austria:** Capital: Vienna. Population: 8.1 million. Currency: euro. Language: German.
- **Switzerland and Austria** are small but beautiful countries mostly in the Alps mountains.
- **Both Switzerland and Austria** make a great deal of money from tourists who come to walk and ski here.
- **Switzerland** has long been 'neutral', staying out of all the major wars. This is why organizations like the Red Cross and World Health Organization are based there.
- **Switzerland is** one of the richest countries in terms of GDP per person ($38,680). Luxembourg's is $45,320.
- **People from** all over the world put their money in Swiss banks because the country is stable politically and its banking laws guarantee secrecy.
- **Switzerland is famous** for making small, valuable things such as precision instruments and watches.

- **Vienna** was once the heart of the great Austrian Empire and the music capital of Europe.
- **Austrians** rely on mountain-river hydroelectricity for much of its power.

◀ Austria earns more than a sixth of its income from tourists who come to enjoy the Alpine scenery.

New England

▲ New England is famous for the stunning colours of its trees in 'fall' (autumn), when the leaves turn reds, golds and ambers.

- **New England** is six states in northeast USA – Maine, Vermont, New Hampshire, Massachusetts, Rhode Island and Connecticut.
- **New England** was one of the first areas of North America settled by Europeans in the 1600s.

- **The USA's** oldest buildings are in New England.
- **New England** is famous for its attractive small towns with pretty 18th- and 19th-century white clapperboard houses and elegantly spired churches.
- **Vermont's** name means 'green mountain' and it has fewer urban inhabitants than any other state.
- **Basketball** was invented in Massachusetts in 1891.
- **Route 128** in Massachusetts is famed for its cutting-edge electronic technology factories.
- **Boston** is one of the USA's oldest, most cultured cities. It also has a large number of educational and research institutes. Harvard University is at Cambridge nearby. Yale is in Connecticut.
- **New Hampshire** is famous for its scenery.

★ STAR FACT ★
Rhode Island is the smallest state in the USA, which is why it is often called 'Little Rhody'.

1000
THINGS
YOU SHOULD KNOW ABOUT

PLANTS

KEY

 How plants work

 Flowers

 Biomes

 Mosses and fungi

 Trees

 Plants and humans

Perennial flowers

▲ *Chrysanthemums are among the most popular perennials.*

- **Garden perennials** are flowers that live for at least three years.

- **Perennials** may not bloom in the first year, but after that they bloom every year.

- **Since they bloom** for many years, perennials do not need to produce as many seeds to survive.

- **Some perennials** are herbaceous – that is, they have soft stems. The stems wither at the end of each summer and new stems grow next spring.

- **Woody perennials** have woody stems. Their stems don't wither, but most shed their leaves in autumn.

- **Perennials** from temperate (cool) regions, like asters, irises, lupins, wallflowers, peonies and primroses, need a cold winter to encourage new buds to grow in spring.

- **Tropical perennials** such as African violets, begonias and gloxinias cannot survive winters outdoors in temperate climates.

- **Most perennials** spread by sending out shoots from their roots which develop into new stems.

- **Some perennials** such as columbines and delphiniums last for only three or four years.

- **Gardeners** spread perennials by taking cuttings – that is, pieces cut from stems or roots.

Oak trees

- **Oaks** are a group of over 450 different trees. Most belong to a family with the Latin name *Quercus*.

- ***Quercus* oaks** grow in the northern half of the world in temperate regions or high up in the tropics.

- **Southern oaks,** such as the Australian and Tasmanian oaks, don't belong to the *Quercus* family.

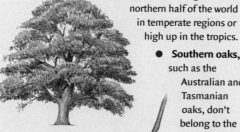

◄ *Oaks have leaves with four or five pairs of lobes. They grow fruits called acorns in a little cup.*

> ★ STAR FACT ★
> The bark of cork oaks in Portugal and Spain is made into corks for bottles.

- **Most oaks** from warmer places, such as the holm oak, are evergreen.

- **When a nail** is driven into freshly cut oak, it creates a blue stain as tannin in the wood reacts with the iron.

- **Tannin from oak bark** has been used for curing leather since the days of Ancient Greece.

- **Oak trees** can live a thousand years or more and grow up to 40 m. In Europe, oaks are the oldest of all trees.

- **Oak wood** is very strong and durable and so was the main building wood for centuries – used for timber frames in houses and for building ships.

- **Oak trees** are divided into white oaks like the English oak and red oaks like the North American pine oak according to the colour of their wood.

Spices

- **The Phoenicians** traded in spices 2500 years ago.

- **The great voyages** of exploration of the 1400s, like those of Columbus, were mainly to find ways to reach sources of spices in southeast Asia.

- **The Molucca Islands** in Indonesia were known as the Spice Islands because they were the main source of cloves, nutmeg and mace.

- **Sesame** was used by the Ancient Chinese for ink and by the Romans as sandwich spread. Arabs thought it had magical powers. In *Ali Baba and the 40 Thieves*, Ali says, 'open sesame' to magically open a door.

- **Cinnamon** is the inner bark of a laurel tree native to Sri Lanka. It was once more valuable than gold.

▲ *Spices made from fragrant tropical plants have long been used to flavour food.*

- **Allspice** is the berries of a myrtle tree native to the West Indies. It gets its name because it tastes like a mixture of cloves, cinnamon and nutmeg.

- **In Ancient Greece and Rome** people often paid their taxes in peppercorns.

- **Cloves are the dried buds** of a large evergreen tree that grows in the Moluccas.

- **From 200 BC** Chinese courtiers sucked cloves to make their breath smell sweet for the Emperor.

- **Saffron** is the yellow stigmas of the purple saffron crocus, used as a dye by Buddhist priests. It is the most costly of all spices. It takes 170,000 flowers to make just 1 kg.

Marine plants

- **Plants in the sea** can only live in the sunlit surface waters of the ocean, called the photic zone.

- **The photic zone** goes down about 100 m.

- **Phytoplankton** are minute, floating, plant-like organisms made from just a single cell.

- **Almost any marine plant** big enough to be seen with the naked eye is called seaweed.

- **Seaweeds** are anchored by 'holdfasts' that look like roots but are really suckers for holding on to rocks.

- **Seaweeds** are red, green or brown algae. Red algae are small and fern-like and grow 30–60 m down in tropical seas. Brown algae like giant kelp are big and grow down to about 20 m, mostly in cold water.

- **Some seaweeds** such as the bladderwrack have gas pockets to help their fronds (leaves) float.

- **The fastest growing** plant in the sea is the giant kelp, which can grow 1 m in a single day. Giant kelp can grow up to 60 m long.

- **The Sargasso Sea** is a vast area of sea covering 5.2 million sq km east of the West Indies. Gulfweed floats so densely here that it looks like green meadows.

- **The Sargasso Sea** was discovered by Christopher Columbus in 1492.

◄ *Seaweeds don't have roots, stems, leaves or flowers, but they are plants and make their food from sunlight (see photosynthesis).*

Gardens

- **The Ancient Chinese and Greeks** grew fruit trees, vegetables and herbs in gardens for food and for medicines.

- **In the 1500s** there were five famous botanical gardens in Europe designed to study and grow herbs for medicine.

- **The first botanical gardens** were at Pisa (1543) and Padua (1545) in Italy.

▲ *Gardening has become one of the most popular of all pastimes.*

- **Carolus Clusius** set up a famous flower garden in Leiden in Holland in the late 1500s. Here the first tulips from China were grown and the Dutch bulb industry began.

- **The most famous gardener** of the 17th century was John Evelyn who set up a beautiful garden at Sayes Court in Deptford near London.

- **The Royal Botanic Gardens** at Kew near London were made famous by Sir Joseph Banks in the late 1700s for their collections of plants from around the world.

- **Today Kew Gardens** has 33,400 classes of living plants and a herbarium of dried plants with 7 million species – that's 98% of the world's plants.

- **Plants** such as rubber plants, pineapples, bananas, tea and coffee were spread around the world from Kew.

- **Lancelot 'Capability' Brown** (1716-83) was a famous English landscape gardener. He got his nickname by telling clients their gardens had excellent 'capabilities'.

- **Ornamental gardens** are ordinary flower gardens.

Cones

> ★ STAR FACT ★
> The largest cones are those of the sugar pine which can grow over 65 cm long.

- **Cones** are the tough little clusters of scales that coniferous trees carry their seeds in.

- **The scales** on a cone are called bracts. The seeds are held between the bracts. Bracts are thin and papery in spruces and thick and woody in silver firs.

- **Pine cone bracts** have a lump called an umbo.

- **All cones** are green and quite soft when they first form, then turn brown and hard as they ripen.

- **Cones stand upright** on the branch until they are ripe and ready to shed their seeds.

- **Most cones** turn over when ripe to hang downwards so that the seeds fall out.

- **The cones of cedars** and silver firs stay upright and the bracts drop away to release the seeds.

- **Long, hanging cones** like those of the pine and spruce hang throughout winter then release seeds in spring.

- **The monkey puzzle** tree has a unique, pineapple-shaped cone with golden spines and edible seeds.

▼ *These Scots pine cones are brown and were fertilized about three years ago. Younger cones further out on branches would have been fertilized last spring and would still be green.*

Lichen

- **Lichens** are a remarkable partnership between algae and fungi.

- **The algae** in lichen are tiny green balls which make the food from sunlight to feed the fungi.

- **The fungi make a protective** layer around the algae and hold water.

- **There are 20,000** species of lichen. Some grow on soil, but most grow on rocks or tree bark.

- **Fruticose lichens** are shrub-like, foliose lichens look like leaves, and crustose lichens look like crusts.

- **Lichens only grow** when moistened by rain.

- **Lichens can survive** in many places where other plants would die, such as the Arctic, in deserts and on mountain tops.

- **Some Arctic lichens** are over 4000 years old.

- **Lichens are very sensitive** to air pollution, especially sulphur dioxide, and are used by scientists to indicate air pollution.

▲ Lichens are tiny and slow-growing – some growing only a fraction of a millimetre a year. But they are usually long-lived.

- **The oakmoss lichen** from Europe and North Africa is added to most perfumes and after-shaves to stop flower scents fading. Scandinavian reindeer moss is a lichen eaten by reindeer. It is exported to Germany for decorations.

Spores and seeds

▶ New sycamore trees grow from their tiny winged seeds (top). Mushrooms (below right) grow from spores.

- **Seed plants** are plants that grow from seeds.

- **Seeds** have a tiny baby plant inside called an embryo from which the plant grows plus a supply of stored food and a protective coating.

- **Spores contain** special cells which grow into new organisms. Green plants like ferns and mosses, and fungi like mushrooms, produce spores.

- **All 250,000 flowering plants** produce 'enclosed' seeds. These are seeds that grow inside sacs called ovaries which turn into a fruit around the seed.

- **The 800 or so** conifers, cycads and gingkos produce 'naked' seeds, which means there is no fruit around them.

- **Seeds** only develop when a plant is fertilized by pollen.

- **The largest seeds** are those of the double coconut or coco-de-mer of the Seychelles which can sometimes weigh up to 20 kg.

- **30,000 orchid seeds** weigh barely 1 gm.

- **The world's biggest tree,** the giant redwood, grows from tiny seeds that are less than 2 mm long.

- **Coconut trees** produce only a few big seeds; orchids produce millions, but only a few grow into plants.

Parts of a tree

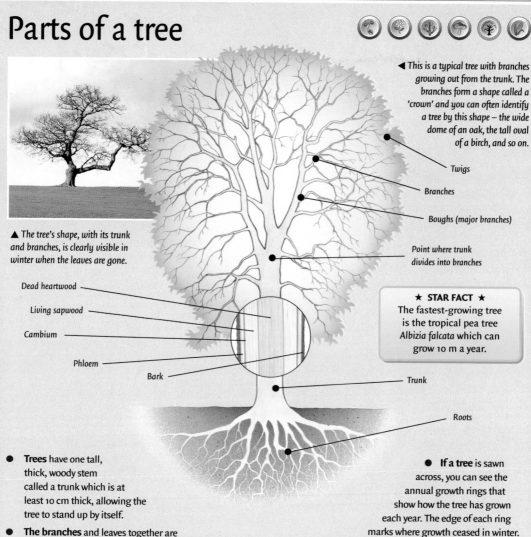

◀ This is a typical tree with branches growing out from the trunk. The branches form a shape called a 'crown' and you can often identify a tree by this shape – the wide dome of an oak, the tall oval of a birch, and so on.

Twigs

Branches

Boughs (major branches)

Point where trunk divides into branches

▲ The tree's shape, with its trunk and branches, is clearly visible in winter when the leaves are gone.

Dead heartwood

Living sapwood

Cambium

Phloem

Bark

Trunk

Roots

★ STAR FACT ★
The fastest-growing tree is the tropical pea tree *Albizia falcata* which can grow 10 m a year.

- **Trees** have one tall, thick, woody stem called a trunk which is at least 10 cm thick, allowing the tree to stand up by itself.

- **The branches** and leaves together are called the crown. The trunk supports the crown and holds it up to the sun.

- **The trunks of conifers** typically grow right to the top of the tree. The lower branches are longer because they have been growing longest. The upper branches are short because they are new. So the tree has a conical shape.

- **Trees with wide flat leaves** are called broad-leaved trees. They usually have crowns with a rounded shape.

- **The trunk and branches** have five layers from the centre out: heartwood, sapwood, cambium, phloem and bark.

- **If a tree** is sawn across, you can see the annual growth rings that show how the tree has grown each year. The edge of each ring marks where growth ceased in winter. Counting the rings gives the age of the tree.

- **Heartwood** is the dark, dead wood in the centre of the trunk. Sapwood is pale living wood, where tiny pipes called xylem carry sap from the roots to the leaves.

- **The cambium** is the thin layer where the sapwood is actually growing; the phloem is the thin food-conducting layer.

- **The bark** is the tree's protective skin of hard dead tissue. Bark takes many different forms and often cracks as the tree grows, but it is always made from cork.

Roses

- **The rose** is one of the most popular of all garden flowers because of its lovely perfume and beautiful blooms.

- **Wild roses** usually have small flowers and have a single layer of five petals. Garden roses usually have big flowers with multiple sets of five petals in two or more layers.

- **There are 100 species** of wild rose, but all today's garden roses were created by crossing 10 Asian species.

- **There are now over 13,000** official varieties of garden rose altogether.

- **Some experts divide garden roses** into groups by when they bloom: old roses bloom once a year in early summer; perpetual roses bloom in early summer, then again in autumn; and everblooming hybrids bloom all summer.

- **Old roses** include yellow briers, damask roses and many climbing roses.

- **Perpetuals** include what are called hybrid perpetuals.

- **Everblooming hybrids** include floribundas, hybrid teas,

▶ Roses often look their best just after they begin to open, when the petals are still in a tight, velvety cluster.

gloribundas and polyanthas.

- **Hybrid teas** such as the Peace are the most popular of all roses. They were created by crossing everblooming but fragile tea roses with vigorous hybrid perpetuals.

- **Attar of roses** is a perfume made from roses, especially damask roses.

Rice

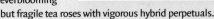

- **Rice** is a cereal grain that is the basic food of half the world's population. It is especially important in SE Asia.

- **The wild rice** or Indian rice collected by North American Indians for thousands of years is not related to rice.

- **Like other cereals,** rice is a grass, but it grows best in shallow water in tropical areas.

- **Rice growers** usually flood their fields to keep them wet. The flooded fields are called paddies.

> ★ STAR FACT ★
> A lot of wheat is fed to livestock, but 95% of all rice is eaten by people.

- **The rice seeds** are sown in soil, then when the seedlings are 25–50 days old they are transplanted to the paddy field under 5–10 cm of water.

- **Brown rice** is rice grain with the husk ground away. White rice is rice grain with the inner bran layer ground away as well, and is far less nutritious.

- **Rice-growing** probably began in India about 3000BC.

- **In 1962** researchers in the Philippines experimented with hybrids of 10,000 strains of rice. They made a rice called 'IR-8' by crossing a tall, vigorous rice from Indonesia and a dwarf rice from Taiwan.

- **IR-8** sometimes gave double yields, and was called 'miracle rice', but it did not grow well in poor soils .

◀ To keep paddies flooded, fields on hillsides are banked in terraces.

Mushrooms

▲ *Like other fungi, mushrooms cannot make their own food and feed off hosts such as trees.*

- **Mushrooms** are umbrella-shaped fungi, many of which are edible.

- **Mushrooms** feed off either living or decaying plants.

- **Poisonous mushrooms** are called toadstools.

- **The umbrella-shaped** part of the mushroom is called the fruiting body. Under the surface is a mass of fine stalk threads called the mycelium.

- **The threads** making up the mycelium are called hyphae (said hi-fi). These absorb food.

- **The fruiting body** grows overnight after rain and lasts just a few days. The mycelium may survive underground for many years.

- **The fruiting body** is covered by a protective cap. On the underside of the cap are lots of thin sheets called gills which are covered in spores.

- **A mushroom's** gills can produce 16 billion spores in its brief lifetime.

- **The biggest mushrooms** have caps up to 50 cm across and grow up to 40 cm tall.

- **Fairy rings** are rings of bright green grass once said to have been made by fairies dancing. They are actually made by a mushroom as its hyphae spread outwards. Chemicals they release make grass grow greener. Gradually the mycelium at the centre dies while outer edges grow and the ring gets bigger.

Forestry

▲ *The signs of pollarding are easy to see in these trees in winter when the leaves are gone.*

- **Forests** provide fuel, timber, paper, resins, varnishes, dyes, rubber, kapok and much more besides.

- **Softwood** is timber from coniferous trees such as pine, larch, fir and spruce. 75–80% of the natural forests of northern Asia, Europe and the USA are softwood.

> ★ **STAR FACT** ★
> Every year the world uses three billion cubic metres of wood – a pile as big as a football stadium and as high as Mt Everest.

- **In vast plantations** fast-growing conifers are set in straight rows so they are easy to cut down.

- **Hardwood** is timber from broad-leaved trees such as oak. Most hardwood forests are in the tropics.

- **Hardwood trees** take over a century to reach maturity.

- **Tropical hardwoods** such as mahogany are becoming rare as more hardwood is cut for timber.

- **Pollarding** is cutting the topmost branches of a tree so new shoots grow from the trunk to the same length.

- **Coppicing** is cutting tree stems at ground level to encourage several stems to grow from the same root.

- **Half the world's remaining** rainforests will be gone by 2020 if they are cut down at today's rate.

Sugar

- **Sugars** are sweet-tasting natural substances made by plants and animals. All green plants make sugar.
- **Fruit and honey** contain a sugar called fructose. Milk contains the sugar lactose.

▼▶ *Crystals of demerara sugar are made from the sugary juice from the stems of the tropical sugar cane.*

- **The most common sugar** is called sucrose, or just sugar – like the sugar you sprinkle on cereal.
- **Sugar is made** from sugar cane and sugar beet.
  - **Sugar cane** is a tropical grass with woody stems 2–5 m tall. It grows in places like India and Brazil.
    - **Sugar juice is made** from cane by shredding and crushing the stems and soaking them in hot water to dissolve the sugar.
    - **Sugar beet** is a turnip-like plant that grows in temperate countries.
    - **Sugar juice is made** from beet by soaking thin slices of the root in hot water to dissolve the sugar.
- **Sugar juice** is warmed to evaporate water so crystals form.
- **White sugar** is sugar made from sugar beet, or by refining (purifying) cane-sugar. Brown sugars such as muscovado and demerara are unrefined cane-sugar. Molasses and black treacle are by-products of cane-sugar refining.

Leaves

- **Leaves** are a plant's powerhouse, using sunlight to join water and carbon dioxide to make sugar, the plant's fuel.
- **Leaves are** broad and flat to catch maximum sunlight.
- **Leaves are** joined to the stem by a stalk called a petiole.
- **The flat part** of the leaf is called the blade.
- **The leaf blade** is like a sandwich with two layers of cells holding a thick filling of green cells.
- **The green** comes from the chemical chlorophyll. It is this that catches sunlight to make sugar in photosynthesis.
- **Chlorophyll** is held in tiny bags in each cell called chloroplasts.
- **A network** of branching veins (tubes) supplies the leaf with water. It also transports the sugar made there to the rest of the plant.
- **Air containing** carbon dioxide is drawn into the leaf through pores on the underside called stomata. Stomata also let out water in a process called transpiration.
- **To cut down water loss** in dry places, leaves may be rolled-up, long and needle-like, or covered in hairs or wax. Climbing plants, such as peas, have leaf tips that coil into stalks called tendrils to help the plant cling.

▶ *A hugely magnified slice through a leaf, showing the cells and veins.*

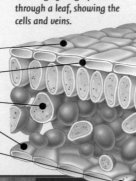

Waterproof wax coat

Upper skin of leaf

Green cells

Lower skin of leaf

Leaf pores (stomata)

Leaf veins containing tiny tubes

Rotting trees

- **Trees** are dying in forests all the time.

- **In the past** foresters used to clear away dead trees or chop down those that were dying, but it is now clear that they play a vital part in the woodland ecosystem.

- **When a tree falls** it crashes down through the leaves and opens up a patch of woodland, called a glade, to the sky.

- **In the glade** saplings (new young trees) can sprout and flourish in the sunlight.

- **Many other woodland plants** flourish in the sunshine of a glade.

- **Flowers** such as foxgloves and rosebay willowherbs often spring up in a glade.

- **Bracken and shrubs** such as brambles grow quickly in a glade.

- **The rotting tree trunk** provides food for fungi such as green-staining and candle snuff fungus.

- **Many insects** such as beetles find a home in the rotting wood.

- **As the rotting tree is broken down** it not only provides food for plants, insects and bacteria; it enriches the soil too.

▶ Rotting trees provide a home for many kinds of plants, such as these tiny green liverworts, growing on an old stump.

Tulips

▲ Huge numbers of tulips are now grown in the fields in Holland.

- **Tulips** are flowers that bloom in spring from bulbs.

- **Tulips are** monocots and produce one large, bell-shaped bloom at the end of each stem.

- **There are about** 100 species of wild tulip, growing right across Asia to China.

- **Tulips** come in most colours but blue. Reds and yellows are common, but they vary from white to deep purple.

- **There are over 4000** garden varieties.

- **Most tulips** are 'late bloomers' with names like breeders, cottages and parrots.

- **Mid-season bloomers** include Mendels and Darwins.

- **Early season** bloomers include single-flowereds and double-flowered earlies.

- **Tulips** were introduced to Europe in 1551 by the Viennese ambassador to Turkey, Augier de Busbecq. But Holland became the centre of tulip-growing early in the 1600s, when Europe was gripped by 'tulipmania'. At this time, people would exchange mansions for a single tulip bulb. Holland is still the centre of tulip growing.

> ★ STAR FACT ★
> The word tulip comes from the Turkish for 'turban', because of their shape.

Herbs

- **Herbs** are small plants used as medicines or to flavour food.

- **Most herbs** are perennial and have soft stems which die back in winter.

- **With some herbs** such as rosemary, only the leaves are used. With others, such as garlic, the bulb is used. Fennel is used for its seeds as well as its bulb and leaves. Coriander is used for its leaves and seeds.

- **Basil** gets its name from the Greek *basilikon* or 'kingly', because it was so highly valued around the Mediterranean for its strong flavour. In the Middle Ages, judges and officials used to carry it in posies to ward off unpleasant smells.

- **Rosemary** is a coastal plant and gets its name from the Latin *ros marinus*, meaning 'sea dew'. People who study herbs – herbalists – once thought it improved memory.

- **Bay leaves** are the leaves of an evergreen laurel tree. They were used to make crowns for athletes, heroes and poets in Ancient Rome. It is said that a bay tree planted by your house protects it from lightning.

- **Oregano** or marjoram is a Mediterranean herb used in Italian cooking. The plant gave its name to the American state of Oregon where it is now very common.

- **Sage** is a herb thought by herbalists of old to have special healing qualities. Its scientific name *Salvia* comes from the Latin word *salvere*, 'to save'.

- **St John's wort** is a perennial herb with yellow flowers which was said to have healing qualities given by St John the Baptist. The red juice of its leaves represented his blood. Now many people use it to treat depression.

> ★ **STAR FACT** ★
> The root of the mandrake was supposed to have magical properties. Anyone who uprooted one was said to die, so people tied the root to a dog's tail to pull it up.

▶ These are just some of the more common herbs used in cooking, either fresh or dried. The flavour comes from what are called 'essential oils' in the leaves. Parsley, thyme and a bay leaf may be tied up in a piece of muslin cloth to make what is called a bouquet garni. This is hung in soups and stews while cooking to give them extra flavour, but is not actually eaten.

Thyme

Rosemary

Mint

Dill

Parsley

Bay

Fennel

Sage

Chives

Monocotyledons

- **Monocotyledons** are one of the two basic classes of flowering plant. The other is dicotyledons.
- **Monocotyledons** are plants that sprout a single leaf from their seeds.
- **Monocotyledons** are also known as monocots or Liliopsida.
- **There are about** 50,000 species of monocots – about a quarter of all flowering plants.
- **Monocots** include grasses, cereals, bamboos, date palms, aloes, snake plants, tulips, orchids and daffodils.
- **Monocots** tend to grow quickly and their stems stay soft and pliable, except for bamboos and palms. Most are herbaceous.

▲ *Daffodils are typical monocots, with long lance-like leaves and petals in threes.*

- **The tubes or veins** in monocot leaves run parallel to each other. They also develop a thick tangle of thin roots rather than a single long 'tap' root, like dicots.
- **The flower parts of monocots** such as petals tend to be set in threes or multiples of three.
- **Unlike dicots,** monocot stems grow from the inside. Dicots have a cambium, which is the layer of growing cells near the outside of the stem. Monocots rarely have a cambium.
- **Monocots** are thought to have appeared about 90 million years ago, developing from water lily-like dicots living in swamps and rivers.

Medicinal plants

▲ *Aspirin is the painkiller most widely used today. It first came from the bark of willow trees.*

- **Prehistoric neanderthal people** probably used plants as medicines at least 50,000 years ago.
- **Until quite recently** herbaceous plants were our main source of medicines. Plants used as medicines were listed in books called herbals.

- **An Ancient Chinese** list of 1892 herbal remedies drawn up over 3000 years ago is still used today.
- **The famous illustrated herbal** of Greek physician Dioscorides was made in the 1st century BC.
- **The most famous English** herbalist was Nicholas Culpeper, who wrote *A Physical Directory* in 1649.
- **Most medicines,** except antibiotics, come from flowering plants or were first found in flowering plants.
- **Powerful painkilling** drugs come from the seeds of the opium poppy.
- **Digitalis** is a heart drug that came from foxgloves. It is poisonous in large doses.
- **Garlic** is thought to protect the body against heart disease – and vampires!

★ STAR FACT ★
Vincristine is a drug made from the Madagascar periwinkle that helps children fight cancer.

Pine trees

- **Pine trees** are evergreen conifers with long needle-like leaves. They grow mostly in sandy or rocky soils in cool places.

- **Pines** are the largest family of conifers.

- **There 90–100 species of pine** – most of them coming originally from northern Eurasia and North America.

- **Pines grow** fast and straight, reaching their full height in less than 20 years – which is why they provide 75% of the world's timber.

- **Some pines** produce a liquid called resin which is used to make turpentine, paint and soap.

- **Soft or white pines**, such as sugar pines and piñons, have soft wood. They grow needles in bundles of five and have little resin.

- **Hard or yellow pines**, such as Scots, Corsican and loblolly pines, have harder wood. They grow needles in bundles of two or three and make lots of resin.

◀ Like all conifers, Corsican pines produce cones. The cones look very different from flowers but serve the same purpose – making the seeds from which new trees grow.

- **Eurasian pines** include the Scots pine, Corsican pine, black pine, pinaster and stone pine.

- **North American pines** include the eastern white pine, sugar pine, stone pines, piñons, Ponderosa pine, and Monterey pine.

- **The sugar pine** is the biggest of all pines, often growing up to 70 m tall and 3.5 m thick. The eastern white pine has valuable fine white wood.

Tropical fruit

- **Tropical fruits** grow mainly in the tropics where it is warm because they cannot survive even a light frost.

- **The best-known tropical fruits** are bananas and pineapples. Others include guavas, breadfruit, lychees, melons, mangoes and papayas.

- **Banana plants** are gigantic herbs with trunks that grow 3–6 m high.

- **Alexander the Great** saw bananas in India in 326BC. Bananas were taken to the Caribbean from the Canaries c. 1550. They are now one of the main Caribbean crops.

- **There are hundreds** of varieties of banana. Most widely used is the Gros Michel. Plantains are cooking bananas.

- **Pineapples** come from Central America, and were seen by Columbus and Sir Walter Raleigh.

- **The Portuguese** took pineapples to India about 1550. Thailand is now the world's leading producer.

- **Mangoes** grow on evergreen trees of the cashew family in Burma and India.

- **The mango** is sacred to Buddhists because the mango groves provided welcome shade for Buddha.

- **Melons** are a huge group of big, round fruit with soft, juicy flesh, including canteloupes. They grow on trailing vines. Watermelons are not true melons.

▼ Bananas are picked green and unripe, shipped in refrigerated ships, then artificially ripened with 'ethylene' gas to turn them yellow.

Tropical rainforest

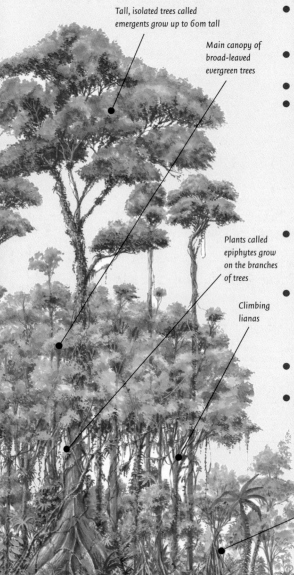

Tall, isolated trees called emergents grow up to 6om tall

Main canopy of broad-leaved evergreen trees

Plants called epiphytes grow on the branches of trees

Climbing lianas

Dense understorey of shrubs

- **Tropical rainforests** are warm and wet, with over 2,000 mm of rain a year and average temperatures over 20°C. This is why they are the world's richest plant habitats.

- **Flowering plants** (angiosperms) originated in tropical rainforests. Eleven of the 13 oldest families live here.

- **Most rainforest trees** are broad-leaved and evergreen.

- **Trees** of the Amazon rainforest include rosewood, Brazil nut and rubber, plus myrtle, laurel and palms. Trees in the African rainforest include mahogany, ebony, limba, wenge, agba, iroko and sapele.

> ★ STAR FACT ★
> One 23 hectare area of Malaysian rainforest
> has 375 species of tree with trunks
> thicker than 91 cm.

- **Many rainforest plants** have big, bright flowers to attract birds and insects in the gloom. Flowers pollinated by birds are often red, those by night-flying moths white or pink and those by day-flying insects yellow or orange.

- **The gloom** means many plants need big seeds to store enough food while they grow. So they grow fragrant fruits that attract animals to eat the fruit and spread the seed in their body waste. Fruit bats are drawn to mangoes. Orang-utans and tigers eat durians.

- **Many trees** grow flowers on their trunks to make them easy for animals to reach. This is called cauliflory.

- **Rainforest trees** are covered with epiphytes – plants whose roots never reach the soil but take water from the air.

- **Many plants are parasitic** including mistletoes and Rafflesia. They feed on other plants.

◄ Most tropical rainforests have several layers. Towering above the main forest are isolated emergent trees up to 60 m tall. Below these, 30–50 m above the ground, is a dense canopy of leaves and branches at the top of tall, straight trees. In the gloom beneath is the understorey where young emergents, small conical trees and a huge range of shrubs grow. Clinging lianas wind their way up through the trees and epiphytes grow high on tree branches and trunks where they can reach daylight.

The first crops

> ★ STAR FACT ★
> Beans, bottle gourds and water chestnuts were grown at Spirit Cave in Thailand 11,000 years ago.

- **The first crops** were probably root crops like turnips. Grains and green vegetables were probably first grown as crops later.

- **Einkorn and emmer** wheat and wild barley may have been cultivated by Natufians (stone-age people) about 7000BC at Ali Kosh on the Iran-Iraq border.

- **Pumpkins** and beans were cultivated in Mexico c.7000BC.

- **People** in the Amazon have grown manioc to make a flat bread called *cazabi* for thousands of years.

- **Corn** was probably first grown about 9000 years ago from the teosinte plant of the Mexican highlands.

- **Russian botanist** N. I. Vavilov worked out that wheat and rye came from the wild grasses of central Asia, millet and barley from highland China and rice from India.

- **Millet** was grown in China from c.4500BC.

- **In N. Europe** the first grains were those now called fat hen, gold of pleasure and curl-topped lady's thumb.

- **Sumerian** farmers in the Middle East c.3000BC grew barley along with wheat, flax, dates, apples, plums and grapes.

▲ Emmer wheat is one of the oldest of all cereal crops. It was probably first sown deliberately from wild grass seeds about 10,000 years ago.

Magnolia

▲ Magnolias have a single large typically white or pink flower at the end of each stem. This is the evergreen Magnolia kobus.

- **Magnolias** are evergreen shrubs, climbers and trees.

- **Magnolias** are named after the French botanist Pierre Magnol (1638-1715).

- **They produce** beautiful large white or pink flowers and are popular garden plants.

- **Nutmegs, custard** apples, ylang-ylangs and tulip trees are all kinds of magnolia.

- **There are** over 80 different kinds of magnolia.

- **Magnolias may be** the most ancient of all flowering plants. Their fossil remains have been found in rocks 120 million years old – when the dinosaurs lived.

- **A seed 2,000 years old,** found by archaeologists (people who study ancient remains) in Japan was planted in 1982. It grew and produced an unusual flower with eight petals.

- **The most popular** garden magnolia was bred in a garden near Paris, France, from a wild Japanese kind (*Magnolia liliiflora*) and a wild Chinese kind (*Magnolia denudata*).

- **Magnolia trees** have the largest leaves and flowers of any tree outside the tropical forests.

- **The cucumber tree** –a kind of magnolia – is named after its seed clusters, which look like cucumbers.

Tundra

▲ In spring the tundra bursts into glorious colour as flowers bloom to take advantage of the brief warm weather.

- **Tundras** are regions so cold and with so little rain that tall trees cannot grow.

- **Tundras** are typically covered in snow for at least half the year. Even in summer the soil 1 m or so below the ground may be permanently frozen.

- **The frozen ground** stops water draining away and makes tundras marshy and damp.

- **Winter temperatures** in the tundra can drop to -40°C. Even summer temperatures are rarely above 12°C on average.

- **Mosses and lichens**, grasses and sedges, heathers and low shrubs grow in tundra. Trees only grow in stunted forms such as dwarf willows and ash trees.

- **In spring** tundra plants grow quickly and bright wildflowers spread across the ground.

- **Arctic tundra** occur in places like northern Siberia and Canada.

- **Alpine tundras** occur high on mountains everywhere.

- **Arctic flowers** include saxifrages, Arctic poppies, fireweeds, cinquefoil, louseworts and stonecrops.

- **Alpine flowers** are often the same as Arctic flowers. They include mountain avens, gentians, saxifrages and snowbells.

Coffee and tea

- **Coffee** comes from the glossy, evergreen *Coffee arabica* shrub which originally grew wild in Ethiopia. Coffee is now grown in tropical countries around the world.

- **The coffee plant** is a mountain plant and grows best from about 1000 to 2500 m up.

- **Coffee beans** are not actually beans at all; they are the seeds inside red berries.

- **Coffee plants** can grow over 6 m tall, but they are usually pruned to under 4 m to make picking easier.

- **A coffee plant** yields only enough berries to make about 0.7 kg of coffee each year.

- **Coffee berries** are picked by hand then pulped to remove the flesh and finally roasted.

> ★ STAR FACT ★
> Legend says Ethiopian goatherds discovered coffee when they saw their goats staying awake all night after eating the berries of the coffee plant.

▲ Coffee berries appear green at first, then turn yellow and eventually bright red as they ripen.

- **Tea** is the leaves of the evergreen tea plant that grows in the tropics, mostly between 1000 and 2000 m.

- **Tea plants** have small, white, scented flowers and nuts that look like hazelnuts.

- **Tea plants** grow 9 m tall but they are pruned to 3 m.

Maple trees

- **Maples** are a huge group of trees belonging to the Acer family.

- **Maples grow** all over the temperate regions of the northern hemisphere, but especially in China.

- **Many maple tree leaves** turn brilliant shades of red in autumn.

◀ All maple trees have winged seeds called samaras or keys. Many also have three-lobed leaves, like these of the sugar maple.

- **Several North American maple trees,** including the sugar maple and the black maple, give maple syrup.

- **Maple syrup** is 'sweet-water' sap. This is different from ordinary sap and flows from wounds during times of thaws when the tree is not growing. Syrup is collected between mid January and mid April.

- **Maple syrup** was used by the Native Americans of the Great Lakes and St Lawrence River regions long before Europeans arrived in North America.

- **About 30 litres** of sap give 1 litre of maple syrup.

- **The leaf of the sugar maple tree** is Canada's national symbol.

- **Many small maples** are grown as garden plants. Japanese maples have been carefully bred over the centuries to give all kinds of varieties with different leaf shapes and colours.

- **The red maple** is planted in many North American cities for its brilliant red autumn leaves.

Wildflowers

- **All flowers** were originally wild. Garden flowers have been bred over the centuries to be very different from their wild originals.

- **Wildflowers** are flowers that have developed naturally.

- **Most wildflowers** are smaller and more delicate than their garden cousins.

- **Each** kind of place has its own special range of wildflowers, although many wildflowers have now been spread to different places by humans.

- **Heathlands** may have purple blooms of heathers, yellow gorse and scarlet pimpernel.

- **In meadow grass** flowers like buttercups, daisies, clover, forget-me-nots and ragged robin often grow.

- **In deciduous woodlands** flowers like bluebells, primroses, daffodils and celandines grow.

- **By the sea** among the rocks, sea campion and pink thrift may bloom, while up on the cliffs, there may be birdsfoot trefoil among the grasses.

- **As humans** take over larger and larger areas of the world, and as farmers use more and more weedkillers on the land, many wildflowers are becoming very rare. Some are so rare that they are protected by law.

- **The lady's slipper orchid** grows in parts of Europe, Asia and America, usually in moist, woodland areas.

▶ There are now very few meadows with rich displays of wildflowers like this.

Arctic plants

- **The Arctic circle** is icy cold and dark for nine months of the year, but for a few months in summer it is daylight almost all the time.

- **Over 900 species** of plants cope with the Arctic climate.

- **Full-size trees** are rare in the Arctic; but grasses and sedges, mosses and lichens are common.

- **Willow trees** grow in the Arctic, but because of the cold and fierce wind, they grow less than 10 cm tall, spreading out along the ground instead.

- **Many Arctic** plants are evergreen so they are ready to make the most of the brief summer.

- **Many small** flowers are specially

adapted to survive Arctic conditions, such as saxifrages, avens, stonecrops, snowbells and willowherbs.

- **The Arctic poppy** is the flower that blooms nearest the North Pole.

- **Butterflies and bees** are rare in the Arctic, so many plants, like mustard, rely on the wind for pollination.

- **The soil is so poor** in the Arctic that seeds make the most of any animal corpse, such as that of a musk ox. Arctic flowers often spring up inside skulls and near bones.

- **Some plants** have dark leaves and stems to soak up the sun's warmth quickly and so melt the snow.

◀ In summer, the Arctic bursts into brief life with tiny flowers and ground berries like bilberries.

Pollination

- **For seeds** to develop, pollen from a flower's male anther must get to a female stigma.

- **Some flowers are** self-pollinating and the pollen moves from an anther to a stigma on the same plant.

- **In cross-pollinating** flowers, the pollen from the anthers must be carried to a stigma on a different plant of the same kind.

- **Some pollen** is carried by the wind.

- **Most pollen** is carried on the bodies of insects such as bees or by birds or bats that visit the flower.

- **Insect-pollinated flowers** are often brightly coloured and sweet-smelling to attract bees and butterflies.

- **Bees and butterflies** are also drawn by the flower's sweet juice or nectar. As they sip the nectar, they may brush pollen on to the stigma, or take some on their bodies from anthers to the stigma of other flowers.

- **Bees and butterflies** are drawn to blue, yellow and pink flowers. White flowers draw night-flying moths.

- **Many flowers** have honey guides – markings to guide the bees in. These are often invisible to us and can only be seen in ultraviolet light, which bees can see.

- **The cuckoopint** smells like cow-dung to attract the flies that carry its pollen.

◀ Many flowers rely on attracting bees to carry their pollen.

The farming year

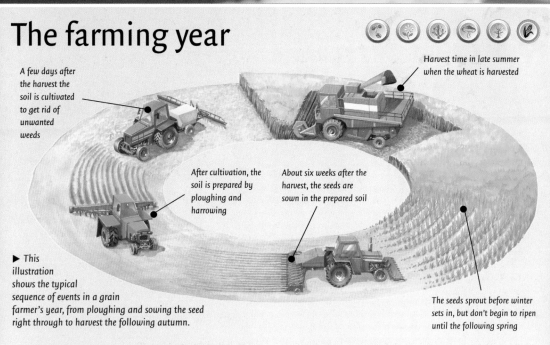

A few days after the harvest the soil is cultivated to get rid of unwanted weeds

Harvest time in late summer when the wheat is harvested

After cultivation, the soil is prepared by ploughing and harrowing

About six weeks after the harvest, the seeds are sown in the prepared soil

▶ This illustration shows the typical sequence of events in a grain farmer's year, from ploughing and sowing the seed right through to harvest the following autumn.

The seeds sprout before winter sets in, but don't begin to ripen until the following spring

- **The farming year** varies considerably around the world, and farmers do different tasks at different times of year in different places.

- **In temperate regions** the crop farmer's year starts in autumn after the harvest. Once the straw has been baled and the surplus burned, the race starts to prepare the soil for next year's crops before snow and frost set in.

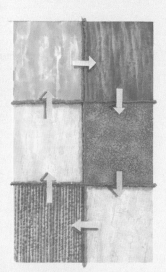

◀ Without artificial fertilizers, the soil is quickly exhausted if grain crops are planted year after year. So in the past, farmers rotated fields with different crops to allow the soil to rest. Rotation systems varied, but usually included grain, green plants, and 'rest' crops. The earliest systems had just two alternating fields. Medieval farmers used three fields. From the 1700s, rotations became more complex.

- **A tractor** drags a cultivator (like a large rake) across the field to make weeds 'chit' (germinate). A few days later the soil is cultivated again to uproot the seedlings.

- **Next the soil** is ploughed to break up the soil ready for the seed to be sown, then harrowed to smooth out the deep furrows made by the plough.

- **Within six weeks** of the harvest if the weather holds, winter wheat or barley seed is sown, fertilizer is applied and the seed soon sprouts like a carpet of grass.

- **In winter,** the farmer turns to tasks like hedge-cutting, ditching and fencing.

- **In spring** potatoes, oats and spring wheat and barley are planted, and winter crops treated with nitrogen fertilizer. In spring and summer, many farmers treat crops with 30 or more pesticides and weedkillers.

- **As the summer wears on** the wheat turns gold and is ready for harvesting when the electronic moisture metre shows it contains less than 18% moisture.

- **If the summer** is damp, the grain's moisture content may not go down below 25%, making harvesting difficult. But warm sun can quickly rectify the situation.

- **The farming year** ends with the harvest. In the past this used to be separated into various stages – harvesting, threshing, winnowing and baling. Now combine harvesters allow the farmer to complete them all at one go.

Boreal forest

- **Forests in cool regions** in the north of Asia and North America, bordering on the Arctic circle, are called boreal forests. The word *boreal* means 'northern'.

- **Winters** in boreal regions are long and cold. Days are short and snow lies permanently on the ground.

- **In Russia and Siberia** boreal forest is called *taiga*, which is Russian for 'little sticks'.

- **Boreal forests** are mostly evergreen conifers such as pine – especially Scots pine – spruce, larch and fir.

- **In Europe** boreal forests include Norway spruce and Sukaczev larch. In Siberia, there are trees such as Siberian larch and fir, chosenia and Siberian stone pine.

- **North American** forests include balsam firs, black spruces, jack pines and lodgepole pines.

▶ *Boreal forests cover 17% of the Earth's land area. For nine months of the year they are cold and dark, but they spring to life in the three-month summer.*

- **Boreal forest floors** are covered with carpets of needles. Twinflowers, calypso orchids, lingonberries, baneberries, and coral roots are among the few plants that will grow.

- **Boreal forest trees** are good at recovering after fire. Indeed jack pine and black spruce cones only open to release their seeds after a fire.

- **The Black Dragon Fire** of 1987 in the boreal forests of China and Russia was the biggest fire in history.

> ★ STAR FACT ★
> Half the ground under conifers is covered in moss and lichen.

The Green Revolution

- **Since ancient times** farmers have tried to improve crops. They brushed pollen from one species on to another to gain desirable qualities in the next generation of plants.

- **In 1876** Charles Darwin discovered that inbreeding – pollinating with almost identical plants – made plants less vigorous. Cross-breeding between different strains produced healthier plants.

- **In the early 1900s** American scientists found that they could improve the protein content of corn by inbreeding – but the yield was poor.

- **In 1917** Donald Jones discovered the 'double-cross', combining four strains (not the normal two) to create a hybrid corn giving high yield and high protein.

▶ *Forty years ago, many farmers abandoned traditional wheat seeds and began planting big 'superwheat' seeds.*

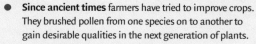

- **Hybrid corn** changed US farming, raising yields from 2000 litres per hectare in 1933 to 7220 in 1980.

- **In the 1960s** US farmers began growing wheat crosses such as Gaines, developed by Norman Borlaug from Japanese dwarf wheats.

- **Gaines and Nugaines** are short-stemmed wheats that grow fast and give huge yields – but they need masses of artificial fertilizers and pesticides.

- **In India and Asia** new dwarf wheats and rices created a 'Green Revolution', doubling yields in the 1960s and 1970s.

- **The Green Revolution** means farmers now use ten times as much nitrogen fertilizer as in 1960.

- **The huge cost** of special seeds, fertilizers and pesticides has often meant that only big agribusinesses can keep up, forcing small farmers out of business.

Mosses

- **Mosses** are tiny, green, non-flowering plants found throughout the world. They form cushions just a few millimetres thick on walls, rocks and logs.
- **Unlike other plants** they have no true roots. Instead, they take in moisture from the air through their stems and tiny, root-like threads called rhizoids.
- **Mosses reproduce** from minute spores in two stages.
- **First** tadpole-like male sex cells are made on bag-like stems called antheridae and swim to join the female eggs on cup-like stems called archegonia.
- **Then** a stalk called a sporophyte grows from the ova. On top is a capsule holding thousands of spores.
- **When the time** is right, the sporophyte capsule bursts, ejecting spores. If spores land in a suitable place, male and female stems grow and the process begins again.
- **Mosses** can survive for weeks without water, then soak it up like a sponge when it rains.

▶ Mosses grow on rocks in damp places everywhere. They take in the moisture they need to grow from the air, but to reproduce, they need to be completely soaked.

- **The sphagnum or peat moss** can soak up 25 times its own weight of water.
- **Male cells** can only swim to female cells if the moss is partly under water. So mosses often grow near streams where they get splashed.
- **Spanish moss** was often used as a filler in packing cases and to pad upholstery.

Rhododendrons

- **Rhododendrons** are a big group of 800 different trees and shrubs which belong to the heath family.
- **The word 'rhododendron'** means 'rose tree'.
- **Most rhododendrons** came originally from the Himalayas and the mountains of Malaysia where they form dense thickets.

- **Many rhododendrons** are now widely cultivated for their big red or white blooms and evergreen leaves.
- **There are over 6000** different cultivated varieties of rhododendron.
- **The spectacular June blooming** of the catawba rhododendron or mountain rosebay in the Great Smoky Mountains, USA, is now a tourist attraction.
- **The Dahurian** is a famous purply pink rhododendron from Siberia and Mongolia.
- **The Smirnow** was discovered in the 1880s high up in the Caucasus Mts on the Georgian–Turkish border.
- **Smirnows** have been bred with other rhododendrons to make them very hardy.
- **Azaleas** were once considered a separate group of plants, but they are now classified with rhododendrons.

◀ Rhododendrons have thrived so well in places where they have been introduced that many people now consider them weeds.

Carnivorous plants

- **Plants that trap** insects for food are called carnivorous plants. They live in places where they cannot get enough nitrogen from the soil and so the insects provide the nitrogen.

- **There are 550 species** living in places from the high peaks of New Zealand to the swamps of Carolina.

- **The butterwort** gets its name because its leaves ooze drops that make them glisten like butter. These drops contains the plant's digestive juices.

◀ Pitchers hang on long tendrils that grow high into the branches of tropical rainforests. Some pitchers are tiny and can trap nothing bigger than an ant. The pitchers of the Nepenthes rajah are big enough for a rat.

- **The sundew** can tell the difference between flesh and other substances and only reacts to flesh.

- **The sundew's** leaves are covered in tentacles that ooze a sticky substance called mucilage.

- **The sundew** wraps up its victims in its tentacles and suffocates them in slime in under ten seconds.

- **A Venus fly-trap's** trap will only shut if touched at least twice in 20 seconds.

- **Insects** are lured on to many carnivorous plants by sweet-tasting nectar – or the smell of rotting meat.

- **The juice** of a pitcher plant will dissolve a chunk of steak to nothing in a few days.

- **The bladders** of bladderworts were once thought to be air sacs to keep the plant afloat. In fact, they are tiny traps for water insects.

The fly touches hairs that send an electrical signal to cells on the side of the trap

◀ Insects are lured into the jaw-like leaf trap of the Venus fly-trap with nectar. Once the insect lands, the jaws clamp shut on the victim in a fraction of a second. At once the plant secretes juices that drown, then dissolve, the insect.

▼ Like the Venus fly-trap, the Sarracenia is a native of North America. But instead of actively capturing its prey, it provides a deep tube for them to fall into. Insects drawn to the nectar round its rim slide in and are unable to climb out.

When triggered, cells on the outside of the trap expand instantly and cells on the inside contract, pulling the trap shut

Tentacles covered in drops of sticky mucilage

◀ When an insect lands on the sticky tentacles of a sundew, it struggles to free itself – but this struggling stimulates the tentacles to tighten their grip. Soon the tentacles exude a digestive juice that dissolves the victim.

Temperate fruit

- **Fruits of temperate regions** must have a cool winter to grow properly.

- **The main temperate fruits** are apples, pears, plums, apricots, peaches, grapes and cherries.

- **Apples were eaten** by the earliest Europeans hundreds of thousands of years ago. They were spread through the USA by Indians, trappers and travellers like Johnny 'Appleseed' Chapman.

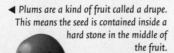

- **The world** picks 32 million tonnes of apples a year, half are eaten fresh and a quarter are made into the alcoholic drink cider. The USA is the world's leading producer of cider apples.

◀ Plums are a kind of fruit called a drupe. This means the seed is contained inside a hard stone in the middle of the fruit.

◀ Pears are the second most important temperate fruit after apples. The leading producer is China.

- **The world's most** popular pear is the Williams' Bon Chrétien or Bartlett. The best is said to to be the Doyenné du Comice, first grown in France in 1849.

- **New pear trees** are grown not from seeds but by grafting branches on to roots such as those of quinces.

- **Plums** came originally from the Caucasus Mountains in Turkey and Turkey is still the world's major plum grower. The damson plum came from Damascus.

- **Plums** are dried to make prunes.

- **The peach** is 87% water and has far fewer calories than fruit like apples and pears.

- **Grapes are grown** in vineyards to make wine. Grape-growing or viticulture is described in detail in Ancient Egyptian hieroglyphs of 2400BC.

Evergreen trees

★ STAR FACT ★
The best-known evergreen is the Christmas tree – typically a Douglas fir or spruce.

- **An evergreen** is a plant that keeps its leaves in winter.

- **Many tropical broad-leaved trees** are evergreen.

- **In cool temperate regions** and the Arctic, most evergreen trees are conifers such as pines and firs. They have needle-like leaves.

- **Old needles** do turn yellow and drop, but they are replaced by new needles (unless the tree is unhealthy).

- **Evergreens** may suffer from sunscald – too much sun – in dry, sunny spots, especially in early spring.

- **Five coniferous groups,** including larches and cypresses, are not evergreen.

- **Many evergreens** were sacred to ancient cultures. The laurel or bay was sacred to the Greek god Apollo and used by the Romans as a symbol of high achievement.

- **Yews are grown** in many European churchyards – perhaps because the trees were planted on the sites by pagans in the days before Christianity. But the bark of the yew tree and its seeds are poisonous.

- **The sakaki** is sacred to the Japanese Shinto religion, and entire trees are uprooted to appear in processions.

▼ In cool northern climates where the summers are brief, conifers stay evergreen to make the most of the available sunshine.

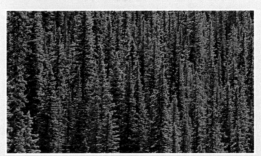

Fertilizers

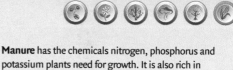

▲ Once the soil is broken up by ploughing, fertilizers are applied to prepare the soil for planting.

- **Fertilizers** are natural or artificial substances added to soil to make crops and garden plants grow better.

- **Natural fertilizers** such as manure and compost have been used since the earliest days of farming.

- **Manure** comes mostly from farm animals, though in some countries, human waste is used.

- **Manure** has the chemicals nitrogen, phosphorus and potassium plants need for growth. It is also rich in humus, organic matter that helps keep water in the soil.

- **Artificial fertilizers** are usually liquid or powdered chemicals (or occasionally gas), containing a mix of nitrogen, phosphorus or potassium. They also have traces of sulphur, magnesium and calcium.

- **Nitrogen fertilizers**, also called nitrate fertilisers, are made from ammonia which is made from natural gas.

- **The first fertilizer** factory was set up by Sir John Lawes in Britain in 1843. He made superphosphate by dissolving bones in acid. Phosphates now come from bones or rocks.

- **Potassium fertilizers** come from potash dug up in mines.

- **The use of artificial** fertilizers has increased in the last 40 years, especially in the developed world.

- **Environmentalists** worry about the effects of nitrate fertilizers entering water supplies, and the huge amount of energy needed to make, transport and apply them.

Flower facts

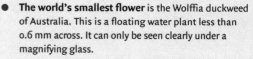

- **The world's tallest** flower is the 2.5 m Titan arum which grows in the tropical jungles of Sumatra.

- **The Titan arum** is shaped so that flies are trapped in a chamber at the bottom.

- **The world's biggest flower** is Rafflesia, which grows in the jungles of Borneo and Sumatra. It is 1 m in diameter and weighs up to 11 kg.

- **Rafflesia** is a parasite and has no leaves, root or stems.

- **Rafflesia** and the Titan arum both smell like rotting meat to attract the insects that pollinate them.

▶ Rafflesia was 'discovered' by British explorer John Arnold in 1818 and named by him after the famous British colonialist Stamford Raffles.

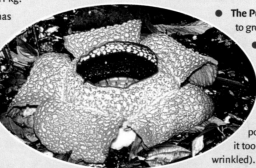

- **The world's smallest flower** is the Wolffia duckweed of Australia. This is a floating water plant less than 0.6 mm across. It can only be seen clearly under a magnifying glass.

- **The biggest flowerhead** is the *Puya raimondii* bromeliad of Bolivia which can be up to 2.5 m across and 10 m tall and have 8000 individual blooms.

- **The Puya raimondii** takes 150 years to grow its first flower, then dies.

- **Two Australian orchids** bloom underground. No-one knows how they pollinate.

- **Stapelia flowers** not only smell like rotting meat to attract the flies that pollinate them – they look like it too (all pinky-brown and wrinkled).

Fruit

▶ There are three kinds of cherries – sweet, sour, and 'dukes', which are sweet-sour cross. We eat mainly sweet cherries like these.

● **Scientists** say a fruit is the ovary of a plant after the eggs are pollinated and grow into seeds. Corn grains, cucumbers, bean pods and acorns are fruit as well as apples and so on.

● **Some fruits** such as oranges are soft and juicy. The hard pips are the seeds.

● **With some fruits** such as hazelnuts and almonds, the flesh turns to a hard dry shell.

● **Fleshy fruits** are either berries like oranges which are all flesh, aggregate fruits like blackberries which are made from lots of berries from a single flower or multiple fruits like pineapples which are single fruits made from an entire multiple flowerhead.

● **Legumes** such as peas and beans are soft, dry fruits held in a case called a pod.

● **Berries** and other juicy fruits are called 'true fruits' because they are made from the ovary of the flower alone.

● **Apples and pears** are called 'false fruits' because they include parts other than the flower's ovary.

● **In an apple** only the core is the ovary.

● **Drupes** are fruit like plums, mangoes and cherries with no pips but just a hard stone in the centre containing the seeds. Aggregate fruits like raspberries are clusters of drupes.

● **Walnuts and dogwood** are actually drupes like cherries.

Roots

● **Roots are** the parts of a plant that grow down into soil or water, anchoring it and soaking up all the water and minerals the plant needs to grow.

● **In some plants** such as beetroots, the roots are also a food store.

● **When a seed** begins to grow, its first root is called a primary root. This branches into secondary roots.

> ★ STAR FACT ★
> The roots of the South African wild fig tree can grow 120 m down into the ground.

● **Roots** are protected at the end by a thimble-shaped root cap as they probe through the soil.

● **On every root** there are tiny root hairs that help it take up water and minerals.

● **Some plants,** such as carrots, have a single large root, called a taproot, with just a few fine roots branching off.

● **Some plants** such as grass have lots of small roots, called fibrous roots, branching off in all directions.

● **Some kinds of orchid** that live on trees have 'aerial' roots that cling to the branches.

● **Mistletoe** has roots that penetrate its host tree.

◀ A tree blown over in a gale reveals some of the dense mat of roots it needs to get enough water and nutrients.

Harvesting grain

- **When grain** is ripe it is cut from its stalks. This is called reaping.
- **After reaping** the grain must be separated from the stalks and chaff (waste). This is called threshing.
- **After threshing** the grain must be cleaned and separated from the husks. This is called winnowing.
- **In some places** grain is still reaped in the ancient way with a long curved blade called a sickle.
- **In most developed countries** wheat and other cereals are usually harvested with a combine harvester.
- **A combine harvester** is a machine that reaps the grain, threshes it, cleans it and pours it into bags or reservoirs.
- **The first horse-drawn** combine was used in Michigan in 1836, but modern self-propelled harvesters only came into use in the 1940s.
- **If the grain is damp** it must be dried immediately after harvesting so it does not rot. This is always true of rice.

▲ Combine harvesters driven by a single man have replaced the huge teams of people with sickles of ancient times.

- **If the grain is too damp** to harvest, a machine called a windrower may cut the stalks and lay them in rows to dry in the wind for later threshing and cleaning.
- **A successful harvest** is traditionally celebrated with a harvest festival. The cailleac or last sheaf of corn is said to be the spirit of the field. It is made into a harvest doll, drenched with water and saved for the spring planting.

Desert plants

▲ Surprisingly many plants can survive the dryness of deserts, including cactuses and sagebushes.

- **Some plants** find water in the dry desert with very long roots. The Mesquite has roots that can go down as much as 50 m deep.
- **Most desert plants** have tough waxy leaves to cut down on water loss. They also have very few leaves; cactuses have none at all.
- **Pebble plants** avoid the desert heat by growing partly underground.
- **Window plants** grow almost entirely underground. A long cigar shape pokes into the ground, with just a small green window on the surface to catch sunlight.
- **Some mosses and lichens** get water by soaking up dew.
- **Resurrection trees** get their name because their leaves look shrivelled brown and dead most of the time – then suddenly turn green when it rains.
- **The rose of Jericho** is a resurrection plant that forms a dry ball that lasts for years and opens only when damp.
- **Daisies** are found in most deserts.
- **Cactuses and ice plants** can store water for many months in special water storage organs.

> ★ STAR FACT ★
> The quiver tree drops its branches to save water in times of drought.

Fungi

- **Fungi** are a huge group of 50,000 species. They include mushrooms, toadstools, mould, mildew and yeast.

- **Fungi** are not plants, because they have no chlorophyll to make their food. So scientists put them in a group or kingdom of their own.

- **Because fungi** cannot make their own food, they must live off other plants and animals – sometimes as partners, sometimes as parasites.

- **Parasitic fungi** feed off living organisms; fungi that live off dead plants and animals are called saprophytic.

- **Fungi** feed by releasing chemicals called enzymes to break down chemicals in their host. The fungi then use the chemicals as food.

▶ These are some of the tens of thousands of different fungi, which are found growing everywhere from rotting tree stumps to inside your body.

- **Cheeses** like Camembert, Roquefort, Stilton and Danish Blue get their distinctive flavours from chemicals made by moulds added to them to help them ripen. The blue streaks in some cheeses are actually moulds.

- **Fungi are made** of countless cotton-like threads called hyphae which absorb the chemicals they feed on. Hyphae are usually spread out in a tangled mass. But they can bundle together to form fruiting bodies like mushrooms.

- **Some fungi** grow by spreading their hyphae in a mat or mycelium; others scatter their spores. Those that grow from spores go through the same two stages as mosses.

- **Truffles** are fungi that grow near oak and hazel roots. They are prized for their flavour and sniffed out by dogs or pigs. The best come from Perigord in France.

The field mushroom, grown wild or cultivated, is the mushroom most widely eaten

Honey mushrooms belong to the Armillaria genus of fungi, which includes the world's largest and oldest living organisms

Fungi can grow in all kinds of shapes, earning them names like this orange peel fungi

The destroying angel is the most poisonous of all fungi, and usually kills anyone who eats one

The water-measure earthstar grows in soil or on rotting wood in grassy areas or woods

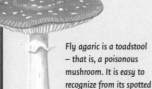

Fly agaric is a toadstool – that is, a poisonous mushroom. It is easy to recognize from its spotted red cap

The chanterelle is a sweet-smelling, edible amber-coloured mushroom. But it looks very like the poisonous jack o'lantern

Puffballs have big round fruiting bodies that dry out and puff out their spores in all directions when burst

Heathlands

▲ *Heather and other heathland plants are usually pollinated by bees and birds like sunbirds.*

- **Heathland** goes under many different names, including scrubland, shrubland and chaparral.
- **Heathlands** occur where the soil is too dry or too poor for trees to grow – typically in Mediterranean regions or areas of sandy soil.

- **Many heathlands** are not natural, but places where human activity has so changed the environment that trees can no longer grow.
- **The most common** heathland shrub is heather. Underneath grasses, sedges and flowers like daisies and orchids grow.
- **Many heathland shrubs** like gorse are thorny to stop animals eating them.
- **The maquis** are the heathlands of the Mediterranean, dominated by tough evergreen shrubs and small trees.
- **Many maquis** plants are aromatic (have a strong scent) – such as mints, laurels and myrtles.
- **Spring blossoms** in the mallee heaths of Australia are so spectacular that they are a tourist attraction.
- **Mallee** is a kind of eucalyptus tree typical of the area.
- **Chaparral** is heathland in California. The climate is Mediterranean, with mild winters and warm summers. The main plants are sages and small evergreen oaks.

Timber

- **Timber** is useful wood. Lumber is a North American term for timber once it is sawn or split.
- **Lumberjacks** are people who cut down trees using power saws or chainsaws.
- **Round timbers** are basically tree trunks that have been stripped of their bark and branches and cut into logs.
- **Round timbers** are used for fencing and telegraph poles or driven into the ground as 'piles' to support buildings and quays.
- **Lumber** is boards and planks sawn from logs at sawmills. At least half of lumber is used for building.

▲ *Tree surgeons stripping branches from a felled tree with chainsaws.*

- **Before lumber** can be used, it must usually be seasoned (dried) or it will shrink or twist. Sometimes it is dried in the open air, but more often it is warmed in a kiln or treated with chemicals.
- **Sometimes** planks are cut into thin slices called veneers.
- **Plywood** is three or more veneers glued together to make cheap, strong wood. Chipboard is wood chippings and sawdust mixed with glue and pressed into sheets.
- **Softwod lumbers** come from trees such as pines, larches, firs, hemlocks, redwoods and cedars.
- **MDF** or medium density fibreboard is made from glued wood fibres.

Symbiosis

- **Living things** that feed off other living things are called parasites.

- **Living things** that depend on each other to live are called symbiotic.

- **Many tropical rainforest trees** have a symbiotic relationship with fungi on their roots. The fungi get

▼ *Leaf-cutter ants cut up leaves and line their nests – not for themselves, but for the fungi which grow on the leaves. The ants eat the fungi.*

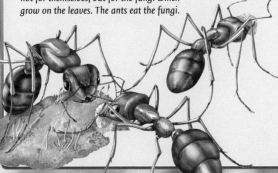

★ STAR FACT ★
Many plants rely on bees and butterflies to spread their pollen. In return, they give nectar.

energy from the trees and in return give the trees phosphorus and other nutrients.

- **A phyte is a plant** that grows on another plant.

- **Epiphytes** are plants that grow high up on other plants, especially in tropical rainforests (see epiphytes).

- **Saprophytes** are plants and fungi that depend on decomposing material, not sunlight, for sustenance.

- **Most orchids** are saprophytic as seedlings.

- **Corsiaceae orchids** of New Guinea, Australia and Chile are saprophytic all their lives.

- **Various ants,** such as leaf-cutter and harvester ants in tropical forests, line their nests with leaves which they cut up. The leaves provide food for fungi which, in turn, provide food for the ants.

Tree flowers

- **All trees have flowers,** but the flowers of conifers are usually tiny compared with those of broad-leaved trees.

- **Flowers** are a tree's reproductive organs.

- **Some flowers are male.** Some are female.

- **Sometimes the male** and female flowers are on separate trees. Sometimes, as in willows and some conifers, they are on the same tree.

- **'Perfect' flowers** like those of cherry and maple trees have both male and female parts.

- **Pollen** is carried from male flowers by insects or the wind to fertilize female flowers.

- **A blossom** can be any flower, but often refers especially to the beautiful flowers of fruit trees such as cherries and apples in spring.

- **Many blossoms** are pink and get their colour from what are called anthocyanin pigments – the same chemical colours that turn leaves red in autumn.

- **Washington DC** is famous for its Cherry Blossom Festival each spring.

- **Omiya** in Japan is famous for its park full of cherry trees which blossom in spring.

▼ *Apple blossoms are usually pink. They bloom quite late in spring, after both peach and cherry blossoms.*

Parts of a plant

All plants that grow from seeds have flowers, although not all are as bright and colourful as these

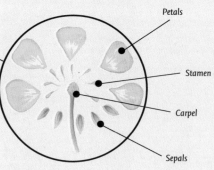

Petals

Stamen

Carpel

Sepals

Flowers usually open only for a short time. Before they open, they are hidden in tight green buds

The leaves are the plant's powerhouses, using sunlight to make sugar, the plant's fuel

◀ Plants come in many shapes and sizes from tiny wildflowers to giant trees 100 m tall. But they all tend to have the same basic features – roots, stem, leaves and flowers.

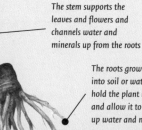

The stem supports the leaves and flowers and channels water and minerals up from the roots

The roots grow down into soil or water. They hold the plant in place, and allow it to draw up water and minerals

- **The first plants** to appear on land were simple plants such as liverworts, ferns and horsetails. They grow from tiny cells called spores.

- **Today, most plants** grow not from spores but from seeds. Unlike primitive plants, seed-making plants have stems, leaves and often roots and flowers.

- **The stem of a plant** supports the leaves and flowers. It also carries water, minerals and food up and down between the plant's leaves and roots.

- **A terminal bud** forms the tip of each stem. The plant grows taller here.

- **Lateral buds** grow further back down the stem at places called nodes.

- **Some lateral buds** develop into new branches. Others develop into leaves or flowers.

- **The leaves** are the plant's green surfaces for catching sunlight. They use the sun's energy for joining water with carbon dioxide from the air to make the sugar the plant needs to grow (see photosynthesis).

- **The roots** are the parts of the plant that grow down into soil or water. They anchor the plant in the ground and soak up all the water and minerals it needs to grow.

- **The flowers** are the plant's reproductive organs. In gymnosperms – conifers, cycads and gingkos – the flowers are often small and hidden. In angiosperms (flowering plants) they are usually much more obvious.

Tropical trees

◀ *Mangrove trees are famous for their dangling pods which can drop like a sword on passersby.*

● **Nearly all tropical trees** are broad-leaved trees.

● **Most tropical trees** are evergreen. Only where there is a marked dry season in 'monsoon' regions do some trees loose their leaves to save water.

● **Most tropical trees** are slow-growing hardwoods such as teak and mahogany. Once cut down, they take many years to replace.

> ★ STAR FACT ★
> Balsa wood from Central America is the lightest and softest wood of all.

● **Mahogany** is a tall evergreen tree with beautiful hard wood that turns red when it matures after a century or so.

● **Most mahogany** wood comes from trees such as the African *Khaya* or the *Shorea* from the Philippines.

● **The best mahogany** is from the tropical American *Swietenia macrophylla*.

● **Balsa** is so light and such a good insulator that it is used to make passenger compartments in aircraft.

● **Teak** is a deciduous tree from India. It is one of the toughest of all woods and has been used to construct ships and buildings for more than 2000 years.

● **Chicle** is a gum drained from the Central American sapota tree in the rainy season. It is the main ingredient in chewing-gum. The best comes from Guatemala.

Dandelions and daisies

● **Dandelions and daisies** are both members of a vast family called *Asteraceae*.

● **All Asteraceae** have flower heads with many small flowers called florets surrounded by leaf-like structures called bracts.

● **There are over 20,000** different *Asteraceae*.

● **Garden Asteraceae** include asters, dahlias and chrysanthemums.

● **Wild Asteraceae** include burdock, butterbur and ragweed, thistles and sagebrush.

▶ *Daisies look like a single bloom, but they actually consist of many small flowers. Those around the edge each have a single petal.*

● **Lettuces, artichokes** and sunflowers are all *Asteraceae*.

● **The thistle** is the national emblem of Scotland.

● **Dandelions** are bright yellow flowers that came originally from Europe, but were taken to America by colonists. Unusually, their ovaries form fertile seeds without having to be pollinated, so they spread rapidly.

● **The name dandelion** comes from the French *dent de lion*, meaning lion's tooth – because its leaves have edges that look like sharp teeth.

● **The daisy** gets its name from the Old English words 'day's eye' – because like an eye its blooms open in the day and close at night.

Berries

- **Berries** are fleshy fruit which contain lots of seeds. The bright colours attract birds which eat the flesh. The seeds pass out in the birds' droppings and so spread.

- **Bananas**, tomatoes and cranberries are all berries.

- **Strawberries**, raspberries and blackberries are not true berries. They are called 'aggregate' fruits because each is made from groups of tiny fruit with one seed.

- **Gean, damson and blackthorn berries** contain a single seed. Holly berries and elderberries contain many.

- **Cloudberries** are aggregate fruits like raspberries. The tiny amber berries grow close to the ground in the far north, and are collected by Inuits and Sami people in autumn to freeze for winter food.

◀ *Most berries are shiny bright red to attract birds.*

- **Cloudberries** are also known as salmonberries, bakeberries, malka and baked appleberries.

- **Cranberries** grow wild on small trailing plants in marshes, but are now cultivated extensively in the USA in places such as Massachusetts.

- **Wild huckleberries** are the American version of the European bilberry. But the evergreen huckleberry sold in florists is actually a blueberry.

- **The strawberry tree's** Latin name is *unedo*, which means 'I eat one'. The red berries are not as tasty as they look.

- **A Greek myth** tells how the wine-red mulberry was once white but was stained red by the blood of the tragic lovers Pyramus and Thisbe, whose story is retold in Shakespeare's *Midsummer Night's Dream*.

Ash trees

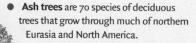

- **Ash trees** are 70 species of deciduous trees that grow through much of northern Eurasia and North America.

- **Ash trees** are among the most beautiful of all trees and are prized for their wood. It was once used to make oars and handles for axes and tennis rackets and for skis.

- **The tallest of all flowering plants** is the Australian mountain ash which grows over 100 m tall.

◀ *The leaves of the ash grow opposite each other in groups of five to nine and have tooth edges. The clusters of flowers are small and often showy.*

- **Ash trees** are part of the olive family.

- **The Vikings** worshipped the ash as a sacred tree. Yggdrasil, the Tree of the World, was a giant ash whose roots reached into hell but whose crown reached heaven.

- **In Viking myth** Odin, the greatest of the gods, created the first man out of a piece of ash wood.

- **The manna ash** got its name because it was once thought that its sugary gum was manna. Manna was the miraculous food that fell from heaven to feed the Biblical Children of Israel in the desert as they fled from Egypt.

- **The mountain ash** is also known as the rowan or quickbeam. In America it is known as dogberry. It is not related to other ash trees.

- **Rowan trees** were once linked to witchcraft. The name may come from the Viking word *runa*, meaning charm. Rowan trees were planted in churchyards, and the berries were hung over doors on May Day, to ward off evil.

- **Rowans** grow higher up mountains than any other tree.

Dicotyledons

▲▶ Dicots, like the Japanese maple above, all begin life as a pair of leaves growing from a seed, like those on the right.

- **Dicotyledons** are one of two basic classes of flowering plant. The other is monocotyledons.

- **Dicotyledons** are also known as dicots or Magnoliopsida.

- **Dicots** are plants that sprout two leaves from their seeds.

  - There are about **175,000** dicots – over three-quarters of all flowering plants.

  - **Dicots** include most garden plants, shrubs and trees as well as flowers such as magnolias, roses, geraniums and hollyhocks.

  - **Dicots** grow slowly and at least 50% have woody stems.

- **The flowers** of dicots have sets of four or five petals.

- **Most dicots** have branching stems and a single main root called a taproot.

- **The leaves of dicots** usually have a network of veins rather than parallel veins.

- **Dicots** usually have a layer of ever-growing cells near the outside of the stem called the cambium.

Orchids

> ★ STAR FACT ★
> To attract male bees, the bee orchid has a lip that looks just like a female bee.

- **Orchids** are a group of over 20,000 species of flower, growing on every continent but Antarctica.

- **In the moist tropics** many grow on the trunks and branches of trees and so are called epiphytes.

- **A few,** such as the Bird's nest orchid, are saprophytes, living off rotting plants in places where there is no light.

- **Some species** are found throughout the tropics, such as *Ionopsis utricularioides*. Others grow on just a single mountain in the world.

- **Orchids** have a big central petal called the lip or labellum. It is often shaped like a cup, trumpet or bag.

- **The fly orchid** of Ecuador has a lip shaped like a female tachinid fly to attract male flies.

- **The flavour vanilla** comes from the vanilla orchid.

- **Ancient Greek** couples expecting a baby often ate the roots of the early purple orchid. They believed that if the man ate the flower's large root the baby would be a boy. If the woman ate the small root, the baby would be a girl.

- **In Shakespeare's** *Hamlet*, the drowned Ophelia is covered in flowers, including the early purple orchid, famous as a love potion. Hamlet's mother says that 'cold maids' call the flowers 'dead men's fingers'.

▶The early purple orchid was said to have grown beneath Christ's cross and the red spots on its leaves were said to be left by falling drops of Christ's blood.

Cycads and gingkos

- **Cycadophytes and gingkophytes** were the first seed plants to appear on land. The cycads and gingkos of today are their direct descendants.
- **Like conifers,** cycads and gingkos are gymnosperms. This means their seeds do not develop inside a fruit like those of flowering plants or angiosperms.
- **Cycads** are mostly short, stubby, palm-like trees. Some are many thousands of years old.
- **Cycads have** fern-like leaves growing in a circle round the end of the stem. New leaves sprout each year and last for several years.
- **The gingko** is a tall tree that comes from China.
- **The gingko** is the only living gingkophyte.
- **The gingko** is the world's oldest living seed-plant.
- **Fossil leaves** identical to today's gingko have been found all over the world in rocks formed in the Jurassic period, 208–144 million years ago.

▲ *The gingko is a remarkable living fossil – the only living representative of the world's most ancient seed plants.*

- **Scientifically,** the gingko is called *Gingko Biloba*. It is also called the maidenhair tree.
- **All today's** gingkos may be descended from trees first cultivated in Chinese temple gardens 3000 years ago.

River plants

▲ *Water crowfoots are buttercups that grow in water. They may have both round floating leaves like these and feathery submerged leaves.*

- **Some aquatic (water) plants** are rooted in the mud and have their leaves above the surface like water lilies.
- **Some water plants** grow underwater but for their flowers, like water milfoils and some plantains. They may have bladders or air pockets to help keep the stem upright.

- **Tiny plants** called algae grow in red, green or brown films on rivers, lakes and swamps.
- **Water hyacinths** are purple American water flowers. They grow quickly and can clog up slow streams.
- **Giant water lilies** have huge leaves with the edges upturned like a shallow pan to keep them afloat.
- **The leaves** of the royal or Amazon lily can be 2 m across.
- **Papyrus** is a tall, grass-like water plant that grows in the Nile river. Stems were rolled flat by the Ancient Egyptians to write on. The word 'paper' comes from papyrus.
- **Many grass-like** plants grow in water, including reeds, mace, flag and rushes such as bulrushes and cattails.
- **Mangroves, bald cypresses,** cotton gum and other 'hydrophytic' trees are adapted to living in water.

★ STAR FACT ★
Mexico's largest lake, Lake Chapala, is sometimes choked with water hyacinths.

Development of a flower

- **Flowers have both** male parts, called stamens, and female parts, called carpels. Seeds for new plants are made when pollen from the stamens meets the flower's eggs inside the carpels.

- **The carpel** contains the ovaries, where the flower's eggs are made. It is typically the short thick stalk in the middle of the flower.

- **A flower** may have just one carpel or several joined together. Together, they are called the pistil.

- **The stamens** make pollen. They are typically spindly stalks surrounding the carpels.

- **Pollen is made** in the anthers on top of the stamens.

- **Pollen** is trapped on the top of the ovary by sticky stigma.

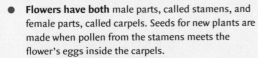

▶ Most flowers rely on bees and butterflies to fertilize them by transferring pollen from the stamens to the carpels. So, like this orchid, flowers have developed wonderful colours and scents to attract the insects to them.

- **Pollen** is carried down to the ovary from the stigma via a structure called the style. In the ovary it meets the eggs and fertilizes them to create seeds.

- **Before the flower opens,** the bud is enclosed in a tight green ball called the calyx. This is made up from tiny green flaps called sepals.

- **The colourful part of the flower** is made from groups of petals. The petals make up what is called the corolla. Together the calyx and the corolla make up the whole flower head, which is called the perianth. If petals and sepals are the same colour, they are said to be tepals.

> ★ STAR FACT ★
> A 'perfect' flower is one which has both stamens and carpels; many have one missing.

1. The fully formed flower is packed away inside a bud. Green flaps or sepals wrap tightly round it

2. Once the weather is warm enough, the bud begins to open. The sepals curl back to reveal the colourful petals

3. The sepals open wider and the petals grow outwards and backwards to create the flower's beautiful corolla

▶ At the right time of year, buds begin to open to reveal flowers' blooms so that the reproductive process can begin. Some flowers last just a day or so. Others stay blooming for months on end before the eggs are fertilized, and grow into seeds.

4. The flower opens fully to reveal its bright array of pollen sacs

Deciduous trees

◀ In autumn, the leaves of deciduous trees turn glorious browns, reds and golds and then drop off. New leaves grow in the spring.

- **Deciduous trees** are trees that lose their leaves once a year.

- **In cool places,** deciduous trees lose their leaves in autumn to cut their need for water in winter when water may be frozen.

- **In the tropics** deciduous trees lose their leaves at the start of the dry season.

- **Leaves fall** because a layer of cork grows across the leaf stalk, gradually cutting off its water supply.

- **Eventually the leaf** is only hanging on by its veins, and is easily blown off by the wind.

- **Leaves go brown** and other colours in autumn because their green chlorophyll breaks down, letting other pigments shine through instead.

- **Among the most spectacular** autumn colours are those of the sweet gum, brought to Europe from Mexico c.1570.

- **The main deciduous trees** in cool climates are oaks, beeches, birches, chestnuts, aspens, elms, maples and lindens.

- **Most deciduous trees** are broad-leaved, but five conifer groups including larches are deciduous.

- **Some tropical evergreen trees** are deciduous in regions where there is a marked dry season.

Tree leaves

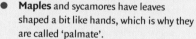

- **Trees** can be divided into two groups according to their leaves: broad-leaved trees and conifers with needle-like leaves.

- **The leaves** of broad-leaved trees are all wide and flat to catch the sun, but they vary widely in shape.

- **You can identify** trees by their leaves. Features to look for are not only the overall shape, but also: the number of leaflets on the same stalk, whether leaflets are paired or offset and if there are teeth round the edges of the leaves.

- **Trees such as birches** and poplars have small triangular or 'deltoid' leaves; aspens and alders have round leaves.

- **Limes** and Indian bean trees have heart-shaped or 'cordate' leaves.

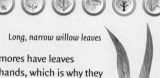

Hand-shaped leaf of a horse chestnut

Long, narrow willow leaves

- **Maples** and sycamores have leaves shaped a bit like hands, which is why they are called 'palmate'.

- **Ash and walnut trees** have lots of leaflets on the same stalk, giving them a feathery or 'pinnate' look.

- **Oaks and whitebeams** have leaves indented with lobes round the edge.

- **Many shrubs,** like magnolias and buddleias, and trees like willows, cherries, sweet chestnuts and cork oaks, have long narrow leaves.

- **Elms, beeches,** pears, alders and many others have oval leaves.

Lobed leaves of the English oak

Pinnate or feather-shaped walnut leaves

Root vegetables

▲▶ *Potatoes and carrots are important root vegetables. Carrot is a source of vitamin A, potatoes are sources of many vitamins, such as C.*

- **Vegetables** are basically any part of a plant eaten cooked or raw, except for the fruit.

- **Root vegetables** are parts of a plant that grow underground in the soil.

- **Turnips, rutabaga,** beets, carrots, parsnips and sweet potatoes are the actual roots of the plant.

- **Potatoes and cassava** are tubers or storage stems.

- **Potatoes** were grown in South America at least 1800 years ago. They were brought to Europe by the Spanish in the 16th century.

- **Poor Irish** farmers came to depend on the potato, and when blight ruined the crop in the 1840s, many starved.

- **Yams are tropical roots** similar to sweet potatoes. They are an important food in West Africa. A single yam can weigh 45 kg or more.

- **Mangel-wurzels** are beet plants grown mainly to feed to farm animals.

- **Tapioca** is a starchy food made from cassava that once made popular puddings.

- **Carrots came** originally from Afghanistan, but were spread around the Mediterranean 4000 years ago. They reached China by the 13th century AD.

Poisonous fungi

- **Many fungi** produce poisons. Scientists call poisons 'toxins' and poisons made by fungi 'mycotoxins'.

- **Some poisonous fungi** are very small microfungi which often form moulds or mildew. Many are either 'sac' fungi (*Ascomycetes*) or 'imperfect' fungi (*Deuteromycetes*).

- **Ergot** is a disease of cereals, especially rye, caused by the sac fungus *Claviceps purpurea*. If humans eat ergot-infected rye, they may suffer an illness called St Anthony's Fire. Ergot is also the source of the drug LSD.

- *Aspergillus* is an imperfect fungus that may cause liver damage or even cancer in humans.

- **False morel** is a poisonous sac fungus as big as a mushroom. True morels are harmless.

- **About 75 kinds** of mushroom are toxic to humans and

⭐ **STAR FACT** ⭐
Athlete's foot is a nasty foot condition caused by a fungus.

so called toadstools. Most belong to the Amanita family, including destroying angels, death caps and fly agarics.

- **Death caps** contain deadly phalline toxins that kill most people who eat the fungus.

- **Fly agaric** was once used as fly poison.

- **Fly agaric** and the *Psilocybe mexicana* mushroom were eaten by Latin American Indians because they gave hallucinations.

▶ *Fly agaric contains the poison muscarine. It rarely kills but makes you sick and agitated.*

Broad-leaved woodlands

▲ *Avenues of broad-leaved trees form shady paths in summer but are light in winter when the trees are bare.*

- **Forests** of broad-leaved, deciduous trees grow in temperate regions where there are warm, wet summers and cold winters – in places like North America, western Europe and eastern Asia.

- **Broad-leaved deciduous** woods grow where temperatures average above 10°C for over six months a year, and the average annual rainfall is over 400 mm.

▼ *Plenty of light can filter down through deciduous trees – especially in winter when the leaves are gone – so all kinds of bushes and flowers grow in the woods, often blooming in spring while the leaves are still thin.*

- **If there are** 100 to 200 days a year warm enough for growth, the main trees in broad-leaved deciduous forests are oaks, elms, birches, maples, beeches, aspens, chestnuts and lindens (basswood).

- **In the tropics** where there is plenty of rainfall, broad-leaved evergreens form tropical rainforests.

- **In moist western Europe,** beech trees dominate woods on well-drained, shallow soils, especially chalkland; oak trees prefer deep clay soils. Alders grow in waterlogged places.

- **In drier eastern Europe,** beeches are replaced by durmast oak and hornbeam and in Russia by lindens.

- **In American woods,** beech and linden are rarer than in Europe, but oaks, hickories and maples are more common.

- **In the Appalachians** buckeye and tulip trees dominate.

- **There is a wide range** of shrubs under the trees including dogwood, holly, magnolia, as well as woodland flowers.

> ★ STAR FACT ★
> Very few woods in Europe are entirely natural; most are 'secondary' woods, growing on land once cleared for farms.

Cut flowers

◀ *Holland is still famous for its flower markets.*

- **Cut flowers** are flowers sold by the bunch in florists.

- **The cut flower** trade began in the Netherlands with tulips in the 1600s.

- **In 1995** 60% of the world's cut flowers were grown in Holland.

- **Latin American countries** like Columbia, Ecuador, Guatemala and Costa Rica are now major flower-growers. So too are African countries like Kenya, Zimbabwe, South Africa, Zambia and Tanzania.

- **In China** the growing popularity of St Valentine's day has meant huge areas of China are now planted with flowers.

- **After cutting,** flowers are chilled and sent by air to arrive in places like Europe and North America fresh.

- **Most of the world's** cut flowers are sold through the huge flower market in Rotterdam in Holland.

- **By encouraging** certain flowers, flower-growers have made cut flowers last longer in the vase – but they have lost the rich scents they once had. Scientists are now trying to reintroduce scent genes to flowers.

- **A corsage** is a small bouquet women began to wear on their waists in the 18th century.

- **A nosegay** was a small bouquet Victorian ladies carried in their hands. If a man gave a lady a red tulip it meant he loved her. If she gave him back a sprig of dogwood it mean she didn't care. Various pink flowers meant 'no'.

Wheat

> ★ **STAR FACT** ★
> The world grows enough wheat a year to fill a line of trucks stretching a quarter of the way to the Moon.

- **Wheat grows** over more farmland than any other crop and is the basic food for 35% of the world's population.

- **Wheat was** one of the first crops ever grown, planted by the first farmers some 11,000 years ago.

- **Today** there are over 30 varieties. Among the oldest are emmer and einkorn.

- **Spring wheat** is planted in spring and then harvested in early autumn.

- **Winter wheat** is planted in autumn and harvested the following summer.

- **Wheat** is a kind of grass, along with other cereals.

- **Young wheat plants** are short and green and look like ordinary grass, but as they ripen they turn golden and grow between 0.6 and 1.5 m tall.

- **Branching from the main stem** are stalks called tillers. Wrapped round them is the base or sheath of the leaves. The flat top of the leaf is called the blade.

- **The head of the corn** where the seeds or grain grow is called the ear or spike. We eat the seed's kernels (core), ground into flour to make bread, pasta and other things.

▼ *An ear of wheat with the seeds which are stripped of their shells or husks before being ground to make flour.*

Annuals and biennials

▲ Foxgloves are typical biennials, flowering in their second summer, then dying back.

- **Annuals** are plants that grow from seed, flower, disperse their seeds and die in a single season.

- **Some annuals' seeds** lie dormant in the ground before conditions are right for germination.

- **With an annual,** forming flowers, fruits and seeds exhausts the plant's food reserves so the green parts die.

- **Many crops** are annuals, including peas and beans, squashes, and cereals such as maize and wheat.

- **Annual flowers** include petunias, lobelias, buttercups and delphiniums.

- **Biennials** live for two years.

- **In the first year** the young plant grows a ring of leaves and builds up an underground food store such as a bulb or taproot like beetroots and carrots. The food store sustains the plant through the winter.

- **In the second year** the plant sends up a stem in spring. It flowers in the summer.

- **Many vegetables** are biennials, including beetroot, carrots and turnips.

- **Biennial flowers** include wallflowers, carnations, sweet williams and evening primroses.

Bamboo

- **Bamboos** are giant, fast-growing grasses with woody stems.

- **Most bamboos** grow in east and southeast Asia and on islands in the Indian and Pacific oceans.

- **Bamboo stems** are called culms. They often form dense thickets that exclude every other plant.

- **Bamboo culms** can reach up to 40 m and grow very fast. Some bamboos grow 1 m every three days.

- **Most bamboos** only flower every 12 years or so. Some flower only 30–60 years. *Phyllostachys bambusoides* flowers only after 120 years.

- **Pandas** depend on the *Phyllostachys* bamboo, and after it flowers they lose their source of food.

▲ Bamboo looks like trees with its tall woody stems and big leaves, but it is actually grass.

- **The flowering** of the muli bamboo around the Bay of Bengal every 30–35 years brings disaster as rats multiply to take advantage of the fruit.

- **The Chinese** have used the hollow stems of bamboo to make flutes since before the Stone Age. The Australian aboriginals use them to make droning pipes called didgeridoos.

- **Bamboo** is an incredibly light, strong material, and between 1904 and 1957 athletes used it for pole-vaulting. American Cornelius Warmerdam vaulted 4.77 m with a bamboo pole.

- **Bamboo** has long been used to make paper. The Bamboo Annals, written on bamboo, are the oldest written Chinese records, dating from the 8th century BC.

Citrus fruit

- **Citrus fruits** are a group of juicy soft fruits covered with a very thick, waxy, evenly coloured skin in yellow, orange or green.

- **Citrus** fruits include lemons, limes, oranges, tangerines, grapefruits and shaddocks.

▼ *Orange trees are planted in groves. The fruit are green when they first appear, but turn orange as they ripen.*

> **★ STAR FACT ★**
> Citrus fruits are richer in Vitamin C than any other fruit or vegetable.

- **Inside the skin,** the flesh of a citrus fruit is divided into clear segments, each usually containing one or several seeds or pips.

- **Citrus fruits** grow in warm Mediterranean climates, and they are very vulnerable to frost.

- **Some citrus** fruit-growers warm the trees with special burners in winter to avoid frost-damage.

- **The sharp tang** of citrus fruits comes from citric acid.

- **Lemons** were spread through Europe by the crusaders who found them growing in Palestine.

- **Columbus** took limes to the Americas in 1493.

- **Scottish physician** James Lind (1716-1794) helped eradicate the disease scurvy from the British navy by recommending that sailors eat oranges and lemons.

Parasites

- **Parasitic plants** are plants that get their food not by using sunlight but from other plants, at the others' expense.

- **In the gloom of** tropical rainforests, where sunlight cannot penetrate, there are many parasitic plants growing on the trees.

- **Lianas** save themselves energy growing a trunk by climbing up other trees, clinging on with little hooks.

- **Rafflesia,** the world's biggest flower, is a parasite that feeds on the roots of lianas.

- **Figs** begin growing from seeds left high on branches by birds or fruit bats.

- **Fig roots** grow down to the ground around the tree, strangling it by taking its water supply. The tree then dies away, leaving the fig roots as a hollow 'trunk'.

- **Mistletoes** are semi-parasitic plants that wind round trees. They draw some of their food from the tree and some from sunlight with their own leaves.

- **Viscum album** mistletoe was held sacred by Druids 2000 years ago.

- **The druid** belief in the magic power of mistletoe survives in the tradition of kissing under the mistletoe at Christmas.

- **Broomrapes** grow on sugarcane roots; witchweeds grow on maize and rice roots.

◄ *Mistletoe, with its distinctive white berries, grows on apple and poplar trees in Eurasia and oaks in America.*

Epiphytes

- **Epiphytes** are plants that grow high above the ground in tropical rainforests, on tree branches.

- **Epiphytes** are often known as air plants because they seem to live on air – attached neither to the ground nor to any obvious source of nutrients.

- **Epiphytes** get their water and minerals from rain water, and from debris on the branch.

- **Various** orchids, ferns and bromeliads are epiphytes in tropical forests.

- **There are also epiphytes** in cooler places, including lichens, mosses, liverworts and algae.

- **Bromeliads** belong to a big family of plants called the pineapple family. At least half of them are epiphytes.

- **The pineapple fruit** is the best-known bromeliad.

- **All but one bromeliad** come from America, but they live in a huge range of habitats, living anywhere from on cacti in deserts to moist forests high up mountains.

▲ *Trees in tropical rainforests are often covered in epiphytes festooned on every bough and branch.*

- **The smallest bromeliads** are moss-like *Tillandsia bryoides*, just a few centimetres long.

- **The biggest bromeliad** is *Puya raimondii*, with a stem up to 4 m long and a flower over 4 m tall.

Seeds and nuts

- **Seeds are the tiny** hard capsules from which most new plants grow.

- **Seeds** develop from the plant's egg once it is fertilized by pollen.

- **Each seed** contains the new plant in embryo form plus a store of food to feed it until it grows leaves.

◀ *Neither Brazil nuts nor coconuts are true nuts. Coconuts (right) are not true nuts, but the stones of drupes. Brazil nuts (left) are just large seeds.*

- **The seed** is wrapped in a hard shell or testa.

- **Some fruit** contain many seeds; nuts are fruit with a single seed in which the outside has gone hard.

- **Acorns and hazelnuts** are true nuts.

- **Cola drinks** get their name from the African kola nut, but there are no nuts in them. The flavour is artificial.

- **Some nuts**, such as almonds and walnuts, are not true nuts but the hard stones of drupes (fruit like plums).

- **Brazil nuts** and shelled peanuts are not true nuts but just large seeds.

- **Nuts are** a concentrated, nutritious food – about 50% fat and 10–20% protein. Peanuts contain more food energy than sugar and more protein, minerals and vitamins than liver.

▶ *Almonds come from trees native to SW Asia but are now grown all over the world*

Photosynthesis

- **Plants use** sunlight to chemically join carbon dioxide gas from the air with water to make sugary food. The process is called photosynthesis.

- **Photosynthesis** occurs in leaves in two special kinds of cell: palisade and spongy cells.

- **Inside the palisade** and spongy cells are tiny packages called chloroplasts. A chloroplast is like a little bag with a double skin or membrane. Each is filled with a jelly-like substance called the stroma in which float various structures, such as lamellae. The jelly contains a chemical called chlorophyll which makes leaves green.

- **The leaf** draws in air containing the gas carbon dioxide through pores called stomata. It also draws water up from the ground through the stem and veins.

- **When the sun** is shining, the chlorophyll soaks up its energy and uses it to split water into hydrogen and oxygen. The hydrogen released from the water combines with the carbon dioxide to make sugar; the oxygen goes out through the stomata.

- **Sugar is transported** around the plant to where it is needed. Some sugar is burned up at once, leaving carbon dioxide and water. This is called respiration.

> ★ STAR FACT ★
> The oxygen in the air on which we depend for life was all made by plants during photosynthesis.

- **Some sugar is combined** into large molecules called starches, which are easy for the plant to store. The plant breaks these starches down into sugars again whenever they are needed as fuel.

- **Starch** from plants is the main nutrient we get when we eat food such as bread, rice and potatoes. When we eat fruits, cakes or anything else sweet, the sweetness comes from sugar made by photosynthesis.

- **Together** all the world's plants produce about 150 billion tonnes of sugar each year by photosynthesis.

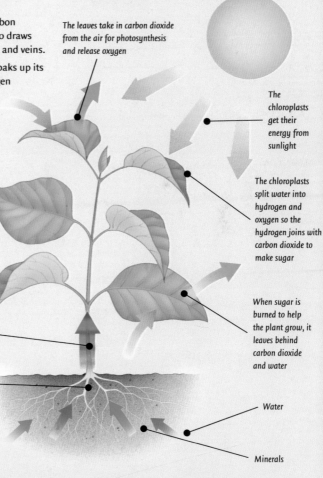

The leaves take in carbon dioxide from the air for photosynthesis and release oxygen

The chloroplasts get their energy from sunlight

The chloroplasts split water into hydrogen and oxygen so the hydrogen joins with carbon dioxide to make sugar

When sugar is burned to help the plant grow, it leaves behind carbon dioxide and water

The minerals are carried up through the plant dissolved in the water

The plant takes up water and minerals from the soil through the roots

Water

Minerals

▶ *Every green plant is a remarkable chemical factory, taking in energy from the sun and using it to split water into hydrogen and oxygen. It then combines the hydrogen with carbon dioxide from the air to make sugar, the fuel the plant needs to grow.*

Tree facts

▲ General Sherman in California is the biggest living tree. It is a giant sequoia over 83 m tall and with a trunk 11 m across.

- **The biggest tree** ever known was the Lindsey Creek Tree, a massive redwood which blew over in 1905. It weighed over 3300 tonnes.

- **The tallest living tree** is the 112 m high Mendocino redwood tree in Montgomery State Reserve, California.

- **The tallest tree** ever known was a Eucalyptus on Watts River, Victoria, Australia, measured at over 150 m in 1872.

- **The great banyan** tree in the Indian Botanical Garden, Calcutta has a canopy covering 1.2 hectares.

- **Banyan trees** grow trunk-like roots from their branches.

- **A European chestnut** known as the Tree of the Hundred Horses on Mt Etna in Sicily had a girth (the distance round the trunk) of 57.9 m in the 1790s.

- **A Moctezuma baldcypress** near Oaxaca in Mexico has a trunk over 12 m across.

- **The world's oldest plant** is the King's Holly in southwestern Tasmania, thought to be 43,000 years old.

- **The ombu tree** of Argentina is the world's toughest tree, able to survive axes, fire, storms and insect attacks.

> ★ STAR FACT ★
> The 'Eternal God' redwood tree in Prairie Creek, California is 12,000 years old.

Poisonous plants

◀ Every single part of the deadly nightshade is highly poisonous and eating a berry will kill you. But in the 1500s ladies would drop extracts in their eyes to make their eyes widen attractively, earning it the name 'belladonna'.

- **There are thousands** of plants around the world that are poisonous at least in parts.

- **Some parts** of edible plants are poisonous, such as potato leaves and apricot and cherry stones.

- **Some plants** are toxic to eat; some toxic to touch; some create allergic reactions through the air with their pollen.

- **The rosary pea** has pretty red and black seeds often used to make bracelets. But eating one seed can kill a man.

- **Oleanders** are so poisonous that people have been killed by eating meat roasted on an oleander stick.

- **Poison ivy** inflames skin badly if touched.

- **Hemlock** belongs to the parsley family but is highly poisonous. It was said to be the plant used to kill the Ancient Greek philosopher Socrates.

- **Birthwort** is a poisonous vine, but its name comes from its use in the past to help women in childbirth.

- **Crowfoots** such as aconite and hellebore, and spurges such as castor-oil and croton are poisonous.

- **Many useful drugs** are poisons extracted from plants and given in small doses including digitalis from foxgloves, morphine from poppies, atropine from deadly nightshade, quinine, aconite, strychnine and cocaine.

Ferns

- **Ferns** belong to a group of plants called feather plants or pteridophytes, along with club mosses and horsetails.

- **Featherplants** are among the world's most ancient plants, found as fossils in rocks 400 million years old.

- **Coal is made** largely of fossilized featherplants of the Carboniferous Period 360-286 million years ago.

- **There are now** 10,000 species of fern living in damp, shady places around the world.

- **Some ferns** are tiny, with mossy leaves just 1 cm long.

- **Rare tropical tree ferns** can grow up to 25m tall.

- **Fern leaves** are called fronds. When new they are curled up like a shepherd's crook, but they gradually uncurl.

- **Ferns** grow into new plants not from seeds but from spores in two stages.

- **First** spores are made in sacs called sporangia. These are the brown spots on the underside of the fronds. From these spores spread out. Some settle in suitable places.

▶ Most ferns grow on the ground in damp, shady places, but some grow on the leaves or stems of other plants.

- **Second** spores develop into a tiny heart-shaped plant called a prothallus that makes male and female cells. When bathed in rain, the male cells swim to the female cells, fertilizing them. A new root and stem then grow into a proper fern frond and the tiny prothallus dies.

Maize or corn

- **Maize or corn** is the USA's most important crop, and the second most important crop around the world after wheat. Rice is the third.

- **Corn,** like all cereals, is a kind of grass.

- **Corn** was first grown by the Indians of Mexico over 7000 year ago and so came to be called Indian corn by Europeans like Columbus.

- **In the USA** only varieties that give multi-coloured ears are now called Indian corn.

- **The Corn Belt** of the USA grows 40% of the world's corn.

- **American corn** grows up to 3 m tall

- **The ear or head** of a corn plant is called a cob and is covered with tightly packed yellow or white kernels of seeds. The kernels are the part of the plant that is eaten.

◀ Ears of mature American corn are typically 20 cm or so long. The core or cob is covered with 18 rows of yellow or white kernels.

- **There are seven main kinds** of corn kernel: dent corn, flint corn, flour corn, sweet corn, popcorn, waxy corn and pod corn.

- **Some corn** is ground into flour; some is eaten whole as sweet corn; some is fed to livestock.

- **Popcorn** has no starch, unlike most other corn. When heated, moisture in the kernels turns to steam and expands or pops rapidly.

Cereals

▶ Harvesting wheat and using it to make flour is a surprisingly complex process. The process is still done with simple tools in some parts of the world. But in the developed world, the entire process is largely mechanized.

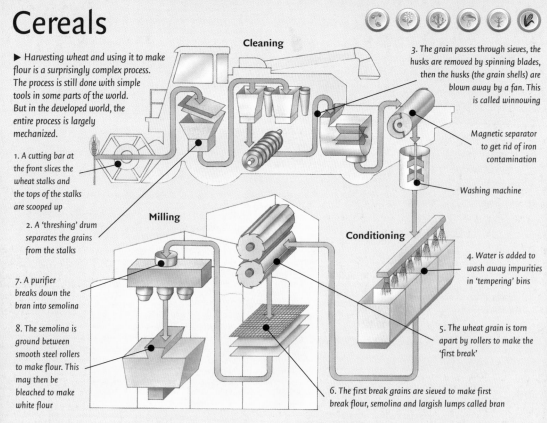

Cleaning

3. The grain passes through sieves, the husks are removed by spinning blades, then the husks (the grain shells) are blown away by a fan. This is called winnowing

Magnetic separator to get rid of iron contamination

Washing machine

1. A cutting bar at the front slices the wheat stalks and the tops of the stalks are scooped up

2. A 'threshing' drum separates the grains from the stalks

Milling

Conditioning

4. Water is added to wash away impurities in 'tempering' bins

7. A purifier breaks down the bran into semolina

5. The wheat grain is torn apart by rollers to make the 'first break'

8. The semolina is ground between smooth steel rollers to make flour. This may then be bleached to make white flour

6. The first break grains are sieved to make first break flour, semolina and largish lumps called bran

- **Cereals** such as wheat, maize, rice, barley, sorghum, oats, rye and millet are the world's major sources of food.

- **Cereals are grasses** and we eat their seeds or grain.

- **The leaves and stalks** are usually left to rot into animal feed called silage.

- **Some grains** such as rice are simply cooked and eaten. Most are milled and processed into foods such as flour, oils and syrups.

- **In the developed world** – that is, places like North America and Europe – wheat is the most important food crop. But for half the world's population, including most people in Southeast Asia and China rice is the staple food.

- **Many grains** are used to make alcoholic drinks such as whisky. A fermentation process turns the starch in the grains to alcohol. Special processing of barley creates a food called malt, which is used by brewers to make beer and lager.

- **Oats** have a higher food value than any other grain.

- **Rye** makes heavy, black bread. The bread is heavy because rye does not contain much gluten which yeast needs to make bread rise.

- **Russia** grows more oats and rye than any other country.

- **Millet** gives tiny seeds and is grown widely in dry regions of Africa and Asia. It was the main crop all over Europe, Asia and Africa in ancient and medieval times.

▶ Wheat flour is used to make everything from pasta to bread.

Cactus

- **Cactuses** are American plants with sharp spines, thick, bulbous green stems and no leaves.

- **Most cactuses** grow in hot, dry regions but a few grow in rainforests and in cold places such as mountain tops.
- **Cactuses** in deserts have a thick, waxy skin to cut water loss to the bare minimum.

◄ The huge saguaro cactus grows only in the dry foothills and deserts of southern Arizona, southeast California and northwest Mexico.

- **The fat stems** of cactuses hold a lot of water so that they can survive in hot, dry deserts.
- **Because of their moist stems**, cactuses are called succulents.
- **Cactuses have spines** to protect themselves from animals which eat any moist vegetation.
- **Cactuses** have to pollinate just like every flowering plant. So every few years, many produce big colourful blooms to attract insects quickly.
- **Most cactuses** have very long roots to collect water from a large area. The roots grow near the surface to collect as much rainwater as possible.
- **The biggest cactus** is the saguaro, which can grow up to 20 m tall and 1 m thick.

Plankton

- **Plankton** are tiny floating organisms (living things) that are found in both the sea and ponds and lakes.
- **The word 'plankton'** comes from a Greek word meaning 'wandering'.
- **Plankton** is a general term that includes every marine organism too small and weak to swim for itself.
- **The smallest algae** are called plankton, but large floating algae (seaweeds) are not called plankton.
- **Plankton** can be divided into phytoplankton, which are tiny plants, and zooplankton, which are tiny animals, but the division is blurred.
- **Most phytoplankton** are very tiny indeed and so called nannoplankton and microplankton. Zooplankton are generally bigger and called macroplankton.
- **Green algae** that give many ponds a bright green floating carpet are plankton.

- **Phytoplankton** get their energy by photosynthesis just like other plants.
- **Countless puffs** of oxygen given out by plankton early in Earth's history gave the air its vital oxygen.
- **Plankton** is the basic food of all large ocean animals.

▼ Diatoms are at the beginning of the ocean food chain. They use the Sun's energy for growth.

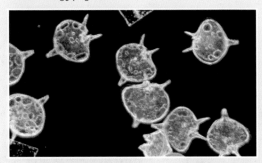

Garden flowers

▲ *Most gardens now have a mix of trees and shrubs, mixed beds of herbaceous flowers and early-flowering bulbs such as crocuses.*

- **All garden flowers** are descended from plants that were once wild, but they have been bred over the centuries to produce flowers quite unlike their wild relatives.

- **Garden flowers** like tea roses, created by cross-breeding two different species, are called hybrids.

- **Garden flowers** tend to have much bigger blooms and last for longer than their wild cousins.

- **By hybridization** gardeners have created colours impossible naturally, such as black roses.

- **Ornamentals** are flowers cultivated just for show.

- **Gardeners** try to mix flowers that bloom at different times so that the garden is always full of colour.

- **18th century botanist** Carl Linnaeus made a clock by planting flowers that bloomed at different times of day.

- **The earliest flowerbeds** were the borders of flower tufts Ancient Persians grew along pathways.

- **A herbaceous border** is a traditional flowerbed planted with herbaceous perennial flowers like delphiniums and chrysanthemums. It flowers year after year.

> ★ STAR FACT ★
> Herbaceous borders were invented by Kew gardener George Nicolson in the 1890s.

Cocoa

- **Cocoa beans** are the fruit of the cacao tree.

- **Cocoa beans** are called cocoa beans and not cacao beans because of a spelling mistake made by English importers in the 18th century when chocolate first became popular.

- **Cocoa beans** are the seeds inside melon-shaped pods about 30 cm long.

- **Cacao trees** came originally from Central America. Now they are grown in the West Indies and West Africa too.

- **Chocolate** is made by grinding the kernels of cocoa beans to a paste called chocolate liquor. The liquor is hardened in moulds to make chocolate.

- **Cooking chocolate** is bitter. Eating chocolate has sugar and, often, milk added.

◄ *The cacao tree is a tall tropical tree growing up to about 8 m. The seeds used to make cocoa are small beans inside the melon-sized pod.*

- **Cocoa powder** is made by squeezing the cocoa butter (fat) from chocolate liquor then pulverizing it.

- **When Spanish explorer** Hernán Cortés reached the court of Moctezuma (Aztec ruler of Mexico in 1519) he was served a bitter drink called *xocoatl*. The people of Central America had regarded *xocoatl* as a sacred drink since the time of the Mayans.

- **In the 1600s** Europeans began to open fashionable chocolate houses to serve *xocoatl* as hot chocolate sweetened with sugar. In the 1700s, the English began adding milk to improve the flavour.

- **'Cacao'** is a Mayan word for 'bitter juice'; chocolate comes from the Mayan for 'sour water'.

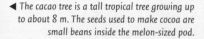

Plants and water

- **Plants cannot survive** without water. If they are deprived of water, most plants will wilt and die very quickly – although some desert plants manage to get by on very little indeed.

- **Nearly all plants** are almost 70% water, and some algae are 98% water.

- **In plants** water fills up the tiny cells from which they are made, and keeps them rigid in the same way as air in a balloon.

- **For a plant** water also serves the same function as blood in the human body. It carries dissolved gases, minerals and nutrients to where they are needed.

▲ *Plants need regular watering to keep them fresh and healthy.*

- **Some water** oozes from cell to cell through the cell walls in a process called osmosis.

- **Some water** is piped through tubes called xylem. These are the fine veins you can often see on leaves.

- **Water in xylem** is called sap and contains many dissolved substances besides water.

- **Plants lose water** by transpiration. This is evaporation through the leaf pores or stomata.

- **As water is lost** through the stomata, water is drawn up to replace it through the xylem.

- **If there is too little** water coming from the roots, the cells collapse and the plant wilts.

Algae

- **Algae** are simple organisms that live in oceans, lakes, rivers and damp mud.

- **Some algae** live inside small transparent animals.

- **Algae vary** from single-celled microscopic organisms to huge fronds of seaweed (brown algae) over 60 m long.

- **The smallest** float freely, but others, such as seaweeds, need a place to grow like a plant.

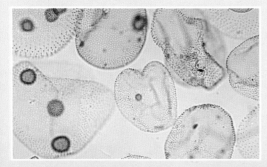

- **Algae** are so varied and often live very differently from plants, so scientists put them not in the plant kingdom but in a separate kingdom called the *Proctista*, along with slime moulds.

- **The most ancient** algae are called blue-green algae or cyanobacteria and are put in the same kingdom as bacteria. They appeared on Earth 3 billion years ago.

- **Algae** may be tiny but they are a vital food source for creatures from shrimps to whales, and they provide most of the oxygen water creatures need for life.

- **Green algae** are found mostly in freshwater. The green is the chlorophyll that enables plants to get their energy from sunlight.

- **Green algae** called *Spirogyra* form long threads.

- **Red or brown algae** are found in warm seas. Their chlorophyll is masked by other pigments.

◄ *Volvox are green algae that live in colonies about the size of a pinhead, containing up to 60,000 cells.*

Grapes

- **Grapes** are juicy, smooth-skinned berries that grow in tight clusters on woody plants called vines.
- **Grapes** can be black, blue, green, purple, golden or white, depending on the kind.
- **Some grapes** are eaten fresh and some dried as raisins, but 80% are crushed to make wine.
- **Grapes** are grown all round the world in places where there are warm summers and mild winters, especially in France, Italy, Spain, Australia, Chile, Romania, Georgia, South Africa and California.
- **Among the best wine grapes** are the Cabernet Sauvignon and Chardonnay for white wine and the Pinot Noir for red wine.

◄ Grapes have been cultivated since the earliest times. Purple grapes like these will be used to make red wine.

- **The Ancient Egyptians** made wine from grapes 5000 years ago.
- **Grapes are made** into wine by a process called fermentation.
- **Grapes** for eating fresh are called table grapes and are bigger and sweeter than wine grapes. Varieties include Emperor, red Tokay, green Perlette and black Ribier.
- **Grapes grown** for raisins are seedless. The best known is Thompson's seedless, sometimes called the sultana.
- **Grapevines** are grown from cuttings. They start to give fruit after three or four years and may bear fruit for a century. Each vine usually gives 10-35 kg of grapes.

Growing from seed

▶ This illustration shows some of the stages of germination, as a plant grows from a seed – here a bean seed.

1. The seed lies dormant until conditions are right

- **When seeds mature**, they contain the germ (embryo) of a new plant and the food needed to grow it.
- **The seed lies dormant** (inactive) until conditions are right for it to germinate (grow into a plant) – perhaps when it begins to warm up in spring.

2. The seed sends a root down and a shoot up

- **Poppy seeds** can lie buried in soil for years until brought to the surface by ploughing, allowing them to grow.
- **Scientists once grew** plants from lotus seeds that were 10,000 years old.
- **A seed needs** water and warmth to germinate.
- **When a seed germinates** a root (or radicle) grows down from it and a green shoot (or plumule) grows up.

- **The first leaves** in the sunflower to come up are the seed-leaves or cotyledons, of which there are two.
- **Only certain parts** of a plant, called meristems, can grow. These are usually the tips of shoots and roots.
- **Because** a plant grows at the tips, shoots and roots mainly get longer rather than fatter. This is called primary growth.
- **Later in life** a plant may grow thicker or branch out.

3. The shoot bursts into the air and grows cotyledons (seed leaves)

4. The stem and roots grow longer, and the plant soon begins to grow new leaves

Prairie and steppe

- **Grasslands in cool parts** of the world are called prairies or steppes. There is not enough rain all year round for trees to grow.

- **Prairies** are the grasslands of North America. Steppes are the grasslands of Russia. Every region has its own name for grasslands, such as the veld in South Africa and pampas in South America. But now grasslands anywhere with tall grass are usually called prairies and grasslands with shorter grass are usually called steppes.

- **Hundreds of kinds** of grass grow in prairies. In moist areas in North America, there are grasses like switch grass, wild rye, Indian grass and big bluestem. In drier areas, the main grasses are dropseeds, little bluestem, June grass, needlegrass and blue grama. Slough grass grows in marshland. The state of Kentucky is famous for its bluegrass.

▼ When European pioneers first saw the American prairies in the 19th century, they described them as 'a sea of grass, stretching to the horizon'. Now, corn and wheat fields and cattle ranches cover most of them. Wild prairies like this are now very rare.

- **Meadow grass** is the most common of all grasses, found on grasslands all over the world – and in garden lawns.

- **Shrubs** such as prairie roses often grow amid the grass, while oaks, cottonwoods and willows grow near rivers.

- **The many prairie flowers** include blazing stars, coneflowers, sunflowers, asters and goldenrods.

- **Eurasian grasslands** bloom with vetches, trefoils, worts, orchids and many herbs.

- **Grasslands cover** nearly a quarter of the Earth's land surface.

- **When grasslands** are destroyed by farming, the soil can be blown away by the wind as in the dust bowl of N. America in the 1900s.

> ★ STAR FACT ★
> Prairies and steppes typically have very dark soils such as chernozems. The word *chernozem* is Russian for 'black earth'.

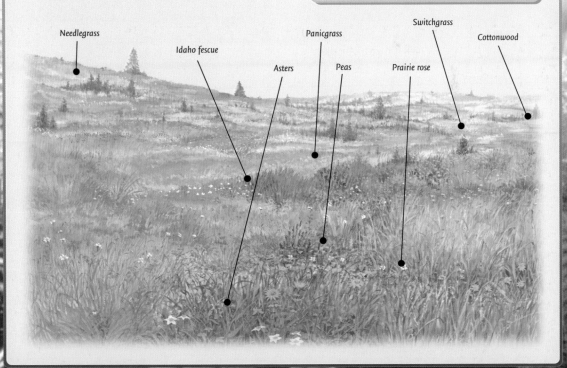

Needlegrass

Idaho fescue

Asters

Panicgrass

Peas

Switchgrass

Prairie rose

Cottonwood

Palm trees

▶ *Date palms produce several clusters of 600-1700 dates towards the end of the year, each year, for about 60 years.*

Palm tree

Date

Raffia Palm

- **Palms** are a group of 2780 species of tropical trees and shrubs.

- **Palms** have a few very large leaves called fronds.

- **The fronds** grow from the main bud at the top of a tall thin trunk.

- **If the main bud** at the top of the trunk is damaged, the tree will stop growing and die.

- **Palm trunks** do not get thicker like other trees; they simply grow taller.

- **Some palms** have trunks no bigger than a pencil; others are 60 m high and 1 m across.

- **Palm fruits** vary enormously. Some are no bigger than a pea. The fruit of the coco-de-mer coconut palm is the biggest seed in the world, growing over 60 cm across.

- **Palm trees** are a very ancient group of plants, and fossil palms have been found dating back 100 million years to the time of the dinosaurs.

- **Date palms** have been cultivated in the hottest parts of North Africa and the Middle East for at least 5000 years. Muslims regard it as the tree of life.

> ★ **STAR FACT** ★
> The world's largest leaves are those of the Raffia palm, which grow up to 20 m long.

Coastal plants

- **Plants** that grow on coasts must be able to cope with exposure to wind and salt spray, and thin, salty soils.

- **Plants** that can tolerate salt are called halophytes.

- **Spray halophytes** can tolerate occasional splashing.

- **True halophytes** can tolerate regular immersion when the tide comes in.

◀ *Sea pinks are also known as thrift because they 'thrive' all the year round on the most exposed cliffs.*

- **The annual seablite** is a true halophyte that lives in between the tides. The word 'blite' comes from an old English word for spinach.

- **The rock samphire's** name comes from St Pierre (St Peter) who was known as the rock. The plant clings to bare rock faces. Samphire was once a popular vegetable and poor people risked their lives to collect it from cliffs.

- **The droppings** of sea birds can fertilize the soil and produce dense growths of algae and weeds such as dock.

- **Lichens** on rock coasts grow in three colour bands in each tidal zone, depending on their exposure to salt.

- **Grey 'sea ivory' lichen** grows above the tide; orange lichens survive constantly being splashed by waves; black lichens grow down to the low water mark.

- **On pebble and shingle beaches** salt-tolerant plants like sea holly, sea kale and sea campion grow.

Lilies

▲ Lilies are one of the most popular garden flowers and have been cultivated in a wide range of colours.

- **Lilies** are one of the largest and most important flower families, containing about 4000 species.

- **Lilies** are monocots (which means a single leaf grows from their seeds) and give their name to the entire group of monocots – liliopsidae.

- **The lily family** includes many flowers called lilies but also asparagus and aloes.

- **Hyacinths** belong to the lily family.

- **Lilies** grow from bulbs to produce clusters of bright trumpet-shaped flowers on tall stems. Each flower has six petals.

- **Lily-of-the-valley** has tiny white bell-shaped blooms. According to superstition, anyone who plants it will die within a year.

- **Lilies-of-the-valley** are famous for their fragrance. They are used to scent soaps and perfumes.

- **Easter lilies** are large trumpet-shaped white lilies that have come to symbolize Easter.

- **Leopard lilies** grow in the western coastal states of the United States. They have red-orange flowers spotted with purple.

- **The Madonna lily** is a lily planted in August that lives throughout the winter.

Cotton

- **Cotton** is a fibre that comes from the cotton plant.

- **The cotton plant** is a small shrub that grows in tropical and subtropical climates.

- **Cotton plants** are annuals and are planted fresh each spring.

- **Cotton plants** grow seed pods called bolls, containing 20–40 seeds – each covered with soft, downy hairs or fibres.

- **As bolls ripen** they burst open to reveal the mass of fluffy fibres inside.

- **When separated** from the seeds, the fluff is known as cotton lint.

- **Cotton seeds** are processed to make oil, cattle cake and fertilizer.

- **There are 39 species** of cotton plant, but only four are cultivated: the upland, Pima, tree and Levant.

- **Upland plants** give 90% of the world's cotton.

▲▶ The bolls picked for cotton develop from the seed pod left when the petals of the cotton flower drop off in summer.

- **Upland** and Pima both came from the Americas, unlike tree and Levant, which are from the Middle East and Africa.

Eucalyptus trees

- **Eucalyptus trees** make up a group of over 400 species of Australian trees. They grow fast and straight, and often reach tremendous heights.

- **Eucalyptus trees** grow best in warm places with marked wet and dry seasons.

- **In winter** eucalyptus trees simply stop growing and produce no new buds.

- **Eucalyptus trees** in California were grown originally from seeds that came from Tasmania.

- **Australians** often call eucalyptus trees gum trees or just gums.

- **Eucalyptus leaves** give eucalyptus oil, used as vapour rubs for people with colds.

◀ *Eucalyptus trees have long, narrow, leathery leaves which are cut, pressed and then steamed to make eucalyptus oil.*

- **The most important** tree grown for oil is the Blue mallee or blue gum. Blue gum trees are the most widespread in North America.

- **Some eucalyptus trees** give Botany Bay kino, a resin used to protect ships against worms and other animals that make holes in their hulls.

- **The jarrah** is an Australian eucalyptus that gives a red wood rather like mahogany. Other eucalyptus woods are used to make everything from boats to telegraph poles.

> ★ STAR FACT ★
> Eucalyptus trees can grow to over 90 m tall – taller than any trees but Californian redwoods.

Green vegetables

- **Green vegetables** are the edible green parts of plants, including the leaves of plants such as cabbages and the soft stems of plants like asparagus.

- **Cabbages** are a large group of green vegetables called the brassicas.

- **Cabbages were** originally developed from the sea cabbage (*Brassica oleracea*) which grew wild near sea coasts around Europe.

- **Kale and collard** are types of cabbage with loose, open leaves.

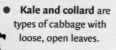

◀ *Lettuces are among the most popular green salad vegetables, used in everything from the famous 'Caesar salads' to garnishes with fast food.*

- **Common and savoy** cabbages are cabbages with leaves folded into a tight ball. Brussel sprouts are cabbages with lots of compact heads.

- **Cauliflower and broccoli** are cabbages with thick flowers. Kohlrabi is a cabbage with a bulbous stem.

- **The leaves of green vegetables** are rich in many essential vitamins including vitamin A, vitamin E and folic acid (one of the B vitamins).

- **Spinach** looks a little like kale, but it is actually a member of the goosefoot family, rich in vitamins A and C, and also in iron. The discovery of the iron content made spinach into the superfood of the cartoon hero Popeye in the mid 20th century.

- **Asparagus** belongs to the lily family. Garden asparagus has been prized since Roman times.

- **In Argenteuil** in France, asparagus is grown underground to keep it white. White asparagus is especially tender and has the best flavour.

Marshes and wetlands

- **There are two kinds of marsh:** freshwater marshes and saltwater marshes.
- **Freshwater marshes** occur in low-lying ground alongside rivers and lakes where the water level is always near the soil surface.
- **Freshwater marshes** are dominated by rushes, reeds and sedges.
- **Sedges** are like grass but have solid triangular stems. They grow in damp places near the water's edge.
- **Rushes** have long cylindrical leaves and grow in tussocks in damp places along the bank.
- **Reeds** are tall grasses with round stems, flat leaves and purplish flowers. They grow in dense beds in open water.
- **Free-floating** plants like duckweed and frogbit are common in marshes. In rivers they'd be washed away.
- **Water horsetails** are relics of plants that dominated the vast swamps of the Carboniferous Period some 300 million years ago.

▲ *Reeds and floating duckweed thrive in open water in marshes.*

- **Saltwater marshes** are flooded twice daily by salty seawater. Cordgrasses and salt-meadow grass are common. Reeds and rushes grow where it is least salty.
- **Where mud is firm,** glasswort and seablite take root. Further from the water sea aster and purslane grow. On high banks, sea lavender, sea plantain and thrift bloom.

Bulbs and suckers

- **Annuals and biennials** only grow once, from a seed. Many perennials die back and grow again and again from parts of the root or stem. This is called vegetative propagation.
- **Plants such as lupins** grow on the base of an old stem. As the plant ages, the stem widens and the centre dies, leaving a ring of separate plants around the outside.

  Bulb

  - **Plants such as irises** sprout from thick stems called rhizomes. These grow sideways beneath the ground.

    - **If the end** of a rhizome swells up it forms a lump called a tuber.

      - **Potatoes** are the tubers of the potato plant.

- **Flowers like crocuses** and gladioli have a bulbous base to their stem. This is called a corm.
- **Bulbs like those** of tulips, daffodils and onions look like corms, but they are actually made of leaf parts rather than the stem. This is why they have layers.
- **Garlic bulbs** are separated into four or five segments called cloves.
- **In winter,** rhizomes, tubers, corms and bulbs act as food stores. In spring they provide the energy to grow new leaves.
- **Plants can also** propagate (grow new plants) by sending out long stems that creep over the ground called runners or under the ground (suckers).

Corm

Tuber

Rhizome

Seed dispersal

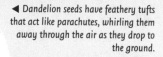

◄ Dandelion seeds have feathery tufts that act like parachutes, whirling them away through the air as they drop to the ground.

● **After maturing** seeds go into a period called dormancy. While they are in this state they are scattered and dispersed.

● **Some scattered seeds** fall on barren ground and never grow into plants. Only those that fall in suitable places will begin to grow.

● **Some seeds** are light enough to be blown by the wind. The feathery seed cases of some grasses are so light they can be blown several kilometres.

● **Many seeds and fruits** have wings to help them whirl through the air. Maple fruits have wings. So too do the seeds of ashes, elms and sycamores.

● **Seeds** like dandelions, cottonwoods and willows have fluffy coverings, so they drift easily on the wind.

● **Some seeds** are carried by water. Coconut seeds can float on the sea for thousands of kilometres.

● **Many fruits and seeds** are dispersed by animals.

● **Some fruits** are eaten by birds and other animals. The seeds are not digested but passed out in the animal's body waste.

● **Some seeds** stick to animal fur. They have burrs or tiny barbs that hook on to the fur, or even a sticky coating.

● **Some fruits,** like geraniums and lupins, simply explode, showering seeds in all directions.

► Sycamore seeds have wings to help them spin away on the wind.

Mountain plants

● **Conditions get colder,** windier and wetter higher up mountains, so plants get smaller and hardier.

● **On lower slopes** conifers such as pines, firs, spruces and larches often grow.

● **Above a certain height,** called the tree-line, it gets too cold for trees to grow.

● **In Australia,** eucalyptus trees grow near the tree-line. In New Zealand, Chile and Argentina southern beeches grow.

> ★ STAR FACT ★
> On Mt Kenya in Africa, huge dandelion-like plants called giant groundsels grow as big as trees.

● **Above the tree-line** stunted shrubs, grasses and tiny flowers grow. This is called alpine vegetation.

● **Alpine flowers** like purple and starry saxifrage have tough roots that grow into crevices and split the rocks.

● **There are few insects** high up, so flowers like saxifrage and snow gentian have big blooms to attract them.

● **To make the most** of the short summers, the alpine snowbell grows its flower buds the previous summer, then lets the bud lie dormant through winter under snow.

● **Alpine flowers** such as edelweiss have woolly hairs to keep out the cold. Tasmanian daisies grow in dense cushion-shapes to keep warm.

◄ As you go higher up a mountain, the trees of the lower slopes thin out. At the top, only mosses and lichens grow.

Tropical grassland

- **Tropical grasslands** are regions in the tropics where there is not enough rain half the year for trees to grow.

- **Grasses** in tropical grasslands tend to grow taller and faster than grasses in cooler regions.

- **Grass stalks** may be eaten by grazing animals, burned by bush fires or dry out, but roots survive underground.

- **In Africa** grasses include 3 m-tall elephant grasses. In Australia, they include tall spear grass and shorter kangaroo grass. In South America, there are plants called bunch grasses and species such as Briza.

- **Most tropical grasslands** are scattered with bushes, shrubs and trees. In Africa, typical trees include hardy broad-leaved trees such as curatella and byrsonima.

- **Many grassland trees** are said to be sclerophyllous. This means they have tough leaves and stems to save water.

- **In drier regions** acacias and other thorn trees are armed with spines to protect them against plant-eating animals. The thorns can be up to 50 cm long.

▲ In East Africa, the grassland is called savanna, and this name is often used for tropical grassland everywhere.

- **In damper places** palm trees often take the place of the thorn trees.

- **Baobab trees** are East African trees with massive trunks up to 9 m across which act as water stores.

- **Baobab trees** look so odd that Arab legend says the devil turned them upside down so their roots stuck up in the air.

Conifers

- **Conifers** are trees with needle-like, typically evergreen leaves that make their seeds not in flowers but in cones.

- **With gingkos and cycads** they make up the group of plants called gymnosperms, all of which make their seeds in cones.

- **The world's tallest tree,** the redwood, is a conifer.

- **The world's most massive tree,** the giant sequoia, is a conifer.

- **One of the world's oldest trees** is the bristlecone pine of California and Nevada, almost 5000 years old.

- **The world's smallest trees** are probably conifers including natural bonsai cypresses and shore pines which reach barely 20 cm when fully grown.

- **Many conifers** are cone-shaped, which helps them shed snow in winter.

- **The needle-like shape** and waxy coating of the leaves helps to save water.

- **The needles of some pines** can grow up to 30 cm long. But the biggest needles ever were those of the extinct *Cordaites*, over 1 m long and 15 cm wide.

- **Conifers** grow over most of the world, but the biggest conifer forests are in places with cold winters, such as north Siberia, northern North America and on mountain slopes almost everywhere.

◄ Most conifers are instantly recognizable from their conical shapes, their evergreen, needle-like leaves and their dark brown cones.

Bahrain 402
bailey 314
Baku 391
balance 211, 223, 244
bald cypress trees 458, 468
baleens 164
Balkans 370, 415
Ballard, Robert 346
ballistic missiles 356
ballonets 354
balloons 341, 354
balsa wood 455
balsam firs 444
Baltic Sea 388
Baluchitherium 170
Bamako 395
bamboo 436, 464
bananas 428, 437, 456
banded coral shrimp 157
bandicoot 156
baneberries 444
Bangkok 368
Bangladesh 100, 112, 406, 422
Banks, Sir Joseph 428
banyan trees 468
baobab trees 481
barbel 165
barbs 165
barchans 86
barley 439, 443, 470
barnacles 137, 160
barometer 129
Bartholdi, Frédéric-Auguste 339
Barton, Otis 346
baryons 280
basal ganglia 199, 211
basal layer (skin) 230
basal slip 90
basal weathering front 88
basalt 93, 115, 130
bascule bridges 338
base 233, 304
basil 435
Basilisk lizard 137
basophils 236
Basque people 418
bathyal zone 160
bathyscaphe 346
bats 139, 142, 147, 152, 154, 157, 178
batteries 190, 263
Battle of Britain 322, 364

battlements 314
Bauhaus 350
bauxite 86, 256
Bavaria 392
bay 103, 435, 447
Bay of Bengal 103
beaches 99, 103, 113
beak 138, 141, 155, 165, 174, 186
beans 439, 449, 464
bear 142, 146, 152, 156, 180, 184
beavers 142, 152, 174, 184
Becquerel, Antoine 279
becquerels 302
Bedouin people 402
bee orchid 457
Beebe, William 346
beech trees 460, 462, 480
beefeaters 336
bees 146, 149, 178
beetles 141, 149, 173, 184
beetroots 164, 449, 446
begonias 426
Beijing 372, 408
Beirut 414
Belarus 385
Belfast 413
Belgium 409
Belgrade 415
Belize 390
Bell, Alexander Graham 296, 340
Ben Nevis mountain 413
bends, the 305
benign 206
Benin 395
Benioff, hugo 98
Benioff-Wadati zones 98
Bennett, Bill 329
benthic 160
Bentley, W. A. 108, 333
Benz, Berta 323
Benz, Karl 323
benzene 262, 286
Berber people 378
bergschrund 90
Berlin 380, 392
Berne 423
Berners-Lee, Tim 294
berries 440, 449, 456, 474
Bertin, Jean 343
beryl 269
Best Friend 313

beta rays 273
Beta star 27
Betelgeuse 34
Bethlehem, Star of 51
bicarbonate 224
biceps 235
bicycle 348
biennials 464, 479
Big Bang 28, 41, 57, 58, 67, 282, 306
Big Ben 334
Big Dipper 27
bilberries 442
bile 209, 212, 229, 238
bilharzia 191
bill 141, 147, 148, 163, 165, 173, 186, 190
binary stars 50, 71
biome 109
biostratigraphy 127
biplanes 322, 361
birch trees 460, 462
bird's nest orchid 457
birds 137, 138, 141, 144, 147, 148, 150, 155, 157, 162, 165, 168, 172, 178, 181, 184, 187, 190, 245
birds of prey 138, 165, 186
birdsfoot trefoil 441
birth 158, 203
birthwort 468
bison 162
bivalves 182
black dwarf stars 28
Black Forest 392
black hole 23, 24, 46, 63, 65, 74, 281, 282, 300
black ice 97
black maples 441
black pines 437
Black Sea 385, 391, 402
black smokers 101
black spruces 444
black widow spider 149, 182
blackberries 449, 456
blackthorn 456
bladder 200, 227, 238
bladderworts 446
bladderwrack 427
Blarney castle 320
blenny 137, 175
Blériot, Louis 341, 343
Bloemfontein 391

F

Acknowledgements

**The publishers would like to thank the following sources
for the photographs used in this book:**

p25 (T/R) Genesis photo library; p42 (B/L) Genesis photo library; p65 (T/R) Genesis photo library; p68 (T/R) Genesis photo library; p74 (B/R) Corbis; p81 (T/C) Corbis; p83 (T/R) Corbis; p101 (C/L) Corbis; p117 (T/C) Corbis; p126 (B/L) Corbis; p136 (B/R) Corbis; p149 (B/R) Corbis; p172 (T/C) Science photo library; p234 (B) Science Photo Library; p238 (T/R) The Stock Market; p243 (T/R) The Stock Market; p265 (C/R) Science Photo Library; p269 (C) Corbis; p273 (T/R) The Stock Market; p277 (T/L) Science Photo Library; p288 (B/L) The Stock Market; p296 (T/R) Science Photo Library; p313 (T/R) CORBIS; p315 (T/L) Steve Lindridge, Eye Ubiquitous/CORBIS; p318 (B/L) Richard T. Nowitz/CORBIS; p329 (B/L) CORBIS; p342 (B/L) Jim Sugar Photography/CORBIS; p345 (B/R) Joseph Sohm, ChromoSohm Inc./CORBIS; p347 (T/R) In-press photography; p353 (T/R) Wolfgang Kaehler/CORBIS p370 (T/L) Wolfgang Kaehler/CORBIS; p370 (B/L) Patrick Johns/CORBIS; p373 (B/L) Wolfgang Kaehler/ CORBIS; p376 (B/C) Paul A. Souders/CORBIS; p378 (T/C) Guy Stubbs, Gallo Images/CORBIS; p383 (B/R) Panos Pictures; p388 (B/L) Catherine Karnow/CORBIS; p395 (T/R) Ted Atkinson, Eye Ubiquitous/CORBIS; p401 (B/L) John Batholomew/CORBIS; p402 (B/L) Panos Pictures; p403 (B/R) Guy Stubbs, Gallo Images/CORBIS; p406 (T/L) David Cumming, Eye Ubiquitous/CORBIS; p409 (B/C) Jeffrey L. Rotman/CORBIS; p411 (C/L) Daewoo Cars Ltd.; p412 (B/L) Owen Franken/CORBIS; p413 (T/R) London Aerial Photo Library/CORBIS; p415 (B/R) Fancoise de Mulder/CORBIS; p418 (B/L) Charles & Josette Lenars/CORBIS. p430 (T/L) Jo Brewer; p434 (T/R) Gunter Marx/CORBIS; p439 (T/R) Bob Gibbons/Holt Studios; p439 (B/L) Jo Brewer; p440 (T/L) Raymond Gehman/CORBIS; p442 (T/C) Scott T. Smith/ CORBIS; p444 (T/R) Woflgang Kaehler/CORBIS; p445 (T/R) Jo Brewer; p448 (B/C) John Holmes, Frank Lane Picture Agency/CORBIS; p449 (B/L) Jo Brewer; p452 (T/L) Sally A. Morgan, Ecoscene/CORBIS; p455 (T/L) Richard T. Nowitz/CORBIS; p458 (T/R) Jo Brewer; p458 (B/L) Steve Austin, Papilio/CORBIS; p466 (T/R) Wayne Lawler, Ecoscene/CORBIS; p471 (B/R) Douglas P. Wilson, Frank Lane Picture Agency/CORBIS; p477 (B/R) Roger Wood/CORBIS.

All other photographs are from MKP Archives